BUSINESS LAW

BUSINESS LAW

General Editor
Joanne Cox

OXFORD
UNIVERSITY PRESS

OXFORD

UNIVERSITY PRESS

Great Clarendon Street, Oxford, OX2 6DP,
United Kingdom

Oxford University Press is a department of the University of Oxford.
It furthers the University's objective of excellence in research, scholarship,
and education by publishing worldwide. Oxford is a registered trade mark of
Oxford University Press in the UK and in certain other countries

Third Edition 2005
Fourth Edition 2009
Fifth Edition 2012

Impression: 3

Published in the United States of America by Oxford University Press
198 Madison Avenue, New York, NY 10016, United States of America

British Library Cataloguing in Publication Data

Data available

Library of Congress Control Number: Data available

ISBN 978-0-19-967865-5

Printed in Great Britain by
Ashford Colour Press Ltd, Gosport, Hampshire

PREFACE

This textbook is designed to support the teaching of the Business Law module on the Law Society of Ireland's Professional Practice Course. The book aims to equip trainees with a knowledge and understanding of those areas of business law which trainees are most likely to come across at the outset of their legal careers. Recent legal developments and the issues most frequently encountered in practice are clearly explained by leading experts in the field.

The text is not designed to be a comprehensive exposition of business law. It is however hoped that the work will be of interest to all who find that business law touches upon their practice, whether in the public or private sector.

The book covers: Chapter 1: Company Incorporation (James Heary); Chapter 2: Conversion and Re-registration (Dáibhí O'Leary); Chapter 3: Officers of a Company (Neil Keenan); Chapter 4: Company Decision-making (Dominic Conlon); Chapter 5: Share Capital (Lorcan Tiernan and David O'Mahony); Chapter 6: Shareholders' Agreements (Paul Robinson); Chapter 7: Financial Statements, Annual return, and Audit (Sean Nolan); Chapter 8: Company Law Enforcement (Aillil O'Reilly); Chapter 9: Commercial Borrowing (Kevin Hoy and Neil Campbell); Chapter 10: Transactions with Directors (Lindsay Stevens); Chapter 11: Corporate Restructuring and Insolvency (Fergus Doorly); Chapter 12: Buying and Selling a Business (Stephen Keogh); Chapter 13: Financial Assistance (Piaras Power); Chapter 14: Partnership Law (Dr Michael Twomey); Chapter 15: Income Tax (Michelle McLoughlin); Chapter 16: Capital Gains Tax (Michelle McLoughlin); Chapter 17: Corporation Tax (Michelle McLouglin); Chapter 18: Consumer Law (Paul Keane and Elaine McGrath); Chapter 19: Commercial Drafting (Jeanne Kelly); Chapter 20: Terms and Conditions of Trading (Paul Robinson and Robert O'Beirn); Chapter 21: Intellectual Property Law (Carol Plunkett); Chapter 22: Information Technology (Rob Corbet, Philip Nolan and Oisín Tobin); Chapter 23: Competition Law (Dr Vincent Power).

This book aims to reflect the law as of 1 June 2015.

While every effort has been made to ensure that this text is accurate, neither the authors, the editors, nor the Law Society of Ireland accept legal liability for any errors, omissions or mis-statements of law.

Joanne Cox
June 2015

AUTHORS

Neil Campbell is a partner in Mason Hayes & Curran, Solicitors. Neil studied law at Trinity College Dublin. Neil works in the Financial Services Department where he advises on all aspects of banking and financial services law and advises institutional and private clients, both international and domestic, on a range of practice areas including secured lending, commercial real estate lending, debt finance structures, corporate restructuring and loan portfolio acquisitions, and disposals in the context of bank deleveraging programmes.

Dominic Conlon is a partner in Leman Solicitors, where he leads their corporate and commercial department. He qualified as a solicitor in 1995. Dominic's practice is primarily focused on Mergers and Acquisitions, Corporate Restructurings, Outsourcings and Commercial Contracts. He is a leading practitioner in the Payments industry, advising many international and domestic financial institutions, payments service providers, and related technology companies. Dominic has lectured and published on Mergers & Acquisitions, Shareholder arrangements, Venture Capital, Corporate Governance, Outsourcing, and Commercial Contracts, including at the Law Society

Rob Corbet is a partner in Arthur Cox, where he heads the Technology & Innovation Group. He qualified as a solicitor in 1999. Rob's practice is primarily focused on technological innovation, where he has extensive Intellectual Property and IT Law experience. He has a leading practice in data protection, advising many of Ireland's largest organisations in this area. He is also a leading adviser in the area of betting and gaming and in broader aspects of online innovation. Rob has been widely published on IT, IP and related matters both domestically and internationally. He has lectured and published internationally on technology law, data protection, open source, betting and gaming regulation and intellectual property, including at the Law Society.

Joanne Cox qualified as a solicitor in England in 1999. Joanne holds an LLB from Warwick University and a Post Graduate Certificate in Higher Education from Nottingham Trent University. She practised in Commercial Litigation before becoming a Senior Lecturer at Nottingham Law School. Since August 2007, Joanne has been the Course Manager responsible for the Law Society's PPC I and PPC II Business Law Courses. Joanne was admitted to the Roll of Solicitors in Ireland in 2009.

Fergus Doorly is a partner in William Fry, Solicitors. He practises in all aspects of insolvency, corporate recovery, and commercial litigation. He has extensive experience in advising liquidators, receivers, examiners and others in all aspects of insolvency law. Fergus has lectured and tutored on the business law course at the Law Society.

James Heary is Associate Director in the Company Compliance and Governance Group of Arthur Cox. An affiliate of the Association of Chartered Certified Accountants and a member of the Institute of Chartered Secretaries and Administrators, he has also completed the UCD Michael Smurfit Graduate Business School Diploma in Corporate Governance. James advises Irish companies in both the private and public sector across a range of company secretarial and corporate governance matters including but not limited to incorporations, share movements, appointments and resignations of board members, voluntary strike offs, annual and extraordinary general meetings, and attendance and minute taking at board meetings.

Kevin Hoy is a partner in Mason Hayes & Curran, Solicitors, where he leads the Real Estate Department, having previously been Head of Financial Services. His work includes development financing and project financing, as well as advising public sector clients and numerous charities. Kevin is a member of the Conveyancing Committee of the Law Society and previously he was the Examiner in Contract Law for the FE 1 examination.

Paul Keane is the managing partner of Reddy Charlton Solicitors, practising in the area of corporate law, contract law, and insolvency. He is the chairman of the Business Law Committee of the Law Society, a member of the Council of the Law Society, and a member of the CCBE Private Law Committee. He co-wrote the Irish contribution on International Taxation and E-commerce published by Kluwer.

Neil Keenan is the managing partner of LKG Solicitors, Glasthule, Co. Dublin and specialises in company and commercial law and business turnaround. Neil has worked on many large and high profile corporate transactions and has written and lectured extensively on company and commercial law related topics. He is a member of the Business Law Committee of the Law Society of Ireland and lectures on the Law Society's Diploma in Corporate Law and Governance.

Jeanne Kelly is a partner in Mason Hayes & Curran, Solicitors. Jeanne studied law at University College Dublin and at the Université de Haute Normandie, Rouen, France. She advises both public and private clients in relation to data protection, contract, communications, information technology, and intellectual property issues. In addition to this edition of *Business Law*, Jeanne has also co-authored books on technology law and data protection law. Jeanne is a guest lecturer in commercial drafting and information technology at the Law Society. She also teaches at UCD Smurfit Business School, on its MBA Course on IP and IT law issues, and is a member of UCD Smurfit Business School Advisory Board on Innovation.

Stephen Keogh is a partner in William Fry, Solicitors, and the Head of its London Office. He practises in the Corporate Department where he specialises in mergers and acquisitions, venture capital investments and also advises on a range of other commercial and company law matters. Stephen has lectured at the Law Society and has served as both an internal and external examiner on the Business Law module.

Elaine McGrath is a partner and European Trade Mark Attorney with Reddy Charlton, Solicitors, since 2006. She holds a Degree in Law & European Studies from University of Limerick and a Postgraduate Diploma in Business & IT from Dublin Business School. Elaine practises corporate and commercial law with a particular interest in commercial contracting and intellectual property. She has lectured on a variety of topics including consumer law, data protection, and bankruptcy.

Michelle McLoughlin qualified as a solicitor in 1999 and has her own commercial law firm M. McLoughlin & Co., Solicitors. She practises commercial, employment, intellectual property, and taxation law. She has particular interest in taxation law. She is a lecturer and tutor with the Law Society in the areas of business law, employment law, and taxation for PPC I and PPC II and masterclasses. Michelle is a co-author of *Capital Taxation for Solicitors* published by Oxford University Press in conjunction with the Irish Law Society's Law School.

Philip Nolan is a partner and Head of the Commercial Department at Mason Hayes & Curran. He also leads Mason Hayes & Curran's Technology, Media and Communications team and the Privacy and Data Security team. Philip specialises in privacy and data security and has advised in the most high profile data security breaches in Ireland in recent years. Philip speaks regularly on data protection and cyber security issues. He holds a BCL from University College Dublin and the University of Oxford.

Sean Nolan is a partner in Kerman & Co Solicitors, Dublin where he practises commercial law, M&A, inward investment, joint ventures, shareholders' agreements, and IP. Formerly he was a partner at one of Dublin's other leading international firms. He is qualified as a solicitor in both England and Ireland, having attended University College London (LL.B) and London Metropolitan University (LL.M). He is co-author of *Buying and Selling a Business-Tax and Legal Issues* published by the Irish Institute of Taxation and *M&A – Protecting the Purchaser* published by Kluwer Law International. He is a member of the Business Law Committee of the Law Society of Ireland and has published various articles on business law subjects in professional journals. He has also lectured at the Law Society on company law.

Robert O'Beirn is a Senior Legal Counsel at UDG Healthcare plc. Robert advises several businesses across the group in connection with a broad range of matters including their day to day commercial contracting requirements and is also involved in the management of the group's acquisition and disposal activities. He previously practised in the Corporate Department of Arthur Cox, Solicitors.

Dáibhí O'Leary is an associate in the Company Compliance and Governance Group in Arthur Cox, having previously trained as a chartered accountant with KPMG. Dáibhí has contributed the chapter on Financial Statements, Accounts and Annual Return to Courtney, The Law of Companies (3rd edition, 2012), contributed a chapter to Bloomsbury Professional's Guide to the Companies Act 2014 (2015), and contributed to MacCann and Courtney, Companies Acts 1963-2012. Dáibhí has addressed the Annual Conference of Chartered Accountants Ireland in relation to the Companies Act, and has had articles on the Act published in its online journals. He also lectures on the Act on the Law Society of Ireland Professional and Diploma courses. Dáibhí's practice in Arthur Cox primarily involves advising on company law and other legislation, particularly in relation to financial statements and corporate governance matters.

David O'Mahony is a solicitor in the Corporate Department of Dillon Eustace. He advises on a wide range of matters for both public and private companies including mergers and acquisitions, commercial contracts, and corporate governance. David has tutored in the area of business law in the Law Society.

Aillil O'Reilly has 15 years' experience as a barrister, focused largely on commercial litigation. During the past six years, his work has been dominated by the consequences of failed investment, acting mainly for financial institutions and insurance companies. Since 2010 he has acted in relation to numerous and sizeable debt litigation and asset tracing for a total value of in excess of €2 billion, including the complicated and protracted litigation with the family of former customers of Anglo Irish Bank (*IBRC v Quinn*). He has direct experience of Corporate Enforcement litigation having been instructed by a succession of liquidators (and directors) in relation to asset swelling, restriction/disqualification and fraud. He also acted in the investigation of DCC plc after the Supreme Court found that it had brought about an €80 million insider trade. Since 2013 his practice has increasingly concerned litigation in pursuit of transferred assets and professional negligence, including large-scale professional negligence proceedings (against former tax advisers). Between 2002 and 2004 he was an external member of the Company Law Review Group 'drafting and consolidation' sub-committee to draft heads of bill for the Companies Consolidation and Amendment Heads of Bill, under the chairmanship of Tom Courtney. He was an external editor on Lyndon MacCann S.C. and Tom Courtney's annotated Companies Acts from its publication in 2007 until 2014. He is the only external contributor to the forthcoming 3rd edition of the textbook *Civil Proceedings and the State*, Thomson Roundhall, Anthony Collins S.C. and James O'Reilly S.C. He has lectured and tutored at the Law Society and the Kings Inns.

Carol Plunkett is a partner in William Fry, Solicitors. She practises in intellectual property law, is known in particular for advising on contentious matters, and has acted in many of the patent, copyright, trade mark, and passing-off cases which have come before the courts in recent years. Carol lectures in the area of business law at the Law Society and has written extensively on the law of intellectual property.

Piaras Power is a partner in Eversheds, Solicitors, where he works in the Banking and Financial Services Department. Piaras advises both Irish and international financial institutions and agencies on a wide range of areas including acquisition finance, real estate and development finance and general secured and unsecured lending transactions. He has extensive experience in advising clients on debt restructuring, workouts and recovery related issues in addition to banking issues relating to insolvency, loan and security documentation. Piaras has lectured on a variety of banking topics both on the Law Society's Professional Practice Courses and its Diploma Programme as well as to members of the Dublin Solicitor's Bar Association.

Dr Vincent Power is a partner in A&L Goodbody and heads the firm's acclaimed EU, Competition & Procurement Unit (shortlisted as among the top five in Europe in the 2015 Global Competition Review Awards). He is a graduate of UCC (College Scholar) (BCL) and University of Cambridge (Evan Lewis Thomas Law Student at Sidney Sussex) (LL.M. and Ph.D.). He has written or edited seven books including *Competition Law and Practice, Irish Competition Law,* and *EU Shipping Law* (winner of the Comité Maritime International Law's Albert Lilar Prize for the best shipping law book in the world in the previous five years). He won the Inaugural Commercial Lawyer of the Year at the Irish Law Awards. He is Adjunct Professor of Law at University College Cork and European Union Centre for Excellence Visiting Professor of Law at Dalhousie University in Canada. He is on the editorial board of, and a contributor to, a number of law journals internationally. He has been involved in many of the leading EU, competition and State aid cases in Ireland over the last twenty years.

Paul Robinson is a partner in Arthur Cox's Corporate and M&A Group and has extensive experience advising on a wide range of corporate and commercial transactions. He has a particular focus on mergers and acquisitions, joint ventures, emerging and growth companies, private equity, corporate reorganisations, and general commercial agreements. Paul has lectured and tutored in the area of business law at the Law Society and has been the external examiner for the Law Society in the area of corporate transactions.

Lindsay Stevens is a solicitor and manager in the Financial Solutions legal team in AIB, dealing with all aspects of restructuring and refinancing distressed debt. Lindsay has worked for three of the 'Big Five' firms in Ireland, and is also qualified in the UK, where she practised for a time. Lindsay has lectured to the DSBA and regularly lectures and tutors on the Business Law module of the Professional Practice Course 1 and the Banking Law and Conveyancing Law modules of the Professional Practice Course 2 at the Law Society of Ireland. Her most recent published works in addition to this book include an article on personal guarantees published in Business Ireland.

Lorcan Tiernan is a partner in Dillon Eustace. His main areas of practice are mergers and acquisitions, corporate finance, corporate insolvency, and financial services. He has written a number of articles in international publications and in legal textbooks and has lectured to the Institute of Bankers in Ireland, the National College of Ireland as well as to the Law Society of Ireland. Lorcan is a graduate of University College Dublin and the University of London.

Oisín Tobin is a Senior Associate in Mason Hayes & Curran, where he specialises in technology and data privacy law. Oisín advises and represents international technology companies in complex cross-border matters and counsels high potential start-ups. Oisín holds an LL.B., with first class honours, from Trinity College Dublin and a BCL, with distinction, from the University of Oxford. Oisín frequently lectures on technology and data protection law at the Law Society of Ireland.

Dr Michael Twomey is the author of Twomey, *Partnership Law,* (Bloomsbury Professional, 2000). He specialises in partnership law, advising law firms on their own behalf, and on behalf of their clients, in relation to all aspects of partnerships. He lectures at the Law Society of Ireland and has previously lectured in partnership law at Trinity College Dublin and been a member of the Business Law Committee of the Law Society of Ireland.

OUTLINE CONTENTS

DETAILED CONTENTS

PART 4   TRADING ISSUES

TABLE OF CASES

TABLE OF LEGISLATION

Irish Statutory Instruments

UK Legislation

Statutes

European Legislation

Treaties and Conventions

PART 1

PRIVATE COMPANIES LIMITED BY SHARES

CHAPTER 1

COMPANY INCORPORATION

1.1 Why Incorporate a Company?

The law governing companies is primarily set out in the Companies Act 2014 (the '2014 Act'). In Ireland, the private company limited by shares has become by far the most common type of corporate entity used by business. Of the 187,139 companies on the register as at 31 December 2013, 86% were private companies limited by shares; less than 1% were public limited companies with the balance being made up primarily of guarantee companies and unlimited companies. The 2014 Act, and this book, accordingly focuses on the new model private company limited by shares (referred to in this chapter as an 'LTD'). All of the law relating to LTDs is set out in Volume 1 of the 2014 Act. Volume 2 of the 2014 Act sets out modifications and additional provisions which apply to other company types. This emphasis marks a significant change from the Companies Acts 1963–2013.

There are a number of distinct and tangible benefits of incorporation:

(a) a company has a separate and distinct legal personality from that of its member(s);

(b) the member(s) of a limited company may avail of limited liability;

(c) a company has perpetual succession until it is either wound up or struck off the register of companies;

(d) a company may sue and be sued; and

(e) a company has the ability to hold property in its own name.

1.1.1 SEPARATE AND DISTINCT LEGAL PERSONALITY

Once a company has been incorporated it acquires its own separate and distinct personality. A partnership or other unincorporated association is merely the sum of its individual parts. If, for example, an unincorporated association incurs a debt, the debt is owed directly by the members of the association. A company has its own legal identity.

1.1.2 LIMITED LIABILITY

Limited liability is an extremely significant benefit of incorporation as a limited company and one of the principal reasons for forming such a company. Members of a limited company have their liability limited to the amount, if any, unpaid on the shares they hold if the company is wound up. As the name implies, limited liability does not apply to the members of unlimited companies.

1.1.3   PERPETUAL SUCCESSION

From the date of incorporation denoted on a certificate of incorporation, the subscribers to the constitution, together with such other persons as may from time to time become members of a company, shall be a body corporate with the name contained in the constitution, having perpetual succession.

This means that even though its members may change or leave (or die) from time to time, the company itself will continue in existence (even if it no longer has any of its original members) until such time as it is dissolved.

1.1.4   MAY BE SUED BY CREDITORS AND IN TURN MAY ITSELF SUE DEBTORS

As a company has its own separate legal personality it can sue and be sued in its own right. For example, it can pursue debtors in its own name (and if creditors take legal proceedings to recover an amount owed by a limited company, those proceedings will be against the company rather than the members). A company may also be prosecuted for criminal offences although some offences by their very nature may only be committed by natural persons and therefore cannot be committed by a corporate body.

1.1.5   HOLDING OF PROPERTY

A company may hold property in its own right and therefore the property belongs to the company and not to its members. If damage is done to a company's property, then the cause of action lies with the company itself and not with its members, whether singly or collectively.

1.2   Procedure for Forming a Private Limited Company ('LTD')

An LTD may be formed for any lawful purpose by any person or persons subscribing to a constitution and complying with the registration requirements of the 2014 Act. An LTD shall not be formed however, unless it appears to the Registrar of Companies that the company, when registered, will carry on an activity in the State.

There are three main ways of forming an LTD:

(a)   by lodging all the forms on the 'ordinary list' in the Companies Registration Office ('CRO');

(b)   the '*Fé Phráinn*' method; or

(c)   the CRODISK method.

Historically, there has also been the option of purchasing a ready-made 'shelf company', if available, from a company formation agent. However this has been significantly obstructed by the provision in the Companies (Amendment) (No.2) Act 1999 that a company may not be formed unless it appears to the Registrar of Companies that it will carry on an activity in Ireland, which includes a requirement that it name the place(s) in Ireland where it will carry on that activity. This obligation has been restated in s 18 of the 2014 Act.

1.2.1   THE ORDINARY LIST

Incorporation of an LTD by means of the ordinary list can take up to three weeks, depending on the existing workload of the CRO at the time of the incorporation paperwork being lodged. The incorporation paperwork which must be lodged to form a company is set out at **1.3** below.

1.2.2   THE COMPANY INCORPORATION SCHEME

The Fé Phráinn or 'Emergency' Scheme has become the standard way for participants (mainly large law/accountancy firms) to have companies incorporated within ten working days of the incorporation paperwork being lodged in the CRO. In order to be able to avail of this scheme the participant must have a 'model' constitution pre-approved and pre-registered by the CRO, which becomes the standard constitutional document for all companies registered by that participant. This permits the CRO to work on the assumption that the incorporation paperwork submitted is in order.

No amendments may be made to a participant's 'model' constitution without the express prior approval of the CRO.

1.2.3   THE CRODISK SCHEME

Under the electronic 'CRODISK' incorporation scheme, incorporation is guaranteed within five working days provided the terms and conditions are met. This Scheme is open to members of the Fé Phráinn Scheme, who may log onto the CRO website and through their web portal, Companies Online Registration Environment ('CORE'), input the details for the proposed company i.e. name, company type, registered office, director details, share capital, and shareholder details. This saves CRO staff from having to do so upon receipt of the original incorporation paperwork. Once the relevant information has been uploaded, an electronic version of the Form A1 (see **1.3.2** below) is produced and must be duly executed by each proposed director, secretary, and shareholder. The electronic version cannot be amended by hand in any way prior to execution.

1.3   Incorporation Paperwork for an LTD

To incorporate an LTD, the following shall be delivered to the Registrar for registration:

- the constitution of the company;

- a Form A1 which sets out the directors, secretary, registered office, place of central administration, and related details, as well as confirming compliance with the Act, and that the company will carry on an activity in the State; and

- the appropriate fees.

Where applicable the following must also be delivered:

- a s 137 bond (if there are no EEA directors upon incorporation); and/or

- a s 23 statement (if a proposed director is disqualified in another State).

1.3.1   CONSTITUTION OF AN LTD

The Companies Acts 1963–2013 provided that a company's constitution comprised two documents, being the memorandum and articles of association. The memorandum contained a number of obligatory clauses: the name clause; the objects clause; the limited liability clause; the capital clause; and the association clause. The articles of association set out the rules for the management of the company's internal affairs and dealt with such matters as the appointment and removal of directors, the powers to be exercised by them, the holding of meetings of the members and the allotment, transfer, and transmission of shares. The articles of association also set out any special rights to be attached to the different classes of shares, e.g. ordinary and preference shares.

An LTD as registered under Part 2 of the Act, will have a one-document constitution in place of what was the memorandum and articles of association. The constitution will retain a number of the same obligatory clauses, the major omission being that of an objects clause. This is addressed at **1.4.1** below.

In respect of the articles of association, many standard provisions which would have been included in a company's articles of association have now been enshrined in the 2014 Act itself, and apply save to the extent that the LTD's constitution states otherwise. To this end, it is envisaged that an LTD's constitution can be a much shorter and succinct document, which can be as short as one page if a company so wishes. If an LTD wishes to include bespoke provisions – such as those attaching different rights to different classes of shares – it will of course be necessary to set these out expressly. The form of constitutional documents for company types other than the LTD is discussed in **chapter 2, 'Conversion and Re-registration'** at **2.3**.

The constitution of an LTD must be in the prescribed form and will include the following clauses:

1.3.1.1 Company name

This clause must confirm the full name of the company, including the relevant suffix. In the case of an LTD, the suffix will be 'limited', 'teoranta', 'ltd', or 'teo' (whether capitalised or not). The CRO implements an online name reservation facility through CORE, which permits an applicant to reserve a company name for a new company for a period of at least 28 days. There is also the option to apply for a once-off extension, which if permitted, will allow an additional 28-day reservation period i.e. 56 days in total.

The CRO charges a fee for a name reservation, which is redeemable against the filing fee for incorporating a company with that name within 28 days. The subsequent fee for the once-off extension is not refunded in any way. Names of companies are discussed in more detail **chapter 2, 'Conversion and Re-registration'** at **2.2**.

1.3.1.2 Company type

In the case of an LTD, this clause shall confirm that the company is a private company limited by shares registered under Part 2 of the Act.

1.3.1.3 Liability clause

In the case of an LTD, this will confirm that the liability of the members is limited.

1.3.1.4 Capital clause

Under s 19 (1)(d) of the 2014 Act, an LTD shall either state:

(i) the total amount of share capital with which the company proposes to carry on business (similar to the existing concept of an 'authorised share capital') and the division of that capital into a specified number of shares of a fixed amount, e.g. 'The share capital of the Company is €1,000,000 divided into 1,000,000 ordinary shares of €1.00 each'; *or*

(ii) the nominal value of the share capital (without stating the full amount or number of shares), e.g. 'The share capital of the Company is divided into ordinary shares of €1.00 each.'

1.3.1.5 Association clause

The subscriber(s) must sign and date the subscriber pages, confirming that they are thereby forming a company, and the signature(s) must be attested by at least one witness. The subscriber pages shall also set out the number of shares for which the subscriber(s) is/are subscribing.

An LTD may additionally elect to include supplemental regulations in its constitution, for example in relation to the allotment of shares, but such provisions are not compulsory.

1.3.2 FORM A1

The following information is required to complete the Form A1:

(a) the name of the company (including any relevant suffix);

(b) the type of company that is being proposed for registration;

(c) the registered office address of the company. This must be in Ireland and may not be a PO Box number. If the proposed registered office is in the care of a specified agent, being an agent who has an office in the State and is approved by the Registrar to provide such service, the agent's name and registered number must also be provided;

(d) a company email address to which the CRO can issue the certificate of incorporation (and other correspondence) in electronic format;

(e) whether the company is applying for an exemption from the requirement to include the relevant suffix (see **chapter 2, 'Conversion and Re-registration'**, at **2.2.2**);

(f) if the company is proposing to use certain restricted words in its name and, confirmation that permission from the relevant party has been sought (see **chapter 2, 'Conversion and Re-registration'**, at **2.2.1**);

(g) the names, residential addresses (unless an exemption has been received), nationality, date of birth, occupation, residence (EEA or otherwise), and current and past worldwide directorships over the preceding five years of each proposed director. LTD's may have a sole director. If none of the proposed directors are resident in the EEA a bond pursuant to s 137 of the 2014 Act will be required (see **1.3.3**);

(h) the name, date of birth, and residential addresses of the person(s) being appointed as the secretary, deputy secretary, assistant or joint secretaries of the company. If a corporate entity is to be appointed the entity's corporate name, registered office address, and company number must be disclosed; and

(i) the signatures of the subscriber or subscribers to the constitution. Details of the proposed authorised and issued share capital must also be disclosed.

Another required element of the Form A1 is that a director or secretary, or a solicitor engaged in the formation of the company must confirm:

(a) that all of the requirements of the 2014 Act in respect of the registration of the company (and incidental matters) have been complied with;

(b) that the company shall carry on an activity in Ireland;

(c) the type of activity to be carried on by the company in Ireland;

(d) the place(s) in Ireland where it is proposed to carry on such activity; and

(e) the place where the central administration of the company will normally be carried on.

The 2014 Act has removed the previous requirement that the declaration of compliance be made under oath.

1.3.3 SECTION 137 BOND

Where an LTD does not have a director resident in the EEA, the company must put in a place a bond in the prescribed form to the value of €25,000. The bond provides that, in the event of a failure by the company to pay the whole or part of each (if any) fines or penalties imposed on the company by the Revenue Commissioners or Registrar the bond will be used to offset those fees.

A copy of the bond must be appended to the incorporation paperwork delivered to the Registrar (previously it was required to file the original bond).

Where an existing company does not have an EEA-resident director, it may avoid the requirement for a bond by obtaining a continuous link certificate, being a written statement from the Revenue Commissioners that they have reasonable grounds to believe that the company has a real and continuous link with one or more activities being carried on in Ireland. The company must lodge the original statement with the Registrar along with the appropriate form, within two months of receipt. It generally takes the CRO 7–10 working days from the date of receipt of the application to issue a continuous link certificate. This exemption will obviously not apply to a company being newly incorporated, as it will not have established a continuous link with any activity, whether in Ireland or otherwise.

1.3.4   SECTION 23 STATEMENT

If a proposed director is a person who is disqualified under the law of another state (whether pursuant to an order of a judge or a tribunal or otherwise) from being appointed or acting as a director or secretary of a body corporate or an undertaking, that person has an obligation to ensure that an additional statement in the prescribed form is lodged at the CRO. The statement must be signed by him or her and must specify:

(a) the jurisdiction in which he or she is so disqualified;

(b) the date on which he or she became so disqualified; and

(c) the period for which he or she is so disqualified.

1.3.5   EFFECT OF REGISTRATION

Once the incorporation paperwork submitted to the CRO has been reviewed and the Registrar is satisfied that (i) the requirements of the 2014 Act have been observed; (ii) the proposed name of the company is available; (iii) the necessary fee has been paid; and (iv) the applicant has adhered to all of the associated statutory requirements, the constitution shall be registered. On the registration of the constitution of an LTD, the Registrar shall certify in writing that the company is incorporated and shall issue to the company a certificate of incorporation in respect of it, stating its date of incorporation.

The date of incorporation is equivalent to a company's date of birth. The certificate of incorporation is conclusive evidence that the company has been duly registered under the 2014 Act.

1.4   Corporate Capacity and Authority

1.4.1   CORPORATE CAPACITY

Under the Companies Acts 1963–2013, every company was required to include in its memorandum of association an objects clause, which set out the purposes for which it had been established and delimited the activities it could carry out. Where a company purported to act outside its objects clause, such action was void and unenforceable, being ultra vires (outside the powers of) the company.

LTDs will no longer be subject to the doctrine of ultra vires because they will no longer be required (or permitted) to have an objects clause. An LTD shall have *'full and unlimited capacity to carry on and undertake any business or activity, do any act or enter into any transaction'* and full powers, rights, and privileges for those purposes (2014 Act, s 38 (1)). Even if an LTD purported to prescribe a limitation on its capacity in its constitution, such limitation would be ineffective. Although this does not of course mean that an LTD will be allowed to carry out illegal activities, an LTD will have the same capacity as a natural person. This is unquestionably one of the most significant reforms to the law of private limited companies.

1.4.2 CORPORATE AUTHORITY

Of course the next question that then arises is whether the people who purport to act for an LTD have the authority to do so?

Section 40 of the 2014 Act provides that the board of directors of an LTD shall be deemed to have authority to exercise any power of the company and to authorise others to do so. This is consistent with the key corporate governance provision set out in s 158 of the 2014 Act, which states that the day-to-day business of a company shall be managed by its directors.

The Act further adds that any persons registered under s 39 of the Act shall also be deemed to have such authority. This reflects an existing provision under reg 6 of the European Communities (Companies) Regulations 1973. However given that a person will only be so registered where they are authorised to bind the company without restriction, it is not thought that this provision will be widely used.

1.4.3 POWERS OF ATTORNEY

In addition, the directors of an LTD may appoint an attorney to act on behalf of the company. A deed signed by such attorney on behalf of the company shall bind the company and have the same effect as if it were under its common seal. Previously there was some ambiguity as to whether the power of attorney had to be executed under the common seal of the company, but the wording of s 41 of the Act appears to imply that this is no longer the case.

1.5 Contracts and the Company Seal

A company, being a legal entity, can enter into contracts as an individual can. As set out above, the limitation that previously applied whereby a company could not enter into a contract which was beyond its objects (ultra vires), has now been removed by the Act in respect of an LTD.

Section 42 (1) of the 2014 Act states that contracts may be entered into on behalf of an LTD as follows:

(a) if a contract would, if made between natural persons, by law be required to be in writing and under seal, it may be made on behalf of the company in writing under the common seal of the company;

(b) if a contract would, if made between natural persons, by law be required to be in writing and signed, it may be made on behalf of the company in writing, signed by any person acting under its authority, express or implied;

(c) if a contract would, if made between natural persons, by law be valid although made only orally, and not set out in writing, it may be made orally on behalf of the company by any person acting under its authority, express or implied.

1.5.1 CONTRACTS UNDER SEAL

Contracts which must be executed by an individual under seal must be executed by an LTD under its common seal. Relatively few contracts are required to be under seal, examples of which include:

(a) the creation or conveyance of a legal estate or interest in land;

(b) an agreement to give a valid release or discharge of a right in personal property or cause of action; and

(c) a guarantee where there is no valuable consideration.

Every Irish company must have a common seal. In essence this is a metal device with two opposing plates on which the name of the company will be engraved. When the two plates are pressed together on a sheet of paper, it will leave the name of the company clearly embossed thereon.

The statutory default (save as otherwise provided by a company's constitution) is that a company's seal shall be used only by the authority of its directors, or of a committee of its directors so authorised by its directors. Section 43 (2)(b) of the 2014 Act also requires that any document to which a company's seal shall be affixed shall be:

(i) signed by a director (or a registered person) of it or by some other person appointed for the purpose (by its directors or by a foregoing committee of them); and

(ii) countersigned by the secretary or by a second director of it or by some other person appointed for the purpose (by its directors or by a foregoing committee of them).

1.5.2 CONTRACTS IN WRITING

Contracts that must be in writing (but not under seal) include:

(a) contracts that are not intended to be performed within one year;

(b) consumer lending contracts; and

(c) legal assignment of the benefit of a contract.

Where a contract is to be made or evidenced in writing, the person authorised by the LTD should sign the contract 'for and on behalf of' the company.

1.5.3 ORAL CONTRACTS

Any contracts that may be made orally by an individual may also be made orally on behalf of an LTD by its agent, most usually a director of the company (duly authorised by resolution of the directors acting as a board).

1.6 Post Incorporation Requirements e.g. Letterheads, etc.

The 2014 Act sets out a number of obligations governing the publication of an LTD's name and disclosure of details about its name, management, registered office, and corporate status in its communications with the public.

1.6.1 PUBLICATION OF COMPANY NAME

An LTD must display its name in a conspicuous position (in easily legible letters) at both its registered office address and also any other address at which it carries on business.

1.6.2   BUSINESS LETTERS

Section 151 (1) of the 2014 Act states that all business letters in which the company's name appears shall also include the following particulars for each director of the company:

    (a)   his or her present forename, or the initials thereof, and present surname;

    (b)   any former forename and surnames of him or her; and

    (c)   his or her nationality, if not Irish.

In addition, the letterhead must also record:

    (a)   the name of the company and the company's legal form;

    (b)   the place of registration and the registration number of the company; and

    (c)   the registered office address of the company.

If there is a reference to the share capital of the company the reference must be to the paid-up share capital.

Section 151(5) of the 2014 Act allows the Minister, in special circumstances, to grant a company an exemption from having to disclose the particulars of their directors on business letters.

1.6.3   WEBSITE

All details which are applicable to a business letter shall also be displayed on a company's website, in a prominent and easily accessible place (2014 Act, s 151 (4)).

1.6.4   NOTICES, PUBLICATIONS, BILLS OF EXCHANGE, AND INVOICES

Under s 49 (b) of the 2014 Act an LTD must have its name mentioned in legible characters on each of the following:

    (a)   all notices and other official publications of the company;

    (b)   all bills of exchange, promissory notes, endorsements, cheques, and orders for money or goods purporting to be signed by or on behalf of the company; and

    (c)   all invoices, receipts, and letters of credit of the company.

1.6.5   PENALTIES

If an LTD fails to comply with the requirements outlined above the company and every officer who is in default shall be guilty of a category 4 offence. An officer may also be found personally liable, for example if they authorise the issuance of an invoice or cheque on which the company's name is not properly described.

CHAPTER 2

CONVERSION AND RE-REGISTRATION

2.1 Types of companies under the Companies Act 2014 and the Companies Acts 1963–2013

Just as under the Companies Acts 1963–2013, there are a number of different company types under the Companies Act 2014 (the '2014 Act'). The new proposed company types correspond as follows to the previously existing company types:

Companies Act 2014 (the '2014 Act')	Companies Acts 1963–2013
New model private company limited by shares (referred to in this chapter as the 'LTD')	Private company limited by shares
Designated activity company ('DAC') limited by shares	Private company limited by shares
DAC limited by guarantee	Private company limited by guarantee and having a share capital
Public limited company ('PLC')	Public limited company (i.e. limited by shares)
Company limited by guarantee ('CLG')	Public company limited by guarantee and not having a share capital
Unlimited company ('UC')	Unlimited company

This chapter considers in some depth the decision that every existing private company limited by shares will have to make, between becoming an LTD and becoming a DAC.

This chapter also seeks to set out some of the distinguishing characteristics between the types of companies generally, and to address how a company can change from one type of company to another. Key characteristics of each company type are discussed at **2.1.1–2.1.5**.

2.1.1 NEW PRIVATE COMPANY LIMITED BY SHARES ('LTD')

The key characteristic of a company limited by shares (an LTD, DAC, or PLC) is that the liability of its shareholders is limited to any amount unpaid on their shares; in most cases shares will be fully-paid up on issue, and the shareholders will have no outstanding liability.

The major difference between an LTD and any other type of company (including the private company limited by shares under the Companies Act 1963–2013) is that the LTD has full and unlimited capacity, in that it does not have an objects clause. In addition, it will have a one-document constitution, as opposed to the other company types, which will have a two-document constitution (see **2.3** below).

An LTD may have just one director, unlike any other type of company under either the Companies Acts 1963–2013 or the 2014 Act.

An LTD cannot act as a credit institution or insurance undertaking, and cannot have, or apply to have, debt securities publicly listed.

2.1.2   DAC (LIMITED BY SHARES OR BY GUARANTEE)

A DAC can have any number of members. However, even if it has just a single member, it must have two directors (as is the case for every company other than the LTD). In the (very rare) case of a DAC limited by guarantee (which will be a company limited by guarantee and having a share capital), the liability of a member will be limited to any amount outstanding on their shares and the amount which they have guaranteed.

2.1.3   PUBLIC LIMITED COMPANY ('PLC')

The key difference between a PLC and other company types is that a PLC is free to have any securities listed (whereas a DAC, for example, can have only debt securities listed, and an LTD may not have any securities listed). Therefore a PLC is the only type of company that can have shares listed on a stock exchange. Unlike the LTD or DAC, the PLC is required to have a minimum level of share capital (€25,000 – previously the minimum requirement was €38,092), of which at least a quarter must be paid up. Previously a PLC was required to have a minimum of seven members, but it is now permitted to have any number of members.

2.1.4   COMPANY LIMITED BY GUARANTEE ('CLG')

In a company limited by guarantee and not having a share capital, the liability of members is limited to the amount which they have guaranteed (typically a very small amount). As the members of such a company are not shareholders and do not have a distinct economic interest in their capital, it is the preferred form of company used by sports and social clubs and by charities. A CLG will only need to have one member (currently, the minimum is seven).

2.1.5   UNLIMITED COMPANY ('UC')

The defining feature of a UC is that if on its being wound up, it is unable to pay its debts, its current members (and certain past members) will be liable to make good the shortfall. This potential liability for members will tend to be a significant reason for not becoming a UC. Under the 2014 Act, a UC will again need to have one member (currently, the minimum is two).

2.2   Names of Companies

2.2.1   CHOICE OF NAME

Where a new company is looking to incorporate with a particular name, or an existing company to change its name, that name must be acceptable to the Registrar of Companies. The Registrar will generally not allow a name to be adopted if it is too similar to a name already on the register of companies, or if it is undesirable on any of the following grounds:

(a)   if it is offensive;

(b)   if it would suggest State sponsorship;

(c)   if it contains the word 'bank' (or similar words, or their Irish equivalent), unless permission has been granted by the Central Bank;

(d)   if it contains the word 'insurance', 'assurance', or 'reinsurance', unless permission has been granted by the Central Bank;

(e)   if it contains the words 'society', 'co-operative', or 'co-op', unless permission has been granted by the Register of Friendly Societies;

(f)   if it contains the words 'university', 'institute of technology', or 'regional technical college', unless permission has been granted by the Department of Education and Skills;

(g)   if it contains the word 'charity' or 'group', unless this is justified; or

(h)   if it contains the words 'standard', 'credit union', or 'building society'.

Where a name is considered too similar to an existing name, the Registrar will not accept words such as 'company', 'holding', 'group', 'Dublin', 'Ireland', 'Eire', or 'international' as being sufficient to differentiate between the name of one company from another. In addition, it is the practice of the Companies Registration Office (the 'CRO') not to allow the use of the name of a dissolved company until 20 years have passed since the date of dissolution.

However, a company will be allowed to use a name similar to that of an existing company if the latter company provides a letter confirming that it does not object to the name change. This will often arise where there is a group of companies.

2.2.2   REQUIRED SUFFIX

Just as is the case under the Companies Acts 1963–2013, the 2014 Act prescribes that a company's name must generally end with a particular suffix, signifying the company type adopted. The table below sets out the suffixes acceptable for each company type; in each case, where an abbreviation is stated, a capitalised form of that abbreviation is also acceptable. Therefore in the case of a public limited company, as well as listed abbreviations such as 'p.l.c.' or 'plc', the abbreviations 'P.L.C.' or 'PLC' would be equally acceptable.

Company type	Acceptable suffixes
LTD	'limited', 'teoranta', 'ltd.', 'teo.'
DAC (whether limited by shares or guarantee)	'designated activity company', 'cuideachta ghníomhaíochta ainmnithe', 'd.a.c.', 'dac', 'c.g.a.', 'cga'
PLC	'public limited company', 'cuideachta phoiblí theoranta', 'p.l.c.', 'plc', 'c.p.t.', 'cpt'
CLG	'company limited by guarantee', 'cuideachta faoi theorainn ráthaíochta', 'c.l.g.', 'clg', 'c.t.r.', 'ctr'
UC	'unlimited company', 'cuideachta neamhtheoranta', 'u.c.', 'uc', 'c.n.', 'cn'

A few additional points should be kept in mind. Firstly, a not-for-profit company established for the promotion of commerce, art, science, education, religion, or charity has been allowed under the Companies Acts 1963–2013 to avail of an exemption from including 'limited' (or some equivalent) in its name. A DAC or LTD that meets the corresponding conditions will similarly be exempted under the 2014 Act from including the relevant suffix in its name.

Secondly, there has until now been no requirement for an unlimited company to include the words 'unlimited company', or indeed any other words or letters, as a suffix. This is therefore a new obligation. However the 2014 Act allows for a transitional measure whereby, during the 18-month period following commencement of the 2014 Act, an existing unlimited company may omit the words 'unlimited company' or 'cuideachta neamhtheoranta' from its name. From the end of this transition period, if an existing unlimited company has not already changed its name to include the required suffix, the name of that company shall be deemed to be altered by the addition of 'unlimited company' or 'cuideachta neamhtheoranta' at the end of its name, and the Registrar of Companies shall issue a certificate of incorporation so altered. There is a provision whereby the Minister may grant an exemption to a UC from including the relevant suffix in its name, but it remains to be seen how often this will be granted.

Finally, the suffix 'designated activity company' (or its Irish equivalent, or any acceptable abbreviation) is likely (at least initially) to be generally unfamiliar – particularly outside Ireland – and this may be a reason for a company not to become such a company, and rather to become an LTD; or where this is not possible, some other type of company.

2.3 The Form of Constitutional Documents for Company Types other than the LTD

As set out in **2.1.1**, an LTD will have a one-document constitution. However every other type of company will have a constitution comprised of two documents, being its memorandum of association and its articles of association.

2.3.1 MEMORANDUM OF ASSOCIATION

The memorandum of association is the fundamental constitutional document of a company (other than an LTD) and sets out the basis on which the company is being established. The 2014 Act sets out a prescribed form for the memorandum of each company type, but the main elements are that the memorandum must state:

(a)   the company's name;

(b)   (its status, i.e. that it is (as applicable):

   (i)   a DAC having the status of a private company limited by shares registered under Part 16 of the 2014 Act;

   (ii)   a DAC having the status of a private company limited by guarantee and having a share capital registered under Part 16 of the 2014 Act;

   (iii)   a PLC registered under Part 17 of the 2014 Act;

   (iv)   a CLG registered under Part 18 of the 2014 Act;

   (v)   a private unlimited company registered under Part 19 of the 2014 Act; or

   (vi)   a public unlimited company registered under Part 19 of the 2014 Act;

(c)   its objects;

(d)   that the liability of its members is limited (or in the case of a UC, that its members have unlimited liability);

(e)   in the case of a company having a share capital, the amount of share capital with which it proposes to be registered and the division thereof into shares of a fixed amount;

(f)   in the case of a company limited by guarantee, that each member undertakes that if the company is wound up while they are a member, or within one year after their ceasing to be a member, they will contribute to the assets such amount – not exceeding an amount to be specified in the memorandum – as may be required for payment of the debts and liabilities etc. of the company.

As previously noted, a key difference between the constitution of an LTD and that of any other company type is that the latter is required to include an 'objects clause', which delimits the purposes for which the company was established and the activities that it can pursue.

Under the Companies Acts 1963–2013, where a company acted other than in furtherance of its objects, such act was said to be ultra vires ('beyond its powers') and void. Where the company acted outside its objects, even where the members would have approved the act, it was not possible for the members to subsequently approve the act. Accordingly companies have tended to include:

(a)   a multitude of objects and powers, so as to cover every imaginable activity;

(b)   an 'independent objects' clause, stating that each object is to be read separately, and that no object is to be treated as merely ancillary to any other object; and

(c)   a 'Bell Houses' clause (so called after a case of that name) giving the company the capacity to pursue any business which the directors believe would benefit the company.

The 2014 Act provides that if a company acts outside its objects, the act may be subsequently ratified by a special resolution of the company. Moreover even if the company does not ratify the act, the validity of the act shall not be called into question on the ground of lack of capacity by reason of anything in the company's objects clause; although in such a case, the directors will be guilty of a breach of duty. Therefore although the directors will still need to have regard to the objects, it will be possible to 'fix' a situation where the company has acted outside those objects. It remains to be seen if this will impact on the form or length of objects clauses.

2.3.2   ARTICLES OF ASSOCIATION

The articles of association set out a company's internal rules.

The 2014 Act states as statutory defaults a number of provisions which until now would have been set out in the articles of association; these are expressed as applying 'save to the extent that the company's constitution provides otherwise'. Therefore where a company is adopting standard provisions, it will no longer be necessary to set these out in the articles of association. It is therefore envisaged that companies will be able to adopt articles of association that are significantly shorter than the articles that companies have typically adopted under the Companies Acts 1963–2013.

For example, almost all companies will previously have included a provision in their articles to the effect that the 'business of the company shall be managed by its directors'. Section 158 of 2014 Act now provides that this will automatically be the case, save to the extent that the company's constitution provides otherwise. Therefore a company will no longer need to set out this standard provision in its articles.

It is likely that the articles of association of existing companies will have included a number of references to provisions of the Companies Acts 1963–2013. For example, existing companies are likely to have adopted, to some extent, one of the 'model' sets of articles set out in the First Schedule to the Companies Act 1963. Although the 2014 Act includes 'savers' for such references, such companies may prefer to amend their articles of association to remove such out-of-date references, and also to avoid any possible ambiguity where the existing articles duplicate, or overlap with, statutory defaults under the 2014 Act.

2.3.3   EFFECT OF THE MEMORANDUM AND ARTICLES OF ASSOCIATION

Section 31 of the 2014 Act states that a company's constitution binds the company and the members of it to the same extent as if it had been signed and sealed by each member, and contained covenants by the company and each member to observe all the provisions of the constitution and the Act as regards the governance of the company. The constitution therefore comprises a statutory contract between the members and the company, and among the members. This is equally the case in respect of an LTD.

2.4   Conversion of Existing Private Companies

2.4.1   EXISTING PRIVATE COMPANIES FACE A DECISION

As is clear from the table at **2.1** above, every existing private company limited by shares will face a decision on commencement of the 2014 Act: whether it wishes to be a private limited company under the new regime set out in Parts 1 to 15 of the 2014 Act (an 'LTD'), or prefers to become a designated activity company ('DAC') or, indeed, some other type of company.

In summary, an existing private company limited by shares has the following options under Chapter 6 of Part 2 of the 2014 Act:

(a) it can, within the 18 months following commencement, 'opt in' to the new regime and decide to become an LTD;

(b) it can, during the 15 months following commencement, 'opt out' and decide to become a DAC, or some other type of company;

(c) if it fails either to opt in or opt out it will, at the end of the 18-month period, be deemed to have become an LTD (but its directors will be in breach of their obligation under s 60 of the 2014 Act, effectively to proactively 'opt in' or 'opt out').

In the last three months of the transition period, a company can still re-register as a DAC, or some other type of company, but will need to do so under Part 20 under re-registration rather than under the simpler transitional procedure under Part 2. During the transition period, or until it opts to become some type of company other than a DAC, an existing private company will be subject to the law applicable to DACs.

2.4.2   WHETHER TO BECOME AN LTD OR ANOTHER TYPE OF COMPANY

It would seem advisable that most existing private companies would take action before the end of the transition period. The reasons for taking positive action include:

(a) for companies which want to opt in, it would seem preferable to have the certainty of an early application of the new regime set out in Parts 1 to 15 of the 2014 Act;

(b) statutory defaults are generally better avoided, especially when a new bespoke constitution can be adopted so easily;

(c) directors can avoid the obligations which would otherwise arise where the members do nothing (as discussed below), by proactively putting a new constitution to the members to adopt;

(d) until such time as an existing private company 'opts in', the applicable law will be the more complicated law contained in Part 16, and Parts 1 to 14 as disapplied, modified, or supplemented by Part 16, which applies to DACs; and

(e)   for companies, such as joint ventures, which may want to retain their objects clauses and avoid re-negotiating their bespoke articles of association, it will be important to take action and opt out, to prevent the application of the default constitution.

A significant proportion of the reforms set out in the 2014 Act apply only to the LTD, and so it is thought that, save where there is a specific reason for an existing private company to choose to become a company type other than an LTD, that it will prefer to become an LTD.

An existing private company might however choose not to become an LTD in the following circumstances:

(a)   where the company is a credit institution or insurance undertaking: an LTD shall not be permitted to carry on such activity (2014 Act, s 68(2)), so an existing private company limited by shares that carries on such activity will need to become some other type of company;

(b)   where the company has, or wishes to have, debt securities (or interests in them) admitted to trading or to be listed on a regulated market: again, an LTD shall not be permitted to carry on such activity (2014 Act, s 18(2)); accordingly, an existing private company that carries on, or wishes to carry on, such activity will need to become some other type of company;

(c)   Where it is important to the company that it would retain its objects clause: an LTD will have full and unlimited capacity to carry on and undertake any business or activity (save as set out in (a) and (b) above), do any act or enter into any transaction; in certain cases, it may be preferable that the company would in fact be restricted in respect of the activities it may undertake (for example in the case of certain joint ventures), and in such cases, it will be necessary that the company would adopt some form other than an LTD.

It is envisaged that an existing private company limited by shares which chooses not to become an LTD for one of these reasons would most likely choose to become a DAC. However they would alternatively have the option of becoming some other type of company (e.g. a PLC), subject to meeting the relevant requirements for that type.

2.4.3   THE APPLICABLE LAW DURING THE TRANSITION PERIOD

During the transition period (or until an existing private company re-registers as another type of company), the law applicable to an existing private company limited by shares will be that applicable to a DAC (being, as previously mentioned, that contained in Part 16, and Parts 1 to 14 as disapplied, modified, or supplemented by Part 16) (2014 Act, s 58). This law adheres relatively closely to the current law applicable to existing private limited companies, with the result that, during this transition period, existing private limited companies will have an opportunity to accustom themselves to the changes proposed by the new regime.

This will mean, however, that the advantages that will accrue to the LTD under Parts 1 to 15 will be denied to companies until the end of the transition period, or unless and until they elect to opt in to the new regime. Existing companies which have adopted in whole or in part the regulations contained in Table A of the Companies Act 1963 will continue during this transition period to be governed by those regulations notwithstanding the repeal of the Companies Act 1963.

2.4.4   STEPS IN CONVERTING TO THE NEW LTD

The 2014 Act provides for three ways in which an existing private company limited by shares can become an LTD:

(a)   the members may adopt a new constitution in the prescribed form by special resolution and deliver it to the CRO for registration (2014 Act, s 59(1));

(b) if the members fail to do so, and the company is neither proceeding, nor required, to re-register as another company type, the directors are obliged to draft a constitution in the prescribed form based on the existing memorandum and articles and to deliver a copy of it to each member and to the CRO for registration (2014 Act, s 60); or

(c) where neither the members nor the directors (in breach of their obligations) take any action, then on expiry of the transition period, the company will be deemed to have a one-document constitution comprising its existing memorandum and articles (except certain clauses) (2014 Act, s 61).

For most companies, the optimal course of action will be for the directors to discuss the options with members and either proactively 'opt in' under (a) above, or 'opt out'. Otherwise, should the members do nothing, the directors will be obliged to amend the company's constitutional documents, and risk having members complain that such exercise has adversely affected their rights.

2.4.4.1 Adoption of constitution by resolution of the members

The simplest way for an existing private company to convert to an LTD is that the members pass a special resolution to adopt a new constitution in substitution of the existing memorandum and articles of association.

The new constitution must be in the prescribed form, as referred to in s 19 of the 2014 Act (see **1.3.1**).

Although many of the provisions currently contained in a company's articles of association will now apply as statutory defaults unless the constitution otherwise provides, companies would be well advised to review their articles of association and ensure that tailored provisions, such as those dealing with pre-emption on transfer, are reflected in the new constitution. Upon delivery of the new constitution so passed to the CRO, the company will become an LTD, a new certificate of incorporation will be issued, and Parts 1 to 15 of the 2014 Act will apply to it.

2.4.4.2 Adoption of constitution by the directors

Unless the shareholders have adopted a new constitution, or the company is going to re-register as a DAC or other type of company – whether by choice, pursuant to a court order under s 57 of the 2014 Act requiring that it re-register as a DAC, pursuant to notice in writing under s 56 of the 2014 Act requiring that it so re-register, or because the company has debt securities admitted to trading or listed on a regulated market – the directors of an existing private company have an obligation, before the expiry of the transition period, to prepare a constitution for the company, deliver a copy to each member, and deliver a copy of it to the CRO (2014 Act, s 60).

The 2014 Act prescribes the information to be included in such a constitution, stating that the provisions of that constitution must consist solely of the company's existing memorandum of association, excluding its objects clause and any clause that prohibits the alteration of the memorandum and articles of association, and its articles of association.

The risk is that the members may claim that the directors have failed to carry out this exercise correctly, causing their rights to have been adversely affected. In addition, any references in the existing memorandum and articles to the Companies Acts 1963–2013 will carry over into the new constitution so adopted and give it an anachronistic appearance.

2.4.4.3 Company deemed to have adopted constitution

Where neither the members, nor the directors (in breach of their obligations) take any action (whether to adopt a new constitution or to opt out by re-registering as a DAC or some other type of company), the 2014 Act also sets out a default provision. In such an event, upon the expiry of the transition period, the existing private company shall be deemed to have, instead of its existing memorandum and articles of association, a one-document constitution comprised of its existing memorandum of association (excluding its objects clause and any clause that prohibits the alteration of any provision of its memorandum and articles of association) and its existing articles of association (2014 Act, s 55). It will also be deemed to have become a new LTD to which Parts 1 to 15 of the 2014 Act apply and the CRO will issue it with a new certificate of incorporation, attesting to its status as such.

While it might seem attractive just to wait for the default to apply, there are a number of disadvantages to taking such an approach. Firstly, the result will be that the company's publicly available constitutional documents will on their face include provisions – such as the objects clause – which will be deemed no longer to apply to it. In addition, to the extent that the company has previously adopted any model regulations from the First Schedule to the Companies Act 1963, such provisions will only apply to the extent that they are not inconsistent with any mandatory provision of the 2014 Act, and the deemed constitution is likely to refer to provisions of the previous Companies Acts which will have been repealed by the 2014 Act. Finally, as so many of the regulations currently found in the First Schedule to the Companies Act 1963 (and either adopted by reference or restated in the current articles of association of many private companies) are included in the 2014 Act and will apply unless a company's constitution provides otherwise, there are likely to be many unnecessary provisions in the resulting deemed constitution. In all of the above respects, this will result in a lack of clarity for users of those constitutional documents.

2.4.5   RE-REGISTRATION AS A DAC

Alternatively, an existing private company limited by shares may 'opt out' of the new regime and elect to become a DAC. Up to three months prior to the expiry of the transition period, there are two re-registration options:

(a)   An existing private company may re-register as a DAC by passing an ordinary resolution to that effect (2014 Act, s 56). Where the directors agree with the members that conversion to a DAC is appropriate, this approach will be the most convenient.

(b)   Alternatively, where the directors are not willing to convene a members' meeting to put such a resolution to the members, a member or one or more of its members holding more than 25% of the voting rights in the company can serve a notice in writing on the company requiring it to re-register as a DAC (2014 Act, s 56(2)).

Finally, where an existing private company does not re-register as a DAC before the end of the transition period (whether obliged to do so or not), a member or members holding at least 15% in nominal value of its issued share capital (or of any class thereof), or a creditor or creditors holding at least 15% of its debentures entitling them to object to alterations in its objects clause, may apply for a court order directing the company to re-register as a DAC, and the court shall, unless cause is shown to the contrary, make the order sought or such other order as seems just.

However the above change is effected, it will cause the company's memorandum of association to state that the company is to be a DAC (2014 Act, s 63(2)). The most obvious change that will be required is that the name of the DAC must (as set out at **2.2.2** above) end with 'designated activity company' or its Irish equivalent, or some acceptable abbreviation, save where the company is exempted under the Act from that requirement. The company must file the resolution, the new memorandum and articles of association, a declaration of compliance and the prescribed form with the CRO.

2.4.6   PROTECTING MEMBERS AND CREDITORS

Without limiting the provisions concerning minority shareholder oppression (2014 Act, s 212), if any member considers that his rights or obligations have been prejudiced by the exercise or non-exercise of any power under the Chapter dealing with conversion, or its exercise in a particular manner, by the company or its directors, the member may apply to court for an order under s 212, and the court may grant such relief to the applicant(s) as the court thinks just (2014 Act, s 62).

2.5   Re-registration

The 2014 Act sets out a simplified procedure for a company to convert from one company type to another; the provisions were previously scattered across a number of different sections of the Companies Acts 1963–2013.

The basic requirement is that every company which wishes to re-register as a different company type must file in the CRO:

(a)   a copy of a special resolution altering the company's constitution (in the case of an LTD, or memorandum and articles in the case of any other company type) so that it:

  (i)   states that the company is to be the type as which it wishes to be re-registered;

  (ii)   conforms with the requirements for the resultant company type; and

  (iii)   meets any other requirements in the circumstances;

(b)   a copy of the constitution, etc., as altered;

(c)   an application in the prescribed form signed by a director or the secretary;

(d)   a compliance statement, signed by a director or the secretary, that the re-registration conditions have been met (the contents will vary depending on the company type involved).

Once satisfied that the documentation is in order, the Registrar shall issue a certificate of incorporation on re-registration that reflects the new company type, and the law applicable to the new company type shall apply to it from the date of the certificate.

Previously, the Companies Acts 1963–2013 restricted a company from changing back and forth between limited and unlimited. That is, where a private limited company had re-registered as unlimited, it was barred from re-registering as limited; and where an unlimited company had re-registered as a private limited company, it was barred from re-registering as unlimited. The 2014 Act removes this restriction, but prevents a company from using its unlimited status to avoid filing financial statements by including specific provision in this regard.

Another key change is that whereas until now, there has been no statutory mechanism for a company limited by shares to re-register as a company limited by guarantee, or vice versa, the 2014 Act allows such re-registration, provided that the necessary conditions are met.

CHAPTER 3

OFFICERS OF A COMPANY

3.1   Introduction

The officers of a company are essentially its directors, secretary, and auditors. This chapter will primarily deal with the roles, functions, duties, and responsibilities of the directors and the company secretary of a private company limited by shares. Any reference in this chapter to a company is a reference to the new model private company limited by shares as governed by Volume 1 of the Companies Act 2014 (the '2014 Act') unless stated otherwise.

In considering the officers of a company it is important to have regard to the wider area of corporate governance which essentially deals with:-

(a)   the composition, functions, powers, and authorities of the various stakeholders within a company such as the board of directors, company secretary, shareholders, and internal and external auditors;

(b)   the relationship between the various stakeholders and how this is managed;

(c)   the necessary reporting and control systems within a company to ensure proper checks and balances exist; and

(d)   that robust risk management procedures are in place.

The development of modern corporate governance arose from a variety of reports in the UK in the late-1990s which led to the Combined Code (first published in 1998). The Combined Code has been replaced with the UK Corporate Governance Code which sets out principles of good governance and provides directors with a checklist against which to assess their corporate governance standing. Companies which are listed and traded on the Irish Stock Exchange must either comply with this code or explain why they have not done so. In the case of public bodies, they are subject to the Code of Practice for the Governance of State Bodies.

It is clear that in recent years there have been significant failures in corporate governance at all levels, including in public bodies, banks, and some public and private companies. This has occurred despite increased regulatory requirements and a focus in company law on compliance and enforcement since the early part of the millennium, including the establishment of the Office of the Director of Corporate Enforcement (the 'ODCE') in 2001. Companies need to learn the lessons of the recent past and consider how to improve their corporate governance processes, and this is where a solicitor can add significant value.

Any organisation looking at corporate governance should consider not just the legal and regulatory requirements that apply to it but also its own requirements as an organisation and what level of corporate governance is appropriate to it. The advantages of good corporate governance include:

(a)   that a business is run properly and more efficiently and effectively;

(b) there is improved corporate performance;

(c) there is a clear reporting structure and division of responsibilities;

(d) potential risk factors are identified and addressed at an early stage; and

(e) there is improved transparency and accountability.

While there may be a cost in putting these processes in place, it should be possible to demonstrate that the advantages outweigh the costs. It is also important to recognize that corporate governance procedures need to be reviewed frequently so as to accommodate changes in legal and regulatory requirements as well as changes in the structure and business of the organisation itself.

The role of corporate governance is increasingly important now that the 2014 Act has introduced some important new duties and requirements on company directors (including in larger private companies and public limited companies the requirement for a public directors' compliance statement).

Part 4 of the 2014 Act specifically deals with corporate governance and has codified the various directors' duties, which were previously to be found through a myriad of Companies Acts 1963–2013 and common law, into statute so they are now easily identifiable.

Shareholders also have an important role to play in the corporate governance processes within a company. Whilst the directors supervise and manage the business, they are, ultimately, accountable to and, along with the auditors, can be appointed and removed by the shareholders. Shareholders should, therefore, satisfy themselves that the appropriate governance structures are in place. In many smaller companies, however, this distinction is artificial given that the directors and the shareholders are often one and the same.

The most important officers of a company are the directors. This chapter therefore focuses on the directors, their duties and responsibilities and also that of the company secretary. The relationships of the directors with other stakeholders within a company and their rights and responsibilities will also be examined. The auditor is also an officer of the company and the role of the auditor and the area of audit and accounts is dealt with in **chapter 7, 'Financial Statements'**.

3.2 Key Legislation

It is important that the various officers within a company should understand their role and be aware of and discharge their duties and obligations. There are a number of different roles and responsibilities among the officers of a private company that need to be considered and understood. Not all of these roles will be relevant to smaller private companies.

There are also some important provisions in the 2014 Act which should be noted:

(a) s 223 of the 2014 Act imposes an overall duty on each director to ensure that the requirements of the 2014 Act are complied with by a company;

(b) s 225 of the 2014 Act requires directors of public companies and larger private companies to provide a public statement acknowledging that they are responsible for compliance with 'relevant obligations' being certain aspects of company law and tax law and market abuse and prospectus law and setting out a compliance policy statement. Such a statement can only be given if effective corporate governance procedures are in place; and

(c) ss 223 to 235 of the 2014 Act set out the general duties of directors and secretaries and their liability and that of other officers.

3.3   Types of Director

3.3.1   EXECUTIVE DIRECTOR/NON-EXECUTIVE DIRECTOR

No reference is made within the Act to 'executive' or 'non-executive' directors and, in fact, this distinction is one which has arisen in practice and in corporate governance procedures. Essentially, executive directors are directors who have an executive responsibility within the company. Such persons participate in the day-to-day management of the company and are usually employed by the company on a full-time basis and are in receipt of a salary. As an executive director holds this dual role in the company (director and employee), his/her removal from the company will necessarily involve removal from both positions. In this regard, it is important to ensure that this dual removal is done and that all applicable procedures are duly followed and naturally the director will have employment law rights in relation to their executive position as an employee of the company.

On the other hand, non-executive directors are those who are not involved in the day-to-day running of the company. Such persons are not employed in the business and do not report to the CEO/Managing Director. Essentially, their role is one which is confined to the boardroom. Notwithstanding this, their input into the board decision-making process is invaluable, given their expected impartiality, objectivity, and independence. Their role includes contributions in the development of strategy and monitoring management performance and activity. There is no legal obligation for private companies to appoint such directors and many smaller companies would not do so. All companies can, however, benefit from the involvement of such directors. Whether a person is an executive or non-executive director, he/she has the same powers to manage the business of the company. Such directors also have the same legal duties and responsibilities to the company as the executive directors.

3.3.2   NOMINEE DIRECTOR

A nominee director is a person who is appointed to the board by a shareholder or a particular group of shareholders with a view to representing and safeguarding their interests within the company. Notwithstanding their brief, such nominee directors must, nonetheless, act in the best interests of the company. Nominee directors have the same duties and responsibilities as the other directors; however, this provision was amended in the 2014 Act by s 228 referred to below whereby nominee directors can have regard to the interests of the shareholder which appointed them pursuant to the company's constitution or a shareholders' agreement.

3.3.3   ALTERNATE DIRECTOR

An alternate director is a person who is appointed to act in place of a director when that person is unable to act. Section 165 of the 2014 Act allows for the appointment of such a person by notice in writing to the company. It should be noted that an alternate director does not hold office in his/her own right. His/her appointment as alternate director will only last as long as he/she is appointed or as his/her appointer is a director (whichever the earlier). An alternate director has the same responsibilities and duties as the director appointing him/her.

3.3.4   SHADOW DIRECTOR

A shadow director is a person who is not formally appointed as a director but who, nonetheless, is deemed to be a director and in certain circumstances may have provisions of the Companies Acts applied to him/her as if formally appointed as a director. Shadow directors are provided for in s 221 of the 2014 Act. A shadow director is defined as 'a person in accordance with whose directions or instructions the directors are accustomed to act' (s 221 (1) 2014 Act). It should be noted, however, that there is an exemption for persons like solicitors who provide advice in a professional capacity to directors.

3.3.5   DE FACTO DIRECTOR

A de facto director is a person who occupies the position of and acts and is 'held out' as if he/she was a director when in fact that person was either not validly or, indeed, ever actually appointed. This person will, nonetheless, be deemed to be a director and have the provisions of the 2014 Acts applied to him/her as if properly appointed as a director (2014 Act, s 222).

3.4   Directors' Powers

The power of management of a company is delegated to directors by virtue of s 158 of the 2014 Act which provides that the business of a company 'shall be managed by its directors...who may exercise all powers of the Company as are not, by the Act or by its constitution, required to be exercised in general meeting'. This will be subject to:

(a)   any regulations contained in the company's constitution;

(b)   the provisions of the 2014 Act; and

(c)   such directions, not being inconsistent with the foregoing regulations or provisions as the company in general meeting may (by special resolution) give.

This provision is broadly similar to the old reg 80 of Part I of Table A to the Companies Act 1963 which delegated powers of management to directors. The directors' powers may be usurped by a court-appointed examiner by way of application to the court. The general rule is that powers given exclusively to directors in the constitution may not be altered by the members in general meeting unless there is a specific provision in the constitution allowing members to do so. However, the power to dismiss directors may not be taken away from the members by any provision in the constitution (2014 Act, s 146). The powers granted to directors enable them to conduct and manage the day-to-day business of the company under s 158 would include such powers as borrowing money, using the company seal, recruiting employees, and entering into contracts. The directors may also delegate that authority to any of their number or to employees or other persons but the board of directors retains responsibility and supervision. Directors generally speaking do not have an authority to act individually unless authorised by the board of directors or registered as a person authorised to bind the company under s 39 of the 2014 Act.

3.4.1   DELEGATION OF POWERS BY DIRECTORS

3.4.1.1   Chairperson

The board may appoint a chairperson. Many smaller private companies, will, however, not have a person acting in this capacity. This person is essentially head of the board and is responsible for managing both directors' and members' meetings. In the context of the board, the chairperson is responsible for leadership of the board, regulating the proceedings of the board meetings, and setting the board agenda. The chairperson should ensure that the directors receive accurate, timely, and clear information and, in the context of meetings, should ensure constructive relations between and, as far as possible, effective contributions from all directors. It is also usual that the chairperson would have a second or a casting vote at board meetings.

3.4.1.2   CEO/Managing Director

Essentially the terms 'CEO' and 'Managing Director' can be used interchangeably in the sense that this is the person who is responsible for the day-to-day running of a company's business, under delegation from the board. The CEO/Managing Director is also responsible for implementing the board's policies and strategies. No reference to the term 'CEO' is made in the 2014 Act but, instead s 159 of the 2014 Act allows for the directors to appoint one of their number to the office of managing director (*by whatever name called*), to whom powers of management of the company's business may be delegated. Accordingly, where the term 'CEO' is preferred to that of 'Managing Director', references in s 159 would be to the CEO. The duties, powers, and remuneration of the Managing Director/CEO are not fixed by law but are set out by the board. The Managing Director/CEO is both an officer and employee of the company. In many organisations which have a chairperson and a CEO, the same person might carry out both functions. Good corporate governance would, however, see both roles carried out separately to ensure that no one person has unfettered powers of decision-making within an organisation.

3.4.1.3   Board Audit Committee

The Board Audit Committee is a committee of the board which links the board with the company's auditors independently of the company's management which is responsible for the accounting system. The role of the Board Audit Committee includes monitoring the integrity of the financial statements and reviewing the company's internal financial control systems and risk management systems. This Board Audit Committee also monitors and reviews the effectiveness of the company's internal audit function and discusses the scope and results of the audit, in addition to overseeing the relationship with the external auditors. The Board Audit Committee should ensure the integrity of the audit process. In private companies, it would be unusual to have a Board Audit Committee. However, under s 167 of the 2014 Act, directors of large private companies limited by shares (those which have a balance sheet total of over €25,000,000 and turnover of greater than €50,000,000) will be required (when the provision is in force) to either establish an Audit Committee on the basis set out in that legislation or explain in the annual report why such a committee has not been established. Section 167 requires at least one independent non-executive director who has an accountancy competency to be on the Board Audit Committee.

3.4.1.4   Board Remuneration Committee

The Board Remuneration Committee is the committee which decides on remuneration of the executive directors. Every company which has a proper corporate governance procedure in place should have a remuneration committee which should consist of non-executive directors and which will decide on the remuneration package of the executive directors. The remuneration structures of senior executives in both public and private organisations has been a source of controversy in recent years and the executive directors should not be deciding on their own pay and benefits packages and the purpose of the Board Remuneration Committee is so that there is independent decision-making on this issue. The matters which the Board Remuneration Committee will consider will include pay of senior executives, pension entitlements, awards of share options, and bonuses. A Remuneration Committee will have to take account of norms within the sector in which the company operates as well as market data and the contribution and performance of individual executives in deciding to make awards of remuneration.

3.4.1.5   Internal Audit Function

The Internal Audit Function is part of the management control systems in a company. Its purpose is to provide independent objective assurance. In this regard, its function is to examine, evaluate, and report on the adequacy of the internal controls which are established to prevent the impacts of risks which threaten a company's strategy and business objectives. Given its remit, the Internal Audit Function should be provided with unrestricted access within a company's operation. In some situations, companies which do not have the resources to establish an Internal Audit Function outsource this function. There is no requirement to have an Internal Audit Function and many small private companies will not have one.

3.5   General Provisions Relating to Directors

3.5.1   QUALIFICATION OF DIRECTORS

A private company limited by shares must have at least one director. Other types of companies such as the designated activity company and public limited companies must have at least two directors.

A body corporate or an unincorporated body of persons may not be a director, unlike in the United Kingdom where it is possible to have corporate directors.

Persons under 18 years of age may not be appointed as directors or secretary of a company.

An Irish company must have at least one EEA resident director. This will not apply if the company holds a bond in the prescribed form (see **chapter 1, 'Company Incorporation'** at **1.3.3**).

The court may disqualify persons from acting or being appointed as, inter alia, directors, auditors, or managers for a five-year period, or such other period as the court may order, if they are convicted of any indictable offence in relation to a company or an offence involving fraud or dishonesty or their conduct makes them unfit to be involved in managing a company. Directors may also voluntarily elect to become disqualified.

In addition, undischarged bankrupts cannot become company directors or secretaries and the Director of Corporate Enforcement has powers under s 133 of the Act to enquire into the solvency status of a director if the Director of Corporate Enforcement has reason to believe that a director or secretary is an undischarged bankrupt.

3.5.2   APPOINTMENT OF DIRECTORS

The first directors of a company shall be those persons determined in writing by the subscribers of the company's constitution or a majority of them. Save to the extent that the company's constitution provides otherwise, any subsequent directors of the company must be appointed in the manner set out in s 144 of the 2014 Act and will usually be appointed by members or by the existing directors either to fill a casual vacancy or as an addition to the existing directors. Any purported appointment of a director without the consent of that director shall be void.

The company must keep a register of directors and secretaries under s 149 of the 2014 Act and must notify the Registrar of Companies of all changes (Form B10). The company constitution may prescribe a maximum number of directors. There is no statutory maximum. The constitution of the company may also require directors to hold qualification shares but the 2014 Act does not require a shareholding qualification. If the constitution does contain a share qualification then the director shall vacate office if he or she does not obtain the necessary share qualification within two months (or any shorter time fixed by the constitution) or ceases to hold the required qualification. A director who has vacated office for not holding a share qualification cannot be re-appointed until they hold the necessary share qualification.

A person cannot at any time be a director of more than 25 private companies limited by shares or 25 companies one or more than one of which is a private company limited by shares and one or more than one of which is a company capable of being wound up under the 2014 Act. Public limited companies and companies that have a certificate confirming they have 'a real and continuous link with economic activity in the State' (see **chapter 1, 'Company Incorporation'** at **1.3.3**) will be counted as one company as will companies within a group of companies. Certain regulated companies such as those which are the holder of a licence as a financial institution can also not be counted towards the 25 directorship limit.

3.5.3   VACATION OF OFFICE

The circumstances in which a director can be deemed to have vacated office are set out in s 148 of the 2014 Act (save where the constitution provides otherwise) and includes resignation, vacation on health grounds which result in the director being no longer capable of possessing adequate decision-making capacity, conviction for an indictable offence, and being absent for more than six months from meetings of directors held during that period without permission of directors.

3.5.4   REMOVAL OF DIRECTORS

The directors of a company may be removed by an ordinary resolution of the company in general meeting (2014 Act, s 146). Unless the directors are directors of a private company holding office for life, this provision may not be altered by the constitution or any agreement between the company and the director. At least 28 days' notice must be given of a resolution proposing to remove a director and a director must have an opportunity to make representations at the meeting and must receive a copy of the notice of the resolution. The director whose removal is being sought is allowed to make representations in writing to the company (not exceeding a reasonable length) upon receipt of the notice of the resolution and such representations must be provided to the members.

Removal under this provision of the 2014 Act does not deprive the director concerned of right to damages etc., irrespective of any claim under employment protection legislation.

The constitution adopted by a company may include a special article facilitating the removal of a director. This would apply for instance in the case of a subsidiary company, where the holding company may be entitled to appoint or remove a director by notice in writing to the secretary or by leaving notice at the registered office.

The constitution may be modified to confer loaded voting rights on a director where it is proposed to pass a resolution to dismiss him, thus enabling the director to remain in office (*Bushell v Faith* [1970] AC 1099).

3.5.5   REGISTER OF DIRECTORS AND SECRETARIES

Section 149 of the 2014 Act provides that a company must keep a register of its directors and secretaries and, if any, its assistant and deputy secretaries. Full details on the information to be kept in the register are set out in that section; it should be noted that details of other directorships of the director during the preceding five years must be included. Any changes must be notified to the Registrar of Companies on the Form B10.

3.6   Controls on Directors

To prevent them from abusing their position, directors are subject to a considerable number of corporate governance controls largely set out in Part 5 of the 2014 Act.

3.6.1   REMUNERATION

The remuneration of directors of a company shall be determined by the directors and the remuneration shall be deemed to accrue from day to day and travelling, hotels, and other expenses may be paid to them (2014 Act, s 155). There are also provisions in s 156 of the 2014 Act to prevent tax-free payments to directors.

3.6.2 DIRECTORS' SERVICE CONTRACTS

Section 154 of the 2014 Act requires that a company must keep at either its registered office, the place where its register of members is kept if other than its registered office, or its principal place of business:

(a) in the case of each director whose contract of service is in writing, a copy of that contract;

(b) in the case of each director whose contract of service with the company is not in writing, a written memorandum setting out the terms of that contract;

(c) in the case of each director who is employed under a contract of service with a subsidiary of the company, a copy of that contract or, if that is not in writing, a written memorandum setting out the terms of that contract; and

(d) a copy or written memorandum, as the case may be, of any variation of any contract of service referred to in sub-paragraphs (a), (b), and (c) above. Members of the company may inspect such documents during normal business hours. Breach of these provisions is a category 3 offence.

These requirements do not apply to the unexpired portion of the term of the service contract if that is less than three years, or where the company may, within the next three years, terminate the contract without payment of compensation.

3.6.3 DIRECTORS' AND SECRETARIES' INTERESTS

Companies must maintain a separate register of the interests of directors, their spouses, and minor children and of 'connected persons', in the company's shares.

Chapter 5 of Part 5 of the 2014 Act deals with disclosure of directors' and secretaries' interest in shares and replaces Part V of the Companies Act 1990. Any person who is a director or secretary and is aware of having an interest themselves or their spouse, civil partner, or child having a disclosable interest in shares in a company or another company which is a member of the same group must notify the company of that disclosable interest.

A duty to notify the company arises if a director or secretary of the company (or that person's spouse, civil partner, or child):

(a) holds shares or debentures in such company or any other company within its group at the date of commencement of the Act and that interest was not previously notified under Part V of the Companies Act 1990 (must be notified within eight days);

(b) has acquired or ceased to hold shares or debentures in the relevant company or member of the group (must be notified within 30 days if by way of transfer otherwise within eight days);

(c) is an existing holder of shares or debentures and subsequently becomes an officer (must be notified within eight days);

(d) is granted by another group company a right to subscribe for shares or debentures in that group company (must be notified within eight days);

(e) is granted by another body corporate of the same group a right to subscribe for shares or debentures in that other body corporate or exercises such a right (must be notified within five days); and/or

(f) assigns or enters into a contract to sell shares or debentures or another group company (must be notified within five days).

The disclosure obligations do not apply to shares in companies which are subsidiaries of other companies or to a director or secretary who receives a share option.

In addition, the disclosure obligations do not apply where the rights arise due to the director being appointed as an attorney or proxy for some other person who has an interest in the shares or debentures or interests of less than 1% (this exception does not apply to public limited companies).

Very importantly if there is a failure to make these notifications within the relevant time frames no right or interest in the shares or debentures will be enforceable by the director or secretary concerned. There are, however, some exceptions:

(a)   There is a right to apply to court for relief if the failure was inadvertent or on just an equitable grounds.

(b)   If the details are entered on the statutory register within 30 days.

(c)   A resolution can be passed in general meeting that (i) the notification provisions have been complied with in relation to the relevant shares or debentures and (ii) the registered holder is entitled to deal with the shares or debentures registered in his or her name. A third party may rely on such a resolution.

(d)   Very usefully, if there was a failure to notify under the old provisions of the 1990 Companies Act, the board of directors can within 18 months of the commencement of the Companies Act resolve that any default in complying with s 53 of the 1990 Act shall cease to operate if the officer concerned presents evidence to the board and the board is satisfied that the default concerned was inadvertent.

3.7   Directors' Duties

Directors are key within the corporate governance structure and need to ensure that they are aware of, and are fulfilling, their responsibilities. In this regard, directors owe a wide range of duties to their company. These duties are to be found both in statute (including company law, health and safety, and environmental legislation, etc.) and common law, arising from the fiduciary position of directors. Importantly, the key directors' duties at company law have now been codified so that they are all set out in Part 5 of the 2014 Act; however, case law and common law principles are still of relevance to directors' duties. Very important provisions are s 223, which provides for the overall duty of each director to comply with the 2014 Act, and s 228, which sets out the principal fiduciary duties of directors. Whilst the general rule is that these duties are only owed to the company, case law has seen this modified in certain situations (e.g. directors owing a duty to a company's creditors when a company is insolvent). Section 224 of the 2014 Act provides that directors can have regard to the interests of the company's employees in general as well as the interest of its members.

The case of *Re City Equitable Fire Insurance Co Ltd* [1925] Ch 407 is the leading case on directors' duties in the context of negligence. It held that the standard of care appropriate to a director is a subjective standard. There will, consequently, be a higher expectation of directors with professional qualifications.

It is important that as potential directors or as legal advisers to directors, solicitors are aware of and can advise on directors' duties. This is a separate topic in itself and there are plenty of materials available on this subject.

Along with the myriad of directors' duties, also comes the possibility of directors' liabilities. Today, more than ever, there is a big demand for directors' and officers' insurance (known as D&O insurance). As its name suggests, this is an insurance policy normally taken out by companies for the benefit of their directors and officers which insures them in respect of their potential liabilities as directors and officers. The policy may also reimburse the companies themselves to the extent that they have lawfully indemnified the directors and officers. These policies are expressly permitted by s 235 of the 2014 Act.

The key new statutory duties in the 2014 Act to be cognisant of are set out below.

3.7.1   COMPLIANCE WITH THE 2014 ACT

Under s 223 of the 2014 Act each director has a duty to ensure that the 2014 Act is complied with. Breach of this duty shall not affect the enforceability of contracts.

3.7.2   DIRECTORS' COMPLIANCE STATEMENTS

Section 225 of the 2014 Act sets out the obligations on directors to give a public compliance statement. The obligation to prepare this statement applies to private companies where both the balance sheet total is greater than €12,500,000 and the turnover is greater than €25,000,000. Directors' compliance statements are dealt with in more detail in **chapter 7, 'Financial Statements'**.

3.7.3   NATURE OF DIRECTORS' DUTIES

Section 227 of the 2014 Act sets out that directors' duties are fiduciary duties and, subject to certain other provisions in the 2014 Act, are owed to the company and the company alone. A breach of duty does not of itself affect the validity of any contract or other transaction or the enforceability (other than with respect to proceedings being brought against the director in breach) of a contract or other transaction.

3.7.4   PRINCIPAL FIDUCIARY DUTIES

Section 228 of the 2014 Act sets out a statement of the principal fiduciary duties of directors which shall have effect (except for (b) and (h) below) in place of common law rules and principles, however, they shall be applied in the same way as common law rules and principles and regard shall be had to common law rules and equitable principles. This means that the case law on these duties will still be relevant. Under s 228 a director shall:

(a)   act in good faith in what the director considers to be the interests of the company;

(b)   act honestly and responsibly in relation to the conduct of the affairs of the company;

(c)   act in accordance with the company's constitution and exercise his or her powers only for the purposes allowed by law;

(d)   not use company property, information, or opportunities for his or her own or anyone else's benefit unless expressly permitted by the constitution or the use has been approved by a resolution of the company in general meeting;

(e)   not to agree to restrict to exercise the directors' power of independent judgement unless expressly permitted by the company's constitution, the director considers in good faith that it is in the interests of the company for a particular transaction or engagement to be entered into and carried into effect, or the directors agreeing to such has been approved by shareholders in general meeting;

(f)   to avoid any conflict between the directors' duties to the company and the directors' other (including personal) interests unless the director is released from his or her duty to the company in relation to the matter concerned by its constitution or a shareholders resolution in general meeting;

(g)   to exercise the care, skill, and diligence which would be exercised in the same circumstances by a reasonable person having both the knowledge and experience that may reasonably be expected of a person in the same position as the director and the knowledge and experience which the director has; and

(h)   to have regard to the interests of its members.

Duties (b) and (h) are new statutory duties and are not traditional common law directors' duties. Directors are now also permitted to have specific regard to the interests of a member who has nominated or appointed that director under the company's constitution or a shareholders' agreement.

3.7.5   OTHER INTERESTS

Section 229 of the 2014 Act confirms that a director of a company may be or become a director or other officer of or otherwise interested in any company promoted by the company or in which the company may be interested as shareholder or otherwise and shall not be accountable to the company for remuneration or other benefits received unless the company otherwise directs.

3.7.6   PROFESSIONAL CAPACITY

Under s 230 of the 2014 Act a director may act in a professional capacity for a company and shall be entitled to remuneration for professional services as if they are not a director. A director cannot be a statutory auditor.

3.7.7   DISCLOSURE OF INTERESTS

Section 231 of the 2014 Act obliges directors to disclose to the company interests that they directly or indirectly have in a contract with the company and to declare their interest at a meeting of the directors of the company. It is now provided that such disclosure is not required if the interest cannot reasonably be regarded as likely to give rise to a conflict of interest. Any such interests declared must be kept in a book kept for that purpose by the company which must be made available to the Director of Corporate Enforcement upon request.

3.7.8   COMPANY SECRETARY

The directors have a duty to ensure that the person they appoint as secretary has the skills necessary to enable him or her to maintain (or procure the maintenance) of non-financial records. Secretaries will have to consent and acknowledge their legal duties (2014 Act, s 226). In addition, under s 129 (4) of the 2014 Act the directors have a duty to ensure that the person appointed has the skills necessary to discharge his or her statutory and other legal duties and such other duties as may be delegated to the secretary by the directors.

3.7.9   RELEVANT AUDIT INFORMATION

Directors have an obligation to include in their directors' report of a company, which has to prepare audited accounts, a statement to the effect that there is no relevant audit information of which the company's statutory auditors are unaware and the director has taken all the steps that he or she ought to have taken as a director in order to make himself or herself aware of any relevant audit information and to establish that the auditors are aware of that information (2014 Act, s 330). 'Relevant audit information' means information needed by the statutory auditors of the company in preparing their report.

3.7.10   BREACH OF DUTIES/OFFICERS IN DEFAULT

Where a director is in breach of the duties mentioned under (a), (c), (d), (e), (f), or (g) set out in s 228 he or she shall be liable to account to the company for any gain which he or she makes directly or indirectly from the breach of duty in question and/or indemnify the company for any loss or damage resulting from that breach (2014 Act, s 232). Directors who authorised breaches of the restrictions on loans, credit transactions, and certain other transactions between the company and its directors and connected persons can also be liable to account or to jointly and severally indemnify along with any other persons who authorised such transactions.

Section 233 of the 2014 Act allows a court to grant relief against any proceedings against a director for breach of duty if the court is satisfied that the director acted honestly and reasonably and that having regard to the circumstances of the case (including those connected with their appointment) he or she ought fairly to be excused for the wrong concerned.

In any legal proceedings it shall be presumed that officers permitted a default if it is proved that they were aware of the basic facts concerning the default concerned unless they can show that they took all reasonable steps to prevent it or that by reason of circumstances beyond their control they were unable to do so (2014 Act, s 271). This provision was amended as the 2014 Act progressed through the legislative process to provide that proof of basic awareness is required to be deemed to be permitting a default. This provision applies to all officers not just directors.

Section 235 of the 2014 Act prevents a company entering into any arrangement with its officers to exempt them from liability and provides that such an indemnity will be void. An indemnity can be given for any criminal proceedings in which the director is acquitted or proceedings in which relief is granted to the director by the court and s 235 will allow a company to purchase D&O insurance.

3.8   Company Secretary

In advance of considering the duties and responsibilities of the company secretary, a few general points should be noted. Every company must have a company secretary who may be one of the directors but where the company has one director that person may not also be the secretary (2014 Act, s 129). Unlike a director, a body corporate can be a company secretary and, indeed, it is not uncommon for accounting and solicitors' practices to carry out company secretarial services. Whilst a director can act, and in the case of smaller private companies often acts, as the company secretary, s 134 of the 2014 Act should be noted. This provides that where any matter needs to be done by the director and the secretary, it cannot be done by the same person. The company secretary is appointed and removed by the directors for such term, at such remuneration, and under such conditions as the directors think fit.

The duties of the secretary (other than the legal responsibilities already provided in the 2014 Act) are those as are delegated by the board from time to time (2014 Act, s 226 (1)). Unlike a public company, there are no formal requirements to be eligible to be a company secretary of a private company. This will not, however, take away from the duties and responsibilities which a company secretary owes. As noted above in **3.7.8** directors have a duty, when appointing a secretary, to ensure that the person appointed has the skills necessary to discharge his or her statutory and other legal duties and such other duties as may be delegated to the secretary by the directors (s 129 (4) of the Act) and a duty to ensure that the person appointed as secretary has the skills necessary so as to enable him or her to maintain (or procure the maintenance of) the records (other than accounting records) which have to be kept under the Act. When appointing a secretary, directors will need to consider carefully whether the person or entity involved has the necessary skills and minute their deliberations.

Notwithstanding that the function of the company secretary is administrative as opposed to managerial, the company secretary in reality will have extensive duties and responsibilities. A company secretary is the principal legal administrative and compliance officer within a company. Ex officio, the company secretary has no decision-making functions.

Accordingly, whilst a company secretary may commonly attend board meetings, he/she cannot take part in the decision-making process. Companies legislation, unfortunately, does not expressly set out the duties of the company secretary. Instead, these are stated only obliquely in company law. Few tasks are, however, the sole responsibility of the company secretary. Most tasks are to be performed by the company secretary and a director.

Many provisions in the 2014 Act which criminalise default by a company further provide that any officer of the company (which would include the company secretary) who is in 'default' will also be so liable (see **3.7.10**).

The duty in s 223 of the 2014 Act to ensure that the Act is complied with does not apply to company secretaries; the equivalent duty under the previous Companies Acts 1963–2013 did apply to the secretary.

Given the importance of the role of the company secretary, we set out in some detail the extent of the duties and responsibilities which it is usual for a company secretary to undertake. The ICSA (the Institute of Chartered Secretaries and Administrators) sees the role of the company secretary as providing advice and guidance to directors as to their obligations and responsibilities under the company's own constitution (the memorandum and articles of association), under company law, and corporate governance guidelines. The company secretary will have a large degree of involvement in both board and shareholder meetings. In this regard, the company secretary will usually convene these meetings and circulate relevant papers, will keep minutes of meetings, and will ensure that procedures are followed and applicable rules and regulations complied with at such meetings. The company secretary is particularly relevant in the context of board meetings. The company secretary will be responsible for preparing agendas for meetings and ensuring the timely circulation of information to directors. The company secretary is often the point of contact for management to feed through proposals to the board. Following the outcome of a board deliberation, the company secretary is also often responsible for communicating such outcome throughout the company. The company secretary should be responsible for organising inductions for new directors and future training for all directors, where necessary. In addition, the company secretary should provide advice or provide access to advice for the directors. The company secretary will normally maintain the statutory registers and minute book and will ensure completion and timely filing of forms in the Companies Registration Office (the 'CRO'), in addition to having custody and control over the use of the seal. The company secretary will, in carrying out his/her responsibilities, owe a duty of skill, care, and diligence, in addition to a duty of fidelity and confidence. Both the ODCE and the CRO set out useful publications on the duties of the company secretary which are available from their websites.

3.9   Risk Management

3.9.1   INTRODUCTION

Risk management is becoming an increasingly important part of good corporate governance procedures.

Many solicitors' firms will have had to review their risk management procedures in recent years to satisfy their insurers and to minimise the risk of future claims. It is something that is being addressed in other industries as well.

The economy and the business environment have become increasingly uncertain. Uncertainty increases business risk. Uncertainties can include risks of liability as a result of defective products or negligence in the provision of services, loss of customers, loss of key suppliers, negative publicity, regulatory action, strikes, employee claims, cashflow issues and lack of capital, pension underfunding, and potential tax liabilities.

Risk management is essentially the identification, assessment, and management of risk exposures to allow uncertain events to be managed and protect the directors and management in the event of a risk exposure or claim arising by enabling them to demonstrate that appropriate procedures were in place.

3.9.2   WHAT TYPES OF COMPANIES SHOULD BE CONCERNED ABOUT RISK MANAGEMENT?

Arguably all companies and businesses should be addressing risk management. However, clearly the risk in a small proprietor-owned business where the proprietor is involved in decision-making and processes will be quite different from the procedures necessary in a larger organisation. It can be of particular relevance to growing companies where the initial proprietors or founders wish to involve a wider group of managers in decision-making and need to ensure that decision-making within the organisation is sustainable and controlled.

There will always be a conflict between ensuring effective risk management and making sure the business does not become too inflexible through too many procedures which prevent effective decision-making, and this can be a problem in larger organisations.

3.9.3   DEVELOPING A RISK MANAGEMENT SYSTEM

A risk management system is not a one-size-fits-all analysis and will have to be tailored to the particular business or organisation involved in the same way as overall corporate governance procedures have to be. Some of the issues that need to be looked at in developing a risk management system are as follows:

(a)   the nature of the business and activities of the business;

(b)   the outlook for the industry or sector in which the business operates;

(c)   what changes in the nature of a business are likely to arise from changing market conditions;

(d)   what are the most material legal and regulatory obligations to which the business is subject and what are the consequences of breach of these obligations;

(e)   what are the threats, uncertainties, and opportunities that impact on the future value of the business;

(f)   an analysis of the management and reporting structures within the business;

(g)   an analysis of training within the business and existing procedures to ensure compliance and prevent risk; and

(h)   how much auditing – both internal and external – of procedures is required.

Objective and transparent goals as part of a risk management process should be set and appropriate expert advisers should be engaged.

Risk management is about looking into the future and identifying the factors that could impact on a business achieving its goals and which could result in lack of legal or regulatory compliance, potential liability, or negative PR and then putting in place processes to minimise those risk factors.

There will also need to be a materiality analysis. It would not be possible or feasible to put in place procedures to guard against every risk or potential breach, no matter how minor, so the consequences of a breach or a risk factor arising need to be analysed. If, for example, the consequence of a particular breach is that the business will lose a regulatory authorisation or will result in such negative PR that there will be a significant loss of customers, then more robust procedures will be required to prevent such a breach than will be required for a more minor breach or one with less consequence.

3.9.4   INCREASING IMPORTANCE OF RISK MANAGEMENT

There is no doubt that the 2014 Act has increased regulation and enforcement and there is an enhanced obligation on directors to take responsibility for compliance with legal, regulatory, and taxation matters (as is evidenced by the directors' compliance statement which is required for larger private companies and PLCs). These obligations are likely to increase into the future and coupled with business uncertainty and a litigious culture, means that no properly managed business can afford to ignore risk management and must ensure that the necessary procedures are in place.

CHAPTER 4

COMPANY DECISION-MAKING

4.1   Roles and Responsibilities

The division of decision-making powers and responsibilities between the members and directors of any company type is essentially the same. This chapter however focuses on the division of roles and responsibilities in a private company limited by shares as governed by Volume 1 of the Companies Act 2014 (the '2014 Act'). Any reference to a company in this chapter is therefore a reference to a private company limited by shares unless stated otherwise.

The persons who have a role in the management and affairs of a company are:

(a)   the member(s) of a company – (who are the owners);

(b)   the director(s) of a company – (who are the managers of the day-to-day business of the company);

(c)   the Managing Director(s);

(d)   the chairperson;

(e)   committees of the board of directors; and

(f)   the company secretary.

The two most significant groups involved in the running of an Irish company are its members and its directors. The same person can very often be both a member and a director, but the 2014 Act provides for, and requires, the separation of the powers and responsibilities of each role. This means that although the same person is entitled to be both a director and a member of a company, they must make certain decisions wearing their director 'hat', and others wearing their member 'hat', and record the consideration and making of those separate decision classes accordingly.

The member(s) of the company are the people/entities which have subscribed for shares in, or membership of, the company, and who own/have an interest in the company itself (it is important to be aware that the members of the company only have a contractual ownership interest in the company itself and do not own the company's assets directly).

Certain fundamental decisions, largely relating to the structure of the company, and the parameters within which the directors can manage the company, and issue its shares are reserved to the members, for example, changes to the company's constitution, or name. It is important to be aware that a company limited by shares (private and public) can issue different classes of share, each such class carrying different rights for the member holding each such class of share. This means that when reviewing the rights of a particular member it is always necessary to review the constitution of the company in question (and any shareholders' agreement entered into between the members) to confirm the actual rights enjoyed by each such member, as a member of the company in question.

Under s 158 (1) of the 2014 Act, the day-to-day management of a company is delegated to the directors who may exercise all such powers of the company save for those powers reserved for the members by the 2014 Act or by the company's constitution. The powers of directors which are conferred by the provisions of the 2014 Act are subject to amendment (where permissible) by the company's constitution and by the members specifically directing otherwise (either by special resolution or by provision in a shareholders' agreement to which the company is a party).

Section 158 (2) of the 2014 Act, however, provides that no direction given by the members shall invalidate the prior act of the directors, if such act was valid prior to that direction from the members.

Directors' powers are exercisable collectively by a board of directors. These powers can be delegated by the board to a registered person or individual/committees within the company. Further information about the delegation of directors powers can be found at **4.3.1**.

The ability of members to remove and appoint the directors is the principal power which the members have to influence the day-to-day operation and management of the company (see below).

The Decision-making Process

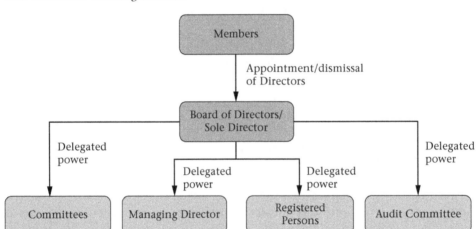

4.2   Decisions Reserved For Members

The 2014 Act sets out a number of decisions which are reserved for the members of the company. The rationale for holding back certain matters from directors for decision by the members reflects the fact that the members are the 'owners' of the company, and that certain fundamental decisions regarding the form and activities of the company should indeed be reserved for decision by those owners.

Decisions reserved for Members include, by way of example, the decision to:

(a)   amend the company's constitution (2014 Act, s 32 (1));

(b)   change the company's name (with the approval of the Registrar) (2014 Act, s 30 (1));

(c)   re-register the company as another type of company (e.g. re-registering an LTD as a DAC) (2014 Act, s 1285);

(d)   vary its share capital (2014 Act, s 83);

(e) authorise the redemption of redeemable shares by the company (2014 Act, s 108 (1));

(f) authorise the acquisition by the company of its own shares (2014 Act, s 105 (4));

(g) give directions to the directors as to the management of the company's affairs (2014 Act, s 158 (1)); and

(h) approve any of the seven restricted activities which can only be engaged in by a company with the approval of the new Summary Approval Procedure (2014 Act, ss 200–211).

Case law has established that where the members have delegated power to make certain decisions to the directors, it is not generally open to the members to challenge the decisions of the board, and where those directors act within their powers, and don't act in an 'oppressive' manner, they may take decisions which conflict with the wishes of some or all of the members. If the members are unhappy with the decisions being made by the board of directors their remedies are to resolve to amend the company's constitution (specifically reserving certain decisions for themselves), to replace the directors on the board in accordance with the provisions of the 2014 Act, or to bring an action on behalf of the company against the directors claiming that they have breached their duties as directors under s 228 of the 2014 Act. Part 5, Chapter 4 of the 2014 Act requires the directors, at s 231, to declare any interests they have in contracts etc., to the other directors. Part 4 also sets out a list of types of transaction (e.g. loans to or from the directors), which the directors can only enter into with the company where they have met the specific requirements of that Part in so doing.

4.3 Rules Governing Directors' Meetings

Part 4, Chapter 4 of the 2014 Act (ss 157 to 167 inclusive) sets out the law relating to directors' proceedings. These provisions will apply unless the specific constitution of the company in question provides otherwise (other than the provisions of s 166 dealing with minutes of directors' proceedings and s 167 on Audit Committees, which are mandatory).

Directors have flexibility to decide how they meet to manage the company's affairs. Section 160 (1) of the 2014 Act provides that the directors may 'meet together for the dispatch of business, adjourn and otherwise regulate their meetings as they think fit'.

4.3.1 THE ESTABLISHMENT OF COMMITTEES

Section 160 (9) of the 2014 Act provides that the directors may establish one or more committees consisting in whole or in part of members of the board of directors. This means that non-directors can sit on the board of a committee.

The directors can (without prejudice to s 40 of the 2014 Act which deals with the power of the board and 'registered persons' to bind a company) (collectively) delegate any of their powers to such person or persons as they think fit, including committees (2014 Act, s 158 (4)). Any committee which has been delegated powers by the board must conform to any restrictions imposed by the board on such delegated powers. This means that it is necessary to check any relevant board minutes and any document setting out the powers and remit of a committee to confirm the committee's authority in each case.

A committee may elect a chairperson of its meetings and may meet and adjourn as it thinks proper. The committee makes its decisions by majority of votes of committee members present (which means non-attending committee members are not included) and where there is an equality of votes, the chairperson shall have a second or casting vote.

Information about Board Audit and Board Remuneration Committees is provided in **chapter 3, 'Officers of a Company'** at **3.4.1.3** and **3.4.1.4** respectively.

4.3.2 THE APPOINTMENT OF A MANAGING DIRECTOR

The directors may appoint one or more of *themselves* as Managing Director(s) of the company and can confer any of the powers exercisable by them (collectively) on the Managing Director, upon such terms and with such restrictions as they think fit (2014 Act, s 159 (4)). These powers may either also be exercised concurrently by the board, or may only be exercised by the Managing Director to the exclusion of their own such powers) (the 2014 Act, s 159).

A Managing Director's appointment shall cease upon him/her ceasing to be a director of the company.

Under s 39 of the 2014 Act, where the board of directors of a company have authorised a person to generally bind the company (such as an M.D., an Attorney, or a 'registered person'), the company *may* make an appropriate filing notifying the Registrar of Companies of the fact of such general binding authorisation, where it will be publically available in the CRO.

Section 40 of the 2014 Act also provides that when deciding whether someone has power to bind a company the board of directors of a company, and any registered person, shall be deemed to have authority to exercise any power of the company, and to authorise others to do so. This effectively gives a statutory basis to the doctrine of ostensible authority.

4.3.3 NOTICE REQUIREMENTS FOR BOARD MEETINGS

The 2014 Act does not specify a minimum period of notice which must be given for directors' meetings, but instead states that all directors are entitled to reasonable notice (2014 Act, s 160 (4)). This recognises that sometimes business reality requires the directors to meet on very short notice to deal with emergencies. The 2014 Act does state, however, that notice must be given to all directors and case law has clearly established that if notice is not so given to all the directors then the relevant meeting will be deemed to be irregular and any business purported to have been transacted at that meeting will be void. Interestingly, the 2014 Act doesn't require the notice of a directors' meeting to specify the business proposed to be carried out at the relevant meeting. Case law has however established that where a director feels that he was misled by the failure to explain the business proposed to be carried out, or indeed, the business actually carried out is different from that detailed in the relevant notice, then if the director/directors who feel they were so misled could have blocked the passing of the relevant resolution had they attended the meeting, the business actually transacted can be declared invalid and not binding. Case law has also established that resolutions passed at an invalid board meeting can subsequently be cured by a subsequent valid board meeting.

Section 160 (3) of the 2014 Act provides that a director may, and the secretary on the requisition of a director shall, at any time summon a meeting of the directors. This means that one director can call a directors' meeting at any time. If the directors so resolve, it shall not be necessary to give notice of a meeting of directors to any director who, being resident in the state, is for the time being absent from the state (2014 Act, s 160 (4)).

Section 160 (5) of the 2014 Act provides that nothing in subsection 160 (4) or any other provision of the 2014 Act enables a person, other than a director of the company concerned, to object to the notice given for any meeting of the directors. This means that no non-director can challenge the validity of a meeting due to lack of notice.

4.3.4 VOTING AT BOARD MEETINGS AND THE ROLE OF THE CHAIRPERSON OF THE BOARD

It is open to the members of a company to modify the voting provisions set out in the 2014 Act in its constitution. It is therefore always necessary to review a company's specific constitution when working out the directors' voting rights e.g. it is not uncommon where a company is a joint venture vehicle for the constitution to be amended to provide that directors appointed by certain members must vote on certain types of transaction in order for them to be validly passed.

The directors may elect a chairperson of their meetings and determine the period for which he or she is to hold office (see **chapter 3, 'Officers of a Company'** at **3.4.1.1**), but if no such chairperson is elected, or, if at any meeting the chairperson is not present within 15 minutes after the time appointed for holding it, the directors present may choose one of their number to be chairperson of the meeting.

Directors shall decide questions arising at directors' meetings by a majority of votes, (i.e. more than 50% of the directors voting at that meeting – not more than 50% of all the directors of the company). The chairperson will have a second or casting vote (where there is an equality of votes (2014 Act, s 160 (2)).

The chairperson of the directors does not, however, have a casting vote on written resolutions (2014 Act, s 161 (4)).

Section 161 (6) of the 2014 Act allows for telephonic/video board meetings and provides that if the directors are not concentrated in a group, the meeting will be deemed to be held where the chairperson is.

Board minutes signed by the chairperson of the meeting, or by the chairperson of the next succeeding meeting, shall be evidence of the proceedings (2014 Act, s 166 (3)).

Subject to the other provisions of the 2014 Act (such as s 231 – duty of directors to disclose interests in contacts made by the company) a director may vote in respect of any contract, appointment, or arrangement in which he or she is interested, and he or she shall be counted in the quorum present at the meeting (2014 Act, s 161 (7)).

4.3.5   DIRECTORS ACTING BY MEANS OF WRITTEN RESOLUTION

Written resolutions are usually used where it is logistically more convenient to circulate a written resolution to all the directors than to convene a directors' meeting. A resolution in writing signed by *all* the directors of a company, or by *all* the members of a committee of them, and who are for the time being entitled to receive notice of a meeting of the directors or, as the case may be, of such a committee, shall be as valid as if it had been passed at a meeting of the directors, or committee, duly convened and held (2014 Act, s 161 (1)). Note that the provisions of s 194 of the 2014 Act which allow the members to pass written resolutions signed by a majority only of the members, does not apply for directors' written resolutions. Where one or more of the directors is not, by reason of: (i) the 2014 Act; (ii) the company's constitution; or (iii) a rule of law, permitted to vote on a resolution, then the written resolution will be valid where signed by all the other directors (provided (pursuant to s 161 (3) of the 2014 Act) the resolution states the name of each non-signing director, and the basis on which they did not sign).

Written directors' resolutions may consist of several documents in like form, each signed by one or more directors, and shall take effect from the time it is signed by the last director (2014 Act, s 161 (5)). A date should not therefore be printed on the face of a written resolution when it is circulated for signature, as that printed date might be different from the date upon which the last director signs, thereby creating confusion.

4.3.6   QUORUMS FOR MEETINGS OF THE BOARD

In order for a directors' meeting to be valid, the minimum number of directors specified in the company's constitution (in most cases the quorum of a company is set by the default incorporation of s 161 of the 2014 Act into its constitution) (the 'quorum') must be present (in person, by telephonic means (or indeed by representation by a duly appointed alternate)) at that meeting.

Section 160 (6) of the 2014 Act provides that the quorum for the transaction of the business of the directors may be fixed by the directors, and unless so fixed shall be two but, where the company has only one director, the quorum shall be one. Where a company is a joint venture vehicle it is common for its constitution to be amended to provide for a higher quorum, requiring each member's nominee to be present to form a quorum.

Where the number of directors falls below that number fixed by the 2014 Act as the necessary quorum of directors, the continuing directors or director may act for the purpose of increasing the number of directors to that number, or of summoning a general meeting of the company, but for no other purpose (2014 Act, s 160 (7)).

A director may be counted in the quorum present at any meeting at which he or she is appointed as director (but may not vote on such appointment) (2014 Act, s 163).

4.3.7   TELEPHONIC, VIDEO, OR ELECTRONIC MEETINGS OF THE BOARD

Directors can conduct meetings by telephone or video conference etc. Section 161 (6) of the 2014 Act states that a meeting of the directors (or of a committee), may consist of a conference between *some* or all of the directors (or members of the committee), who are not all in one place, but each of whom is able (directly by means of telephonic, video, or other electronic communication) to speak to each of the others and to be heard. A director or member of a committee taking part in such a conference shall be deemed to be present in person at the meeting and shall be entitled to vote and be counted in the quorum accordingly. Such a meeting shall be deemed to take place:

(a)   where the largest group of those participating in the conference is assembled;

(b)   if there is no such group, where the chairperson of the meeting then is;

(c)   if neither (a) or (b) applies, in such location as the meeting itself decides.

The location of board meetings is important for establishing where a company is managed and controlled for tax purposes.

4.3.8   MINUTES OF PROCEEDINGS OF THE BOARD

All companies are obliged to keep minutes of their director and committee meetings and written resolutions. Section 166 (1) of the 2014 Act provides that a company shall cause minutes to be entered in books kept for that purpose of:

(a)   *all appointments of officers made by its directors;*

(b)   *the names of the directors present at each meeting of its directors and of any committee of the directors;*

(c)   *all resolutions and proceedings at all meetings of its directors and committees of directors.*

Minutes should be entered in the relevant appointment and meeting minute books *as soon as may* be after the appointment concerned is made, the meeting concerned has been held, or the resolution concerned has been passed. Minutes, if purporting to be signed by the chairperson of the meeting, or by the chairperson of the next succeeding meeting, shall be evidence of the proceedings. Section 166 (4) of the 2014 Act provides that where minutes have been made in accordance with s 166 then, until the contrary is proved, the relevant meeting will be deemed to have been duly held and convened, all proceedings had at the meeting shall be deemed to have taken place, and all appointments of officers made by the directors shall be deemed to be valid.

Under ss 166 (5) and (6) of the 2014 Act, a company shall, if required, produce its minute books to the Director of Corporate Enforcement, and allow the Director to inspect and take copies of such records, and if a company fails to keep the prescribed books, or to produce them to the Director, the company, and any officer in default, shall be guilty of a category 4 offence.

Sections 215 to 218 of the 2014 Act deal with the inspection of registers. Minutes of meetings (etc.) must be kept in the State, and the company must notify the Registrar if those records are not kept at the companies registered office. Under s 216 of the 2014 Act the company's members (but not its directors) may request a copy of the minutes of its meetings.

4.4   Rules Governing Members' Meetings

The law relating to meetings and resolutions of a company's members is set out in Part 4, Chapter 6 of the 2014 Act (ss 175 to 199).

4.4.1   THE REQUIREMENTS FOR AND PURPOSE OF AN ANNUAL GENERAL MEETING

A company must, in addition to any other general meetings of its members held in that year, hold an annual general meeting of its members (the 'AGM') and shall specify such meeting as the company's AGM in the notice sent convening such meeting each year.

The first AGM must be held within 18 months of the date of incorporation of the company, and not more than 15 months may elapse between the date of one AGM of a company and that of the next.

Section 175 (3) of the 2014 Act provides that physical AGMs will be optional for all private companies limited by shares – even where they have more than one member. Under the Companies Acts 1963–2013, a private company could only opt out of holding a physical AGM where it had only one member. Under the 2014 Act, a private company limited by shares need not hold an AGM where all the members entitled to attend and vote at such general meeting sign, before the latest date for the holding of that meeting, a unanimous written resolution under s 193 of the 2014 Act:

(a) *acknowledging receipt of the financial statements that would have been laid before an AGM;*

(b) *resolving all such matters as would have been resolved at the AGM; and*

(c) *confirming no change is proposed in the appointment of the person (if any) who, at the date of the resolution is the statutory auditor of the company.*

Where a provision of the 2014 Act requires that a thing is to be done at an AGM then, if it is dealt with in the written resolution dispensing with the AGM, that requirement shall be regarded as having been complied with (2014 Act, s 175 (4)). This means that if the text of the written resolution resolves to adopt the company's statutory financial statements and the report of the directors, then they are indeed so adopted.

Section 176 (1) of the 2014 Act now allows a company to hold its meetings (including its AGM) either within or outside the State. Sections 176 (2) and (3) go on to provide that where any general meeting (including an AGM) is held outside of the State then, unless all of the members entitled to attend and vote consent in writing to its being held outside of the State, the company has a duty to ensure, at the company's own expense, that members can by technological means participate in any such meeting without leaving the State.

A general meeting (including an AGM) can now be held in two or more venues (whether inside or outside the State) at the same time, using any technology that provides members as a whole with a reasonable opportunity to participate (2014 Act, s 176 (4)).

Section 186 of the 2014 Act sets out the business to be transacted at each AGM, which must include:

(a) *the consideration of the company's statutory financial statements and the report of the directors and, unless the company is entitled to and has availed itself of the audit exemption under section 360 or 365, (being group companies and dormant companies) the report of the statutory auditors on those statements and that report;*

(b) *the review by the members of the company's affairs;*

(c)   *save where the company's constitution provides otherwise:*

    (i)   *the declaration of a dividend (if any) of an amount not exceeding the amount recommended by the directors (this is an important control for the directors when running the business of the company and its finances); and*

    (ii)   *the authorisation of the directors to approve the remuneration of the statutory auditors (if any);*

(d)   *where the company's constitution so provides, the election and re-election of directors. (As already discussed this is an important control for the members);*

(e)   *save where the company is entitled to and has availed itself of the exemption referred to in paragraph (a) above, the appointment or re-appointment of statutory auditors;*

(f)   *where the company's constitution so provides, the remuneration of the directors.*

In addition to the above, the members may of course also pass other ordinary or special resolutions proposed at the AGM.

Section 341 (1) details the financial statements and reports which the directors are obliged, in respect of each financial year, to lay before the members at an AGM (see **chapter 7, 'Financial Statements'**):

4.4.2   THE RIGHTS OF DIRECTORS, MEMBERS, AND THE COURT TO CONVENE EXTRAORDINARY GENERAL MEETINGS

All general meetings of a company, other than the AGM, are known as extraordinary general meetings ('EGMs'). Section 177 (2) of the 2014 Act now allows the directors of a company to, whenever they think fit, convene an EGM. This power is not stated as being subject to the company's constitution so is an absolute right of the directors. Section 177 (3) provides that where there are insufficient directors capable of acting to form a quorum for a directors' meeting, then any director of the company, or any member, may convene an EGM in the same manner as nearly as possible as that in which general meetings may be convened by the directors. This is a useful provision allowing a sole remaining director to call an EGM – for the purposes of having the members appoint another director(s) for example, to bring the board back up to any specified quorum minimum.

Section 178 of the 2014 Act sets out the rights of members to convene an EGM, or to cause an EGM to be convened. This includes a new directly enforceable right allowing one or more members holding not less than 50% (or such other percentage as may be specified in the constitution) of the paid-up share capital of the company carrying the right to vote at general meetings to convene an EGM. It should be noted that this right can be disapplied entirely, or modified, by altering the '50% or more of' threshold up or down, in a company's constitution. It is therefore necessary to check a company's constitution when advising on the ability of its members to directly convene an EGM.

Section 178 (3) of the 2014 Act sets out the right of one or more members holding not less than 10% of the paid-up voting share capital of the company to require the directors to 'forthwith' convene an EGM. The 'requisitionists' must sign a requisition, stating the objects of the EGM, and that if the directors do not, within 21 days from the date of such requisition by the member(s) in question, convene the EGM (to be held within two months) then the requisitionists (or at least half of them) may themselves convene the EGM. This right is absolute because s 178 (1)(b) of the 2014 Act states that it shall have effect notwithstanding anything in the constitution of the company.

Section 179 (1) of the 2014 Act has increased the power of the court to convene a general meeting. A director or voting member (or the personal representative of such a member, or the assignee in bankruptcy of such a bankrupt member) can apply to the court for an order requiring a general meeting to be called, held, and conducted in any manner that it thinks fit. An order will be made if the court is satisfied that for any reason it is impractical or otherwise undesirable for any person to call a general meeting in any manner in which meetings of that company may be called, or to conduct a general meeting of the company in any manner provided by the 2014 Act or the constitution. A court can also make such an order of its own volition.

4.4.3   NOTICE REQUIREMENTS FOR GENERAL MEETINGS

Section 180 (1) of the 2014 Act sets out a definitive list of the persons who have the right to receive notice of general meetings of a company. This section is not prefaced with the words 'save where constitution provides otherwise' so these persons enjoy an inalienable statutory right to such notice. Those persons are: (a) every member (whether or not the constitution entitles them to vote at that meeting, with s 180 (2) providing that where a share is jointly held, notice may be given by giving notice to the first named joint holder in the register of members); (b) the personal representative of a deceased 'voting' member of the company; (c), the assignee in bankruptcy of a bankrupt 'voting' member; and (d) the directors and secretary of the company. Interestingly s 180 (5) of the 2014 Act allows a company's constitution to be modified to include provisions requiring notice to also be given to additional persons in addition to those specified above.

Section 180 (6) of the 2014 Act provides that where a company has auditors they too shall be entitled to attend any general meeting of the company and to receive all notices of and other communications relating to general meetings, and to be heard at general meetings on any part of the business of that meeting which concerns them as auditors.

Section 181 (1) of the 2014 Act provides that, unless a company's constitution provides for greater notice, the minimum notice for a general meeting is:

(a)   not less than 21 days for each of: (i) AGMs; and (ii) EGMs for the passing of a special resolution; and

(b)   not less than seven days for any other type of EGM.

Occasionally it is necessary to call an EGM on short notice to deal with unexpected urgent business so s 181 (2) allows the calling of general meetings on shorter notice than that prescribed by s 181 (1) where each of: (i) all the members entitled to attend and vote; and (ii) (where there are auditors) the auditors, all so agree. This requirement for the consent of all members means that an EGM or AGM cannot be held on short notice if one or more members won't 'play ball'.

It is important that the logistics of delivering general meeting notices are also taken into account when calculating compliance with and diarising the 21/7-day notice periods. Section 181 (3) of the 2014 Act provides that where a notice is posted (in ordinary prepaid post), it is deemed to have been delivered 24 hours after posting. Section 181 (4) gives a clear statutory basis to the requirement to factor in and add two 'clear days' to the minimum 21/7-day notice periods. In calculating the required notice it is therefore necessary to add a day to those periods for each of: (i) the day on which the notice is served; and (ii) the day of the meeting itself. Effectively this means that 23 and nine days' notice are required (and if posted the periods are 24 and ten days) respectively.

Section 181(5) of the 2014 Act now sets out the information that each general meeting notice must specify, being:

(a)   the place, date, and time of the meeting;

(b)   the general nature of the business to be transacted at the meeting;

(c)   the text or substance of any special resolution (text of ordinary resolutions is not required to be detailed in the notice, but good corporate governance practice would suggest that it should be); and

(d)   with reasonable prominence a statement that:

(i)   a member entitled to attend and vote is entitled to appoint a proxy (or where allowed proxies) to attend, speak, and vote instead of him/her;

(ii)   a proxy need not be a member; and

(iii) the time by which the proxy must be received by the company.

A precedent draft EGM notice is attached to the end of this chapter.

Section 181 (6) of the 2014 Act provides that, unless the constitution provides otherwise, the accidental omission to give notice of a general meeting to, or its non-receipt by, any person entitled to receive it shall not invalidate proceedings at that meeting. The words 'unless the constitution provides otherwise' means that it is open to the members to specify a stricter invalidation for accidental omission regime if they so choose.

Section 218 of the 2014 Act sets out how a company may serve notice on its members and includes the ability to serve notice by electronic means where the company's constitution specifically allows, and the receiving member has consented to receiving notices by electronic means.

4.4.4   QUORUM FOR GENERAL MEETINGS

Business should not be transacted at any general meeting unless a quorum of members is present at the time the general meeting proceeds to business (2014 Act, s 182 (1)). Section 182 (2) of the 2014 Act provides that, save: (i) to the extent that its constitution provides otherwise; or (ii) where the company is a single-member company, two members of a company, present in person, or by proxy, at a general meeting shall be a quorum. Where the relevant company is a single-member company, one member present in person or by proxy at a general meeting shall be a quorum (2014 Act, s 181 (3)). Where a company has a disparate group of members, with different interests (such as where the company is a joint venture vehicle), it would be usual to insert a specifically tailored quorum requirement in its constitution ensuring that the members cannot have a general meeting unless some, or all, of the various different members are present. Such arrangements can be a double-edged sword, and unless appropriate failsafes are included in the drafting could lead to disgruntled member(s) effectively blocking the ability of the other members to hold a general meeting by refusing to turn up when notice is given. In those circumstances the new majority written resolution procedure (discussed at paragraph **4.4.10.2** below) may provide a solution.

Sections 182 (4) and (5) of the 2014 Act together provide that, unless the relevant company's constitution provides otherwise, if within 15 minutes after the time appointed for the relevant general meeting to take place a quorum is not present, then:

(a)   where the general meeting had been convened by the members it shall be dissolved; and

(b)   in any other case, the general meeting will stand adjourned to the same day in the next week, at the same time and place or to such other day, and at such other time and place as the directors determine; and if at the adjourned meeting a quorum is not present within half an hour after the time appointed for the general meeting, the members present shall be a quorum.

4.4.5   PROXIES

Under s 183 of the 2014 Act a member of a company entitled to attend and vote at a meeting of the company shall be entitled to appoint another person (whether a member or not) as his or her proxy to attend and vote instead of him or her. A proxy shall have the same right as the member who appointed that proxy to speak and vote (on a show of hands and on a poll) at the relevant general meeting. The right to appoint a proxy, and the proxy's right to speak and vote, cannot be altered by a provision in the relevant company's constitution, so it is therefore an inalienable statutory right of each such member.

Section 183 of the 2014 Act also specifies what form the instrument of proxy should take and how, when, and where it should be deposited.

In addition to being entitled to appoint a proxy, a body corporate, where it is a member of a company, may, pursuant to s 185 of the 2014 Act, by resolution of its directors, or other governing body, authorise such person (an 'authorised person') as it thinks fit to act as its representative at any general, or class, meeting of the members of that company in which it is a member. The authorised person is entitled to exercise the same powers on behalf of its appointor as that appointor could exercise if it were an individual member of the company. The chairperson of any meeting is entitled to require a person claiming to be an authorised person to produce such evidence of their authority as the chairperson may reasonably specify, and if such evidence is not produced, the chairperson may exclude such person from the meeting. Unlike the case for proxies, the 2014 Act does not require an authorised person's evidence of authorisation to be lodged with the company 48 hours in advance of the relevant general meeting. Therefore if a corporate member has missed the 48-hour proxy deadline, it can still appoint an 'authorised person' immediately before such general meeting.

4.4.6 PROCEEDINGS AT GENERAL MEETINGS

Section 187 of the 2014 Act provides that each of the following requirements will apply to proceedings at general meetings of a company, save to the extent that such company's constitution provides otherwise:

(a) the chairperson (if any) of the board of directors will preside as chairperson of every general meeting of the company, or if there is none, or if he or she is not present within 15 minutes after the time appointed for holding the general meeting, or is unwilling to act, the directors present will elect one of their number to chair the general meeting;

(b) if no director is willing to act, or if no director is present within 15 minutes after the time appointed for holding the general meeting, the members will choose one of their number to chair that general meeting;

(c) the chairperson may, with the consent of a quorate general meeting, and shall if directed, adjourn the general meeting from time to time and place to place;

(d) if a general meeting is adjourned then only unfinished business from the original meeting can be transacted at the adjourned meeting;

(e) when a general meeting is adjourned for 30 days or more, notice of the adjourned meeting shall be given as in the case of the original meeting, but otherwise it is not necessary to give notice of an adjournment or the business to be transacted at an adjourned meeting;

(f) unless a poll is demanded (dealt with at **para 4.4.8** below), voting at any general meeting shall be decided on a show of hands and a declaration by the chairperson as to whether a resolution has been carried, or carried unanimously, or by a particular majority, or lost; and an entry in the minute book to that effect, is conclusive evidence of that fact; and

(g) where there is an equality of votes, whether on a show of hands, or a poll, the chairperson shall have a second or casting vote. (This provision is very often amended in a joint venture scenario.)

4.4.7 VOTING

Section 168 of the 2014 Act defines a member as the subscribers, and thereafter every person who has agreed to become a member and whose name is entered in the register of members of the company. Importantly, s 188 of the 2014 Act deals with voting mechanisms, and states that its provisions apply 'save to the extent the company's constitution provides otherwise'. This again means that it will always be necessary to check a company's constitution to confirm that the below provisions have not been modified for that specific company.

Under s 188 (2) where a matter is being decided:

(a) on a show of hands, every member present in person and every proxy shall have one vote, but no individual member shall have more than one vote; and

(b) on a poll,

every member (whether present in person or by proxy) shall have one vote for each share held, or for each €15 of stock held by him or her. This is subject to the rights or restrictions attaching to any class of shares.

In the case of joint holders, the vote of the senior holder (first holder named on the register) who tenders a vote (whether in person or by proxy) shall be accepted (2014 Act, s 188 (3)).

Members of unsound mind, who have made an enduring power of attorney or in respect of whom an order has been made by a court having jurisdiction in cases of unsound mind, may vote by his or her committee, donee, receiver, guardian, or other court-appointed person (2014 Act, s 188 (4)).

A member cannot vote at a general meeting unless all calls or other sums immediately payable in respect of his or her shares have been paid (2014 Act, s 188 (6)).

An objection cannot be raised about the qualification of any voter except at the meeting, or adjourned meeting, at which the vote objected to is cast, and every vote not disallowed at such meeting shall be valid. Any objection made to a member's qualification at the relevant meeting shall be decided upon by the chairperson, whose decision is final and conclusive (2014 Act, ss 188 (7) and (8)). This means that votes cannot subsequently be set aside for lack of qualification unless a company's constitution is specifically amended to provide otherwise.

4.4.8   RIGHT TO DEMAND A POLL

A poll may be demanded at a general meeting in relation to a matter, whether before, or on, the declaration of the result of the show of hands relating to the matter which the member wants decided on the basis of a poll. This right has been recognised as an important protection for members and consequently is a mandatory provision which the constitution cannot vary (2014 Act, s 189 (1)).

Under s 189 (2), the following persons may demand a poll:

(a)   the chairperson of the relevant meeting;

(b)   at least three members (they do not have to be voting members), present in person or by proxy;

(c)   any member or members, present in person or by proxy, representing not less than 10% of the total voting rights of all the members of the company having the right to vote at the meeting; and

(d)   any member or members holding shares in the company conferring the right to vote at the meeting, being shares on which an aggregate sum has been paid up equal to not less than 10% of the total sum paid up on all the shares conferring that right.

A demand for a poll may be withdrawn by the person(s) who made the original demand. If a poll is demanded it is to be taken in such a manner as the chairperson directs. A poll demanded with regard to the election of a chairperson, or on a question of adjournment, must be taken immediately. A poll demanded on any question other than the election of the chairperson, or adjournment, shall be taken at such time as the chairperson of the relevant general meeting directs, and any business other than that on which a poll is demanded may go ahead pending the taking of the poll. The chairperson therefore has a degree of flexibility as to how and when to take a poll. If advising at a contentious meeting, it is prudent to ensure that clear and transparent logistics for taking a poll have been worked out in advance.

Section 190 of the 2014 Act states that:

> On a poll taken at a meeting of a company, or a meeting of any class of members, a member, whether present in person or by proxy, who is entitled to more than one vote need not, if he or she votes:
>
> (a)   use all of his or her votes; or
>
> (b)   cast them all in the same way.

This is often relevant where a shareholder is merely a nominee for a number of different beneficial owners, some of which require their beneficially owned shares to be voted in favour of a resolution, and others require their beneficially owned shares to be voted against the same resolution.

4.4.9   ORDINARY AND SPECIAL RESOLUTIONS

Two types of resolution may be passed by a company's members in general meeting – 'ordinary resolutions' and 'special resolutions'. An ordinary resolution is normally used for routine, non-contentious business; conversely, a special resolution is normally used for fundamental issues concerning the company and its structure – such as amending the company's name or constitution, or approving one of the 'restricted' activities pursuant to the Summary Approval Procedure (see **chapter 10, 'Transactions with Directors'**). Consequently, the default position is that members are given longer notice (21 days, as opposed to seven, unless the requirements for shorter notice are met), and a higher number of member votes in favour of the relevant special resolution is required to approve its passing (75% as opposed to 50.01% for an ordinary resolution).

Section 191 (1) of the 2014 Act defines an ordinary resolution as 'a resolution passed by a simple majority (50.01% or more) of the votes cast by members of a company as, being entitled to do so, vote in person or by proxy at a general meeting of the company'. It is important to note that the 50.01% test for resolutions passed at a physical general meeting is for 50.01% or more of the votes actually cast at that meeting – not 50.01% or more of the votes capable of being cast (i.e. not 50.01% or more of the issued shares). An ordinary resolution may be passed by way of written resolution (see **4.4.10**). When a resolution is passed as a written resolution, it is an ordinary resolution if it is described on its face in the text of the written resolution as being an ordinary resolution (regardless of the number of members who sign).

A special resolution is defined in s 191 (2) of the 2014 Act as a resolution that:

(a)   is referred to as such in the 2014 Act, or is required (whether by the 2014 Act or by a company's constitution or otherwise) to be passed as a special resolution; and

(b)   is passed by not less than 75% of the votes cast by such members of the company concerned as, being entitled to do so, vote in person or by proxy at a general meeting; and

(c)   is passed at a meeting of which 21 days' notice has been given and which complies with the requirements of s 181 (1) (a) and (5) (i.e. requirements detailed above in relation to place, date, time, nature of business, text of the special resolution).

A special resolution can also be passed by way of a written resolution. Again, if a written resolution is to be a special resolution it must be described as such on its face.

A special resolution can be passed at a general meeting called at short notice. Section 191 (4) of the 2014 Act provides that, despite the 21-day notice requirement, a resolution may still be proposed and passed as a special resolution at a meeting of which less than 21 days' notice has been given if a majority in number of the members having the right to attend and vote at any such meeting, (being a majority either:

(a)   together holding not less than 90% in nominal value of the shares giving that right; or

(b)   together representing not less than 90% of the total voting rights at that meeting of all the members),

agree to such short notice. It should be noted that the 90% test at (b) above is satisfied by just 90% of the voting shares held by members attending at the relevant meeting. This means that a minority of the shareholders of a company can pass a special resolution on short notice where that majority constitutes 75% or more of the voting members at that meeting.

The terms of any resolution (whether special or otherwise) before a general meeting may be amended by ordinary resolution moved at the meeting, provided that the terms of the resolution as amended will still be such that adequate notice of the intention to pass the same can be deemed to have been given (2014 Act, s 191 (6)). It is not possible, however, to amend a resolution so as to fundamentally alter its nature, or to introduce a new resolution unless all the members are present.

4.4.10   UNANIMOUS AND MAJORITY WRITTEN RESOLUTIONS

The 2014 Act retains the ability for members to avoid having to meet together and hold a physical general meeting, and instead pass resolutions by way of written resolution. However, the law has been tweaked in that, formerly, written resolutions were only available where the power to pass them was specifically included within a company's articles of association. Now s 193 (1) of the 2014 Act provides that the default position is that companies can pass a resolution by way of a written resolution. It is not, however, possible to use the written resolution procedures to remove a director or a statutory auditor from an office (except for single member companies).

Under the Act, a written resolution will be effective, provided that all members entitled to attend and vote have been circulated with the proposed text of the relevant resolution and an explanation of it and it has been signed by the requisite majority (more than 50% of members for an ordinary resolution, or 75% or more for a special resolution); however, any such written resolutions will not take effect until, in the case of an ordinary resolution, seven days after the last member signs it, or for a special resolution, 21 days after this date, unless this period is waived by all members entitled to vote on the resolution. This 'cooling-off period' reflects the statutory notice periods required to convene a meeting to pass such resolutions. Private unlimited companies and designated activity companies will also be able to avail of this procedure, save where their constitution provides otherwise. Majority written resolutions are discussed in greater detail at paragraph **4.4.10.2** below.

4.4.10.1   Unanimous written resolutions

A resolution in writing signed by all of the members of a company entitled to attend and vote on such a resolution at a general meeting (or being bodies corporate by their duly appointed representatives) is as valid and effective for all purposes as if it had been passed at a general meeting duly convened and held, and if described as a special resolution it shall be deemed to be a 'special resolution' (2014 Act, s 193 (1)).

A unanimous written resolution may consist of several documents in like form, each signed by one or more members. A unanimous written resolution shall be deemed to have been passed at a meeting held on the date on which it was signed by the last member to sign; and where a signature is dated, that shall be prima facie evidence that it was signed on that date. The signatories of a written resolution must deliver it to the company within 14 days of its passing and where a resolution is not contemporaneously signed, the company must notify the members of its passing within 21 days of the company itself having received all the signed documents constituting the resolution from all the members. The company must retain the written resolution sent to it as if they constituted minutes of a meeting. A failure to comply with the delivery and notice requirements does not, however, invalidate the relevant written resolution.

Section 193 (11) provides that (as was the case under pre-existing statute), a unanimous written resolution cannot be used for the removal of a director or of a statutory auditor (although the sole member of a single member company can in fact remove a director).

4.4.10.2   Majority written resolutions

The ability to pass a majority written resolution did not exist before the 2014 Act.

Sections 194 (1) and (3) of the 2014 Act provide that a resolution in writing that is:

(a)   described as being an ordinary resolution; and

(b) signed by a member or members who alone or together, at the time of the signing, represent more than 50% of the total voting rights of all the members who would have the right to attend and vote at a general meeting at that time; and

(c) the proposed text of which, and an explanation of its main purpose, has been circulated, by the directors or the other person proposing it, to all the members of the company who would be entitled to attend and vote on the resolution,

shall be as valid and effective for all purposes as an ordinary resolution as if the resolution had been passed at a general meeting of the company duly convened and held.

Section 194 (4) provides that where a written resolution is:

(a) described as being a special resolution; and

(b) is signed by a member or members representing 75% of the total voting rights; and

(c) the proposed text of which, and an explanation of its main purpose, has been circulated, by the directors or the other person proposing it, to all the members of the company who would be entitled to attend and vote on the resolution,

it will be as valid and effective for all purposes as a special resolution as if it had been passed at a general meeting.

Majority written resolutions may also consist of several documents in like form, each signed by one or more members.

One important feature of this new majority written resolution mechanism is that s 194 (9) imposes a delayed effect on the coming into force of such majority written resolutions. An ordinary resolution passed as a majority written resolution shall be deemed to have been passed at a meeting held seven days after the date on which it was signed by the last member to sign, and a special resolution passed as a majority written resolution shall be deemed to have been passed at a meeting held 21 days after the date on which it was signed by the last member to sign. The mandatory delayed effect shall be waived where all of the members who are entitled to attend and vote on the resolution state, in a written waiver signed by each of them, that the period of delay is waived (2014 Act, s 194 (10)).

The members who sign a written resolution must deliver the documents constituting the written resolution to the company. Within three days of the date of delivery of the resolution to the company, the company must notify every member of:

(a) the fact that the resolution was signed by the requisite majority; and

(b) the date that it will be deemed to be passed.

The company is required to retain the documents constituting the written resolution as if they were minutes of a meeting (s 195 (4)). A majority written resolution is of no effect unless and until it is delivered to the company in accordance with s 195 (3) of the 2014 Act, but non-compliance by the company with notification and retention requirements does not affect the validity of the relevant written resolution.

4.5   Post Decision Requirements

Section 198 (1) of the 2014 Act provides that a copy of every resolution or agreement to which that section applies, including:

(a) all special resolutions;

(b) some ordinary resolutions;

(c) alterations in share capital;

(d) resolutions conferring authority for the allotment of shares;

(e) resolutions that a company be wound up voluntarily passed under s 580;

(f)   resolutions attaching rights or restrictions to any share;

(g)   resolutions varying any such right or restriction; and

(h)   resolutions classifying any unclassified share,

must be forwarded by each company to the Registrar of Companies within 15 days after the date of their passing or making. The documents required to be filed under the 2014 Act have altered slightly from those applying prior to its coming into force.

As previously stated, s 199 of the 2014 Act provides that each company must, as soon as may be after the holding or a meeting or passing of a resolution, cause minutes and the terms of all resolutions to be entered in books kept for that purpose.

4.5.1   OTHER FILINGS

Other provisions of the 2014 Act also require that additional filings are so made in relation to matters such as (i) changes in the directors or secretary of the company or in their particulars (e.g. change of address); (ii) allotment of shares; and (iii) change in registered office.

4.6   The Summary Approval Procedure ('SAP')

The 2014 Act provides for a new summary approval procedure for the approval of seven different restricted activities which the company would otherwise generally be prohibited from undertaking. The SAP is, in many respects, similar to the old White Wash Procedure. Most of the SAP will be the same regardless of which of the seven restricted activities is being approved (so we will largely have one baseline validation procedure) with certain different requirements applying depending on which restricted activity is being approved. The SAP is dealt with in more detail in **chapter 10, 'Transactions with Directors'**.

SPECIMEN BOARD MINUTES CONVENING AN EGM

[*NAME*] LIMITED

(COMPANY NUMBER [•][1])

(THE 'COMPANY')

MINUTES OF A MEETING OF THE DIRECTORS OF THE COMPANY
DULY CONVENED, CONSTITUTED, AND HELD AT
[*ADDRESS*] AT [*TIME*] AM/PM ON [*DATE*]

Present: [*Director Name*]

                       [*Director Name*]

In attendance: [•]

Apologies: [•]

1.   CHAIRPERSON AND OPENING OF MEETING

     It was agreed that [*Chairperson Name*] would act as chairperson of the meeting and the Chairperson declared the meeting open.

2.   NOTICE AND QUORUM

     The Chairperson NOTED that all of the Directors [had received due notice of the meeting]/[were present in person and that notice of the meeting had been waived by all of the Directors]/[,and [NAME]] being in communication by [telephone] link that he had satisfied himself that all of the Directors taking part in the meeting could hear each other speak,] *[Amend as appropriate]*   and that the meeting was quorate and, accordingly, the meeting could proceed to business. *[Check the company's constitution to confirm that the procedure for calling meetings of directors and quorum requirements set out in s 160 (1) and s 160 (6) (quorum) have not been specifically altered.]*

3.   DISCLOSURE OF INTERESTS

     [Check the constitution of the company to determine whether the provisions of s 161 (7) and s 163 of the Act allowing an interested director to vote and be counted in the quorum present at the meeting has been modified.]

The Chairperson NOTED that:

each Director confirmed that he was not disqualified from participating in this meeting and/or the considerations, the determinations and resolutions to be made hereunder, and he had disclosed to the Secretary of the company, in writing, the manner (if any) in which he was interested in the matters to be considered at this meeting, whether as a director of the company or otherwise, for the purposes of section 231 of the Companies Act, 2014 (the '2014 Act') *[Check the constitution of the company for disclosure requirements.]* It was noted that pursuant to [Section 161 (7) of the Companies Act, 2014] OR [Regulation [NUMBER] of the company's constitution] [each Director was permitted to participate in and vote at the meeting notwithstanding such interests;] OR [the Director[s] so interested would not vote or count as part of a quorum on any of the matters in which they were [respectively] interested and that, nevertheless, there would be a quorum for all items of business to be transacted by the meeting;] *[Delete this paragraph if the directors do not have any interests to disclose.]*

pursuant to section 137 of the Companies Act, 2014, at least one of the Directors of the company is resident in the European Economic Area and that no Director present individually held more than twenty-five directorships for the purposes of section 142 of the 2014 Act and the Directors were therefore eligible to vote on all board resolutions brought before the meeting; and

no person who is the subject of a declaration under section 819 of the 2014 Act (restriction orders) or an order under sections 839 to 842 inclusive of the 2014 Act (disqualification orders) is appointed or acts in any way, directly or indirectly, as a director or secretary of the company.

4.   [PURPOSE OF THE MEETING]

The Chairperson NOTED the business of the meeting concerned [set out details] (the Transaction).

5.   EXTRAORDINARY GENERAL MEETING

The Chairperson EXPLAINED that the steps required to [approve the entry by the company into the Transaction] would require the passing of [special resolutions for the purpose of [Details] and ordinary resolutions in order to [Details], and that an extraordinary general meeting of the company would have to be convened to pass those resolutions.

6.   IT WAS RESOLVED that:

(a)   an Extraordinary General Meeting of the company be convened for [Date] [on the basis that the necessary consents to short notice would be given] (the 'EGM');

(b)   the draft notice convening the EGM, which was submitted to this meeting, be and is hereby approved; and

(c)   the Secretary be instructed to serve notice convening the EGM on each of: (i) the members (including the personal representatives of deceased members (if any) and the assignee in bankruptcy of any members who are bankrupt (if any)); (ii) all the directors; (iii) the secretary; and (iv) the auditors, of the company [and to obtain written consent from all the shareholders entitled to attend and vote, and the auditors, to the holding of the EGM at short notice].

7.   CLOSE OF MEETING

There being no further business, the meeting then terminated.

_____

CHAIRPERSON

APPENDIX 2

SPECIMEN NOTICE OF AN EGM

[NAME] LIMITED

(COMPANY NUMBER)

(THE 'COMPANY')

NOTICE is hereby given that an Extraordinary General Meeting of the company will be held at [ADDRESS] on [DATE] at [TIME] am/pm for the purpose of considering and, if thought fit, passing the following Resolution[s] of which [Resolution[s] number [   ] [and [   ]] will be proposed as a[n Ordinary]/[Special] Resolution[s] [and Resolution number [   ] and [   ]] will be proposed as a[n   Ordinary]/[Special] Resolution].

---

1. AS A SPECIAL RESOLUTION:

   THAT, subject to the approval of the Registrar of Companies, the name of the Company shall be changed to [*NAME*] Limited

2. AS AN ORDINARY RESOLUTION:

   That each of the [*Class*] Shares of €[1.00] in the capital of the Company be and is hereby subdivided into [*Number*] shares of €[*Amount*] each

3. AS A SPECIAL RESOLUTION:

   That Regulation 4 in the Company's constitution be and is hereby altered by the deletion of regulation 4 and the substitution of the following regulation therefore:

   '4. The share capital of the company is € [•] divided into [•] ordinary shares of € [•] each.'

4. AS AN [ORDINARY]/ [SPECIAL] RESOLUTION:

   A.   [•].

BY ORDER OF THE BOARD

[NAME]

Secretary Registered Office:

[ADDRESS]

Date: [DATE]

APPENDIX 3

SPECIMEN PROXY FOR AN EGM

[NAME] LIMITED

(THE 'COMPANY')

EXTRAORDINARY GENERAL MEETING FORM OF PROXY

*I/We [*name of member*] (the Member) of [*address of member*] being a holder(s) of [•] [ordinary] shares of €[*Amount*] each in the company and entitled to vote, hereby appoint [*name and address of proxy*] or failing *him/her [*name and address of alternative proxy*] or failing him/her the Chairperson of the meeting, as the proxy of the Member to attend, speak and vote for the Member on behalf of the Member at the Extraordinary General Meeting of the company to be held at [*address*] on [*date*] at [*time*] am/pm, and at any adjournment of the meeting.

The Proxy is to vote as follows:

Voting Instructions to Proxy (choice to be marked with an 'x')			
NUMBER OR DESCRIPTION OF RESOLUTION:	In Favour	Abstain	Against
1. [CLASS] RESOLUTION			
2. [CLASS] RESOLUTION:			
3. [CLASS] RESOLUTION:			
Unless otherwise instructed the proxy will vote as he or she thinks fit.			
SIGNATURE OF MEMBER:...			
Dated: [date]..			

*Delete as appropriate.

NOTES:

In the case of a corporate shareholder, this instrument may be either under its common seal or under the hand of an officer or attorney authorised in that behalf.

For omnibus/nominee shareholders, who without going to underlying investors do not have the authority to vote, please indicate how you wish your proxy/representative to vote by inserting the aggregate number of underlying investor votes 'for' and/or 'against' and/or 'abstain' in the relevant box.

If you wish to appoint a proxy other than the Chairperson of the meeting, please insert his/her name and address and delete 'the Chairperson of the meeting'.

If this instrument is signed and returned without any indication of how the person appointed proxy shall vote, he will exercise his discretion as to how he votes and whether or not he abstains from voting.

In the case of joint holders, the vote of the senior who tenders a vote whether in person or by proxy, shall be accepted to the exclusion of the votes of the other joint holders and for this purpose seniority should be determined by the order in which the names stand in the register of members in respect of the joint holding.

Any alterations made to this form must be initialled.

The address to which the proxy form should be returned is:

[ADDRESS]

APPENDIX 4

SPECIMEN APPOINTMENT
OF REPRESENTATIVE AT EGM

[NAME] LIMITED

(COMPANY NUMBER [•])

(THE 'COMPANY')

EXTRAORDINARY GENERAL MEETING APPOINTMENT OF REPRESENTATIVE

We [Name of corporate shareholder] of [Registered Office] being a member of the company HEREBY CONFIRM that we have appointed [NAME] as our representative to act on our behalf at and in connection with the Extraordinary General Meeting of the company to be held at [ADDRESS] on [DATE] at [TIME] am/pm and every adjournment thereof.

[And we consent to the notice [and other documents] being sent to the members less than [Number] days before the meeting.]

Dated: [DATE]

SIGNED for and on behalf of

[CORPORATE SHAREHOLDER COMPANY NAME]:

)

)

Duly Authorised Signatory

)

Name:

)

)

Title:

)

APPENDIX 5

SPECIMEN CONSENT TO SHORT NOTICE OF EGM (SHAREHOLDERS)

[NAME] LIMITED

(COMPANY NUMBER [●])

(THE 'COMPANY')

MEMBERS' CONSENT TO SHORT NOTICE OF EXTRAORDINARY GENERAL MEETING

I/We the undersigned, being a member/members of the Company having a right to attend and vote at the meeting, HEREBY CONSENT to the Extraordinary General Meeting convened for [DATE] being held on less than the normal statutory period of notice.

DATED: [*DATE*]

SIGNED for and on behalf of   )

[CORPORATE SHAREHOLDER
COMPANY NAME]:   )   _____

                                                              Duly Authorised Signatory

)

)
                                                              Name:

)   _____

)
                                                              Title:

)   _____

SIGNED by [SHAREHOLDER name]:   )

)   _____

)

APPENDIX 6

SPECIMEN CONSENT TO SHORT NOTICE OF EGM (AUDITORS)

[NAME] LIMITED

(COMPANY NUMBER [•])

(THE 'COMPANY')

**AUDITORS' CONSENT TO SHORT NOTICE OF
EXTRAORDINARY GENERAL MEETING**

We, being the Auditors of the company HEREBY CONSENT to the Extraordinary General Meeting convened for [DATE] being held on less than the normal statutory period of notice.

DATED: [DATE]

SIGNED for and on behalf of [AUDITOR name]:   )

)   _____

                                                 Duly Authorised Signatory

)

)   Name:

)   _____

)   _____

APPENDIX 7

SPECIMEN MINUTES OF AN EGM

[NAME OF COMPANY]

(COMPANY NUMBER [•])

(THE 'COMPANY')

MINUTES OF THE EXTRAORDINARY GENERAL MEETING
OF THE COMPANY HELD AT [ADDRESS] ON [DATE] AT [TIME] AM/PM.

Present: [*Name*] [(as proxy for the shareholders mentioned below)] (in the Chair)

[*Name*] [(as proxy for the shareholders mentioned below)].

1.   CHAIRPERSON/QUORUM/NOTICE

There being a quorum present [*Name*] was appointed Chairperson. The notice convening the meeting was [read by the Chairperson]/[with the consent of the meeting, taken as read.] [*Delete as appropriate*].

2.   CONSENT TO SHORT NOTICE

[IT WAS NOTED that all the members entitled to attend and vote, and the Auditors had agreed to accept shorter notice of the meeting than the period of notice prescribed by Section 181 (1) of the Companies Act 2014.] [*Delete if meeting not being held on short notice*]. OR

[IT WAS NOTED that the only business to be conducted at the meeting is the consideration of [a] Special Resolution(s) and, in accordance with the provisions of Section 191 (4) of the Companies Act 2014 that a majority in number of the members having the right to attend and vote at any general meeting, (being a majority [together holding not less than 90% in nominal value of the shares giving that right] or [together representing not less than 90% of the total voting rights of all the members at this general meeting] had agreed to accept shorter notice of the meeting than the period of notice prescribed by Section 181 (1) of the Companies Act 2014.] [*Delete if meeting not being held on short notice*].)

3.   [PROXY FORMS/REPRESENTATIVES]

Proxy forms duly completed by [*Name*] in favour of [*Name*] and [*Name*] in favour of [*Name*] were produced and noted.]

[It was noted that [*Name*] was in attendance as the authorised representative of [*Name*] having been properly appointed.]

4.   RESOLUTIONS

IT WAS RESOLVED as a Special Resolution that, subject to the approval of the Registrar of Companies, the name of the Company shall be changed to '[*Name*] Limited'.

IT WAS RESOLVED as an Ordinary Resolution that each of the [*Class*] Shares of €[1.00] in the capital of the Company be and is hereby subdivided into [*Number*] shares of €[*Amount*] each.

IT WAS RESOLVED as a Special Resolution Regulation 4 in the Company's constitution be and is hereby altered by the deletion of regulation 4 and the substitution of the following regulation therefore:

'4.   The share capital of the company is € [•] divided into [•] ordinary shares of € [•]each.'

IT WAS RESOLVED as a[n Ordinary]/[Special] Resolution [*Detail*]

[REPEAT AS APPROPRIATE].

5.   CLOSE OF MEETING

_____

CHAIRPERSON

APPENDIX 8

SPECIMEN MEMBERS' WRITTEN RESOLUTION

[COMPANY] LIMITED

(COMPANY NUMBER [•])

(THE 'COMPANY')

[SPECIAL]/[ORDINARY] *[delete as appropriate]* [UNANIMOUS]/[MAJORITY ORDINARY]/ [MAJORITY SPECIAL])*[delete as appropriate]* WRITTEN RESOLUTIONS OF THE MEMBERS OF THE COMPANY

RESOLVED: pursuant to section [193 (1)]/[194(1) and (3)]/[194 (4)] *[delete as appropriate]* of the Companies Act 2014:

1. AS A SPECIAL RESOLUTION:

   THAT, subject to the approval of the Registrar of Companies, the name of the Company shall be changed to [*Name*] Limited.

2. AS AN ORDINARY RESOLUTION:

   That each of the [*Class*] Shares of €[1.00] in the capital of the Company be and is hereby subdivided into [*Number*] shares of €[*Amount*] each.

3. AS A SPECIAL RESOLUTION:

   That Regulation 4 in the Company's constitution be and is hereby altered by the deletion of regulation 4 and the substitution of the following regulation therefore:

   '4. The share capital of the company is € [•] divided into [•] ordinary shares of € [•] each.'

4. AS ORDINARY RESOLUTIONS:

   a. THAT the Company enters into a [DETAILS OF AGREEMENT]

      together with any and all other documents which the directors consider to be necessary or desirable in connection with the transactions contemplated therein, the 'Transaction Documents'.

b.   THAT the terms of, and the transactions contemplated by, the Transaction Documents to which the Company is a party be and are hereby approved;

c.   THAT the directors of the Company be and are hereby authorised to settle and approve any amendments or variations to the Transaction Documents as they, in their sole discretion, think necessary and appropriate;

d.   THAT the directors of the Company are instructed to take any action in connection with the negotiation, execution, delivery and performance of the Transaction Documents to which the Company is a party as they shall deem necessary and appropriate and where any Transaction Document is to be executed under seal, the common seal of the Company be affixed to the Transaction Document and the Transaction Document be executed under seal in accordance with the Articles of Association of the Company and, where any Transaction Document is to be executed under hand, any of the directors be authorised to sign the Transaction Document under hand on behalf of the Company; and

e.   THAT the transactions contemplated by the Transaction Documents and the various confirmations, undertakings, obligations and other matters on the part of the Company set out in the Transaction Documents are in the best interests of the Company and its members and the entry by the Company into the proposed transactions substantially on the terms set out in the Transaction Documents is to the commercial benefit and advantage of the Company.

DATED

[This [These] Resolution[s] may be executed in any number of counterparts, and by the several members on separate counterparts, each of which when so executed will constitute an original but all of which together will evidence the same resolution[s].]

*[in the case of a unanimous written resolution]*NB: [This] [These] resolution[s] [is/are] not effective until signed by all of the members. The effective date will be the date on which the last member signs. *OR*

*[in the case of majority ordinary written resolution]*NB: [This] [These] ordinary resolution[s] [is/are] not effective until the date which is 7 days after the date upon which [it]/[they] [is/are] signed by all of the members]. *OR*

*[in the case of majority special written resolution]*NB: [This] [These] special resolution[s] [is/are] not effective until the date which is 21 days after the date upon which [it]/[they] [is/are] signed by all of the members].

SIGNED by the following being [together all of the members entitled to attend and vote on the resolution[s] at a general meeting of the company (or being bodies corporate by their duly authorised representatives.)]/[together more than 50% of the total voting rights of all the members entitled to attend and vote on the above ordinary resolution[s] at a general meeting of the company (or being bodies corporate by their duly authorised representatives.)/[together more than 75% of the total voting rights of all the members entitled to attend and vote on the above special resolution[s] at a general meeting of the company (or being bodies corporate by their duly authorised representatives).]/[the sole member entitled to attend and vote on the resolution[s] at a general meeting of the company.] *[delete as appropriate]*

SIGNED for and on behalf of   )
[SHAREHOLDER COMPANY NAME]:

)
                                                  _____

                                                  Duly Authorised Signatory

)

)
                                                  Name:

)

)
                                                            _____

                                                  Title:

)
                                                            _____

SIGNED by [SHAREHOLDER NAME]:   )

)
                                                  _____

)

SIGNED by [SHAREHOLDER NAME]:   )

)
                                                  _____

)

APPENDIX 9

SPECIMEN DIRECTORS' WRITTEN RESOLUTION

[NAME OF COMPANY]

(COMPANY NUMBER [•])

(THE 'COMPANY')

RESOLUTIONS OF THE DIRECTORS OF THE COMPANY

NOTED: [*Set out background to the resolutions and include declaration of interests, if thought appropriate*]

RESOLVED: pursuant to [Section 161 of the Companies Act 2014] *OR* [regulation [•] of the company's constitution]:

1. Application having been received for the allotment of [•] [ordinary] shares of € [•] each and the subscription price having been received, that [•] [ordinary] shares of € [•] each be and are hereby allotted to [•] for cash at par credited as fully paid up.

2. That a share certificate be issued as follows and the common seal affixed thereto:

Shareholder	No. and Class of Shares
[•]	[•] [Ordinary] Shares of € [•] each.

DATED: [*DATE*] at [*TIME*]am/pm

[This]/[These] Resolution[s] may be executed in any number of counterparts, and by the several Directors on separate counterparts, each of which when so executed will constitute an original but all of which together will evidence the same resolution[s].

NB: [This] [These] resolution[s] [is/are] not effective until signed by all of the Directors. The effective date will be the date on which the last Director signs.

SIGNED by the following being [together all of the Directors of the company

SIGNED by [DIRECTOR NAME]:   )

)   _____

)

SIGNED by [DIRECTOR NAME]:   )

)   _____

)

CHAPTER 5

SHARE CAPITAL

5.1 Introduction

This chapter considers private companies limited by shares and every reference to a company is in reference to a private company limited by shares. The members of these companies own the companies through their ownership of shares, and are therefore known as 'shareholders'.

This chapter will examine some of the most important issues that surround shares and share ownership, both for the company and the shareholders.

5.2 What is Share Capital?

Share capital is the amount of money that a company raises by issuing shares and is dealt with in more detail below.

5.3 Maintenance of Capital

The maintenance of share capital is one of the main principles of company law and comes up time and time again in daily practice. This principle underpins many of the concepts that you will come across in this book and is driven by the primacy given under Irish company law to the protection of creditors.

Share capital is the fund available to creditors for the payment of debts owed to them and as a result it must generally be maintained. In other words paid-up share capital must generally not be returned to shareholders, and there should be no reduction to their liability for share capital not paid up on shares. This is particularly important because the liability of shareholders in a company is limited (in other words shareholders cannot generally be sued for the obligations or debts of the company).

As a result, shareholders of a company, having bought shares in the company, cannot normally return their shares to the company in exchange for the consideration they originally provided. In order to realise their investment in the company, they must sell their shares to another shareholder or investor.

5.4 Allotting and Issuing Shares

The allotment of new shares is often known as 'equity finance'. The company will typically receive money from subscribers and in exchange will issue them with shares. The company can then use the money received for the company's business to buy equipment, to pay for stock, to pay for marketing campaigns, and so on. The other main way in which companies raise finance is through borrowing money – either from banks or the capital markets through bond issuances. The allotment of shares is different from a transfer of existing shares, where an existing shareholder sells or gives his or her shares to another person.

The board of directors of a company will determine the price and number of shares to allot. In larger companies, an investment bank or firm of accountants will usually advise on the amounts needed and the price per share. The directors of a typical private company though will arrive at an amount without the need for external professional assistance. This will often be based on a business plan and set of financial projections.

A solicitor's job will be to ensure the allotment is carried out correctly and to draft the necessary documents. All companies big and small, private and public will allot shares at some point during their life.

Typically an allotment is triggered when someone applies to the company for shares, usually having been asked to do so by the board (in private companies there will be significant cross-over between the directors and shareholders so in practice allotments do not arrive out of the blue for shareholders). This person (the 'subscriber') will receive the shares following a resolution of the directors. The subscriber will be given a share certificate evidencing his or her shares. Finally, but critically, the company secretary will enter the subscriber's name in the share register. This last step is critical as a company's share register is the authoritative evidence of title to shares.

Under the Companies Act 2014 (the '2014 Act'), the board may be required to obtain various resolutions from the shareholders prior to resolving to allot the shares. This is because an allotment will potentially affect each existing shareholder's shareholding as a percentage of ownership of the company (known as dilution). An allotment may significantly alter the existing shareholders' voting power on resolutions and may also result in the existing shareholders getting reduced dividends, since the profits available for distribution as dividends will have to be split among a greater number of shares. As a result proposed allotments of shares can be quite contentious in practice with minority shareholders putting up resistance to any form of dilution. This is particularly the case if the minority shareholder is a professional investor such as a venture capital fund. The powers surrounding allotments can therefore be heavily negotiated in shareholders' agreements.

The resolutions under the 2014 Act concern the need for the directors to have authority to allot shares for a particular time period (2014 Act, s 69 (3)) and statutory pre-emption rights, i.e. a right of first refusal given to existing shareholders (2014 Act, s 69 (6)). There may also be restrictions under the constitution of the company or in a shareholders' agreement.

Students should be aware that the two words 'allotting' and 'issuing' are often used interchangeably. Strictly speaking, shares are allotted to someone (i.e. allocated) when that person acquires an unconditional right to be included on the company's register of members in respect of that share (2014 Act, ss 70 (6) and 169). When the name of the shareholder has been entered on the company's register of members then the shares may be said to have been issued by the company (*Re Heaton's Steel and Iron Co, Blyth's case* (1876) 4 ChD 140). However, both 'allotting' and 'issuing' are frequently used to describe the whole process by which a shareholder takes shares in a company.

5.4.1 SHARE CAPITAL

The share capital is the amount of money which a company raises by issuing shares. The authorised share capital is a 'ceiling' on the number of shares which a company can allot.

Under the 2014 Act a private company limited by shares may however dispense with this requirement (2014 Act, s 19 (1)(d)). A private company limited by shares is simply required to make a statement of capital and the number of shares taken by each subscriber when the company was incorporated. For example, a new company is often formed with 100 ordinary shares of a nominal value (par value) of €1 each, and this information would be included in its constitution on incorporation. Alternatively, s 19 (1)(d)(ii) of the 2014 Act provides that on incorporation, a company can elect not to state an authorised share capital but instead can state that its share capital will be divided into shares of a fixed amount specified in the constitution. This therefore represents the company's share capital.

If the company wishes to raise additional finance by issuing more shares, it must follow the procedure under the 2014 Act and in its constitution. In some cases the shareholders will need to give their prior approval to issuing more shares above the amount with which the company was formed.

It is possible for a company to include a restriction in its constitution on the number of shares which it can issue. If the company wishes to raise money by issuing shares in excess of any limit imposed by the constitution of the company, then the company can only proceed if the shareholders first pass a special resolution under s 32 of the 2014 Act to amend the constitution of the company to remove the limit.

5.4.2   DIRECTORS' POWER TO ALLOT SHARES

At the first board meeting of a new company the board will usually want to allot shares in the company, and may subsequently wish to issue more shares to raise additional finance.

No shares may be allotted by a company unless the allotment is authorised, either specifically for a particular allotment or pursuant to a general authority, by ordinary resolution or by the constitution of the company (2014 Act, s 69 (1)). Where a new company is formed, it is useful if the authority is contained within the constitution of the company so that the matter does not have to be considered at a general meeting or by written resolution.

In the case of a company whose constitution states an authorised share capital, no shares may be allotted by the company unless those shares are comprised in the authorised but unissued share capital of the company.

Regardless of how the necessary authority is given, it must state the maximum number of shares the directors have authority to allot. The authority may provide for the directors to allot just one batch of shares, or it may be given generally, allowing them to issue any number of shares up to the amount of the authorised share capital.

An authority, whether conferred by an ordinary resolution or the constitution, may also give the period of time for which the authority is to last, in which event any shares issued outside of that time period will not have been properly authorised.

Save to the extent the constitution of a company provides otherwise, the directors of a company may allot, grant options over, or otherwise dispose of shares to such persons, on such terms and conditions and at such times as they may consider to be in the best interests of the company and its shareholders (2014 Act, s 69 (4)).

If the authority to allot shares is contained in a company's constitution, an ordinary resolution is sufficient to remove this authority (2014 Act, s 70 (5)). This is unusual as normally a special resolution is required in order to amend a company's constitution.

Under s 70 of the 2014 Act, a return of allotments must be filed with the Companies Registration Office (the 'CRO') within one month of the date of the allotment in the prescribed form. This ensures that the public record always gives an up-to-date view of the company's capital.

5.4.3   STATUTORY PRE-EMPTION RIGHTS

Regardless of the fact that the directors may have authority to issue shares, and of the rights conferred under s 69 (4) of the 2014 Act, the directors should first investigate as to whether any pre-emption rights exist over unissued shares in the company. Sections 69 (6) and 69 (7) of the 2014 Act provide that where shares are being issued for cash payment, those shares must first be offered to the existing shareholders of the company. The percentage of shares each current shareholder holds will dictate the number of shares that he or she is offered. Only if the present shareholders decline to take up the shares, having been given a minimum of 14 days to take up the offer, can they be offered to a 'non-member'.

This right to be offered shares by the company is known as a 'pre-emption right' or 'statutory pre-emption rights' (as the right is conferred by statute).

If the directors do not wish to apply the pre-emption rights to allot the shares to the existing shareholders in accordance with their current shareholdings, they should check the constitution of the company to see whether the statutory pre-emption rights have been removed. If not removed by the constitution, the members will be required to pass a special resolution to dispense formally with the need to offer the shares to the present shareholders. Alternatively shareholders can be asked to waive their pre-emption rights. This is usually done by way of a short letter addressed to the company secretary.

The 2014 Act provides various ways in which the pre-emption rights may be disapplied (i.e. excluded). Depending on the method used, the pre-emption rights may be dispensed with either generally or for just one particular issue of shares.

Under s 69 (12) of the 2014 Act, pre-emption rights shall not apply in the following circumstances:

(a)   where the pre-emption rights have been disapplied (either generally or in relation to a particular allotment or class of allotments) by the constitution of the company, a special resolution, or the terms of issue of already allotted shares;

(b)   where shares are allotted for consideration wholly or partly paid for, otherwise than in cash (say, a piece of land). It would not be necessary to disapply statutory pre-emption rights in this case, as there would not be any pre-emption rights in the first place. The constitution should however be checked carefully as it may include pre-emption rights even where the consideration is non-cash;

(c)   to allotments of shares to the subscriber or subscribers to the company's constitution upon the company's incorporation, being the shares taken by that subscriber or those subscribers before such incorporation;

(d)   to allotments of shares to persons under the terms of an employee's share scheme established by the company; and

(e)   to the allotment of bonus shares.

Under s 69 (8) of the 2014 Act, pre-emption provisions in the constitution of a company will override the statutory provisions in s 69 (6) of the 2014 Act, though the notice provisions in s 69 (6)(b) still apply unless they too have been excluded in the constitution.

5.4.4   PROCEDURE

Shares in a company may be allotted to third parties who are not already shareholders using one of two separate procedures, depending on whether shareholder approval is required.

5.4.4.1   Shareholder approval needed

(a)   A board meeting must be called by any director on reasonable notice.

(b)   Directors must check:

(i)   whether there are any restrictions on the allotment of shares in the constitution of the company which need to be revoked by a special resolution;

(ii)   whether they have authority to allot the shares, under the constitution or under the 2014 Act, or whether the shareholders must first either amend the constitution or pass an ordinary resolution authorising the allotment; and

(iii)   whether there are any pre-emption rights in place which require that the shares be offered to the current shareholders first.

(c)   If the number of shares which can be issued is restricted and/or authority is required and/or pre-emption rights need to be disapplied then the constitution will need to be amended as appropriate. The directors will need to pass a board resolution to call an extraordinary general meeting ('EGM') or propose written resolutions for the shareholders to agree. 21 clear days' notice is required for the EGM in the usual way. Notice in writing must be sent to all shareholders, and short notice may be consented to by the shareholders.

(d)   If the requisite majority vote in favour then the EGM will be held and the resolutions passed.

(e)   The directors will then reconvene the board meeting (or call a second board meeting) and the directors will pass a board resolution to allot the shares in accordance with the amended constitution.

(f)   Private companies are not in general permitted to offer their shares to members of the public. Therefore, it is necessary that the offer to buy comes from the prospective shareholders and that that offer is accepted by the company. The directors will then resolve to issue the shares to those persons who have made a written application for them.

(g)   The directors will resolve to seal the share certificates and will instruct the secretary to enter the name of the new members on the register of members. The sealed share certificates must also be complete and ready for delivery to the new shareholders within two months of the date of the allotment or of the date the transfer is lodged with the company unless the conditions of issue of the shares provides otherwise. They will also instruct the company secretary to notify the CRO in the prescribed form, within 30 days of the allotment, that new shares have been issued.

5.4.4.2   Shareholder approval not needed

(a)   A board meeting must be called by any director on reasonable notice.

(b)   Directors must check:

(i)   the constitution of the company and the 2014 Act to see whether they have authority to allot the shares; and

(ii)   whether there are any pre-emption rights in place which require that the shares be offered to the current shareholders first.

(c)   Assuming that the directors have authority to allot the shares and no shareholder approval is needed, and that no pre-emption rights exist over the shares, the directors will simply need to pass a board resolution to allot the shares. No shareholder involvement is required and so no EGM or written resolution is needed. The board will resolve to issue the shares to those persons who have made written application for them.

(d)   The directors will resolve to seal the share certificates and will instruct the secretary to enter the name of the new members on the register of members. The sealed share certificates must also be complete and ready for delivery to the new shareholders within two months of the date of the allotment or of the date the transfer is lodged with the company unless the conditions of issue of the shares provides otherwise. They will also instruct the secretary to notify the Registrar of Companies in the prescribed form, within 30 days of the allotment, that new shares have been issued.

5.4.5 PAYMENT FOR SHARES

A prospective shareholder may provide non-cash consideration (which can include good-will and expertise) only if the board agrees. Otherwise he or she must pay for shares in cash (which is the more usual form of consideration).

5.4.6 PARTLY-PAID SHARES

Usually, a prospective shareholder will pay for the shares which are to be issued to him or her. For example, if a prospective shareholder offers to buy 100 €1 shares at €1 each, the directors will expect him or her to pay the company €100 (or they may agree to accept assets worth €100 in payment for the shares). However, it is possible, if the directors agree, for the prospective shareholder to be issued shares for which he or she has only partly paid. This means that although the full price of the shares must be paid eventually, it does not have to be paid immediately. For example, the directors might issue 100 €1 shares on the basis that 50c per share is payable on issue and the remaining 50c per share is payable 12 months later. The directors of the company may from time to time make calls on share-holders to pay up any outstanding amount. In the event of the insolvency of the company shareholders will be liable to pay to the liquidator any amount unpaid on their shares.

5.4.7 SHARES ISSUED AT A PREMIUM

The nominal value of each share is also known as the par value (e.g. €1.00 par value each). Depending on their market value (i.e. the actual value of the company as re-flected in its share price), shares may be issued at a price higher than their nominal value (e.g. for €1.50). This is common in private companies as the price of the share will normally reflect the value of the business. If this happens, the excess amount of con-sideration paid above the nominal value of the shares (e.g. 50c) must not be treated as part of the company's trading profit and must be recorded in a separate share premium account (2014 Act, s 71 (5)). It is treated as share capital, and thus is subject to the same rules governing the maintenance of the paid-up share capital of the company. Specific restrictions apply to any such account in the instance of mergers (2014 Act, s 72), group reconstructions (2014 Act, s 73), and in the case of shares allotted in return for the acquisition of issued shares of a body corporate (2014 Act, s 75).

5.4.8 SHARES ISSUED AT A DISCOUNT

There is a general prohibition on the issue of shares for less than their nominal value (2014 Act, s 71 (2)). If this happens, the shareholder is obliged to pay the amount of discount to the company with interest (2014 Act, s 71 (3)).

5.5 Classes of Shares

A company may decide to restrict the rights held by certain shareholders (for example employees who receive shares under an employee incentive scheme) and therefore create different classes of shares. The typical type of share is known as an ordinary share, but there may be more than one class of ordinary shares within the company. For example, two different classes of ordinary shares may carry different voting rights or dividend rights (2014 Act, s 66). This way, directors can raise capital by issuing shares to new or existing shareholders, while still retaining control of the company by not attaching any voting rights to the newly issued shares. Usually differing classes of shares are distinguished al-phabetically, e.g. 'A Ordinary Shares' and 'B Ordinary Shares'. The rights attaching to a share are dependent on the constitution of the company. If no separate rights attach to a particular class of shares, the common law rule is that all shares are presumed, prima facie, to rank equally (*Birch v Cropper* [1889] 14 App Cas 525 at 543 (HL), *Scottish Insurance Corp Ltd v Wilsons & Clyde Coal Co Ltd* [1949] AC 462).

The different classes of shares and the rights attaching to them must be included in the constitution of the company which is lodged at the CRO when the company is formed (2014 Act, s 19). Types of shares may include those discussed in **5.5.1** to **5.5.3** below.

5.5.1   ORDINARY SHARES

Ordinary shares usually carry the primary voting rights of the company, the right to a dividend if declared, and rights to participate in a surplus in a winding up, however this will depend on the constitution of the company and the rights and dividends attaching to shares are matters for the company.

As set out above, unless stated otherwise in the constitution of the company, it is assumed that all shares have the same rights. If, for example, the constitution states that the capital of the company is to be €100 divided into 100 shares of €1 each, the shares all have the same, unrestricted rights. It is not necessary to classify them as ordinary shares since there are no others. But there is no objection to doing so.

A company is entitled to attach special rights to different shares, for example as regards dividends, return of capital, voting, or the right to appoint a director. It is always necessary to check the company's constitution when seeking to establish what rights apply.

5.5.2   PREFERENCE SHARES

Preference shares are any shares which are specified as having priority over the ordinary shares. The priority is usually in relation to capital and dividends, though neither of these is required to be a priority for a share to be deemed a preference share. There are often express differences between preference and ordinary shares, though none are implied.

The dividend applying to preferential shares may be cumulative (i.e. it rolls up), or it may be payable only out of the profits of each year. The dividend will generally be a fixed one, i.e. it is expressed as a fixed percentage of the par value of the share. There is no right for a preferential shareholder to compel the company to pay the dividend if it declines to do so. You may come across this in practice if, rather than using profits to pay a dividend, the company decides to make a provision in its accounts for a liability or loss.

Preference shares are often issued to investors in a company, with Enterprise Ireland being an example of an investor that will quite often invest in preference shares.

Preference shares are often used as an alternative to lending money to the company. The benefit being that preference shareholders will have priority over any profits of the company at a fixed rate, and the dividend is usually paid periodically (say annually). Preference shares are usually also redeemable, which allows the investor the opportunity to exchange the shares for cash at some stage in the future.

There are four main kinds of preference shares:

(a)   cumulative;

(b)   non-cumulative;

(c)   participating; and

(d)   convertible.

'Cumulative' means that, if the preference share dividend has not been paid on a preceding occasion, the preference shareholder has to be paid any missed dividends as well as the current dividend. This takes priority over the payment of dividends to the ordinary shareholders. 'Non-cumulative' therefore means that no such priority is given and an unpaid dividend will not be paid in future years in the event that there are insufficient profits to pay a dividend in any given year.

In addition to the fixed preference rights, participating shareholders have a further right to participate in profits or assets. For example, there could be a right to an additional payment to the preference shareholders in the event that the ordinary shareholders are paid a dividend above a specified amount. Convertible preference shares may be exchanged for ordinary shares at a specified price and after a specified date. The rights of a preference shareholder will be set out in the constitution of the company (or possibly in a negotiated shareholders' agreement, depending on the facts).

5.5.3 REDEEMABLE SHARES

Sections 102–112 of the 2014 Act govern the purchase by a private company of its own shares. Shares that are designed specifically to be bought back by the company are called redeemable shares. In order for the directors to issue redeemable shares, there must be a specific regulation in the company's constitution, setting out details of the terms and conditions of issue. For example, shares may be redeemable at the option of the shareholder, or of the company, or of either.

The constitution may also provide for the terms and manner of the redemption, or alternatively, if they are authorised by a special resolution of the members (excluding the shares being proposed to be redeemed), the directors of a company can decide the conditions of redemption. Generally, redeemable shares have to be redeemed from distributable profits or from the proceeds (i.e. money received by the company) from a fresh issue of shares to new or existing subscribers.

Redeemable shares can ensure a straightforward exit route from the company for investors and as such are sometimes used by venture capital investors. Prior to investing, they will usually seek to agree a structured and easy exit from the company after a three to five-year period, at which point they can (hopefully) realise a profit to return, in turn, to their investors (or reinvest).

5.6 Distributions

A distribution, or dividend, (an income payment on shares) can only be paid if there are 'profits available' for this purpose (2014 Act, s 117). Initially, the directors will decide whether or not to recommend that the company pay a distribution to shareholders. The directors will first have to ascertain whether there are profits available. This is done by deducting from all the realised profits of the company to date all the realised losses to date. The balance, or profit, left after doing this, if any, is available to pay a dividend. The directors will make this calculation based on the latest set of audited accounts. It should be noted that, as the audited accounts will usually apply to the previous year's trading, a company may be able to pay a dividend based on previous year's profits even if the company has not made a profit in the current year (as the current year's audited accounts will not be finalised). It is open to the directors to draw up 'interim' financial statements to allow them to form the reasonable view that there are sufficient profits available if the previous year's financial statements do not show a profit available to make a distribution.

Any shareholder who has received the dividend must refund it to the company if he or she knows or has reasonable grounds for believing that the payment is unauthorised (2014 Act, s 122). A director of a company may be personally liable to repay a dividend paid by a company where that director has authorised the payment of the dividend otherwise than out of distributable profits. This applies regardless of whether or not the director was a shareholder (*Bairstow v Queens Moat Houses plc* [2000] 1 BCLC 549).

The constitution of the company determines the power to declare a dividend. The directors may recommend the amount of the dividend if they decide that the company has sufficient funds. However, the dividend may only be declared by the shareholders in a general meeting (2014 Act, s 124). The shareholders cannot vote to pay a dividend in excess of what the directors have recommended; however, they could decide that a smaller amount was more appropriate. The dividend will usually be in a form pro rata to the shareholders shareholding, for example, 5c in the Euro, which means that for every €1 share they hold, they receive a dividend of 5c.

5.7   Transfer of Shares

Shares are transferred if the shareholder who owns them, or someone on his or her behalf, sells them or gives them to another person.

5.7.1   PROCEDURE FOR TRANSFER

A stock transfer form is the document used to evidence the transfer of a share or shares. The seller or donor of the shares ('the transferor') should complete and sign a stock transfer form, which he or she should then give to the buyer or recipient ('the transferee') (2014 Act, ss 94–101). There is no need for the transferee to sign the stock transfer form or for the signature of the transferor to be witnessed. The share certificate should also be handed over to the transferee. It should be noted that the stock transfer form is not a CRO form and should not be filed with the CRO. It should be filed with the Revenue Commissioners only. If the shares are being sold for more than €1,000, the buyer must pay stamp duty (currently charged at 1%) on the stock transfer form. The transferee should then send the share certificate and stock transfer form to the company who should, within two months, send the new shareholder a new share certificate in his or her name, and should also ensure that his or her name is entered on the register of members (2014 Act, s 99). The change in the composition of the membership of the company is notified to the CRO on the company's next annual return.

5.7.2   RESTRICTIONS ON TRANSFER

The 2014 Act governs the ability of the shareholders of a company to transfer their shares to whomever they choose. Under s 95 of the 2014 Act directors have an absolute discretion on the registration of transfers and may, save where the constitution of the company provides otherwise, decline to register the transfer of any share. This power, to decline to register a transfer, shall cease to be exercisable on the expiry of two months after the date of delivery to the company of the instrument of transfer of the share and the directors must notify the transferee of its refusal within this 2 month time frame. The directors may also decline to register any instrument of transfer unless: a fee of €10 (or such lesser sum as the directors may require) is paid to the company in respect of it; the instrument of transfer is accompanied by the certificate of the shares to which it relates and such other evidence as the directors may reasonably require to show the right of the transferor to make the transfer; and the instrument of transfer is in respect of one class of share only.

Under s 169 of the 2014 Act, a company shall keep a register of its members. The register of members shall be prima facie evidence of any matters directed or authorised to be inserted in it by the 2014 Act (2014 Act, s 171). The register of members should be updated within 28 days after the date of conclusion of the agreement with the company by the new shareholder to become a member or, in the case of a subscriber of the constitution, within 28 days after the date of registration of the company, or in the case of a person ceasing to be a member, within 28 days of the date when that person ceased to be a member. If the name of any person is, without sufficient cause, entered in the register of members or omitted from it, or not removed from it as appropriate, the person aggrieved, or any member of the company, or the company, may apply to court to rectify the register. Where an application is made for rectification, the court may either refuse the application or may order rectification of the register and payment by the company of compensation for any loss sustained by any party aggrieved.

A company may, without application to the court, at any time rectify any error or omission in the register but such a rectification shall not adversely affect any person unless he or she agrees to the rectification made. If any such rectification is made, the company shall notify the registrar if the error referred to also occurs in any document forwarded by the company to the registrar.

The court will generally not interfere with the directors' operation of the company, for example if directors exercise their discretion and refuse to register a new shareholder. However this will not be the case if the transferee can show that the directors did not act in good faith.

5.8   Transmission of Shares

Transmission is the process by which shares automatically pass on the death or bankruptcy of a shareholder. When a shareholder dies, his or her shares immediately pass to his or her personal representatives (PRs). If a shareholder is declared bankrupt, his or her shares automatically vest in his or her Official Assignee in Bankruptcy. When either event happens, the PRs or the Official Assignee shall not be entitled to exercise the votes which attach to the shares as they are not members of the company; however, they will be entitled to any dividend declared on the shares (2014 Act, ss 96 (8) and (9)).

The PRs of a deceased shareholder must produce to the company any document which is by law sufficient evidence of probate of the will or letters of administration of the estate of a deceased person to establish their right to deal with the shares as PRs of the estate (2014 Act, s 96 (12)), but they then have a choice:

(a)   They may elect to be registered as shareholders themselves. The entry on the register of members will not show that they hold the shares in a representative capacity. All of the limitations, restrictions, and provisions of the 2014 Act relating to the right to transfer and the registration of a transfer of a share (as dealt with above) shall be applicable to a notice to transfer from any person becoming entitled on the death or bankruptcy of a member (2014 Act, s 96 (7)). The directors cannot prevent the PRs from acquiring the shares by transmission in their capacity as PRs, but they can prevent their being registered as shareholders. If the PRs are registered as shareholders of the company, they can then deal with the shares in the usual way, either transferring them to the beneficiary under the deceased member's will or selling them to a third party for the benefit of the deceased member's estate.

(b)   They can transfer the shares directly to the ultimate beneficiary or to a third party in their representative capacity without being registered as a shareholder in the interim.

Likewise, the Official Assignee in Bankruptcy may elect to be registered as a shareholder and then sell the shares; alternatively, he or she can sell them directly in his or her representative capacity. He or she must establish his or her right to deal with the shares by producing the court order concerning his or her appointment.

5.9   Nominee/Beneficial Ownership of Shares

Quite often the ultimate beneficial owner of shares will elect not to be the registered owner. This could be for a number of reasons: confidentiality and convenience being the main ones. In such an instance, the beneficial owner of the shares will appoint a 'nominee' to act on his or her behalf pursuant to a simple nominee agreement and the shares will be registered in the name of the nominee. Most stockbroking firms provide a nominee service as standard for shareholders in public companies and while it is less common in private companies, it is not unusual.

From a company's perspective it cannot and does not recognise the trust relationship created pursuant to a nominee relationship and it can only recognise the name registered on the share register as the shareholder. Under s 66 (6) of the 2014 Act the company shall not be bound or compelled in any way to recognise, even where the company has notice of it, any equitable, contingent, future, or partial interest in any share, or any interest in any fractional part of a share. Likewise, unless the 2014 Act or another law provides otherwise, the company may not be bound or compelled to recognise any other rights in respect of any share, except the absolute right of the holder of that share to the entirety of it. However, this does not prevent a company from requiring a member or transferee of shares to furnish the company with information which the company may reasonably require as to the beneficial ownership of any share (2014 Act, s 66 (7)).

CHAPTER 6

SHAREHOLDERS' AGREEMENTS

6.1 Introduction

The operation of the Companies Act, 2014 (the '2014 Act') as regards the balance between the rights of shareholders in a company may not be appropriate for every situation. In particular, the 2014 Act (as did its predecessors) offers very limited protection for minority shareholders (i.e. shareholders holding less than 50% of the shares) in a private company. Accordingly, it is typical to find that the minority shareholders seek the inclusion of special protective provisions in either the company's constitution and/or a separate agreement entered into between the shareholders (and sometimes the company itself), i.e. a shareholders' agreement. Majority shareholders can also benefit from provisions included in the shareholders' agreement, which apply to all shareholders who sign it.

The best shareholders' agreement is one that, when signed, is put away and never looked at again because of the good relations between the parties. However, it may be that the very existence of this agreement is what promotes and protects a relationship between the parties as it sets the boundaries to behaviour, which would otherwise form the basis of future disputes. The expense incurred at the outset of a venture on a shareholders' agreement is typically money well spent giving the costly, time-consuming, and damaging disputes that can arise when shareholder relationships go wrong. The goal of the shareholders' agreement should be to prevent disputes rather than to resolve them if they arise.

Part 4, Chapter 8 of the 2014 Act deals with the protection of minorities. This provides a remedy where the affairs of the company are conducted, or powers of the directors are exercised in a manner oppressive to them or in disregard of their rights (2014 Act, s 213). While this section provides wide discretion to the court to make orders ending the oppression, recourse to s 213 is a costly and sometimes protracted option and one that should be exercised as a last resort. It can take a year or more from presenting the petition to the ultimate resolution by the court.

There is no legal requirement either for a shareholders' agreement or for all shareholders in the company to be party to a shareholders' agreement. The company's constitution also governs relationship between all the shareholders and there is often overlap between it and any shareholders' agreement put in place. As anything included in the constitution will be in the public domain (as the constitution must be filed in the Companies Registration Office), commercially sensitive provisions are typically found only in the shareholders' agreement.

In situations where a shareholders' agreement is entered into, care should be taken that it does not conflict with the constitution and that all necessary shareholders are party to it (and so bound by its provisions). Shareholders' agreements are almost always made between shareholders in private companies, as shareholders in listed companies can easily sell their shares if they do not agree with how the company is being operated. As such, this chapter focuses on shareholders' agreements as they relate to private companies and any reference to a company is a reference to a private company limited by shares.

The form and content of a shareholders' agreement depends on the circumstances pertaining to the company and its shareholders and while certain provisions are commonly found, whether they are included and how they are included is typically a matter for negotiation between the parties. While there is no standard form, this chapter is concerned with typical provisions that one may find in a shareholders' agreement in a private limited company.

6.2   Principal Uses

Most of the provisions found in a shareholders' agreement could be included in the constitution, however there are circumstances when it is preferable or required to include them in a shareholders' agreement instead. The principal uses for shareholders' agreement include the following:

(a)   to confer rights on shareholders which would not be possible or appropriate to include in a company's constitution;

(b)   to include rights/obligations other than in the capacity as a shareholder (for example, the obligation to lend money or to provide services to the company) – the constitution binds members in their capacity as members;

(c)   to enshrine minority shareholder rights that could otherwise be varied by a change in the constitution; and

(d)   to preserve confidentiality as the shareholders' agreement is not a public document.

6.3   Main Provisions

Typically a shareholders' agreement will deal with some or all of the following:

6.3.1   PROVISIONS RELATING TO SHARES

It is common for the following provisions to be dealt with in a shareholders' agreement (although some or all may be mirrored in the company's constitution). In fact, it may be advisable to also include certain of these in the constitution so that any prospective purchaser of shares will be on notice of the provisions when they acquire or seek to acquire shares in the company.

6.3.1.1   Pre-emption rights

Rights on issue of shares

These rights can be statutory (the 2014 Act), contract (shareholders' agreement), or constitution based, and allow a shareholder to buy shares in the company at such a level that allows him/her to maintain his equity percentage if he or she so wishes to participate in the share issuance. In many cases shareholders will want to supplement or vary the statutory pre-emption rights (which in any event can be disapplied) in the shareholders' agreement. The purpose of these types of rights is that any shareholder who takes up the rights to buy shares does not get diluted when new shares are issued by the company.

Rights on transfer of shares

These pre-emption rights would be either contract or constitution based and allow a shareholder to acquire shares proposed to be sold by other shareholder(s) so that, if all pre-emption rights are exercised, the remaining shareholders will be the only shareholders in the company (avoiding a new person becoming a shareholder) and no shareholder will increase his/her relative equity percentage, provided the other shareholders take up their full pro rata entitlement to buy the shares offered for sale.

6.3.1.2   Drag-along rights

Drag-along rights usually benefit the majority shareholders and operate to allow certain shareholders (holding a certain level of shares e.g. 60%), on receipt of a qualifying offer for their shares, to compel all of the other shareholders to also sell their shares (typically on the same terms) to the proposed buyer. Such rights are desirable where shareholders want to force a sale when an attractive offer is made, as often such an offer will only be made where a prospective purchaser can acquire all of the shares in the company. In the event that all of the shareholders of the company are not party to the shareholders' agreement such a provision could also be included in the constitution. It is much preferable that all shareholders would agree to a sale and sign the relevant documents, rather than be contractually dragged into it.

6.3.1.3   Tag-along rights

Tag-along rights (sometimes also referred to as piggy-back rights) enable certain shareholders (usually minority shareholders) to force other shareholders, who are selling their shares, to procure that an offer is also made by the buyer to the minority shareholders (typically on the same terms) for their shares. Such rights will go some way to protecting a minority shareholder from being excluded or left behind in the company by the majority shareholders, who sell some or all of their shares to a third party. Again, a consensual purchase of the minority shares is preferable.

6.3.1.4   Compulsory sales

It is not uncommon that a shareholders' agreement will provide for compulsory offering for sale of shares held on the occurrence of certain events. In such circumstances it will be necessary to put in place a structure and mechanism to fix the price and the transfer mechanics. The rationale for such compulsory sale provisions is that the shareholders have agreed who they wish to conduct their affairs with as shareholders, and therefore wish to retain control as to the ownership of the shares in the event of the following:

Departure of an employee (Good Leaver/Bad Leaver)

Where an employee is offered certain share ownership incentives in connection with his/her role in the company, it is common to provide for a compulsory offering for sale of his/her shares in the event the employee ceases their employment with the company. The price payable for such shares will usually be dependent on the circumstances surrounding the termination of their employment. It is usual to find disincentive provisions which apply where the employee is deemed a bad leaver, for example, if she/he resigns and takes up a position with a competitor. In such circumstances he/she would typically not get full market value for his/her shares. In the case of retirement, such a person would be a good leaver and get full market value for their shares.

Death or incapacity of a shareholder

As the relationship between the shareholders is often a personal one (and often one where certain shareholders operate in an executive capacity in the company), it is often provided that in the case of the death of a shareholder, his/her estate is required to offer the shares held to the other shareholders. A similar situation can apply in relation to the incapacity of a shareholder and the compulsory offering for sale of the relevant shares. It would be unusual if there were a discount applied to fair market value of the shares in these circumstances.

An insolvency event in the case of a shareholder

In such circumstances the other shareholders in the company would not be dealing with a person or persons who they may be comfortable with, but rather the liquidator or trustee, and given the effective change in relationship, it is not uncommon for compulsory sale provisions to apply in such circumstances. It would be unusual if there were a discount applied to fair market value of the shares in these circumstances.

Deemed transfer on breach of agreement

It may be the case that a shareholder repeatedly (deliberately or otherwise) breaches the agreed terms of the shareholders' agreement. In such circumstances it may be appropriate to include provisions that, unless the breach or breaches are remedied (usually after a warning is given), the shares which were held by the shareholder in breach are involuntarily and automatically made available for sale (usually at a discount to market value) to the other non-breaching shareholders.

6.3.1.5   Lock in

It is common that shareholders may agree not to sell their shares in the company for a certain time, or until the other shareholders agree. In such scenarios there are often carve-outs (permitted transfers) whereby shares can be transferred to certain family members or family trusts, or when a certain type of consent is achieved (from the other shareholders or the board). From a perspective of a corporate shareholder, intra-group transfers are often allowed provided and to the extent that the transferee remains in the original group (otherwise compulsory sale provisions may apply).

6.3.1.6   Exit/Realisation

Often the shareholders in a company do not wish to hold the shares forever and expect a sale of the company, or at least a sale of their shares at some time in the future (a 'Realisation'). Such provisions require careful negotiation as expected timescales for Realisations (and value) can differ greatly from one shareholder to another. In particular, it may force the sale of the company at a time when other shareholders (including majority shareholders) do not want to sell. Realisation provisions may include, for example:

(a)   a best endeavours obligation to realise the investment by a certain time;

(b)   the appointment of corporate financiers to find a buyer for the company;

(c)   a public listing of the company, which typically allows the shareholders who do not want to sell to retain their shares in the company; and

(d)   a put option in favour of the minority shareholders to force the majority to buy the minority shares in the company, or an obligation to procure that the company itself buys or redeems the minority shares.

In circumstances of a put option sale, great attention needs to be focused on how the shares are to be valued and whether it is appropriate that any discounts (such as a minority discount) should be applied to the relevant shares.

6.3.2   PROVISIONS RELATED TO OPERATIONS AND DAY-TO-DAY MANAGEMENT OF A COMPANY

6.3.2.1   Board composition and quorum

Details of the composition of the board, i.e. how many directors can be appointed and by whom, are typically included in the shareholders' agreement. A minority shareholder by law does not have a right to appoint or remove a director but the shareholders' agreement may provide that certain shareholders (for example the minority shareholders holding a certain percentage or a particular investor) may have the right to appoint one or more directors and to remove or replace those persons. The appointment of directors is an important right for minority shareholders, given the access to information and the participation in management that a director is entitled to by law.

Certain shareholders' agreements include the right to appoint non-voting 'observers' to attend board meetings. This is not a position that is statutorily recognised and any observer needs to ensure that he is not in fact acting as a 'shadow director' or 'de facto director' as that has consequences under the 2014 Act.

Details of the quorum necessary for a board or shareholder meeting to be validly held should be included in the shareholders' agreement as well as the constitution. If a shareholder has the right to appoint a director (and has so appointed one), it is likely that they will want their nominated director to form part of the quorum for any board or shareholder meeting. The 2014 Act provides (unless disapplied by the constitution), that an EGM can be convened at short notice by the majority shareholders.

It will also need to be considered whether a chairperson (independent or otherwise) should be appointed and whether the chairperson should have the casting vote at meetings.

The shareholders' agreement will also usually set out how frequently board meetings should be held and the information which should be circulated to the directors in advance of any meetings, such as a detailed agenda and related papers.

6.3.2.2   Conflict of interest

Historically, directors were held by common law to owe fiduciary duties to the company and were required to ensure that their own personal interests did not conflict with those of the company. These duties have now been given a statutory footing and are contained in Part 5, Chapter 2 of the 2014 Act. This is particularly relevant where a director is also a shareholder in the company as he must act in the best interests of the company and not fetter his discretion.

6.3.2.3   Information

In addition to the very limited commercial information which shareholders are entitled to under the 2014 Act (being annual accounts), the shareholders' agreement will typically provide that minority shareholders are entitled to certain specific information with pre-scribed time periods. This may include monthly or quarterly management accounts, for example, (within three weeks of the period end), annual (audited) accounts when signed by the directors, budgets, and other information reasonably required. It is also common for a provision to be included to give shareholders access to the company's premises and records on reasonable notice and during normal business hours to take copies of relevant company information. These rights may be predicated on the shareholder holding a certain minimum percentage of the issued share capital of the company (for example 5%) and are particularly relevant for a minority shareholder who may not have a nominated director on the board and so may not have very limited visibility on the affairs of the company. From the company's perspective, it should ensure that compliance with these rights is not overly burdensome on it. Linked to the right to receive information will be a confidentiality provision requiring it be kept secret and used only for the permitted purpose.

6.3.2.4   Vetoes

It is common for the shareholder's agreement to include a restricted transactions section which provides that the company cannot carry out certain actions unless the consent of shareholders (or a certain level of shareholders) is obtained or alternatively the consent of a particular nominated director on the board is obtained. This provides protection for minority shareholders and ensures that the company cannot undertake certain actions against their legitimate interests. The list of restricted transactions should be tailored to the company in question and the nature of its business so that it is not unduly restrictive to its day-to-day 'ordinary course' operations. Depending on the nature of the restriction, certain provisions may need to be drafted as obligations of the shareholders, rather than the company, as the company cannot fetter its statutory powers. Set out below are some common examples of what might be included in a veto section:

(a)   restrictions on issuing any new shares (or creating a new class of shares);

(b)   restrictions on granting options or other securities convertible into shares;

(c)   restrictions on the remuneration of executives;

(d)   restrictions on amending the company's constitution;

(e)   restrictions on granting security over the company's assets;

(f)   restrictions on making loans and incurring borrowings;

(g)   restrictions on changing the nature of the business; or

(h)   restrictions on disposing of or acquiring substantial assets.

6.3.2.5   Dividend policy

The dividend policy of the company is also a matter commonly dealt with in a shareholders' agreement, as shareholders (particularly minority shareholders) are often eager to ensure they get a return on their investment while they hold the shares. The agreement may provide that, at a minimum, a certain level of the profits available for distribution are distributed annually amongst the shareholders. Alternatively, the agreement may provide that dividends are a matter for the board (or a particular committee of the board) to determine at its discretion.

6.3.2.6   Financing

The shareholders' agreement often details how the company is to be financed initially and sets parameters as to how it is to go about seeking ongoing and future financing. This can be important to stop a shareholder getting diluted by other shareholders with deeper pockets when third party financing is readily available. Alternatively, the agreement may include an obligation on the existing shareholders to provide financing to the company on a pro rata basis or otherwise. However, this is unusual and it is more common for the agreement to state that the shareholders are not under any obligation to provide future funding to the company. The granting of any security or guarantees by the company in connection with third party financing are often matters covered in the restricted transactions section.

6.3.2.7   Audit and remuneration committees

One of the main tensions in a company is between those running the company and those who have made an investment in it. In this regard, in the absence of information on what is going on from day-to-day, it can be useful and give comfort to have an audit committee to oversee the financial and internal reporting and control processes in the company. The audit committee should have written terms of reference which deal clearly with its authority and duties. Ideally it would consist of non-executive directors or at least a majority of non-executive directors.

Given that often some shareholders are employed in an executive capacity and others are not, sometimes shareholders' agreements provide for the establishment of a remuneration committee to deal with their employment and incentive packages. The remuneration committee's function is usually to establish a formal and transparent procedure for developing policy on executive remuneration and for fixing the remuneration and incentive packages of individual executives. No person should be involved in deciding his or her own remuneration or anyone related to them. The committee should have access to professional advice outside the company and, where appropriate, maintain contact with non-executive shareholders about executive remuneration in the same way as the company does for other matters (see **chapter 3, 'Officers of a Company', 3.4.1.3** and **3.4.1.4** for further information on establishing audit and remuneration committees).

6.3.3 DISPUTE RESOLUTION AND DEADLOCK

6.3.3.1 Deadlock

Depending on the share structure, it is possible that a deadlock may occur at either shareholder or board level and a mechanism is sometimes included in a shareholders' agreement to address this. In particular, this is very important in joint venture arrangements where the shareholdings are held in equal proportions (50:50). If a dispute arises, it may not be practical for the shareholders to remain in business with each other. Sometimes the only solution, in the event that a deadlock cannot be resolved, involves one shareholder buying the other out. This is obviously a drastic solution and should only be used as a last resort. It is also possible that the agreement provides that the company be wound up if the shareholders can no longer work together and a deadlock ensues. However, this can destroy value in a company and should be a last resort.

6.3.3.2 Russian Roulette

Where a deadlock arises, this mechanism provides that one shareholder (Shareholder A) can offer to buy all of another shareholder's (Shareholder B's) shares at a specified price. Once the offer is made, Shareholder B must either: (a) sell all of its shares to Shareholder A at the price offered; or (b) buy Shareholder A's shares at that price. This encourages a fair price to be offered by Shareholder A, as it could be reversed by Shareholder B.

6.3.3.3 Texas/Mexican Shoot Out

This is a variation of the Russian Roulette deadlock resolution procedure. Shareholder A offers to buy Shareholder B's shares at a specified price. Shareholder B then has a period of time to serve a counter notice on Shareholder A stating it is prepared to sell at the price offered by Shareholder A or stating that it wishes to buy Shareholder A's shares at a higher price. If both parties wish to buy the shares of the other, then a sealed bidding process will ensue with the person who bids the highest being successful.

6.3.4 OTHER MATTERS

6.3.4.1 Restrictive covenants

To protect the goodwill of the company, it is common to include a provision in the shareholders' agreement which restricts the shareholders from competing with the business of the company or from soliciting customers, suppliers or employees of the company away from it while the shareholder holds shares in the company and sometimes for a limited period of time thereafter. Restrictive convents are only enforceable if they are limited in time, geographical location, and scope to the extent necessary to protect the business. If they are not so limited, a court may deem them unenforceable. Accordingly, it is important that a severance clause be included in the shareholders' agreement so that in the event a court finds a particular provision overly restrictive, the remainder of the provision may still be valid and enforceable.

6.3.4.2 Interaction and conflict with the constitution

As there is a significant overlap between the shareholders' agreement and the constitution, it is important to ensure that both are consistent and do not conflict with one another. A clause is usually included in the shareholders' agreement, to provide that in the event of a conflict between the two, the shareholders' agreement shall prevail, given it has been negotiated by the parties and is more likely to correctly reflect what has been agreed. This clause should also state that, in the event of a conflict, the shareholders shall amend the constitution so that it conforms with the shareholders' agreement.

6.3.4.3   Duration/Term

It is important to specify the duration of the agreement and how and when it might terminate. It should cease to apply to a shareholder once he ceases to hold shares in the company (other than with respect to provisions which are expressed to survive termination, for example confidentiality or restrictive covenants). It might also be terminated by the agreement in writing of a certain percentage of shareholders, although this has obvious dangers for minority shareholders. The agreement would typically cease to have effect on a Stock Market listing.

6.3.4.4   Confidentiality

This is an important provision in a shareholders' agreement to ensure that any commercially sensitive company information divulged to shareholders is protected and not passed to third parties, who may use it to their advantage to the detriment of the company. There are usually exceptions where disclosure is permitted, for example, if required by law or regulation.

6.3.4.5   Assignment, new shareholders, and deeds of adherence

A provision is often included which provides that shareholders may assign their rights under the agreement to third parties who acquire their shares and sign a deed of adherence. Pursuant to the deed of adherence, they agree to be bound by the provisions of the shareholders' agreement and acquire the rights and obligations of the shareholder who sold the shares to them.

6.3.4.6   Company as a party

Where the company has a high degree of autonomy from individual shareholders, it is useful that it is bound by and party to the shareholders' agreement (in particular as regards the restricted actions outlined in the vetoes section (see **6.3.2.4**). There may also be particular obligations that are properly obligations of the company, such as the provision of information to shareholders. The key point is that where the company is bound as a party, it is not bound in such a way so as to fetter its statutory powers, as such obligations may not be enforceable against the company (but may be enforceable as between the shareholders if set out in that manner).

6.4   Advantages/Disadvantages

As noted above, many of the provisions in a shareholders' agreement could be included solely in the constitution and accordingly, discussion and consideration needs to be given as to where to include them.

A key advantage of a shareholders' agreement is that, unless it provides otherwise, it cannot be amended without the consent of all parties to it. This is distinct from the constitution, which can be amended by the passing of a special resolution. Another key advantage of a shareholders' agreement over the constitution is that the constitution is a publicly available document, where a shareholders' agreement is private and confidential.

However, there are disadvantages to the shareholders' agreement as, unlike the constitution, it does not automatically bind all the shareholders of a company once they become shareholders. Related to this, in companies with a large number of shareholders, it may not be practical to have each one sign up to a shareholders' agreement, in which case it is more appropriate to deal with the rights of the shareholders, as far as is possible, in the constitution.

6.5   Subscription and Shareholders' Agreement

Sometimes a shareholders' agreement is combined with a subscription agreement, being an agreement where a person or persons invest (subscribe) for new shares in a company thereby providing financing for it. In such agreement there would be customary provisions relating to the investment, including warranties from the company (and sometimes the current shareholders) in favour of the investor, and the usual mechanics to provide for the issue of the relevant number of shares.

6.6   General Provisions/Boilerplate

Most commercial agreements, including shareholders' agreements, contain generic or 'boilerplate' provisions. Most boilerplate appears at the end of an agreement and is usually uncontroversial. Certain boilerplate provisions such as assignment, severability, and 'no partnership' are of added importance in a shareholders' agreement given that the ability to assign rights to a person, to sever unenforceable provisions of a restrictive covenant, and to ensure the arrangement is not a legal partnership can have material implications in the relationship between shareholders.

CHAPTER 7

FINANCIAL STATEMENTS, ANNUAL RETURN, AND AUDIT

7.1   Accounting Records: Introduction

Section 281 of the Companies Act 2014 (the '2014 Act') requires a private company limited by shares (referred to in this chapter as 'a/the company') to keep, or cause to be kept, 'adequate accounting records'. 'Adequate accounting records' are defined by s 282 of the 2014 Act as being those that are:

(a)   sufficient to correctly record and explain the transactions of the company;

(b)   enable at any time the assets, liabilities, financial position and profit or loss of the company to be determined with reasonable accuracy; and

(c)   enable the directors to ensure that any statutory financial statements required to be prepared under s 290 (paragraph **7.7** below) or s 293 (paragraph **7.7.7** below) of the 2014 Act and any directors' report required to be prepared under s 325 of the 2014 Act (paragraph **7.8** below) comply with the requirements of the 2014 Act and enable those financial statements of the company to be audited by the statutory auditors.

'Adequate accounting records' shall be deemed to have been maintained by a company if they comply with the above requirements, the additional requirements set out in s 282 (3) of the 2014 Act, and explain the company's transactions and facilitate the preparation of financial statements that give a 'true and fair view' of the assets, liabilities, financial position, and profit or loss of the company and, if relevant, the group of which it forms part.

7.2   Form of Accounting Records

The 'adequate accounting records' required by s 281 of the 2014 Act to be kept may be in written form (in English or Irish) or in another medium so as to enable the records to be readily accessible and readily convertible into written form. Thus, the accounting records may be kept on a computer. Where the accounting records are kept on a computer that computer is required to be kept in the State unless the accounting records are kept outside the State. The Minister may, by regulation, impose requirements on such a company to keep its accounting records in such a manner that will provide for effective access to those records (see ss (5) (6) and (7) of s 282 of the 2014 Act).

7.3   Where Accounting Records are to be Kept

Section 283 of the 2014 Act provides that a company's accounting records may be kept at its registered office or at such other place as the directors think fit. Where the accounting records are kept at a place outside the State the company is required to ensure that there shall be sent to and kept at a place in the State, such information and returns relating to the business dealt with in the accounting records as will disclose with reasonable accuracy the assets, liabilities, financial position, and profit and loss of that business. Such information is required to be sent at intervals not exceeding six months. The information must also be sufficient to enable the preparation of statutory financial statements under ss 290 or 293 of the 2014 Act and the directors' report required by s 325 of the 2014 Act.

7.4   Access to Accounting Records

Section 284 of the 2014 Act requires that the accounting records and any information and returns (referred to in paragraph **7.3** above) are required to be made available (in English or in Irish) at all reasonable times for inspection without charge by the officers of the company and by other persons entitled pursuant to the 2014 Act to inspect the accounting records of the company. If the accounting records, relevant information, and returns are kept on a computer the company is required to secure that such are capable of being converted without charge into written form upon request by the person having such a right of inspection. Section 284 (3) of the 2014 Act introduced helpful clarity into the law to the effect that members (other than those who are also directors) have no general right to inspect the accounting records and financial statements of a company except where that right is conferred by statute or the company in general meeting. In this regard the directors are required from time to time to determine whether and to what extent and at what times and places and under what conditions or regulations the financial statements and accounting records of the company shall be open to inspection of its members other than those members who are directors of the company. See also *Healy v Healy Homes Limited* [1973] IR 309. Section 386 of the 2014 Act provides the company's statutory auditors with a right of access at all reasonable times to the accounting records of the Company.

7.5   Retention of Accounting Records and Offences

The accounting records maintained under s 281 and the information or returns referred to in s 283 (2) of the 2014 Act are required to be preserved by the company concerned for a period of least six years after the end of the financial year containing the latest date to which the record, information, or return relates.

A company that contravenes the obligations referred to in paragraphs **7.1** to **7.4** above is guilty of a category 2 offence. Similarly, a director of a company who fails to take all reasonable steps to secure compliance by the company with the requirements referred to in paragraphs **7.1** to **7.4** above or who has by his or her own intentional act been the cause of any default by the company shall be guilty of a category 2 offence. A category 2 offence carries a maximum fine of €50,000 and term of imprisonment of five years.

More onerous sanctions apply, and the offence is elevated to a category 1 offence, (which carries a maximum fine of €500,000 and imprisonment of ten years) where (a) the contravention arose in relation to a company that is subsequently wound up where that company is unable to pay its debts and the contravention has contributed to the company's inability to pay all of its debts or resulted in substantial uncertainty as to the assets and liabilities of the company or substantially impeded the orderly winding up of the company; or (b) the contravention persisted during a continuous period of three years or more; or (c) the contravention involved a failure to correctly record and explain one or more transactions of the company the value or aggregate value of which exceeded €1m or 10% of the net assets of the company, whichever is the greater (2014 Act, ss 286 (3) (4) (5) and (6)).

In any such proceedings against such a director consisting of a failure to take reasonable steps to secure compliance by the company with the said obligations it is a defence for the director to prove that he or she had reasonable grounds for believing and did believe that a competent and reliable person was charged with the duty of undertaking that those requirements were complied with and that the discharge of that duty by such competent and reliable person was monitored by the director by means of reasonable methods properly used.

7.6   The Concept of the 'Financial Year'

Sections 287–288 of the 2014 Act contain various technical rules concerning the commencement and termination of a company's 'financial year' and provisions regarding the frequency with which and the methodology whereby a company may change its 'financial year end date'. A company's first financial year begins with the date of its incorporation and must end on a date no more than 18 months after that date of incorporation. Each subsequent financial year begins on a day immediately after the end of the previous financial year and continues unless changed for a period of 12 months, give or take seven days either side of that time period. A company may by notice in the prescribed form given to the Registrar of Companies alter its current financial year end date or its previous financial year end date. A change in its financial year end date may not be made if this would result in the financial year being in excess of 18 months. Subject to certain exceptions a company may only change its financial year end date where a period of five years has elapsed from the previous change of the financial year end date.

7.7   Statutory Financial Statements

Part 6, Chapter 4, of the 2014 Act deals with the obligation of the directors of a company to prepare statutory financial statements for the company known as 'entity financial statements' (where the company is a member of a group there is an obligation to prepare 'group financial statements' for the holding company and its 'subsidiary undertakings' which are addressed separately in s 293 and in Part 6, Chapter 5 of the 2014 Act). Save where a company prepares 'group financial statements' a company's 'statutory financial statements' are its 'entity financial statements'.

A company has a choice whereby it may elect to prepare its entity financial statements under two alternative financial reporting frameworks. The first framework is that of the 'Companies Act entity financial statements' prepared in accordance with s 291 and sch 3 of the 2014 Act. The second framework is the 'IFRS entity financial statements' which are entity financial statements prepared in accordance with international financial reporting standards and s 292 of the 2014 Act. The latter are international standards which are progressively replacing the many different national accounting standards. A consideration of which of the two financial reporting frameworks is applicable to a company is outside the scope of this chapter.

7.7.1   COMPANIES ACT ENTITY FINANCIAL STATEMENTS

Companies Act entity financial statements are required by s 291 of the 2014 Act to comprise a balance sheet as at the financial year end date, a profit and loss account for the financial year and any other additional statements and information required by the financial reporting framework adopted in relation to the company. Such financial statements are required to give a 'true and fair view' of the assets, liabilities, and financial position of the company as at the financial year end date and of the profit or loss of the company for the financial year. The requirement that the financial statements give a true and fair view is of crucial importance. Where compliance with accounting principles and other requirements of sch 3 of the 2014 Act would not be sufficient to result in the Companies Act entity financial statements giving a true and fair view the necessary additional information is required to be given in the entity financial statements or in a note thereto. Similarly, if in special circumstances compliance with any provision of the 2014 Act is inconsistent with the requirement to give a true and fair view the directors are required to depart from that provision to the extent necessary to give a true and fair view and a note to that effect is required to be given in a note to the financial statements.

The significance of the fundamental principle that the financial statements give a true and fair view is copper-fastened by s 289 of the 2014 Act which prohibits the directors from approving financial statements unless they are satisfied that they give a true and fair view of the assets, liabilities, and financial position and profit and loss of the financial statements. Similarly, the statutory auditors of the company in performing their functions in relation to the company's statutory financial statements are required to have regard to the directors' said duty under s 289 of the 2014 Act.

Schedule 3 of the 2014 Act sets out in 83 paragraphs the accounting principles, format, and content of Companies Act entity financial statements. Section A of Part II of sch 3 sets out the general rules applicable to the required balance sheet and profit and loss account. Section B of Part II of sch 3 sets out the format of the required balance sheet. Two alternative formats are prescribed, being Format 1 and Format 2. A summary of the items to be included in Format 1 are set out below.

7.7.2 BALANCE SHEET (FORMAT 1)

A. Fixed Assets
   I. Intangible assets (e.g. goodwill)
   II. Tangible assets (e.g. land and buildings, or plant and machinery)
   III. Financial assets (e.g. shares in group undertakings)

B. Current Assets
   I. Stocks (e.g. raw materials, consumables, and work in progress)
   II. Debtors (e.g. trade debtors)
   III. Investments (e.g. shares in group undertakings)
   IV. Cash at bank and in hand

C. Creditors: amounts falling due within one year (e.g. bank loans and overdrafts)

D. Net current assets (liabilities)

E. Total assets less current liabilities

F. Creditors: Amounts falling due after more than one year (e.g. bank loans and overdrafts)

G. Provisions for liabilities

H. Capital and reserves

   Examples include the following:
   I. Called-up share capital presented as equity
   II. Share premium account
   IV. Revaluation reserve
   V. Other reserves
   VI. Profit and loss account

Section B also sets out four alternative formats of a profit and loss account. Format 1 requires inclusion of the following:

7.7.3   PROFIT AND LOSS ACCOUNT (FORMAT 1)

1. Turnover
2. Cost of sales
3. Gross profit or loss
4. Distribution costs
5. Administrative expenses
6. Other operating income
7. Income from shares in group undertakings
8. Income from participating interests
9. Income from other financial assets
10. Other interest receivable and similar income
11. Amounts written off financial assets and investments held as current assets
12. Interest payable and similar charges
13. Tax on profit or loss on ordinary activities
14. Profit or loss on ordinary activities after taxation
15. Extraordinary income
16. Extraordinary charges
17. Extraordinary profit or loss
18. Tax on extraordinary profit or loss
19. Other taxes not shown under the above items
20. Profit or loss for the financial year

Section A of Part III of sch 3 contains specific cardinal principles which must be applied in the preparation of the Companies Act entity financial statements including an assumption that the company shall be presumed to be carrying on business as a going concern, that accounting policies shall be applied consistently from one financial year to the next, and that the amount of any item in the financial statements shall be determined on a prudent basis. In particular only profits realised at the financial year end date shall be included in the profit and loss account and all liabilities which have arisen in the course of the financial year shall be taken into account even if such liabilities only become apparent between the financial year end date and the date on which the financial statements are signed.

It should be noted that the concept of 'realised' profits plays an important role from a legal perspective. Whether or not a profit is or is not realised is highly relevant in the context of whether a company has sufficient distributable profits to declare a dividend or otherwise make a distribution. Section 276 makes it clear that whether a profit is realised is to be determined in accordance with generally accepted accounting principles.

Where it appears to the directors that there are special reasons for departing from any of the principles stated in Section A of Part III in preparing the company's financial statements they may depart therefrom but particulars of the departure and the reasons for it and its effect on the balance sheet and profit and loss account are required to be stated in a note to the financial statements.

7.7.4   NOTES TO THE BALANCE SHEET AND PROFIT AND LOSS ACCOUNTS

Part IV of sch 3 prescribes the information which is to be included in the financial statements by way of notes thereto. The following subject matter is required by paragraphs 45 to 61 to be stated by way of a note to the balance sheet:

(a)   debentures;

(b)   fixed assets;

(c)   financial assets held as current assets;

(d)   information about fair valuation of assets and liabilities;

(e)   information where investment property and living animals and plants are included at fair value;

(f)   dividends, reserves, and provisions for liabilities;

(g)   provision for taxation;

(h)   details of indebtedness;

(i)   guarantees and other financial commitments; and

(j)   miscellaneous matters.

7.7.5   NOTES TO THE PROFIT AND LOSS ACCOUNT

The profit and loss account is required by paragraphs 62 to 66 to be supplemented by notes relating to the following subject matter:

(a)   separate statement of certain items of income and expenditure;

(b)   particulars of tax;

(c)   particulars of turnover; and

(d)   miscellaneous matters.

Material related party transactions concluded otherwise than under normal market conditions must also be disclosed in the notes to the financial statements.

Part V contains special provisions applicable where a company is a holding company or a 'subsidiary undertaking'. Where a group situation arises it is important to ensure that the financial statements are not misrepresented by, for example, the inclusion of assets and liabilities attributable to group members. Accordingly, Part V requires the specific inclusion of, for example, guarantees and other financial commitments which are undertaken on behalf of or for the benefit of holding and subsidiary undertakings.

A specimen profit and loss account and a balance sheet are set out in the Appendix to this chapter. For ease of presentation, the examples do not include the auditors' and directors' report and some other information customarily included in financial statements.

7.7.6   IFRS ENTITY FINANCIAL STATEMENTS

Where a company elects to prepare its entity financial statements under the international financial reporting standards framework it is required to prepare IFRS entity financial statements in accordance with s 292 of the 2014 Act. Essentially, IFRS entity financial statements are required to contain the information required in Part 6 of the 2014 Act except the information required by schs 3 and 4 of the 2014 Act (which only apply to Companies Act entity financial statements). IFRS standards do not require the financial statements to reflect a true and fair view. They require that the financial statements present fairly the assets, liabilities, financial position, financial performance, and cash flows. This is deemed to be equivalent to the true and fair view standard required in relation to

Companies Act entity financial statements. Where the directors prepare IFRS entity financial statements, s 292 requires that they shall comply with all IFRS and the notes thereto must contain an unreserved statement that they have been prepared in accordance with IFRS. A consideration of the format of the financial statements which are required to be prepared where a company elects to adopt IFRS is outside the scope of this chapter.

7.7.7 GROUP FINANCIAL STATEMENTS

Subject to certain exceptions, s 293 of the 2014 Act requires that where a company is a holding company, as well as preparing entity financial statements for the financial year of that company it shall also be required to prepare group financial statements for the holding company and all its subsidiary undertakings for that financial year. A detailed consideration of this obligation and the exemptions therefrom is outside the scope of this chapter and practitioners are referred to ss 293 to 304 of the 2014 Act.

7.7.8 DISCLOSURE OF DIRECTORS' REMUNERATION AND TRANSACTIONS

In addition to the information which must be contained in the notes to the financial statements referred to in sch 3 of the 2014 Act (see paragraph **7.7.4** and **7.7.5** above) additional information containing directors' remuneration and transactions and arrangements between the company and its directors is required to be stated in the notes (see 2014 Act, Part 6, Chapter 6). These obligations apply to both Companies Act entity financial statements and IFRS entity financial statements.

7.7.9 ADDITIONAL DISCLOSURE REQUIREMENTS RELATING TO THE NOTES TO THE FINANCIAL STATEMENTS

Part 6, Chapter 7 of the 2014 Act requires that the notes to the financial statements include particulars of the following additional information including, but not limited to, (1) details of authorised share capital, allotted share capital, and movements; (2) information about related undertakings; and (3) particulars about staff.

7.7.10 APPROVAL OF THE STATUTORY FINANCIAL STATEMENTS

Part 6, Chapter 8 of the 2014 Act addresses the process concerning the approval and signing of the statutory financial statements by the board of directors. Section 324 of the 2014 Act requires that where the directors are satisfied that the statutory financial statements give a true and fair view and otherwise comply with Art 4 of the IAS Regulation (EC No. 1606/2002 of the European Parliament and of the Council), those statements shall be approved by the board of directors and signed on their behalf by two directors where there are two or more directors in the company. A similar obligation applies where the company has a sole director. Where the statutory financial statements are approved which do not give a true and fair view every director of the company who is a party to their approval and who knows that they do not give such a 'true and fair view' or otherwise comply with the 2014 Act or is reckless as to whether that is so is guilty of a category 2 offence.

7.8 The Directors' Report

Part 6, Chapter 9 of the 2014 Act imposes an obligation on the directors of a company to prepare a directors' report dealing with the following matters:

(a) the names of the persons who at any time during the financial year were directors of the company;

(b) the principal activities of the company during the course of the year;

(c)   a statement of the measures taken by the directors to secure compliance with the requirements of ss 281 to 285 of the 2014 Act with regard to keeping accounting records and the location of those records;

(d)   the amount of any interim dividends paid by the directors during the year and the amount, if any, that the directors recommend should be paid by way of final dividend;

(e)   particulars of any important events affecting the company which have occurred since the end of the financial year;

(f)   an indication of the activities, if any, of the company in the field of research and development;

(g)   an indication of the existence of branches of the company outside the State;

(h)   political donations made during the year that are required to be disclosed by the Electoral Act 1997;

(i)   the use of financial instruments concerning financial risk management and related information;

(j)   a business review including a fair review of the business of the company and a description of the principal risks and uncertainties facing the company and related particulars as set out in s 327 of the 2014 Act;

(k)   information on the acquisition or disposal of own shares in accordance with the particulars required by s 328 of the 2014 Act;

(l)   information on the directors' and the secretary's interests in shares and debentures in the company and group companies in accordance with the particulars required by s 329 of the 2014 Act; and

(m)   a statement to the effect that as far as each of the directors is aware there is no relevant audit information of which the company's statutory auditors are unaware and each director has taken all the steps necessary to make himself/herself aware of any relevant audit information and to establish that the company's statutory auditors are aware of that information.

The above requirements are in addition to any other requirements concerning the establishment of an audit committee in the case of a large private company and the obligation under s 225 of the 2014 Act for the directors to issue a directors' compliance statement (see **7.9** below).

The directors' report must be approved by the board of directors comprising those who made the report and signed on their behalf by two directors where there are two or more directors or by one director where the company has a sole director.

7.9   The Directors' Compliance Statement

The requirement for an annual directors' compliance statement to be included in an Irish company's financial statements was originally enacted by s 45 of the Companies (Auditing & Accounting) Act 2003. Its purpose was to foster a greater culture of Irish corporate compliance. However, in response to concerns from the business community that the benefits would be outweighed by a disproportionate cost for business, the Government held back and in 2005 referred the issue to the Company Law Review Group to examine and to report back to Government. Following compromise proposals recommended by the Company Law Review Group, the requirement for directors' compliance statements has been re-enacted in a modified form in s 225 of the 2014 Act.

Section 225 of the 2014 Act provides that private limited companies, designated activity companies, and guarantee companies which have a balance sheet total exceeding €12.5m and a turnover exceeding €25m and all PLCs will be required to issue a directors' compliance statement. Unlimited companies and investment companies are excluded from the obligation, as will other categories of company if designated by the Minister for Jobs, Enterprise and Innovation.

Essentially, the directors of those companies within the scope of the section are required to include a statement in the directors' report to be annexed to the financial statements which (a) acknowledges that they are responsible for securing the Company's compliance with its 'relevant obligations'; and (b) with respect to each of the three matters specified below confirms that the matters have been done, or if they not been done, it specifies the reasons why they have not been done. The three matters mentioned are:

(a)   The drawing up of a statement (a 'Compliance Policy Statement') setting out the company's policies that in the directors' opinion are appropriate to the company respecting compliance by the company with its 'relevant obligations'.

(b)   Putting in place of appropriate arrangements or structures that are in the directors' opinion designed to secure material compliance with the company's 'relevant obligations'.

(c)   Conducting a review during the relevant financial year to which the directors' report relates of any arrangements or structures referred to in paragraph (b) that have been put in place.

Section 225 operates on a 'comply or explain' basis, i.e. it does not in fact require a Compliance Policy Statement to be drawn up, or for the directors to put in place arrangements or structures that are designed to secure material compliance with the company's relevant obligations, or to conduct a review of the arrangements or structures. However, if the company is not in a position to confirm that these matters have been done, the directors' compliance statement must specify the reasons why they have not been done. Given that s 225 only applies to companies with a balance sheet total of €12.5m and a turnover of €25m, it is considered that such a company must be in a position to provide a credible reason in support of any decision not to prepare a Compliance Policy Statement.

'Relevant obligations' in relation to a company are those obligations under the 2014 Act where a failure to comply would constitute a category 1 offence (one which on a summary conviction carries a sanction of imprisonment not exceeding 12 months or on indictment a term not exceeding ten years) or a category 2 offence (one which on a summary conviction carries a sanction of imprisonment not exceeding 12 months or on indictment a term not exceeding five years), a serious market abuse offence or a serious prospectus offence and obligations under tax law, which broadly includes all obligations relating to tax imposed under the Taxes Acts (as defined). The new restrictive definition of relevant obligations represents a significant dilution of the former definition in the 2003 Act. The former definition included *all* obligations under the Companies Acts, tax law, and 'any other enactments that provide a legal framework within which the company operates and that may materially affect the company's financial statements' (this latter catch-all having introduced considerable uncertainty into the scope of a directors' compliance statement under the former provision).

The arrangements or structures referred to above may, if the directors of the company so decide, include reliance on the advice of one or more persons employed by the company or retained by it under a contract of services being a person who appears to the directors to have the requisite knowledge or experience to advise the company on its compliance with its relevant obligations. Thus, it would be possible for a company to outsource some of the arrangements and structures which are designed to ensure that the company is in material compliance with its relevant obligations.

7.10   The Obligation to Have Statutory Financial Statements Audited

The directors of a company must arrange for the statutory financial statements for the financial year to be audited by statutory auditors unless the company is entitled to and has elected to avail itself of an audit exemption. The audit exemptions are addressed in paragraphs **7.14** and **7.15** below. If an audit exemption is availed of s 335 of the 2014 Act it requires the inclusion of a statement in the balance sheet to that effect and the provision of certain other particulars.

Part 6, Chapter 11 of the 2014 Act sets out the obligations which fall on the statutory auditors to issue a report on the statutory financial statements which are laid before the company in general meeting. Note that under s 391 the statutory auditors of a company are required to make a statutory auditors' report to the members on all statutory financial statements laid before the members. The requirements relating to the statutory auditors' report is set out in s 336 of the 2014 Act.

7.11   The Publication of Financial Statements

Section 338 of the 2014 Act requires that a copy of the statutory financial statements, directors' report, and statutory auditors' report on those financial statements shall be sent to every member of the company, every holder of debentures of the company, and all other persons who are entitled to receive them not less than 21 days before the date of the general meeting of the company at which those documents will be laid before the members.

Where all the members that are entitled to attend and vote at the general meeting consent to short notice then copies of the documents may be sent less than 21 days before the date of the meeting. Copies of those documents may be sent by way of electronic communication where a notification of an address has been furnished to the company. Where the company and recipient have agreed that documents may be made available on a website s 338 (5) permits disclosure by such means provided that they are made available throughout the entire 21 days before the meeting and notification has been made to the persons entitled not less than 21 days before the meeting of their availability.

Section 339 of the 2014 Act creates a statutory right of the members of a company and of holders of debentures in a company to be given on demand a copy of the company's 'statutory financial statements' for the most recent financial year, the directors' report, and the statutory auditors' report for that year.

Section 341 requires the directors to lay the 'statutory financial statements' of the company for each financial year together with the directors' report and statutory auditors' report before the company in general meeting not later than nine months after the financial year end date.

7.12   The Annual Return and Documents Annexed to it

Section 343 (2) of the 2014 Act requires a company to deliver to the Registrar of Companies an annual return containing prescribed particulars in relation to the company. The annual return must be in the prescribed form and contain the prescribed information and be made up to a date that is not later than its annual return date. For companies incorporated before the commencement of s 345 of the 2014 Act, a company's annual return date is its existing annual return date as determined under the Companies Acts 1963–2013 and the anniversary thereof. For those companies incorporated on or after the commencement of s 345 of the 2014 Act, a company's annual return date is the date which is six months after the date of its incorporation. A company may alter its annual return date in accordance with s 346.

Under s 347 of the 2014 Act the following copy documents shall be attached to the annual return:

(a)   the statutory financial statements of the company as laid before the general meeting;

(b)   the directors' report; and

(c)   the statutory auditors' report on those financial statements and that directors' report.

It is anticipated that the form of the annual return and the prescribed information to be contained therein will be issued by way of Regulation under the 2014 Act.

7.13   Exclusions, Exemptions, and Special Arrangements with Regard to Public Disclosure of Financial Information

Part 6, Chapter 14 of the 2014 Act contains important exemptions from the obligation to disclose by way of attachments to the annual return some of the information in the financial statements. If a company satisfies two or more of the following requirements it will fall to be treated as a 'small company'. The requirements are that:

(a)   the amount of the turnover of the company does not exceed €8.8 million;

(b)   the balance sheet total of the company does not exceed €4.4 million; and

(c)   the average number of employees of the company does not exceed 50.

A company which qualifies as a small company is exempt from the requirement to annex to the company's annual return the statutory financial statements, the directors' report, and the statutory auditors' report and in lieu thereof it may file abridged financial statements which comply with the requirements of s 353 of the 2014 Act which essentially entitles the company to avoid filing a profit and loss account.

A company will qualify as a 'medium company' if it satisfies two or more of the following requirements:

(a)   the amount of the turnover of the company does not exceed €20 million;

(b)   the balance sheet total of the company does not exceed €10 million; and

(c)   the average number of employees of the company does not exceed 250.

Where a company qualifies as a medium company it will be entitled to attach to its annual return 'abridged financial statements'. These are similar to a full set of financial statements except that certain information relating to the profit and loss account need not be disclosed, for which see s 354 of the 2014 Act.

Where a small or medium company avails itself of the above exemptions the abridged financial statements must be specifically approved by the board of directors and must contain certain prescribed particulars as set out in s 355 and a report by the auditors is required under s 356 of the 2014 Act.

Under s 357 of the 2014 Act, where a company is a subsidiary undertaking of a holding undertaking that is established under the laws of an EEA State it is exempt from the requirement to annex financial statements to its annual return if its holding undertaking has provided a guarantee over the liabilities in the financial statements of the subsidiary for the whole of that financial year. This exemption applies provided the conditions set out in s 357 are met.

7.14   Exemption from Statutory Requirement for an Audit for Small Companies

Part 6, Chapter 15 of the 2014 Act allows small private limited companies to claim exemption from the requirement to have their financial statements audited. The company must satisfy certain criteria to avail of this exemption, and must satisfy two of the following conditions:

(a)   a balance sheet total not exceeding €4.4 million;

(b)   a turnover not exceeding €8.8 million per annum; and

(c)   a number of employees not exceeding 50 persons.

Under s 362 the exemption is not available if the company holds a banking licence, insurance licence, or is one of the financial services companies listed in sch 5 to the 2014 Act (other than one referred to in paragraphs 5 or 16 of that schedule). A company which has claimed the audit exemption will still have to prepare annual financial statements and submit them to the members at a general meeting. The annual return of the company and the unaudited financial statements must still be furnished to the Companies Registration Office in compliance with the requirement of s 343 of the 2014 Act within 28 days of the annual return date. Many companies lose their audit exemption due to being late in filing their annual returns. If the exemption is available, the appointment of an auditor may be terminated for so long as the exemption may be claimed.

Section 334 creates an important right for minorities in that a member or members holding one-tenth or more of the voting rights in a company may serve notice on the company that they do not wish the audit exemption under Chapter 15 to be availed of.

7.15   Exemption from Statutory Requirement for an Audit for Dormant Companies

Dormant companies can claim an exemption from the requirement to have their financial statements audited. For these purposes 'dormant' means that during the relevant year the company has had no significant accounting transaction and its assets and liabilities comprise only permitted assets and liabilities being investments in shares of and amounts due to or from other group undertakings.

7.16   Revision of Defective Statutory Financial Statements

Part 6, Chapter 17 of the 2014 Act addresses the situation where the directors have approved statutory financial statements or a directors' report and they subsequently identify that there has been an error or deficiency in those statutory financial statements or the directors' report. Section 366 of the 2014 Act entitles the directors to voluntarily prepare revised financial statements or a revised directors' report in respect of that year. This provision creates a new entitlement which was not formerly contained in the Companies Acts 1963 to 2013.

7.17   Statutory Auditors

Part 6, Chapters 18, 19, and 20 of the 2014 Act regulate the appointment of statutory auditors, the rights, obligations and duties of statutory auditors and the removal and resignation of statutory auditors. Essentially, s 380 of the 2014 Act requires one or more statutory auditors to be appointed in accordance with Chapter 18 for each financial year of a company. The first statutory auditors of a company may be appointed by the directors at any time before the first annual general meeting of the company. Subsequent appointments are required to be made at each subsequent annual general meeting whereby the auditors will hold office from the conclusion of that meeting until the conclusion of the next annual general meeting. Where a casual vacancy arises in the office of statutory auditors the directors are under an obligation to appoint statutory auditors to fill the vacancy.

Chapter 19 sets out the principal obligations of the statutory auditors. As noted in paragraph **7.10** above, s 391 of the 2014 Act sets out the principal obligation of the statutory auditors which is to make in the form set out in s 336 of the 2014 Act a report on the financial statements. Sections 386 and 387 of the 2014 Act provide the statutory auditors with a right of access at all reasonable times to the accounting records of the company and to require from the officers of the company such information and explanations as appear to the auditors to be within the officers' knowledge or can be procured by them and which the statutory auditors think necessary for the performance of their duties. A strict two-day period applies in relation to the production of such information and explanations. Specific rules apply in relation to companies which form part of a group, which are contained in s 388 of the 2014 Act. Under s 389 of the 2014 Act, an officer of a company who knowingly makes a statement to the statutory auditors which conveys or purports to convey any information or explanation which they require under the 2014 Act which is misleading or false in a material particular or makes such a statement being reckless as to whether it is so commits a category 2 offence.

Auditors are, under s 390 of the 2014 Act, subject to a statutory duty to carry out the audit services concerned with professional integrity. The auditors are, under ss 392 and 393 of the 2014 Act, also under a statutory duty to report certain contraventions of the 2014 Act to the Director of Corporate Enforcement. Chapter 20 regulates the removal and resignation of statutory auditors, and Chapters 21, 22, and 23 of Part 6 of the 2014 Act regulate the duty of an auditor to notify the Irish Auditing and Accounting Supervisory Authority regarding the cessation of his/her office or his/her becoming disqualified.

SPECIMEN FINANCIAL STATEMENTS

'X' LIMITED

FINANCIAL STATEMENTS

FOR THE YEAR ENDED 31ST DECEMBER 2014

(EXCLUDING DIRECTORS' REPORT AND AUDITOR'S REPORT)

'X' LIMITED

PROFIT AND LOSS ACCOUNT FOR THE YEAR ENDED 31ST DECEMBER 2014

	Note	2014 €	2013 €
Turnover		2,669,300	2,501,548
Variation in Work in Progress		(75,500)	(285,117)
Management Fee		0	60,000
Other Income		939	117,369
Staff Costs	1	(1,334,933)	(1,257,448)
Depreciation		(21,516)	(22,254)
Other Operating Charges		(1,282,445)	(1,197,109)
Profit/(Loss) on Ordinary Activities before Taxation	2	(14,155)	(83,011)
Interest Payable & Similar Charges	3	(1,258)	(1,565)
		(15,413)	(84,576)
Tax on Profit/(Loss) On Ordinary Activities	4	(0)	(1,509)
Profit/(Loss) on Ordinary Activities after Taxation		(15,413)	(86,085)
Reserves Brought Forward		2,372,043	2,957,798
		2,356,630	2,871,713
Distributable Reserves Used to Repurchase Shares		(0)	(499,670)
Distributable Reserves Carried Forward		2,356,630	2,372,043

Turnover and operating profit arose solely from continuing operations. There were no recognised gains or losses other than those recognised in the profit and loss account

Approved by the Board on 19 January 2015

On behalf of the Directors

_____   _____

   DIRECTOR   **DIRECTOR**

'X' LIMITED

BALANCE SHEET AS AT 31ST DECEMBER 2014

	Note	2014 €	2013 €
FIXED ASSETS			
Intangible Assets	5	25,182	20,063
Tangible Assets	6	16,344	18,959
		41,526	39,022
CURRENT ASSETS			
Debtors	7	2,134,940	2,048,008
Cash		1,819,615	1,810,347
		3,954,554	3,858,355
CREDITORS (amounts falling due within one year)	8	1,638,510	1,524,394
NET CURRENT ASSETS		2,316,044	2,333,961
TOTAL NET ASSETS		2,357,570	2,372,983
CREDITORS (Greater than one Year)	9	0	0
TOTAL ASSETS LESS LIABILITIES		2,357,570	2,372,983
CAPITAL & RESERVES			
Share Capital	10	940	940
Distributable Reserves		2,356,630	2,372,043
		2,357,570	2,372,983

Approved by the Board on 19 January 2015

On behalf of the Directors

_____   _____

   DIRECTOR   **DIRECTOR**

'X' LIMITED

NOTES ON THE ACCOUNTS FOR THE YEAR ENDED 31st DECEMBER 2014

1. EMPLOYEES AND REMUNERATION

	2014	2013
	€	€
Technical	29	24
Administration	3	3
	32	27

The staff costs are comprised of:	2014	2013
	€	€
Wages & Salaries	1,153,493	1,079,745
Social Welfare Costs	146,181	135,739
Pension Cost	35,259	41,964
	1,334,933	1,257,448

2. PROFIT(LOSS) ON ORDINARY ACTIVITIES BEFORE TAXATION

The profit/(loss) on ordinary activities before taxation is stated after charging:

	2014	2013
	€	€
Directors' Remuneration	188,873	232,502
Directors' Pensions	20,285	81,299
Auditors Remuneration	14,500	17,650
Operating Lease Rentals	0	0
Depreciation	21,516	22,254

3. INTEREST PAYABLE AND SIMILAR CHARGES

	2014	2013
	€	€
Bank overdraft interest & charges repayable within five years otherwise than by instalments	802	1,218
Finance lease interest	456	347
	1,258	1,565

4. TAX ON PROFIT (LOSS) ON ORDINARY ACTIVITIES

The charge based on the profit on ordinary activities comprises:-

	2014	2013
	€	€
Corporation Tax @ 12.5 %	0	0
S.441 Surcharge	0	1,509

Adjustment relating to prior years	0	0
	0	1,509

Factors affecting tax charge for year

Profit on ordinary activities before tax	(15,413)	(84,576)
Corporation Tax @ 12.5 %	(1,927)	(10,572)
Effects of		
Expenses not allowable for tax purposes	3,046	3,461
Items not chargeable for tax purposes	(396)	(515)
Capital Allowances	(3,267)	(3,188)
Losses Carried Forward	2544	10,814
Current tax charge for year	0	0

5.   INTANGIBLE FIXED ASSETS

	2014	2013
	€	€
The cost of interests in other companies held by X Limited is as follows		
49 Ordinary Shares – 49% in Y Limited 1 Ordinary Share	62	62
- 50% in JV Limited	1	1
	63	63
Goodwill	25,120	31,400

'X' Limited purchased the business of Blue Coat & Partners during 2013. This goodwill will be amortised over a five year period.

6.   TANGIBLE FIXED ASSETS

	Office Equipment & Furniture	Premises	Goodwill	Total
COST	€	€	€	€
At 1 January	743,773	66,420	20,063	830,256
Additions	12,621	0	11,399	24,020
Cost of Disposal	0	0	0	0
At 31 December	756,394	66,420	31,462	854,276
DEPRECIATION				
At 1 January	724,814	66,420	0	791,234
Charge for period	15,236	0	6,280	21,516
Relating to Disposals	0	0	0	0
At 31 December	740,050	66,420	6,280	812,750

NET BOOK AMOUNTS

31 December 2014	16,344	0	25,182	41,526
31 December 2013	18,959	0	20,063	39,022

7. **DEBTORS**

Amounts falling due within one year	2014	2013
	€	€
Trade debtors & Prepayments	1,418,141	1,321,329
Related Company	342,164	315,483
Work-in-Progress	207,500	283,000
Withholding Tax	167,135	128,196
	2,134,940	2,048,008

8. **CREDITORS**

Amounts falling due within one year	2014	2013
	€	€
Creditors & Accruals	1,546,655	1,384,311
Corporation Tax	1,509	1,509
Other Taxes	90,346	136,294
Leasing	0	2,280
Related Company	0	0
	1,638,510	1,524,394

9. **CREDITORS (CONT'D)**

Other Taxes Compose:	2014	2013
	€	€
PAYE/PRSI	45,835	72,632
VAT	44,511	63,662
	90,346	136,294

10. **BANK LOANS AND OVERDRAFTS**

The Bank of Ireland holds as security for all monies advanced floating debenture over the assets of the company dated 30/08/2000.

11. **CALLED UP SHARE CAPITAL**

	2014	2013
	€	€
Authorised		
1,000,000 shares (Ordinary) at €1.269738 each	1,269,738	1,269,738
Issued		
740 Shares (Ordinary) €1.269738 paid	940	940

12. DIRECTORS

The Directors during the year and their interest in the issued Share Capital of the Company are as follows:-

	Ordinary Shares of €1.269738 each
A. Smith	300
B. Smith	250
C. Smith	190

13. RELATED PARTY TRANSACTIONS

The company owns a 49% share in Related Company and a 50% share in JV Limited. During the year transactions between these companies are set out below

Invoices for Services To	€
JV Limited	0
Related Company	24,748

Invoices for Services From	€
JV Limited	0
Related Company	135,764

Related companies included In Creditors at year end	2014 €	2013 €
Related Company	301,501	152,810
JV Limited	25,481	25,481

Related companies included In Debtors at year end	2014 €	2013 €
Related Company	135,003	110,255
JV Limited	7,623	7,623

'X' LIMITED

REVENUE ACCOUNT FOR THE YEAR ENDED 31ST DECEMBER 2014

	2014		2013	
	€	€	€	€
Fee Income		2,699,300		2,501,548
Opening Work in Progress	(283,000)		(568,117)	
Closing Work in Progress	207,500		283,000	
		(75,500)		(285,117)
		939		177,369
		2,624,739		2,393,800
Directors Remuneration	188,873		232,502	
Staff Salaries	1,047,383		960,655	
Office Salaries	106,110		103,573	
Employers PRSI	146,181		135,738	
Redundancy	0		15,517	
Pension	55,544		123,263	
Consultants	584,584		295,493	
Sub-Contract	70,913		0	
Planning Fees/Hire of Equipment	0		90	
Postage, Printing, Stationery	25,914		27,270	
Motor & Travel	106,974		78,831	
Telephone/Fax	22,928		29,369	
Rent & Rates/Service Charge	168,291		157,940	
Light & Heat	16,965		15,598	
Leasing Interest	456		347	
Repairs & Renewals	2,203		14,033	
Subscriptions/Courses/Seminars	6,987		13,845	
Insurance	116,310		112,107	
Audit & Accountancy	14,500		17,650	
Management Charges	0		2,783	
Bank Interest & Charges	802		1,218	
Canteen & Cleaning	10,540		10,931	
Entertainment	4,446		5,655	
Sponsorship & Donations	1,070		2,580	
Sundry	793		10,398	
Temporary Staff	394		2,647	
Interest on Late Payment	0		587	
Professional Fees	14,576		47329	
Advertising & Promotion	5,228		280	
Technical Books/Courses	8,163		7,564	
Specific Bad Debt Provision	(147,294)		(2,080)	
Carriage Out	0		3,377	
Computer Software/Maintenance	32,650		29,092	
Depreciation:	21,516		22,254	
		2,640,152		2,478,376
Surplus (Loss) for the year		(15,413)		(84,576)

CHAPTER 8

COMPANY LAW ENFORCEMENT

8.1 Introduction

The enforcement of (compliance with) company law has different aspects and is not limited to the powers of the various State agencies involved. The Companies Act 2014 (the '2014 Act') includes many criminal offences. The enforcement of these offences has a public and a private aspect, divided according to its subject matter and the laws in question. Corporate regulation (i.e. the enforcement of company law by the State) is limited in scope and serves the public interest, not any private one. Regulation does not cover all of the possibilities for enforcement, many of which are issues of private law. Companies are subject to the law contained in the 2014 Act as well as certain European Regulations. Officers of all companies are under a general obligation to ensure that *their* companies comply with those laws.

Trading as a company, regardless of its type, brings responsibilities for the company and for its officers (the board of directors). It is important to remain clear about the specific duties of the players (shareholders, directors, and the company itself). The 2014 Act has provided a non-exhaustive list of directors' duties. These duties apply to all directors. There is no distinction in the 2014 Act between those that have been formally appointed, de facto directors, non-executive directors, or shadow directors. Directors' duties are covered in more detail in **chapter 3, 'Officers of a Company'** at **3.7**.

Company law enforcement does not cover EU CFSP (Common Foreign and Security Policy)/ UN sanctions, anti-money laundering or counter-terrorist financing rules. The obligations under those rubrics are separate, cumulative to those covered in this chapter, and almost universally the subject of serious criminal penalties for breach.

Company law serves many masters. It must operate within constitutional norms, which include thereby the law of the European Community. It must be interpreted in accordance with the European Convention on Human Rights, to the extent required by the ECHRA 2003. Its overarching aim was commerce and it provides basic rules for the operation of companies. These laws include those designed to curb excesses and to protect creditors and investors from avoidable loss. Some of these laws may be enforced only by private parties. Those rules, which relate to loss and insolvency and receivership, have been particularly visible during the six years since the collapse of the Irish banking system. The colossal interest in the first wave of prosecutions arising from the failure of the bank formerly known as Anglo Irish Bank has demonstrated the important enforcement role played by the Director of Corporate Enforcement. The Central Bank of Ireland has a separate and vital role to play, but only in relation to bodies supervised or regulated by it, and not companies per se. It is outside of this course of study, but it should be noted that the structure and competences of the Central Bank are different from those of the Irish Financial Services Regulatory Authority ('IFSRA') and the Central Bank prior to September 2008.

8.2   Public Enforcement

The public instruments of corporate enforcement are: (i) The Director of Corporate Enforcement (the 'Director') and the Office of the Director of Corporate Enforcement (ODCE); (ii) The Director of Public Prosecutions ('DPP'); (iii) The Companies Registration Office ('CRO'); (iv) The Irish Auditing and Accounting Supervisory Authority ('IAASA'); and (v) private parties.

All of the exercise of the powers of the Director, the DPP, the CRO, and IAASA is governed by public law (although IAASA is slightly more complicated). Any unauthorised exercise of those powers is subject to judicial review by the High Court. While the ultra vires rule of company law has been repealed in the 2014 Act, administrative law of necessity requires compliance by a public body with the grant of its power: see, for example, the decision of Cregan J in *Flynn v National Asset Loan Management Ltd* ([2014] IEHC 408).

Two highly visible types of enforcement are the prosecution of Companies Acts offences and the collection of information by the State bodies via mandatory reporting rules. Applications for restriction, while related to enforcement, are best dealt with as part of a treatment of restriction and insolvency generally.

8.3   Crimes

The 2014 Act creates four categories of offence:

(a)   Category 1 – a conviction on indictment can result in up to ten years' imprisonment or a fine of up to €500,000 or both. A summary conviction attracts a class A fine or imprisonment for up to 12 months, or both;

(b)   Category 2 – a conviction on indictment can result in up to five years' imprisonment or a fine of up to €50,000 or both. A summary conviction attracts a class A fine or imprisonment for up to 12 months or both;

(c)   Category 3 – This is a summary offence only and can result in up to six months' imprisonment and a 'Class A fine' or both; and

(d)   Category 4 – this is a summary offence only and is punishable by a Class A fine.

A 'Class A fine' is a fine within the meaning of the Fines Act 2010 (a fine not exceeding €5,000).

For offences already committed, or committed during the transitional period (ending 18 months after commencement of the 2014 Act), and for other aspects involving the effect of the previous legislation, or its repeal, it will be necessary to have regard to the limited transitional provisions in the 2014 Act and to the Interpretation Act 2005.

Section 865 of the 2014 Act permits the Director to enforce any breach of the 2014 Act by summary criminal proceedings. The Director is entitled under s 873 of the 2014 Act to deliver a notice (for category 3 or 4 offences) imposing a fine to be paid before a 21-day notice of intention to prosecute expires. If the fine is paid and the default remedied the Director will not prosecute. This section provides a means whereby the Director may, without the institution of court proceedings, levy fines in respect of summary offences in order to avoid the need to prosecute, without denying the person accused of the offence the right to be heard in court.

Section 867 of the 2014 Act states that the time limit for the prosecution of a summary offence is three years from the date of commission. This time limit may be extended if the accused person was outside the jurisdiction, or if the information describing the offence came to the attention of the authorities, after the expiry of the time limit. There is no time limit for the prosecution of indictable offences but, in exceptional circumstances, prosecutorial delay may result in an accused being denied the opportunity of a fair trial.

Section 270 of the 2014 Act provides that an officer who is in default is any officer who authorises or who, in breach of his duty as such officer, permits the default in question. Section 271 of the 2014 Act creates a presumption that where the defendant was aware of the basic facts concerning the default in question, then in the absence of evidence that he took reasonable steps to prevent the default, it shall be presumed that he permitted the default. It is not entirely clear whether this presumption is limited to civil proceedings.

The venue for the prosecution of a summary offence under the 2014 Act may be either the court area in which the offence is charged, the court area in which the accused is arrested or resides, the court area in which the registered office of the company is situated, or a court area specified under s 15 of the Courts Act 1971.Summary offences are those that incorporate a period of imprisonment of 12 months or less. Indictable offences are those carrying a higher tariff. Offences are enforceable by summary prosecution or on indictment at the option of the prosecutor. The DPP or the Director may prosecute all summary offences under the 2014 Act. The CRO may prosecute a limited number of summary offences. The DPP may prosecute all indictable offences.

8.4   Functions of the Regulators

Each regulator has a different focus and statutory bailiwick. It is not uncommon for a given client issue to span a number of regulators. All situations remain subject to general obligations (on the company) to comply and (on its officers) to ensure compliance.

8.4.1   THE DIRECTOR OF CORPORATE ENFORCEMENT

The Director of Corporate Enforcement (the 'Director') was created by s 7 of the Company Law Enforcement Act 2001 and continues in being pursuant to s 945 of the 2014 Act. Section 949 of the 2014 Act states that the functions of the Director are to: (i) enforce and encourage compliance with the 2014 Act; (ii) investigate suspected company law offences; and (iii) where relevant, supervise receivers and liquidators. It also empowers the Director to do such acts or things as are necessary or expedient for the discharge of his functions under the 2014 Act and that he may perform those functions through the staff of the office.

Section 951 of the 2014 Act states that Gardaí seconded to the Director shall remain vested with their usual powers and duties as Gardaí, in addition to any powers that they may exercise as Officers of the Director. Clients should be made aware of this issue when dealing with a Garda that is on secondment as part of the ODCE, especially as regards general powers of arrest, entry, search, and seizure. Of significance, in this regard is the recent change in the extent of the exclusionary rule concerning evidence obtained in inadvertent breach of a person's Constitutional rights, as a consequence of the judgement of the Supreme Court in the *DPP v JC* ([2015] IESC 31.

The Director may refer cases to the DPP (2014 Act, s 949) where he considers that an indictable offence under the 2014 Act has been committed. The Director may refer a case to the DPP, prosecute summarily himself, or impose an instant fine to be paid before the expiry of a notice of intention to prosecute.

The Director can bring disqualification applications under s 842 of the 2014 Act and may relieve a liquidator of his obligation to bring restriction applications against directors of an insolvent company under s 820 of the 2014 Act. These sections penalise transgressions of company law but are more properly dealt with in **chapter 11, 'Corporate Restructuring and Insolvency'**.

Sections 850 and 851 of the 2014 Act provide that a person may provide an undertaking submitting themselves to disqualification. Similarly ss 852 and 853 of the 2014 Act permit a person to provide an undertaking submitting themselves to restriction. Similar to the provision in relation to fines, the opportunity to submit such undertakings is limited to a 21-day notice period. This period may be extended, but only on foot of a request made within the period.

The Director has the power to seek an order restraining an officer of a company from removing from the State, his, or the company's, assets or reducing them where so ever located. The Director may apply to the High Court to compel a company or officer to make good a failure to comply with the Companies Acts or to repay or restore assets in cases of misfeasance.

In addition in a winding up the Director may seek from the court an order to obtain records, to examine an officer, or to arrest an absconding contributory or officer.

8.4.2 THE DIRECTOR OF PUBLIC PROSECUTIONS (DPP)

The DPP was created by the Prosecution of Offences Act 1974 and has authority to prosecute all indictable offences under the 2014 Act. The question of whether the Attorney General retains a residual constitutional right to prosecute (as suggested by Walsh J in *State (Collins) v Ruane* [1984] IR 105) probably does not arise. The DPP has no special role to play other than to decide whether to prosecute on foot of evidence prepared for him.

8.4.3 THE REGISTRAR OF COMPANIES

The Joint Stock Companies Act 1844 established the Registrar of Companies. It operates the filing and registration requirements of the 2014 Act. Its role is to provide essential information about registered companies, to enforce the provisions of company law in relation to filing obligations, and to register the creation of a company in the certificate of incorporation. The Registrar is empowered to prosecute companies summarily for registration offences, to impose fines to be paid before the expiry of a notice of intention to prosecute, and to strike companies off the register of companies.

8.4.4 THE IRISH AUDITING AND ACCOUNTING SUPERVISORY AUTHORITY (IAASA)

IAASA was established in accordance with the provisions of Part 2 of the Companies (Auditing and Accounting) Act 2003, and is continued by s 901 of the 2014 Act. IAASA, pursuant to s 905 of the 2014 Act, supervises prescribed accountancy bodies, whether the accounts of certain classes of companies (private companies meeting certain turnover or balance sheet thresholds and PLCs), and whether companies governed by the laws of the EU that are listed on regulated markets (i.e. certain stock exchanges) have published accounts that comply with the International Financial Reporting Standards (IFRS).

8.5 Reporting

By creating a flow of information to the State bodies the Oireachtas intends to support enforcement. Officers of a company, auditors, liquidators and receivers each have different obligations to make reports to some or all of the State bodies. Those obligations crystallise according to each section creating the requirement. They are dealt with below. These reports are mandatory.

8.5.1 DUTIES ON AUDITORS, LIQUIDATORS, RECEIVERS, AND EXAMINERS

There is a general obligation to comply with the law, including the provisions of the 2014 Act. There are extra duties imposed on certain designated persons. The duties consist of reports that must be made to those statutory bodies. There is an extra duty in the case of a liquidator, who must bring restriction proceedings against all the directors of a company in liquidation (2014 Act, s 820). This is dealt with in **chapter 11, 'Corporate Restructuring and Insolvency'**.

8.5.2   AUDITORS' DUTIES

An auditor's responsibility is to report to the shareholders on the truth and fairness of the financial statements presented at the annual general meeting. An auditor shall report all category 1 or 2 offences arising from the 2014 Act believed to have been committed by the company, or its agents, to the Director. The obligation does not affect legal or professional privilege, but client confidentiality (or other legal duty) may be breached. An auditor cannot be held liable for damage caused by compliance with the 2014 Act.

An auditor's responsibility has been described as onerous but according to Lopes LJ (in *Re Kingston Cotton Mill Co (No 2)* [1896] 2 Ch 279 at 288) the law regards an auditor as 'a watchdog, not a bloodhound'. This statement should be used with care. Accounting standards have developed greatly since that century and have long included investigation of suspected non-compliance with the Companies Acts.

Section 393 of the 2014 Act states that:

> *Where, in the course of, and by virtue of, their carrying out an audit of the accounts of the company, information comes into the possession of the statutory auditors of a company that leads them to form the opinion that there are reasonable grounds for believing that the company or an officer or agent of it has committed category 1 or 2 offence, the statutory auditors shall, forthwith after having formed it, notify that opinion to the Director and provide the Director with particulars of the grounds on which they have formed that opinion.*

The obligation arises 'in the course of, and by virtue' of an audit. The use of the conjunctive 'and' between 'in the course of and by virtue of' in s 393 could mean that the duty does not arise if the accountant is carrying out non-audit work solely. If an auditor forms a belief, after the discharge of his duties, that allows him to form a view that an offence has been committed he does not appear to be obliged to report it. If the information indicates, post facto, that the audit is not a 'true and fair' view of the books and records then the audit 'sign-off' should be withdrawn at that point. If it indicates that an offence has been committed, but that the audit itself remains a true and fair view then arguably the duty to report the evidence to the Director does not arise as the audit was completed.

8.5.3   EXAMINERS' DUTIES

Examinership is the protection afforded by the court while it appoints an examiner to investigate a company's affairs and to report on its commercial prospects of survival.

An examiner is subject to regulation by the ODCE to the extent that an examiner is subject to the 2014 Act. An examiner is required by s 519 of the 2014 Act to act with utmost good faith in relation to the conduct of examinership. Section 558 of the 2014 Act requires that where a disciplinary tribunal (however called) of a professional body finds that an examiner has not maintained appropriate records or has reasonable grounds for believing that the examiner has committed a category 1 or 2 offence during the course of the examinership, then the tribunal shall report the matter, giving details of the finding or, the alleged offence, to the Director forthwith. A similar provision exists in respect of liquidators, pursuant to s 688 of the 2014 Act.

8.5.4   LIQUIDATORS' DUTIES

A liquidator is a person appointed to the company to wind it up and cause it to be dissolved. His duties are to gather in and realise the assets of the company and then distribute them to the creditors in accordance with priority.

Under s 682 of the 2014 Act a liquidator appointed to an insolvent company is obliged to report to the Director on the conduct of the directors.

Where a liquidator in a voluntary winding up believes that any past or present member, or officer of the company has been guilty of a criminal offence, that liquidator is obliged to report his belief and the grounds for it to the Director (as well as the DPP). A liquidator shall furnish such information, and facilitate access or copies for the ODCE, as the Director may require.

On request from the Director a liquidator must provide his books for inspection. Liquidations that have been completed more than six years ago are exempted from this requirement. The liquidator must also answer any queries or provide such reasonable assistance as required. A liquidator is also required to make certain filing returns to the CRO.

8.5.5   RECEIVERS' DUTIES

A receiver is a person appointed on foot of a debenture (or sometimes by a court order) who is responsible for gathering in the charged assets, realising their value, and applying the proceeds to discharge the debt. He has no general duty to inform the company of how business is going. After a receiver has ceased to act, he must send to the Registrar of Companies a statement of opinion as to whether the company is solvent.

Pursuant to s 446 of the 2014 Act, the ODCE may request a receiver to produce his books for inspection. The receiver faces an identical compulsion to a liquidator and must provide his books for inspection. Receiverships that have been completed for more than six years are exempt from this requirement. The receiver must answer any queries or provide such reasonable assistance as required.

Section 447 of the 2014 Act requires that where a receiver believes that any past or present member, or officer of the company has been guilty of a criminal offence, that receiver is obliged to report his belief and the grounds for it to the ODCE (as well as the DPP). The liquidator is required to furnish such information, and facilitate access or copies for the Director as he may require.

8.6   Information Gathering

A company inspector may be appointed by the Director or the court. Strictly speaking, he is not a part of any regulatory body, but he is subject to the supervision of the High Court. He is best seen as an intrusive form of information gathering. When dealing with the statutory power to investigate company law abuses the courts have repeatedly pointed to the privilege conferred by incorporation and the need to protect creditors and the general public. Murray J (in *Dunnes Stores Ireland Co v Ryan* [2002] 2 IR 60) described the purpose of the powers of inspection as being:

> 'to ensure, inter alia, that companies who have availed of the right to incorporate and register under the Acts and the advantages which such incorporation confers, do not abuse those advantages to the detriment of their shareholders, creditors and, in particular, the public interest.'

A company inspection is not required to accord with the rules of natural and constitutional justice until it reaches a point at which adverse conclusions are to be drawn against a person. Murphy J in *Chestvale v Glackin* ([1993] 3 IR 35) speaks of the entry of a verdict against an investigated party as a condition precedent to the procedural rights identified in *Re Haughey* [1971] I.R. 217). Shanley J followed this logic when ruling on the legality of the process of inquiry adopted in *Re National Irish Bank (No. 1)* ([1999] 3 IR 145). The learned judge decided that a mere information gathering exercise did not attract rights of natural justice.

Kelly J in *Re National Irish Bank and National Irish Bank Financial Services* ([1999] 3 IR 190) further analysed the inspection process, and confirmed that the making of an allegation under oath does not elevate an information gathering process unless the inspectors admit such allegation as evidence or if its admission as evidence may give rise to adverse conclusions being drawn against the accused party.

As made clear by Barrington J in *Re National Irish Bank (No 1)* in the Supreme Court, the privilege against self-incrimination did not apply to officers or agents of the company being examined under oath by the inspector.

There are two types of company inspections inspectors. The first is appointed by the Director to determine the true ownership or control of a company or its shares. The second is appointed by the court to investigate and report on the affairs of a company.

8.7   Private Enforcement

Private parties may participate in enforcement to the extent that they possess locus standi. High Court litigation for non-compliance is commonly not justified by the bulk of instances of non-compliance. As stated above, a member, creditor, or director may apply through s 797 of the 2014 Act to enforce compliance with the 2014 Act by that company.

Oppression suits under s 212 of the 2014 Act can include a comparison of the corporate compliance sins of the various litigants. Examples of compliance breaches may establish that the powers of a company are being exercised in an oppressive fashion, but the mere fact that an action is illegal does not render it an act of oppression. The corollary is true of legal act, which is not necessarily benign merely because it is permitted by the 2014 Act. On hearing an oppression suit the High Court may make such order 'as it thinks fit', which can encourage litigants to identify non-compliance so as to detract from the merits of the other party's argument.

Keep in mind the limits of any derivative action (a company should sue for wrongs committed against it (*Foss v Harbottle* [1843] 2 Hare 461). A derivative action may be taken if an illegal act is perpetrated; if more than a bare majority is required to ratify the wrong complained of; if the members' personal rights are infringed; where a fraud has been perpetrated on a minority; or where the justice of the case permits it.

Insolvency-type situations are not strictly relevant here. They tend to move into a search for missing assets and knowledge where compliance is only of relevance if it facilitates asset recovery, either by providing information, or by making available the funds of persons responsible for the losses.

8.7.1   ENFORCEMENT OF DUTY TO COMPLY WITH THE 2014 ACT

Under s 797 of the 2014 Act if a request has been made to a company, or an officer thereof, to remedy a breach of the provisions of the 2014 Act and the default remains uncorrected for a further 14 days, an application may be made to the High Court. This application can be made by the members of the company, creditors of the company, the CRO, or the Director.

No rules are provided for the application. In such circumstances application may be made by way of originating motion. The court appears to have jurisdiction to make an order once a valid notice is served and failure to remedy the default complained of has been adduced. The section does not apply where the wrong in question constitutes one done to the company that, in general law, is maintainable by the company alone. The relief is also not available if the default in question amounts, in the opinion of the court, to the commission of an offence. No existing litigation is needed to invoke this section, which in those circumstances, would proceed by way of originating notice of motion.

8.7.2   PRIVATE CRIMINAL PROSECUTIONS FOR BREACH OF THE COMPANIES ACTS

On the criminal side, jurisdiction exists for a private party (not a company) to prosecute summary offences as a 'common informer'. The continuation of this jurisdiction as 'an important common law right that has survived the Constitution' was reaffirmed by the Supreme Court in *Cumann Luthchleas Gael Teo v Windle* ([1994] 1IR 525).

CHAPTER 9

COMMERCIAL BORROWING

9.1　Introduction

The principal ways in which a business can obtain access to the capital it needs to operate and grow are:

(a)　by issuing bonds;

(b)　by issuing shares; and

(c)　by borrowing.

Issuing bonds is effectively only available to very large businesses and is not considered further here. In general, shareholders invest to participate in the profits and/or capital appreciation of the business in exchange for their investment. Accordingly, they accept a relatively high level of risk and (in many private companies) expect to participate in the management of the business. Lenders get interest on the funds provided, with no expectation of obtaining an increased level of return if the business does well. Accordingly, lenders require a much lower level of risk and will generally seek to take security over the assets of the business.

The choice of whether to raise money by issuing shares or by borrowing or both is often governed by the availability of funds. Assuming that funds are available from both sources, the main trade-off is between (i) the dilution of existing rights regarding dividends and capital appreciation of the business (when issuing shares) and (ii) the obligation to pay interest (when borrowing).

The first part of this chapter deals with different types of borrower and the different types of financial facilities which may be offered, with primary focus on private companies limited by shares. The second part analyses different forms of security and the usual checks to be carried out when the borrower is a company incorporated under the Companies Acts, 1963–2009 or the Companies Act 2014 (the '2014 Act'). The third part deals with registration issues. Any reference to a company in this chapter is reference to a private company limited by shares unless stated otherwise.

The chapter confines itself primarily to situations where the lender of the money is a financial institution. Intra-group lending is common, but tends to be surrounded by such informality that solicitors are often not part of the process. Nevertheless, issues of permissible borrowing (particularly in the context of financial assistance as dealt with in **chapter 13, 'Financial Assistance'** and the solvency of the companies) may arise in the intra-group situation. Practitioners need to be alert to the legal consequences of proposed structures, even or perhaps particularly, when the client regards the matter as straightforward.

9.2   Who is the Borrower?

This review examines individuals, partnerships, companies, corporate entities, and State boards. Each is examined in terms of capacity, authorisation, and applicable legislation. Although this chapter focuses primarily on a private company limited by shares there are many other forms of business entities and very often companies, partnerships, and individuals borrow jointly or guarantee each other's liabilities.

9.2.1   INDIVIDUALS

9.2.1.1   Capacity

An individual may do anything unless prohibited by law. If the borrower is an individual, the issues which may affect capacity are:

(a)   is the person 18 or older? If not, the law relating to contracts with minors applies;

(b)   is the person a bankrupt or capable of being made a bankrupt? A search in the Bankruptcy Office and the Judgments Office will assist. If the transaction which is being funded is at less than market value, a declaration of solvency may be useful; and

(c)   is the person of sound mind?

9.2.1.2   Authorisation

Individuals may authorise others to act on their behalf. A power of attorney is usually required to prove the authorisation in any borrowing transaction. Some matters are peculiarly within the knowledge of the individual. Because of this, most solicitors advising lenders would be very reluctant to accept, for example, a family home declaration made by an attorney. In the context of valid execution it is worth noting that requirements for a deed by a private individual have been amended by the provisions of the Land & Conveyancing Law Reform Act 2009 (the 'Land Act 2009'), removing the requirement for sealing.

9.2.1.3   Applicable law

Consumer legislation and regulations are drafted in broad, sometimes inconsistent, terms. Individual borrowers and guarantors have various protections. The European Communities (Unfair Terms in Consumer Contracts) Regulations 1995 (SI 27/1995) as amended by the European Communities (Terms in Consumer Contracts (Amendment) Regulations 2000 (SI 307/2000) and the Consumer Credit Act 1995 circumscribe freedom of contract by imposing procedural and substantive obligations on a party dealing with a consumer. The latter is a person acting outside his trade, business, or profession. Legal advisers to financial institutions lending to individuals constantly face the question of whether an individual borrower is a consumer. The Consumer Protection Code 2012 (as amended by the inclusion of Chapter 13 which is effective from 1 January 2015), The Code of Conduct for Business Lending to Small and Medium Size Business 2012, and the Code of Conduct on Mortgage Arrears 2013 may all be relevant. If so, the consequences for the documentation are fundamental. General domestic legislation, such as the Family Home Protection Act 1976 and the Civil Partnership and Certain Rights and Obligations of Cohabitants Act 2010 (the 'Civil Partnership Act 2010') impact on commercial lending. For example, many sole traders live on the business premises, be it a farm, pub, or shop.

If the loan is revolving (being drawn, repaid, and drawn again), as will often be the case in small businesses where the loan is filling cashflow gaps, the Supreme Court decision in *Bank of Ireland v Purcell* [1989] IR 327 necessitates ensuring family home and related legislation compliance each time the redrawing takes place.

Floating charges are generally only available to companies. However, the Agricultural Credit Act 1978 allows individual farmers to create floating charges on agricultural stock.

Farming income tends to be seasonal with a high capital requirement to acquire stock or buy seed and then income coming in during another part of the year. The stocking and restocking facilities in particular would be cumbersome if security had to be taken each time, so the floating charge is useful.

9.2.2   PARTNERSHIPS

9.2.2.1   Capacity

While the Partnership Act 1890 and the Limited Partnerships Act 1907 provide a framework for entities to come together with a view to profit, the law does not recognise the partnership as having any legal personality which is separate from the partners. Therefore, questions of capacity of partnerships are really questions about the capacity of each partner.

9.2.2.2   Authorisation

An analysis of the partnership deed and the partnership legislation will disclose who may act for the partnership. Often, one partner may bind all, but in some circumstances the lender requires all partners to sign regardless, so that there is no possibility of any subsequent dispute about authority.

9.2.2.3   Applicable law

The Partnership Act 1890 is enabling, not mandatory. Parties are free to depart from the parameters set out in that Act. No separate legal entity is created and limited liability is not granted, so the law is comfortable with the partners deciding themselves how to regulate their venture.

Limited partnerships (under the Limited Partnerships Act 1907) bestow limited liability, but only on passive partners. The Investment Limited Partnerships Act 1994 made some further changes, primarily to encourage collective investment schemes.

To avail of tax reliefs, partnerships became popular vehicles for investments in assets as diverse as hotels, nursing homes, car parks, life policies, and equipment. Successive Finance Acts have limited the tax efficacy of partnerships and so the frequency with which partnership structures will appear in financing transactions in the future has been substantially reduced.

9.2.3   COMPANIES

9.2.3.1   Capacity

Most commercial lending transactions involve companies borrowing. As an artificial legal entity, a company may only do what the law permits. The 2014 Act introduces a fundamental change to Irish private company law as private companies limited by shares will have general power to do whatever an artificial entity could do instead of the previous approach which was based on being empowered to do whatever the memorandum of association permitted. A designated activity company on the other hand will retain an objects clause and its capacity to borrow must therefore be ascertained.

Does the company exist without a fundamental infirmity?

(a)   The certificate of incorporation proves that the company was incorporated on a particular day. It does not guarantee ongoing existence. The certificate will also confirm the company number. Using the company number in documents such as a guarantee and a mortgage may assist in identifying the corporate borrower in spite of any subsequent name change.

(b)   A company might be struck off the register. The Companies Registration Office ('CRO') has powers of strike off to encourage companies to file annual returns and accounts. Under the State Property Act 1954 when a company has been dissolved (including by reason of strike off) its assets vest in the Minister for Finance. A company, or indeed a creditor, may apply to the High Court for reinstatement of the company to the register. Once restored, the company is deemed to have continued in existence as if it had never been struck off. The Registrar may restore the company if application is made within one year of strike off (2014 Act, Part 12, Chapter 2).

(c)   A company may have been placed in receivership, under the protection of the court (examinership), or in liquidation.

A search in the Companies Registration Office ('CRO') is an important first step when dealing with a borrower which is a company. The information is not exhaustive or necessarily conclusive, but it may avoid subsequent embarrassment at completion if, for example, the company has been struck off.

May the company borrow?

Under the 2014 Act, a private company limited by shares will be empowered to enter into any transaction. This will substantially reduce the risk of any ultra vires activity. Previously the objects of the company have been set out in the memorandum of association and this will continue to be the case for designated activity companies. Generally, borrowing and granting security were not regarded as objects, but rather as powers to be used to further the objects of the company. Therefore, matching the borrowing to a permissible business objective was important and will continue to be important for designated activity companies.

Because incorporation as a limited company provides not only a separate legal entity but also limited liability, the legislation contains various protections so that this special privilege is not abused to the detriment of third parties. Two of the major issues which arise in this area, namely financial assistance and dealings with directors or connected persons, are considered in more detail in **chapter 13, 'Financial Assistance'** and **chapter 10, 'Transactions with Directors'** respectively.

9.2.3.2   Authorisation

Because a company is an artificial entity, it has to deal with the world through others. The 2014 Act and the company's constitution set out how the internal management is regulated. Usually, the board of directors will have day-to-day control. Sometimes the shareholders/members will have to consent, either because of a specific legislative requirement (e.g. s 238 of the 2014 Act) or because of bank policy (e.g. where there is a potential conflict of interest between a director's own affairs and those of the company).

In addition, s 41 of the 2014 Act provides that a company may appoint an attorney, although this usually only arises for transactions abroad.

9.2.4   OTHER CORPORATE ENTITIES

While much commercial activity is carried on through companies, partnerships, and sole traders, other legal forms of business organisation also exist. Foreign corporates may operate branches in Ireland rather than establishing separate subsidiaries. Specific legislation deals with friendly societies and cooperatives. The cooperative movement has been particularly successful in Ireland in the agriculture and agribusiness areas.

9.2.4.1   Capacity

Sometimes the question of whether the co-op has the power to borrow at all, never mind how much it may borrow, may arise.

9.2.4.2   Authorisation

The committee of a co-operative may have to go to the members to approve borrowing or the granting of security.

9.2.4.3   Applicable law

The Industrial and Provident Societies Acts and the Friendly Societies Acts belong to a different era, and need a major overhaul. Some changes were made by the Registration of Title Act 2006.

9.2.5   STATE BOARDS

Many State commercial enterprises are incorporated under the Companies Acts 1963–2013, e.g. Bórd na Móna plc. However, others which have separate legal existence are creatures of a tailor-made statute, e.g. the Electricity Supply Board and the National Asset Management Agency. In the latter category, one must check the specific legislation to ascertain whether the body may borrow, what protection third parties are given in relying on a decision of the board or its equivalent, and whether any third party consent (often that of the Minister for Finance) is needed for the transaction to be effective. Various public bodies must get the consent of the Minister for Finance under recent credit stabilisation legislation.

9.3   Types of Facilities

9.3.1   OVERDRAFTS

Overdrafts are usually negotiated for a period of up to one year and are repayable on demand. Often the bank will require that an account with the benefit of an overdraft nevertheless has a credit balance for a minimum aggregate period (e.g. a month) during the year.

9.3.2   TERM LOAN

Term loans comprise loans which are repayable by negotiated amounts over a period. As these loans are not repayable on demand (unlike overdrafts), the events of default which enable the bank to require early repayment are important.

9.3.3   REVOLVING CREDIT FACILITIES

Revolving loans comprise loans which are rolled over after specified periods with an original or renegotiated maturity. Loans which are repaid may be drawn again.

These may be demand facilities, without events of default, or may be term loans with events of default.

9.3.4   PROVISION OF GUARANTEES TO THIRD PARTIES

Financial institutions may provide guarantees, indemnities, or undertakings to third parties at the request of a company. A typical example of such a guarantee would be a performance bond on a building contract or on a planning permission condition. The bank will require a counter-indemnity from the company so that it can clearly reclaim such sums from the company.

9.3.5   FACTORING

Factoring, strictly speaking, does not constitute a lending service by banks. However, companies that factor their debts to banks usually see factoring as a financial facility comparable to borrowing. Factoring, in practical terms, constitutes the offering by a company to a finance company of an option whereby the finance company may acquire the debts invoiced by the company for particular sums of money and those debts are paid to the finance company rather than to the company. Factoring in the ordinary course of business is exempt from stamp duty.

9.3.6   LEASING

Leasing, again, whilst not constituting the giving by a bank of a loan, nonetheless enables companies to acquire assets by making periodic payments tapering down to nominal payments. The bank buys an asset and leases it for a primary leasing period which may be anything from two to eight years. After the expiry of the primary leasing period, a secondary leasing period for an indeterminate time proceeds, at the start of which the rental payment is reduced to a nominal amount.

9.4   Types of Security

Why do banks require security? What do the buzzwords mean? What types of security are sought? The main focus of this section is on companies borrowing from, and granting security to, lending institutions and the implications for the companies of granting such security.

9.4.1   PURPOSE–PRIORITY ON INSOLVENCY

The purpose of a bank taking security is to ensure a quicker and more assured payout in the event that a company goes into receivership, examinership, or liquidation (see **chapter 11, 'Corporate Restructuring and Insolvency'** at **11.5.4** which sets out the priorities which will be applied in an insolvency situation).

9.4.2   LEGAL TERMINOLOGY

9.4.2.1   Debenture

The term debenture has three meanings:

(a)   'An instrument, often but not necessarily under seal, issued by a company or public body as evidence of a debt or as security for a loan of a fixed sum of money upon which interest is payable. It is usually called a debenture on the face of it and it contains a promise to pay the amount mentioned on it.' (*Murdoch's Dictionary of Irish Law*)

(b)   In the context of borrowing by a company, the word debenture usually means a document which contains a covenant by the company to pay all sums due or to become due by the company to the lender and which contains a charge (fixed and/ or floating) in favour of the lender.

(c)   On the money markets, a debenture usually means a debt security (whether secured or unsecured). Under s 2 (1) of the 2014 Act 'debenture' includes debenture stock, bonds, and other securities of a company whether constituting a charge on the assets of the company or not.

9.4.2.2   Mortgage

The historical method of creating a legal mortgage prior to commencement of the Land Act 2009, in a real property context, was by way of transferring or conveying the interest in the real property to the mortgagee/lender. The creation of a legal mortgage over unregistered land has now been brought into line with the law for registered land and as and from 1 December 2009 operates by way of charge. This change has been introduced to reflect the realities of modern usage of a mortgage as security for a loan. As of 1 December 2009 the only method of creating a legal mortgage is by charge by deed. Many provisions of the Land Act 2009 appear to apply to mortgages created after 1 December 2009. As such a 'dual' system of law governing mortgage has developed. The Land and Conveyancing Reform Act 2013 clarified that the benefit of certain provisions of previous legislation which had been repealed by the Land Act 2009 continued to apply, thereby removing the doubt highlighted by the decision of the High Court in *Start Mortgages Limited v Gunn* 2011 IEHC 275.

The Land Act 2009 does not abolish the equitable mortgage. Such a mortgage passes only an equitable estate or interest, either because the form of transfer or conveyance used is an equitable one, i.e. operates only as between the parties to it and those who have notice of it (such as an equitable mortgage by deposit of title deeds or an equitable mortgage of shares by deposit of the share certificates), or because the mortgagor's estate or interest is equitable, that is, it consists merely of the right to obtain a conveyance of the legal estate.

9.4.2.3   Charge

A charge is the form of security for the repayment of a debt or performance of an obligation consisting of the right of a creditor to receive payment out of some specific fund or out of the proceeds of the realisation of specific property. In the real property context, a charge is now taken on both Registry of Deeds and Land Registry property and is registered in the Registry of Deeds or as a burden on the folio in the Land Registry.

9.4.2.4   Pledge

A pledge arises where goods or documents of title for goods are delivered by the pledgor to the pledgee to be held as security for the payment of a debt, or for the discharge of some other obligation. The subject matter of the pledge will be restored to the pledgor as soon as the debt or other obligation is discharged. Where a definite time for payment has been fixed, the pledgee has an implied power of sale upon default. If there is no stipulated time for payment, the pledgee may demand payment and, if the pledgor does not pay, the pledgee may exercise the power of sale after giving notice to the pledgor.

This form of security is relevant in the case of items the ownership of which may be transferred by delivery.

9.4.2.5   Hypothecation

Hypothecation is the creation of a charge on a chattel as security for payment of a sum of money where the property remains in the possession of the debtor.

9.4.2.6   Lien

The definition of mortgage in the Land Act 2009 includes a lien, except in Part 10 where the meaning is limited to a legal mortgage by charge by deed after 1 December 2009.

A lien is the right to hold the property of another as security for the performance of an obligation.

9.5   Principal Securities Delivered by Companies

9.5.1   FLOATING CHARGE OVER UNDERTAKING

A floating charge usually constitutes a charge over all the assets of the borrower company as acquired from time to time. The company remains free to deal with its assets in the ordinary course of its business. The charge only becomes a fixed charge upon crystallisation. On the appointment of a receiver or liquidator, the floating charge is fixed on all assets in the ownership of the company at that time.

The main elements of floating charges include:

(a)   *The covenant to pay.* This usually extends to cover all sums due or to become due whether as principal or as surety, whether alone or jointly with any person, company, or other entity.

(b)   *The charging clause or provision.* This will usually be a charge on *'all the undertaking property and assets of the company whatsoever and wheresoever present and future including its uncalled capital for the time being and goodwill'.*

(c)   *Negative pledge/restrictions on other charges.* There will usually be a restriction on the company creating any other charge ranking *pari passu* (equal) with or in priority to the floating charge. In the absence of such a provision, the company could create a fixed mortgage or charge on particular property in favour of another lender.

(d)   *Continuing security/the rule in* Clayton's Case. The rule in *Clayton's Case* (1816) 1 Mer 572 stated that sums paid into a borrower's account go to reduce or extinguish the secured debt and left the bank unsecured with regard to subsequent advances. Therefore, this rule is specifically excluded if the charge is to constitute continuing security and is not to be satisfied by any interim repayments. The rule in *Clayton's Case* was considered in *Tom Grace, Anglo Irish Bank fund and Anglo Irish Nominees Ltd Applicants v Stephen Pearson and Others* [2007] 4 IR 1 where it was held that it could be displaced in the particular circumstances of a case where its application would result in injustice between investors.

(e)   *Further assurance and power of attorney.* The company will undertake to deliver such further documents as the lender may require to ensure that the charge created continues to be valid. It is usual also for the security document to contain a power of attorney by way of security, whereby the lender is authorised to do whatever is necessary in order to perfect the security and do other things in the name of the company.

(f)   *Events of default and power to appoint receiver.* Events of default are essential in a term facility. The power to appoint a receiver is the most important practical power that a lender has to enforce its security.

9.5.2   MORTGAGE/CHARGE/EQUITABLE MORTGAGE OVER LAND

The Land Act 2009 greatly simplifies the method of creating a legal mortgage over unregistered land, aligning it with the Land Registry system. The holder of such a charge is entitled to exercise the powers of sale set out in the charge itself or under the Land Act 2009. For pre 1 December 2009 mortgages the position is unclear.

An equitable mortgage is created by the deposit on behalf of the company of relevant documents of title to property. Unusually, an equitable mortgage may be created by deed if the interest being mortgaged by the borrower company is an equitable interest only.

9.5.3   MORTGAGE OF PLANT AND MACHINERY

A company may create a specific mortgage over its plant and machinery (as well as charging such plant and machinery in the general sense by way of floating charge). Frequently, such a document is described as a 'chattel mortgage'. This expression should not be confused with a chattel mortgage under the Agricultural Credit Act 1978.

9.5.4 CHATTEL MORTGAGE UNDER AGRICULTURAL CREDIT ACT 1978

An individual, a company, or for that matter any other entity may create a chattel mortgage in favour of a 'recognised lender' (most of the Irish licensed banks are recognised lenders) of 'stock' under the Agricultural Credit Act 1978. Stock is agricultural produce or machinery used in processing or distributing it. This is dealt with in greater detail below. The chattel mortgage may include fixed and/or floating charges over such stock.

9.5.5 ASSIGNMENT OF THE BENEFIT OF AN INTEREST UNDER MATERIAL CONTRACTS

The assignment of the benefit of the interest under a contract/agreement is often a component part of a debenture or mortgage but can be a stand-alone document.

9.6 Taking Security over Particular Assets

9.6.1 LAND INCLUDING LICENSED PREMISES

Formalities for taking mortgages over land are dealt with in the Conveyancing module of the Professional Practice Course to which you should cross-refer for necessary materials.

A company is entitled to hold a licence for the sale of intoxicating liquor although it has to be said that many district judges are happier to see a company's licence held in the name of an individual nominee of a company. The licence to sell intoxicating liquor is not transferable.

Instead, it is usual for a collateral deed of covenant to be delivered to the bank by the licence holder, be it the company or the individual nominee. The covenantor undertakes to do everything to preserve the licence and to do everything necessary so as to vest the licence in the bank's nominee should the occasion arise on an enforcement of security.

9.6.2 STOCK-IN-TRADE

Stock-in-trade is usually charged by the floating charge in a debenture. Stock may be charged by way of fixed charge, but then such assets would cease to be 'stock-in-trade' in the accepted sense as a specific release would be required every time the particular stock was sold. Retention of title in favour of suppliers is a relevant factor.

9.6.3 PLANT AND MACHINERY

Plant and machinery, if moveable or not substantial, will often be charged simply by the floating charge provisions of a debenture. However, in cases of substantial machinery, e.g. valuable printing machines or packing machines, fixed charges (sometimes in the form of a chattel mortgage) will be taken. Sufficient information should be included in the mortgage clearly to identify the property.

A lender will have to satisfy itself that the items are not subject to any hire purchase or leasing agreements and that any reservation of title clauses in the contracts of supply have been waived. Alternatively, an auditor's certificate to this effect will be sought, or a letter from the supplier.

9.6.4   SHIPS AND AIRCRAFT

Ship mortgages are a particular discipline in themselves. These must conform to a particular format and, when delivered, there is usually a collateral deed of covenant between mortgagor and lender. Fishing vessels are frequently mortgaged as security and appropriate specific covenants should be included in the deed of covenant.

Aircraft may be mortgaged by chattel mortgage in the same way as plant and machinery save that such chattel mortgages are likelier to be more 'big ticket' (in other words, of greater monetary value) than plant and machinery chattel mortgages.

9.6.5   'STOCK' (AGRICULTURAL CREDIT ACT 1978)

Stock is defined by the Agricultural Credit Act 1978 (the 'Agricultural Credit Act'), as including:

(a)   animals and birds of every kind and the progeny and produce of such animals and birds;

(b)   insects and fish of every kind and the progeny and produce of such insects and fish;

(c)   agricultural crops (whether growing on or severed from the land);

(d)   trees (whether growing on or severed from the land);

(e)   any product derived from any of the foregoing; and

(f)   machinery, implements, vehicles, fixtures, fittings, and materials used in or for the production, manufacture, processing, preparation for sale, or marketing of any agricultural or fishery produce.

There are certain powers given to a chattel mortgagee, such as the right of inspection, the making of an inventory, and the possibility of crystallising a floating charge before the appointment of a receiver, specifically under the terms of the Agricultural Credit Act.

9.6.6   SHARES AND DEBENTURES

It is common for lenders to take security over stocks and shares. More often than not, security will be taken over quoted shares and debentures which are securities of public companies. Security over shares in unquoted companies is less attractive because of the lack of a ready market for sale and, in private companies, restrictions on transferability. The three principal categories of shares to be considered in the context of taking security are set out below.

9.6.6.1   Bearer shares

The title to bearer securities passes by delivery and share warrants can be fully negotiable instruments.

9.6.6.2   Registered shares

Most securities are 'registered', i.e. the names and addresses of the holders are entered in a register which shows the amount of stock or the number of shares which they hold. As proof of such registration, a share certificate or stock certificate is issued. However, the advent of the CREST system of dematerialised shares has changed this for certain quoted companies.

9.6.6.3   Inscribed shares

Inscribed stock involves the persons named being entered in the inscription books of the registration authority. No certificate is supplied but instead a stock receipt or certificate of inscription is issued. This stock receipt (unlike a stock certificate) does not have to be produced when the stock is sold. The stock is transferable in the books of the registration authority on the personal attendance of the holder or of a duly appointed attorney, who is normally a solicitor or banker.

The usual forms of securities offered as security to lenders are:

(a) debenture stock (a loan to the company which may or may not be secured on the assets);

(b) preference shares/stock (these will usually rank before the ordinary shares with regard to payment of dividend and capital);

(c) ordinary shares/equity capital (these shares constitute the 'real' ownership of a company); and

(d) deferred shares (these are rarely issued these days and would rank last for payment of dividend and capital).

Stocks and shares in quoted companies have certain advantages as security:

(a) these are easy to value;

(b) there are few formalities when transferring them;

(c) these may easily be sold; and

(d) there is full negotiability in the case of bearer securities.

Unquoted shares have their own disadvantages. There may be difficulty in valuing the shares or in finding a purchaser. Even if the bank finds a purchaser, it may be that the directors in the exercise of the power conferred on them by the articles may decline to register a transfer in the lender's favour or in favour of the lender's nominee or purchaser. In certain cases, the company's constitution may prevent the bank taking a legal mortgage over the shares in the first place.

9.6.6.4 CREST (uncertified securities)

The Companies Act 1990 (Securities) Regulations 1996 (SI 68/1996) came into effect on 24 January 1997. The Regulations have since been amended by the Companies Act 1990 (Uncertificated Securities) (Amendment) Regulations 2005 (SI 693/2005). The Regulations provide for the holding of shares of a class in uncertificated form if they are to be a 'participating security' for the purposes of the Regulations. On a voluntary basis, quoted companies may apply to Euroclear Limited (a company established under the Regulations to operate the CREST system in Ireland) for admission of their shares as participating security. It is not possible to take an equitable deposit over uncertificated marketable shares (because there are no share certificates).

9.6.7 CASH, DEBTS RECEIVABLE

It is possible to take a fixed charge over credit balances at a bank or to take fixed charges over debts receivable.

In the case of charges over cash, the House of Lords in *Morris v Agrichemicals* [1997] 3 WLR 909 confirmed that it is possible for a bank to obtain a charge over a credit balance of a borrower with itself. The bank will often look to obtain rights of set-off against that deposit in addition to the banker's right of set-off. As to fixed charges on book debts, the provisions of the Taxes Consolidation Act 1997, s 1001 require careful consideration. There is limited protection to lenders if a copy of the Form C1 is sent to the Collector General (currently at Sarsfield House, Limerick) within 21 days of the creation of the charge.

9.6.8   GOODS AND BILLS OF LADING

In the case of exports of goods, a bank may be required to open a letter of credit to facilitate the transaction. The bank will take a pledge of the relevant goods upon receipt of the documents of title to those goods which, in certain contracts, will typically be an invoice, an insurance policy, and a bill of lading.

A bill of lading is a document signed by the ship's owner or by the master or other agent of the ship's owner which states that certain goods have been shipped on a particular ship and sets out the terms on which those goods have been delivered to and received by the ship's owner.

9.7   Supporting Security

9.7.1   GUARANTEE

9.7.1.1   Meaning

A contract of guarantee is a contract by one person to be answerable for the debt or default of another. Pursuant to s 2 of the Statute of Frauds (Ireland) 1695, a guarantee must be evidenced in writing.

There are three parties concerned and two contracts:

(a)   the first contract involves the principal creditor ('lender') and the principal debtor ('borrower'); and

(b)   the contract of guarantee involves the principal creditor (lender) and the guarantor or surety. The guarantee is a collateral security and there must be primary liability in some person other than the guarantor, the guarantor being liable only secondarily, i.e. if the principal debtor (borrower) does not pay.

An indemnity is different from a guarantee in that the person giving the indemnity is primarily liable on foot of the indemnity and there is no secondary liability. An indemnity is a more onerous obligation than a guarantee. Even though the principal may escape, the indemnifier remains liable. One distinction between a guarantee and indemnity is that, whereas a guarantee must be in writing, an indemnity need not be. In practice, frequently in a guarantee document, there is an indemnity to require payment by the guarantor if the guarantee provisions in the guarantee fail.

9.7.1.2   Termination of liability of guarantor

The guarantor is a favoured debtor and may insist on rigid adherence to the terms of the guarantee. A guarantor's liability does not arise until the principal debtor has made default. Although only secondarily liable for the debt, it is not necessary for the creditor to request the debtor to pay or to sue the debtor before taking proceedings against the guarantor. It has been held that, in the absence of a specific provision to the contrary, a guarantor is discharged from liability under a guarantee in the following circumstances:

(a)   if the transaction is void as between the principal debtor and the creditor;

(b)   if the principal debtor is discharged or if the creditor releases the principal debtor from liability;

(c)   if there is any material variation of the terms of the contract between the creditor and the principal, e.g. allowing the principal debtor extra time to pay;

(d)   if there is any change in the constitution of the persons to or for whom the guarantee was given (e.g. changes in partnerships). This rule was embodied as far as partnerships were concerned in the Partnership Act 1890, s 18.

9.7.1.3   Usual clauses found in guarantees

Most guarantees contain a clause permitting the creditor, without the consent of the guarantor, to vary the form of security, which it has in respect of the principal debtor's debt, and to grant the principal debtor extra time for payment.

The guarantee will also contain a clause whereby the guarantor undertakes not to protect himself by taking security from the principal debtor. The reason for this is to ensure that if the debtor becomes bankrupt and part of his liability is unsecured, his free assets will not be depleted to the detriment of the creditor as a result of charges created in favour of the guarantor.

The guarantee should also contain a clause indicating that the security will be a continuing security and that it will remain in full force until all obligations of the principal debtor have been discharged. This is inserted in order to exclude the operation of the rule in *Clayton's Case* (1816) 1 Mer 572. If the rule was not excluded, each sum paid into the principal debtor's account, in the case of a bank after the execution of the guarantee, would reduce the guarantor's liability, while each debit to the account would create a fresh advance for which the guarantor would not be liable. The case of *Triodos Bank NV v Dobbs* [2005] EWCA Civ 630 [2005] 2 Lloyd's Reports 588 has brought about a practice of retaking guarantees when new funds are being advanced and having guarantors sign an acceptance of any facility letter or variation letter. In *Danske Bank A/S trading as National Irish Bank v McFadden* [2010] IEHC 116 Clarke J found a guarantee could well cease to have effect where a material alteration had taken place in the contract under which the principal debt was owed save in circumstances where the guarantor could be said to have assented to that change. The guarantor will be prohibited from suing the debtor in respect of any money paid on foot of the guarantee, until such time as the entire debt due to the creditor has been discharged in full. If this clause were not included, it could prejudicially affect the creditor.

The operative clause whereby the guarantor agrees to guarantee the debt usually contains a provision that the guarantor will pay the principal debt on demand. By inserting this provision, one may avoid the Statute of Limitations 1957 running until such time as demand is made. For example, where a debtor has a running account with the bank for a number of years, this could be relevant. The guarantee should also contain a provision as to what will constitute the service of the demand and this will usually be contained in a notice clause.

It is usual for the guarantee to include a provision permitting the creditor and the principal debtor to vary the contract, even if the liability of the guarantor is thereby increased.

9.7.1.4   Guarantees by partnerships

Unless it may be shown that the giving of guarantees is necessary for the carrying on of the business of a particular partnership in the ordinary way, one partner has no implied authority to bind the firm by executing a guarantee (Partnership Act 1890, s 5).

9.7.1.5   Guarantees by limited companies

Under the 2014 Act in the case of a designated activity company it will be necessary to check the company's memorandum of association to establish whether the company has the power to execute a guarantee, but private companies limited by shares (properly so called) will be able to enter into any transaction.

9.7.1.6   Assignment of life policy

Companies often take out life assurance policies on the lives of key personnel. These life policies may be given as security by the company. The life policies are assigned to the lender by means of a deed of assignment.

A life policy is a chose in action (property which cannot be reduced to physical possession). As with all charges over choses in action, the creditor/bank must protect its priority by giving notice of its security to the obligor, in this case the assurance company.

9.7.2   COLLATERAL ISSUES

Frequently, the controller of a company will create a charge over his/her individual property to support a guarantee or indemnity obligation. In these circumstances, it is important that the provisions of relevant family and consumer credit legislation are considered.

For example, if the managing director of a company is guaranteeing the company's borrowings and granting security over the family home his wife should obtain independent legal advice with regard to the transaction. The borrower and the bank will need advice on whether this security amounts to a housing loan within the Consumer Credit Act 1995 and the Land Act 2009.

9.7.3   SET-OFF

It is usual, in conjunction with the taking of security over companies (or for that matter on the opening of accounts of the companies in the case of certain banks), for 'Letters of Lien, Appropriation and Combination' to be signed on behalf of a borrowing company entitling the bank to combine accounts at will. The banks want to assert that the net sum due by the company to the bank is what must be repaid only, with any other sums due being written off against credit balances.

9.8   Secretarial Considerations and Requirements

9.8.1   INCORPORATION

The fact of incorporation of the company must always be proven. 'Does the company (still) exist (under its supposed name)' may seem a very basic question, but it is one which must always be addressed by searches in the CRO.

9.8.2   POWER OF THE COMPANY TO BORROW, DELIVER SECURITY, AND GIVE GUARANTEES

A certified copy of the constitution of the company, as well as confirmation of its status if incorporated before the commencement of the 2014 Act, are essential. As discussed above, private companies limited by shares do not have an objects clause, and subject to the provisions of the company's constitution have the power to borrow and provide security. In the case of a designated activity company, it will be necessary to check the company's objects clause.

9.8.3   DIRECTORS' POWERS TO EXERCISE THE COMPANY'S POWERS

The constitution of the company or, in the case of a designated activity company, the articles of association of the borrower company, will need to be examined to determine whether there are any limitations on the borrowing power of directors.

A special resolution approving borrowing, delivery of security, or the giving of a guarantee needs to be passed by the company in general meeting if the provisions of s 82 or s 239 of the 2014 Act apply to the proposed borrowing, delivery of security, or giving of a guarantee (see **chapters 10, 'Transactions with Directors'** and **13, 'Financial Assistance'**).

Sometimes, in the case of transactions where a company is guaranteeing the obligations of third parties, lenders will seek the passing of a resolution of the company in general meeting noting that the giving of the guarantee is bona fide in the best interests of the company, noting some consideration received by the company for the giving of the guarantee, and resolving that the board of directors be authorised and directed to attend to the delivery of a guarantee.

9.8.4   RESOLUTION OF THE BOARD OF DIRECTORS

As a general rule, a lender will look for a resolution of the board of directors whereby the directors resolve to borrow the money and, if relevant, deliver the relevant security in accordance with their powers.

Where a document is to be a deed, it will be sealed in accordance with the provisions of the company's constitution. The seal should be affixed on documents only by the authority of a resolution of the board of directors with the relevant document being signed by a director and countersigned by another director, the secretary, or some other person appointed by the directors for the purpose.

9.8.5   COMPLETION OF A BORROWING TRANSACTION — DOCUMENTS TABLED/HANDED OVER TO LENDER'S SOLICITOR

9.8.5.1   Certificate of incorporation

The original certificate of incorporation, any certificate(s) of incorporation on change of name, and an up-to-date CRO search will be required. The latter demonstrates the continued incorporation of the company under its purported name.

The original certificate of incorporation and any certificates of incorporation on change of name will be required in connection with delivery of any charge document to the Land Registry.

9.8.5.2   Constitution/Memorandum of association

A copy of the constitution (or memorandum and articles of association in the case of a designated activity company) certified as being a true copy of the current document incorporating all amendments will be required. Authentication of such a document under the companies legislation may be effected by a director or the secretary.

9.8.5.3   Members' resolutions

If the directors' borrowing powers are restricted under the company's constitution, a certified copy of any members' resolutions approving the borrowing will be required together with evidence that the resolutions have been delivered to the CRO. If the Summary Approval procedure applies, then a certified copy of the director's statutory declaration and a special resolution of the members will be required.

9.8.5.4   Directors' resolution

A certified copy of the resolution of the meeting of the board of directors approving borrowing/delivery of security/giving of guarantee will be required. As a general rule, a certified copy resolution will be signed by either the chairperson or the secretary although the chairperson should be the signatory in view of s 166 (3) of the 2014 Act.

9.8.5.5   Security documents

The following additional documents may be needed, depending on the security:

Charge of land	All documents of title to land
Mortgage over plant and machinery	Auditors' certificate as to no reservation of title/HP or leasing
Charge over shares	Share warrant or share certificate memorandum of deposit, executed incomplete stock transfer form
Assignment of life policy	original life policy, letter confirming no lapse or cancellation of life policy, birth certificate of life assured (if age not admitted on the policy)

9.8.5.6   Form C1 for security documents containing charges

Prescribed particulars of charges must be delivered to the Registrar of Companies (CRO) within 21 days of the creation of a charge. If the security includes a fixed charge on book debts, then a copy should also be sent to the Collector General within the same 21-day period.

9.8.5.7   Registry of Deeds filings

Up to July 2008 a document known as a memorial, essentially an abstract of the charge, was filed in the Registry of Deeds. Documents are now lodged for registration by use of a standardised application form. Even if a debenture contains merely a floating charge in general terms over the undertaking, property, and assets of the company, an application form regarding that debenture may be lodged for registration in the Registry of Deeds provided there is general charge wording.

9.8.5.8   Certificate of company secretary as to certain corporate details

It is common, on completion, to obtain a certificate from the company secretary:

(a) certifying the identity of the directors, the secretary, and the location of the registered office;

(b) confirming that no other charges have been executed, that no resolution has been circulated to put the company into receivership, liquidation, or court examination, and that no petition is pending to put the company into receivership, liquidation, or court examination and that no judgment has been obtained capable of being converted into a judgment mortgage; and

(c) confirming that the company is not subject to any agreement, order, or trust whereby its powers of borrowing or delivering security are in any way impaired.

It is unclear what redress a lender will obtain from a secretary who has misstated any of these facts, but it does at least provide some comfort that these matters have in fact been investigated.

9.8.5.9   Particulars of insurance

Frequently, lenders will look for evidence of non-life insurance, which is relevant for a borrower's business, e.g. insurance of particular key assets or buildings.

Generally, lenders will require that their interest be noted on the insurance policies. At the very least, a letter is sought from the insurance company undertaking that it will not let the policies lapse or be cancelled without prior written notice to the lender. This will be so as to enable the lender to pay the premiums to preserve the insurance if the lender believes that that is important. Increasingly, lenders are requiring that they be joint beneficiaries or sole loss payee.

9.8.5.10   Searches

Searches with satisfactory explanations of acts appearing will be required to be handed over by the borrowing company.

Office	Will disclose
Companies Registration Office	Charges, insolvency, dissolution of company, restriction and disqualification of directors, timing of annual returns
Judgments Office	Registered money judgments
Sheriff's Office	Unexecuted execution orders against goods, rates certificates
Revenue Sheriff's Office	Unexecuted Revenue certificates
Registry of Deeds	Documents affecting any interest in heritable property
Land Registry	Burdens on registered property, pending dealings, registered owner

In certain cases searches on overseas registers will be required.

9.9   Post-completion Procedures

9.9.1   STAMP ALL STAMPABLE DOCUMENTS

Stamp duty ceased to be payable on security documents such as mortgages on 7 December 2006. Prior to this, the rate was €1 per €1,000 secured, subject to a maximum of €630 on a document where the amount secured was more than €250,000. Collateral and counterpart documents were stamped at €12.50 each.

Note that documents transferring an interest in real or leasehold property and certain asset sale agreements must be stamped at various rates depending on the nature of the property and other factors. As stamp duty law in the residential sector is regularly amended, practitioners must be particularly careful to ensure documents have the relevant statutory certificates and sufficient money is held to pay applicable stamp duty.

9.9.2   REGISTRATION OF A CHARGE

9.9.2.1   Companies Registration Office

When a company executes a charge, particulars of the charge must be delivered to the Registrar within 21 days from the date of its creation (2014 Act, s 409).

Section 408 of the 2014 Act states that the prescribed particulars of all mortgages and charges, whether arising from written or oral agreements must be registered save for five exceptions, namely security on cash, on bank accounts, on shares, on certain financial instruments, and on rights related to any of these exceptions.

Failure to do so renders the charge void against the company, any liquidator, or creditor. Registration of a charge on an Irish company's property is undertaken by lodging a

Form C1. In the case of a foreign company, a similar procedure using a Form F8 is required, whether or not the company has registered on the External Register. Part 21, Chapter 2 of the 2014 Act applies in relation to external companies and registration under s 409 will be relevant to those external companies which have registered.

If the applicant for registration is the company itself, the form must be verified by some person interested in the charge otherwise than on behalf of the company, setting out such interest. Generally, the solicitor for the lending institution will verify the particulars. If particulars are not filed within the appropriate period, application may be made to court under s 417 of the 2014 Act, for an order extending the time for registration or rectifying the error in the application. The court must be satisfied that the omission to register was accidental.

If the charge becomes void under s 409 of the 2014 Act by failure to register on time, the money secured becomes immediately payable and the lender may immediately sue for the debt. A new security document may be executed and the appropriate particulars filed within the appropriate time. The difficulty which could arise here is in respect of s 597 of the 2014 Act in that in the case of a floating charge, the charge could be rendered invalid if the borrower is wound up within 12 months of the creation of the charge as no cash is paid to the company at the time of, or in consideration for, the granting of the charge.

It should be noted that if a property subject to an existing mortgage is acquired by a company, the new purchasing company must file Form C3, as the existing charge now represents a charge on its property. It should also be noted that practice of the CRO is to reject any forms delivered outside the 21-day period even if the form had been delivered originally within the period with inadvertent errors only.

Certain charges created by non-Irish companies over assets in Ireland were registered on the 'Slavenburg Register'. This arose because of the mismatch between the Companies Act 1963, s 111 and Part XI of that Act. The thinking was that external companies having an established place of business in Ireland should have delivered appropriate particulars to the CRO so that a file may be opened in their name in the CRO to register charges. Section 111 applied the rules as to registration of charges to companies having an established place of business in Ireland whether or not they have so registered. The practice developed of delivering Forms 8E to the CRO of such companies and these were put on a (non-indexed) 'Slavenburg Register' (named after the case of that name which highlighted the issue in England). Under the 2014 Act, this will be discontinued as it will only be registered external companies which have the obligation to file using the new Form F8.

In addition, s 410 of the 2014 Act introduces a new two stage procedure whereby one may register an intention to create a charge and thereby gain priority for that charge from the date of first filing, provided that one files the prescribed particulars of charge within 21 days of that first filing date. The applicable forms will be C1a and C1b. If the latter filing does not take place then the Registrar is to reject the first filing. A similar procedure (Forms 8a and 8b) will be available for foreign companies which are registered on the external register.

The filings under the 2014 Act can be made online.

It will no longer be permissible to file negative pledge details and there is a new obligation to register prescribed particulars of a judgment mortgage within 21 days of the deemed receipt of notice from the Property Registration Authority of registration of a judgment mortgage (three days after the issuing of the notice to the creditor being deemed to be the date of receipt). The new form is C10.

9.9.2.2   Land Registry/Registry of Deeds (Property Registration Authority)

Normal registration in the Registry of Deeds and Land Registry proceeds where title is unregistered and registered land respectively. The Land Act 2009 amends s 62 (2) of the Registration of Title Act 1964 which had required that a charge over registered land must be 'in the prescribed form (or an instrument as may appear to the Registrar to be sufficient to charge the land, provided that such instrument shall expressly charge or reserve out of the land the payment of the money secured)'.

The Land Act 2009 deletes the words in brackets. All of the banks revised their standard documentation in line with the Property Registration Authority requirements. It is important when using the banks' standard documentation that it is the updated 2009 Act compliant version as otherwise the Property Registration Authority will refuse to register it.

In the case of registered land, debentures incorporating floating charges only are not ordinarily registered against folios although it should be noted that in 1986 an amendment to the Land Registry Rules 1972 (SI 230/1972) was enacted making crystallised floating charges registrable charges under the provisions of the Registration of Title Act 1964.

There have been other significant developments on foot of the Registration of Title Act 2006. Filings can now be pre-lodged on line. eDischarges can now be lodged by the bank directly online, removing the need to lodge a deed of release with a Form 17.

9.9.2.3   County Registrar (Agricultural Credit Act chattel mortgages)

A charge over stock must be registered with the appropriate County Registrar under the Agricultural Credit Act 1978, within one month from the date of its creation. The registration requirement arises wherever the 'land' of the borrower is situate. Land is defined as any land used for the purpose of the business of the company. Frequently registration has to be effected in more than one county. If more than one registration is to be effected, careful checking of each registrar's requirements is advisable. For example, does the Registrar require presentation of a stamped original?

9.9.2.4   Port of ship

A mortgage on a ship must be registered at the port of registration of the ship.

9.9.2.5   Notification to other lending institutions

If there is a prior mortgage or charge and the security is to rank second, notice should be served on the first mortgagee that a second mortgage or charge is being created.

If there is a sharing arrangement between two or more banks, it should be evidenced in writing and agreed on by the various lenders setting out the sum of money lent by each lender for which the security will be shared. Priority may be regulated in a priority agreement.

9.9.2.6   Notice to assurance company

When a life policy is assigned as security, notice should be served on the assurance company that the policy has been assigned. The notice should also request particulars of any prior notice of charge to the assurance company. A statutory fee of 32c may be payable but is rarely if ever required.

9.9.2.7   Company-filing requirements

Declarations required under the Summary Approval Procedure

The filing requirements in relation to declarations required under the summary approval procedure are dealt with in **chapters 10, 'Transactions with Directors'** and **13, 'Financial Assistance'**.

Special resolutions

Generally, under s 198 of the 2014 Act, special resolutions must be filed in the CRO within 15 days.

Where a charge document charges assets situated in a foreign jurisdiction (e.g. Northern Ireland or the UK), filing on a foreign companies or commercial register may be needed. If there is any element of foreign law to be considered, whether because of the location of assets or the place of incorporation of the borrower, appropriate legal advice should be obtained from a lawyer qualified to practise in that jurisdiction.

Write up register of debenture holders

Section 418 of the 2014 Act requires a company to keep a register of debenture holders. The register should be written up by the company secretary.

Have copy charge document available

Section 216 (10) of the 2014 Act requires a company to have copies of documents creating charges available for inspection by creditors.

Put members'/directors' resolution in minute book

Section 199 of the 2014 Act requires the keeping of minute books. Appropriate minutes should be put in the appropriate books.

9.9.3   RELEASE OF SECURITY

9.9.3.1   Floating charge

A release of a floating charge may be effected by deed or by letter returning the original floating charge. If the floating charge has been registered in the Registry of Deeds, then it is usual for there to be a deed of release and for an application for release to be furnished. In a conveyancing transaction, a non-crystallisation letter is handed over.

9.9.3.2   Mortgage on real/leasehold property

A mortgage is released by a deed of release or by receipt under the Housing Act 1988.

9.9.3.3   Charge registered in the land registry

A charge registered in the Land Registry is released by means of a deed of discharge in the appropriate Land Registry Form 71A or B.

9.9.3.4   Equitable mortgage by deposit of title deeds

An equitable mortgage by deposit of title deeds is released by a simple letter of release.

9.9.3.5   Notification of release

Unusually, it is the company which notifies the CRO that a charge has ceased to affect the company's property or that it has been discharged. A Form C6 or a Form C7, as appropriate, is submitted to the CRO. The Registrar serves notice on the relevant lending institution that a form has been filed and that the charge will be struck off within a certain period, unless notice to the contrary is served by the lending institution on the CRO.

The Property Registration Authority as of 9 March 2009 introduced an eDischarge system (Application in electronic form for cancellation of charges) for banks.

CHAPTER 10

TRANSACTIONS WITH DIRECTORS

10.1 Introduction

Part III of the Companies Act 1990 (the '1990 Act') has traditionally dealt with transactions between an Irish company (the 'company' for the purposes of this chapter) and its directors. The legislation, an extension of the capital maintenance rules, was put in place to curtail persons in positions of power from siphoning away the assets of the company, and putting such assets beyond the reach of creditors and shareholders. The interpretation of Part III of the 1990 Act has been famously problematic and has made transactions involving directors much more complex than they were ever intended to be. Some commentators have also noted that despite elevating the cost and administration of doing business in Ireland, the 1990 Act has not had the preventative effect intended and that those inclined to improper activity of this nature have succeeded to some degree in continuing it, regardless of the legislation.

The Companies Act 2014 (the '2014 Act'), the biggest overhaul of Irish company law in a number of decades, rose to the challenge of dealing with the difficulties being experienced by practitioners in this arena. Part 5, Chapter 4 of the 2014 Act deals with transactions between the company and its directors and is more streamlined than its predecessor. Although enacted, several sections of the 2014 Act, including Part 5, have not been commenced at the time of writing (commencement is scheduled for June 2015). A comparative table highlighting the key changes between the legal position as set out in the 1990 Act and the 2014 Act is set out at Appendix 1 to this chapter.

10.2 Prohibitions on a Company on Loans/Quasi-loans/Credit Transactions and Related Security with Directors and 'Connected Persons'

10.2.1 WHAT IS PROHIBITED?

Section 239 of the 2014 Act (which mirrors, almost exactly, the wording of its predecessor s 31 of the 1990 Act) provides that a company shall not:

(a) make a loan or a 'quasi-loan' to a director of a company or to a director of its holding company or to a person 'connected' with such a director;

(b) enter into a 'credit transaction' as creditor for such a director or a person so connected; or

(c) enter into a guarantee or grant security in connection with a loan, quasi-loan, or credit transaction made by any other person for such a director or a person so connected.

In order to fully understand the ambit of the prohibition, it is important to appreciate what each of the above terms means. The meaning of most of the terminology used in s 239 is enshrined within the legislation itself, which we will now consider.

An 'at a glance' step plan for assessing whether or not s 239 applies to a transaction is set out for ease of reference at Appendix 2 to this chapter.

10.2.2   WHAT IS A COMPANY?

The meaning of 'company' is key to the understanding of s 239. Section 239 sits within Part 5 of the 2014 Act, an area of the legislation dealing with directors' duties. For Part 5 of the 2014 Act notes that the term 'company' is to be understood as a private company limited by shares (both formed under the 2014 Act and existing). For the sake of good order, the practitioner should note that under the structure of the 2014 Act, parts of the legislation applicable to private limited companies will also apply to designated activity companies ('DACs') and public limited companies ('PLCs') unless specifically disapplied or modified, as set out in s 964 of the 2014 Act (in the case of DACs) and s 1002 of the 2014 Act (in the case of PLCs). Neither section specifically disapplies s 239 (nor s 238, dealt with below) and so the restrictions on transactions involving directors will also apply for companies of these types. However, for the purposes of this chapter we will assume that we are dealing with a private company limited by shares.

The first step in the s 239 step plan is therefore to ask:

> **Is an Irish company involved?**

10.2.3   HOW SHOULD LOAN, QUASI-LOAN, CREDIT TRANSACTION, GUARANTEE, OR SECURITY BE UNDERSTOOD?

The term 'loan' was deemed self-explanatory by the Irish legislators and no definition of the word is contained in the 2014 Act. The word therefore has its ordinary meaning of being an amount of money that is given to one person by another for a period of time with a promise that it will be paid back at a future date.

Section 219 of the 2014 Act deals with other relevant definitions. A 'quasi-loan' is defined as a transaction whereby the creditor company agrees to pay or pays (otherwise than in pursuance of an agreement) a sum of money for a borrower, or reimburses expenditure incurred on behalf of a borrower, in each case in circumstances where there is an obligation on the borrower to reimburse the creditor company. So if a company was to pay its director's credit card bill with an understanding that the director would repay the company at a later date, this would be considered a 'quasi-loan'.

Section 237 of the 2014 Act should be highlighted at this juncture. It provides that in civil proceedings concerning the prohibition on transactions of this kind, if the terms of an arrangement are not in writing, or are wholly or partially in writing but ambiguous, it shall be presumed that the arrangement is *not* a loan or quasi-loan. This is a helpful clarification for the legal practitioner.

A 'credit transaction' is defined as a transaction under which the creditor supplies any goods or sells any land, enters into a hire purchase or conditional sale agreement, leases or licenses the use of land, hires goods in return for periodical payments or otherwise disposes of land, or supplies goods or services, with the understanding that payment is to be deferred. The most obvious circumstance where this arises in practice is a company leasing a car or real property to its director. There is a 'carve-out' in s 219 (4) of the 2014 Act for leases of land reserving a nominal annual rent of not more than €100, where the company is granting the lease for a capital payment or premium representing the open market value of the property in question. Such lease arrangements will not be considered a credit transaction. This replaces the very similar exception contained in s 25 of the 1990 Act. The primary difference in the two is the value of nominal annual rent required for the exception to apply. In the 1990 Act, the threshold is much lower: €12.70.

An important point to note is that a credit transaction will only be caught under s 239 where the company is the **creditor** i.e. the party owed the money under the arrangement. So the following scenario:

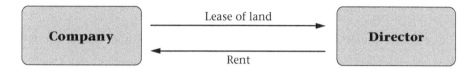

would be caught by s 239 because the person owed the money under the lease is the company, who is therefore the creditor. However, the following scenario:

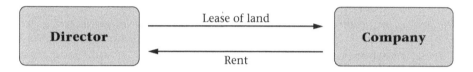

would **not** be caught by s 239 as the creditor in this instance is the director rather than the company.

The meaning of the term 'guarantee' was again deemed self-evident by the Irish legislators and no definition is included in the 2014 Act. The term will therefore have its ordinary meaning i.e. a contract by one person to take responsibility for the debt of another. Section 219 of the 2014 Act makes clear that a guarantee will also include an indemnity. Similarly 'security' is not defined in the legislation and so all forms of security can be understood to be prohibited by s 239 including liens, pledges, mortgages, mortgage debentures, charges, and security assignments.

The next step in the s 239 step plan is therefore:

> **Is the company:**
> 　　　(a) **Making a loan;**
> 　　　(b) **Making a quasi-loan;**
> 　　　(c) **Entering into a credit transaction**
> 　　　　　 **AS CREDITOR?**
> 　　　(d) **Giving a guarantee in relation to a loan,**
> 　　　　　 **quasi-loan or credit transaction of another?**
> 　　　(e) **Giving security in relation to a loan,**
> 　　　　　 **quasi-loan or credit transaction of another?**

10.2.4   WHO IS A DIRECTOR?

Section 2 of the 2014 Act defines a 'director' as including 'any person occupying the position of director by whatever name called'. This definition is wide enough to catch not only lawfully appointed directors but also de facto directors and shadow directors.

10.2.5   WHO IS A CONNECTED PERSON?

Section 220 of the 2014 Act defines a 'connected person' to a director. The definition is a wide one and covers family relationships (the director's spouse, civil partner, parent, brother, sister, and child will all be caught), the trustee of any trust the principal beneficiaries of which are the director, his spouse or civil partner, or his children, and anyone in partnership with the director. Importantly, it also covers a relationship which might be less immediately obvious to the unobservant practitioner. Section 220 (3) of the 2014 Act provides that: 'A body corporate shall also be, for the purposes of this Part, connected with a director of a company if it is controlled by that director or by another body corporate that is controlled by that director.' The measure of 'control' under the 2014 Act is if the director, together with any other director or directors of the body corporate or any person or persons connected with any director or directors:

(a)   is interested in one half or more of the equity share capital of that body; or

(b)   controls or is entitled to control one half or more of the voting power at general meeting of the company.

Section 7 of the 2014 Act defines the equity share capital of a company as meaning its issued share capital (excluding any part thereof which neither as regards capital or dividends carries any right to participate beyond a specified amount in a distribution).

Therefore, for the purposes of this section of legislation a connected person can in fact be a **company**. It is important to note that the directors and any persons connected to them are considered **together** in making the assessment of whether or not a company is controlled by them. The following examples may be helpful in illustrating the point.

Example:

Joe Bloggs is a director and 50% shareholder of A Limited with his wife Sarah Bloggs, who is also a director and holds the other 50% of the shares in A Limited.

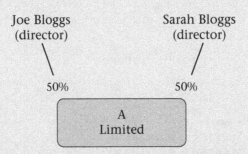

Joe also has a 49% shareholding in another company, B Limited. Sarah has no involvement whatsoever with B Limited. The other 51% of the shares in B Limited are held by Joe's friend James Brown. A Limited is giving a €500,000 loan to B Limited, whose shares are owned as follows:

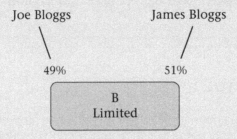

Using the step plan, a s 239 (s 31) issue may exist:

1.   **Is an Irish company involved?** A Limited is an Irish company active in the transaction so this does apply.

2.   **Is it carrying out one of the prohibited transactions?** A Limited is making a loan, one of the prohibited activities, so again, this does apply.

3. **Is it making the loan to a director or person connected to a director?** A Limited is not making the loan to a director, but we need to consider whether borrower B Limited is connected to Joe by reason of his shareholding in B Limited. Based on the facts, Joe holds only 49% of the issued share capital in B Limited and Sarah has no involvement in B Limited. This isn't sufficient for Joe to be considered to 'control' B Limited. The loan from A Limited to B Limited would not therefore contravene s 239 of the 2014 Act as B Limited the recipient of the loan is neither a director nor a connected person.

Example:

Joe Bloggs is a director and shareholder of C Limited with his friend Michael Hall and Michael's daughter Sally Field, who does not hold any role with C Limited beyond her shareholding.

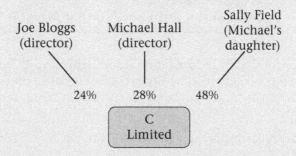

C Limited is providing a €500,000 loan to D Limited, which is owned as follows:

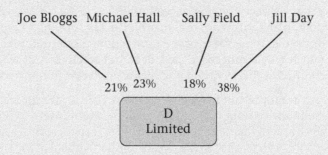

Jill Day is a friend of Joe and Michael's but is not related or connected in any way to any of the other parties.

Using the s 239 step plan, a s 239 (s 31) issue may exist:

1. **Is an Irish company involved?** C Limited is a company of this kind and it is making a loan to D Limited, so this does apply.

2. **Is it carrying out one of the prohibited transactions?** C Limited is making a loan, one of the prohibited activities, so the answer to this question is yes.

3. **Is it making the loan to a director or person connected to a director?** C Limited is not making the loan to a director, but we need to consider whether D Limited is connected to Joe, Michael, or Sally by reason of their shareholding in D Limited. Joe does not by himself meet the legislative threshold as he only holds 21% of the shares, but his 'interest' in the shares of D Limited must be added to that of Michael, also a director of C Limited. Joe and Michael's shareholding only amounts to 44% of the overall shareholding of D Limited, but, as Sally is a person connected to C Limited's

(continued)

other director Michael, being his daughter, we must **also** add her shareholding to Joe and Michael's shareholding. Together the three are 'interested in' 62% of the shares in D Limited and so the required measure of 'control' is there. D Limited therefore is a person connected to Joe (and, for that matter, to Michael) for the purposes of the prohibition. A loan from C Limited to D Limited in these circumstances will therefore breach the section. The obvious fact that directors are not typically legal experts and may not necessarily volunteer all of the information about their connections and relationships (because they may not be aware of its relevance) should be pointed out here. It is the job of the legal practitioner to diligently seek all of the facts, when trying to establish whether a party is connected to a director for the purposes of the legislation.

The next step in working out whether s 239 applies is therefore:

> **Is the transaction to or for the benefit of:**
>
>   **(a) a director?**
>   **(b) a person connected to that director?**

If the answer to each of the above listed transaction steps is 'yes', then the company has acted in contravention of the prohibition **unless** one of the exemptions noted in the legislation applies.

10.2.6 EXEMPTIONS TO SECTION 239

10.2.6.1 Minor transactions

Because various day-to-day transactions i.e. the payment of personal expenses, with the understanding that a director will eventually reimburse the company **are** caught within the s 239 prohibition and this is not the 'mischief' s 239 is trying to prevent, s 240 sets out a de minimis threshold. If the value of the transaction in question is below that threshold, a transaction which would otherwise have been in breach of s 239 will not be deemed to infringe it. Section 32 of the 1990 Act includes a similar de minimis exemption.

The threshold set is a transaction value of less than 10% of the company's relevant assets. The 2014 Act helpfully sets out that a company's 'relevant assets' are to be determined by reference to the last set of financial statements laid before the annual general meeting, and if none are available, by reference to the called-up share capital of the company (this largely mirrors what is already contained in the 1990 Act). It should be noted that where there are or have been a number of transactions entered into by the company with a director or connected person, the transaction value is considered to be the **total** amount outstanding under the arrangement **and** those other arrangements (including past arrangements).

Where, within two months of the date the directors were aware or ought reasonably to have become aware of the situation, an arrangement below the *de minimis* threshold suddenly falls outside this exemption i.e. because the value of the company's relevant assets has fallen, and the transaction value now **exceeds** 10% of the company's relevant assets, the 2014 Act imposes further obligations with a view to 'anti-avoidance'. Section 241 provides that it is the duty of the company, the directors, and any persons for whom the arrangements were made to amend the arrangements so that they once again fall within the s 240 exemption. Failure to do so means that the arrangements are voidable at the instance of the company. This two month 'fix up' period really is a trap for the unwary and severely limits the scope of the exemption. Third party institutions dealing with the company would do well to note.

10.2.6.2 Summary Approval Procedure

In a departure from the 1990 Act, s 242 of the 2014 Act sets out that **any** prohibited transaction with a director or connected person, be it a loan, quasi-loan, credit transaction where the company is creditor, or a guarantee or security from the company in connection with any such prohibited transaction is capable of being whitewashed using the Summary Approval Procedure ('**SAP**'). The 1990 Act had restricted the application of the whitewash procedure, contained in s 34, to use only where the company was giving a guarantee or security for a prohibited transaction.

This departure from its predecessor means that under the 2014 Act a much wider spread of transactions will be capable of being 'blessed'.

The SAP in regards to transactions with directors under the 2014 Act is different from the whitewash procedure set out in s 34 of the 1990 Act. At the outset, it should be noted that under the 2014 Act the SAP is not unique to transactions with directors, but can be used to 'bless' a number of specified restricted activities under the 2014 Act, which would otherwise be prohibited without it. This is a change to the existing position under the 1990 Act where different restricted activities had different whitewash procedures.

A particular point of difficulty under s 34 of the 1990 Act was the fact that the whitewash procedure, which required: (i) a statutory declaration of solvency from a majority of directors; and (ii) a special resolution of the members of the company approving the transaction, **also** required (iii) an independent auditor's report confirming that the directors' statutory declaration (that the company would be in a position to meet its debts as they fall due) was a reasonable one. This is essentially an open-ended blessing by auditors of the company's solvency (no time limit as to the solvency of the company was to be included in the directors' declaration) with which the Institute of Chartered Accountants ('**ICA**') was very uncomfortable. It resulted in a recommendation issuing from the ICA to their members that auditors should not provide the report required as part of the s 34 whitewash procedure. The impact on the ground was that this procedure was seldom used as a 'fix'. Instead, borrowers and financial institutions often had little option but to structure transactions differently.

The SAP in respect of transactions involving directors, set out in s 203 of the 2014 Act, is more simplistic than its predecessor, does not contain any requirement for the problematic auditor's report, gives a finite period for the directors' declaration of solvency, and effectively makes the whitewashing of transactions involving directors a genuine possibility once more. Its essential elements are as follows:

(a)   A declaration of the directors of the company setting out the prescribed information in respect of the restricted activity including: (i) the circumstances in which the transaction was entered into; (ii) the nature of the transaction or arrangement; (iii) the persons to or for whom the transaction is to be made; (iv) the purpose of the transaction; (v) the nature of the benefit accruing to the company (whether directly or indirectly), and finally a statement that the declarants have made full inquiry into the affairs of the company and that having done so have formed the opinion that the company, having entered into this transaction, will be in a position to meet its debts as they fall due **for the next 12 months following the relevant act**. The highlighted point represents a key change from the open-ended form of declaration set out at s 34 of the 1990 Act.

(b)   Such declaration being delivered to the Companies Registration Office ('CRO') within 21 days of the restricted activity taking place.

(c)   A special resolution of the members of the company being passed not more than 12 months prior to the restricted activity, authorising the directors to carry out the activity. This too must be filed in the CRO.

This more streamlined approach to blessing restricted activities is to be greatly welcomed. It should be noted that Ireland stopped short of the approach taken in the UK where the Companies Act 2006 removed a huge amount of the whitewash process and effectively provided that restricted activity transactions were capable of being dealt with at board level.

10.2.6.3   The group exemption

The 'group' exemption, set out at s 243 of the 2014 Act, lifts the restrictions on transactions with directors where the company carrying out the activity and the company benefiting from the action as a person 'connected' to one of the directors, are companies in the same group for company law purposes i.e. a holding company and subsidiary. 'Subsidiary' is defined in s 7 of the 2014 Act (a similar but much more expansive definition to that contained in s 155 of the Companies Act 1963) and sets out inter alia that a company will be a holding company of another if it holds more than half in nominal value of the equity share capital of that company, holds more than half in nominal value of the shares holding voting rights, or holds a majority of the shareholders' voting rights.

Section 243 picks up on an anomaly created by s 35 of the 1990 Act which provides that the group exemption applies to a company making a loan or quasi-loan, entering into a credit transaction as creditor, or giving a guarantee or security in relation to any of the above for 'any **company** which is its holding company, subsidiary, or a subsidiary of its holding company'. The word 'company' in the context of the 1990 Act is defined and means, as discussed at **10.2.2** above, an Irish limited company.

Some concern had therefore developed among practitioners that where the transaction was for a subsidiary company which was a non-Irish company, the exemption could not be availed of. Section 243 makes clear that the exemption applies, regardless of whether the subsidiary or holding company is Irish, by using the phrase 'body corporate' instead of the word 'company'. Section 243 therefore reads:

Section 239 does not prohibit a company from:

(a) *making a loan or quasi-loan to any **body corporate** which is its holding company, subsidiary or a subsidiary of its holding company, or*

(b) *entering into a guarantee or providing any security in connection with a loan or quasi-loan made by any person to any **body corporate** which is its holding company, subsidiary or a subsidiary of its holding company.*

(c) *entering into a credit transaction as creditor for any **body corporate** which is its holding company, subsidiary or a subsidiary of its holding company, or*

(d) *entering into a guarantee or providing any security in connection with any credit transaction made by any other person for any **body corporate** which is its holding company, subsidiary or a subsidiary of its holding company.*

clearing up the previous confusion which had existed in practice as to the breadth of the exemption.

10.2.6.4   Ordinary course of business

Section 245 of the 2014 Act provides that transactions which are in the ordinary course of business of the company and on arm's length terms will not be caught within the prohibition. The value of the transaction must not be greater nor the terms more beneficial for the person for whom the transaction was made, than that which the company offers ordinarily. Note that when assessing whether an activity is within the ordinary course of business of the company, a **factual** assessment will require to be carried out. If a company is not as a matter of fact ordinarily carrying out the activity, it will be extremely difficult to fit within the exemption.

10.2.6.5   Directors' expenses

Section 244 of the 2014 Act provides that where a director has incurred properly vouched expenditure, there is nothing in the prohibition to prevent the company putting the director in funds to that amount.

The final step in assessing whether or not s 239 has been breached is therefore:

> **Do any of the listed exemptions apply to the transaction?**

If the answer to the above question is 'no', then s 239 has been breached. The legislation sets out various consequences of a breach, both civil and criminal.

10.2.7   CONSEQUENCES OF A BREACH OF SECTION 239

10.2.7.1   Voidability

Section 246 of the 2014 Act provides that if a company enters into a transaction or arrangement in contravention of s 239, such transaction will be voidable at the instance of the company (which will include any liquidator of the company), mirroring the provision set out in s 38 (1) of the 1990 Act. Purchasers for value without actual notice take precedence. This provision is debatably of greatest concern to any financial institution funding the transaction. It runs a risk that any guarantees or security given by the company for the deal will be unenforceable.

10.2.7.2   Personal liability

Section 247 of the 2014 Act (which replaces s 38 (2) of the 1990 Act, which was harsher in tone) provides that on the winding up of the company if a court considers that an arrangement in contravention of s 239 has contributed materially to the inability of the company to meet its debts as they fall due, the court may declare that any benefiting director or connected person can be made personally liable to the company, without any limitation of liability, for any gain made and must indemnify the company for any loss suffered.

Section 210 of the 2014 Act (which relates specifically to the SAP and, loosely, replaces s 34 (5) of the 1990 Act) provides that where a director makes the declaration forming part of the SAP without having reasonable grounds for the opinion, on the application of certain specified persons (including a liquidator, creditor, member, or the Director of Corporate Enforcement), a court may declare that director personally responsible, without any limitation to liability for all or any of the debts or other liabilities of the company. If a company winds up within 12 months of such a declaration being made, there will be a rebuttable presumption that the director did not have reasonable grounds for making the declaration.

10.2.7.3   Criminal liability

Section 248 of the 2014 Act provides that any officer of a company in contravention of s 239 shall be guilty of a category 2 offence. This means that such an officer can potentially be liable on summary conviction to a class A fine, imprisonment for up to 12 months, or both and on conviction on indictment to a fine of up to €50,000, imprisonment of up to five years, or both. This is broadly similar to the penalties under the 1990 Act.

The DPP has historically prosecuted a number of directors in respect of contraventions of the prohibition. In *The Director of Public Prosecutions v Stuart Fogarty* (Circuit Court, unreported, 28 May 2008) the Court imposed on the offending director a fine of €34,000 and also imposed a two-year suspended sentence along with 240 hours' community service.

Any legal practitioner advising a company and its directors on compliance with s 239 should ensure that the genuine possibility of jail time is strongly emphasised in their advices.

10.3   Prohibitions on a Company in Relation to Substantial Property Transactions with Directors and Connected Persons

10.3.1   WHAT IS PROHIBITED?

Less severe restrictions are imposed by legislation where interest in property is transferring between a company and its directors. Nevertheless compliance with the relevant legislation, s 238 of the 2014 Act, is important. Once again, the consequences of non-compliance can result in the transaction being voidable at the instance of the company and this is of primary concern to financial institutions providing the funding.

Section 238 sets out that a company shall not enter an arrangement where:

(a)   a director of such company or its holding company, or a person connected with such a director, acquires or is to acquire, one or more non-cash assets of the requisite value from such a company, or

(b)   such company acquires or is to acquire, one or more non-cash assets of the requisite value from such a director or a person so connected, **unless** the arrangement is first approved (i) by a resolution of the relevant company in general meeting, and (ii) if the director or connected person is a director of its holding company or a person connected with such a director, by a resolution of the holding company in general meeting.

The s 238 step plan is set out at **Appendix 3** to this chapter. As s 238 applies to a 'company' as defined, the first question to ask is:

> **Is an Irish company acquiring or disposing of an interest in something?**

The same understanding of 'company' applies here as to s 239.

10.3.2   WHAT IS A NON-CASH ASSET?

Section 238 of the 2014 Act clarifies for the practitioner what is meant by a non-cash asset. Subsection (8) (which mirrors the existing s 29 (9)(a) of the 1990 Act) sets out that a 'non-cash asset' means any property or interest in property other than cash, which can include foreign currency. The next step in the s 238 step plan is therefore:

> **Is a non-cash asset involved in the acquisition/disposal?**

10.3.3   WHAT IS THE REQUISITE VALUE?

Section 238 (2) of the 2014 Act provides that to be of the requisite value to be caught by the section, the non-cash asset must be of a value in excess of €65,000 or 10% of the company's relevant assets. This represents a slight amendment to s 29 of the 1990 Act, which required the non-cash asset to exceed €63,486.90 or 10% of the amount of the company's relevant assets. The assessment of the company's relevant assets is as it was for s 239 of the 2014 Act and the value of the relevant assets are to be assessed by looking at the most recently audited financial statements for the company, and if none such is available, 10% of the called-up share capital of the company. The next step in the s 238 step plan is therefore to ask:

> **Is the non-cash asset of the requisite value?**

10.3.4   WHO IS A DIRECTOR OR PERSON CONNECTED TO A DIRECTOR?

The same analysis as to who constitutes a person connected to a director applies to s 238 as discussed above for s 239. The next step in the step plan is to ask:

> **Is the transaction with (i) a director (ii) a person connected to a director?**

10.3.5   EXEMPTIONS TO SECTION 238

There are much fewer legislative exemptions to s 238 than the harsher s 239. They are laid out in the body of s 238 itself.

10.3.5.1 Group exemption

Section 238 (4) of the 2014 Act provides that transactions between companies in the same group will be exempt (mirroring the position under the 1990 Act).

10.3.5.2 Ordinary resolution

The legislation provides that in order to avoid the restriction imposed by s 238 the company must **first** obtain the approval of the shareholders of the company by way of ordinary resolution. The same is true if the person with whom the transaction is being carried out is a director or is connected to a director of the company's holding company.

However, failure to approve the transaction in advance will not be fatal. Section 238 (3) (c) (which replaces s 29 (3)(c) of the 1990 Act) sets out that a company will have fulfilled its obligations under Section 238 if it affirms the arrangement in question by a resolution of the company in general meeting within a reasonable period of time after the date on which the arrangement is entered into. The 2014 Act does not clarify what a 'reasonable' time frame might be to 'fix up' a situation that would otherwise offend the legislation. At the time of writing and shy of definitive case law, it is difficult to see what a practitioner advising the company would lose in arranging to have put in place an affirming resolution as soon as the breach is realised.

10.3.5.3 Baby, it's a two way thing

Practitioners can often miss the fact that the legislation relating to substantial property transactions is 'two way'. It not only prohibits the company acquiring an asset **from** its director or a person connected, but it also prohibits a company from disposing of an asset *to* a director or person connected. In a transaction involving two companies who are caught within the section by reason of one being 'connected' to the director of the other, this can be easy to overlook. An example is set out below.

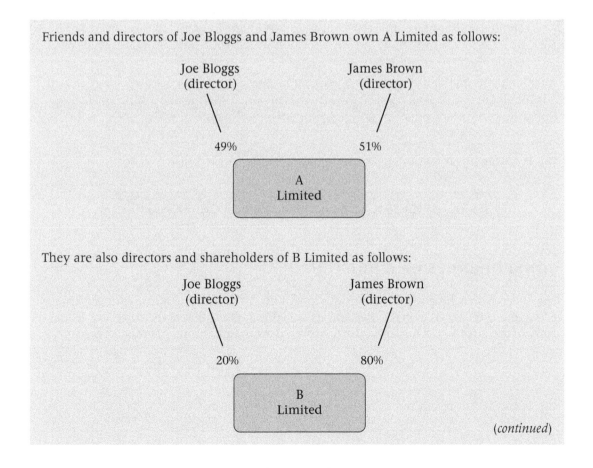

Friends and directors of Joe Bloggs and James Brown own A Limited as follows:

Joe Bloggs (director) — 49% — A Limited

James Brown (director) — 51% — A Limited

They are also directors and shareholders of B Limited as follows:

Joe Bloggs (director) — 20% — B Limited

James Brown (director) — 80% — B Limited

(continued)

If A Limited was to purchase a business property in Blackhall Place, Dublin from B Limited at a price of €200,000, s 238 (s 29) would be an issue for both companies.

To follow the s 238 step plan in respect of A Limited to assess, a practitioner should ask:

1. **Is an Irish company doing a relevant action i.e. acquiring/disposing?** The transaction involves an Irish limited company, A Limited, 'doing' one of the relevant actions i.e. acquiring a property.

2. **Is a non-cash asset involved in the acquisition/disposal?** The acquisition involves a non-cash asset, being the business premises at Blackhall Place.

3. **Is the non-cash asset of the requisite value?** The non-cash asset is of the requisite value as it exceeds the legislative threshold of €65,000. The purchase price is €200,000.

4. **Is the transaction with a director or person connected to a director?** A Limited is acquiring a non-cash asset from B Limited. B Limited is connected to A's director James Brown for the purposes of the legislation because he holds 80% of the shares in B Limited.

A Limited will therefore need to pass an ordinary resolution at general meeting approving the transaction in order to comply with s 238.

However, as there are two Irish companies in the deal, we also need to apply the above analysis to B Limited. A practitioner should therefore also ask:

1. **Is an Irish company doing a relevant action i.e. acquiring/disposing?** B Limited is likewise 'doing' one of the relevant actions i.e. disposing of the Blackhall Place property.

2. **Is a non-cash asset involved in the acquisition/disposal?** B Limited is disposing of the non-cash asset Blackhall Place.

3. **Is the non-cash asset of the requisite value?** As discussed, above, the value of Blackhall Place, €200,000 means it is of the requisite value.

4. **Is the transaction with a director or a person connected to a director?** B Limited is disposing of the non-cash asset to A Limited. A Limited is connected to B's director James Brown for the purposes of the legislation because James holds 51% of the shares in A Limited.

B Limited will therefore **also** need to pass an ordinary resolution at general meeting in relation to the transaction, because the activities of both disposing and acquiring of a non-cash asset of a certain value are caught by the 'two way' nature of s 238.

The final step in the s 238 step plan is therefore to ask:

> **Do any of the listed exemptions apply to the transaction?**

10.3.6   CONSEQUENCES OF A BREACH?

The effect of breaching the provisions of s 238 of the 2014 Act (also a consequence under s 29 of the 1990 Act) is to make the contract voidable at the option of the company. Unlike s 239 of the 2014 Act, a breach of the provision does not carry criminal sanctions.

APPENDIX 1

KEY CHANGES BETWEEN THE POSITION UNDER THE 1990 ACT AND THE 2014 ACT

	1990 Act	2014 Act
Prohibition on loans, quasi-loans, credit transactions and related guarantees, and security with directors and connected persons		
Prohibition	Section 31	Section 239
Definition of quasi-loans and credit transactions	Section 25	Section 219
Definition of connected persons	Section 26	Section 220
De minimis exemption	Section 32	Section 240
Whitewash procedure	Section 34	Section 242 and 203 (known as a 'Summary Approval Procedure')
Group exemption	Section 35	Section 243
Directors' expenses exemption	Section 36	Section 244
Ordinary course of business exemption	Section 37	Section 245
Consequences of a breach	Sections 34(5), 38, 39, and 40	Sections 210, 246, 247, and 248
Prohibition on substantial property transactions with directors and connected persons		
Prohibition	Section 29	Section 238
Definition of non-cash asset	Section 29 (9)(a)	Section 238 (8)
Definition of requisite value	Section 29 (2)	Section 238 (2)
Definition of connected persons	Section 26	Section 220
Ordinary resolution/Affirmation within a reasonable period	Section 29 (1) and Section 29 (3)(c)	Section 238 (1) and Section 238 (3)(c)
Consequences of a breach	Section 29 (3)	Section 238 (3)

APPENDIX 2

SECTION 239 STEP PLAN

Section 239 Step Plan

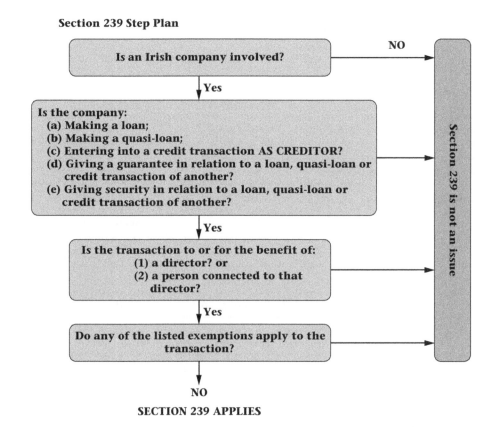

APPENDIX 3

SECTION 238 STEP PLAN

Section 238 Step Plan

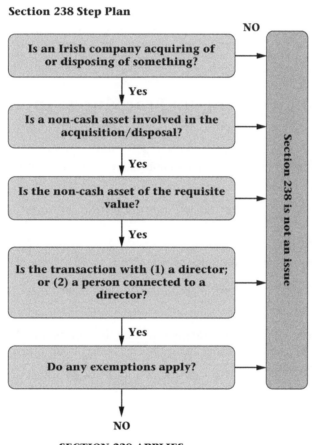

CHAPTER 11

CORPORATE RESTRUCTURING AND INSOLVENCY

11.1 Introduction

This chapter is an introduction to corporate restructuring and insolvency law in Ireland.

11.2 Insolvency and Winding-up Procedures Applicable to Companies

The insolvency and winding-up procedures applicable to companies are:

(a) receivership;

(b) schemes of arrangement;

(c) examinership;

(d) members' voluntary winding up;

(e) creditors' voluntary winding up; and

(f) compulsory liquidation.

The application of these procedures are governed by the Companies Act 2014 (the '2014 Act'), the National Asset Management Act 2009 (the 'NAMA Act'), the Rules of the Superior Courts. and case law.

11.3 Receivership

The appointment of a receiver is a remedy available to a secured creditor for the enforcement of security. A receiver is usually appointed on foot of a debenture, wherein the secured creditor is entitled to appoint a receiver for the purposes of taking possession of and realising the assets secured by the debenture. A receiver is usually appointed where the company has defaulted in the repayments on the secured loan, or where some other event of default, as specified in the debenture, has arisen.

Irish law provides for different types of receivership (including the appointment of a receiver by the court and the appointment of a statutory receiver by NAMA under the NAMA Act). However, the most common type of receivership occurs where a secured creditor appoints a receiver under contractual powers granted by the borrower in a debenture. Where there is no such contractual power contained in the debenture, the creditor can apply to the High Court for the appointment of a receiver under the Conveyancing Act

1881 or the Land and Conveyancing Law Reform Act 2009 (depending on the date of the mortgage), the court's equitable jurisdiction pursuant to the Supreme Court of Judicature Act (Ireland) 1877, or under the Rules of the Superior Courts. The debenture is a contractual document and the powers of the debenture holder and the receiver are usually provided for in this document. A number of statutory provisions are contained in Part 8 of the 2014 Act (ss 428–448).

Section 437 of the 2014 Act sets out the powers of a receiver. These powers are in addition to any powers contained in any court order or in any debenture. The powers contained in s 437 of the 2014 Act include the power to lease or dispose of property of a company.

A receiver can be appointed only over those assets which have been charged to the debenture holder. Although the directors cease to control the assets over which the receiver has been appointed, their normal powers and duties continue in respect of any other assets and liabilities of the borrower.

A receivership can in some limited cases be a temporary condition affecting a company, which, unlike liquidation, does not necessarily lead to the company's dissolution. After a receiver has been discharged, the directors resume their normal functions in relation to all of the company's affairs, unless a liquidator has been appointed in the meantime.

In practice, many receiverships result in the disposal of the company's assets and business. A receiver and liquidator may act concurrently in respect of the same company but a liquidator is unable to deal with those assets under a receiver's control.

Where loans have been transferred to NAMA it has the power to appoint a statutory receiver pursuant to the powers contained in the NAMA Act or pursuant to the securities which it has acquired from a participating institution.

11.4   Examinerships

Examinership procedure is a procedure for the rescue of companies in financial difficulties. Examinerships are governed by Part 10 of the 2014 Act (ss 508–558). A summary of the main provisions of the examination process is set out below.

11.4.1   APPOINTMENT OF AN EXAMINER

Where a company is, or is likely to be, unable to pay its debts and has not been wound up, a petition may be presented to the Circuit Court or the High Court seeking the protection of the court and the appointment of an examiner pursuant to s 512 (4) of the 2014 Act. Where a receiver has been appointed to the company for a continuous period of at least three days prior to the presentation of the petition, the court may not hear the petition. Under the NAMA Act, where a statutory receiver has been appointed to assets of a company, the appointment of an examiner to that company does not displace the statutory receiver or affect his or her powers.

A petition to appoint an examiner may be presented by any of the following:

   (a)   the company;

   (b)   the directors of the company;

   (c)   any secured, unsecured, contingent, or prospective creditor (including an employee); or

   (d)   members representing 10% or more of the paid-up capital of the company.

In making an order to appoint an examiner, the court must be satisfied that there is a reasonable prospect of the survival of the company and the whole or any part of its undertaking as a going concern.

11.4.2   EFFECT OF COURT PROTECTION

Section 534 (3) of the 2014 Act provides that for a period of 70 days from the date of the petition (which period can be extended in certain circumstances by a further 30 days), the creditors of the company are prevented from taking action to enforce any judgments or any security against the company. During the period of court protection, no winding-up proceedings may be commenced, no receiver can be appointed, no attachment or execution against assets, nor any attempt to repossess goods under a hire purchase or retention of title agreement will be allowed. No steps can be taken against any third party who has guaranteed the liabilities of the company.

11.4.3   ROLE OF AN EXAMINER

The role of an examiner is to formulate proposals for a compromise or a scheme of arrangement in respect of the company, its creditors, and members and to report to the court on the viability of the company. The proposals for a compromise or a scheme of arrangement are put to the shareholders and to the different classes of creditors and are deemed to be accepted by the creditors if passed by a majority in number and value of any class whose interests or claims would be impaired by the proposals.

Once the examiner's proposals have been voted upon by the members and creditors, he or she must again report to the court on the outcome of those meetings. If the proposals are not accepted the court will usually bring the examinership to a conclusion and a receiver or liquidator may be appointed. If the proposals have been accepted, a hearing date is set for the court to consider the proposals. At this court hearing, any creditor or member whose claim or interest would be impaired if the proposals were implemented may appear and be heard. The court has a discretion to confirm, confirm subject to modifications, or refuse to confirm the proposals.

If the court decides to confirm the proposals, it fixes a date for the implementation of the proposals, which will not be later than 21 days (2014 Act, s 542 (3)) from the date of its confirmation. The date of the implementation of the proposals will be the date on which the company comes out of court protection and the role of the examiner ceases. The proposals for a compromise or scheme of arrangement then become binding on the company, its members, and creditors, including members or creditors who may have not approved of the proposals.

If the proposals are not confirmed by the court, then it can make such order as it deems fit which in most cases is likely to be an order for the winding up of the company.

11.4.4   ARRANGEMENTS AND RECONSTRUCTIONS

Section 450 of the 2014 Act provides, inter alia, that, where a compromise or arrangement is proposed between a company and its creditors, the court may, on the application of the company, or of any creditor or member of the company order a meeting of the creditors or members, as the case may be, to be summoned in such manner as the court directs.

If the majority of the creditors or members representing at least three-quarters in value of that class, vote in favour of the resolution agreeing to any compromise or arrangement, the compromise or arrangement shall, if sanctioned by the court, be binding on all the creditors.

This section is a very rarely used provision and has in practice been largely superseded by the process of examinership.

11.5   Winding Up

There are three forms of winding-up procedure applicable under Irish law pursuant to the 2014 Act. The winding up of a company may be:

(a)   by the court; or

(b)   voluntary.

11.5.1   VOLUNTARY WINDING UP

The voluntary winding up of a company may be a member's voluntary winding up in accordance with the summary approval procedure or in circumstances where s 580 of the 2014 Act applies. Section 580 applies to companies of a fixed duration on the expiry of the period provided for by its constitution, or where an event occurs and the company's constitution provides that the company is to be dissolved.

11.5.2   MEMBERS' VOLUNTARY WINDING UP

The provisions applicable to members' voluntary winding up are contained in ss 207, 208, 210, and 578–584 of the 2014 Act. A members' voluntary winding up is a form of winding up applicable only to a solvent company. If the circumstances outlined in s 202 of the 2014 Act apply this procedure can be implemented by following the summary approval procedure. When this procedure is being used the declarations referred to in s 207 of the 2014 Act must be obtained. Where the summary approval procedure is used, the members of the company pass a special resolution that the company be wound up and that a liquidator be appointed. Strictly speaking, it is not an insolvency procedure because the company must be solvent.

11.5.2.1   Declaration of solvency (s 207 or s 580 of the 2014 Act)

To avail of the members' voluntary winding-up procedure, the directors of the company (or where the company has more than two directors, a majority of them) must meet and make a declaration that they have made a full enquiry into the affairs of the company and that, having done so, they have formed the opinion that the company will be able to pay its debts (including any contingent or prospective liabilities) in full within a period not exceeding 12 months from the commencement of the winding up. The declaration must be sworn at a meeting of directors before a practising solicitor or any other person before whom a statutory declaration can be made.

11.5.2.2   Statement of assets and liabilities

The declaration must embody a statement of the company's assets and liabilities as at the latest practicable date before the making of the declaration, and in any event at a date not later than three months before the making of the declaration.

11.5.2.3   Report of independent person

The declaration must be accompanied by a report made by a person qualified to be the statutory auditor of the company, stating whether in his or her opinion the declaration is not unreasonable

11.5.2.4   Personal liability (s 210 of the 2014 Act)

It is important that the directors be advised that if it is subsequently proved that the company is unable to pay its debts within the period specified in the declaration of solvency, a court may declare that any director who is party to the declaration without having reasonable grounds for the opinion that it would be able to pay its debts in full within the

12-month period specified will be personally liable, without any limitation of liability, for all or any of the debts or the liabilities of the company.

11.5.2.5   Resolution to wind up voluntarily

A company can pass a resolution for its winding up pursuant to (a) a special resolution where the summary approval procedure is used, or (b) s 580 (1). Where it does so the company must publish a notice of the resolution in Iris Oifigúil.

11.5.2.6   Matters following the commencement of the winding up

A voluntary winding up is deemed to commence at the time of the passing of the winding-up resolution. The company will then cease to carry on business, except in so far as is necessary to facilitate the liquidation.

The liquidator's function is to wind up the affairs and distribute the assets of the company. The appointment of the liquidator usually puts an end to the directors' powers.

Where a members' voluntary winding up continues for a period in excess of one year, the voluntary liquidator must with 28 days after the anniversary, and in each succeeding year, summon a general meeting of the company and lay before this meeting an account of his or her acts and dealings and of the conduct of the winding up during the preceding year.

If at any time the liquidator forms the opinion that, contrary to the directors' declaration of solvency, the company is unable to pay its debts in full, he or she must publicly advertise and call a meeting of the company's creditors. The liquidation will then no longer be a members' voluntary winding up, but will proceed as a creditors' voluntary winding up. It would be in these circumstances that the question of directors' personal liability may arise.

11.5.2.7   Final meeting of members

When the company's assets have been collected and all creditors and shareholders are paid, the liquidator convenes a final meeting of members and provides an account of the winding up, showing the receipts and disbursements in the period of the liquidation, and showing how the property of the company has been disposed of, either by realisation for cash or by way of distribution *in specie* to the shareholders.

This meeting must be called by advertisement in two daily newspapers circulating in the district where the registered office of the company is situated, and must be published 28 days before the meeting is held.

Once the meeting is held, a copy of the liquidator's account, together with a return of the holding of the final meeting, must be sent to the Registrar of Companies. The company is deemed to be dissolved three months following the Registrar receiving these documents.

11.5.3   CREDITORS' VOLUNTARY WINDING UP

This is a liquidation, which is commenced by resolution of the shareholders. The procedure is used for companies that are insolvent or where a declaration of solvency has not been sworn by the directors of the company. It is also the procedure which applies where a members' voluntary winding up is converted to a creditors' voluntary winding up, where the company could not discharge its liabilities in full or where the summary approval procedure has not been employed correctly.

The procedure to implement a creditors' winding up is summarised as follows:

(a)   The board of directors of the company decides that steps should be taken to implement a creditors' voluntary liquidation and to appoint a liquidator.

(b) The board instructs the secretary to convene a meeting of shareholders for the purpose of passing an ordinary resolution pursuant to s 586 (2) of the 2014 Act. The resolution passed for a creditors' voluntary winding up is that 'the company cannot, by reason of its liabilities, continue its business and that it be wound up as a creditor's voluntary winding up'.

(c) At the meeting of members, the members must pass the resolution for the winding up of the company and for the appointment of a liquidator. It is at this meeting that a liquidator is appointed by the members of the company.

(d) Section 587 (1) of the 2014 Act states that a meeting must also be convened of all creditors of the company, to be held on the same day or the day immediately following the day on which the members' meeting is held. The purpose and agenda of the creditors' meeting is as follows:

   (i)   to inform the creditors of the winding-up resolution passed by the members;

   (ii) pursuant to s 587 (7) of the 2014 Act, to present the directors' statement of affairs to the creditors;

   (iii) to confirm the appointment of a liquidator. (If creditors representing a majority in value of those present personally or by proxy and voting at the creditors' meeting, vote for a liquidator other than the liquidator appointed by the members, that liquidator nominated by the creditors shall prevail. Otherwise, the liquidator nominated by the members remains appointed (2014 Act, s 588 (2)); and

   (iv) the election, if required, of a committee of inspection. (There is no mandatory requirement to elect a committee of inspection and its function, if elected, is typically to supervise the liquidation and to be available for consultation by the liquidator.)

(e) All creditors must be given at least 10 days' notice of the creditors' meeting. The holding of the creditors' meeting must be advertised in two daily newspapers circulating in the district in which the company carried on business. This timetable cannot be shortened.

(f) The function of the liquidator once appointed is to realise all of the assets of the company. The liquidator will then distribute the proceeds of sale of the assets to creditors, in accordance with the priorities contained in the Companies Acts.

The liquidator conducts the liquidation independently of all parties and reports on the conduct of the liquidation to meetings of the members and creditors held at the end of each year following his or her appointment.

11.5.4   COMPULSORY WINDING UP

Under s 569 of the 2014 Act, the High Court has power to order the winding up of a company and appoint a liquidator. The parties who may petition the court for such an order include creditors, members, the Director of Corporate Enforcement, or the company itself. The most common petitioner is the creditors' petition.

If a creditor presents a petition to the High Court to wind up a company, the court must determine that the company is insolvent and unable to pay its debts as they fall due or that it is just and equitable that the company be wound up.

The grounds upon which a petition may be presented are listed in s 569 (1) of the 2014 Act. The two most common grounds are:

(a) that a company is unable to pay its debts (para (d) of s 569). The circumstances in which a company is deemed to be unable to pay its debts are set out in s 570; and

(b) that it is just and equitable that the company should be wound up (in the opinion of the court) (para (e) of s 569).

On hearing the petition, the court may dismiss it, adjourn it, or make a winding-up order. Where a winding-up order is made the order places the company into liquidation and appoints the official liquidator. The directors' powers cease on the appointment of the official liquidator.

The court can, on sufficient urgency being shown, appoint a provisional liquidator prior to the winding-up order for the purpose of continuing the company's business or protecting its assets up until the appointment of an official liquidator.

The procedure in a compulsory liquidation is broadly similar to that outlined above in relation to the conduct of a voluntary liquidation, save that the appointment arises, not from meetings of members, but by order of the High Court.

Where a court orders a liquidation it will thereafter be conducted in broadly the same fashion as a creditor's voluntary liquidation. The requirement for the liquidator to report to the High Court periodically and to submit matters such as the adjudication of the claims of all creditors to the High Court Examiner has been abolished. The liquidator's remuneration will now be approved, not by the court, but by the Committee of Inspection, or a meeting of the creditors.

The obligations of the liquidator, in voluntary and compulsory liquidations, is to take control of all the property and assets of the company, to realise the assets in such a way as to discharge the company's liabilities to creditors. If it is not possible to pay all the creditors, there are statutory provisions setting out the priorities to be applied. In summary, those priorities are as follows:

(a)   fixed charges in order of priority of their creation;

(b)   costs and expenses of the winding up;

(c)   fees, costs, and expenses of an examiner;

(d)   fees due to the liquidator;

(e)   claims under the Social Welfare Consolidation Act 1981;

(f)   preferential debts pursuant to s 621 of the 2014 Act [s 285 Companies Act, 1963], ranking *pari passu* with each other;

(g)   uncrystallised floating charges in order of their creation;

(h)   unsecured debts ranking *pari passu* with each other; and

(i)   deferred debts ranking *pari passu* with each other.

The liquidator is charged with certain statutory duties and powers, including carrying on the business of the company as far as may be necessary for the beneficial winding up. To that end, he or she is empowered to continue contracts to which the company is a party, but only insofar as it is for the benefit of the winding up.

11.6   Consequences of Insolvent Liquidation

11.6.1   FUNCTIONS OF A LIQUIDATOR

11.6.1.1   Functions

A liquidator is appointed to wind up the affairs of a company. This involves the realisation and distribution of assets. His or her duties include examining the affairs of a company to establish if there are assets which were improperly transferred by the company. In exceptional circumstances, directors can be held personally liable for the debts of the company.

The following is an introduction to the provisions of the 2014 Act, which can be invoked in practice in the context of an insolvent liquidation of a company.

11.6.1.2   Post-commencement dispositions

Section 602 of the 2014 Act provides that:

> (1)   *This section applies to each of the following acts in any winding up of a company:*
>
>   (a)   *any disposition of the property of the company;*
>
>   (b)   *any transfer of shares in the company; or*
>
>   (c)   *any alteration in the status of the members of the company, made after the commencement of the winding up.*
>
> (2)   *Without prejudice to subsection (3), an act to which this section applies that is done without the sanction of—*
>
>   (a)   *the liquidator of the company, or*
>
>   (b)   *a director of the company who has, by virtue of section 677(3) retained the power to do such act, shall, unless the court otherwise orders, be void.*

Accordingly, payments out of a company's bank account after the appointment of a liquidator will be void.

11.6.1.3   Improper transfer of assets

A liquidator may apply to the High Court for the return of property disposed of by the company if the liquidator is of the opinion that the *effect* of such a disposal was to perpetrate a fraud on the company, its members, or creditors. Where the court is satisfied of this, it may order the return of the property or the proceeds of sale on such terms as it sees fit (2014 Act, s 608).

11.6.1.4   Unfair preference

Section 604 of the 2014 Act, provides, inter alia, that any payment or disposal of property of a company, which at the time is unable to pay its debts as they fall due, in favour of any creditor, within six months of the commencement of the winding up, with a view to giving the creditor a preference over the other creditors, shall be deemed to be an unfair preference of its creditors and will be invalid. Where a payment or disposal of the asset was made in favour of a connected person, the period of six months is replaced with a period of two years and there is a presumption that an intent to prefer existed.

11.6.1.5   Invalidating floating charges

Section 597 (1) of the 2014, provides that:

> *Where a company is being wound up, a floating charge on the undertaking or property of the company created within 12 months before the date of commencement of the winding up shall, unless it is proved that the company immediately after the creation of the charge was solvent, be invalid.*

If a floating charge is declared to be invalid, the creditor becomes an unsecured creditor in the liquidation of the company.

11.6.1.6   Fraudulent trading

Section 722 of the 2014 Act provides that:

> *If any person is knowingly a party to the carrying on of the business of a company with intent to defraud creditors of the company or creditors of any other person or for any fraudulent purpose, the person shall be guilty of a category 1 offence.*

Section 871 of the 2014 Act provides for a maximum penalty of imprisonment for a term not exceeding ten years or a fine not exceeding €500,000, or both. Under s 610 of the 2014 Act, any person found guilty of fraudulent trading can also be held personally liable without limitation of liability for all or any part of the debts or other liabilities of the company as the court may direct. In order to impose this civil liability, it is necessary to show *fraudulent intent* on the part of directors. There have been only a limited number of reported cases, the most important ones being: *Kellys Carpetdrome Limited (In Liquidation)* [1984] ILRM 418, *Hunting Lodges Limited* [1985] ILRM 75, *Re Aluminium Fabricators Limited* [1984] ILRM 399, *Corran Building Services Limited (In Liquidation)* 18 March 2004, District Court, (unreported), and *PSK Construction Ltd v Companies Acts* [2009] IEHC 538. In this last case, the court held that a decision taken by a director to underdeclare and underpay the Revenue Commissioners in order to continue trading was taken for a fraudulent purpose, this purpose being to induce the Revenue Commissioners to believe that the amount due by the company in respect of PAYE/PRSI deducted from employees' wages and RCT was the amount declared, rather than the true amount.

11.6.1.7   Reckless trading

Section 610 (1)(a) provides that personal liability can be imposed where it appears that a person was, when an officer of the company, 'knowingly a party to the carrying on of any business of the company in a reckless manner'.

Without prejudice to the general concept of recklessness, the section contains a deeming provision, so that the following are deemed instances of recklessness:

(a)   where a person was a party to the carrying on of the business and having regard to the general knowledge, skill, and experience that may reasonably be expected of a person in his or her position, he/she ought to have known that his/her actions or those of the company would cause loss to the creditors of the company or any of them; or

(b)   he was a party to the contracting of a debt by the company and did not honestly believe on reasonable grounds that the company would be able to pay the debt when it fell due for payment, as well as all its other debts (taking into account the contingent and prospective liabilities).

The test is an objective one and accordingly any director who assumes such a position must meet certain standards of knowledge, skill, and experience.

Since the introduction of the concept of reckless trading, there have been very few reserved judgments on this section. The leading case is the case of *Re Hefferon Kearns Limited* [1992] ILRM 51. In this case, there was evidence that the directors were aware of the fact that the company was insolvent, but continued to trade and incur certain debts in an effort to rescue the company. On the facts, the Court found in favour of the defendant directors, but the judgment contains a number of important statements about the concept of reckless trading:

(a)   The section does not impose collective responsibility. It operates independently, individually, and personally against the officers and the onus is on a plaintiff to prove in relation to each director and officer that his or her conduct falls within the ambit of conduct prohibited.

(b)   The inclusion of the word 'knowingly' in the section requires that the director is a party to the carrying on of the business in a manner which the director knows very well involves an obvious and serious risk of loss or damage to others and yet ignores that risk because he or she does not really care whether others suffer loss or damage, or because his/her selfish desire to keep his/her own company alive overrides any concern he or she might have for others.

This judgment is the main Irish judgment on the section. The critical feature of reckless trading, and the most common basis for proving such conduct, is if it can be shown that the directors have caused or permitted the company to continue to incur liabilities without having reasonable grounds to believe that the company would be able to pay its debts so incurred as they fall due.

11.6.1.8 Failure to keep adequate accounting records

Section 281 of the 2014 Act requires every company to keep adequate accounting records. Section 286 prescribes the liability of officers of the company where proper books of account are not kept. If the company is being wound up and is unable to pay all its debts and has contravened ss 281–285 of the 2014 Act and the court considers that such contravention has contributed to the company's inability to pay all of its debts, or has resulted in substantial uncertainty as to the assets and liabilities of the company, or has substantially impeded the orderly winding up thereof, then under s 286 of the 2014 Act criminal liability can be imposed, including a fine of up to €500,000 or a term of imprisonment of up to ten years, or both. Under s 609 (2) of the 2014 Act, in an insolvent liquidation, the court has power to declare that any officer so in default shall be personally liable without limitation of liability for all or such part as may be specified by the court of the debts of the company.

Each of these sections provides for a defence that where a director took all reasonable steps to secure compliance by the company with ss 281–285 or had reasonable grounds for believing and did believe that a competent and reliable person acting under the supervision or control of a director of the company who has been formally allocated such responsibility was charged with the duty of ensuring that that section was complied with and was in a position to discharge that duty.

The leading case on this remedy is the case of *Mantruck Services Limited: Mehigan v Duignan* [1997] 1 ILRM 171. In that case, the Court held there would have to be established a causal link between the failure complained of, in this case the failure to keep proper books of account, and the loss suffered by the creditors. The Court held that the director concerned should be held personally liable for that portion of the costs, fees, and expenses associated with the winding up of the company, which was directly attributable to the failure to maintain proper books and records. In a recent case, *Dev Oil and Gas Ltd v Companies Acts* [2008] IEHC 252, the Court ruled that the directors' failure to keep proper books of account of the company, recording accurately the debts due to the company, including the names and addresses of the persons from whom the debts were due, hindered the company significantly in recovering those debts. One of the directors was held personally liable for €425,864, representing approximately 68% of the debts of the company. The official liquidator had given evidence that the debtor recovery rate of less than 2% was directly attributable to this director's failure to keep proper books and records.

11.6.1.9 Misfeasance

Section 612 of the 2014 Act provides that where it appears that an officer or other party has misapplied assets of the company or been guilty of 'misfeasance or breach of duty or breach of trust', the court may make an order compelling him or her to restore the property or assets concerned or to contribute to the assets of the company by way of compensation in respect of the misapplication of assets. The section is not confined to directors and officers, but applies to any person who has taken part in the formation or promotion of the company.

11.6.2 CONSEQUENCES OF INSOLVENT LIQUIDATION FOR DIRECTORS OF A COMPANY

11.6.2.1 Restriction

Section 819 of the 2014 Act provides that the court can, upon application, make an order restricting a director of an insolvent company from acting as a director of another company for a period of five years.

Section 683 of the 2014 Act provides that the liquidators of all insolvent companies are obliged to bring such an application, unless the liquidator is relieved of this obligation by the Director of Corporate Enforcement.

A restriction order means that any company to which the director is subsequently appointed must meet capital requirements such as that the nominal value of the allotted share capital of the company shall:

(a)   in the case of a public limited company, be at least €500,000; and

(b)   in the case of any other company, be at least €100,000.

There are also specific rules regarding the maintenance of share capital. To defend a restriction application, the respondent must demonstrate that they acted honestly and responsibly in relation to the conduct of the affairs of the company and that there is no other reason why it would be equitable that a restriction order be made. The onus of establishing that the person has acted honestly and responsibly is on the director concerned. There have been numerous judgments on the provisions of s 150 and the meaning of the terms 'acting honestly and responsibly'.

Most of the decided cases concerning this section have focused on the question of what is meant by acting 'responsibly', it having been accepted that there was no evidence of dishonesty. However, there have been some reported judgments where the courts have considered whether the directors of a company have acted honestly. In the case of *Re Outdoor Advertising Services Limited* [1997] IEHC 201, Costello J held that the directors had not acted honestly or responsibly as they had consciously and deliberately sought to benefit themselves personally at the expense of the insolvent company's creditors.

In *La Moselle Clothing Limited* [1998] ILRM 345, the court held that the simple fact that the business failed is not evidence of a lack of responsibility or of dishonesty. The Court identified the considerations which should be taken into account in determining whether a director has acted 'responsibly'. These considerations were approved by the Supreme Court in *Re Squash (Ireland) Limited*, and are as follows:

(a)   The extent to which the director has or has not complied with any obligation imposed by the Companies Acts.

(b)   The extent to which his or her conduct could be regarded as so incompetent as to amount to irresponsibility.

(c)   The extent of the director's responsibility for the insolvency itself.

(d)   The extent of the director's responsibility for the net deficiency in the assets disclosed at the date of the winding up.

(e)   The extent to which the director has in his or her conduct of the affairs of the company displayed a lack of commercial probity or want of proper standard.

The court also considered that it may take into account any relevant conduct after the commencement of the winding up such as failure to cooperate with the liquidator.

In *Re Tralee Beef & Lamb Limited* [2008] 2 ILRM 420, it was held that the court should also have regard to the duties imposed on a director at common law. This judgment has been overturned by the Supreme Court in a judgment that was critical of the legislation governing restriction orders. However, in considering the conduct of directors, it is possible in future cases that the court will have regard to the common law duties of directors.

11.7   Disqualification

Under ss 839 and 842 of the 2014 Act, the grounds for the making of a disqualification order include the following:

(a)   that the person has been convicted of an indictable offence or has been guilty of any fraud or dishonesty in relation to a company, its members, or creditors;

(b)   breach of duty;

(c)   having a declaration of personal liability made under s 610 of the 2014 Act (i.e. fraudulent or reckless trading);

(d)   conduct making him or her unfit to be concerned in the management of a company;

(e)   persistent default in relation to the 'relevant requirements'. These are primarily requirements concerning the filing of company returns, but they now include having been found guilty of two or more offences under s 286 of the 2014 Act;

(f)   being a person disqualified under the law of another State from being appointed to act as a director or officer in cases where the court is satisfied that if the conduct concerned had arisen in this State, it would have been proper to make a disqualification order; and

(g)   being a director of a company that is struck off the register pursuant to s 733 of the 2014 Act.

In *Re C.B. Readymix Limited (In Liquidation): Cahill v Grimes* [2002] 1 IR 372, the Court referred to English case law which ruled that the purpose of disqualification is not to punish the individual but to protect the public against directors whose conduct has shown them to pose a danger to creditors and ordinary commercial misjudgement is not in itself sufficient to justify disqualification. In *Re Clawhammer Limited Director of Corporate Enforcement v McDonnell and others* [2005] 1 IR 503, it was stated that in determining a period of disqualification, the court must have regard to the fact that the Oireachtas intended disqualification to be a more serious sanction than restriction under s 150 of the Act of 1990. In *PSK Construction Ltd v Companies Acts* [2009] IEHC 538, the period of disqualification for a director who was found guilty of fraudulent trading was seven years.

11.7.1   SHADOW DIRECTORS

The remedies and sanctions discussed in this section apply to 'shadow directors'. There are a number of cases arising from the old s 150 in which the court has had to consider whether persons have become shadow directors and as such should be the subject of restriction or disqualification orders. Section 221 of the 2014 Act, defines a shadow director as:

> *a person in accordance with whose directions or instructions the directors of a company are accustomed to act (in this Act referred to as a 'shadow director') shall be treated for the purposes of this Part as a director of the company unless the directors are accustomed so to act by reason only that they do so on advice given by him or her in a professional capacity.*

In the case of *Re Vehicle Imports Limited,* 23 November 2000, High Court, (unreported), the court held that the company's accountant and auditor was in the particular circumstances a shadow director. There was evidence that the accountant advised the client as to which cheques to write and which payments to make from time to time. He advised the client to sign blank cheques, which were then left with the accountant to determine, *as part of his auditing role*, which suppliers of the company were to be paid. As such, the accountant/auditor was in substantial control of all of the financial lodgements. Finally, the accountant concerned had also given advice to the directors concerning the signing of personal guarantees.

The case of *Gasca Limited* [2001] IEHC 20 concerned a company in which the only two directors had resigned some time prior to the liquidation. The shareholder appointed two persons to act as managers of the company and to run the company's affairs on a day-to-day basis. They were not appointed directors. McCracken J considered that there was sufficient evidence to show that the principal shareholder of the company was in effect controlling the affairs of the company by giving direct instructions to the managers concerned. As such, he had become a shadow director and a restriction order was made in respect of him.

11.7.2   DE FACTO DIRECTORS

The issues discussed in this chapter can also apply to persons who have not been formally appointed to the board of directors of a company. Section 222 of the 2014 Act defines a de facto director to 'a person who occupies the position of director of a company but who has not been formally appointed as such director shall, subject to subsection (4), be treated, for the purposes of this Part, as a director of the company'.

The question of a person, other than a shadow director, being deemed to be a de facto director, was considered for the first time in the case of *Re Lynrowan Enterprises Limited (In Liquidation)* [2002] IEHC 90, which arose from an application by the liquidator of the company for restriction orders pursuant to the old s 150 Companies Act 1990. In this case, the liquidator named as a respondent to the application a person, Mr James V Mealy, who had never been validly appointed a director of the company. The Court held that:

'a person although not validly appointed a director of a company may nonetheless be said to be a *de facto* director and thus deemed to be a "a director" within the meaning of s 2 (1) Companies Act 1963 and thus amenable to the restriction contained in s 150 Companies Act 1990 in the following circumstances:

(a)   where there is clear evidence that that person has been either the sale person directing the affairs of the company, or

(b)   is directing the affairs of the company with others equally lacking in valid appointment, or

(c)   where there were other validly appointed directors that he was acting on an equal or more influential footing with the true directors in directing the affairs of the company.'

11.7.3   OTHER POWERS OF THE DIRECTOR

The 2001 Act also enabled the Director of Corporate Enforcement to initiate actions, which previously were only available to liquidators and individual creditors, such as misfeasance proceedings against directors, promoters, liquidators, receivers, or examiners under s 298 Companies Act 1963.

Finally, the 2001 Act also granted the Director the power to initiate certain proceedings that could previously only be initiated by directors. Section 251 Companies Act 1990 provided that where a company which is insolvent and is not being wound up and the only reason why it is not being wound up is the insufficiency of its assets, the liquidator of the company could bring a number of applications such as proceedings to hold directors personally liable for fraudulent or reckless trading or misfeasance proceedings or proceedings to hold directors personally liable for failure to keep proper books of account of the company. The 2001 Act extends the power to commence such proceedings to the Director of Corporate Enforcement. These powers are retained in the 2014 Act.

11.8   EU Council Regulation No. 1346/2000 on Insolvency Proceedings

Before this Regulation was enacted, liquidators who were appointed to companies that operated across the EU encountered difficulties in ensuring that their appointment and powers were recognised in other Member States. The Brussels Convention on Jurisdiction of Courts and Enforcement of Judgments in Civil and Commercial Matters expressly exempted bankruptcies, the winding up of insolvent companies, judicial arrangements, compositions, and analogous proceedings from its operation. Consequently, courts of different Member States were forced to adopt an ad hoc and frequently inconsistent approach towards the recognition of liquidators on a cross-border basis.

These problems were addressed by Regulation No. 1346/2000, which came into force on 31 May 2002 and which applies where the company concerned has its main centre of interests within a Member State of the EU. While the Regulation does not attempt to harmonise substantive bankruptcy and insolvency laws across the EU, it does establish a regime for improving the efficiency of the conduct of cross-border insolvencies. The Regulation creates a system whereby basic orders relating to the appointment of liquidators and other officials, or the invocation of remedies typically available to them, that are made in one Member State may be recognised and enforced across all other Member States. The Regulation also establishes a regime for the management of asset realisation and processing of creditor claims.

One of the most important decisions relating to the interpretation of the Regulation is the Irish case of *Eurofood IFSC Limited*. Any students interested in cross-border insolvency matters should read the judgment in that case.

As a regulation passed at EU level, the position was only altered in so far as Member States were concerned. Denmark has opted out of the Regulation and accordingly the rules for recognition and enforcement, which previously applied to that State and to non-EU Member States, remain unchanged.

11.9   Insolvency Regulation Review

The European Commission, following a review of the Insolvency Regulation, identified a number of shortcomings in its operation. In particular, the Commission recommended that revisions were needed in relation to the scope of the Regulation, the concept of Centre of Main Interest (COMI), the availability of information on insolvency proceedings, the control of secondary proceedings, and the coordination of group insolvencies.

On 5 February 2014, the European Parliament voted in favour of the main elements of the EU Commission's Recommendations including:

- expanding the Regulation to cover rescue proceedings;
- the creation of an EU-wide system of web-based insolvency registers;
- the possibility of avoiding the opening of multiple proceedings; and
- new rules dealing with the insolvency of groups of companies.

At the time of writing, the proposed changes are going through the European legislative process, which requires both the Council and the Parliament to agree a final text. It is expected that the proposals will be formally approved in the first half of 2015 and will then enter into force 24 months later.

11.10   Recent Developments Affecting Insolvency Law and Practice

11.10.1   NAMA ACT 2009

On 21 December 2009, the NAMA Act established the National Asset Management Agency ('NAMA') to deal with certain loan portfolios on the balance sheets of Irish banks. The NAMA Act provides that the purpose of NAMA is to address the serious threat to the economy, to secure the stability of credit institutions, and to deal with the need for the maintenance and stabilisation of the financial system in the State. NAMA is an asset management company that acquires good and bad loans from participating institutions. It manages these assets (hold, dispose, develop, or enhance them) with the aim of achieving the best possible return for the taxpayer on the acquired loans and on any underlying assets over a seven- to ten-year time frame.

The effect of transferring bank assets to NAMA is to confer on NAMA all the rights and remedies available to the participating financial institution against the borrower, under original loan agreements, facilities, and security instruments.

NAMA also has a number of additional remedies under the NAMA Act including the power to appoint a statutory receiver. One of the most important decisions relating to NAMA which has been made by the Irish courts is the *McKillen* [2011] IESC 14 judgment given in relation to the challenge by developer Paddy McKillen of the decision of NAMA to acquire his loans. The Supreme Court ruled that the decision made to acquire Mr McKillen's portfolio of loans had no legal effect as it was taken by an interim team on 11 December and 14 December in 2009, before the establishment of NAMA on 21 December of that year.

The NAMA Act is having and will continue to have a significant effect on insolvency law and practice.

11.10.2 EXAMINERSHIP FOR SMALL COMPANIES

Examinership for small companies in the Circuit Court was introduced into Irish law by the Companies (Miscellaneous Provisions) Act 2013. This allows a 'small company' to apply directly to the Circuit Court for examinership protection. The provisions of the Companies (Miscellaneous Provisions) Act 2013 are replicated in Part 10 of the 2014 Act, with s 509 (7)(b) conferring jurisdiction on the Circuit Court.

To be eligible to apply to the Circuit Court, a company must satisfy at least two of the following criteria set out in s 350 (5) of the 2014 Act:

(i)   turnover of less than €8.8 million;

(ii)   a balance sheet total not exceeding €4.4 million; and/or

(iii)   an average number of employees not exceeding 50.

Eligible companies must apply to the relevant circuit where its registered office is located or, if there is no registered office and its principal place of business is outside the State, in the Dublin circuit.

The purpose of these changes was to make examinership more accessible for small companies, who may previously have been dissuaded by the higher costs associated with the traditional High Court process.

CHAPTER 12

BUYING AND SELLING A BUSINESS

12.1   Introduction

This chapter explains the principal features of transactions under which businesses are purchased and sold – commonly called mergers and acquisitions. Strictly speaking, a merger arises where two or more separate corporate entities combine to form one corporate entity. By contrast, an acquisition arises where a target corporate entity or business is bought by an acquirer, without any change occurring to the legal form of the parties or the target. In the case of share purchases (i.e. where a company is being acquired) the descriptions in this chapter generally assume that 100% of an Irish private company limited by shares is being acquired ('the target company' or 'target') and accordingly the features discussed in this chapter are the standard features of a share purchase agreement for the entire issued share capital of such a target company.

It is of course possible to effect a share purchase on the basis of a much simpler form of agreement, particularly in the purchase of a small shareholding or a transaction between related parties where the most basic form of a share purchase agreement, a share transfer form, may be all that is completed.

The role of the corporate lawyer in mergers and acquisitions transactions generally includes advising on the optimum transaction structure to be employed by your client, drafting and negotiating initial Heads of Agreement, examining the legal affairs of the target with a view to identifying any areas of material legal risk or liability, drafting and negotiating a main purchase agreement and ancillary agreements, and attending to the formalities of the change of ownership, as more fully described in this chapter.

12.2   Structuring of Transactions

12.2.1   GENERAL CONSIDERATIONS

When a transaction is first proposed, careful consideration needs to be given as to how best to structure the transaction. Most often, this comes down to a choice between a purchase of the shares of a target company from the target company's shareholders or the purchase of some or all of the business (i.e. the assets and liabilities) of that company from the company itself. In many cases a share purchase is most suitable for the parties. A key advantage can be the fact that all assets (including trading contracts) automatically pass with the target company to the purchaser. However, this is an issue which should be considered at the outset of every transaction. The matters to consider include those set out below.

12.2.2   CHOICE OF ASSETS AND LIABILITIES

The advantage of being able to choose specific assets and liabilities is a common reason for a purchaser electing for an asset purchase rather than share purchase. This choice may be taken, in particular, where the company has uncertain liabilities, such as a pending legal claim. The purchaser will require only the assets and will not want to take on liabilities which could turn out to be substantial. In such an instance, the purchaser should be conscious that if the liability is subsequently not met by the company, the creditor may seek to challenge the transaction. Therefore, it is important that the transaction be carried out at arm's length and that the price be demonstrably fair. Careful thought is also required as to how the sale proceeds will be disbursed because, if a purchaser is in any way complicit in an arrangement where a creditor is being prejudiced, they may have difficulty if the transaction is subsequently challenged. The choice might also be made if there are assets in the target company which the purchaser does not want and for some reason it is not possible to extract those assets from the target company in advance of completing the transaction, for example, due to the creation of excessive tax liabilities on extraction. In these circumstances, it is usually a question of assessing whether the taxation liabilities are more onerous if the assets are extracted or if the assets and relevant liabilities are sold by the target company.

By way of contrast, a purchaser of the shares in a target company will take the target company with all of its known and unknown assets and liabilities.

12.2.3   STAMP DUTY

Stamp duty at a rate of 1% is payable by a purchaser on the transfer of shares. On a transfer of assets, the rate of stamp duty depends on the type of assets. For example, the transfer of certain types of intellectual property (including patents, trade marks, copyright, and directly attributable goodwill) is exempt from stamp duty. Assets such as stock and loose plant and machinery may, if the transaction is properly structured, pass by delivery and attract no stamp duty charge. However, on assets such as property, goodwill, or book debts, stamp duty is payable usually at the rate of 2%. It is always necessary to check the stamp duty rates currently in force when assessing the benefits of an asset purchase over a share purchase as there may be a material cost differential for the purchaser depending on the chosen structure.

12.2.4   TAX LOSSES

If a target company is acquired that has ongoing tax losses, it may be possible for the share purchaser to utilise those tax losses in the future trading of the target company (there are some restrictions on this which prevent significant changes in the nature of the business). If a business is acquired by way of asset purchase, it is regarded as extremely difficult to transfer tax losses.

12.2.5   KEY LEGAL AND PRACTICAL DIFFERENCES

Share purchase	Asset purchase
All assets and liabilities pass to purchaser	Purchaser has flexibility to choose assets and liabilities. Specific asset transfer documents in addition to the main purchase agreement may be required (e.g. conveyancing deeds)
Stamp duty is levied at a rate of 1%	Stamp duty may be levied at a rate of 2% (although some assets such as intellectual property may be exempt or pass by delivery)

Tax losses pass, subject to anti-avoidance legislation	Difficult to secure tax losses
Employees pass automatically	May be some flexibility not to take employees, but this is rendered difficult by European Communities (Protection of Employees on Transfer of Undertakings) Regulations 2003 (SI 131/2003)
Consideration paid to vendor shareholders	Consideration paid to target company

12.2.6   CONSIDERATION

The proceeds of sale in a share purchase are paid to the shareholders of the target company, who are subject to taxation if they have made a gain on the sale of those shares. On the other hand, if the assets are purchased from the target company, the target company receives the proceeds and is the chargeable entity rather than its shareholders. If the target company then wishes to pass the sale proceeds to its shareholders, there will be tax payable by those shareholders on what they receive from the target company. There are, therefore, two possible tax events on an asset purchase, whereas the share sale will involve only one taxable event. An added complication with an asset purchase is that the target company, depending on its trading position, may be prohibited by financial prudence requirements from immediately handing over the sale proceeds to its shareholders. Thus, for example, if there are significant liabilities in the target company which are unquantified, it may be appropriate to await quantification of those liabilities before the target company distributes the proceeds to its shareholders.

12.2.7   EMPLOYEES

If the shares in a target company are purchased, the legal status of the employees of the target company will be unaffected as they will remain employed by the target company (albeit indirectly for the purchaser). In an asset purchase scenario, under the European Communities (Protection of Employees on Transfer of Undertakings) Regulations 2003, there is an automatic transfer of the rights and obligations of the target company towards its employees to the purchaser on a transfer of an undertaking or business. There are, however, possible situations where the Regulations do not apply. For example, if the assets being purchased form part of a distinct business within the target company, it may be permissible to take only those employees who relate to that business. Special rules also operate in respect of pension entitlements. This is a specialist area on which there is a considerable volume of case law.

12.2.8   NAME

If the target company's shares are purchased, the name of the target company is obviously automatically acquired. If, on the other hand, the transaction is conducted by way of asset purchase and it is intended to continue trading under the target company's name, it would be necessary for the purchase vehicle to change its name (and for the target company also to change its name).

12.3   Heads of Agreement

When the parties have reached agreement on the basic principles of the deal (such as structure and price), it is common to record these in a short document sometimes called a Heads of Agreement (or Term Sheet, Letter of Intent, Memorandum of Understanding, etc.). This is designed to ensure that the fundamental terms are indeed agreed, in advance of the parties devoting resources to due diligence (see below) and negotiation of the purchase agreements.

Heads of Agreement are generally stated to be non-binding save in respect of any confidentiality provisions and any exclusivity provisions (where the vendor agrees not to negotiate with anyone else for a limited period). Alternatively, stand-alone confidentiality agreements and/or exclusivity agreements (also called lock-out agreements) will sometimes be used and be expressly legally binding on the parties. When advising clients on confidentiality agreements it is prudent to remind them that enforcing such agreements can be challenging, not least because it is often difficult to prove a breach by the counterparty.

Less commonly, parties to a transaction sometimes consider entering into 'lock-in' agreements, meaning an agreement to negotiate until the deal has been agreed. Such agreements are highly likely to be unenforceable as a matter of Irish law.

12.4   Due Diligence

12.4.1   GENERALLY

One of the first things an intending purchaser will do is carry out of a number of commercial, financial, and legal investigations on the assets or company being acquired, usually referred to as 'due diligence'. This should usually include some or all of the following:

 (a) accounting due diligence;

 (b) general legal due diligence (commercial contracts, litigation, etc.);

 (c) Companies Registration Office/statutory books review;

 (d) investigation of title;

 (e) actuarial due diligence;

 (f) insurance review;

 (g) environmental review; and

 (h) areas specific to the target company.

The level of detail of these investigations will depend on the nature of the target and the attitude of the purchaser. As a general principle, the level of investigation will be greater where the purchase price is greater, but this would not always apply. For example, a company acquired for €1 may have very significant liabilities and a very extensive investigation to quantify these may be appropriate. When the investigations are complete, the purchaser's advisers will sometimes compile the results in a formal due diligence report.

Due diligence is often initiated by way of a general due diligence checklist prepared by the purchaser's lawyer, to be responded to by the vendor and its advisers. Vendors will usually seek to facilitate the process by collating the relevant documentation in a Data Room, either physical (e.g. at its solicitor's office) or, more commonly, online. Sometimes, particularly if there is more than one potential purchaser, the vendor will even instruct its own advisers to complete the due diligence report, which is then shared with the purchaser. This is known as 'vendor due diligence'.

12.4.2   ACCOUNTING DUE DILIGENCE

It is important that every acquisition of a target company be the subject of some form of accounting review. This is usually carried out by a financial adviser to the purchaser. In a simple case, this may involve reviewing the last few sets of audited accounts and reviewing projections for a future period. In a more complex situation, a very detailed accountants' report would be prepared pointing out any accounting deficiencies of the target company and very detailed work would be done on the future position. The scope of this work is largely outside the territory of the legal adviser, but it is critical that a legal adviser should advise the client to make sure that this matter is attended to as it is likely to be the most fundamental review that requires to be carried out. The accounting review should also cover the tax affairs of the target company, in particular where the target company is a member of a group, as leaving a group (upon completion of the transaction) often crystallises tax liabilities.

12.4.3   GENERAL LEGAL DUE DILIGENCE

It is good practice, at an early stage in an acquisition, to look for a copy of all significant legal documentation which has been entered into by a target company. Apart from areas specifically dealt with below, this would include a review of key trading contracts, employment contracts, distribution/agency agreements, agreements relating to trade marks, patents, and other intellectual property rights, hire purchase/leasing agreements, and conditions of sale. Given the increasing importance of technology and the increasing frequency with which technology companies are acquired, particular attention needs to be paid to intellectual property rights. It is critical to establish that the target company either owns or has proper licences for all of its intellectual property to avoid litigation by third parties alleging breach. Furthermore, in a company that supplies technology, there must be a full understanding of the basis on which that technology is made available to others, with particular focus on arrangements where exclusive licences have been agreed or where the licence arrangements permit the customer to sub-license the technology or a product incorporating same.

12.4.4   COMPANIES REGISTRATION OFFICE/STATUTORY BOOKS REVIEW

The legal adviser should at an early stage conduct a Companies Registration Office (the 'CRO') search against the target company and its subsidiaries. Consideration should also be given to searching against any company with a similar name, as this may disclose potential passing off problems or issues about the name of the target company. It may also be appropriate to check domain names and trade mark registrations. The CRO search gives the purchaser's solicitor useful information at an early stage such as a list of registered charges, a list of the directors as filed in the CRO, and the other information contained in the last annual return. This may indicate deficiencies in paperwork. It is useful at an early stage also to obtain a copy of the memorandum and articles of association of the target company and its subsidiaries. This will highlight issues which may need to be dealt with in the course of the acquisition such as the waiver of pre-emption rights on share transfers or specific quorum requirements relevant to the completion board meeting of the target. The due diligence in this regard should also cover a review of the statutory books of the target company and its subsidiaries. This is often left until the last moment, but in practice should be conducted as early as possible in the transaction, as clearly the entries in the statutory books should mirror details in the share purchase contract and in the Companies Registration Office.

12.4.5   INVESTIGATION OF TITLE

Where valuable lands and buildings are being acquired (either directly or within a target company), it is critical that some form of title investigation is carried out. The most usual format of investigation involves raising requisitions on title and enquiries in the same way as if the property itself is being bought and getting various documents on completion in the same way as the completion of a property transaction. A possible (but less common) alternative is to have the vendor's solicitors certify the title. A certificate of title may be the only practical way to proceed if there are a significant number of properties and there is a commercial urgency in completing the transaction. An alternative to investigation or certificate of title is to rely on the warranties given by the vendor as part of the share purchase agreement. This is sometimes done when the properties are comparatively insignificant in value compared to the target company as a whole or where there are a lot of properties, none of which individually is particularly material, and where the purchaser has some degree of confidence that they have been acquired and managed in a competent fashion. As in a property transaction, it is of course always advisable that a purchaser should conduct a survey of the property. A purchaser should always be advised that this is an appropriate course of action. It is a commercial decision for a purchaser to then weigh up the cost of the survey as against the benefits.

12.4.6   ACTUARIAL DUE DILIGENCE

If a target company has set up a pension scheme, it is important that some form of investigation (usually known as an actuarial investigation) be carried out into the pension scheme. This will specifically focus on whether the assets of the pension scheme are sufficient to meet its liabilities. If it is found that a pension scheme is inadequately funded, there is often an adjustment in the purchase consideration to reflect this. There are two different types of schemes: defined benefit schemes (where the members are promised a definitive amount based on their salary when they retire, e.g. one-half of final salary) and defined contribution schemes (where the members receive whatever their aggregate contributions will buy at the time of retirement). Defined benefit schemes have become rarer but are often problematic and generally require more thorough investigation than defined contribution schemes. Both would need to be reviewed by specialists in the area. The review should also encompass any promises that have been made to employees in relation to their pension. A recent trend has been for nearly all new schemes to be defined contribution schemes and for some existing defined benefit schemes to be converted into defined contribution schemes. The mechanics of such a conversion (including whether beneficiary consent is required) can be very complex and it is an area to be focused on during the actuarial due diligence review.

12.4.7   INSURANCE REVIEW

The purchaser should review the insurances put in place by a target company because if the purchaser completes the purchase, and the insurance turns out to be inadequate, it is the purchaser who will suffer the loss. This task is usually carried out by handing over a schedule of insurance policies to the purchaser's insurance brokers. The review should generally at least cover property and public liability insurance, employers' liability, product liability, and directors' and officers' insurance.

12.4.8   ENVIRONMENTAL REVIEW

Given the increasing legislative importance that is being placed on care of the environment, it may be important, particularly with a target company which has a significant environmental impact, that an environmental assessment be carried out. This may involve a thorough review (similar to a survey) carried out by appropriately qualified personnel. The focus would be on whether the target company causes air, water, noise, or other pollution, how waste products are disposed, of and compliance with any existing licences which the company has. Particular attention may need to be paid as to whether the land on which the company operates has been historically contaminated as this may give rise to problems in the future which could be expensive to remedy. While not specifically an environmental area, thought should also be given to issues concerning the safety of employees as the internal environment may give rise to as many problems as the external environment.

12.4.9   OTHER ISSUES

While the above headings enumerate the principal issues which need to be looked at as a part of due diligence, thought should always be given to the particular circumstances of the target company. Depending on the business the target company is engaged upon, there may be further issues that require consideration. For example, if a company is heavily involved in the processing of data, compliance with the data protection legislation becomes enormously relevant; if a company is involved in mineral exploration, compliance with appropriate legislation and with mining licences is critical. The purchaser should be readily able to identify the areas that are likely to require focus, based on the specifics of the target company.

12.5   Pre-conditions to a Purchase Agreement

12.5.1   GENERALLY

Although the commercial details of a purchase agreement may be agreed, it is sometimes the case that it is not possible for the parties to proceed immediately to complete the transaction because of the necessity to get the consent of one or more third parties (often a State entity such as the Competition and Consumer Protection Commission). The device which is used in these circumstances to enable the parties to commit to their agreement (unlike the heads of agreement (see above) which are generally non-binding) is the insertion in the purchase agreement of a number of pre-conditions. This enables the parties to sign and therefore be bound by their agreement subject only to these appropriate pre-conditions being satisfied.

A distinction should be drawn between conditions precedent to the agreement itself and conditions precedent to completion of the agreement. In the case of conditions precedent to an agreement, the parties wait for the fulfillment of certain conditions either of them may have stipulated during negotiations before they form their contract. In the case of conditions precedent to completion, the parties have decided they want the certainty of a contract in place between them, albeit that there may be some issues to be resolved before completion of the purchase takes place. In this case the parties have signed a binding contract but have the right to rescind if the pre-conditions are not fulfilled. The parties may, therefore, incur contractual obligations to each other even though the contract is never completed.

12.5.2   STANDARD CONDITIONS PRECEDENT

The most common issues giving rise to conditions precedent are the need to obtain:

(a)   consent of shareholders;

(b)   consent of a grant authority such as Enterprise Ireland;

(c)   consent of bankers or other parties having a contract with the target company containing change of control provisions; or

(d)   clearance from the Competition and Consumer Protection Commission.

These are discussed in detail below at **12.5.5**.

12.5.3   'NEGATIVE' CONDITIONS PRECEDENT

If conditions precedent of the type listed above are being inserted into a contract, there will inevitably be a delay between signing and completion while the various anticipated matters are dealt with. If any other matter should negatively affect the business during this time period, the purchaser may wish to abandon the deal or to renegotiate the purchase price. Accordingly, consideration needs to be given to the insertion of other 'negative' conditions precedent, such as a condition that no substantial damage should occur to the assets of the company and a condition to the effect that there should be no substantial breach of warranty between the date of signing and completion. Clearly, a purchaser faced with the situation where a premises has burnt down or substantial litigation against a target company has been initiated after signing but before completion will want to be able to elect not to proceed with the contract. Purchasers may also seek conditions concerning a due diligence process, such as a condition to the effect that they should be satisfied with the due diligence process in general or certain aspects thereof. This, like most negative pre-conditions, is normally resisted by the vendor as it gives the purchaser too much room to decide not to proceed with the contract. Perhaps the most hotly contested negative pre-condition is the pre-condition sometimes sought by purchasers that no material adverse change has occurred in relation to the target between signing and completion.

12.5.4   END DATE

If a contract contains pre-conditions, there is a possibility that third parties who have to give the relevant consents/approvals may take some considerable length of time to do so, or indeed may never do so. It is also possible that by the time they issue their approval or consent, circumstances will have radically changed. It is, therefore, common practice to include a latest date by which all of the conditions are to be satisfied. This means that either of the parties is free not to proceed with the contract if the pre-conditions are not satisfied by that date. While there is no set practice for the length of time involved, normally a reasonable estimate as to how long it is going to take to fulfil the conditions will be made and a short period added to this to allow for slippage.

12.5.5   SUBSTANTIVE CONDITIONS PRECEDENT

12.5.5.1   Merger control

The Competition and Consumer Protection Act 2014 gave jurisdiction over mergers control (both investigations and decision-making) to the Competition and Consumer Protection Commission. Transactions may require prior clearance from the Competition and Consumer Protection Commission before they can be completed. This is an important consideration as it can affect the timetable for completion. In addition, if the transaction raises serious competition issues, there may be a risk that the Authority will prohibit the transaction or clear it only subject to conditions (e.g. requiring the purchaser to divest of a competing business).

12.5.5.2   Consent of grant authority

Many Irish companies, particularly those in the manufacturing sector, will have received grant assistance from grant authorities. The grant agreements used by these bodies typically provide that the controlling interest in a grant-aided target company may not change hands without the grant authority's consent or else the grant will be recalled. Therefore, it is necessary on a share purchase to get a prior written consent from the authority involved. This is a fairly simple procedure which involves liaising with the authority concerned, usually by the target company or the vendor. However, it is prudent to make an application for this as early as possible in the acquisition process, as the matter may require formal board approval of the grant authority and this may take several weeks.

12.5.5.3   Banking consent and change of control clauses

If the target company has banking facilities, it is quite possible that the bank may have provided, in its banking facilities, that its consent is required to a change of control and if it is not obtained that this amounts to an event of default. It is important in these circumstances that bank consent is obtained as, even if the bank is aware of the situation, it is unsatisfactory to create technical defaults. The purchaser should make enquiries into this matter at an early stage in the transaction. Obviously, if a search as part of the due diligence process indicates there is a charge registered by a bank against the target company, an enquiry should immediately be made as to whether bank consent is required.

In a way similar to banks, other persons who contracted with the target company may impose a condition which allows that party to take certain action if control of the company changes. For this reason, it is prudent to establish that none of the important contracts to which the company is a party, is subject to such a change of control clause. This is often done by way of warranties, which will then be disclosed against (see below at **12.7**). Again if there is such a change of control clause, the necessary consent should be obtained and this may be included in a pre-condition to the contract.

12.5.5.4 Consent of shareholders

In some cases, the consent of the shareholders of the vendor and/or the purchaser will be required. This in particular arises:

(a) in large transactions for publicly quoted companies as required by the Stock Exchange rules; and

(b) where the purchaser or the vendor is a director or connected with a director, in which event it may be required by the Companies Act 2014 or by Stock Exchange rules.

12.6 Warranties and Indemnities

12.6.1 GENERALLY

Warranties are statements by a vendor concerning the company or assets it is selling. By far the most substantive part of a typical purchase agreement is the section dealing with this. The warranties tend to be the aspect of the agreement which gives rise to the most negotiation between the parties at contract stage and accordingly they should be regarded as being of great significance.

12.6.2 WHY SHOULD A PURCHASER SEEK WARRANTIES?

If a purchaser acquires a target company or target assets without the benefit of warranties, the principle of *caveat emptor* applies. Thus, for example, if it emerges after completion that a target company is subject to a substantial undisclosed litigation claim which arose before the transaction was concluded, the purchaser may have no recourse to the vendor. It is accordingly commonplace, in most purchase transactions, for the purchaser to seek fairly extensive statements in relation to the target, amounting to a series of promises to the effect that the target is virtually perfect. Exceptional situations do arise where, as a matter of contractual negotiations, no warranties are given. In particular, this can arise in:

(a) situations where one shareholder in a target company is buying the shares of other shareholders;

(b) management buyouts (because management already has in-depth knowledge of the company's affairs);

(c) share purchases for very nominal consideration (although in these instances, the purchaser ought to be conscious of the possibility that there could be very substantial liabilities); and

(d) an acquisition of a listed or quoted company where, because of the large number of shareholders in the target, it is impractical to get warranties.

It is sometimes argued by vendors that, where a very extensive due diligence process has been carried out, warranties should not be given or should be significantly watered down. This is usually resisted by a purchaser, as no matter how extensive the due diligence process is, it is no substitute for warranties from those people who know the target best.

12.6.3   WHO SHOULD GIVE THE WARRANTIES?

In most situations, the vendor or, if there is more than one, all of the vendors will give the warranties. However, care should be taken to ensure that the warranties are not being given by a 'man of straw' as no matter how strong the warranties are, they are of no benefit if they are not given by a person or entity with sufficient means to satisfy a warranty claim.

Particular care should be taken when acquiring from a corporate vendor which is a member of a group of companies. Ideally in these circumstances, the most appropriate warrantor may be the holding company within the group, although it may be prudent to get warranties from the vendor company and perhaps other group companies with substantial assets. Alternatively the purchaser may seek a parent company guarantee in respect of the selling subsidiary's potential liability as warrantor.

If there is more than one vendor, the purchaser will normally seek to have warranties given on a joint and several basis. This means that the purchaser may make his warranty claim against every vendor and may choose to enforce against any (or all) of them. Conversely, vendors will sometimes seek to have liability established on a several basis only, with each particular vendor liable only for a proportion of any claim. This is unsatisfactory from a purchaser's viewpoint, as it may mean that the purchaser may only recover part of their loss, in the event that some of the warrantors turn out to be difficult to locate or of inadequate means.

12.6.4   MEASURE OF DAMAGES

The measure of damages which may be obtained, should there be a breach of warranty in relation to a target company, is a matter which gives rise to much debate. The prevailing view is that a court should assess the market value of the target company taking account of the circumstances giving rise to the breach of warranty, and compare this with the market value had the position been as warranted. This can be a difficult exercise and, from the point of view of the purchaser, the damages recovered will not necessarily be enough to put the target company in the position that it would have been in, had the breach of warranty not taken place. In some instances, to cover this point, the purchaser may seek a provision that the measure of damages should be sufficient to effect restitution—however, this would usually be resisted by vendors as effectively amounting to an indemnity. Universal indemnification in respect of warranty claims is not standard practice in Irish share purchases (similar to the position in the United Kingdom but unlike the position in the United State of America where general indemnification is standard practice).

12.6.5   SUBJECT MATTER OF WARRANTIES

The subject matter of warranties is discussed in greater detail below at **12.6.8–12.6.12**. They will usually cover every conceivable aspect of the target company's affairs, including its accounts, its taxation affairs, matters relating to its employees, its assets, debtors, and any litigation against the company. A considerable number of warranties are intended to elicit detailed information in relation to the target company through the disclosure letter (discussed at **12.7** below), rather than seeking to represent that there are no issues which may result in substantial liability.

12.6.6   PREPARATION FOR POTENTIAL WARRANTY CLAIM

If a purchaser has some concern that warranty claims may arise, there are a number of possible further steps that should be taken. One possibility is for the purchaser to seek to retain a portion of the purchase price which is only to be paid over in the future if no warranty claims have been asserted by a certain point in time. This is sometimes referred to as a 'retention amount'. It may also be possible to get insurance cover against warranty claims (although this is relatively rare). This is normally something which is obtained by a vendor and involves giving a copy of the agreement and the underlying disclosure letter to the insurer who is then in a position to assess the premium payable for taking the risk.

12.6.7   LIMITS ON WARRANTIES

If a vendor gives warranties, he is potentially exposed to risk of being sued for breach of warranty for as long as the Statutes of Limitations permit. In addition, he could be exposed to a claim for an amount greater than he received for the target company or could be subjected to trivial claims being asserted by a purchaser. For this reason, it is usual for a vendor to seek to negotiate limits on warranties. Typical variations which a vendor will seek are set out below.

(a) A vendor may seek a provision that any warranty claim must be notified in writing to the vendor by the purchaser within an agreed time scale. It is common practice in this area to distinguish between claims relating to tax and other claims. In the case of tax claims, the time limit agreed is usually somewhere between three and six years (having regard for the number of years for which the Revenue Commissioners are entitled to audit a company's prior tax returns). In the case of non-tax claims, a vendor will seek a shorter period of liability and in this instance periods in the order of one year to two years are common. From a purchaser's point of view, it is often considered that two separate audits which are finished after completion should be sufficient to bring to light any warranty claims and in negotiating a limiting period, a purchaser may therefore seek sufficient time to complete two full audits post completion.

(b) A vendor will usually seek to cap the aggregate liability which may arise on foot of the warranties. Quite frequently, the cap is the purchase consideration. The purchaser should, however, always be advised that in extreme circumstances their loss may be considerably greater than the purchase price and they will obviously lose the benefit of an alternative use to which they could have put the money. Care should also be taken by purchasers when the purchase price is relatively low. If there are provisions for increasing or varying the consideration, this should be considered when agreeing any limit.

(c) The vendor will usually seek to negotiate a minimum threshold which claims must exceed before they may be brought. This is often known as a 'de minimis' provision and the level will vary from transaction to transaction. A vendor will sometimes seek to have this amount constitute an excess, so that if a claim arises the amount below this threshold is a cost for the purchaser. This is not normally acceptable to a purchaser. The vendors will also sometimes seek to rule out any individual claim which falls below a certain amount. From a purchaser's point of view, this practice is dubious as it is possible that there could be a very large number of very small claims which, in the aggregate, would have a significant financial effect.

(d) Where there is more than one vendor, the vendors may seek to apportion liability on a several basis. This is discussed at **12.6.3** above.

(e) The vendor may seek to avoid responsibility for claims which arise due to a change in the law after completion. This is normally acceptable.

(f) The vendor may seek to be relieved of liability if the warranty claim arises as the result of any action by the purchaser after completion. The purchaser will often resist this and try and confine it, if agreed, to actions outside the normal course of business.

(g)   The vendor will try and exclude matters which are covered by a provision or reserve in the company's accounts. To the extent that something is specifically provided for or reserved (as opposed to merely noted), this should be acceptable, on the basis that it has very likely been taken into account in arriving at the agreed valuation of the company.

(h)   The vendor will try and exempt liability for anything which is covered by a policy of insurance maintained by the company; again this is normally acceptable, although the insurance premium may increase as a result of the insurance claims being made.

(i)   A vendor will sometimes seek to reduce its level of exposure in a warranty, by giving the warranty 'to the best of their knowledge, information, and belief' or 'so far as the vendor is aware'. The qualification of warranties by these words is often the subject of considerable debate in the context of a purchase transaction but is generally resisted by a purchaser except for fairly trivial warranties.

(j)   The limits are often expressly disapplied in case of fraud or wilful concealment by the vendor.

A line of English cases (including *Eurocopy plc v Teesdale* [1992] BCLC 1067 and *Infiniteland Ltd and John Stewart Aviss v Artisan Contracting Ltd* [2005] EWCA Civ 758) suggest that if before signing a purchase agreement a purchaser is aware of circumstances giving rise to a breach of warranty (and distinctions will be made between different levels of awareness, such as actual knowledge, constructive knowledge, or imputed knowledge), the purchaser may not be entitled to a remedy for a breach of warranty. In such circumstances indemnities may be particularly important to the purchaser – see further below at **12.6.14**.

12.6.8   FINANCIAL MATTERS

Warranties which may be sought on financial matters related to a target company include those set out below.

(a)   A warranty that the latest set of audited accounts comply with all applicable laws and with generally accepted accounting principles and that they give a true and fair view of the assets and liabilities and financial position of the target company may be sought. This is commonly regarded as the most essential warranty obtained on any share purchase, and if this warranty is obtained, it may well give coverage against the bulk of claims which are likely to arise even in the absence of any other warranties. If a company has a trading record, it is important to focus on whether accounts are consistent with previous accounting periods and if not, why not.

(b)   It is usual to seek some comfort that, apart from transactions in the ordinary course of business, there have been no material changes since the date to which the last audited accounts have been made up. This is a particularly important matter to cover if the last audited accounts are relatively old. In addition, if the last audited accounts are quite old, the vendor may be asked to warrant management accounts.

(c)   Extensive provision is usually made in warranties to deal with taxation. These warranties principally focus on whether the company has paid all of its tax which has become due prior to the date of completion. They also focus on whether the company is registered for all taxes for which it is liable and whether it has made returns on time. The warranties frequently focus on points of detail within the tax code, for example, whether the company has claimed roll-over relief under the capital gains legislation and whether it has ever incurred balancing charges. For trading companies with employees, the warranties should focus very clearly on VAT, PAYE, and PRSI, as non-payment of these taxes may, quite quickly, give rise to very substantial financial liability.

(d)   Warranties are usually given as to the borrowing facilities available to the company, whether these are guaranteed or otherwise secured by the vendor, and the level of borrowing which has been incurred up to completion.

(e)   It is not unusual to seek a warranty to the effect that the net assets of the company are not less than a stated figure. If such a warranty is given at completion of the transaction, it acts as an assurance that there have not been any major negative changes since the end of the last audited accounting period.

12.6.9   CONSTITUTION OF TARGET COMPANY

Warranties relating to the constitution of a target company include warranties:

(a)   that the memorandum and articles of the target company are as supplied;

(b)   as to the identity of directors and secretary;

(c)   as to returns to the Companies Registration Office;

(d)   as to who owns the share capital;

(e)   that proper records including statutory books are being kept by the company;

(f)   that no petition has been presented to wind up the company;

(g)   as to dividend payments; and

(h)   as to whether there have been any breaches of the Companies Acts.

12.6.10   ASSETS OF TARGET COMPANY

The various warranties described below focus on matters relating to assets:

(a)   Warranties are frequently sought as to the ownership of intellectual property (e.g. trade marks, patents, and copyrights) used by a target company. In a target company which is substantially dependent upon intellectual property, material issues to consider include whether it has the right to use all the intellectual property which it is using. If the target company is selling a product which incorporates intellectual property, it is important to ensure that the target company's right to use the intellectual property covers the right to incorporate that intellectual property in the product sold. It is also important to ascertain that such a company has not given any exclusive licence to one party, which would preclude the company from providing the product to other parties.

(b)   The warranties will focus on whether a target company is party to any unusual agreements such as long-term contracts or guarantees.

(c)   The warranties will focus on whether a target company owns all of its assets and whether they are subject to lease, hire purchase, etc.

(d)   Warranties will often focus on the state of the assets and whether they are in good repair or are likely to require replacement. These warranties are often resisted by a vendor who might require purchasers to take their own view on assets.

(e)   A warranty is usually sought that stock-in-trade is in good condition and, somewhat more controversially, that stocks are not excessive or slow moving or obsolete.

(f)   A warranty is frequently sought that the book debts of a target company will be collected in the normal course and within a set time period after completion. This is frequently the subject of debate between vendor and purchaser, as the vendor will not want to guarantee their collectability.

(g)   It is not unusual that extensive warranties would be given in relation to the properties occupied by a target company. This would normally focus on the target company having good and marketable title to the property and any encumbrances which may exist. The warranties would also cover the planning on the property and any notices which have been served affecting the property.

(h)   There is usually a warranty as to whether the assets include amounts owed to a target company by the vendor or its associates. These will usually be collected at completion.

(i)   A warranty is usually sought that a target company has all the licences it needs to carry on its business.

(j)   A warranty will be sought as to distribution and agency agreements to which a target company is party.

(k)   Warranties are usually sought as to the insurance held by a target company. This is frequently disclosed against by producing all of the insurance policies and requiring the purchaser to take its own view as to the appropriateness of same.

12.6.11 LIABILITIES OF TARGET COMPANY

Warranties will also address liabilities of a target company. Examples are set out below:

(a)   A warranty will usually focus on any litigation to which the target company may be subject. Issues addressed include:

    (i)   whether there is any litigation in which the target company is involved or litigation which is contemplated;

    (ii)   whether the target company has been in breach of any environmental law, in particular those relating to air pollution, water pollution, noise, and waste; and

    (iii)   whether it has sold defective products.

(b)   There is usually a warranty to the effect that the target company has complied with its statutory obligations generally without any specific statute being averted to.

(c)   There is usually a warranty seeking to establish whether the target company has any grants. If this is the case, there may be a liability to repay if there is default (e.g. a change of control).

(d)   There is sometimes a warranty focusing on whether customers or suppliers have indicated that they are going to cease dealing with the target company or are winding down their level of dealing.

(e)   There is usually a warranty seeking to ascertain whether the target company owes any money to the vendors or persons associated with them. If there is a disclosure against this, the money is often discharged at completion.

12.6.12 EMPLOYEE-RELATED MATTERS

There is usually a section of the warranties focusing on the status of employees. This would include a warranty:

(a)   containing a list of employees and details of their benefits, including salary;

(b)   that no one is entitled to an unusually long notice period;

(c)   that there are no liabilities or claims pending for unfair dismissal or redundancy;

(d)   that there are no trade disputes;

(e)   that all employee safety legislation has been complied with; and

(f)   that there are pension schemes in place for employees and that they are properly funded.

12.6.13   OTHER ISSUES

There is usually concern on the part of the purchaser that, notwithstanding the details of all of the specific warranties set out above, there are other issues of which they ought to be aware. It is not unusual to find a warranty to the effect that the vendor has disclosed to the purchaser any matter which would render any information otherwise given as untrue or misleading, or any matter which ought to be disclosed to an intending purchaser of shares in the company. The inclusion of this type of warranty is generally resisted by the vendor.

12.6.14   INDEMNITIES

In order to succeed with a warranty claim (including claims made pursuant to the tax warranties), a purchaser must overcome the hurdles of proving that the circumstances giving rise to a breach of warranty exist (and were not adequately disclosed) and must also prove that it has suffered a loss. It is generally accepted by the parties to a sale and purchase transaction that the remedies available to a purchaser should be enhanced in the case of any unexpected pre-completion tax liabilities of a target company. The parties will typically agree that in the event of such a tax liability arising, the purchaser is automatically entitled to recover the amount of the liability (and its associated costs) from the seller. An indemnity is used to achieve this – it is a commitment to reimburse the buyer on a euro for euro basis in respect of a particular liability, should it arise. For this purpose a separate deed of tax indemnity is usually employed as one of the transaction documents, although the indemnification provisions can equally be included within a share purchase agreement. The extent to which the various limits on liability which have been agreed to apply to the warranties should also apply to the tax indemnity is very often the subject of negotiation.

In a similar way, if prior to signing the purchaser becomes aware of any specific circumstances which it is concerned may give rise to a material liability for the target company after completion, rather than have to rely on a warranty claim the purchaser will often seek specific indemnification in relation to those circumstances in order to ease the process of compensation and in particular to try to avoid any complications involved in demonstrating its loss or any difficulties arising regarding recovery by virtue of the purchaser's prior awareness of the issue. Such indemnities, if applicable, are usually incorporated in the share purchase agreement as opposed to being in a stand-alone deed. Again, there will usually be some negotiation over limitations but in general in this situation purchasers will be much less inclined to concede exclusions of the seller's liability. The typical exceptions to this are a time limit for taking claims and a financial cap on liability, neither of which would be uncommon.

It should be clearly expressed in the transaction documents that the disclosure letter has no bearing on the tax indemnities or any other indemnities as, if the concept of indemnification has been agreed by the parties, the purchaser's prior knowledge of the relevant circumstances should not be a bar to its right to recovery.

12.6.15   CONCLUSION

The warranties which are typically given vary to some extent from transaction to transaction. While most legal advisers to a purchaser tend to have their own typical list of warranties, thought should always be given to whether additional warranties are needed in the context of the transaction. For example, if a target company's assets largely consist of intellectual property, it may be prudent to expand the intellectual property warranties over and above those which appear in a standard type of list of 'off the shelf' warranties. If a target company has substantial involvement with data, it may be appropriate to look carefully at legislation such as the Data Protection Acts and draft specific warranties to ensure compliance.

12.7   Disclosure Letter

In every share purchase transaction where there are warranties, the net effect of those warranties is to state that the company is 'perfect'. Clearly no company will reach the state of perfection suggested by the warranties and the vendor is therefore given an opportunity to set out, in a contemporaneous letter, where the company deviates from perfection. This is known as the disclosure letter. This is an extremely important document from the vendor's point of view and must be prepared with enormous care. The preparation of the letter involves the vendor being taken through each of the warranties by his solicitor and being asked whether there are any matters associated with the target company which would be a deviation from those warranties. Specialist areas such as accounts warranties, tax warranties, and pension warranties are usually referred to the target company's accountants and tax and pension advisers for their comment.

While this list can only be regarded as being indicative, typical disclosures would include:

(a)   banking facilities available;

(b)   Companies Registration Office filings not being up to date;

(c)   litigation by or against the company;

(d)   details of all of the company insurance policies;

(e)   disputes concerning employees;

(f)   assets which are leased by the company;

(g)   details of the company's pension affairs;

(h)   issues with title to property;

(i)   non-compliance with legal obligations;

(j)   arrears of taxation or past occasions when taxation was discharged late; and

(k)   areas where there might be a doubt as to the tax payable.

It is normal that the disclosure letter be prefaced by a number of general disclosures. These may be quite contentious (as between vendor and purchaser) as some standard general disclosure may be construed as putting the purchaser on notice of matters that he could ascertain by inspection. Therefore, disclosures of Companies Registration Office records and statutory registers which are actually given to a purchaser would be regarded as acceptable. However, a disclosure of everything which might be ascertained by inspecting the premises and records of the target company is normally regarded as inappropriate as this would put a purchaser on notice of everything that might be in the company's filing cabinets or anything that might be found out about the property as a result of a survey.

The disclosure letter is usually written by the vendor to the purchaser. It is occasionally written on behalf of the respective clients by the firms of lawyers involved, in which event it should be clearly stated by the vendor's lawyers that it is based on instructions from their client and that they themselves disclaim the contents.

A body of case law has developed over what degree of disclosure in relation to particular facts or circumstances is required in order to serve as an effective qualification, pursuant to the terms of the relevant share purchase agreement, of the seller's liability under the warranties. In some cases, courts have determined that the purported disclosure was not fulsome enough to enable a reasonable purchaser to understand the relevant issue and accordingly failed to amount to an effective disclosure pursuant to the requirements of the relevant share purchase agreement. In order to reduce uncertainty in this area, parties will frequently attempt to define in the share purchase agreement the applicable standard of disclosure that they agree is required, e.g. 'fair' disclosure, 'full' disclosure, 'accurate' disclosure, 'reasonable' disclosure etc... or some combination of the foregoing (e.g. *Daniel Reeds Limited v Chemists Limited* [1995] EM ESS CLC).

12.8 Consideration Payable under Share Purchase Agreement

12.8.1 GENERALLY

There are a number of ways in which the consideration payable under a share purchase agreement may be discharged. The principal forms of consideration are as follows:

(a) cash;

(b) allotment of shares in the purchaser company; and

(c) loan notes.

12.8.2 PAYMENT IN CASH

Payment in cash is the simplest and most common form of consideration and it applies in most transactions.

12.8.3 ALLOTMENT OF SHARES IN PURCHASER

Allotment of shares in the purchaser company is somewhat unusual but it arises occasionally, most often where the purchaser is a listed public limited company. It is settled law that a company must not issue its shares at a discount. However, historically this has not created any particular problem where a purchaser was issuing shares because, except in the most extreme of circumstances, shares in the target company would represent sufficient consideration to pay up the shares being allotted. However, the Companies Act 2014 at Part 17, Chapter 3 contains an important qualification to this principle. This limits the circumstances in which a public limited company may allot shares paid up otherwise than in cash. Subject to an exception, which is dealt with below, a public limited company may not generally allot shares without a valuation of the consideration for those shares from a person qualified to be the auditor of the company. A valuation report must be made to the company during the six months immediately preceding the allotment of the shares and a copy of that report must be sent to the proposed allottee. If the allottee does not receive a report or, to the knowledge of the allottee, there is some other contravention, the allottee is liable to pay the company the nominal value of the shares together with any premium plus interest.

An important exception to the provision is contained in s 1028 (2) of the Companies Act 2014. This provides that the valuation procedure does not apply where there is an arrangement providing for the allotment of shares in a plc, on terms that the whole or part of the consideration for the shares allotted is to be provided by the transfer to that company of all or some of the shares of a particular class in another company. However, the arrangement to take newly allotted shares must be available to all the holders of the shares in the target company.

12.8.4 LOAN NOTES

A possible method of paying consideration, otherwise than by cash, is by way of loan notes. The vendors need to focus on whether the loan notes are secured or unsecured and whether they are guaranteed by a relatively financially stable third party such as a bank.

12.8.5 OTHER RELEVANT FACTORS RELATING TO THE CONSIDERATION

12.8.5.1 Deferred consideration

A device which is commonly used in share purchase transactions is to defer the payment of part of the consideration. Frequently, the amount which is deferred is uncertain and is computed by reference to future events, most notably the financial performance of the target company (called an 'earn-out'). If a vendor agrees to payment of deferred consideration, which is dependent upon the financial performance of the target company, considerable thought needs to be given to controls placed on the purchaser in relation to the target company's behaviour during the period by reference to which the deferred consideration is computed. The vendor would want to ensure that profits are calculated on a basis consistent with past practice. The vendor is also likely to insist on a right to have an independent review of the basis on which the calculation is made and a right to appeal to a third party, in the event that they are dissatisfied with the results as produced by the purchaser's auditors. Deferred consideration is also somewhat unsatisfactory from the point of view of the vendor, in that it may seem convenient to the purchaser to withhold payment of deferred consideration if there is any issue of warranty claims arising. For this reason, there are sometimes extensive negotiations if the vendor looks for a specific assurance from the purchaser in the agreement, that payment will not be withheld on account of pending warranty claims. As a further comfort to vendors, deferred consideration is sometimes paid on completion into an escrow account under the joint control of the purchaser and the vendor (or their respective advisers) and subject to strict rules concerning withdrawals.

12.8.5.2   Form CG50A

Section 980 of the Taxes Consolidation Act 1997 contains provisions intended to stop the avoidance of capital gains tax on the disposal of land in Ireland and on the disposal of certain other assets. If land in Ireland is being disposed of, it is necessary for the purchaser to either get a clearance (known as a Form CG50A) of the vendor from capital gains tax or, alternatively, to withhold 15% of the purchase price at source.

Clearly, it would be easy to avoid this particular provision by putting land into a company and then selling the shares in the company. The Revenue has, therefore, extended this principle to shares in a company, the value of, or the greater part of whose value is, derived from land situated in Ireland and also from certain other assets, most notably mineral and exploration rights. The Revenue Commissioners have a fairly liberal interpretation of what constitutes 'deriving the greater part of the value of shares in a company from land'. It is therefore necessary to look very closely at the target company's accounts to determine whether this requirement applies. If in doubt, the purchaser should insist on a CG50A certificate. In practice, any target company which owns substantial lands is one to which the provision may apply and it is usually prudent to seek a CG50A clearance. This should be obtained by the vendor. It is usually dealt with fairly quickly by means of an application to the inspector of taxes who deals with the vendor's affairs (although complications arise with foreign vendors).

If a transaction is completed in which a Form CG50A ought to have been obtained and was not, the purchaser may subsequently be called upon by the Revenue to pay over 15% of the sale proceeds to the Revenue Commissioners. It is therefore a serious problem for a purchaser not to obtain such a certificate when one is required. This procedure does not apply to small transactions, with the current threshold being fixed at €500,000.

12.8.5.3   Financial assistance

Section 82 of the Companies Act 2014 prohibits a target company from giving financial assistance for the purpose of an acquisition by any person of shares in the company (or its holding company). This does not give rise to any problem where a purchaser is proposing to fund a purchase entirely from within its own resources. However, if the purchaser intends in some way to use the financial resources of the target company to fund the purchase, the provisions of s 82 will require consideration. Section 82 renders it unlawful for a company to give such financial assistance, whether directly or indirectly, and whether by means of a loan, guarantee, the provision of security, or otherwise.

The section most commonly arises where the purchaser is using a bank loan to fund the purchase and the bank proposes to secure the facilities, not only on the purchaser and its assets, but also on the assets of the target company or companies. The security being given by the target company or companies would constitute financial assistance and is unlawful unless the Summary Approval Procedure for derogating from s 82 is carried out. In general terms, this procedure involves the swearing of a statutory declaration as to solvency by the directors and the passing of a special resolution permitting the financial assistance by the members. If s 82 is an issue, it should be flagged early in the transaction as the derogation procedure will require cooperation from the vendor. The derogation procedure is not available to public limited companies.

It is critical for the vendor to satisfy itself that s 82 is not breached, as any transaction in breach of the section is voidable by the company as against a person who had notice of the facts which constitute the breach. It is extremely likely that the vendor would have notice of such facts and would be so caught. Section 82 is dealt with in more detail in **chapter 13, 'Financial Assistance'**.

12.9 Restrictive Covenants

A share purchase agreement usually includes a clause restricting the vendors from competing with the company. The validity or otherwise of this is governed by the Competition and Consumer Protection Act 2014 (with both civil and criminal consequences in the case of infringement). As a general principle the Competition and Consumer Protection Commission holds the view that where the agreement involves the sale of the goodwill of the business such restrictions are not in breach of the Competition and Consumer Protection Act and should therefore be enforceable. This is provided that the restrictions are limited in terms of duration, geographical coverage, and subject matter, to what is necessary to secure the adequate transfer of goodwill.

12.10 Signing and Completion of Share Purchase Agreements

12.10.1 INTRODUCTION

One of the common practical difficulties with share purchase agreements is the concept of the signing of a share purchase agreement and the concept of completion of such an agreement. While the distinction may be difficult to grasp, from a lawyer's point of view it is similar to the concept which arises in a property transaction, where a contract is signed on one day and some time later there is a completion. However, in many share purchase transactions, and particularly where no pre-conditions are involved, the signing will take place contemporaneously with completion.

12.10.2 SIGNING

The central feature of signing for a share purchase agreement is that a document has been agreed that contains all of the relevant commercial details. This would cover not only the share purchase agreement, but also ancillary documents such as the disclosure letter, a deed of tax indemnity, and documents dealing with any other relevant issues such as distribution agreements, employment agreements, etc. It is common practice that documents such as a deed of tax indemnity and the ancillary documents mentioned above, would be in agreed form at the time of signing but would not in fact be signed until completion takes place.

With increasing frequency, parties are opting for 'virtual' signings and completions, where some or all of the signatories are not physically together at a meeting, relying instead on their solicitors to exchange emails attaching executed agreements. The 2008 UK case of *R*

(Mercury Tax Group and Another) v HMRC [2008] EWHC 2721 illustrates some of the potential dangers of this. The safest course in this scenario (and assuming that the agreement contains a counterparts clause) is for each principal to receive an email attaching a pdf of the final version of the entire agreement and for each principal then to sign and return to his solicitor by email a pdf of the final version of the entire agreement as signed by him, authorising its release to the other side. The respective solicitors should then agree the precise manner in which they will formally exchange the signed contracts. Other possible options (and dangers inherent in 'virtual' signings/completions) are identified in the current Law Society Guidance On The 'Virtual' Execution of Documents.

12.10.3 COMPLETION

If completion of a transaction is to be delayed for some time, there are a number of matters with which the purchaser and, to a lesser extent, the vendor must concern themselves. These matters are considered below.

12.10.3.1 Completion date

A firm completion date must be set or, alternatively, a date by which completion must take place. If this is not met, it is usually provided that either party may walk away from the transaction. This is important, for the reasons outlined in more detail under pre-conditions at **12.5.4** above, as the parties would not want to be bound to a course of action for an indefinite time while waiting for pre-conditions to be fulfilled.

12.10.3.2 Business between signing and completion

If there is to be a gap between signing and completion, it is critical, from the purchaser's point of view, that between signing and completion the company operates strictly in the ordinary course of business. Consequently, the purchaser will usually seek to insert a clause insisting that it must agree any course of action other than trading in the normal course of business. These clauses would usually restrict the target company from issuing new shares, paying dividends, making acquisitions or disposals, hiring and firing an employee, granting mortgages, incurring significant capital expenditure, and entering a number of other unusual types of transactions. The inclusion of such a provision is important from the point of view of a purchaser because, if the owners of the target company were free to take all manner of actions between signing and completion, the purchaser may find that the target company (and its financial position) had radically changed over a short period of time.

12.10.3.3 Repetition of warranties

If there is a gap between signing and completion, the purchaser will want the warranties repeated at completion. If the vendor accepts this, the vendor is likely to want the ability to add extra disclosure items to the disclosure letter because issues could arise between signing and completion which cause one or more warranties to become incorrect. If this is agreed by the purchaser, it is usually on the basis that they have the right to walk away from the transaction should they not like the particular additional disclosures. This is a matter which should always be considered when there is a gap between signing and completion.

12.10.4 FORMALITIES OF COMPLETION

In practice, completion generally involves a meeting between the purchaser and vendor. The purchaser will arrive at a completion meeting ready to pay the purchase consideration and the vendor will arrive at the meeting with a set of papers, which are handed over to the purchaser.

The set of completion papers will vary from transaction to transaction but will include the following:

(a)   share transfer forms for the shares in the target company and the appropriate share certificates (if a share certificate is lost an indemnity in place of the lost certificate will usually suffice);

(b)   any necessary pre-emption waivers in relation to these transfers;

(c)   if there is a group of companies involved in the target, all shares in subsidiaries which are not owned by other group companies should be covered by a share transfer form and appropriate share certificate;

(d)   a copy duly executed by the vendor and the target company of ancillary documents such as the deed of tax indemnity and ancillary contracts;

(e)   the statutory books and registers of the target company;

(f)   the directors' minute book of the target company;

(g)   the seal of the target company;

(h)   the certificate of incorporation of the target company;

(i)   title documents to any properties owned by the target company (although if these are mortgaged to a bank and the mortgage is being left in place, they may not be presented at a completion);

(j)   a certificate of title in relation to properties (if this has been agreed);

(k)   any letters of consent required from third parties such as grant-aiding authorities, banks, mergers consent, etc. (these are discussed in more detail in relation to pre-conditions above);

(l)   CG50A clearance (if this is required);

(m)   a certified copy of the memorandum and articles of association of each target company;

(n)   mandates that have been put in place for the target company (there may be a need to amend the mandates at completion and having a copy of the mandates enables the necessary changes to be identified and made);

(o)   letters of resignation of the directors and secretary (if it is agreed that they should resign). The letters of resignation should ideally include a confirmation that they have no outstanding claims against the target company. If this is not done, there is a danger from the purchaser's point of view that a claim could be asserted by such people;

(p)   repayment of loans between target company and the vendor/his associates;

(q)   tax registration numbers of the vendors (required by the purchaser for the stamp duty payment process); and

(r)   any other documents that may be required depending on the circumstances.

12.10.5 BOARD MEETING

A second important component of the completion of a transaction, which needs to be organised by the vendor, is the holding of board meetings of each target company, duly convened in accordance with all applicable requirements. Handing over the above documents it is not sufficient to complete the transaction. Some of them must be processed and approved by the board of the target company. In particular, the following must be dealt with:

(a)   transfer forms must be approved for registration;

(b)   resignations of directors must be approved and new directors appointed;

(c)   resignation of the secretary must be approved and a new secretary appointed;

(d)   the resignation of the auditors must be noted and new auditors appointed;

(e)   changes to the bank mandates should be effected; and

(f)   if the registered office is to be changed, a resolution to this effect must be adopted.

With regard to the transfer of shares, the board of the target company should satisfy itself that it has an absolute power to register the transfers without any consent being required from any shareholder. Alternatively, if shareholders have some form of pre-emption rights on the transfer of shares, these pre-emption rights should have been properly waived. In the context of the appointment of new directors, the target company should obtain the consent of the new directors in the form of the usual Companies Office Form B10 (it is desirable but not strictly necessary to deal with this at completion).

Once the various documents required are handed over to the purchaser and the board meetings are held, the purchaser then completes the transaction by formally handing the consideration over to the vendor.

12.10.6   ITEMS TO BE ACTIONED POST-COMPLETION

There are a number of matters which must be attended to after completion takes place. In particular, the issues outlined below must be considered.

12.10.6.1   Stamping

Share transfers must be presented for stamping within 30 days of completion of the transaction. Stamp duty is levied at the rate of 1% of the market value of the shares being acquired. In case there are delays with the stamping process it is appropriate to include in the terms of the share purchase agreement a provision under which the vendor agrees to cooperate with the purchaser in voting the shares in whatever way the purchaser wishes. This is because it is not permissible to enter the name of the purchaser onto the register of members until stamping is completed. Thus, for example, if stamping is to take six months and an AGM of the target company takes place four months after completion, the persons strictly entitled to be represented at the AGM are the outgoing vendors. The share purchase agreement should contain a power of attorney in favour of the purchaser to enable the purchaser to represent the vendor and control the votes on the shares at the AGM.

12.10.6.2   CRO returns

Various returns to the CRO need to be made. It is not necessary to return particulars of the new shareholders to the CRO, although this detail will in due course be included in the next annual return. However, if there are changes concerning company officers or the company's registered office, then particulars of the changes should be filed within 14 days from completion. A new bank mandate should be given to the bank as soon as possible.

12.10.6.3   Directors' interests

Under s 261 of the Companies Act 2014, directors and company secretaries must formally notify their company if they acquire or dispose of shares in the company. If the vendor is a director, or an entity controlled by a director, the target company should be notified of the disposal. If the purchaser is a director, or a party connected with a director, a notice should also be given to the target company of the acquisition of the shareholding interest. Failure to give this notice in the case of an acquisition may result in any right or interest, of any kind, in respect of selling the shares not being enforceable directly or indirectly by action or legal proceedings (Companies Act, 2014, s 266 (2)). It is also an offence to fail to comply with such a requirement.

12.10.6.4 Tax returns

The vendor may be required to file a capital gains tax return following completion.

12.10.6.5 Name change

If a target company is a member of a group or has a name which identifies it with the vendor, it will almost certainly be provided in the agreement that the target company must change its name. Again, this is a matter which must be actioned post completion. It is often the case that if this arises, a special resolution providing for the change of name will be adopted at the time of completion, and it is therefore a matter of processing this through the Companies Registration Office following completion.

12.10.6.6 Access to records

The vendor may need access to the records of the target company after completion and may seek the inclusion of such a clause in the share purchase agreement. This may be acceptable to the purchaser, but should be subject to a stringent confidentiality obligation, which only allows for disclosure of information if it is required by law.

12.11 Analysis of Typical Share Purchase Agreement

A typical share purchase agreement consists of the following components:

(a) parties;

(b) recitals;

(c) definitions;

(d) pre-conditions;

(e) consideration provision;

(f) warranties and indemnities (if any);

(g) restrictive and other covenants;

(h) completion;

(i) miscellaneous provisions; and

(j) schedules (including schedule of warranties).

12.11.1 PARTIES

It is standard to set out the names and addresses of the parties at the front of the document. If any of the parties are companies, it may be useful to list their registered numbers as no matter how many times a company changes its name, it can always be identified by reference to the registered number.

12.11.2 RECITALS

It is standard in a commercial contract, such as a share purchase agreement, to set out recitals. These broadly set out brief details of the target company, including its registered number and issued share capital, and then recite that the vendor has agreed to sell the shares and that the purchaser has agreed to purchase the shares. Recitals are useful in that they describe the target company and give an idea as to the broad subject matter of the agreement.

12.11.3   DEFINITIONS

It is conventional in a share purchase agreement, as with other commercial documents, that terms which are frequently used are defined for all purposes of the agreement. This section may appear in different parts of the agreement, but usually, it is found at the opening section of the agreement. However, it may appear at the end of the main body of the agreement or sometimes in a schedule.

12.11.4   PRE-CONDITIONS

This section of the agreement covers the matters which are referred to in detail in 'Pre-conditions to a Purchase Agreement' at **12.5**. Specifically the section will identify:

(a)   the substantive conditions precedent;

(b)   relevant 'negative' conditions precedent; and

(c)   an end date.

This section typically provides that the vendor and the purchaser will use their best efforts to secure the satisfaction of the pre-conditions.

12.11.5   CONSIDERATION PROVISION

This provision is the operative provision, which provides that the purchaser will purchase and the vendor will sell the shares in question. It is important that the provision makes it clear that they are being sold free from all encumbrances and with the benefit of all rights attaching to them, otherwise there is a possibility that the purchaser will be deemed to have acquired the shares subject to whatever encumbrances may be attached to them such as equities, options, mortgages, charges, reservation of title, etc.

This provision also sets out the consideration payable. This is fully discussed in 'Consideration Payable under Share Purchase Agreement' at **12.8**.

12.11.6   WARRANTIES

It is usual to include, in the main body of the share purchase agreement, the operative provisions whereby the warrantors agree to give warranties to the purchaser, subject to certain limitations, qualifications and liability exclusions (reviewed in 'Limits on Warranties' at **12.6.7**). The terms of the warranties themselves are normally set out in a separate schedule and typically include items such as the following:

(a)   a warranty that the parties have full power and authority to enter into and perform the share purchase agreement;

(b)   a warranty that the shares being sold constitute all of the shares in the capital of the company and are not subject to encumbrance; and

(c)   warranties covering all aspects of the target company and its business.

12.11.7   RESTRICTIVE AND OTHER COVENANTS

The agreement normally provides for restrictive covenants, which bind the vendor. Such a section may also include other covenants such as covenants concerning a change of name of the target company or the vendor and covenants concerning ancillary agreements.

12.11.8 COMPLETION

A section of the agreement usually provides for the formalities of completion. This will include: the list of documents to be handed over at completion; the agenda for the board meeting to take place at completion; and a covenant that the purchaser will pay the purchase price on completion. If there is to be a gap between signing and completion, it may be appropriate, at this point of the agreement, to make provision to address the issues that arise.

The relevant issues are discussed in 'Signing and Completion of Share Purchase Agreements' at **12.10**. This section may also deal with matters to take place post completion such as stamping of share transfers.

12.11.9 MISCELLANEOUS PROVISIONS

It is usual that the last section of a share purchase agreement consists of general provisions sometimes referred to as 'boilerplate clauses'. Matters typically dealt with in these clauses include: a prohibition on the making of any public announcement concerning the terms of the purchase, except by agreement between the parties; a provision dealing with the assignment of warranties; a provision dealing with who will bear the expenses of the transaction; and a provision dealing with the service of any notices required under the agreement. This usually provides for notices to be served by hand or by post and specifies a time limit after which they are deemed to have been given. It may also provide for methods of communication, such as fax or email. There is usually a clause providing that a once-off waiver by a party of a liability will not be construed as a general waiver and further that an acquiescence in a breach will not be deemed to be a general waiver.

It is often provided, particularly where there are a number of parties involved, that the original agreement may be signed in more than one counterpart. This facilitates signing where parties are in a number of different locations.

It is sometimes provided that the share purchase agreement and identified ancillary documents constitute the entire agreement between the parties. This is helpful, particularly from a vendor's point of view, as it prevents a purchaser from arguing that there are unwritten warranties or representations which form the basis on which they entered into the agreement.

The general clauses at the end will usually deal with the governing law of the contract. If all of the parties are clearly located in Ireland, this should not give rise to a problem if it is omitted. However, if there are parties from different jurisdictions, the omission of a governing law clause may give rise to difficulties and consequently it is important that something should be included. For foreign parties, it may also be appropriate to include a clause under which they submit to the jurisdiction of an Irish court.

12.11.10 SCHEDULES

It is usual to include matters in schedules to cover the detail of items such as warranties, the members of the board of the target company and details of its properties.

CHAPTER 13

FINANCIAL ASSISTANCE

13.1 Introduction

For well over 50 years the statutory prohibition on an Irish company giving financial assistance for the purchase of or subscription for its own shares or those of its holding company was covered under s 60 of the Companies Act 1963 (the '1963 Act'). Section 60, which largely mirrored the UK equivalent legislation, had as its original objective, the prevention of the depletion of a company's capital for the benefit of its creditors. However, the prohibition was widely drafted so as to include direct or indirect assistance whether given by way of a loan, the provision of a guarantee or security or otherwise. As a result, the legislation was notorious for its uncertain language and its wide all-encompassing ambit and many 'innocent' transactions, which it was never intended to prohibit, fell into its clutches. The protection of a company's capital may be of less material importance in today's commercial world given the array of other protections/ restrictions comprised under company law and, in particular, given that a company's paid-up capital and its actual intrinsic value bear little correlation. Perhaps this reduction in importance is reflected in the removal, in 2006, by the UK legislature of their equivalent of s 60.

The Companies Act 2014 (the '2014 Act') contains a number of significant changes to company law in Ireland including important amendments to the financial assistance regime applying to private companies. Rather than deleting the prohibition from Irish company law, it has been carried over into the 2014 Act but with a number of notable changes. The relevant provisions are included in Part 3, Chapter 3 of the 2014 Act, which deals with allotment of shares generally.

The 2014 Act includes a restatement of the existing prohibition on the giving by a company of financial assistance for the acquisition of its shares, subject to some important modifications which can be summarised as follows:

(a)   the scope of the prohibition has been narrowed;

(b)   a number of extensions/clarifications to the exceptions to the prohibition on giving financial assistance including the introduction of a principal purpose and good faith test; and

(c)   the existing 'whitewash' validation procedure has been replaced by new Summary Approval Procedure ('SAP') with some significant changes.

For ease of review, a comparative table highlighting the key changes between the legal position as set out in the 1963 Act and the 2014 Act is set out at the Appendix to this chapter.

13.2 Prohibition on a Company Giving 'Financial Assistance'

The giving by a company of financial assistance for the acquisition of its shares is treated as a 'restricted activity' under the 2014 Act. Section 82 (2) of the 2014 Act sets out the extent of the updated prohibition and provides as follows:

> *It shall not be lawful for a company to give any financial assistance for the purpose of an acquisition made or to be made by any person of any shares in the company, or, where the company is a subsidiary, in its holding company.*

This replaces the more broadly drafted wording under s 60 (1) of 1963 Act which referred to direct and indirect financial assistance whether by way of loan, guarantee, the provision of security or otherwise for the purpose of or in connection with the purchase or subscription of shares. In considering whether financial assistance is relevant, it is necessary to examine carefully each of the principal components of the prohibition to establish whether the prohibition has any application. The relevant components are (emphasis added) as follows:

(a) '...for *a company* to give';

(b) '...any *financial assistance*';

(c) '...for the *purpose of an acquisition*';

(d) '...*made or to be made* by any person';

(e) '...of *shares* in the company'; and

(f) '...or, where the company is a subsidiary, in *its holding company*'.

Therefore, for s 82 (2) to apply, the underlying transaction must involve a company, it must involve the giving of financial assistance of some kind and it must have as its purpose the acquisition of that company's shares or those of its holding company. The reference to 'made or to be made' means that the prohibition captures both transactions or arrangements that have already occurred in addition to those which will occur in the future. The meaning of company/holding company, financial assistance, and acquisition are considered in more detail below.

13.2.1 WHAT IS A COMPANY/HOLDING COMPANY?

The term 'company', when used in the 2014 Act, means a body corporate, including a private company limited by shares, whether formed under the 2014 Act or existing. Accordingly, when considering whether the prohibition under s 82 (2) applies to a particular set of circumstances, the nature and identity of the company giving the financial assistance will be relevant.

Pursuant to the 2014 Act parts of the legislation applicable to private limited companies will also apply to designated activity companies ('DACs') and public limited companies ('PLCs') unless specifically disapplied or modified, as set out in s 964 of the 2014 Act (in the case of DACs) and s 1002 of the 2014 Act (in the case of PLCs). The treatment of PLCs in the context of prohibited financial assistance is considered further below.

Whilst s 82 does not have extra-jurisdictional effect so as to apply to the actions of a company incorporated outside of Ireland, the laws of the jurisdiction of incorporation of such foreign entity may equally contain similar restrictions. Most jurisdictions have a prohibition on the giving of financial assistance in some shape or form, however, not all have a means of circumventing it. Foreign law advice should always be sought in such circumstances.

The prohibition on an Irish company giving financial assistance applies not only with respect to the acquisition of its own shares but also to the shares in its holding company. Section 8 of the 2014 Act provides that a company is another company's holding company if, but only if, that other is its subsidiary.

A detailed definition of 'subsidiary' is contained in s 7 (2) of the 2014 Act. Essentially, a company (referred to, for the purposes of s 7, as a 'lower company') is the subsidiary of another (referred to, for the purposes of s 7, as a 'superior company' respectively) if that superior company:

(i)   *is a shareholder or member of it and controls the composition of its board of directors; or*

(ii)   *holds more than half in nominal value of its equity share capital; or*

(iii) *holds more than half in nominal value of its shares carrying voting rights (other than voting rights which arise only in specified circumstances); or*

(iv)   *holds a majority of the shareholders' or members' voting rights in the lower company; or*

(v)   *is a shareholder or member of it and controls alone, pursuant to an agreement with other shareholders or members, a majority of the shareholders' or members' voting rights;*

or

the superior company has the right to exercise a dominant influence over the lower company:

(a)   *by virtue of provisions contained in the lower company's constitution; or*

(b)   *by virtue of a 'control contract'.*

or

(c)   *the superior company has the power to exercise, or actually exercises, dominant influence or control over the lower company; or*

(d)   *the superior company and the lower company are managed by the superior company on a unified basis; or*

(e)   *the lower company is a subsidiary (by virtue of the application of any of the provisions of Section 7) of any company which is the superior company's subsidiary (by virtue of such application).*

A 'control contract' is a contract in writing conferring such a right which is authorised by the constitution of the company in relation to which the right is exercisable and which is permitted by the law under which that company is established. Under s 7 (3), the composition of the lower company's board of directors shall be regarded as being 'controlled' by the superior company if, but only if, the superior company, by the exercise of some power exercisable by it without the consent or concurrence of any other person, can appoint or remove the holders of all or a majority of the directorships.

The 2014 Act also recognises, in the case of a document created before the commencement of the 2014 Act, if that document defines the expression 'subsidiary' by reference to s 155 of the 1963 Act, then the construction provided in respect of subsidiary by the document is not affected by the 2014 Act in the absence of an agreement to the contrary by the parties to the document.

13.2.2   WHAT CONSTITUTES FINANCIAL ASSISTANCE?

Like its predecessor before it, s 82 of the 2014 Act has not sought to define the term 'financial assistance'. Accordingly, the circumstances which pertain in each transaction or arrangement involving the acquisition of shares need to be carefully considered to determine whether the transaction or arrangement falls within the prohibition's ambit. Consequently, one must look to the commercial realities of each transaction in order to ascertain whether there is any element of financial assistance.

The question of what is meant by 'financial assistance' has been considered in a number of leading English cases.

In the case of *Charterhouse Investment Trust Limited v Tempest Diesels Limited* [1986] BCLC 1, in considering the use of the term under the corresponding English statute, Hoffmann J noted:

Typical Example of Financial Assistance

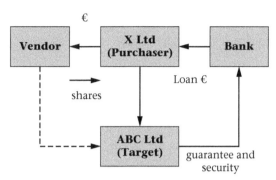

'the words [financial assistance] have no technical meaning and their frame of reference is, in my judgment, the language of ordinary commerce. One must examine the commercial realities of the transaction and decide whether it can properly be described as the giving of financial assistance by the company, bearing in mind that the section is a penal one and should not be strained to cover situations which are not fairly within it.'

Lord Denning M.R., in *Wallersteiner v Moir* [1974] 3 All ER 217, states:

'…you look to the company's money and see what has become of it. You look to the company's shares and see into whose hands they have got. You will soon see if the company's money has been used to finance the purchase.'

A useful rule of thumb to help determine whether an arrangement amounts to 'financial assistance' is to consider whether that arrangement has the effect of reducing the net assets of the company giving such assistance. In other words, is the company doing something and does that something result in the company giving away its assets (including by way of security)? Of course, this is not a definitive test and each case must be considered on its facts.

Financial assistance most frequently arises in leveraged transactions where the shares of a company (often called the target) are being acquired with the purchaser using the assets of the target to finance the acquisition.

In the example above, X Ltd the purchaser is seeking to acquire all of the shares in ABC Ltd (the target) following which ABC Ltd will become its wholly owned subsidiary. X Ltd is borrowing the purchase price from Bank and is proposing to secure those borrowings by way of a guarantee from the target, ABC Ltd, supported by a charge from ABC Ltd over all of its property and assets. This is classic financial assistance terrain. The giving by ABC Ltd of the guarantee and supporting charge constitutes financial assistance prohibited by s 82 (2).

13.2.3   WHAT IS PROHIBITED?

Under the old s 60 regime, the prohibition could apply where the assistance was given 'for the purpose of or in connection with a purchase or subscription made or to be made for any shares in the company…'.

Whilst it may have been relatively straightforward to identify financial assistance given for the 'purpose of' the purchase of or subscription for shares, it was arguably far more difficult to establish where the assistance is given 'in connection with' such a transaction.

For lawyers, another test often used to establish whether assistance was being given in connection with a share acquisition or subscription was to ask whether that purchase or subscription for shares would have proceeded in the absence of such assistance being given. If the answer to the so-called 'but for' test was no, then there is arguably a demonstrable connection between the act constituting the assistance and the share purchase/

subscription. Again, while of assistance to practitioners in weaving their way through the legislation, such a test was not definitive and was far from ideal. More often than not, where any doubt existed as to the application of the prohibition, the default position for many lawyers was simply to validate the transaction in advance using the whitewash procedure.

The 2014 Act has sought to address the issues raised by the uncertain and far-reaching 'in connection with' language by deleting the same. Section 82 (2) makes it clear that the assistance must be 'for the purpose of' an acquisition of shares. Accordingly, in order for a company to provide financial assistance (and fall foul of the prohibition) it must have as its objective assisting an acquisition of shares. It is not sufficient if the assistance is in connection with or ultimately results in an acquisition of shares if it was not the purpose of so doing.

The issue of whether financial assistance was 'for the purpose of' the acquisition of shares was considered in the English case of *Barclays Bank plc v British and Commonwealth Holdings plc.* [1996] 1 BCLC 1. In that case, Aldous J held that even where there is financial assistance in a transaction, it will not breach the statutory prohibition unless it is for the purpose of an acquisition of shares. Arguably, the acquisition of shares does not need to be the dominant purpose in order to come within the prohibition's remit; however, it must nevertheless be one of the purposes of the underlying transaction.

The prohibition on direct or indirect financial assistance has been maintained in s 82 (4) as have the stated categories of assistance by means of a loan or guarantee, the provision of security or otherwise. The inclusion of the or 'otherwise' means that financial assistance is still likely to be construed broadly subject always to the purpose test referred to above.

13.2.4 WHAT IS AN ACQUISITION?

Helpfully, s 82 (1) clarifies the meaning of 'acquisition' as being the acquisition of shares whether by way of a share subscription, purchase, exchange, or otherwise.

Previously, there had been frequent debate among practitioners as to whether certain other transactions involving shares (for example share redemptions) could constitute an acquisition for the purposes of the prohibition under s 60. This has now been clarified by the inclusion of a new exemption under s 82 (6)(d) (which excuses share redemptions made in accordance with s 105) although the inclusion of the words *'or otherwise'* in s 82 (1) could still leave this issue somewhat open to covering other innocent situations.

13.3 Exemptions

Originally, there were only very few exemptions from the prohibition on giving financial assistance under s 60 of the 1963 Act. The enactment of the Investment Funds, Companies and Miscellaneous Provisions Act 2005 (the '2005 Act') introduced a number of additional exempted transactions reflecting some of the problems faced by practitioners over the years when grappling with the prohibition and its applicability to certain cases. Many of these exemptions are repeated under the 2014 Act.

Subsections (5) and (6) of s 82 set out the exemptions which will apply under the new regime. The new principal purpose exemption is considered on its own given that it represents a significant extension of the position under the 1963 Act.

13.3.1 PRINCIPAL PURPOSE

Section 82 (5) of the 2014 Act introduces a significant amendment to the prohibition on financial assistance with the inclusion of a principal purpose and good faith test based largely on the equivalent UK legislation covering financial assistance.

Subsection (2) does not prohibit the giving of financial assistance in relation to the acquisition of shares in a company or its holding company if:

> (a) *the company's principal purpose in giving the assistance is not to give it for the purpose of any such acquisition; or*
>
> (b) *the giving of the assistance for that purpose is only an incidental part of some larger purpose of the company,*

and the assistance is given in good faith in the interests of the company

The section provides therefore, that transactions which are deemed to constitute the giving of financial assistance will be excused from the prohibition if one of the two test under paragraphs (a) and (b) in subsection (5) are met *and* the assistance is given in good faith and in the interests of the company.

While this might seem straightforward enough in its application, unfortunately the concepts of 'principal purpose', 'purpose', and 'good faith and in the interests of the company' as used in subsection (5) are not defined in the 2014 Act. It is therefore likely that practitioners may be faced with challenges when seeking to discern whether this exemption can be relied upon to permit financial assistance to be given in any particular case. Until the provisions of s 82 (5) have been the subject of judicial decision in this jurisdiction, we will have to rely largely on UK cases for guidance.

13.3.2 SUMMARY APPROVAL PROCEDURE

The prohibition under s 82 (2) does not prohibit the giving of financial assistance were such assistance has been approved in advance in accordance with the new Summary Approval Procedure (the 'SAP') laid down in the 2014 Act. This is largely a re-statement of the old 'whitewash' validation procedure detailed under s 60 (2) of the 1963 Act which had the effect of validating what would otherwise have been a prohibited transaction.

However, the SAP, in so far as it applies to prohibited financial assistance under the 2014 Act, differs from the previous 'whitewash' procedure under s 60 (2) in that the SAP is not unique to financial assistance transactions, but is a common validation procedure which may be used to 'bless' a number of specified restricted activities under the 2014 Act.

The SAP as set out in s 203 of the 2014 Act is more simplistic than s 60 (2) in that it gives a finite period for the directors' declaration of solvency. The essential steps to be taken in order to complete the SAP are as follows:

> (a) First, the directors of the company (or a majority of them) must meet to consider its affairs and the nature of the proposed financial assistance, whether it be a loan, the granting of a guarantee or security or some other form of financial assistance (i.e. the 'or otherwise') for the purpose of the acquisition of shares in the company or its holding company and, if satisfied that it is in the best interests of the company to do so, pass the appropriate resolutions approving the transaction or arrangement.
>
> (b) Subject to the directors being satisfied that the company will, after having provided the applicable financial assistance, be able to pay its debts as they fall due, all or a majority of the directors must then make *at the meeting* a declaration of solvency (see paragraph (c) below) confirming that they have carried out a full enquiry into the affairs of the company and, having done so, have formed an opinion that having provided the financial assistance, the company will be able to pay its debts as and when they fall due for the next 12 months.
>
> (c) The declaration of solvency must contain the following prescribed information in respect of the restricted activity:
>
>> (i) the circumstances in which the transaction was entered into;
>>
>> (ii) the nature of the transaction or arrangement;

      (iii)   the person or persons to or for whom the transaction or arrangement is to be made;

      (iv)   the purpose for which the company is entering into the transaction or arrangement;

      (v)   the nature of the benefit accruing to the company (whether directly or indirectly) from entering into the transaction or arrangement; and

      (vi)   critically, a statement that the declarants have made full inquiry into the affairs of the company and that having done so have formed the opinion that the company, having entered into this transaction or arrangement (the 'relevant act'), will be in a position to meet its debts as they fall due for the next 12 months following the relevant act. This reference to 12 months represents a key change from the open ended form of declaration set out under s 60 of the 1963 Act.

(d)   A copy of the declaration of solvency must be given to each shareholder of the company.

(e)   The directors must then seek authority to carry out the restricted activity (the giving of the financial assistance) by means of (i) a special resolution or, (ii) as an alternative, by way of unanimous written resolution of *all* the members of the company (2014 Act, s 193 (1)) which resolution must be passed not more than 12 months prior to the entry into of the restricted activity. In the case of a written resolution, a copy of the declaration of solvency must be annexed thereto (2014 Act, s 202 (1)).

(f)   A copy of the declaration of solvency must then be filed in the Companies Registration Office ('CRO') within 21 days of the restricted activity taking place (i.e. the financial assistance being given) (2014 Act, s 203 (3)).

(g)   A copy of the resolution of the members approving the giving of the assistance (with, in the case of a written resolution, a copy of the declaration of solvency annexed thereto) must be forwarded to CRO within 15 days of the passing or making of the resolution (2014 Act, s 198 (1)).

It is worth considering further the obligations imposed on directors in the context of making the declaration of solvency referred to above. The statement to be given by the directors essentially constitutes an 'opinion' to be formed by them as to the company's solvency going forward following the entry into of the restricted activity. This opinion has always been a source of concern for directors making the declaration and frequently gave rise to queries as to whether such an opinion constituted a 'guarantee' by them of the company's future solvency.

Clearly, this statement was only ever intended to be a reasonable assessment made on the facts and circumstances known to the directors at the time they make the declaration. For this reason, directors often sought to support their opinion with cashflow projections, auditors' reports, or other appropriate financial information which, although not legally required, assisted the declarants in forming the required opinion.

The directors are not being asked to speculate as to what might happen in the future other than by reference to the facts known to them at that time. In making the declaration, they are not guaranteeing that the company will be able to pay its debts in full as they fall due. Directors risk incurring liability only if, having regard to the position at the time they make the declaration, they did not have reasonable grounds for believing that the company, having carried out the transactions, will be able to pay its debts as they fall due.

Section 203 (2) is of further assistance in this regard in that it clarifies that:

For the purposes of a declaration under this section, in determining whether or not a company will be able to pay or discharge its debts and other liabilities in full, the declarants shall not be required to assume (in circumstances where the following are relevant) either that the company will be called upon to pay moneys on foot of a guarantee given or, as the case may be, that security given will be realised

In addition to the obligations imposed on directors with respect to the company's solvency, the SAP also requires the board to consider the nature of the benefit accruing to the company (whether directly or indirectly) from entering into the transaction. This was not expressly set out under the requirements of s 60 (2) but was always an implicit part of the approvals process.

Typically, the passing of the board resolution, the making of the declaration of solvency and the passing of special resolution are all completed on the day the assistance documents are to be completed. There should, in principle, be no logistical reason why this may not be done, provided the timing is right.

Practitioners should note that the SAP must occur *before* the financial assistance is provided, as the procedure cannot be availed of retrospectively. Any financial assistance the subject of the SAP must be given within 12 months of the passing of the special resolution. Otherwise, the procedure must be undertaken *de novo*.

The courts have traditionally required strict compliance with the validation procedure and this is almost certainly likely to continue.

Finally, it is also worth noting that a company with a 'restricted person' as a director or secretary cannot use the SAP except in respect of a voluntary winding up.

13.3.3   OTHER EXEMPTIONS

In addition to the exemptions under the principal purpose and the SAP, other exemptions may also be relevant to facilitating what would otherwise be a prohibited transaction under s 82 of the 2014 Act. These exemptions are detailed in the subsections of s 82.

13.3.3.1   Payment of dividends

The payment by a company of a dividend or making by it of any distribution out of profits of the company available for distribution does not constitute financial assistance (s 82 (6)(b)). Whilst this exception is self-explanatory of course, it requires any dividend intended to be paid to be properly declared and to comply with all technicalities and formalities under the 2014 Act.

13.3.3.2   Payment of debts

The discharge by a company of a liability lawfully incurred by it (s 82 (6)(c)) does not constitute financial assistance. The use of the word 'lawfully' means that unless the obligation is enforceable in the first instance, this exemption cannot be availed of.

13.3.3.3   Share redemptions

The purchase, under s 105, or redemption under ss 105 or 108 of the 2014 Act, of own shares or the giving of financial assistance, by means of a loan or guarantee, the provision of security or otherwise, for the purpose of such purchase or redemption (s 82 (6)(d)) is not prohibited. This addresses the issue which gave rise to queries under s 60 as to whether share redemptions were caught by the prohibition.

13.3.3.4   Ordinary course of business

Where the lending of money is part of the ordinary business of the company, the lending of money by a company in the ordinary course of its business does not amount to financial assistance (s 82 (6)(e)). In general, this exemption is of limited use given that it is applied strictly and, consequently, really only of benefit to banks and other institutions involved in the lending of money in their day-to-day business.

13.3.3.5   Employee share schemes

There is an exemption for the provision by a company, in accordance with any scheme for the time being in force, of money for the purchase of, or subscription for, fully-paid shares in the company or its holding company, being a purchase or subscription of or for shares to be held by or for the benefit of employees or former employees of the company or of any subsidiary of the company including any person who is or was a director holding a salaried employment or office in the company or any subsidiary of the company (s 82 (6)(f)).

13.3.3.6   Loans to employees (non-directors) to acquire shares

The making by a company of loans to persons, other than directors, bona fide in the employment of the company or any subsidiary of the company with a view to enabling those persons to purchase or subscribe for fully-paid shares in the company or its holding company to be held by themselves as beneficial owners thereof is not prohibited (s 82 (6)(g)).

13.3.3.7   Refinancings

There has been considerable discussion amongst practitioners as to whether the existing refinancing exemption contained in s 60 (12)(c) was capable of being relied upon in situations where a 'guarantee' has been given (and previously whitewashed). Unfortunately, the language used in that provision referred to 'security' only whereas the prohibition contained in s 60 (1) referred to the provision of *guarantees* and security. Although it is nonsensical to argue that the legislators sought to distinguish between guarantees and security (particularly when one considers the rationale behind the prohibition in the first place – maintenance of company assets for the benefit of others) nevertheless, many practitioners adopted a cautious approach and in the main were unwilling to rely on the refinancing exemption in order to avoid a re-whitewashing.

This has now been resolved with the new exception (s 82 (6)(h)) which permits the giving of financial assistance:

(a)   by means of a loan or guarantee, the provision of security or otherwise to discharge the liability under, or effect that which is commonly known as a refinancing of, any arrangement or transaction that gave rise to the provision of financial assistance, being financial assistance referred to in subsection (2) *that has already been given* by the company in accordance with the SAP or s 60 (2) of the 1963 Act; or

(b)   by means of any subsequent loan or guarantee, provision of security or otherwise to effect a refinancing of: (A) refinancing referred to subparagraph (a) above; or (B) refinancing referred to in this subparagraph that has been previously effected (and this subparagraph shall be read as permitting the giving of financial assistance to effect such subsequent refinancing any number of times).

13.3.3.8   Representations and warranties in share purchase transactions

Again, this repeats the exemption introduced by the 2005 Act to permit the making or giving by a company of representations, warranties, or indemnities to a person (or any affiliate or connected person) who has purchased or subscribed for, or proposes to purchase or subscribe for, shares in the company or its holding company for the purpose of or in connection with that purchase or subscription (s 82 (6)(i)).

13.3.3.9   Fees and expenses of advisers in subscriptions/acquisitions

Other exemptions introduced by the 2005 Act (and repeated under the 2014 Act) largely dealt with the payment by a company of fees and expenses connected with share purchases/subscriptions. In the case of s 82 (6)(j) this expressly covers fees and expenses of (i) advisers to any subscriber for, or purchaser of, shares in the company that are incurred in connection with his or her subscription for, or purchase of, such shares; or (ii) the advisers to the company or its holding company that are incurred in connection with that subscription or purchase.

13.3.3.10 Expenses in share listings

The incurring of any expense by a company in order to facilitate the admission to, or the continuance of, a trading facility of securities of its holding company on a stock exchange or securities market, including the expenses associated with the preparation and filing of documents required under the laws of any jurisdiction in which the securities in question are admitted to trading or are afforded a trading facility is not prohibited (s 82 (6)(k)).

13.3.3.11 Takeovers

The following situations do not constitute 'financial assistance':

(a) the incurring of any expenses by a company in order to ensure compliance by the company or its holding company with the Irish Takeover Panel Act 1997 or an instrument thereunder or any measures for the time being adopted by the State to implement Directive 2004/25/EC of the European Parliament and of the Council of 21 April 2004 on takeover bids (s 82 (6)(l)); and

(b) the reimbursement by a private limited subsidiary of an offeree (within the meaning of the Irish Takeover Panel Act 1997) of expenses of an offeror (within the meaning of that Act) pursuant to an agreement approved by, or on terms approved by, the Irish Takeover Panel (s 82 (6)(m)).

13.3.3.12 Payment of commissions and fee on allotment of shares by plcs

In connection with an allotment of shares by a parent public company, the payment by a private limited subsidiary of that company of commissions, not exceeding 10% of the money received in respect of such allotment, to intermediaries, and the payment by that subsidiary of professional fees is not prohibited (s 82 (6)(n)).

13.3.3.13 Employee share ownership schemes/trusts

To the extent that provision of this kind is not authorised by paragraph (f) or (g) of subsection (6), the provision of financial assistance by a holding company or a subsidiary of it in connection with the holding company or subsidiary purchasing or subscribing for shares in the holding company on behalf of:

(a) the present or former employees of the holding company or any subsidiary of it;

(b) an employees' share scheme; or

(c) an employee share ownership trust referred to in s 519 of the Taxes Consolidation Act 1997 (s 82 (6)(o)), is not prohibited.

The exemptions in subsection 6 (f), (g) and (o) around employee share schemes broadly mirror the changes brought about by the 2005 Act.

13.4 Consequences of a Breach of Section 82

Failure to comply with s 82 is a criminal offence and any financial assistance granted in breach of s 82 is voidable.

13.4.1   CRIMINAL LIABILITY

Section 82 (11) of the 2014 Act provides that if a company contravenes s 82, the company and any officer of it who is in default shall be guilty of a category 2 offence under the 2014 Act. An officer of the company convicted of a category 2 offence can potentially be liable on summary conviction to a class A fine, imprisonment for up to 12 months, or both and on conviction on indictment to a fine of up to €50,000, imprisonment of up to five years, or both.

The foregoing represents a strengthening of the sanctions faced by officers found guilty of a breach of the section.

13.4.2   VOIDABILITY

Section 82 (9) of the 2014 Act provides that if a company enters into a transaction in contravention of s 82, such transaction shall be voidable at the instance of the company against any person (whether a party to the transaction or not) who 'had notice of the facts' which constitute such contravention.

This is most likely to arise in the context of the liquidation of a company. A liquidator, appointed to the company, will likely review the activities of the company prior to his appointment and will seek to establish whether there have been any breaches of company law.

The question of notice was considered in *Bank of Ireland v Rockfield Limited* [1979] IR 21, High Court, 2 June 1987, where the Court heard that had the bank inspected the documents it would have realised that there was a financial assistance issue. However, it did not do so. The Supreme Court (Kenny J) held that in that case that the bank was required to have actual notice (meaning that the bank had been informed either verbally or in writing that part of the advance was to be used to acquire shares in the defendant company or were aware of facts from which they must have inferred part of the loan advance was to be used for that purpose) of the facts constituting the problem and not constructive notice.

In the case of *Re: Northside Motors, Eddison v Allied Irish Banks Ltd* (unreported, High Court, 24 July 1985), the bank knew the procedure had to be followed, but advanced the money before the financial assistance process was put in place. Thus it was clearly on notice and the transaction was voidable.

In *Lombard and Ulster v Bank of Ireland,* Unreported, High Court, 2 June 1987, the Bank was told that the 'whitewash' procedure had been complied with when in reality it had not. The bank was unaware of this and the company was not allowed to avoid the security created in those circumstances. Costello J held that for the bank to have notice they must have actual notice.

An earlier draft of the Companies Bill proposed that for the purposes of s 82 (9), the criteria for an offending transaction being voidable as against any person be on the basis of 'actual or imputed' notice of the facts constituting the breach rather than 'actual' as indicated in the earlier cases which had considered the issue. However, the reference to 'imputed' was dropped at an early Committee stage and did not make it into the final Bill as enacted.

13.5   Public Limited Companies and their Subsidiaries

There is a general policy against PLCs giving financial assistance in connection with the purchase of their own shares. Other than in very limited circumstances, a PLC cannot give financial assistance. The exemptions afforded to private companies are, in the main, not available to a PLC.

PLCs can only use the SAP to effect a members' voluntary winding up, treatment of pre-acquisition profits, and for the making of loans to directors/connected persons.

Section 82 (7) provides that subject to subsection (8), the SAP cannot be used by a private subsidiary company to provide finance assistance for the purposes of an acquisition of shares in its parent PLC. It is therefore common to include in the declaration of solvency under the SAP a statement to the effect that the company carrying out the restricted activity is not a public company subsidiary.

Subsection (8) allows the Minister for Finance, by regulation, to specify those circumstances in which a private limited company may avail itself of the SAP.

13.6   Conclusion

The provisions of s 82 are complex. Any breach of the section (whether inadvertent or not) may have significant consequences for those participating, be they officers entering into arrangements involving the acquisition of shares or the financial institutions funding them. The financial propriety of companies and the duties and liabilities imposed upon the directors managing them are increasingly coming under the spotlight. All this imposes even greater responsibility on legal practitioners to identify the applicability of s 82 and to successfully guide their clients through the many pitfalls therein contained.

APPENDIX

KEY CHANGES BETWEEN THE POSITION UNDER THE 1963 ACT AND THE 2014 ACT

	1963 Act	2014 Act
Prohibition on the giving of financial assistance		
Prohibition	s 60 (1) - *'for the purpose of or in connection with…'*	s 82 (2) – *'for the purpose of…'*
Definition of 'financial assistance'	Not defined	Not defined
Categories of 'financial assistance'	Loans, guarantees, provision of security or otherwise	Loans, guarantees, provision of security or otherwise
Definition of 'acquisition'	Not defined	s 82 (1) *'acquisition'*, in relation to shares, means acquisition by subscription, purchase, exchange, or otherwise.
Exemptions		
Principal purpose exemption	Not applicable	Yes – s 82(5) – if: (a) company's principal purpose in giving the assistance is not to give it for the purpose of any acquisition; *or* (b) giving of the assistance for that purpose is only an incidental part of some larger purpose of the company, *and* assistance is given in good faith in the interests of company.

'Whitewash' procedure	Yes – s 60 (2) – Sets out s 60 whitewash validation procedure particular to financial assistance transactions.	Yes – s 82 (6)(a)/s 203 Sets out a new 'Summary Approval Procedure' (SAP) used to validate certain restricted activities including financial assistance. Declaration of directors no longer required to be a 'statutory' declaration.
Payment of dividend or distribution	Yes	Yes – s 82 (6)(b) Out of profits available for distribution
Discharge of a lawful liability	Yes	Yes – s 82 (6)(c)
Share redemptions	No	Yes – s 82 (6)(d)/s 105 or 108
Lending of money in ordinary business	Yes	Yes – s 82 (6)(e) Where part of ordinary business of the company
Employee share schemes	Yes	Yes – s 82 (6)(f)
Making of loans to employees, other than directors, to enable them to purchase or subscribe for fully-paid shares	Yes	Yes – s 82 (6)(g)
Refinancings	Yes – Subject to query with respect to 'guarantees'	Yes – s 82 (6)(h)
Making or giving of representations, warranties, or indemnities to a purchaser or subscriber for or of shares	Yes	Yes – s 82 (6)(i)
Payment by a company of fees and expenses of the advisers of any subscriber for shares in the company or its holding company that are incurred in connection with that subscription	Yes	Yes – s 82 (6)(j)
Incurring of fees, commissions, and expenses	Yes	Yes – s 82 (6)(k), (l), (m), (n)

In connection with the holding company or subsidiary purchasing or subscribing for shares in the holding company on behalf of: (i) present or former employees; (ii) an employees' share scheme within the meaning of the Companies (Amendment) Act 1983; or (iii) an employee share ownership trust referred to in s 519 of the Taxes Consolidation Act 1997	Yes	Yes – s82 (6)(o)
Consequences of a breach		
Voidability	Yes Voidable at the instance of the company against any person who had actual notice of the facts.	Yes – s 82 (9) Voidable at the instance of the company against any person who had actual notice of the facts.
Criminal sanctions	Yes Company acts in contravention of section, every officer of the company who is in default shall be liable: (a) on conviction on indictment, to imprisonment for a term not exceeding two years or to a fine not exceeding £500, or to both; or (b) on summary conviction, to imprisonment for a term not exceeding six months or to a fine not exceeding £100, or to both.	Yes – s 82 (11) Company and any officer of it who is in default shall be guilty of a *category 2 offence*. Officer can potentially be liable on summary conviction to a class A fine, imprisonment for up to 12 months, or both and on conviction on indictment to a fine of up to €50,000, imprisonment of up to five years, or both.

PART 2

PARTNERSHIPS

CHAPTER 14

PARTNERSHIP LAW

14.1 Nature of Partnerships

14.1.1 IMPORTANCE OF PARTNERSHIP LAW

14.1.1.1 General

Partnerships occupy an important part of Irish business life for a number of reasons. First, partnership is the default form of business organisation in the sense that any time two or more people carry on a business venture without forming a company, they will invariably be partners. This point is highlighted by the case of *Joyce v Morrissey* [1998] TLR 707 which involved The Smiths, the 1980s rock band. A dispute arose about the sharing of the band's profits between, on the one side, the lead singer (Morrissey) and lead guitar player (Johnnie Marr) and, on the other side, the drummer and bass guitarist. Although the four may never have thought that they were creating a partnership when they formed the band, it was held that they were carrying on business as partners and therefore the rules in the Partnership Act, 1890 (the '1890 Act') about the division of profits applied to them. In that case, it meant that all four were entitled to share the band's profits equally and the court rejected Morrissey's and Marr's claim that as they were the main creative force behind the band, they were entitled to a greater share of the profits.

In most cases, any time two or more people carry on business together without doing it through the medium of a registered company, they constitute a partnership and are subject to partnership law. Indeed, even where two or more companies are involved in business together, they will be subject to partnership law if they do not form a special purpose joint venture company for the project.

The second reason partnerships are important is that they form an integral part of Irish business life because there is a large section of Irish business which is effectively required to use partnerships to operate. This is because professionals such as lawyers, doctors, dentists, vets, and accountants are not allowed to incorporate. Thus, any time two or more such professionals carry on business together, they will invariably be partners.

The final reason why partnerships occupy an important role in Irish business life is because they provide significant tax, accounting, and disclosure advantages over companies. For example, in a company, both corporation tax and income tax are paid in respect of the profits of the enterprise, i.e. corporation tax is paid on the company's profits and income tax is paid on the company's dividends paid to shareholders. However, a partnership is 'see-through' for tax purposes and therefore there is only one point at which tax is payable on the enterprise's profits, i.e. income tax is paid by the partners on the share of the profits received by them and no tax is paid by the partnership. As regards disclosure and accounting advantages, partnerships do not generally have to file their accounts publicly while companies do and it is considerably easier and cheaper for partners to subscribe and withdraw capital from a partnership than it is for shareholders in a limited company, thus making partnerships popular venture capital vehicles.

For the foregoing reasons, it follows that a solicitor, whether in a large corporate practice or a general practice, will encounter clients who either consciously or unconsciously are in business partnerships and who will require advice on the applicable law. In addition, the solicitors themselves may be partners in a law firm, since approximately one out of every four solicitors is a partner in a law firm. Perhaps the most important aspect of partnership law is the fact that the Partnership Act, 1890 implies standard terms into every partnership unless the parties agree otherwise. Since many of these implied terms are inappropriate for modern partnerships, it is imperative that every partner and his legal adviser be aware of those terms and have a written partnership agreement which replaces them with more appropriate terms.

14.1.1.2   Partnership versus company

It is useful at this juncture to compare partnerships with the main form of business association in Ireland, the registered company. A partnership, unlike a company, is not a separate legal entity from its members, thus explaining why a company is taxed separately from its owner shareholders while a partnership is not taxed but the partners are taxed. Similarly, it is to be noted that partnerships are not required to go through any registration process to be formed, while companies have to be registered in the Companies Registration Office. On the other hand, the main advantage that limited companies have over partnerships is that the shareholders have limited liability while partners have unlimited liability. Yet it should be remembered that partners may themselves be limited liability companies and in this way have an effective cap on their liability. In addition, in many companies (particularly in small businesses), limited liability is largely illusory because of the common requirement for directors and often their spouses to provide personal guarantees to banks and other creditors.

In addition, as is noted hereunder (see **14.6** below), there are two other types of partnerships in which some of the partners have limited liability, namely the limited partnership and the investment limited partnership. In this section, however, we concentrate on ordinary partnerships.

14.1.1.3   Why is it important to determine whether a partnership exists?

In this section, we look at the rules for determining whether a partnership has come into existence as well as some of the formalities for the operation of partnerships. The question of whether a partnership exists is important, because a partner is liable for the losses which his co-partner causes in carrying on the partnership business, even though he had no knowledge of his co-partner's activities and this includes situations where the co-partner has defrauded clients of the business. On the other hand, a partner is also entitled to an equal share of the partnership profits and for this reason, in a profitable business, it would be an advantage to be a partner. Another situation where it is important to establish whether a partnership exists is where a potential plaintiff is faced with a penniless defendant. If the defendant is carrying on business with a richer business colleague, it would be useful to establish that his richer business colleague is his partner and therefore jointly liable for the damages suffered by the potential plaintiff. Clearly, in these types of situations the question of whether a partnership exists will be of importance.

14.1.2   RELEVANT LAW

Much of the law relating to partnerships is to be found in the Partnership Act, 1890. The 1890 Act was a codification of the law of partnership as it had developed up to 1890. However, it is important to note that the Act does not provide a complete code of partnership law, and indeed s 46 specifically provides that:

> *The rules of equity and of common law applicable to partnership shall continue in force except so far as they are inconsistent with the express provisions of this Act.*

Therefore, regard must always be had to the case law from both before and after the 1890 Act. Any reference to legislation in this chapter is a reference to the Partnership Act 1890 unless otherwise stated.

14.1.3 DEFINITION OF PARTNERSHIP

14.1.3.1 General

The definition of a partnership is to be found in s 1 (1) of the 1890 Act which states: 'Partnership is the relation which subsists between persons carrying on a business in common with a view of profit'. Where people carry on business in common through the medium of a company, they are specifically excluded from being partners by s 1 (2) of the 1890 Act. It should be noted that a written partnership agreement is not a prerequisite for the existence of a partnership since the court will have regard to the true contract and intention of the parties as appearing from the whole facts of the case.

To satisfy the definition of partnership, two or more persons must actually be carrying on a business. It follows from this that an agreement to run a business in the future does not constitute an immediate partnership, nor does the taking of preliminary steps to enable a business to be run. Similarly, two or more people cannot agree that they were partners retrospectively unless they were actually carrying on business at the relevant time. In *Macken v Revenue Commissioners* [1962] IR 302, the parties signed a partnership agreement in the month of April, but it provided that the partnership 'shall be deemed to have commenced' in January of that same year. The High Court held that the partnership did not commence until the parties actually started carrying on business together which was in the month of April.

The definition of partnership in s 1 (1) also requires the parties to be carrying on business with a 'view of profit'. In *McCarthaigh v Daly* [1985] IR 73, the respondent, a prominent Cork-based solicitor, was involved in a rather clever tax loophole which has since been closed off by the Revenue Commissioners. Under that scheme, Mr Daly agreed to contribute capital of £50 to a limited partnership connected with the Metropole Hotel in Cork in the tax year 1977–78. However, the arrangement was completely uneconomical and was clearly designed to make a loss, rather than a profit, which loss was to be used to reduce the income tax of Mr Daly on his personal income as a solicitor. Mr Daly sought to set off his share of the losses of the limited partnership which amounted to £2,000 against his personal income tax as a solicitor. O'Hanlon J in giving his decision was constrained by procedural rules. It is clear that, if it were not for the constraints of these procedural rules, O'Hanlon J would not have held that this arrangement constituted a partnership because of the absence of the 'view of profit'.

In addition to the definition of partnership in s 1 (1) of the 1890 Act, s 2 of the 1890 Act lays down certain rules for determining the existence of a partnership. These rules include the following:

(a) joint or common ownership of property 'does not of itself create a partnership' even where profits from the property are shared (s 2(1));

(b) the sharing of gross returns does not of itself create a partnership (s 2(2)). The difference between gross returns and net profits is illustrated by the example of a person who sells goods on commission for another. Such a person will receive a percentage of the gross sales or gross returns of the business. However, if he was to receive a percentage of the profits, this would involve the additional step of calculating the costs and overheads which would have to be deducted from the gross returns to calculate the profits, if any, of the business. Thus, a percentage of the gross returns could be valuable while a percentage of the net profits might be nothing; and

(c) the receipt of a share of profits is prima facie evidence of partnership (s 2(3)), but it does not of itself make the recipient a partner.

14.1.3.2   Co-ownership agreements

An important issue in recent times has been the question of the status of co-ownership agreements between investors in property and whether these are in fact partnerships.

The very act of simply co-owning property with another person or company does not of itself constitute the co-owners as partners. Indeed, this principle is enshrined in s 2 (1) of the Partnership Act, 1890.

> *Joint tenancy, tenancy in common, joint property, common property, or part ownership does not of itself create a partnership as to anything so held or owned, whether the tenants or owners do or do not share any profits made by the use thereof.*

However, a considerable amount of confusion has been caused regarding property investments in this country in the past few years because of undue reliance on this section. But s 2 (1) of the Partnership Act, 1890 must not be looked at in isolation. Even the section itself does not state that co-owners of property cannot be partners. It simply says that co-ownership does not of itself lead to partnership. This means that to prove a partnership exists it is not sufficient simply to show that two or more people own property jointly. That is what s 2 (1) means; it does *not* mean that an investment *is prevented* from being a partnership because the investors happen to co-own the property which is the subject of the investment.

To determine whether a partnership exists between people who happen to co-own property, s 2 (1) is only a small part of the equation. The most important thing to consider is whether the property project satisfies the definition of partnership in s 1 (1) of the Partnership Act, 1890. As we have seen at **14.1.3.1**, this simply requires two or more people to be carrying on business in common with a view to profit. The fact that the arrangement or investment may be termed a 'co-ownership' rather than a partnership is irrelevant. In the words of Lord Halsbury in *Adam v Newbigging* (1888) 13 AC 308 at 315:

> If a partnership in fact exists, a community of interest in the adventure being carried on in fact, no concealment of name, no verbal equivalent for the ordinary phrases of profit or loss, no indirect expedient for enforcing control over the adventure will prevent the substance and reality of the transaction being adjudged to be partnership. . . and no phrasing of it by dextrous draftsmen. . . will avail to avert the legal consequence of the contract.

We have noted that s 2 (1) means that co-ownership of property is not sufficient in itself to make the co-owners partners. Therefore, something more is required than simple co-ownership of property for there to be a partnership. However, very little more is required to establish that people who enter a property investment together with a view to making a profit are in fact carrying on a business for the purposes of s 1 (1) so as to be partners.

The real aim of s 2 (1) is to establish that those people who become co-owners almost by chance are not partners just because they happen to be co-owners of property. For example this would apply to people who become co-owners through an inheritance and who are not carrying on any business with the property—the very fact of co-ownership does not make them partners. However, where the property is simply the means by which two or more people carry on business or an investment together, s 2 (1) does not grant them immunity from being partners.

It follows that most co-ownership agreements which are being entered into by investors in the current climate *are* in fact partnership agreements. As such, the default partnership agreement in the Partnership Act, 1890 with all its implied terms (referred to at **14.1.7** below) will apply to them, unless their agreement contracts out of those terms.

14.1.4   NUMBER OF PARTNERS

The Companies Act 2014, s 1435 (1) prescribes that the maximum number of persons who may be members of a partnership is 20. However, pursuant to s 1435 (1)(c) solicitors and accountants are not subject to this limitation and also exempt under this section are limited partnerships if they are formed for the purpose of thoroughbred-horse breeding and also limited partnerships which have no more than 50 partners that are formed for venture capital purposes.

14.1.5 TYPES OF PARTNERSHIPS AND PARTNERS

Every partnership is either a partnership at will (informal partnership) or a formal partnership (or, as it is sometimes called, a fixed-term partnership). A partnership at will is one which may be dissolved by any one partner at any time by notice (see 1890 Act, ss 26 (1) and 32 (c)). Every partnership is presumed to be a partnership at will unless there is an express or implicit agreement to the contrary between the partners (*Murphy v Power* [1923] 1 IR 68). Where there is an express or implicit agreement to exclude the right of a partner to dissolve the partnership by notice, the resulting partnership is known as a formal partnership (fixed-term partnership).

The exclusion of this right is often achieved implicitly, e.g. by the agreement that the partnership will last for a fixed term and the majority of formal partnerships are such fixed-term partnerships.

In addition to there being different types of partnerships, there may also be different types of partners. Two types of partners are worthy of specific mention, i.e. a dormant partner and a partner by holding out. A dormant partner is a partner who plays no active role in the business of the partnership. However, the term has no legal significance since a dormant partner has the same rights and liabilities as any other partner and so he is entitled to an equal share of the profits of the firm, he is equally liable for the losses of the firm and he is entitled to take part in the management of the firm.

A partner by holding out is in fact a contradiction in terms, since he or she is not a true partner but is held out as if he or she were a partner. The most common example of a partner by holding out is a salaried partner. While the term 'salaried partner' is not a term of art and some persons who are called salaried partners may in fact be true partners, usually a salaried partner is not a true partner but is held out as if he or she were a true partner. Typically a salaried partner is a person who operates in the middle rank of professional partnerships between true partners and salaried employees. The salaried partner is held out to the world as a partner yet he receives a salary and sometimes a bonus by way of remuneration, but he does not receive a share of the profits like a normal partner. Typically he is also not entitled to the other rights of partnership, e.g. to vote at partners' meetings, to dissolve the firm etc. However, as regards outsiders who deal with the firm, the salaried partner is as good as a partner. This is because he is held out to be a 'partner' and thus will be liable to third parties who relied on the fact that he was a partner under the principle of holding out as a partner, which is considered below (see **14.3.4**). For this reason, it is advisable for a salaried partner to receive an indemnity from the partners in respect of such potential liabilities to third parties. The case of *McAleenan v AIG (Europe) Limited* [2010] IEHC 128 involved the plaintiff who was an employee of the notorious solicitor, Michael Lynn, who had, at the time of the case, been struck off by the Law Society for fraud and had left the country. During the period of time when Ms McAleenan and Mr Lynn had been in practice together, she had represented herself to the Law Society and the firm's insurers as Mr Lynn's partner, even though he had at all times remained an employee, who was subject to PAYE and employee's PRSI. The case concerned her application for a declaration that the insurers of the practice, AIG, were not entitled to avoid her insurance policy on the grounds of her misrepresentation that she was a partner. In the High Court, Laffoy J considered the law applicable to partners by holding out and the manner in which they are liable as partners:

> 'By so holding himself out, or being held out, [the partner by holding out] may become liable to third parties as a partner, whilst not being a true partner, either by reason of s 14 (1) of the Partnership Act 1890, or by application of the doctrine of estoppel by representation. Twomey, Partnership Law, (2000) (Dublin, Bloomsbury Professional) at para 7.10 explains:

"Like the expression 'salaried partner', the expression 'partner by holding out' is a contradiction in terms, since it is used to describe someone who is not in fact a partner. Rather, this expression denotes a person who, because of his action or in-action, is held to be liable to third parties as if he was a partner."

I would respectfully agree with the above quotation insofar as it refers to a partner by holding out.'

On the facts of the case, Laffoy J held that AIG was entitled to avoid the insurance policy on the grounds of the misrepresentation by Ms. McAleenan of her status in the firm. The Court held that it was a material and reckless misrepresentation, which under the terms of the policy, entitled AIG to avoid the policy.

14.1.6   BUSINESS NAME OF PARTNERSHIP

Partnerships commonly trade under a name other than the names of the partners. This has implications under the Registration of Business Names Act 1963 since if the business of a partnership is carried on under a name which does not consist solely of the surnames of all the partners, then the firm must register this name as a business name (Registration of Business Names Act 1963, ss 3 (1)(a) and (4) and it must publish the true names of the partners on the stationery of the firm (Registration of Business Names Act 1963, s 18).

14.1.7   WHY A WRITTEN PARTNERSHIP AGREEMENT IS ESSENTIAL

The 1890 Act sets out certain basic terms of the partnership agreement which will apply to every partnership, save in so far as they are modified or excluded by the partners. In this sense, the 1890 Act may be viewed as a default partnership agreement whose terms apply to every partnership if they are not excluded. For this reason, it is crucial for partners and their advisers to be aware of all of the rights and duties which are implied by the 1890 Act and then to decide which of them are appropriate for the partnership and which of them should be modified by the terms of the partnership agreement.

This is particularly so because it is fair to say that the majority of the terms of the 1890 Act are wholly inappropriate for most partnerships. It is for this reason that it is crucial that most partnerships have a written partnership agreement and that such a partnership agreement expressly provides terms which are contrary to those contained in the 1890 Act. A few examples will illustrate how inappropriate the 1890 Act is for most partnerships.

(a)   There is no right under the default partnership agreement to expel a partner. Thus, no matter how unprofessional or negligent or belligerent a partner is, his co-partners may not expel him from the partnership in the absence of a right of expulsion.

(b)   In every partnership at will, regardless of the number of partners in the firm, be it two or 32, any one partner in the firm may dissolve the partnership by simply arriving at a partners' meeting and giving notice orally that the firm is dissolved.

(c)   If a partner dies, the firm will automatically dissolve under the terms of s 33 of the 1890 Act and may be wound up at the wish of any one partner. There is no general right in law to acquire a deceased partner's share, so if the surviving partners want the firm to continue, they have to enter negotiations with the deceased partner's estate to purchase this share. Therefore, a written partnership agreement should provide that the death of a partner will not dissolve the firm but instead that the deceased partner's share may be purchased by the surviving partners pursuant to an agreed valuation mechanism.

(d)   There is no general power to retire under partnership law. Thus, the only possibility for a partner who wishes to retire in the absence of a retirement provision is for him to dissolve the partnership. This is a drastic solution and accordingly it is important to have a provision allowing a partner to retire.

These are but four examples of why a carefully drafted partnership agreement is necessary to avoid the full rigours of the 1890 Act (see further Twomey, *Partnership Law,* paras 21.03 *et seq.*). The only way to ensure against these and other rights which may be inappropriate in a partnership is to have a carefully drafted provision in the partnership agreement excluding those rights. Finally, in considering the application of the terms of a partnership agreement to the day-to-day running of a firm, it is important to bear in mind the terms of the 1890 Act, s 19. Section 19 provides that the rights of partners may be varied by express or implied consent. For this reason, in some circumstances, it may be prudent for a partner who is conducting himself contrary to his express rights under the partnership agreement to clarify in writing that such action is not to be construed as an implied variation of the terms of the partnership agreement.

14.2   Partners' Rights *Inter Se*

14.2.1   INTRODUCTION

Once it is established that a partnership is in existence, the next step is to determine the respective rights of the partners *inter se*, and in this section consideration is given to these rights. It has been noted that the 1890 Act operates for partnerships in much the same way that Table A of the Companies Act 1963 operates for companies, since in the absence of any other agreement between the partners, the terms of their partnership agreement may be found in the 1890 Act. It has also been seen that some of these default rules are inappropriate for modern partnerships and therefore the partners may wish to have a written partnership agreement which excludes them. Reference has already been made to one of those default rules, namely the right of any one partner to dissolve the partnership by giving notice. Reference will now be made to the other important default rules in the 1890 Act regarding the internal operations of a partnership.

14.2.2   MANAGEMENT OF THE PARTNERSHIP

Section 24 (5) of the 1890 Act states that, subject to contrary agreement, express or implied, '[e]very partner may take part in the management of the partnership business'. If the management structure of a particular partnership is to be different from the equality of partners presumed by s 24 (5), then express agreement should be made. For example, in the large professional partnerships, it is usual for the partnership agreement to provide for the management of the firm to be delegated to a management committee.

14.2.2.1   Decisions of the partners

Section 24 (8) of the 1890 Act says that (subject to contrary agreement, express or implied):

> *any differences arising as to ordinary matters connected with the partnership business may be decided by a majority of the partners, but no change may be made in the nature of the partnership business without the consent of all the partners.*

It should be noted that the expression 'majority of the partners' means a majority in number and not on the basis of capital contribution, profit-share, or otherwise. It follows that under the default partnership agreement, a simple majority of the partners is required to take a decision regarding ordinary partnership matters. If the partners desire a different voting system, an express term must be put in the partnership agreement. In the case of *Highley v Walker* (1910) 26 TLR 685, the taking-on of one of the partner's sons as an apprentice in the partnership business was regarded as an ordinary matter within the terms of s 24 (8) and therefore it only required a decision of the majority of the partners and not a unanimous decision of the partners. If there is an equality of votes between the partners, the law provides that a decision is deemed not to be taken and the status quo is preserved (*Clements v Norris* (1878) 8 Ch D 129).

14.2.2.2   Restrictions on majority rule

There are two main limitations imposed on the ability of the majority of the partners to bind the whole firm.

First, partners are under a fiduciary duty to each other and so must exercise their powers for the benefit of the firm as a whole. For example, in *Heslin v Fay (No 1)* (1884) 15 LR Ir 431, the partnership agreement for a grocery store in North King Street in Dublin gave one partner, Fay, the power to increase the capital of the firm if it was necessary for carrying on the business of the firm. The agreement also entitled each partner to withdraw the amount of any surplus capital paid by him to the partnership. When one of the partners, Heslin, called on his co-partners to repay the surplus capital which he had paid to the firm, Fay responded by raising the capital of the firm, so as to reduce the amount of the surplus owed to Heslin. It was held that Fay had no right to use his power of increasing the capital for the purpose of resisting Heslin's demand for a return of his surplus capital and, for this reason, Heslin was granted a dissolution of the partnership. Thus, a partner owes a fiduciary duty to his fellow partners and an important aspect of this is the requirement to show the utmost good faith in his dealings with them much like the duty a trustee owes to a beneficiary. This aspect of a partner's fiduciary duty is considered further below at **14.2.4**.

The second main type of limitation on the majority rule is to be found in the following provisions of the 1890 Act:

(a)   Section 24 (8) requires unanimity for a change in the partnership business. This is because a partner who has decided to invest in one particular type of business may not be forced to invest in something else against his wishes.

(b)   Section 24 (7) provides that: '*No person may be introduced as a partner without the consent of all the existing partners*'. Such a rule is vital to the running of a small partnership where each partner will wish to ensure that his fellow partners cannot force him to go into partnership with someone of whom he disapproves. In large firms, it is common to exclude this default rule by allowing for a new partner to be admitted by a vote of 75% or more of the partners.

(c)   Section 25 prevents expulsion of a partner by a majority of the partners unless all the partners have expressly agreed to such a power being conferred. Since there is no right of expulsion under the default partnership agreement, one reason for having a written partnership agreement is to provide the partners with such a right.

Finally, another limitation on majority rule in partnerships is the general common law principle that, like any contract, a partnership contract may not be amended without the consent of all the signatories, although it is possible for an amendment to the partnership agreement to be inferred from a course of dealings by all the partners.

14.2.3   OTHER PROVISIONS OF THE 1890 ACT AFFECTING PARTNERS' RIGHTS *INTER SE*

Other provisions of s 24 which affect the relationship between the partners are as follows:

Section 24 (2) gives a partner a right to be indemnified by the firm in respect of payments made and personal liabilities incurred 'in the ordinary and proper conduct of the business of the firm or in or about anything necessarily done for the preservation of the business or property of the firm'.

Section 24 (9) gives all the partners a right to inspect and copy the partnership accounts.

14.2.4 A PARTNER'S FIDUCIARY DUTY TO HIS CO-PARTNERS

14.2.4.1 Generally

The existence of a partner's fiduciary duty to his co-partners has long been recognised by the courts. It is because they trust one another that they are partners in the first instance and therefore the partners are required not to abuse this trust and this duty between fiduciaries is the primary control of partners' behaviour *inter se*. In the case of *Williams v Harris* [1980] ILRM 237, McWilliam J in the High Court recognised the existence of a partner's fiduciary duty and he noted that 'the mere existence of a partnership creates a fiduciary relationship between the partners'. In addition to this general common law duty, the 1890 Act recognises a number of aspects of the duty in ss 28–30.

14.2.4.2 Duty of partners to render accounts

Section 28 provides that:

> *Partners are bound to render true accounts and full information of all things affecting the partnership to any partner or his legal representative.*

14.2.4.3 Accountability of partners for private profits

Section 29 provides that a partner must account to the firm for any profits made from partnership property in the following terms:

> *(1) Every partner must account to the firm for any benefit derived by him without the consent of the other partners from any transaction concerning the partnership, or from any use by him of the partnership property, name or business connection.*

> *(2) This section applies also to transactions undertaken after a partnership has been dissolved by the death of a partner, and before the affairs thereof have been completely wound up, either by any surviving partner or by the representatives of the deceased partner.*

The principle in s 29 to account for private profits made by partners applies also to 'partnership opportunities' so that if a transaction was entered into by a partner where the opportunity came to him as a result of the partnership and which might have been used to benefit the partnership, he will have to account to his partners for the benefit he derived therefrom unless his partners have consented to the transaction following full disclosure of the circumstances. The concept underlying this principle is that these opportunities are regarded as partnership property and therefore may not be appropriated by one partner for his exclusive benefit.

14.2.4.4 Duty of partner not to compete with firm

Section 30 of the 1890 Act provides that:

> *If a partner, without the consent of the other partners, carries on any business of the same nature as, and competing with that of the firm, he must account for and pay over to the firm all profits made by him in that business.*

In *Lock v Lynam* (1854) 4 Ir Ch R 188, the parties had agreed to enter a partnership for the purpose of obtaining contracts for the supply of meat to British troops based in Ireland. During the operation of this partnership, Lynam entered into similar arrangements with third persons, whereby he was to share in the profits of similar contracts, if obtained by them. Lock sought an account of the profits of these contracts which Lynam had with third parties. Lynam argued that there was no agreement with Lock that he would not enter into similar contracts with third parties. Nonetheless, Lord Chancellor Brady held that such conduct by Lynam was a breach of his duty of good faith to his partner and he ordered that an account of those contracts be taken.

It remains to be observed that there is overlap between s 30 and s 29 (1), since a partner who continues as a partner but at the same time sets up a new business may be held accountable to his partners, because he is competing with his firm *or* because he is using 'the partnership property name or business connection' for his own benefit.

14.2.4.5   No common law restriction on former partner competing with firm

A related issue concerns the position of a former partner. It should be noted that a partner's fiduciary duty to his co-partners does not prevent a *former* partner from competing with his former firm in the absence of an agreement to that effect.

14.2.5   FINANCIAL RIGHTS AND DUTIES OF PARTNERS

14.2.5.1   Capital

The capital of a partnership is the cause of more confusion than most other areas of partnership law. This is caused in part by the confusion between the assets or other property of a partnership on the one hand, and its capital on the other hand. This confusion will be avoided if the capital of a firm is thought of as the sum which is contributed by the partners to establish the firm. The capital of a partner may be contributed in the form of cash or in the form of property (including, for example, business premises or the goodwill of an existing business).

14.2.5.2   Division of profits and sharing of losses

Section 24 of the 1890 Act lays down a number of rules as to division of profits. These rules are default rules since they may be varied by an express or implied agreement of the partners. Nevertheless, even if the default rules are to apply, the partnership agreement should state the ratios in which profits and losses of income and profits and losses of capital are to be divided between the partners, in order to avoid any confusion. The main default provision is to be found in s 24 (1) of the 1890 Act which provides that:

> *All the partners are entitled to share equally in the capital and profits of the business, and must contribute equally towards the losses whether of capital or otherwise sustained by the firm.*

Thus, s 24 (1) provides as regards the sharing of profits that they are to be shared equally. The contribution of capital in unequal shares does not give rise to the implication that profits are not to be shared equally. If a partner is to receive more than an equal share of profits because of his capital contribution or the work he does or for any other reason, this must be specifically agreed to and should be expressly stated in the partnership agreement.

As regards the sharing of losses, s 24 (1) states that the default rule is that losses are shared equally. However, if the partners share profits unequally (because of an express or implied agreement to do so), then losses of capital or of income will also be shared in the same proportion unless there is an agreement to the contrary. This principle is clear from s 44 (a) and s 44 (b)(4) of the 1890 Act and also from the case of *Robinson v Ashton* (1875) LR 20 Eq 25.

14.2.5.3   Redistribution of capital contributions and sharing of capital losses and profits

Section 24 (1) states that 'all the partners are entitled to share equally in the capital'. Particular care should be taken with this phrase since it does not mean that the capital which was contributed unequally by partners is treated as an aggregate fund to be divided between the partners in equal shares. Rather, this reference to 'capital' must be read as being first subject to the requirement in s 44 (b)(3) of the 1890 Act that capital contributions are repaid to the partners rateably according to the amount of their respective contributions. The effect of this part of s 24 (1) is that once the capital contributions have been repaid, the partners share equally in the capital profit or divide the capital losses equally, unless they have agreed a different sharing ratio. If there is no specific agreement regarding capital profits and capital losses, then if the profits or losses of income have been agreed by the partners to be shared unequally, the profits and losses of capital, in the absence of a specific agreement, will be shared in that proportion (1890 Act, s 44 (a) and (b)(4) and *Robinson v Ashton* (1875) LR 20 Eq 25). The partners are, of course, free to agree to any form of division they like and, for example, they may decide that capital profits should be divided in the same ratio as capital was contributed by the partners.

14.2.5.4   Interest on capital

Section 24 (4) provides that in the absence of contrary agreement 'A partner is not entitled . . . to interest on capital'. Where capital is contributed unequally, it may be considered appropriate to make provision in the partnership agreement for interest on capital to be paid to the partners so as to compensate the partner who has contributed more. In such a case, the partnership agreement should specify the rate of interest to be paid. At the end of the firm's financial year, the net profit of the firm is determined and the partners' first entitlement will be to interest on capital and then the remaining net profit will be allocated in accordance with the agreed profit-sharing ratio.

14.2.5.5   Interest on loans

Section 24 (3) also provides a default rule in respect of loans by a partner to his firm. It provides that, in the absence of contrary agreement, a loan by a partner to the partnership carries interest at the rate of 5%. It should be noted that this rate of interest is paid only on 'actual payments or advances'. Interest is not payable under s 24 (3) on a share of profits which is simply left in the business in the shape of undrawn profits of a partner. The partners are, of course, free to agree that interest will be paid on undrawn profits if they wish.

14.2.5.6   Remuneration of partners

Another important default rule regarding partners' financial rights and duties is contained in s 24 (6) which provides that: '*No partner shall be entitled to remuneration for acting in the partnership business*'. In some partnerships, it may be appropriate to override this default rule, e.g. where the division of work between the partners is unequal and the partners agree that some of them are to be paid compensation for the extra work which they do. As with interest on capital, such a sum payable to a partner is merely a preferential appropriation of profit. It is important not to confuse such a partner who receives a preferential appropriation of profit with a 'salaried partner'. The latter is simply an employee of the firm who is held out to the world as a partner. He is not a partner since he is not 'carrying on business in common' with the partners but is employed by them.

14.2.5.7   Drawings

The amount of money which represents a partner's share of the profits of the firm will not be known until the profit and loss account of the firm has been drawn up after the end of the partnership's financial year. For this reason, it is usual for a partnership agreement to provide that the partners have the right to take a specified amount of money on account of their anticipated profits, known as 'drawings'. If at the end of the year the partner has taken less than he was entitled to, he may draw the balance. If he has taken more than his entitlement, the partnership agreement should provide for him to pay back the excess to the firm. Sometimes, the partnership agreement may provide that each partner is to leave undrawn in the business a proportion of his entitlement to profit. This is because businesses normally need to retain funds to meet increased costs of trading and to fund any future expansion.

14.2.6   PARTNERSHIP PROPERTY

In every partnership, it is important to determine which property is owned by the partnership and which property, although it may be used by the partnership, is the property of a partner or partners individually or of some third party. This is because partnership property, unlike the personal property of a partner which is used by the firm, must be used for the purposes of the partnership and so, for example, any increase in its value will accrue to the firm and not to an individual partner. In the case of the personal property of a partner, that partner will be entitled to use it as he wishes and on the bankruptcy of the firm or on his bankruptcy, the property is available for the benefit of his separate creditors, in priority to the firm's creditors.

This crucial question of whether property is partnership property is determined by the agreement and intention of the partners, be that express or implied. If the partners intend that property is to be partnership property, then the fact that it happens to be vested in one partner's name will be irrelevant to a finding that the property belongs to the firm. For this reason, each case must be determined according to its own set of circumstances. However, the 1890 Act assists in this enquiry by providing two rebuttable presumptions regarding the status of property as partnership property. Thus, it is presumed that property which is acquired for the purposes of, and in the course of, the partnership business is partnership property since s 20 (1) of the 1890 Act provides that:

> All property and rights and interests in property originally brought into the partnership stock or acquired, whether by purchase or otherwise, on account of the firm, or for the purposes and in the course of the partnership business, are called in this Act partnership property, and must be held and applied by the partners exclusively for the purposes of the partnership and in accordance with the partnership agreement.

It is also presumed that property which is purchased with partnership funds is partnership property, since s 21 of the 1890 Act provides:

> Unless the contrary intention appears, property bought with money belonging to the firm is deemed to have been bought on account of the firm.

Yet, one must not lose sight of the overriding importance of the intentions of the partners and these presumptions may therefore be rebutted in appropriate circumstances. Case law demonstrates that the term 'partnership business' as used in s 20 (1) of the 1890 Act is not to be interpreted restrictively but rather includes a situation where property is not strictly within the description of partnership business as set out in the partnership agreement, provided that it is held for the benefit of, or on behalf of, the partnership business (*Murtagh v Costello* (1881) 7 LR Ir 428).

To avoid a situation where a court has to decide the intention and agreement of the partners regarding the status of property, the question of which property is partnership property should be clarified where practicable in the partnership agreement. Indeed, sometimes of equal importance is a provision indicating which property is not partnership property.

14.3 Relations between Partners and Third Parties

14.3.1 INTRODUCTION

In the course of carrying on the partnership's business, the partners will invariably incur debts and other obligations. In this section, we look at the nature of the partners' liabilities for these obligations as well as the extent to which an individual partner may bind the partnership as a whole. We will then go on to look at whether it is possible for individuals who are not in fact partners at the time the debt or obligation was incurred to be liable for that debt or obligation (whether because they have been held out as partners or because they are admitted to the partnership subsequently).

14.3.2 NATURE OF LIABILITY OF PARTNERS TO THIRD PARTIES

Partners are liable for the debts and obligations of the partnership without limitation (1890 Act, ss 9 and 10). Their liability is joint in the case of contractual obligations and joint and several in the case of tortious obligations. However, the significance of this distinction between joint and joint and several obligations was much reduced by the Civil Liability Act 1961 which now allows proceedings to be brought successively against persons jointly liable even where there has been an earlier judgment against other persons who were jointly liable for that obligation. Where a firm is unable to pay its debts out of partnership property, the creditor of that firm is entitled to obtain payment from the private estates of the partners. Special rules apply in such cases, so as to attempt to do justice both to the creditors of the firm and to the separate creditors of the individual partners. These rules are contained in the Bankruptcy Act 1988, s 34. It is not intended to deal with these rules in detail (see further Twomey, *Partnership Law*, paras 27.01 *et seq.*). However, they may be summarised as follows:

(a) partnership property is used to pay partnership creditors in priority to the personal creditors of each partner;

(b) personal property of each partner is used to pay his personal creditors in priority to partnership creditors;

(c) if the personal creditors of a particular partner are paid in full from his personal property, then the partnership creditors may resort to the balance of that partner's personal property; and

(d) if the partnership creditors are paid in full from partnership property, the personal creditors of a partner may resort to the balance of his share of the partnership property.

14.3.3 AUTHORITY OF PARTNER TO BIND FIRM

14.3.3.1 Generally

The relationship between partnership law and the law of agency is very close and some of the rules regulating the relationship between a partnership and the outside world may be explained purely in terms of particular applications of agency principles and, in particular, from examining the nature of a partner's authority to bind the firm. In general terms, the partnership as a whole is bound by a partner acting within the scope of his authority. This authority of a partner may arise in three ways, i.e. express authority, implied authority, and ostensible authority.

(a) Express authority is where the authority of the partners is specifically agreed upon by the partners.

(b) Implied authority is implied either from a course of dealings between the partners (which amounts to an actual agreement) or because the authority is a natural consequence of an authority actually given to the partner.

(c) Ostensible authority arises from the fact that a person dealing with a partner is, in certain circumstances, entitled to assume that the partner has authority to bind the firm.

The first two types of authority are categories of actual authority (in the sense that the partner has in fact authority to do the act in question), which distinguishes them from ostensible authority where there is no actual authority but, for the protection of third parties, the partner is deemed to have authority to do the act in question.

14.3.3.2 Express authority

The scope of express authority depends on the agreement between the parties. The partnership agreement may specify what powers the partners individually are to have and may specify that some partners are to have greater powers than others. The extent of express authority is not, in practical terms, of great significance to a person dealing with a partner. This is because, whether or not there is express authority, the third party will usually be able to rely on the ostensible authority of the partner. The outsider need only rely on express authority where the partner has done something which the law does not consider to be within the ostensible authority of a partner.

14.3.3.3   Implied authority

It has been noted that the authority of a partner to do an act may be implied from a course of dealing involving the partners or because the authority is a natural consequence of an authority actually given to the partner. This is called implied authority. The implied powers of partners in a trading partnership are more extensive than the powers of partners in a non-trading partnership. This is because the court recognises the need of the partners and the persons dealing with them to rely on normal trading practices.

Examples of powers assumed to be available to partners in all partnerships include the power to:

(a)   bring or defend legal proceedings in the firm name or the joint names of all of the partners;

(b)   open a bank account in the name of the firm;

(c)   sign cheques on behalf of the firm;

(d)   enter contracts on behalf of the firm within the ordinary course of business of the firm;

(e)   sell goods belonging to the firm; and

(f)   take on employees for the purposes of the partnership business and dismiss such employees.

A partner in a trading partnership will be assumed to have all the above powers and also the power to grant security for borrowings and to draw, accept, or endorse a bill of exchange or promissory note.

14.3.3.4   Ostensible authority

The scope of ostensible authority is not always easy to establish or describe. Such authority may be said to arise from the fact that the partner who is acting on behalf of a firm *appears* to have authority to bind the firm and it is, therefore, reasonable for the outsider to assume such authority. It is for this reason that it is sometimes referred to as apparent authority. The principle underlying ostensible authority is to be found in the 1890 Act, s 5 which provides that:

> *Every partner is an agent of the firm and his other partners for the purpose of the business of the partnership; and the acts of every partner who does any act for carrying on in the usual way the business of the kind carried on by the firm of which he is a member bind the firm and his partners, unless the partner so acting has in fact no authority to act for the firm in the particular matter, and the person with whom he is dealing either knows that he has no authority, or does not know or believe him to be a partner.*

The easiest way to understand the scope of the section is to examine each of the qualifications on a partner's authority which the section recognises. First, it should be noted that the section does not say that *anything* which a partner does binds the firm; rather, to bind the firm the following requirements must be satisfied:

(a)   the act must be done by a partner;

(b)   the act must be done *qua* partner; and

(c)   the act must be within the ordinary course of business of the firm.

The first and second requirement are generally easy to establish, while the requirement that the act be within the firm's ordinary course of business has caused the most difficulty.

14.3.3.5   Act must be done by a partner

Before a firm is bound by the act of its partner, it is perhaps self-evident that the act must be that of a partner and the fact that the partner in question is a dormant partner or a junior partner does not in any way reduce his power to bind his partners (*Morans v Armstrong* (1840) Arm M & O 25). In cases where a partner in a firm does not have the authority to do acts within the ordinary course of business of a firm, the third party must believe that he is dealing with a partner. This is because, under s 5 of the 1890 Act, if the partner does not have authority to do an act which is within the firm's ordinary business, the firm will nonetheless be bound by that act, *unless* the third party did not know or believe that he was a partner. Where the third party does not believe that he is dealing with a partner, he must then be taken to know that the first requirement for the firm to be bound has not been satisfied. If the partner is a partner, with the authority but the third party does not know he is a partner, then the firm will still be bound provided that each of the requirements above is satisfied.

14.3.3.6 Act must be done *qua* partner

The second requirement to be satisfied for a firm to be bound by the actions of a partner is that the act in question must be done by the partner qua partner. It is important to distinguish between this requirement and the fact that the act must be done within the ordinary course of business of the firm. Thus, the act of a partner in an accountancy firm who becomes a company director of his family company, may not be binding on his firm since, although done by a partner and constituting an act which is within the ordinary course of business of an accountancy firm, it may not have been done by him qua partner.

14.3.3.7 Act must be within the firm's ordinary course of business

The third and final condition to be satisfied for a firm to be bound by the acts of its partners is the one which has received the most attention from the courts, namely that the act be within the ordinary course of business of the firm. The classification of a particular act as being within the 'ordinary course of business of the firm' is crucial since in most cases the question of the liability of the firm for the acts of a partner is determined by this fact. For example, a firm of doctors would be liable for the damage caused by the negligent driving of one of the partners where he is involved in a car accident on the way to see a patient. This is because the negligent driving of the partner is an act which is committed by the partner while acting in the ordinary course of business of the firm. On the other hand, the firm of doctors will not generally be liable for the damage caused by one of the partners where, on his way to see a patient, he decides to take a detour and assault an innocent third party. This assault would not be regarded as being 'within the ordinary course of business of the firm' since the partner is acting in a completely unusual manner for his own purposes and not in order to benefit the firm.

Finally, a partner who makes a contract with an outsider without authority will be personally liable to the outsider for breach of warranty of authority where the partnership as a whole is not made liable on the contract. However, where a contract made without authority is ratified by the partnership, it becomes binding on the partners as well as on the outsider. In addition, where the partner's authority to do acts within the ordinary course of business of the firm is restricted, s 8 of the 1890 Act provides that an outsider is not prejudiced since it provides that the third party is not affected by any restriction placed on the powers of the partner unless he has notice of it.

14.3.4 PERSONS HELD OUT AS PARTNERS

So far we have only considered the liability of actual partners vis-à-vis outsiders. A person who holds himself out as a partner or who 'knowingly suffers himself to be represented as a partner' is liable to anyone who 'on the faith of such representation' gives credit to the firm as if he were a partner (1890 Act, s 14). The most common example of the application of this rule is where a 'salaried partner' (who is in fact an employee of the firm, rather than a partner) allows his name to be used by the partnership (e.g. on notepaper). In view of the potential liability under s 14 (1), it is advisable for salaried partners to obtain an indemnity from the 'true' partners in relation to this potential liability. A person cannot be held liable under s 14 (1), unless he has in some way contributed to the mistake made by the person giving credit to the firm, for example, by allowing his name to be given as a partner.

Section 14 (1) only applies where 'credit is given' to the firm by the third party on the basis of the misrepresentation that a person was a partner in the firm. This term is construed widely so that, for example, the apparent partner is liable where goods are delivered, as well as where cash is lent to the firm.

14.3.5   LIABILITY OF NEW PARTNERS

Section 17 (1) of the 1890 Act provides that 'a person who is admitted as a partner into an existing firm does not thereby become liable to the creditors of the firm for anything done before he became a partner'. This provision ensures that an incoming partner is not liable to the existing creditors of the firm merely because he has become a partner in a firm which has a large number of obligations and debts. As between himself and the existing partners, the incoming partner may agree to pay a share of debts owed to existing creditors. This does not make him directly liable to the existing creditors as they are not privy to the contract. The new partner may become directly liable to existing creditors by a novation (that is, a tripartite contract between the old partners, the new partner and the creditor whereby the existing contract between the old partners and the creditor is discharged and replaced by a contract between the new firm, including the new partner, and the creditor). However, this will not be a regular occurrence in modern partnerships because it would necessitate an agreement between a partnership and its creditors every time a partner joins the firm.

14.4   Actions between Partners

14.4.1   INTRODUCTION

Disputes between partners may involve a wide variety of potential actions ranging from a claim for damages to an application for the appointment of a receiver to the firm. However, regardless of the form of action, two important characteristics of the partnership relationship should be borne in mind as these two characteristics will commonly influence the outcome of the litigation. First, one of the grand characteristics of a partnership is the fact that it is not a separate legal entity, but an aggregate of all the partners. For this reason, the partners are not treated as debtors or creditors of the firm while the partnership continues, since to do so would involve the concept of a person owing himself a debt. It is only on a final settlement of accounts between the partners on the firm's dissolution that they are regarded as debtors and creditors. It is for this reason that the courts are reluctant to facilitate a partner in suing his co-partners in respect of a single partnership obligation. Instead, the courts lean in favour of all partnership obligations being determined as part of the general settlement of accounts on the dissolution of the firm.

The second important characteristic of the partnership contract is that it requires a high degree of confidence and trust between the partners. It is, therefore, understandable that the courts would be reluctant to compel an unwilling person to be another person's partner. For this reason, the specific performance of partnerships, while not unheard of, are certainly not granted as a matter of course. For the same reason, the courts favour granting other remedies such as injunctions and appointing receivers/managers as part of the dissolution of partnerships rather than during the life of partnerships. This judicial attitude may be easily justified since the very fact that a court application is being made in the first place indicates that the degree of trust and confidence necessary for the partnership to continue may be absent. Thus, any order which is intended to apply during the life of the partnership may turn out to be futile and clearly the court does not wish to involve itself in making such orders.

In this section, we look at the remedies available to a partner which include dissolution of the partnership, appointment of a receiver, and other remedies which may be available under the terms of the partnership agreement itself. (For further remedies, see Twomey, *Partnership Law*, paras 20.01 *et seq.*)

14.4.2   MEDIATION AND ARBITRATION

'Partnership actions always take a long time and, indeed, are one of the most expensive and unsatisfactory types of action which we have' *per* Kenny J in *O'Connor v Woods*, 22 January 1976, High Court (unreported). This view of partnership disputes was reiterated by the Supreme Court, albeit in the context of quasi-partnerships, when Murphy J observed that they were similar to matrimonial proceedings in *Re Murray Consultants Ltd* [1997] 3 IR 23):

> 'Partnership disputes and family law disputes] both involve an examination of the conduct of the parties over a period of years and usually a determination by them to assert rights rather than solve problems. It may well be that the disparate forms of litigation are frequently fuelled by a bitterness borne of rejection: matrimonial or commercial. In neither discipline can the courts persuade the parties that it is in their best interests to direct their attention to solving their problems rather than litigating them.'

By repeating the observations of the Irish judiciary on the subject of partnership disputes, it is hoped to persuade some partners and their legal advisers to try and solve their problems by mediation or other non-adversarial methods and in particular to include a compulsory mediation clause in their partnership agreement and, failing resolution by mediation, it is suggested that the parties seek to resolve their differences by arbitration. A typical mediation clause along the following lines is recommended:

> All disputes and questions whatsoever which shall either during the term of the Partnership or afterwards arise between the Partners or their representatives or between any Partners or Partner and the representatives of any other deceased Partner touching this Indenture or construction or application thereof or any clause or thing herein contained or any amount valuation or division of assets, debts or liabilities to be made hereunder or as to any act, deed or omission of any Partner relating to the Partnership or as to any other matter in any way relating to the Partnership business or the affairs thereof or the right duties or liabilities of any persons hereunder shall be referred first to a single mediator to be nominated by all the persons in dispute or in default of agreement by the President for the time being of the Law Society. Failing a resolution of the dispute through such mediation to the satisfaction of all the parties, the dispute shall be referred to a single arbitrator to be nominated by all the persons in dispute or in default of agreement by the President for the time being of the Law Society in accordance with and subject to the provisions of the Arbitration Act, 2010 or any statutory modification or re-enactment thereof for the time being in force.

14.4.3   EXPLUSION OF A PARTNER

There is no right under the 1890 Act to expel a partner. Indeed, the contrary is expressly stated by s 25 which reads 'no majority of the partners can expel any partner unless a power to do so has been conferred by express agreement between the partners'.

The absence of a right under general partnership law to expel a partner is an important reason for having a written partnership agreement incorporating such a right, since no matter how unprofessional, negligent, or belligerent a partner becomes, the other partners are not entitled to expel him from the firm in the absence of such a right. The desire of the partners in a firm to expel their co-partner, in the absence of a right to expel, may lead to a general dissolution of that firm. This is because the only recourse for the 'innocent' partners is to apply to court under the 1890 Act, s 35 for a general dissolution of the partnership on the grounds of the partner's misconduct.

Where an expulsion clause is included in the agreement, it will normally state that specific activities (such as fraud) or breaches of certain terms of the partnership agreement (such as requiring a partner not to compete with the partnership or to devote the whole of his time to the business) will justify expulsion. As noted at **14.5.2.3** below, bankruptcy of a partner is a ground for the automatic dissolution of the whole partnership (under the default rules contained in s 33 (1) of the 1890 Act), but in order to avoid the consequences of dissolution it is common for the partnership agreement to override this default rule and provide that a bankruptcy of a partner will not cause dissolution, rather that it will justify expulsion.

14.5 Dissolution of a Partnership

14.5.1 GENERAL DISSOLUTION VS TECHNICAL DISSOLUTION

An important distinction must be made between the general dissolution of a partnership and its technical dissolution. If a partnership is subject to a general dissolution, the partnership will come to an end and its business is wound up. A technical dissolution is where there is a change in the membership of the partnership but no winding up of the 'old' partnership since the business of the partnership continues as before the change in membership, such as where a partner leaves the firm or a partner joins the firm. The same events lead to the technical and general dissolution of a partnership, thus the death of a partner 'dissolves' the partnership that existed between the partners, and thereafter the surviving partners may continue the partnership business as before (in which case there would be a technical dissolution) or they may decide to sell the partnership assets and wind up the business (in which case there would be a general dissolution). In this section, we consider the legal consequences of the occurrence of both a general and a technical dissolution since it is only with the benefit of hindsight (i.e. was the firm wound up or did it continue in business) that one may determine whether a particular event led to the general or the technical dissolution of the firm.

Unless the partnership agreement provides otherwise, the death or bankruptcy of a partner results in the automatic dissolution of the partnership (1890 Act, s 33 (1)), and at that stage any partner may demand that the partnership is wound up, in which case the partnership will go into general dissolution (1890 Act, s 39). General dissolution is such an extreme step that an important reason to have a written partnership agreement is to provide expressly that dissolution is not to occur automatically on the occurrence of the death or bankruptcy of a partner.

14.5.2 DISSOLUTION OF A PARTNERSHIP

14.5.2.1 Dissolution by notice

Under the 1890 Act, ss 26 and 32 (c) and in the absence of any express or implied contrary agreement, any one partner may, at any time, give notice to their fellow partners to dissolve the partnership. This notice takes effect from the date specified in the notice (subject to the fact that the date of dissolution may not be before the date of receipt). If the notice is silent on the point, it takes effect from the date when the notice is received. Once the firm is dissolved under s 26 or 32 (c), any partner is entitled under s 39 of the 1890 Act to demand the sale of the partnership assets in order for the liabilities of the firm to be paid off and in this way to force the general dissolution of the firm. In most cases, this will have disastrous consequences for the partnership business. It is important, therefore, to bear in mind that ss 26 and 32 (c) may be overridden if the partnership agreement contains provisions to the contrary.

As a result many partnership agreements exclude these default rights completely or require a majority vote or a minimum period of notice to be given before the partnership is dissolved. Commonly, the right of a partner to dissolve a partnership is excluded by implication, namely by an agreement between the partners that the partnership shall last for a fixed term.

14.5.2.2   Dissolution by agreement

The partnership agreement may specify circumstances which cause the partnership to be dissolved, such as the occurrence of a particular event. The agreement may also specify the manner in which the partnership will be dissolved.

14.5.2.3   Automatic dissolution

A partnership will be automatically dissolved under the Act on the death or bankruptcy of a partner or in circumstances where a partnership is found to carry out an illegal activity.

Under s 32 (a) and (b) of the 1890 Act, a partnership is dissolved:

(a)   if it was entered into for a fixed term, upon the expiration of that term; and

(b)   if it was entered into for a single adventure or undertaking, upon the completion of that adventure or undertaking.

A provision to the contrary in the partnership agreement overrides s 32 (a) and (b). If the agreement is silent and the partnership continues despite the expiry of the term or the completion of the adventure, the 1890 Act, s 27 provides that a partnership at will, dissolvable by notice, is brought into existence. Such a partnership is subject to the terms of the original agreement to the extent that these terms do not conflict with the incidents of a partnership at will.

14.5.3   DISSOLUTION BY THE COURT

14.5.3.1   Generally

In a formal partnership (i.e. where the partners have excluded the right of a partner to dissolve the partnership by notice), the partners usually agree to remain in partnership together for a fixed term (for this reason, they are sometimes referred to as fixed-term partnerships). It will often occur that some of the partners may wish to bring the partnership to a premature end for a variety of reasons ranging from personality clashes to the wrongful conduct of a partner. Unfortunately, there is no automatic right under the 1890 Act for the partners to expel a partner guilty of misconduct and for this reason, these types of situations often result in an application to court for a dissolution of the partnership under the 1890 Act, s 35. The only other option open to the partner(s) wishing to end the partnership with a difficult partner is to attempt to terminate the partnership in breach of the partnership agreement which is obviously an unsatisfactory solution.

A number of general aspects of s 35 are worthy of mention at this juncture. This section provides for the dissolution of a partnership in circumstances where:

(a)   a partner is of unsound mind;

(b)   a partner is incapable of performing the partnership contract;

(c)   a partner's behaviour is prejudicially affecting business;

(d)   a partner is in breach of a partnership agreement;

(e)   the business is running at a loss; or

(f)   it is just and equitable to do so.

The court has an absolute discretion to order a dissolution in any of the six cases listed in s 35. If for no other reason, this fact should encourage potential litigants to make every effort to resolve their differences amicably since there is no requirement on a court to order or not to order a dissolution, regardless of the conduct of the partners. However, since the courts generally lean against ordering the specific performance of a partnership agreement between unwilling partners, the result of an application to dissolve a partnership often, but not always, is a court dissolution. In addition, partnership disputes usually end up in dissolution because a court in a partnership dispute, unlike the situation in a company dispute, does not have a statutory power to order the expulsion of a partner or the sale of one partner's share to his co-partners. It follows that the parties to a partnership dispute have the added knowledge that a dissolution is more likely than not to result from an application to court under s 35 with the likelihood that the practice or business of the partnership will have to be sold and the consequent loss of goodwill. In general terms therefore, there is a very great incentive for partners to attempt to agree to dissolve amicably without incurring the costs of going to court to obtain an order to dissolve the partnership.

Although s 35 has six separate headings under which a dissolution of a partnership may be claimed, more often than not, a dissolution will be sought under s 35 (f) on the grounds that it is just and equitable for the court to order the dissolution of the partnership. Such an application obviates the need for the petitioner to satisfy the pre-conditions of the other subsections of s 35 such as incapacity, breach of partnership agreement, etc.

14.5.4   CONSEQUENCES OF A DISSOLUTION

14.5.4.1   Generally

The occurrence of one of the events leading to the automatic dissolution of a partnership will cause the partnership to be 'dissolved'. Whether this results in the technical or general dissolution of the firm depends on whether the right to wind up the firm under s 39 of the 1890 Act has been excluded by the partners and, if not, whether a partner wishes to force the general dissolution of the firm by exercising this right under s 39 of the 1890 Act. Section 39 provides:

> On the dissolution of a partnership every partner is entitled, as against the other partners in the firm, and all persons claiming through them in respect of their interests as partners, to have the property of the partnership applied in payment of the debts and liabilities of the firm, and to have the surplus assets after such payment applied in payment of what may be due to the partners respectively after deducting what may be due from them as partners to the firm; and for that purpose any partner or his representatives may on the termination of the partnership apply to the Court to wind up the business and affairs of the firm.

The most common way in which the right under s 39 is excluded is by the partners having a partnership agreement which provides that when a partner leaves the firm, his share shall be purchased by the continuing partner.

Where the firm goes into general dissolution, s 38 provides that, after the dissolution, the authority of each partner to bind the firm (as well as the other rights and obligations of the partners) continues despite the dissolution but only to the extent necessary to wind up the affairs of the partnership, and to complete transactions begun but unfinished at the time of the dissolution.

14.5.4.2   Realisation of partnership assets on general dissolution

Once the firm has been dissolved and the general dissolution begins, the value of the assets owned by the partnership will be ascertained, as will the extent of the debts and liabilities owed to creditors. In so far as it is necessary, the assets will be sold to raise the funds to discharge the debts. These assets will include the 'goodwill' attaching to the business.

Where goodwill is sold, the purchasers will want to protect their investment against the loss of custom arising from the former owners setting up in competition in the same vicinity. Accordingly, the purchaser may wish to include a restrictive covenant in the sale agreement to guard against this possibility

14.5.4.3   Distribution of partnership assets on general dissolution

Once the liabilities of the partnership have been met, any surplus is distributed to the partners. Section 44 (b) of the 1890 Act provides that, in the absence of any contrary agreement, on a general dissolution, the assets of the firm shall be applied in the following order:

(a) debts of the firm to third parties;

(b) repayment of advances made by the partners to the firm;

(c) repayment of the capital contribution made by the partners to the firm; and

(d) balance is divided in the same manner as the profits are divided amongst the partners.

Section 44 (a) of the 1890 Act provides that if the partnership has made losses (including losses of capital), in the absence of any contrary agreement, these shall be met on the general dissolution of the firm in the following order:

(a) from profits;

(b) from capital; and

(c) from the partners in the proportion in which profits are divisible.

Both parts of s 44 are subject to contrary agreement. In particular, the partners may agree to share surplus assets and to contribute to losses in a ratio different from their normal profit sharing. However, the requirement that creditors are paid off first is not subject to variation by the partners.

14.5.4.4 Sharing of losses on general dissolution

Under s 44 (a) and (b), any loss or residue, whether of capital or profits, will be shared between the partners in the proportion in which they share the profits, in the absence of contrary agreement. These subsections are traps for the unwary, as this sharing of the capital losses or capital profits applies irrespective of the manner in which the partners have contributed to the capital of the firm but rather in proportion to the rate at which profits are shared. (See also 1890 Act, s 24 (1); *Ex parte Maude* (1867) 16 LT 577; *Re Weymouth Steam Packet Co* [1891] 1 Ch 66; and *Re Wakefield Rolling Stock Co* [1892] 3 Ch 165.) Therefore, a partner who contributes all the capital of the firm and shares the profits of the firm evenly with his partner, will, in the absence of any agreement to the contrary, share evenly in any capital profit or capital loss on the winding-up of the firm. In some cases, this may come as a surprise to the partner who contributes all the capital and accordingly the terms of the sharing of capital residues or losses require careful consideration in such partnerships.

An example will highlight this issue. A, B, and C contributed capital of €2,000 in the following proportions: €1,000, €500, and €500 respectively, the partners sharing profits and losses equally. On a winding-up there is residual capital of only €1,000, thus leaving a capital loss of €1,000. Under the general rules governing the sharing of capital losses, these are shared in the same proportion as the profit shares (1890 Act, s 44 (a)) so that A, B, and C are required to contribute a third each, i.e. each notionally contribute €333 giving a notional capital of €2,000. This is because such a shortfall in the capital is as much a loss as any other shortfall and is made up in the same way, namely by being shared between the partners. The notional capital is then repaid to the partners in accordance with their capital contributions, since s 44 (b) requires the capital to be repaid to partners 'rateably'. Therefore, they will notionally receive the €2,000 divided in proportion to their capital contributions, i.e. 2:1:1 so that A will notionally receive his €1,000 back and B and C will receive back €500 each. To get the actual amount received by A, deduct his notional contribution of €333 from the notional amount of capital he should receive (€1,000) to give €667 which he actually receives. Similarly for B and C, deduct their notional contribution of €333 from the notional amount of capital, which they were to receive (€500), to give €167, which they will each receive. So, in respect of A's initial capital contribution of €1,000, he gets back €667, and thus he makes a loss of €333. While in respect of B's and C's capital contributions of €500, they get back €167 and thus they also make a loss of €333 each. The same result could have been achieved by dividing the capital loss of €1,000 equally between A, B, and C.

14.5.4.5   Notification of the dissolution

Under s 36 (1) of the 1890 Act, outsiders dealing with the firm after a change in the membership of the firm are entitled to treat all apparent members of the firm as still being members until the outsider has notice of the change. In order to protect themselves from liability for obligations incurred after the dissolution, the partners in the dissolved firm are entitled to publicly notify the fact of the dissolution (1890 Act, s 37) and s 36 (2) of the 1890 Act provides that persons who had no dealings with a firm prior to a change in the membership of the firm are deemed to be on notice of a change in the firm which is advertised in Iris Oifigiúil.

Section 36 (2) only provides that *new* customers of the firm are on notice of the change advertised in Iris Oifigiúil. It does not apply to existing customers of the firm.

To obtain protection from liability for obligations incurred with *existing* customers after the dissolution, the former partners should give notice individually to each of these customers. In the case of a technical dissolution (i.e. where the business of the partnership continues after the departure of a partner), this will be an important issue since the partnership business will continue as before. In practice in larger firms, the former partner may opt to rely on an indemnity from the continuing partners in respect of such liabilities rather than attempting to notify all the clients of the firm that he is no longer a partner.

14.5.5   DEPARTURE OF A PARTNER FROM A FIRM

14.5.5.1   Generally

Partnership agreements can, and should, contain provisions dealing with the departure of a partner from the firm. This is because the 1890 Act does not specifically deal with retirement. Under the 1890 Act the only option available to a partner who wishes to leave a firm is to give notice to dissolve the partnership under s 26, if it is a partnership at will. If a s 26 notice is given the partnership will be dissolved (see **14.5.2.1**); the section does not permit a partner to depart, i.e. retire, without having to dissolve the partnership. To avoid this, suitable provisions must be included in the agreement entitling a partner to leave the firm and usually providing for the continuing partners to purchase his share in the partnership. This section considers the position of a former partner, regardless of how he leaves the firm, whether by retirement or expulsion. The position of a partner who dies is considered at **14.5.6**.

14.5.5.2   Obligations incurred before departure

The mere fact that a partner leaves a firm does not release him from obligations incurred by the firm while he was a partner. Section 17 (2) of the 1890 Act provides that a 'partner who retires from a firm does not thereby cease to be liable for partnership debts or obligations incurred before his retirement'. For this reason, it is common for the former partner to be indemnified by the continuing partners. In the absence of such an indemnity, the former partner is fully liable for all obligations incurred while he was a partner, subject only to the relevant rules on the barring of claims under the Statute of Limitations.

14.5.5.3   Obligations incurred after departure

The general rule is that partners are only liable for debts incurred by the partnership while they are members of the firm. Therefore, ceasing to be a partner prevents the *former* partner becoming liable on future debts as the retirement terminates the agency relationship. However, this general rule is subject to exceptions. Section 36 (1) of the Act states:

> *where a person deals with a firm after a change in its constitution, he is entitled to treat all apparent members of the old firm as still being members of the firm until he has notice of the change.*

It is important to note that s 36 (1) only applies to existing customers of the firm and not to those persons who only began dealing with the firm after the former partner departed.

If the former partner wishes to be absolutely protected from liability for future debts, he should give the existing customers formal notification of his retirement. Although the matter is not beyond dispute, it is thought that actual notice is not required under s 36 (1). A former partner may also be liable for obligations incurred after his departure from the firm under the doctrine of holding out (s 14 (1)).

14.5.5.4 Post-dissolution profits of a firm

Once a partner has left a firm, the partnership agreement should provide for his share in the firm to be purchased by the continuing partners. If there is no agreement, the default right in s 39 of the 1890 Act will apply and the former partner may force the winding-up of the partnership under s 39.

In addition, s 42 (1) of the 1890 Act provides for the situation where a member of a firm ceases to be a partner (including by death) and the continuing partners carry on the business of the firm without any final settlement of accounts as between the firm and the outgoing partner or his estate. Under this section, the outgoing partner or his estate is entitled, subject to contrary agreement, at the option of himself or his personal representatives to claim:

(a) such share of the profits made since the dissolution as the court may find to be attributable to the use of his share of the partnership assets; or

(b) interest at the rate of 5% p.a. on the amount of his share of the partnership assets.

14.5.6 DEATH

Death causes the automatic dissolution of a partnership. In order to avoid inconvenience to the surviving partners, it is common to provide in the partnership agreement that, instead of leading to the general dissolution of the partnership, the surviving partners will continue the partnership business and usually the agreement provides for the deceased partner's share to be purchased by them. In this way, the right of a partner to wind up the partnership under the 1890 Act, s 39 is excluded.

14.5.6.1 Liability of partner's estate for debts

It has already been noted that under the 1890 Act, s 9 every partner is jointly liable for debts and obligations of the firm incurred while he is a partner. In addition, s 9 provides that the estate of a deceased person is severally liable for such debts and obligations so far as they remain unsatisfied but subject to the prior payment of the deceased partner's personal debts. A partnership creditor may, therefore, proceed against the estate of a deceased partner in respect of partnership debts (even after obtaining a judgment against the other partners) provided some part of the debt is unsatisfied. However, partnership creditors are postponed to the deceased partner's own creditors. Section 36 (3) of the 1890 Act provides that the deceased partner's estate is not liable for partnership debts contracted after the death.

14.6 Partnerships with Limited Liability

The main type of partnership in Ireland is the ordinary partnership, which is the main focus of this text. However, there are two other types of partnership under Irish law, the limited partnership and the investment limited partnership, which are governed by the Limited Partnerships Act 1907 and the Investment Limited Partnerships Act 1994. A discussion of these types of partnerships is beyond the scope of this chapter.

PART 3

BUSINESS TAXATION

CHAPTER 15

INCOME TAX

15.1   Business Taxation

The following chapters on taxation will give an overview of the principles and concepts that apply to income tax and capital gains tax for individuals and partners in a partnership, and to corporation tax and chargeable gains for companies.

Tax is a method of collection of money from persons and corporate entities to pay for services provided by the State. Different rules apply to different types of taxes.

The primary source of legislation for income tax and corporation tax is the Taxes Consolidation Act 1997 as amended ('TCA 1997'), the Finance Acts, and various statutory instruments. These chapters have been prepared using the Finance Act 2014 and the taxes may have been amended since this date so the current legislation should always be ascertained and reviewed when addressing and advising on taxation matters.

The government agency responsible for the collection of tax is Revenue Commissioners. The administration and collection of taxation has been gradually moving online using the ROS and PAYE Anytime facilities of Revenue Commissioners. Revenue Commissioners issue a number of guidance notes and briefing on its interpretation of taxation. Much of this information can be obtained on its website (www.revenue.ie).

15.2   An Introduction to Income Tax

Income tax is payable by individuals on annual income (profits and gains of a business and any other sources of income) earned in a tax year.

A tax year runs from 1 January to 31 December.

For an employee, income tax is deducted from salary through the PAYE (Pay as You Earn) system.

Self-employed persons pay their own tax directly to Revenue Commissioners using the self-assessment system and by filing a form 11 with Revenue Commissioners ('Revenue'). The self-assessment system applies to self-employed persons and to other persons who receive income from sources where all of the tax cannot be collected under the PAYE system.

Example:

John's main source of income is his job as a mechanic in a local garage but he also has rental income of €15,000 each year from three apartments he bought in 2010.

His Schedule E source income (income from his employment) is subject to PAYE and his employer deducts income tax, the universal social charge ('USC'), and PRSI at source directly from John's salary. John must separately declare the Schedule D Case V income (rental income) to Revenue and Revenue will determine whether it will deduct this additional tax from him using the PAYE system by making an adjustment to his tax credits and tax bands. If the rental income is not deducted using the PAYE system John will have to file a tax return and pay the tax directly to Revenue using the self-assessment system and completing a form 12 (if specifically requested by Revenue) or form 11 annual tax return. A form 11 will be required if the net assessable non PAYE income is in excess of €3,174 or the person has total gross income from non PAYE sources of €50,000 or more.

15.3   Who Must Pay Irish Income Tax?

The obligation to pay Irish income tax This depends on whether an individual is resident, ordinarily resident, or domiciled in Ireland. An individual who is resident, ordinarily resident, and domiciled in the State is liable to income tax in respect of his/her total worldwide income.

15.3.1   RESIDENCE

A person is resident for Irish tax purposes if they spend:

(a)   183 days in Ireland in a tax year; or

(b)   280 days over two years – (when you count the number of days spent in Ireland in the current and the preceding tax year if it is 280 or more the person will be resident for the current year – if a person spends less than 30 days in Ireland in a tax year then these days are ignored).

A day for the residence test is a day in which the person is in Ireland at any time in a day.

Example:

Anne came to Ireland on 15 December 2013 and left in March 2014. She was not treated as tax resident in Ireland as she had not been present for 183 days in Ireland in either 2013 or 2014. Her time in Ireland in 2013 is ignored as it was for less than 30 days.

If Anne had stayed until 20 March 2015, she would have been tax resident in Ireland in the tax year 2014 as she spent more than 183 days in Ireland in 2014 (365 days). She would also have been tax resident for 2015 as she spent more than 280 days over two years: 365 days in 2014 and 79 days in 2015.

15.3.2   ORDINARY RESIDENT

An individual who has been resident in Ireland for three consecutive tax years becomes ordinarily resident in Ireland from the beginning of the fourth tax year.

Example:

Mark moved to Ireland in February 2012 and remained here until December 2015. He was tax resident for 2012, 2013, and 2014 and he became ordinary resident in Ireland in 2015.

An individual who has been ordinarily resident in Ireland ceases to be so at the end of the third consecutive tax year in which he/she is not resident in Ireland.

Example:

Mark left Ireland on 30 December 2015 and returned to New Zealand. He will not cease to be ordinarily resident in Ireland until the tax year 2019 (as he ceases to be tax resident in 2015).

15.3.3   DOMICILE

Domicile is a legal concept. It is generally interpreted as meaning living in a particular country with the intention of residing permanently in that country.

15.3.4   DOUBLE TAXATION

Generally under a tax treaty, where income is taxable in two different states, either an exemption for tax is provided in one state or alternatively the tax paid in one of the states is permitted as a tax credit against tax in the other state.

For the purposes of this chapter it is assumed that the individuals are resident, ordinarily resident, and domiciled in Ireland.

15.4   Tax Rates

Each year in the budget the Government announce the tax rates for the next tax year. Currently a tax year runs from 1 January to 31 December. The tax rates for the tax year 1 January to 31 December 2015 are as follows (TCA 1997, s 15):

    (a)   For single, widowed, or a surviving civil partner, the first €33,800 of income is taxed at 20% and the balance of income is taxed at 40%.

    (b)   For single, widowed, or a surviving civil partner that qualify for the single person child carer tax credit, the first €37,800 of income is taxed at 20% and the balance of income is taxed at 40%.

    (c)   For married or civil partners where one spouse/civil partner only has income, the first €42,800 of income is taxed at 20% and the balance of income is taxed at 40%.

    (d)   For married or civil partners where both spouses/civil partners have income, the first €42,800 (plus an additional €24,800 maximum or the amount of the second income if less) (i.e. up to €67,600 of income) is taxed at 20% and the balance of income is taxed at 40%.

Examples:

Single – 2015

Mary is single and has employment income of €50,000 payable under the PAYE system. Her income tax is as follows (ignoring all tax credits, allowances, and reliefs):

€33,800 * 20% =   €6,760

€16,200 * 40% =   €6,480

€50,000 results in €13,240 income tax.

(*continued*)

Single and qualify for single person child carer credit in 2015

If Mary had a daughter and qualified for the single person child carer tax credit her income tax is as follows (ignoring all tax credits, allowances, and reliefs):

€37,800 * 20% =   €7,560

€12,200 * 40% =   €4,880

€50,000 results in €12,440 income tax.

Married one spouse with income in 2015

If Mary was married and she was the only spouse working her income tax is as follows (ignoring all tax credits, allowances, and reliefs):

€42,800 * 20% =   €8,560

€7,200 * 40% =   €2,880

€50,000 results in €11,440 income tax.

Married two spouses with income in 2015

If Mary was married and her spouse Ron also earned €50,000 as a self-employed butcher their combined income tax is as follows (ignoring all tax credits, allowances, and reliefs) assuming that Ron is assessed for both their incomes:

€67,600 * 20% =   €13,520

€32,400 * 40% =   €12,960

€100,000 results in €26,480 income tax.

15.4.1 EXEMPTIONS FROM INCOME TAX

An exemption from having to pay income tax applies to persons over 65 years of age that have total income of less than €18,000 if single or widowed or €36,000 if married/civil partners in 2015. These limits are increased for dependent children.

15.5 Tax Credits

Tax credits are available under tax legislation and can be used to reduce the tax payable by an individual. There are numerous credits dependent on certain circumstances and conditions. Some of these credits are detailed below.

15.5.1 PERSONAL TAX CREDITS FOR 2015

This is a tax credit available to every individual tax resident in Ireland and the level of the credit is based on the civil status of the person – whether the individual is single, widowed, married, or a civil partner.

A single person is entitled to a tax credit of €1,650.

Married persons or civil partners who are jointly assessed to tax are entitled to a tax credit of €3,300.

A widowed person or surviving civil partner is entitled to a tax credit:

(a)   in the year of death of the spouse/civil partner the tax credit is €3,300; and

(b)   thereafter if no qualifying children the tax credit is €2,190.

Various rates apply to widowed person or surviving civil partner with a qualifying child, with the rates dependent on the year the person was bereaved.

Examples:

Mary is single and is entitled to a tax credit of €1,650 as a deduction against her income tax liability.

Mary and Ron are married and jointly assessed to tax and are entitled to a tax credit of €3,300 as a deduction against their income tax liability.

Jennifer, who lost her husband Michael in June 2015, is entitled to a tax credit of €3,300 in 2015 and as she has no children, she will be entitled to a tax credit of €2,190 in 2016 and thereafter.

15.5.2   SINGLE PERSON CHILD CARER TAX CREDIT

An individual is entitled to a single person child carer tax credit of €1,650 if the individual is single, a widow or widower, a surviving civil partner, a divorced, separated, or deserted parent or in a dissolved civil partnership, and the individual is the primary carer and has the custody of a child (which includes a stepchild or an adopted child) and the child resides with the individual for the greater part of a year and the individual maintains the child at his or her own expense.

The child must reside with the claimant for the whole or greater part (more than six months) of the year of assessment. If the child was born in the year of assessment, he or she must reside with the claimant for the greater part of the period from when he or she was born. A child can only be the subject of one claim, and a claimant can only make a claim for one child for a year of assessment irrespective of the number of children that reside with him or her.

Example:

Mary is single and has a daughter and qualifies for the single person child carer tax credit. Her income for the year is €50,000 and her income tax is as follows (ignoring allowances and reliefs):

€37,800 * 20% =   €7,560

€12,200 * 40% =   €4,880

€50,000 results in €12,440 income tax.

Less:

Tax credits:

Single: (€1,650)

Single person carer credit   (€1,650)

Net tax   €9,140

15.5.3   PAYE TAX CREDIT

A PAYE tax credit of €1,650 is available for deduction against income that is subject to the PAYE system. If a person has PAYE income of less than €1,650 only an amount equivalent to the actual PAYE income can be deducted as a tax credit.

Example:

Maeve gets a part-time job over the Christmas and receives €800 in payment under the PAYE system. The maximum PAYE tax credit that Maeve can claim is €800.

If Maeve had employment income of €5,000 paid under the PAYE system she will be entitled to the full PAYE credit of €1,650.

Example:

Mary is single, earns €50,000 (subject to PAYE) in 2015 and has a daughter and qualifies for the single person child carer tax credit. Her income tax is as follows:

€37,800 * 20% =	€7,560
€12,200 * 40% =	€4,880

€50,000 results in €12,440 income tax.

Less:

Tax credits:

Single:	(€1,650)
PAYE	(€1,650)
Single person carer credit	(€1,650)
Net tax	€7,490

There are restrictions and conditions on a spouse, civil partners, or child obtaining the PAYE credit when the income is paid by the spouse, civil partner, or parent or a partnership of the spouse, civil partner, or parent.

15.5.4   RENT RELIEF FOR PRIVATE RENTED ACCOMMODATION

Rent relief at a rate of 20% is available for rent paid up to a maximum in 2015 of €600 for single persons (the maximum is €1,200 for 2015 for a person over age 55) and €1,200 in 2015 for married, widowed, or surviving civil partner (the maximum is €2,400 in 2015 for married persons aged over 55). Relief only applies to persons who commenced renting before 7 December 2010.

Example:

Stephen aged 26 pays €6,500 in rent each year. He has been renting since 2009. For the year 2015 he can claim €600 * 20%=€120.

15.5.5   PENSION CONTRIBUTIONS

Tax relief is available; currently against the highest rate of tax payable by a person, for payments into a pension. The relief is based on the age of the taxpayer and is capped at a percentage of a person's net relevant earnings (employment income or self-employed earnings after deduction of losses and capital allowances). There is an overall limit/cap on net relevant earnings of €115,000 (in 2015) that can be used when calculating the tax relief.

Age	% of Net Relevant Earnings
Up to 30	15%
30 up to 40	20%
40 up to 50	25%
50 up to 55	30%
55 up to 60	35%
60 and upwards	40%

Example:

John, a 45-year-old self-employed, dentist has earnings of €225,000 and has paid €60,000 into his pension fund in 2015. He can claim tax relief on 25% of €115,000=€28,750. He will get tax relief of €11,500 on the pension payment (€28,750 * 40%) in 2015.

15.5.6 PROFESSIONAL SERVICES

Income tax at the standard rate (currently 20%) is deducted from payments made for professional services by government departments, State bodies, local authorities, and other specified bodies (TCA 1997, ss 520–529). Legal services provided by solicitors are professional services and tax is deducted, known as professional services withholding tax (PSWT), when an invoice is being paid. A credit for the tax deducted is given against the income tax liability of the year in which PSWT is deducted. In certain hardship circumstances a refund of the PSWT may apply.

15.5.7 OTHER TAX RELIEFS

Other tax reliefs include:

(a) Property-based reliefs;

(b) Medical insurance premiums;

(c) Tax relief on films;

(d) Tax relief for loan interest; and

(e) Medical expenses.

15.6 Types of Income

Different tax rules apply depending on the type of income and how the income is earned. Different types of income are divided into different schedules and within Schedule D into different classes. This chapter will primarily focus on Schedule D and Schedule E income when discussing income tax.

15.6.1 SCHEDULE D

Schedule D covers income tax and sources of income are divided into a number of classes:

(a) Case I – trade income;

(b) Case II – income from a profession;

(c)   Case III – discounts, interest, annual payments (excluding deposit interest received under a deduction of tax (which is taxed under Case IV)), dividends on credit union regular share accounts (special share accounts are taxed under Case IV), and income from foreign securities and possessions that do not suffer Irish tax at source, for example; foreign rental income, dividends and interest, foreign employment;

(d)   Case IV – annual profits or gains not falling into another category as well as shares issued instead of dividends and interest subject to deposit interest retention tax (DIRT) from financial institutions; and

(e)   Case V – rental income within the State.

For the purposes of this chapter Schedule D Case I & II will be dealt with together and will be called income from a business.

15.6.2   SCHEDULE E

Schedule E covers income received from employment and most people will be familiar with this tax if they have ever been an employee. It covers payments received from the employer – for example salary, cash bonus, and benefits in kind, for example, payment of health insurance for the employee and occupational pensions. The employer deducts income tax, PRSI, and the Universal Social Charge from the payment and pays it directly to Revenue Commissioners and the balance remaining is paid to the employee. Details of the deductions are set out in the payslip. Each year Revenue issues a statement of tax credits for each individual and employers are informed of the tax bands and tax credits applicable to employees to facilitate the deduction of the correct tax. Most employees pay tax by deduction under the PAYE (Pay As You Earn) scheme, where the tax is deducted by the employer from the salary and other payments payable to the employee.

15.6.3   SCHEDULE F

Schedule F covers Irish dividend income from an Irish company received by an Irish individual or partnership.

15.7   Deposit Interest & Deposit Interest Retention Tax (DIRT) (Scheduled D Case IV)

For the tax year 2015 the rate of DIRT is 41%.

Generally a financial institution is obliged to deduct DIRT from any interest paid on a deposit account and the saver receives the net interest amount. For taxation purposes the person is taxed on the gross income and can claim a credit for the DIRT deducted against the income tax on the deposit interest.

The deduction of DIRT satisfies the income tax liability of an individual for the income tax payable on the interest received.

Deposit interest that is subject to DIRT is exempt from the USC and it is therefore necessary to exclude deposit interest subject to DIRT when calculating the USC charge. However, gross interest must be included when calculating a person's reckonable income that is used to calculate the amount of PRSI that an individual must pay.

Example:

Emer has been saving to purchase her own home and has a deposit account with a bank in Ireland in 2015 on which she has received net interest of €8,000 as the bank has deducted DIRT of 41% on her gross interest.

For income tax purposes Emer will pay tax on the gross interest received under Schedule D Case IV. The DIRT must be added back to the net interest to calculate the tax payable and Emer will receive a credit for the DIRT amount.

€8,000=59% so €13,559.32 is the gross amount. DIRT is €5,559.32.

A special relief was introduced from 15 October 2014 to provide a refund for DIRT deducted when the savings are used to purchase a first principal private residence. The refund will be available until the end of 2017.

Companies can open a deposit account and receive interest payments without deduction of DIRT.

An exemption from DIRT applies to an individual (or his spouse or civil partner) aged 65 or over and whose total income does not exceed the income tax exemption limit (total income of less than €18,000 if single or widowed or €36,000 if married/civil partners plus an additional amount for dependent children). A declaration to confirm eligibility for the exemption must be made to the financial institution.

Example:

Income Tax for Married Couples – PAYE Income and Deposit Interest in 2015.

In addition to the net deposit interest of €8,000 Emer also has PAYE income of €50,000. She is married and her spouse also works and has PAYE income of €60,000. Emer is jointly assessed for income tax purposes. Assume €20,000 tax has been deducted under PAYE. For the tax year 2015 what is their income tax liability?

Steps:

1. Identify the different sources of income.

2. Identify the relevant tax bands and rates of tax.

3. Ascertain if any tax credits are available.

4. Ascertain if any losses are available.

5. Ascertain if any reliefs or allowances are available.

Sources of income 2015:

Schedule D Case IV – deposit interest

€8,000=59% so €13,559.32 is the gross amount.

DIRT is €5,559.32 (41%)

Schedule E – employment income

PAYE income €50,000 – self

PAYE income €60,000 – spouse

Total   €110,000

Total income:

€13,559.32	Schedule D Case IV	pay tax on gross income
€110,000	Schedule E	
€123,559.32	Total income	

(Continued)

Relevant Tax Band:

Married – 2 incomes – tax year 2015.

For married or civil partners where both spouses/civil partners have income, the first €42,800 (plus an additional €24,800 maximum or the amount of the second income if less) (i.e. up to €67,600 of income) is taxed at 20% and the balance of income is taxed at 40%.

€67,600 * 20%, balance at 40%, Deposit Interest at 41%.

Tax credits available

Married couple	€3,300
PAYE self	€1,650
PAYE spouse	€1,650

Losses – no information

Reliefs/allowances – no information

Tax calculation

Total income: €123,559.32

Taxed as follows:

€67,600 * 20%	€13,520	
€13,559.32* 41%	€5,559.32	
42,400 * 40%	€16,960	
Total		€36,039.32
Less Tax credits:		
Personal credit	€3,300	
PAYE self	€1,650	
PAYE spouse	€1,650	
		€6,600
		€29,439.32
Less DIRT paid		(€5,559.32)
Less PAYE paid		(€20,000.00)
Net income tax payable		€3,880

15.8   Rental Income – Schedule D Case V

In calculating the amount of rental income liable to income tax, certain deductions and expenses are permitted to be deducted from the rental income. Deductions can include any rent paid on the property (the property could be sub-let), any rates payable, goods and services provided to the tenant, maintenance costs, repairs, insurance, capital allowances on fixtures and fittings (at a rate of 12.5%), and interest on money borrowed to purchase, improve, or replace property (the interest on residential property is capped at 75% of the interest) if the property has been registered with the Private Residential Tenancies Board.

Example:

James has invested in two houses and he rents them out to professionals each year. He took out mortgages to pay for the houses and he pays mortgage repayments totalling €30,000 each year of which €10,000 relates to interest on the mortgages. He received rental income of €15,000 in 2015. He spent €3,000 maintaining the houses.

He will be able to claim a deduction of €3,000 in expenses and €7,500 for the interest payment from the income of €15,000 leaving him with a net rental income of €4,500 liable to income tax.

15.9   Income from a Business – Schedule D Case I & II

Schedule D Case I and II relates to the rules on the taxation of the income that arises on a trade/profession (a business).

A person is taxed based on the annual accounts of the business. The annual accounts in the tax year are used and the date of the annual accounts does not matter for an ongoing business – tax is paid on accounts of 12 months ending in a tax year – for example, a year ended 31 March, 30 June, 30 September, 31 December or any other date can be used. Special rules apply on the commencement and cessation of a business (see below).

Tax on other income is based on the income earned in a tax year (1 January to 31 December).

Taxable profits are the business turnover (gross income/sales excluding VAT if VAT registered) less deductible allowable business expenses that are used wholly and exclusively for the business.

15.9.1   PERMITTED DEDUCTIONS AND ADD BACKS

Day-to-day running costs and expenditure and business expenses incurred in making a profit are deductible subject to certain rules. Examples of deductible expenses include; light and heat, telephone, broadband, mobile charges, rent, and accountancy fees.

Pre-trading expenses incurred in the three-year period prior to commencing business are deductible when calculating the business income. They are treated as having been incurred when the business commences.

A claim cannot be made for private expenses – these are expenses not used wholly and exclusively for the business, any personal expenses, and business entertainment expenses. Only certain food and subsistence expenses are allowable. Where expenses relate to both business and private use the amount must be apportioned to exclude the private use.

Capital expenditure is not deductible but instead a capital allowance may be available (see **15.9.4.2**).

Claims can only be made for expenses actually incurred and for which receipts have been retained.

Example:

Aidan is a self-employed software designer. He operates out of an office in his home. He cannot claim a deduction for all of his heating and electricity bills. He will need to apportion the bills between private (home) usage and his office (business) usage.

He cannot seek a deduction for his daily lunch when he is working out of his home office. He may be able to seek a deduction for his food expenses if he is away from the office working on site for a client.

15.9.2   DRAWINGS – HOW CAN A SELF-EMPLOYED PERSON GET MONEY OUT OF THE BUSINESS

An individual pays tax on the net profits of the business without taking account of any drawings removed by the owner from the business.

Drawings cover all payments and items taken by the owner from the business – this would include any salary, bonus, cash, or stock withdrawals.

Drawings are not valid deductions from the income of the business for taxation purposes and must be added back to the profits to calculate the taxable profits of the business.

Drawings are treated as a withdrawal of capital from the business and the drawings will be recorded in the balance sheet of the business.

15.9.3   CALCULATING TAX ON SCHEDULE D CASE I & II INCOME

It is necessary to start with the net profit figure in the financial accounts of the business – the profit and loss account for a 12-month period ending in the tax year (see **15.10.1** and **15.10.2** for special rules on commencement or cessation of a business).

The business expenses should be reviewed to ascertain if all of them are deductible for tax purposes.

If the accounts have made a deduction for depreciation then this deduction will not be allowed for tax purposes and this expense will need to be added back to ascertain the taxable profits. A person may be able to make a claim for capital allowances instead (see **15.9.4.2**).

If the accounts have made a deduction for drawings then this deduction will not be allowed for tax purposes and the drawings will need to be added back to ascertain the taxable profits.

15.9.3.1   Steps

1. Identify the different sources of income.
2. Adjust income for tax purposes if necessary:
   (a)   Are all expenses deductible?
   (b)   Check for depreciation.
   (c)   Check for drawings.
3. Identify the relevant tax bands and rates of tax.
4. Ascertain if any tax credits are available.
5. Ascertain if any losses are available.
6. Ascertain if any reliefs or allowances are available.

Example:

Aidan has made a net profit for the year ended 30 September 2015 of €25,000 having taken a salary of €2,000 each month from his software business. Calculate his income tax liability on the basis that he has no other source of income and he is single aged 25.

Steps:

1. Identify the different sources of income – Schedule D Case I only.
2. Adjust income for tax purposes – €24,000 taken by way of drawings.

3. Identify the relevant tax bands and rates of tax: single: €33,800 * 20%, balance at 40%.

4. Ascertain if any tax credits are available – single €1,650.

5. Ascertain if any losses are available – none.

6. Ascertain if any reliefs or allowances are available – no information.

Schedule D Case I

Net profit:

€25,000

€24,000 add back drawings (€2,000 * 12)

€49,000 adjusted profits for tax purposes

Taxed as follows:

€33,800 * 20%	€6,760
€15,200 * 40%	€6,080
€49,000	€12,840

Less Tax credit

Personal	€1,650
Net tax payable	€11,190

15.9.4 DEPRECIATION V CAPITAL ALLOWANCES

15.9.4.1 Depreciation

Depreciation is a wear and tear allowance calculated using accounting rules to determine the rate at which an asset should be written down in value over the life of an asset. Different rates of depreciation will apply to different assets; for example a building, a motor vehicle, and computer software. A building will last many years while a motor vehicle or a laptop or software may only have a short life.

Deprecation is not a valid deduction for taxation purposes and any deduction for depreciation must be added back to the net profits of the business to calculate the adjusted profits for taxation purposes.

A capital allowance may instead be claimed against the taxable income if certain conditions are satisfied.

15.9.4.2 Capital allowances

Capital expenditure is expenditure on assets that have a lasting use, for example a photocopier or a new office building.

The full capital expenditure cannot be deducted from the trading profits of the business in the year in which it is acquired. Instead an allowance, called a capital allowances, is deductible.

Capital allowances are calculated on different categories of assets at different rates; for example, at 12.5% each year on the cost of plant and machinery.

There is a maximum cap on the net cost of a motor vehicle for capital allowances purposes. The current cap is €24,000 and whether an allowance is available and the amount of capital allowance is linked to the carbon emission level of the vehicle.

When an asset is disposed of a check is done to ascertain if a further allowance is required (a balancing allowance) or whether the taxpayer needs to pay back any capital allowances to Revenue (a balancing charge).

Example:

Máiread runs a retail shop. In January 2015, she purchased machinery for use in the shop at a cost of €12,000.

Capital allowance is calculated on a straight-line basis on plant and machinery at a rate of 12.5% of the net cost of the asset if the asset is used in the business.

Máiread will be able to seek a deduction for capital allowance on the machinery of €12,000 * 12.5%=€1,500 in 2015. She will not be entitled to deduct the full €12,000 in 2015.

15.10   Special Rules

15.10.1   COMMENCEMENT OF A BUSINESS

There are special start-up rules for new businesses that must be followed for the first three years in business.

In the first year of business income tax is payable on the profits from the date of commencement of the business until 31 December in that year (s 66 of the TCA 1997).

In the second year in business the profits to be assessed are those in a set of accounts made up in that tax year for a 12-month period, for example accounts made up to 31 March, 30 June, 30 September in that tax year, or if there are more than one set of accounts those made up to the latest date or, if there are no accounts, the actual profits from 1 January to 31 December in that tax year.

In the third year and onwards in business the profits liable to income tax are those profits assessed on a set of accounts of 12 months ending in a tax year.

A special relief applies in the third year which allows a person to make a claim to have the third year profits reduced by any excess profits in year two (the excess profits are calculated as being profits assessed in year two which exceeded the actual profits in year two if calculated on an actual basis from 1 January to 31 December in year two). A claim for the relief must be made in writing by 31 October following the third year of business, i.e. on the same date as the paper tax return must be filed.

If the excess profits in year two are greater than the taxable profits in year three any remaining year two excess can be carried forward and used against future profits.

15.10.2   CEASING IN BUSINESS

In the final year, tax is payable on profits from 1 January to the cessation date.

In the previous year, the profit situation is reassessed and if the actual profits for the year from 1 January to 31 December exceed the profits in the financial year accounts then the actual profits figure must be used to calculate the income tax payable. The onus is on the taxpayer to do this calculation and pay over the revised tax liability.

15.10.3   SHORT-LIVED BUSINESSES

Where a business only lasts three years (i.e. starts and ceases within three tax years) a special provision is available that allows a taxable person to elect that the taxable profits for the three years cannot exceed the profits earned in the three years.

15.10.4 CHANGE OF ACCOUNTING YEAR END

If a person changes the accounting year end date this must be notified to Revenue. A taxpayer is obliged to review the preceding year under s 65 of the TCA 1997 to ascertain what the profits would have been had the new accounting year end date been used. If the profits using the new date exceed the original profits additional tax must be paid.

15.11 Losses

15.11.1 INCOME FROM A BUSINESS – SCHEDULE D CASE I & II

A loss incurred in a trade or profession in a current tax year can be used as follows in accordance with ss 381 to 390 of the TCA 1997:

(a) against *any other income* chargeable to tax in the same year; and

(b) any remaining unutilised loss can be carried forward and set off against future profits of the *same trade or profession* in the future.

Restrictions on the use of losses to a maximum of €31,750 (or the actual loss if lower) in a year have been introduced in Finance Act 2015 when an individual carries on a trade or profession in a non-active capacity (TCA 1997, ss 381B and 381C).

Examples:

Prior Year Losses

Mark has been in business for many years. He owns two shoe shops but the businesses have been suffering in recent years. He made a loss of €3,000 in 2013 and €4,000 in 2014 and for 2015 he has made a small profit of €10,000.

Mark can utilise the losses that he made in the business in 2013 and 2014 to reduce his taxable income in 2015 leaving him €3,000 liable to income tax (€10,000 – €7,000).

Same Year Losses

Ruth runs a craft shop and she is struggling. Luckily she made some property investments in 2000 and she is generating some rental income of €20,000 in 2015 that she is surviving on as her craft shop has made a loss of €5,000 in the financial year ending 31 October 2015.

Ruth can utilise the loss from her business against the rental income so that only €15,000 of the rental income is liable to income tax.

15.11.2 TERMINAL LOSS RELIEF

In the case of a business that is being shut down and discontinued, special loss rules apply, which are called terminal loss relief rules (TCA 1997, s 385).

Terminal loss relief can be claimed for losses made in the last 12-month period of the trade or profession. How the relief works is that there is a look back at the profits made in the business and the losses can be carried back and set against profits made in the business for the three years of assessment prior to the tax year in which the discontinuance occurs.

Example:

Ryan's business has reduced considerably in 2015 as many other stores closed in the shopping centre and he has very few customers. Ryan decides to shut down his business. He has losses of €20,000 for 2015.

He had made small profits in recent years: €4,000 in 2014, €6,000 in 2013, and €6,000 in 2012.

He can claim terminal loss relief and utilise the €20,000 losses against his profits for 2014, 2013, and 2012. He can utilise €16,000 of these losses to eliminate the profits in these years.

15.11.3   LOSSES AND CAPITAL ALLOWANCES – CONNECTION

Capital allowances can be used to create or to increase a loss in a business if there are any capital allowances remaining after they have been set off against any balancing charges in the same tax year.

15.11.4   SCHEDULE D CASE IV

These losses can only be set against other Schedule D Case IV income or carried forward and can only be offset against future Schedule D Case IV income.

15.11.5   SCHEDULE D CASE V

Rental losses on property in the State are carried forward and can be offset only against rental income from property in the State.

15.12   Tax Incentives for Investors

There are a number of tax incentives in place to encourage investment in business and to encourage the formation of business operating through companies. These include:

15.12.1   EMPLOYMENT AND INVESTMENT INCENTIVE (EII) – INCOME TAX RELIEF

A tax relief applies for making investments in certain qualifying companies. A person can get income tax relief for making an investment in certain corporate trades. Relief is available for each individual of up to €150,000 per annum in each tax year up to 2020.

15.12.2   START-UP RELIEF FOR ENTREPRENEURS (SURE)

A special tax relief is available to individuals who start up and work full-time in his/her own company that engages in a qualifying business. The relief applies by enabling the individual to claim back the income tax paid in the previous six years to invest equity by subscribing for shares in the new company. Up to €100,000 can be recovered in each of the previous six years and €100,000 in the current year.

15.12.3   START YOUR OWN BUSINESS

Currently there is an exemption from income tax (for income up to €40,000) for individuals who have been unemployed for at least 12 months and set up a qualifying, unincorporated business. The relief will apply for the first two years of the new business. USC and PRSI will apply on this income. The scheme runs until 31 December 2016.

15.12.4 OTHER RELIEFS

Other reliefs include tax relief on investments in films and relief for investment in renewable energy generation.

15.12.5 HIGH EARNING RESTRICTIONS

Where an individual is held to be a 'high income individual' restrictions are imposed on certain reliefs that the individual can claim.

The purpose of the legislation is to ensure that high income individuals do not use specified reliefs to reduce significantly the amount of tax that they pay and to ensure that tax at an effective rate of 30% is paid in a tax year.

The restrictions apply to a person who has income of €125,000 and receives specified reliefs totalling €80,000. The specified reliefs are set out in legislation.

15.13 Universal Social Charge (USC)

This is a charge payable on gross income (after a deduction for certain capital allowances and losses) before pension contributions.

An exemption from the USC applies in 2015 where an individual's total income for the year does not exceed €12,012. Once this income threshold is reached all of the income is liable to the USC.

Income that is subject to Deposit Interest Retention Tax (DIRT) is not liable to the USC.

Certain Department of Social Protection payments and similar payments paid by other government departments are also exempt from the USC.

The 2015 USC rates are detailed below.

15.13.1 STANDARD RATE

(a)	Income up to €12,012	1.5%;
(b)	Income from €12,012.01 to €17,576 (€5,564)	3.5%;
(c)	Income from €17,576.01 to €70,044 (€52,468)	7%;
(d)	Income above €70,044	8%.

15.13.2 SPECIAL REDUCED RATE

A special reduced rate applies for individuals aged 70 years and for individuals who hold a full medical card (in each case if their aggregate income for the year is €60,000 or less).

| (a) | Income up to €12,012 | 1.5%; and |
| (b) | Income above €12,012 | 3.5%. |

Regardless of age persons with non-PAYE income above €100,000 pay an extra 3% surcharge on this income (excluding income subject to PAYE) that exceeds €100,000 in a year. This means that a rate of 11% applies to such income in 2015.

Examples:

Catherine, aged 32, earns €60,000 PAYE income and €2,000 gross deposit interest that is subject to DIRT. She does not hold a medical card.

She will have to pay USC on €60,000 calculated as follows:

€12,012 * 1.5% =	€180.18
€5,564 * 3.5% =	€194.74
€42,424 * 7% =	€2,969.68
€60,000	€3,344.60

Joan, aged 72, with a pension of €58,000.

She will have to pay USC on €58,000 calculated as follows:

€12,012 * 1.5% =	€180.18
€45,988 * 3.5% =	€1,609.58
€58,000	€1,789.76

Ciaran, aged 52, earns €160,000 in his own business and €2,000 gross deposit interest that is subject to DIRT.

He will have to pay USC on €160,000 calculated as follows:

€12,012 * 1.5% =	€180.18
€5,564 * 3.5% =	€194.74
€52,468 * 7% =	€3,672.76
€29,956 * 8% =	€2,396.48
€60,000 *11% =	€6,600.00
€160,000	€13,044.16

Edward, aged 72, earns investment income of €120,000.

He will have to pay USC on €120,000 calculated as follows:

€12,012 * 1.5% =	€180.18
€5,564 * 3.5% =	€194.74
€52,468 * 7% =	€3,672.76
€29,956 * 8% =	€2,396.48
€20,000 *11% =	€2,200.00
€120,000	€8,644.16

15.14 Pay Related Social Insurance (PRSI)

PRSI is calculated on an employee's reckonable pay. Reckonable pay is the gross money pay plus notional pay (benefit in kind) if applicable. PRSI applies to all income of a person subject to the exclusions outlined below.

Since 1 January 2014 employees also pay PRSI on non-pay income.

The PRSI contributions for a self-employed person are paid on the person's gross income less capital allowances and allowable pension deductions. Self-employed persons pay PRSI on all sources of income.

While PRSI is collected by Revenue, PRSI is administered by the Department of Social Protection.

15.14.1 RATES OF PRSI

The 2015 rates are as follows:

(a)   For employees – under Category A1 the current rate is 4%.

(b)   An employee is exempt from PRSI if his income is below €352 per week. If the income is above €352 per week, it is all subject to PRSI.

(c)   An employer must also make a PRSI payment for his employees: an employer pays at the rate of 8.5% on income up to €356 per week and 10.75% on income above this level.

(d)   For self-employed persons the rate is 4% for the year 2015 with a minimum amount of €500 payable (if 4% of total income is less than this amount). An exemption applies if total income is less than €5,000.

Example:

Aine is a self-employed hat designer and runs a retail shop selling her hats. She has the following income in 2015:

Income from a retail shop of €40,000

Deposit interest €10,000

Rental income €20,000

Her PRSI liability for 2015 will be €40,000+€10,000+€20,000=€70,000 * 4%=€2,800.

15.15   Administration and Payment of Income Tax

15.15.1 TAX REGISTRATION – REGISTERING FOR TAX

A person (including a company) must notify Revenue Commissioners when he/she/it has started in business.

The form TR1 is the registration form that applies to individuals, partnerships, trusts, or unincorporated bodies to register for income tax, employer's PAYE/PRSI, VAT, and Relevant Contracts Tax.

Information that must be filed in the Form TR1 includes the following:

(a)   General details about the individual: name, address, PPS number, gender, nationality, date of birth, contact details.

(b)   Business details: business address, business details, legal form, commencement date, accounts details, rental details of premises, and adviser details.

(c)   Confirmation of registration for income tax purposes.

(d)   Details for registration of Value Added Tax (VAT).

(e)   Details for registration as an employer for PAYE/PRSI purposes.

(f)   Details for registration for Relevant Contracts Tax (RCT) purposes.

The form TR2 is the registration form that applies to companies to register for corporation tax, employer's PAYE/PRSI, VAT, and Relevant Contracts Tax.

Income tax is the tax payable on the profits of the business.

If a person is to be engaged as an employee of a business the business must register as an employer and register to operate the PAYE system and register for PRSI.

A business must also register for VAT if it is a taxable person and the annual turnover exceeds €75,000 in relation to the supply of goods or €37,500 in relation to the supply of services.

The tax reference for an individual will be the PPS number – Personal Public Service number.

15.15.2 PRELIMINARY TAX

Employees have income tax, PRSI, and USC deducted directly from their salary by their employer. A similar system does not apply for self-employed persons so a different system is used.

Preliminary tax is an estimate of the tax due for the full tax year and must be paid by 31 October (early November, if using ROS to pay and file online) in the tax year. Revenue announce the ROS extension deadline each year.

The payment of preliminary tax must include a payment for PRSI and USC.

To avoid paying interest a certain minimum payment must be made:

(a) 90% of the current year final tax liability (e.g. 90% of 2015 tax liability for the tax year 2015); or

(b) 100% of the preceding year's final tax liability (e.g. 100% of 2014 liability); or

(c) 105% of the year pre-dating the preceding year's final tax liability (e.g. 105% of 2013 liability) if you pay by direct debit and the 105% tax liability was not nil.

Example:

How much preliminary tax does Jane have to pay if she estimates that her tax liability for 2015 is €24,000? Her tax liability for 2014 was €30,000 and for 2013 was €20,000?

Choices:

2015:	€24,000 * 90% =	€21,600;
2014	€30,000 * 100% =	€30,000 or
2013	€20,000 * 105% =	€21,000 and pay by direct debit.

If the 90% formula is used and this estimate becomes incorrect when the final tax is calculated and 90% of the final tax liability is greater than the payment made, the taxpayer will then be *liable to interest* (0.0219% per day or part of a day) on the difference between the payment made and the actual final tax liability. The full tax liability also becomes immediately due and payable from the 31 October preliminary tax date.

Example:

Gerry pays €45,000 in preliminary tax for his 2015 income tax liability. This was calculated based on 90% of his 2015 tax liability which he estimated to be €50,000 (€50,000 * 90%=€45,000). The actual 2015 liability turns out to be €65,000 (90%=€58,500).

This means that he has underpaid the preliminary tax by €13,500.

Interest is due on the underpayment of €13,500 * 0.0219% * number of days from 31 October 2015 until the date the €13,500 plus interest is paid.

The underpayment also triggers the payment of his full 2015 liability as it becomes due and payable from 31 October 2015 and interest will run on the full amount until it is paid.

Some relief is available where the amount is underpaid by less than 5% (or €3,175 maximum) and it is paid by 31 December. Also if the amount underpaid is not more than €635 then interest is not payable as €635 is the permitted margin of error.

It is the taxpayer's responsibility to make the necessary payments and filings under the self-assessment system. The tax payment should be made to the Collector General.

15.15.3 PAY AND FILE SYSTEM – PAYMENT OF TAX AND MAKING A TAX RETURN

A person who has a business and also has PAYE employment income only needs to file one income tax return that covers all sources of income. Proprietary directors and other persons notified by Revenue are also obliged to file a tax return.

Tax law provides for both civil penalties and criminal sanctions for the failure to make a return or making a false return or claiming allowances and relief to which a person is not entitled. See below.

There is a set date for the payment of income tax and the filing of income tax returns. The 'pay and file' date is 31 October in each tax year.

On 31 October a person liable to the self-assessment system must:

(a)   pay preliminary income tax, USC, and PRSI for the current tax year;

(b)   file an income tax and CGT tax return (form 11) for the previous tax year; and

(c)   pay any balance of income tax, USC, and PRSI from the previous tax year.

By paying and filing on ROS the date is extended to early November (date is announced annually by Revenue).

In the tax year 2015 for an ongoing business:

(a)   preliminary tax for the tax year 2015 has to be paid by 31 October 2015;

(b)   the tax return for tax year 2014 must be filed by 31 October 2015; and

(c)   the balance of the tax due for the tax year 2014 must be paid by 31 October 2015.

By paying and filing on ROS the date is extended to 12 November 2015.

15.15.4 METHODS OF FILING A TAX RETURN

Taxpayers can file their returns in a paper or electronic format.

15.15.4.1 ROS

Tax filing can be done electronically and payment can be made electronically using the Revenue On-Line Service (ROS) accessible at www.revenue.ie. Certain taxpayers are obliged to make payments to Revenue and file their tax returns online using the ROS system. The pay and file date is extended as an incentive to those who pay and file using ROS.

15.15.4.2 New business

For a new business extended time is granted for the filing of the first tax return. The tax return for the first year and second year of business can be filed at the same time if the person or his spouse was not carrying on another business in the tax year in which the new business was set up.

15.15.5   LATE FILING OF RETURN – CONSEQUENCES – SURCHARGE

If a person fails to file the tax return by the pay and file date then a surcharge is imposed on the person. The amount of the surcharge depends on the lateness of the return filing date.

If the return is filed within two months of the return filing date (i.e. by 31 December) a surcharge of 5% of the tax up to a maximum of €12,695 is payable in addition to the tax liability for the tax year. If the return is filed more than two months after the return filing date (i.e. after 31 December in the tax year) a surcharge of 10% of the tax up to a maximum of €63,485 is payable in addition to the tax liability for the tax year.

15.15.6   LATE PAYMENT OF TAX – CONSEQUENCES – INTEREST

Interest at a rate of is 0.0219% per day or part of a day is imposed if tax is not paid on time and continues to accrue until the tax is paid. Civil and criminal penalties can also arise in the case of a late filing of a return or a failure to file a return.

Example:

Joe, a sole trader, fails to file and pay his income tax liability for the tax year 2014 by the ROS deadline in November 2015. He has trading income of €60,000; he is single, aged 32, and has no other source of income. Assume that his total income tax, USC, and PRSI liability is €25,000.

What are the consequences?

a.   If he pays by 30 November 2015?

b.   If he pays by 13 January 2016?

Surcharge

a.   If he pays by 30 November 2015?

A surcharge of 5% of the tax up to a maximum of €12,695

€25,000 * 5% =   €1,250

b.   If he pays by 13 January 2016?

A surcharge of 10% of the tax up to a maximum of €63,485

€25,000 * 10% =   €2,500

Interest

Interest at a rate of is 0.0219% per day or part of a day is payable until the tax is paid.

a.   If he pays by 30 November 2015?

Due 31 October 2015 – paid 30 November 2015

30 days * 0.0219% * amount not paid

b.   If he pays by 13 January 2016?

Due 31 October 2015 – paid 13 January 2016

30+31+13=74 days * 0.0219% * amount not paid.

15.15.7   ASSESSMENT

Full self-assessment is required by taxpayers when making the tax return filing. A taxpayer must include a self-assessment of the tax payable for the tax year in the tax return.

An individual has an option to file a tax return by 31 August in advance of the pay and file date to enable Revenue to do the self-assessment for the taxpayer.

If a taxpayer files electronically using ROS and uses the calculation of liability provided by ROS in the self-assessment, interest or penalties will not apply if the assessment is incorrect owing to any error or mistake that might arise from using the ROS calculated assessment figures.

If a person fails to include a tax self-assessment a fixed penalty of €250 will be imposed and a fixed penalty of €100 will be imposed if a person does not amend a self-assessment when this is necessary.

An assessment will issue from Revenue after the return has been submitted. If a person is not happy with an assessment (Revenue decision on the return) he/she can appeal the assessment to the Appeal Commissioners within 30 days of the notice of the assessment.

15.16 Obligations to Keep Records

Every person must keep full and accurate records for tax purposes; this includes records of all businesses from their commencement. The records must be sufficient to enable the taxpayer to make a proper return of income for tax purposes.

The records must include books of accounts that record all purchases and sales of goods and services and all amounts received and all amounts paid out. They should show cash introduced to the business (capital), details of debtors and creditors, as well as all items of expenditure and drawings from the business.

Supporting records for example invoices, bank statements, cheque stubs, and receipts must be retained as well as records of all drawings – all amounts of cash withdrawn from the business or cheques drawn on the business bank account for personal use.

The business prepares its financial statements based on these records: its profit and loss account and balance sheet.

Records must be retained for at least six years.

Failure to keep proper records is an offence with a risk of a fine or imprisonment.

15.17 Expression of Doubt

If a person is unsure about a tax matter when filing a tax return a person may express doubt provided that the return is submitted on time (i.e. by the return filing date for the tax year or if a company for the accounting period involved). The doubt over the tax treatment of the income must be genuine having checked the tax legislation and guidance notes issued by Revenue. If Revenue rejects an expression of doubt a person can appeal against that decision.

If the doubt is genuine and Revenue decides to treat the income in a different manner from the manner that the taxpayer treated the matter, a person will not be penalised as he has pointed out the doubt to Revenue.

15.18 Anti-Avoidance

There are extensive anti-avoidance rules provided for in legislation in Ireland to prevent persons taking certain steps or participating in certain transactions to minimise or avoid paying tax.

15.19   Revenue Powers

Revenue has extensive powers to enforce tax legislation including:

(a)   to carry out inspections;

(b)   to request information from taxpayers and from third parties;

(c)   to enter premises;

(d)   to make enquiries and ask questions;

(e)   to carry out investigations; and

(f)   to carry out audits – to verify returns – income and entitlement to tax credits, reliefs, and allowances.

15.20   Penalties

Both civil penalties and criminal sanctions can be imposed for:

(a)   the failure to make a return;

(b)   the making of a false return;

(c)   facilitating the making of a false return; or

(d)   claiming tax credits, allowances, or reliefs which are not due.

In the event of a criminal prosecution, a person convicted of an offence on indictment may be liable to a fine not exceeding €126,970 and/or to a fine of up to double the difference between the declared tax due and the tax ultimately found to be due and/or to imprisonment.

In addition, various penalties are imposed by Revenue based on when the failure or incorrect return is notified to Revenue, and whether it is a voluntary disclosure, an unprompted, or prompted qualifying disclosure (where the disclosure is made after Revenue notify a taxpayer that an audit is to be carried out). Mitigation of penalties may apply where a taxpayer cooperates with Revenue and penalties are also based on what caused the incorrect return to be filed – was it deliberate behaviour or was it carelessness? The penalties also are determined by the number of notifications a taxpayer has had to make to Revenue – is it a once-off or has the taxpayer a history of having to make disclosures?

15.21   Examples: Income Tax, Universal Social Charge, and PRSI

Example: Self-employed, married one income – 2015

Jamie asks you to prepare his income tax liability – he tells you that his net trading income is €120,000: €50,000 from the new retail shop he set up in March 2015 and €70,000 from his garage. He has no PAYE source income. He has rental income on an investment property of €30,000 in 2015 from which he had to pay €5,000 maintaining and painting the property and gross deposit interest of €10,000 which income was liable to Deposit Interest Retention Tax.

He had taken drawings from the retail shop of €15,000 during 2015 which he had deducted from the gross trading income which would otherwise have been €65,000.

He has losses from 2014 from his garage of €10,000.

He is married, aged 40, and his spouse does not work and they have no children.

Identify preliminary tax.

Identify pay and file dates.

Calculate his income tax, USC, and PRSI for 2015.

Preliminary tax

100% of 2014 tax liability; or

90% of 2015 tax liability – payable by 31 October 2015, 12 November 2015 if paid via ROS.

Pay and file dates.

His 2015 income tax return must be filed by 31 October 2016 (or early November 2016 if he uses ROS and also pays the balance of the tax due through ROS).

Steps:

1.   Identify the different sources of income.

2.   Adjust income for tax purposes if necessary.

3.   Identify the relevant tax bands and rates of tax.

4.   Ascertain if any tax credits are available.

5.   Ascertain if any losses are available.

6.   Ascertain if any reliefs or allowances are available.

Sources of income:

<u>Schedule D Case 1 –</u>

Garage - €70,000

New retail business-commencement rules apply:

50,000 – relates to trade March 2015 to 31 December 2015. If Jamie had produced accounts for a period after 31 December 2015, the income tax would be payable only on the income to 31 December 2015.

Add back drawing €15,000

Total taxable income €65,000.

Schedule D Case I:

Garage	€70,000
Less	
Losses carried forward	<u>(€10,000)</u>
	€60,000
Shop	<u>€65,000</u>
Net taxable	€125,000

Schedule D Case IV

Deposit interest	€10,000	
DIRT	10,000 * 41%	€4,100 deducted by the bank

(Continued)

Schedule D Case V

Gross Rental Income	€30,000
Less expenses	(€5,000)
Net taxable income	€25,000

Tax Credits:

Married: Personal tax credit	€3,300

Tax Paid

Deduction for DIRT	€4,100

Tax: – married – one spouse income – first €42,800 of income is taxed at 20% and the balance of income is taxed at 40%.

Total income

€125,000	net Schedule D Case I
€10,000	Schedule D Case IV
€25,000	Schedule D Case V
€160,000	

Income tax: 2015

€42,800 * 20%	€8,560
€10,000 * 41%	€4,100
€107,200 * 40%	€42,880
Total	€55,540

Less

Tax credits

Personal tax credit	(€3,300)
	€52,240

Less Tax already paid:

Deduction for DIRT	(€4,100)
Net tax payable	€48,140

PRSI

USC – 2015

€160,000 * 4%	€6,400

160,000 – 10,000=150,000 liable to USC:

First €12,012 * 1.5% =	€180.18
Next €5,564 * 3.5% =	€194.74
Next €52,468 * 7% =	€3,672.76
Next €29,956 * 8% =	€2,396.48
Last €50,000 * 11% =	€5,500
	€11,944.16
Total liability	€66,484.16

Example: Self-employed, married two incomes – one PAYE 2015

Jonathan is a businessman with a number of businesses. He has prepared his accounts for 2015 and he estimates that he will have the following income for 2015: He estimates that his net trading profits to 31 December 2015 are €170,000. He has no PAYE source income. He has net rental income on an investment property of €50,000 in 2015 and gross deposit interest of €30,000 which was liable to Deposit Interest Retention Tax.

He had taken drawings from the business of €80,000 during 2015 which he had deducted from the trading income.

The net trading profits include depreciation of €10,000 on a machine purchased for the trading business in 2011 which cost €100,000.

He is married and his spouse earns €30,000 working as a civil servant. He is aged 50 and they have no children. They are jointly assessed for income tax purposes.

Calculate the tax liability (income tax, PRSI, and USC) for 2015.

Steps:

1. Identify the different sources of income.

2. Adjust income for tax purposes if necessary.

3. Identify the relevant tax bands and rates of tax.

4. Ascertain if any tax credits are available.

5. Ascertain if any losses are available.

6. Ascertain if any reliefs or allowances are available.

Sources of income:

Schedule D Case 1 –

€170,000	
€80,000	drawings add back
€10,000	depreciation add back
€260,000	adjusted trading income for tax purposes

Capital allowances €100,000 *12.5% = €12,500.

€260,000	Adjusted trading income
(€12,500)	capital allowance
€247,500	net taxable

Schedule D Case IV – €30,000	
DIRT	€12,300 deducted by the bank
Schedule D Case V	€50,000
Schedule E – €30,000	spouse

Total income

€247,500	Schedule D Case I
€30,000	Schedule D Case IV
€50,000	Schedule D Case V
€30,000	Schedule E spouse
€357,500	

(*Continued*)

Taxed as follows:

Income Tax 2015

€67,600 * 20%	€13,520
€30,000 * 41%	€12,300
€259,900 * 40%	€103,960
	€129,780

Less Tax credits

Personal	€3,300
PAYE spouse	€1,650
	(€4,950)
	€124,830

Less Tax already paid:

DIRT deducted	(€12,300)
PAYE paid	(€6,000) (assumes €30,000 * 20% paid through PAYE)
Net income tax payable	€106,530

PRSI (Jonathan only as spouse would have paid through PAYE system)

€327,500 * 4% = €13,100

USC (Jonathan only as spouse would have paid through PAYE system)

€247,500 + 50,000 = €297,500 (Deposit interest excluded, capital allowance excluded).

€12,012 * 1.5%	€180.18
€5,564 * 3.5%	€194.74
€52,468 * 7%	€3,672.76
€29,956 * 8%	€2,396.48
€197,500 * 11%	€21,725
	€28,169.16

Total: €106,530 + €13,100 + €28,169.16 = €147,799.16 + what spouse has paid in PAYE, PRSI, and USC.

15.22 Taxation of a Partnership

For taxation purposes a partnership is not treated as a separate person that must pay tax. The partnership is not a separate legal entity.

The rules governing the taxation of partnerships are set out in the TCA 1997 as amended and the various Finance Acts.

15.22.1 INCOME TAX

For taxation purposes the partnership prepares its own business accounts – a profit and loss account and a balance sheet for the business of the partnership using the income tax rules as they apply to individuals.

Partnership income is calculated as if the partnership is a separate business.

Expenses incurred wholly and exclusively in operating the partnership trade are deductible business expenses.

The net profit of the partnership is calculated and is then divided between the partners in accordance with whatever profit sharing agreement the partners have made.

Each partner's tax liability will be calculated using the income tax rules outlined earlier in the chapter with the share of the profit of the partnership treated as a separate (several) trade of the individual and this separate trade will be included in the self-assessment return (form 11) of each partner as Schedule D Case I or II income.

The assets of the partnership are treated as the assets of the individual partners apportioned in the same manner as the profit share of the partnership.

The separate trade for a partner commences when the partnership commences to trade (or the partner joins an existing partnership) and ceases when a person ceases to be a partner in the partnership or the partnership ceases to carry on a trade. The commencement and cessation rules outlined earlier in the chapter will apply to this several trade.

15.22.2 CAPITAL ALLOWANCES

A partner is entitled to his/her share of the capital allowances attributable to the partnership trade and is liable to tax on his/her share of the partnership's balancing charges (if any) for each year of assessment in which he/she is a partner.

Capital allowances are calculated for the partnership and then allocated to each partner. The appropriate share of the allowances is the amount computed in accordance with the profit sharing ratio included in the partnership agreement for the tax year.

15.22.3 LOSSES

Losses are allocated to the partners in accordance with the agreed profit/loss share arrangement in the partnership agreement. Each partner is responsible for claiming the loss relief appropriate to his own personal circumstances and may make his/her own decision as to the form of the loss relief claim of his/her several trade. Terminal loss relief may be available on cessation of the partnership as a severable trade.

15.22.4 DRAWINGS

Any drawings or salary of a partner deducted by the partnership in calculating its net profit must be added back as the partners will be taxed on the net profit of the partnership without a deduction for drawings (which would include partnership salaries).

A partner is taxed on his/her share of the net profit of the partnership and not on any drawings taken from the partnership or on a partner's salary.

Any drawings or salary taken from the partnership are treated as a removal of capital from the partnership and are not an income deduction but a capital deduction that should be reflected in the balance sheet of the partnership and the capital accounts of the partnership.

Example:

Adam, Barry, and Caroline are partners in ABC partnership and each took drawings from the partnership of €10,000 in 2015. The net profit of the partnership after deducting the drawings was €60,000.

(Continued)

Calculate Caroline's share of the partnership profits. Under the partnership agreement Caroline is entitled to 30% of the partnership profits.

Partnership profits	€60,000
Add back drawings	€30,000
Adjusted profits	€90,000

Caroline's share of partnership profits is €90,000 * 30% = €27,000.

15.22.5 RETURN

The partnership must file a partnership tax return – a form 1 (firms) providing details of the accounts of the partnership. The individual partners do not then need to file extracts from the same accounts in the form 11 that each partner must file.

The precedent partner is required to make the partnership's return of income before the relevant income tax pay and file deadline for that year (31 October). This is a return of information as no income tax is payable by the partnership.

15.22.6 EXAMPLES

Example:

John is a partner with Marie and Amy and together they operate a dental practice as a partnership. The partnership agreement provides that the income of the partnership is to be allocated as follows: Marie (40%), Amy (30%), and John (30%). The net profits of the partnership for 2015 are €90,000.

John also has rental income of €8,000 from which he had to pay €3,000 in maintaining the property.

John is single and has no PAYE income.

Calculate John's tax liability.

Schedule D Case I

Share of the partnership income is treated as a several trade and John is taxed on such income under Schedule D Case I – as a separate business:

€90,000 adjusted net profits of the partnership.

John's share under partnership agreement = 30% so his income is €27,000.

Several trade   €27,000.

Schedule D Case V – rental interest

€8,000	income
(€3,000)	expenses
€5,000	net income

Total Income:

€27,000

€5,000

€32,000

Income Tax:

32,000 @ 20% =   €6,400

Less Tax Credits

Personal   €1,650

Net   €4,750.00

PRSI

32,000 * 4% =   €1,280.00

USC

First €12,012 * 1.5% =   €180.18

Next €5,564 * 3.5% =   €194.74

Balance €14,424 * 7% =   €1,009.68

USC total   €1,384.60

Total payable   €7,414.60.

Example 2:

Profit and Loss account of ARC Partnership as at 31/8/15

Sales   €800,000

Cost of Sales   (€450,000)

Gross Profit   €350,000

Expenses   (€200,000)

Profit before tax   €150,000

The expenses include depreciation of €50,000 on plant and machinery that was calculated at 20% of the initial cost of €250,000.

Aidan Rooney is a partner in ARC Partnership and he is entitled to 35% of the partnership profits.

Aidan also has rental income of €90,000 from which he had to pay €15,000 in maintaining the property in 2015. Aidan is single, aged 52, and has no PAYE income.

Calculate Aidan's tax liability for 2015.

Partnership profits

Profits before tax as per P & L account   €150,000

Add back depreciation   €50,000

Adjusted profits for tax purposes   €200,000

Available deduction

Less Capital Allowance   (€31,250*)

Taxable amount   €168,750

*Capital allowance is calculated at €250,000 * 12.5% = €31,250 on the plant and machinery – it is calculated at 12.5% on a straight line basis.

(Continued)

Schedule D Case I

Share of the partnership income is treated as a several trade and Aidan is taxed on such income under Schedule D Case I – as a separate business:

€200,000   adjusted net profits of the partnership.

Aidan's share under partnership agreement=35% so his income is €70,000.

Aidan's share of capital allowances=35% so he can claim €31,250 * 35%=€10,937.50 rounded to €10,938.

Several trade	€70,000
Capital Allowance	€10,938

Schedule D Case V – rental interest

€90,000	gross income
(€15,000)	expenses
€75,000	net income

Total Income:

€70,000	several trade
(€10,938)	capital allowance
€59,062	net taxable
€75,000	rental income
€134,062	Net income

Income Tax: 2015

Initial €33,800 @ 20% =	€6,760	
Balance €100,262 @ 40% =	€40,104.80	
Total	€46,864.80	
Less Tax Credits		
Personal	(€1,650)	
Net		€45,214.80

PRSI

€134, 062 (total income less capital allowance) * 4% =   €5,362.48

USC

€134,062 (total income less capital allowance)

First €12,012 * 1.5% =	€180.18	
Next €5,564 * 3.5% =	€194.74	
Next €52,468 * 7% =	€3,672.76	
Next €29,956 * 8% =	€2,396.48	
Last €34,062 * 11% =	€3,746.82	
Total USC		€10,190.98
Total		€60,768.26

15.22.7 CHARGEABLE GAINS – PARTNERSHIP ASSETS

Partners are assessed and charged separately on gains accruing from the disposal of partnership assets. The assets of the partnership are treated as the assets of the partners and disposals by the partnership are treated as disposals by the partners.

Gains that accrue on a disposal of partnership assets are apportioned between the partners and assessed and charged on the partners.

A partnership is required to include in the partnership return (form 1 (firms)) details of its chargeable gains and chargeable assets acquired.

When a partner disposes of his interest in a partnership this is treated as a disposal of a chargeable asset of the partnership and Capital Gains Tax ('CGT') may be payable by the disposing partner. Goodwill is a chargeable asset and any gain accruing to a disposing partner on the disposal of his interest in the partnership that is attributable to goodwill will be chargeable to CGT. Stock-in-trade and work in progress consideration will not be liable to CGT. CGT is covered in more detail in **chapter 16, 'Capital Gains Tax'.**

CHAPTER 16

CAPITAL GAINS TAX

16.1   What is Capital Gains Tax?

Capital gains tax ('CGT') is a tax charged on chargeable gains accruing to a person on the disposal of assets. The rules governing CGT are set out in the Taxes Consolidation Act 1997 ('TCA 1997'), as amended, and the various Finance Acts.

It is a tax on the gain made on the disposal of an asset (TCA 1997, s 28).

Capital gains that arise for persons other than companies are chargeable to CGT and capital gains that arise for companies are generally chargeable to corporation tax (with some exceptions; for example, companies are chargeable to CGT on chargeable gains from disposals of development land). See **chapter 17, Corporation Tax**, for taxation of companies' chargeable gains.

Self-assessment rules apply to CGT for all persons – self-employed and individuals who receive payment under the PAYE system (e.g. employees and recipients of pensions). A person is obliged to pay and file CGT without being requested to do so by Revenue Commissioners.

Assets include all forms of property including land, shares, and buildings (TCA 1997, s 532).

Certain assets are not chargeable assets (e.g. Euro currency or wasting assets) and some gains are not chargeable gains as an exception or relief may apply (e.g. generally no CGT applies on a principal private residence used wholly as residential premises).

16.2   What is a Disposal?

A disposal includes a sale, a transfer, a gift, or any other method by which a person ceases to own or have an interest in an asset. A disposal includes the granting of an option over an asset (TCA 1997, s 534).

Death is not treated as a disposal for CGT purposes (TCA 1997, s 573). The beneficiary (the person acquiring the asset on the death) is treated as acquiring the asset at its market value at the date of death.

16.3   Gift/Disposal not at 'Arm's Length'

When an asset is disposed of otherwise than for full consideration by way of a bargain made at arm's length, for example there is a full or partial gift of the asset, for CGT purposes the transaction is treated as a disposal of the asset for a consideration equal to the asset's market value at that time.

CGT is calculated on the market value of the asset.

16.4   Who Must Pay Irish Capital Gains Tax?

A person who is resident or ordinarily resident and domiciled in Ireland is liable to Irish CGT on the disposal of any asset worldwide.

A person who is resident or ordinarily resident but not domiciled in Ireland is liable to Irish CGT on disposals of Irish assets and also on foreign disposals outside of Ireland on a remittance basis (to the extent that the proceeds are brought into Ireland they are liable to Irish CGT).

A person not resident or domiciled in Ireland is only liable to Irish CGT on the disposal of certain Irish assets (land and buildings in the State, minerals in the State, exploration and exploitation rights in the Continental Shelf, and shares deriving their value from such assets or assets in the State used for the purposes of a business carried on in the State (the 'specified assets for tax clearance purposes')).

16.4.1   RESIDENCE

An individual's residence status for Irish tax purposes is determined by the number of days an individual is present in Ireland during a tax year (1 January to 31 December).

An individual will be tax resident in Ireland in either of the following circumstances:

    (a) if 183 days or more are spent in Ireland for any purpose in the tax year; or

    (b) if a person spends 280 days or more in Ireland for any purpose over two consecutive tax years he/she will be regarded as tax resident in Ireland for the second tax year.

If an individual spends 30 days or less in total in Ireland in a tax year those days will not be taken into account when checking if an individual is resident in Ireland for tax purposes. A day for the residence test is one on which an individual is present in Ireland at any time during the day.

> **Example:**
>
> If Joan, an Australian national, spends 121 days in Ireland in 2014 and 160 days in Ireland in 2015 she will be tax resident in Ireland for 2015. If she had spent just 20 days in Ireland in 2014 these days will not be counted when doing the residence test and she would not be resident in 2015.

16.4.2   ORDINARY RESIDENCE

If an individual has been resident in Ireland for three consecutive tax years he/she will be ordinarily resident from the beginning of the fourth tax year.

> **Example:**
>
> Simon arrived in Ireland from Australia in January 2012 and has remained in Ireland ever since. As he is tax resident in Ireland in 2012, 2013, and 2014 he will be ordinarily tax resident in Ireland from 2015 onwards.

A person will only cease to be ordinarily resident in Ireland if he/she has been non-resident for three consecutive tax years.

16.4.3   DOMICILE

Domicile is a legal concept. It is generally interpreted as meaning living in a country with the intention of residing permanently there. A person is born with a domicile of origin but this can be changed by the actions of a person to a domicile of choice.

16.5   Rate of Tax

CGT is currently charged at a rate of 33% on the gain of most assets disposed of on or after 6 December 2012.

Special rules apply to disposals of foreign life assurance policies and offshore funds which are distributing funds. For certain windfall gains which were attributable to the re-zoning of land the gain was liable to income tax at a rate of 80% if it related to a trade and if it did not relate to a trade to CGT at a rate of 80% until 31 December 2014. Since 1 January 2015 a CGT rate of 33% applies.

16.6   Timing of Payment

The date of payment of CGT is triggered by the date the contract is made (TCA 1997, s 542). If it is a conditional contract then the relevant date is the date the conditions are satisfied.

For the 'initial period' (gains in the period 1 January to 30 November each year) CGT must be paid on or before 15 December in the same year.

For the 'later period' (gains in the period 1 December to 31 December each year) CGT must be paid on or before the following 31 January.

For companies, where gains are chargeable to corporation tax, the due date for payment is determined by reference to the accounting period in which the gain accrues.

Interest applies to any tax not paid on time. Interest at a rate of 0.0219% per day/part day is payable until the tax is paid if a payment is late.

Example:

A contract is signed on 1 October 2015 and the conveyance is executed on 2 December 2015. When is the CGT payable?

As the contract was signed on 1 October 2015 and does not appear to be conditional, this contract falls within the initial period and the CGT must be paid on or before 15 December 2015.

If the contract is not signed until 2 December 2015, CGT would be payable on 31 January 2016.

Payment is made to the Collector General.

16.7   CGT Returns

CGT returns of all chargeable gains and allowable losses must be made by the file date (31 October in the tax year following the date of disposal). The file date is extended if ROS is used – to early November (date announced annually by Revenue). A return must be filed even if no tax is due where a person has used losses or claimed a relief.

Self-employed persons file the income tax self-assessment form (form 11), employees file a form 12, partnerships file a form 1 (firms), and companies file a form CT1 which is also used for corporation tax purposes.

If a person is not required to make an income tax return (for example: a non-resident individual selling their Irish holiday home; a person who is not obliged to submit an income tax return; or a person exempt from income tax) then that person files a form CG1.

If a CGT return is not made when due on the file date (31 October) the following surcharges apply:

(a) If the return is filed up to two months late – 5% of the tax due subject to a maximum of €12,695.

(b) If the return is filed over two months late – 10% of the tax due subject to a maximum of €63,485.

Example:

Audrey fails to file her CGT return by 31 October 2015 in relation to a €7,000 CGT liability that arose from a disposal in 2014. She realises this mistake and files the return by 30 November 2015. As this is within two months of the filing date she is subject to a 5% surcharge calculated as €7,000 * 5% = €350.

Full self-assessment applies. If Revenue raise an assessment and a person is not happy with an assessment (Revenue decision on the return) he/she can appeal the assessment to the Appeal Commissioners within 30 days of the notice of the assessment.

16.8 Calculating CGT

16.8.1 PERMITTED/ALLOWABLE DEDUCTIONS

In calculating CGT certain deductions are permitted from the consideration received (or deemed to be received; e.g. if the disposal was a gift) before the gain or loss is determined (TCA 1997, s 552).

The deductions include:

(a) The costs incurred by the person in disposing of the asset – for example legal and valuation fees.

(b) The original purchase cost (or deemed cost if it was a gift) of the asset (this is known as the base cost). This may be adjusted for inflation if it was acquired prior to 31 December 2002. If an asset was acquired before 6 April 1974 the market value at 6 April 1974 has to be used as the base cost when calculating CGT on a disposal of the asset and not the original price and costs of acquisition. CGT was only introduced in 1974.

(c) The costs of acquiring the asset – for example, legal and valuation fees. This may be adjusted for inflation if the property was acquired prior to 31 December 2002.

(d) Monetary expenses incurred in improving/enhancing the asset. This is known as enhancement expenditure as the work increases the value of the asset (e.g. the building of an extension to a property) rather than an expense that maintains or repairs an asset or deals with the wear and tear of an asset. This may be adjusted for inflation if it was incurred prior to 31 December 2002.

(e) Losses carried forward from previous years.

(f) Losses on other disposals in the current year.

(g) Annual allowance.

Expenditure that is allowable for income tax purposes cannot also be deducted for CGT purposes (TCA 1997, s 554).

16.8.2   INDEXATION

There is an allowance for inflation when calculating the gain for assets which were acquired and certain expenditure (enhancement expenditure) that has been incurred prior to 31 December 2002. This is achieved by multiplying the cost of purchasing the asset and enhancement expenditure by an 'indexation factor' determined by the tax year in which the asset was acquired or the expenditure incurred. The indexation factors are available from Revenue website. No indexation was available prior to 31 December 2002 if you sold a chargeable asset within 12 months of purchasing an asset.

16.8.2.1   Development land

Development land is land with development potential. It is land that has a market value that exceeds its current use value. Indexation does not apply to development land. Property valuations for land have to be split between the current use value and development element to determine the indexation relief to be granted.

There is an exception to this rule where the total consideration receivable by an individual from disposals of development land in any tax year does not exceed €19,050. These gains are treated as if the disposals were not disposals of development land and the restrictions on development land for both indexation relief and losses do not apply.

16.8.2.2   Indexation factors

Each year up to 2003 Revenue Commissioners issued indexation factors which were based on the Consumer Price Index. The indexation factor is based on the tax year in which the asset was acquired (column on left side) and the tax year in which it was sold (top of table).

Indexation was abolished with effect from 31 December 2002 so it can only be used for acquisition costs and expenditure occurred before that date.

16.8.2.3   Restrictions on use of indexation

There are restrictions on the use of indexation. Indexation cannot be used:

(a) to convert a monetary gain into a loss or a monetary loss into a gain – instead the disposal is treated as a no gain-no loss situation; or

(b) to increase a monetary loss – the actual loss is the loss that can be used.

> **Example:**
>
> On a disposal of an asset bought in 2001 Jonathan makes an actual gain of €2,000 but when he calculates his CGT liability using the indexation factors he calculates that he has made a loss of €5,000. Owing to the restriction on the use of indexation in these circumstances Jonathan cannot claim this loss and instead for CGT purposes he is treated as if the disposal of the asset was a no gain-no loss situation.

16.8.3   ANNUAL ALLOWANCE

Each individual is entitled to an annual allowance of €1,270 against all net gains (gains less current year losses and prior year losses carried forward) accruing in a tax year.

The allowance does not apply to companies, trustees, or other non-corporate bodies.

16.8.4 SUGGESTED METHOD

The following outline is a suggested method of calculating tax:

Sale Price

less	Costs of sale
less	Purchase price or market value
	& Costs of purchase
	(indexed to 2003)
less	*Enhancement expenditure*
	(indexed to 2003)
	Total deductions
equals	*loss or gain*
less	*loss relief:*
Losses carried forward	
Current year losses	
less	Annual allowance
= Taxable Gain	

16.8.5 EXAMPLES

Example 1:

Gordon purchased a factory in September 1982. He paid €300,000 for the premises and he incurred €3,000 in legal and other fees in buying the factory. In 1987 Gordon painted the factory at a cost of €5,000. The business expanded and in March 1992 an extension was built onto the factory at a cost of €150,000 to give the business more space. In 1995, there was a leak in the roof in the older part of the factory and it cost Gordon €12,000 to replace part of the roof. The factory was painted again in 1997 (cost €6,000) and 2007 (cost €12,000). A further extension was built in 2003 at a cost of €300,000.

Gordon sells the factory in September 2015 for €2,000,000 and incurred legal and other costs of €10,000 in relation to the sale and he wants to know what, if any, of these expenses are deductible and whether he has to pay any CGT.

Sale Price			€2,000,000
less	Costs of sale	€10,000	
less	Purchase price or market value		
	(Multiplier for 82/83) €300,000 * 2.253 =	€675,900	
	& Costs of purchase		
	(Multiplier for 82/83) €3,000 * 2.253 =	€6,759	
	(indexed to 2003)		

less	*Enhancement expenditure*		
	(Multiplier for 91/92) €150,000 * 1.406 =	€210,900	
	2003 €300,000	€300,000	
	(indexed up to 2003)		
	Total deductions		(€1,203,559)
equals	*loss or gain*		€796,441
less	*loss relief*		nil
less	Annual allowance		(€1,270)
=	Taxable Gain		€795,171
=	Tax @ **33**%		€262,406.43

This tax must be paid by 15 December 2015 and a return of this disposal must be made by 31 October 2016 (based on current tax rules).

Painting the factory would be treated as maintenance expenditure and will not qualify as enhancement expenditure. Also the repair to the roof would be treated as maintenance rather than an enhancement and would not qualify for enhancement expenditure.

Actual gain/loss without indexation:

Sale Price			€2,000,000
less	Costs of sale	€10,000	
less	Purchase price or market value		
	(Multiplier for 82/83)	€300,000	
	& Costs of purchase		
	(Multiplier for 82/83)	€3,000	
	(indexed to 2003)		
less	*Enhancement expenditure*		
	(Multiplier for 91/92)	€150,000	
	2003 €300,000	€300,000	
	(indexed up to 2003)		
	Total deductions		(€763,000)
equals	*loss or gain*		€1,237,000

Use of multiplier reduces the gain which is its purpose so there is no restriction on its use in these circumstances.

Example 2:

Shares were purchased by Jamie on 2 December 1980 for €4,000. Jamie sold the shares on 10 May 2015 for €15,000. The costs of sale were €2,000.

Does Jamie have any CGT liability?

Sale Price		€15,000
Less:		
Costs of sale	€2,000	
Base cost: €4,000		
Multiplied by indexation factor (80/81) * 3.240	€12,960	
Total deductions		(€14,960)
Gain		€40
Less Loss relief carried forward		nil
Less Annual allowance		(€1,270)
Taxable Gain		nil
Tax @ **33%**		nil

Example 3:

John has sold shares for €50,000 on 1 October 2015. The costs of sale were €3,000. John had purchased the shares in February 2000 for €5,000 and the acquisition costs were €1,000.

Calculate any tax payable and identify the pay and file deadline.

Sale Price			€50,000
less	Costs of sale		€3,000
less	Purchase price or market value		
	(99/2000)	€5,000 * 1.193	€5,965
	& Costs of purchase		
	(99/2000)	€1,000 * 1.193	€1,193
	(indexed to 2003)		
less		*Enhancement expenditure*	
total deductions			(€10,158)
equals	*loss or gain*		€39,842
less	*loss relief*		nil
less	Annual allowance		(€1,270)
=	Taxable Gain		€38,572
=	Tax @ **33%**		€12,728.76

This tax must be paid by 15 December 2015 and a return of this disposal must be made by 31 October 2016.

Example 4:

John has sold shares for €10,000 on 1 October 2015. The costs of sale were €3,000. John had purchased the shares in February 2000 for €5,000 and the acquisition costs were €1,000.

Calculate any tax payable and identify the pay and file deadline.

Sale Price			€10,000
less	Costs of sale	€3,000	
less	Purchase price or market value		
(99/2000)	€5,000 * 1.193	€5,965	
& Costs of purchase			
(99/2000)	€1,000 * 1.193	<u>€1,193</u>	
(indexed to 2003)			
less	*Enhancement expenditure*		
total deductions			<u>(€10,158)</u>
equals	*loss or gain*		(€158)

Calculate actual gain/loss without indexation

Sale Price			€10,000
less	Costs of sale	€3,000	
less	Purchase price or market value		
	(99/2000)	€5,000	
	& costs of purchase		
	(99/2000)	<u>€1,000</u>	
	(indexed to 2003)		
less	*Enhancement expenditure*		
total deductions			<u>(€9,000)</u>
equals	*loss or gain*		€1,000

The use of indexation converts a monetary gain into a loss so the use of the multiplier is restricted and John cannot claim a loss. He is treated as making no gain and no loss.

16.8.6   SHARES – SPECIAL RULES

When shares are being disposed of, shares of the same class are treated as if the shares first purchased are the shares first sold; this is known as the 'first in first out' basis (TCA 1997, s 580).

Example:

John holds 20,000 shares in ABC Limited which he has bought over the last ten years, purchasing 2,000 shares at a time since 2002. He decides to sell 5,000 shares. These shares being disposed of will be treated as 2,000 shares bought in 2002, 2,000 shares bought in 2003, and 1,000 shares bought in 2004.

16.9   Losses

No CGT is payable on a loss. All chargeable gains in a tax year are aggregated and losses on disposals of assets in the current tax year can be set off against other gains made in the same tax year (TCA 1997, s 546). A person pays CGT based on the net balance.

Example 1:

Amy sold in 2015 the three apartments that she had purchased as investments and rented out in 2005. She made a gain of €4,000 on apartment A, a gain of €7,000 on apartment B, and a loss of €5,000 on apartment C. When calculating her chargeable gains Amy will be able to deduct the €5,000 loss from the gains of €11,000 and will pay CGT based on the net gain of €6,000.

If a loss cannot be used in the current year (e.g. a person has made a loss and does not dispose of any other asset in the same tax year) the loss can be carried forward and set against future chargeable gains.

Example 2:

Using the same facts as in the Amy example above but this time there is a loss of €15,000 on apartment C.

When calculating her chargeable gains Amy will be able to deduct the €15,000 loss from the gains of €11,000 and there will be no CGT payable in 2015. Amy has unused losses of €4,000 that she can carry forward and set off against future chargeable gains.

Losses on development land can be offset against gains on all disposals. However, gains on development land can only be offset by losses on development land.

Where an asset qualified for capital allowances, a balancing charge or allowance will be calculated at the time the asset is disposed. For CGT purposes any loss on such an asset will only cover any loss not already covered by a capital allowance.

16.10   Anti-Avoidance

There are a number of anti-avoidance measures that must be considered (for example if there is an arrangement and the main purpose or one of the main purposes of the arrangement is to secure a tax advantage the loss may be restricted or disallowed) and there are restrictions on the use of losses arising on disposals to connected persons (TCA 1997, ss 546A and 549).

16.11   Exemptions

There are many exemptions to CGT. The following is an overview of some reliefs:

16.11.1   PRINCIPAL PRIVATE RESIDENCE

CGT relief applies where an individual sells his or her principal private residence (for example an apartment or a dwelling-house). There is relief for any period during which the property has been occupied as a principal private residence.

A gain on the disposal by an individual of their apartment or a dwelling-house (including grounds of up to one acre) is exempt in certain circumstances.

The exemption is available if, throughout the individual's period of ownership, the residence had been occupied by the individual as his/her only or main residence or, in certain circumstances, as the sole residence of a dependent relative. In the case of a married couple or civil partners living together only one residence can qualify as the only or main residence of the spouses or civil partners.

Full exemption may not be available if only part of the residence has been used as the individual's residence. For example, where the residence is used partly for business purposes or where rooms in the residence have been let. If this occurs an apportionment is made between the residential part and the business/let part to calculate the exempt portion of the total gain. The exemption is also restricted where the taxpayer has not lived in the residence for the full duration of ownership.

The following periods of absence from the residence qualify for relief even though the owner may not have been actually living in the property at the time:

(a)   the period of up to 12 months immediately before the disposal is treated as a period of occupation when calculating the relief;

(b)   any period throughout which the individual was employed outside the State; and

(c)   a period of up to four years during which the individual was required by the conditions of his/her employment to reside elsewhere,

provided that, both before and after the periods (in (b) and (c) above), the residence was the owner's only or main residence and throughout those periods he/she had no other residence eligible for exemption as a principal private residence.

When the private residence comprises development land (it includes the disposal of a garden or part of a garden of a principal private residence) and the consideration exceeds €19,050, the private residence relief is restricted to the current use value of the property.

16.11.2   TRANSFER OF A SITE TO A CHILD TO ENABLE THEM TO BUILD A RESIDENCE

No CGT is payable on the transfer of a site by a parent to a child where the site is valued at €500,000 or less and the transfer is to enable the child to build a residence. The site excluding the area on which the house is to be built cannot exceed one acre.

As an anti-avoidance provision, on a subsequent sale the child pays the CGT on the parent site transfer to him/her unless the child has built a residence on the site and has occupied the residence for three years before disposing of the residence.

16.11.3   SPOUSES/CIVIL PARTNERS

Generally there is no CGT on a transfer between spouses or civil partners living together. The acquiring spouse/civil partner takes the base cost and period of ownership of the disposing spouse/civil partner; i.e. the receiving spouse/civil partner is treated as if he/she had originally acquired the asset.

However there are anti-avoidance rules that impose CGT on the transfer where the spouse/civil partner who receives the asset would not be liable to Irish CGT if he/she were to then dispose of the asset.

There is relief from CGT on a transfer between spouses/civil partner not living together, if the transfer relates to a deed of separation or a separation or divorce order/dissolution of a civil partnership.

16.11.4 ACQUISITION RELIEF 2012–14

Where land and buildings in any European Economic Area (including Ireland) was purchased in 2012, 2013, and/or 2014 for market value (or for 75% of market value if purchased from a relative) and held for seven years then there is no CGT for any gain in the seven-year holding period if the property is liable to Irish tax (TCA 1997, s 604A). This relief was only available to acquisitions up to 31 December 2014.

16.11.5 RETIREMENT RELIEF

16.11.5.1 To a child, grandchild, foster-child, or certain nieces/nephews

Once a person is 55 years old he/she can avail of retirement relief on the transfer/disposal of qualifying business assets (e.g. a trade or shares in a family trading company). The relief applies where the person passes the qualifying business assets to a child of the disponer, a child of a deceased child, or to certain nephews/nieces who have worked in the business.

Since 1 January 2014 a cap of €3 million has been imposed on the value of the qualifying business assets for relief where the disponer is over 66 years. There are a number of conditions that apply to the relief and a number of clawback provisions are also applicable.

16.11.5.2 To anyone else

Once a person is 55 years old he/she can avail of retirement relief on the transfer/disposal of qualifying business assets (e.g. a trade or shares in a family trading company) valued at €750,000 or less (this is a lifetime limit).

Since 1 January 2014 this value has been reduced to €500,000 where a disponer is over 66 years. There are a number of conditions that apply to the relief and a number of clawback provisions are also applicable.

Recent Finance Acts have extended the relief to cover certain lands that are leased for five years or more, and disposed of to a person other than a child of the taxpayer on or after 1 January 2014. The relief has also been extended to land leased for 25 years including to disposals to a person other than a child of the taxpayer by 31 December 2016.

A Farm Restructuring Relief is also available.

16.11.6 CGT ENTREPRENEURIAL RELIEF

A tax credit is available for those who invest the proceeds of a disposal after 1 January 2010 in new business assets between 1 January 2014 and 31 December 2018 and hold the new business assets for at least three years. The tax credit will be the lower of 100% of the CGT on the first disposal or 50% of the CGT on the disposal of the new assets (TCA 1997, s 597A).

16.12 Tax Clearance Certificates

A tax clearance certificate (Form CG50A) may be required on the disposal of certain specified assets (see list under who must pay CGT **section 16.4**) where the consideration exceeds €500,000. Otherwise the vendor must withhold 15% from the consideration payment and pay it over (remit it) to the Collector General within 30 days.

16.13 Self-assessment

Full self-assessment applies since 1 January 2013 under which a taxpayer sets out the tax payable for a year as part of the return. (TCA 97, Part 41A, introduced by the Finance Act 2012.)

CHAPTER 17

CORPORATION TAX

17.1 Introduction

This chapter will look at the rules that relate to the taxation of an Irish business that operates through a company. Rather than pay income tax and capital gains tax certain trading income and chargeable gains of a company are liable to corporation tax. The primary source of legislation for corporation tax is the Taxes Consolidation Act 1997 as amended ('TCA 1997'), the Finance Acts, and various statutory instruments.

The starting point for calculating the profits of a company for taxation purposes is the financial statements (profit and loss account and balance sheet) of the company. Certain adjustments are made to the profit and loss account – adding back of non-qualifying deductions and making certain permitted deductions for taxation purposes. Corporation tax is calculated on the adjusted profit figures.

The self-assessment system applies to companies, which means that a company must file a tax return and pay the corporation tax without being requested to do so by Revenue.

Corporation tax covers both income profits and most chargeable gains so the capital gains of a company are calculated in accordance with the capital gains tax rules but are chargeable to corporation tax and are generally not chargeable to capital gains tax.

Disposals of development land are chargeable to capital gains tax.

17.2 Liability to Irish Corporation Tax

If a company is resident in Ireland it is liable to corporation tax. For a non-Irish resident company, under s 25 of the TCA 1997, the income and chargeable gains attributable to a branch or agency in the Republic of Ireland are chargeable to Irish corporation tax. Since 1 January 2015 all companies incorporated in Ireland are Irish tax resident except if it not so regarded under a tax treaty.

An Irish incorporated company will be liable to Irish tax if it is not regarded as tax resident in a tax treaty jurisdiction because it is not incorporated there.

A new s 23A of the TCA 1997 came into effect on 1 January 2015 and provides that all newly incorporated companies will be Irish tax resident if they are incorporated in Ireland except if they are not so regarded under a tax treaty. Companies not incorporated in Ireland but with central management and control of the company in Ireland will also continue to be Irish tax resident.

A transitional period until 31 December 2020 will apply to exiting Irish incorporated non-Irish tax resident companies under old rules. Previously one had to ascertain where the central management and control of the company was to determine tax residency.

17.3 How to Register for Corporation Tax

Companies must take steps to register for tax.

17.3.1 TAX REGISTRATION – FORM TR2

The form TR2 is the registration form that applies to companies to register for corporation tax, employer's PAYE/PRSI, VAT, and Relevant Contracts Tax. It must be completed by a company (and other entities) and filed with Revenue.

It must include the following details:

(a) company name;

(b) registered address;

(c) business address;

(d) contact details;

(e) legal format of the entity;

(f) registration date;

(g) Companies Registration Office number;

(h) commencement date;

(i) accounts date;

(j) type of business;

(k) director details;

(l) company secretary details;

(m) shareholder details;

(n) adviser details;

(o) property rental details; and

(p) tick boxes to register for corporation tax, VAT, PAYE/PRSI, and related information.

A company will be given a taxation reference number by Revenue Commissioners.

A company must register directors and employees for PAYE purposes and deduct PAYE, USC, and PRSI on employee and certain director salary payments.

17.3.2 ADDITIONAL COMPANY FILING ON FORMATION – STATEMENT OF PARTICULARS

A statement of particulars has to be furnished to Revenue under s 882 TCA 1997 (Form 11F CRO) within 30 days of commencing to carry on a business. It must contain the following information:

(a) company name;

(b) address – registered and business addresses;

(c) secretary details;

(d)   commencement date;

(e)   company accounting date;

(f)   nature of the business;

(g)   whether an incorporated company is claiming to be not tax resident; and

(h)   whether it has any related company.

Any material changes must be notified to Revenue within 30 days of the change. A failure to file the statement can result in a notification from Revenue Commissioners to the Companies Registration Office which can result in the company being struck off for failing to comply with this filing obligation.

17.4   Tax Rates

Income tax is not chargeable on the income of a company; instead, a company pays corporation tax on its profits which includes both income and chargeable gains.

12.5% is the standard corporation tax rate for trading companies (TCA 1997, s 21). The 12.5% rate applies to the trading income of a company.

25% is the corporation tax rate for certain designated activities (excepted trades); for example, working minerals, petroleum activities, dealing in or developing lands (TCA 1997, s 21A).

25% is also the corporation tax rate for the following non-trading income:

(a)   Schedule D Case III income – interest not taxed at source, foreign income;

(b)   Schedule D Case IV – royalties and other sources of income; and

(c)   Schedule D Case V income – rental income from land and buildings.

Example:

The profits of Bright Sparks Limited relating to its retail shop will be liable to corporation tax at 12.5%.

If Bright Sparks Limited purchased an office and rented this out to another person, this income would not relate to its trading business and would be taxed as rental income at a rate of 25%.

17.5   Calculation of Corporation Tax

Corporation tax is payable on the taxable profits of a company for an accounting period.

17.5.1   WHAT IS AN ACCOUNTING PERIOD?

An accounting period is determined by tax rules and generally is of 12 months' duration chosen by the company.

An accounting period starts when a company:

(a)   commences to carry on a trade;

(b)   becomes resident in Ireland;

(c)   acquires its first source of income; or

(d)   commences to be wound up.

An accounting period is deemed to end:

(a) 12 months after the period commences;

(b) on a company's specified accounting date;

(c) on a company ceasing to trade; or

(d) on a company being wound up.

Example:

ABC Limited commences to trade on 1 April 2015. This starts an accounting period. If the company wishes to make up its accounts to 31 December 2015, the accounting period ends on that date otherwise the accounting period will end 12 months from the start of the accounting period, 31 March 2016.

17.5.2 COMPANY PROFITS

The starting point to calculating a company's corporation tax is to review the profits of a company for an accounting period and to review the income and expenses to ascertain if all are applicable for corporation tax purposes.

17.5.3 DEDUCTIONS

Expenses wholly and exclusively used for the business of the company and expenses incurred for the purposes of the business are deductible. Personal deductions and other specified deductions are not permitted – for example business entertainment expenses are not deductible. Pre-trading expenses incurred within three years of commencement can be deducted if they were incurred for the purposes of the business. Depreciation is not a qualifying deduction.

17.5.4 DEPRECIATION AND CAPITAL ALLOWANCES

Depreciation does not qualify as a deduction from income for taxation purposes and so the depreciation figure deducted as an expense in the profit and loss account must be added back to the profit figure to determine the profit figure for taxation purposes.

Instead, a deduction is available for capital allowances on capital assets. A tax calculation must be done on the capital assets of the company to ascertain if any of them can avail of capital allowances.

The rates for deductions for capital allowances are set out in tax legislation and are divided into different categories, including, plant and machinery, industrial building, and motor vehicles.

Example:

- A furnace costs €10 million and will last five years. At that time assume the cost of demolition is the same as the value of the material that is left.

- If preparing a five-year set of accounts, the cost of the furnace would be €10 million.

- The use of the furnace is over the five years for €10 million, so €2 million per year would be deductible in the accounts.

- The depreciated value of the furnace after one year shown in the balance sheet is €8 million, after 2 years is €6 million and so on.

(continued)

The €2 million depreciation figure in the profit and loss account must be added back.

The furnace would constitute plant and machinery for capital allowances so the applicable rate is 12.5% for capital allowances.

The capital allowance deductible for taxable purposes for year one will therefore be €10 million * 12.5% = €1, 250,000 and this figure is deductible from the adjusted profits for taxation purposes and not the €2 million in the accounts.

17.5.5   CHARGES ON INCOME

Certain interest payments, royalty payments, and other annual payments are treated as charges on income. They are not deductible as expenses of the company when calculating company profits but are separately deductible as charges from the corporation tax profits.

In certain circumstances the company may have to deduct income tax from the payments and pay it over to Revenue.

17.5.6   REVIEW OF FINANCIAL STATEMENTS: PROFIT & LOSS A/C TO 30/9/15

Sales	€663,000
Cost of sales	(€523,000)
Gross profit	€140,000
Expenses	(€95,000)
Profit before tax	€45,000
Tax on profits	(€8,000)
Profit after tax	€37,000
Dividends	(€10,000)
Retained profits	€27,000

If the figures in the profit and loss account are used the corporation tax on €45,000 * 12.5% would have been €5,625.

This therefore indicates that certain expenses of the company have been added back for taxation purposes (€19,000) as the taxation is €64,000 * 12.5% = €8,000.

17.6   Start-up Exemption

Relief is available for the first three years of trading for trading income and certain gains on new qualifying start-up companies that are commenced up to the end of 2015. The effect of the relief is that a qualifying start-up company can earn €320,000 tax free per year for the first three years if it has paid (or is deemed to have been paid) sufficient employer's PRSI.

Relief from corporation tax and chargeable gains may be available where the total corporation tax liability in any of the first three accounting periods does not exceed €40,000.

Since 2011 the value of the relief is based on the amount of employer's PRSI paid (or deemed paid) by the company in the accounting period. It is based on a maximum of €5,000 PRSI per employee.

If the paid employer's PRSI is less than the corporation tax liability the relief is restricted to match the employer's PRSI paid.

Example:

ZZZ Limited was set up by Aidan in November 2014 as a new business that qualifies for the start-up exemption. It has a corporation tax liability for the accounting period ended 31 October 2015 of €20,000.

ZZZ Limited has paid or been deemed to pay €8,000 in employer's PRSI in the same period.

ZZZ Limited can get an exemption from corporation tax for the PRSI paid and it only has to pay corporation tax on the balance (€20,000 – €8,000) €12,000.

If ZZZ Limited had paid €20,000 or more in employer's PRSI no corporation tax would have been payable.

There are certain conditions that must be complied with for the relief to apply. It will not apply to an existing trade taken over by a new company, it does not apply to service companies, and it does not apply to companies that must pay corporation tax at 25% on trading income.

17.7 Preliminary Tax

Preliminary tax for an accounting period is due on the 21st day of the month preceding when the accounting period ends (except for large companies as outlined below). Generally this is the 21st day of the eleventh month of the accounting period.

To avoid an interest charge the preliminary tax must be 90% of the final tax liability. There is a facility to top up the preliminary tax if there is a disposal of an asset and a chargeable gain arises after the preliminary tax is paid. If payments are made via ROS the payment date is extended by two days to 23rd of the month.

The balance of the tax is due by the 21st day of the ninth month after the accounting period ends. If a company is late paying or pays less than the appropriate preliminary tax amount, the total tax is deemed due from the preliminary tax date.

Example:

Bright Sparks Limited's accounts are made up to 30 September. This means that the preliminary tax must be paid by 21 August (as it is a small company) and the balance of the tax must be paid and the tax return filed by 21 June after the end of the accounting period.

17.7.1 LARGE COMPANY – SPLIT PAYMENT OF PRELIMINARY TAX

A large company is a company which has had a corporation tax liability of more than €200,000 in the previous accounting period.

Preliminary tax is paid in two instalments by a large company. The first payment is due on the 21st day of the sixth month of the accounting period. The payment must be 50% of the corporation tax of the previous accounting period or 45% of the current period's corporation tax liability. The second payment is due on the 21st day of the eleventh month of the accounting period and it must be of such amount that will bring the total payment to 90% of the corporation tax liability of the current period. For an accounting period of less than seven months the large company must pay all of the preliminary tax in one payment.

Example:

IOU Limited is very successful and has had a corporation tax liability of more than €350,000 in its accounting period ended 31 August 2015 so for the accounting period ended 31 August 2016 it will need to pay the following preliminary tax payments:

21 February 2016 – 45% of current accounting period's liability (or 50% of prior year corporation tax liability); and

21 July 2016 – so much as will bring the total preliminary tax payment to 90% of current accounting period's corporation tax liability.

17.7.2   SMALL COMPANY

A small company is a company which had a corporation tax liability of less than €200,000 in the previous accounting period. Such a company can calculate its preliminary tax based on 100% of the prior period's corporation tax liability or to 90% of the corporation tax liability of the current period. The preliminary tax is payable by the 21st day of the eleventh month of the accounting period (or the 21st day of the month before end of accounting period if accounting period is less than 12 months).

17.7.3   START-UP COMPANIES

New or start-up companies with a corporation tax liability of €200,000 or less are not required to pay preliminary tax for the first accounting period and can pay the tax at the same time as filing the tax return which is by the 21st day of the ninth month after the accounting period ends.

Example:

Bright Sparks Limited has a corporation tax liability of €8,000 for its first accounting period and is not required to pay preliminary tax for its first accounting period that ends on 30 September 2015 and it can pay the €8,000 corporation tax when it files the corporation tax return (form CT1) by 21 June 2016.

17.8   Tax Return and Payment of Balance of Corporation Tax

A company must file a tax return, a form CT1 by the 21st day of the ninth month after the accounting period ends. The balance of the tax liability must be paid by this date also. If the return is filed and the tax paid using ROS the deadline is extended to the 23rd day of the ninth month. Generally all companies are obliged to file and pay using ROS.

Example:

ZZZ Limited accounts are made up to 31 October. This means that the preliminary tax must be paid by 21 September (as it is a small company) and the balance of the tax must be paid and the tax return filed by 21 July after the end of the accounting period.

17.8.1   SURCHARGE

If a company fails to file the form CT1 tax return by the due date a surcharge is imposed which is determined by how late the company is in filing the return.

The surcharge is calculated in the same way as it is for income tax:

(a)   if the return is filed within two months of the return filing date a surcharge of 5% of the tax up to a maximum of €12,695 is payable in addition to the tax liability for the tax year; and

(b)   if the return is filed more than two months after the return filing date a surcharge of 10% of the tax up to a maximum of €63,485 is payable in addition to the tax liability for the tax year.

17.8.2   INTEREST

Interest will be payable on any late payment at the rate of 0.0291% per day or part of a day.

17.8.3   FAILURE TO INCLUDE INFORMATION

A surcharge may also be payable if a company fails to include certain information in its return in relation to reliefs that it is claiming and the company becomes aware that it has failed to include the information and fails to provide it to Revenue. The surcharge is calculated at 5% of the tax up to a maximum of €12,695. The surcharge is payable in addition to the tax liability for the tax year.

17.8.4   RESTRICTIONS ON RELIEFS AND ALLOWANCES FOR LATE FILING

If a return is filed late this has consequences on the reliefs and allowances that a company can claim. The reliefs and allowances that are impacted include group relief, trading losses, and certain capital losses.

If the return is filed within two months of the return filing date reliefs and allowances are restricted by 25% subject to a maximum of €31,740 for each relief and allowance. If the return is filed more than two months after the return filing date reliefs and allowances are restricted by 50% subject to a maximum of €158,715 for each relief and allowance.

Example:

XYZ Limited has trading losses of €10,000 and it has other income of €40,000 taxable at 12.5%. It delays in filing its tax return, form CT1 and it files one month later than it should.

The consequences of this will mean that the trading losses will be restricted to €7,500.

In addition XYZ Limited will have to pay a surcharge of 5% of the tax up to a maximum of €12,695 as well as the tax liability for the tax year.

Interest per day or part of a day at 0.0219% on the unpaid tax is also due.

17.9   Trading Losses – Schedule D Case I or II

Losses cannot be set off against other personal income of the shareholders.

For companies with income taxed at 25%, losses may be offset against the company's other profits before charges in the same accounting period and against the company's profits for the *immediately preceding* accounting period of the same length on a Euro for Euro basis (TCA 1997, s 396). Any unused trade loss can be carried forward and can be set against future trading profit of the same trade.

For companies with income taxed at 12.5% losses from income liable to tax at 12.5% may be offset against the company's other trading profits taxable at 12.5% before charges in the same accounting period and against the company's trading profits taxable at 12.5% for the immediately preceding accounting period of the same length on a Euro for Euro basis (TCA 1997, s 396 A). Any unused trade loss can be used against income not taxable at 12.5% on a value basis for the same accounting period and immediately preceding accounting period and any remaining losses can be carried forward and can be set against future trading profit of the same trade.

If the company is a member of a group of companies the losses can be surrendered to other members of the group.

Example:

Bright Sparks Limited made a loss of €50,000 for 31 December 2015. The loss can be set off against other trading income taxable at 12.5% for the 12 months ending 31 December 2015 and the trading income taxable at 12.5% for the 12 months ending 31 December 2014.

Any unused trading loss may be set off against the company's non-trading income but only on a value basis and if any losses remain they can be carried forward against future trade profits.

Example:

Bright Sparks Limited has unused trading losses of €25,000 (this trade is taxable at 12.5%) and it has investment income of €40,000 (taxable at 25%) in 2015. It can get relief for the loss at a rate of 12.5% (€25,000 * 12.5% = €3,125) and deduct this from the investment income of €40,000 leaving €36,875 of investment income to be taxed at 25% = €9,218.75.

17.9.1   ORDER FOR USE OF LOSSES

Generally under the legislation losses must be used in a specific order.

For a trading loss on a trade taxable at 12.5% the following order would be used:

(a)   use losses carried forward from a previous accounting period for the same trade against the profits of the trade;

(b)   then use current period losses for offset against current period trading income taxed at 12.5%;

(c)   if any losses remain carry back against income (in a preceding accounting period of equal length) taxed at 12.5%;

(d)   then use current period losses for offset against current period trading income and gains not taxed at 12.5% on a value basis;

(e)   if any losses remain carry back against income and gains (in a preceding accounting period of equal length) not taxed at 12.5% on a value basis; and

(f)   any remaining losses are available to be carried forward against future profits from the same trade.

17.9.2 TERMINAL LOSS RELIEF

If a company ceased to trade and made a loss in its last accounting period, it can seek to carry this loss back against income from the same trade in the preceding three years.

17.9.3 SCHEDULE D CASE IV

A loss made on Schedule D Case IV income can be set against other Case IV income in the same accounting period and any unused loss can be carried forward against future Case IV income.

17.9.4 SCHEDULE D CASE V

A Schedule D Case V loss can be carried back against Case V income in a preceding accounting period of equal length and any unused loss can be carried forward against future Case V income.

17.10 Group Relief

Group relief may be claimed where companies are members of the same group.

Members of a group may surrender current year trading losses, excess charges on income, excess management expenses (in the case of investment companies), and excess capital allowances in rental property.

A group for group loss relief applies if one company is a 75% subsidiary of the other (i.e. one company owns 75% of the shares in the other company) or two or more companies are 75% subsidiaries of another company. The parent company must be beneficially entitled to not less than 75% of the profits available for distribution and 75% of the assets available for distribution on a winding up.

All the companies must be resident in the Republic of Ireland or in the European Economic Area and be in a country with which Ireland has a tax treaty. Group relief is also available to members of a consortium if the loss making company is owned by the consortium. A company is able to hand over (surrender) its trading loss to another member of the group.

Example:

DE Limited and FG Limited are 100% subsidiaries of ABC Limited.

DE Limited has a loss of €20,000, FG Limited has a loss of €5,000, and ABC limited has a profit of €150,000. Each of the companies make their accounts up to 31 December each year, each of the companies are Irish incorporated, and all of the companies qualify as trading companies that pay tax on their trading income as 12.5%.

DE Limited can surrender the losses of €20,000 to ABC Limited to reduce its profits to €130,000.

FG Limited can also surrender its losses of €5,000 to ABC Limited to further reduce its profits to €125,000.

17.11 Inter Group Payments

A group for inter group payments is a 51% group; if one company is a 51% subsidiary of the other (i.e. one company owns 51% of the shares in the other company) or two or more companies are 51% subsidiaries of another company. A member of a group is permitted to make certain payments to another member of a group without deducting tax in certain circumstances. For example; interest payments and royalties may be paid gross i.e. without deduction of tax if a group relationship exists.

17.12 Taxation of Dividends

17.12.1 IF AN IRISH COMPANY RECEIVES DIVIDENDS

No tax is payable on dividends received from other Irish resident companies.

Dividends received from a foreign company that is tax resident within the EU or in a country with which Ireland has a tax treaty which are paid out of trading profits are liable to corporation tax at 12.5%.

Otherwise foreign dividends are liable to corporation tax at 25%.

17.12.2 IF A COMPANY PAYS A DIVIDEND

If a company declares and pays a dividend the recipients will be liable to income tax on the dividend received.

The company that declares and pays the dividend may have to deduct dividend withholding tax on the dividend (currently at a rate of 20%) and pay this directly to Revenue (before the 14th day after the month of the payment of the dividend). A voucher detailing the dividend withholding tax must be provided to the shareholders.

The company cannot seek a deduction from corporation tax for the dividend paid and the payment must be made out of after tax profits (profits available for distribution) that are subject to company law rules.

Example:

G2G Ltd: Profit & Loss A/c to 30/9/15

Sales	€663,000
Cost of sales	(€523,000)
Gross profit	€140,000
Expenses	(€95,000)
Profit before tax	€45,000
Tax on profits	(€8,000)
Profit after tax	€37,000
Dividends	(€10,000)
Retained profits	€27,000

What are the taxation implications of the payment of the €10,000 in dividends?

G2G Limited does not get any deduction from its profits to pay the dividends.

The company must withhold dividend withholding tax at a rate of 20% when paying the dividends to its shareholders (subject to certain exceptions).

The gross dividend is €10,000. 20% will be withheld as dividend withholding tax (€2,000) and paid over to Revenue Commissioners before the 14th day after the month in which the dividend is made with the balance of €8,000 paid out to the shareholders with a voucher showing the dividend withholding tax deducted that the shareholder can use as evidence of their entitlement to a credit for the dividend tax deducted.

The shareholders in receipt of the dividends are taxed under the income tax rules on the gross dividend paid and they will get a credit for any dividend withholding tax.

17.12.3 PAYMENT OF A SALARY/BONUS V PAYMENT OF A DIVIDEND

Should a shareholder be paid a dividend or a salary/bonus payment? Is there any difference for the company or for the individual?

A tax deduction may be available for the company for the payment of a salary or bonus to an employee or director of the company. However employer's PRSI may also be payable on the salary or bonus except where a payment is made to a proprietary director (a director who controls 15% or more of the shares in the company and who must pay the PRSI him/herself as a self-employed person).

Example:

A company makes a payment of a bonus to Celia, an employee, of €8,000. This payment may be subject to an employer's PRSI payment (PRSI 10.75% * €8,000 = €860).

If Celia was a proprietary director (she is a director and she can control more than 15% of the shares) Celia will pay the PRSI and not the company.

Example:

HHH Limited has pre-tax profits of €10,000 and wishes to make a payment of €2,000 to Alison an employee for all of her hard work in setting up the company and assisting in launching the first product. Alison holds 25% shares in the company and is a director.

Should HHH Limited pay a bonus to Alison or should it declare a dividend?

HHH Limited can only pay a dividend if it has profits available for distribution. It confirms that it has sufficient profits available to make the distribution.

HHH Limited – tax consequences:

	Dividend	Bonus
Pre tax profit	€10,000	€10,000
Less bonus	0	(€2,000)
Taxable profits	€10,000	€8,000
Corporation tax @ 12.5%	€1,250	€1,000
After tax profits	€8,750	€7,000
Dividend paid	(€2,000)	0
Balance	€6,750	€7,000
Tax saving		€250

There is a corporation tax saving of €250 for the company by paying a bonus rather than a dividend as it can take a deduction for the bonus from its trading income which reduces its trading income for corporation tax purposes.

HHH Limited must withhold dividend withholding tax at the standard rate (20%) from the dividend if it decides to pay a dividend. €2,000 * 20% = €400 and pay this over to Revenue.

(*continued*)

Alison – taxation consequences:

It is assumed that she has already fully used all her tax credits and is paying tax on the €2,000 at 40%, USC at 7% and PRSI at 4% (2015 rates).

Bonus:

She receives €2,000 through the PAYE system and after calculation of her income tax, USC plus her own PRSI payment she ultimately receives a net payment of €980 (€2,000 – €1,020). €2,000 * 51% (40% + 4% + 7% = 51%) = €1,020. The tax is €1,020.

Dividend:

She receives €1,600 as a net dividend.

Alison must pay tax of €620 on the dividend. €2,000 gross dividend less income tax (40%), USC (7%) and PRSI (4%) totalling 51% * €2,000 = €1,020 – less the dividend withholding tax credit of €400 = net tax payable €620.

The total tax paid is €400 + €620 = €1,020.

In this example Alison pays the same tax irrespective of whether she receives a bonus or dividend but the company makes a corporation tax saving by paying a deductible bonus rather than paying a dividend.

17.12.4   IS THERE ANY OTHER REASON WHY A COMPANY MAY PAY A DIVIDEND?

Reasons include providing a return for its shareholders or to avoid a close company surcharge.

17.13   Close Company

17.13.1   WHAT IS A CLOSE COMPANY?

A close company is an Irish resident company under the control of its directors who are participators or under the control of five or fewer participators.

A *participator* is someone who has an interest in the income or capital of a company. A participator is deemed to own the shares and interest of his/her associates when determining interests in the company.

An *associate* includes the spouse/civil partner, direct relatives, and partners and trustees of a participator.

17.13.2   RESTRICTIONS ON A CLOSE COMPANY

Corporation tax rules impose a number of restrictions on close companies.

17.13.2.1   Expenses for free benefits

If a company incurs an expense in providing any benefit to a participator, the amount of the expense will not be deductible for corporation tax purposes and instead the benefit will be treated as a distribution by the company to the participator and the participator will have to pay tax on the distribution.

17.13.2.2 Interest payments.

Interest paid to directors or their associates above a specified rate may be treated as a distribution.

17.13.2.3 Loans to participators

There are certain rules and negative consequences on loans provided by a company to participators or their associates. Tax must be deducted on loans provided to participators or their associates and if a loan is forgiven, the grossed-up amount is treated as income of the participator or his associate.

17.13.2.4 Close company surcharge

Surcharges are imposed on a close company that does not make distributions to its shareholders.

If a company has after tax investment income or rental income (passive income) available for distribution to its shareholders and it does not distribute the income within 18 months of the end of the accounting period then a surcharge is imposed on the company if the amount of the undistributed passive income is more than €2,000 and the company is not precluded by law from distributing the income.

The surcharge is 20% of the undistributed investment and rental income. For trading companies the undistributed income can be reduced by 7.5% before the surcharge is calculated.

Example:

ABC Limited is a close company and it has after paying tax, rental income of €20,000 and deposit interest of €10,000 unrelated to the trading income for the year ended 31 July 2015.

As ABC Limited is a trading company the income can be reduced by 7.5% before the surcharge is calculated.

If ABC Limited does not distribute this income by 31 January 2017 it will be subject to a surcharge of €30,000 − 2,250 (30,000 * 7.5%) = €27,750 * 20% = €5,550.

A close company that is a service company (professional company) is also liable to a surcharge that is calculated differently.

The surcharge is 20% of the rental income and investment income (passive income) available for distribution and an additional 15% of half the distributable trading income.

For trading companies the undistributed income can be reduced by 7.5% before the surcharge is calculated.

Example:

ZZZ Limited is an architectural practice operating as a company owned by two brothers and it has €40,000 in after tax rental and investment income and €55,000 trading income for the year ended 30 September 2015. If it does not distribute this income by 31 March 2017 it will be subject to a surcharge:

40,000 − 3,000 (40,000 * 7.5%) = 37,000 = passive income

55,000/2 = €27,500 = half trading income

(continued)

20% * €37,000 = €7,400; and

15% * €27,500 = €4,125.

Total surcharge €11,525.

To avoid the surcharge a company must make a distribution within 18 months of the end of the accounting period if it has profits available for distribution that it can legally distribute.

17.14   Reliefs

There are a number of incentives and reliefs available to encourage and attract businesses to be set up as companies and some reliefs are only available to companies.

For example, a 25% tax credit is available for qualifying research and development expenditure for companies engaged in in-house qualifying research and development undertaken within the European Economic Area. The credit may be set against the company's corporation tax liability and is available on a group basis in the case of a group of companies. The first €100,000 of all qualifying research and development expenditure qualified for a 25% tax credit in 2013 and thereafter. For expenditure in excess of this amount the credit was available only for such research and development expenditure that exceeds the research and development expenditure incurred in the base year 2003 specified in the legislation until 31 December 2014. The 2003 base year restriction was removed from 1 January 2015.

17.15   Companies Chargeable Gains

17.15.1 CHARGEABLE GAINS LIABLE TO CAPITAL GAINS TAX

Gains of an Irish resident company that arise on the disposal of development land are charged to Capital Gains Tax ('CGT').

Gains that arise for a non-resident company on the disposal of certain non-trading assets situated in the State (Republic of Ireland) are liable to CGT.

17.15.2 CHARGEABLE TO CORPORATION TAX

All other gains (i.e. non-development land gains) of an Irish resident company are charged to corporation tax.

Gains accruing to a non-resident company on the disposal of assets situated in Ireland and used for the purpose of a trade carried on by it in the State through a branch or agency are liable to corporation tax.

17.15.3 AMOUNT ON WHICH TAX IS PAID

The amount of the chargeable gain liability is calculated using CGT rules.

As the rate of corporation tax and the rate of CGT are different a notional amount of gain is calculated so that when this notional gain is charged at the rate of corporation tax applicable to the company, the correct amount of chargeable gain liability is assessed.

> **Example:**
>
> XYZ Limited calculates that it has a capital gain in 2015 of €20,000 * 33% = €6,600. The rate of corporation tax for XYZ Limited is 12.5% as it is a trading company.
>
> The amount of the gain to be considered for the corporation tax assessment is an amount that when taxed at 12.5% will equal €6,600.
>
> The notional amount will have to be €52,800 as 12.5% of €52,800 equals €6,600.

17.15.4 PAYMENT OF TAX ON CHARGEABLE GAIN

The liability for a company's chargeable gains is assessed for the accounting period in which the gain accrued and is included in the form C1 as part of the corporation tax return for the accounting period.

17.15.5 LOSSES

17.15.5.1 Trading losses

Trading losses may only be offset against trading income for the same and immediately preceding accounting period of the same length on a Euro for Euro basis. See paragraph **17.9**.

Any unused trading loss may be offset against non-trading income, including chargeable gains, but only on a value basis as different tax rates apply to trading income and chargeable gains.

> **Example:**
>
> ABC Limited has an unused trading loss in 2015 of €200,000 and a chargeable gain of €200,000. ABC Limited can get relief for the loss at the rate of 12.5% against the liability on the chargeable gain.
>
> Tax due on the chargeable gain is €200,000 * 33% = €66,000 and ABC Limited can claim loss relief of €25,000 (€200,000 trading loss * 12.5%) as a deduction against the €66,000 chargeable gain leaving it with a net liability of €41,000 to be paid.

17.15.5.2 Losses on the disposal of assets

Losses of a company on non-development land assets may be offset against chargeable gains (but not development land gains) of the company in the current accounting period. Any unused balance can be carried forward for use against any future chargeable gains.

Losses on the disposal of development land can be offset against gains arising on other assets. Any unused balance can be carried forward for use against any future chargeable gains.

17.15.5.3 Groups

A group for CGT purposes applies if one company is a 75% subsidiary of the other (i.e. one company owns 75% of the shares in the other company) or two or more companies are 75% subsidiaries of another company.

Sales of assets between companies within a group are treated as resulting in a no loss/no gain situation. Instead a company on leaving a group pays the tax on the chargeable gain.

17.16 Corporation Tax Calculation Example

Example:

RS Limited has had a successful year ending 30 June 2015. It has net trading income of €70,000, gross rental income on an office building that it let out of €30,000, and investment income of €20,000.

It sold an asset of the trading business and has a chargeable gain of €20,000.

It deducted depreciation of €5,000 on plant and machinery as part of its expenses for the year to 30 June 2015. Capital allowances on the plant and machinery calculated at 12.5% amount to €4,000.

RS Limited had made a trading loss in the year 30 June 2014 and has losses of €12,000 still available.

RS Limited spent €8,000 maintaining the office building in the year to 30 June 2015.

Calculate RS Limited's corporation tax for the accounting period ended 30 June 2015

Schedule D Case I:

€70,000	income
€5,000	depreciation add back
€75,000	adjusted profits for tax purposes
(€12,000)	losses carried forward s 396 relief
€63,000	taxable Case I income
(€4,000)	Capital allowance deductible
€59,000	income taxable at 12.5%

Schedule D Case III

Investment income €20,000 – income taxable at 25%

Schedule D Case V

€30,000	rental income
(€8,000)	costs
€22,000	net income – taxable at 25%

Chargeable gain

€20,000 = €20,000 * 33% = €6,600

What notional gain would result in tax of €6,600 if taxed at 12.5%?

X * 12.5% = €6,600

€6,600/12.5 * 100 = €52,800

€52,800 * 12.5% = €6,600.

€52,800 is the notional figure to be used for the chargeable gain for corporation tax purposes.

Corporation tax liability:

€59,000 * 12.5%	€7,375	trading income
€52,800 * 12.5%	€6,600	chargeable gain
€42,000 (€20,000 + €22,000) * 25% =	€10,500	
Total Corporation Tax is	€24,475	

Preliminary tax of 90% (€22,027.50) must have been made by 21 May 2015. A form CT1 must be filed and the balance of the corporation tax must be paid by 21 March 2016.

17.17 Comparison of Income Tax and Corporation Tax

Corporation Tax	Income Tax 2015
Applies to companies	Applies to individuals
Tax rates:	Tax rates:
12.5% for trading income	20% standard rate
25% for other income	40% higher rate
No PRSI on income	PRSI @ 4% of income
No USC	USC – possibly up to 11%
Includes chargeable gains	Chargeable gains taxed under CGT
Add back depreciation	Add back depreciation
Capital allowances deductible	Capital allowances deductible
Group relief available for groups	Tax credits available
Close company restrictions	No equivalent
Certain specific reliefs only available to companies	
Losses can be carried back	Carried back only on terminal loss

PART 4
TRADING ISSUES

CHAPTER 18

CONSUMER LAW

18.1 Introduction

Legislative efforts to protect consumers are a patchwork of uncoordinated measures rather than a raiment of coherent pattern. This patchwork sits on top of the common law.

Even in the European legislation, there is great incoherence. Key concepts and terms are differently defined and used in each piece of legislation. The legislation overlaps and is even contradictory in some areas. There is no overarching set of principles which apply in all areas regulated by European law.

The problem is further exacerbated by the tendency in Ireland to adopt the language of directives without seeking to integrate the new law with the existing law. The problem of lack of coherence has been recognised by the European institutions. For a number of years the Commission has been working on this issue. The Commission has published proposals for a Common European Sales Law which can be adopted by parties as the basis for their contracting.

This chapter only deals with the major elements of consumer protection legislation in the area of the sale of goods and supply of services. There are consumer protection provisions to be found in a wide range of sectors in respect of which there is specific legislation. Some of these are noted at the end of this chapter.

18.2 Sale of Goods—The 1893 and 1980 Acts

18.2.1 INTRODUCTION

The Sale of Goods Act 1893 ('the 1893 Act') largely restated the common law in relation to the sale of goods. Although it set out terms that were to be implied in such contracts, it preserved traditional freedom of contract, by permitting such implied term to be varied or negatived (1893 Act, s 55).

The 1893 Act was substantially amended by the Sale of Goods and Supply of Services Act 1980 ('the 1980 Act'). The 1980 Act restricts the ability to contract out of the implied terms and, in addition to dealing with the sale of goods, also deals with the supply of services. References to the 1893 Act are to that legislation as amended by the 1980 Act.

18.2.2 KEY CONCEPTS

18.2.2.1 Goods

Goods include for the purpose of the 1893 Act 'all chattels personal other than things in action and money'. The term includes emblements, industrial growing crops, and things attached to or forming part of the land which are agreed to be severed before sale or under the contract of sale (1893 Act, s 62).

18.2.2.2   Dealing as a consumer

The 1893 Act and the 1980 Act set out specific provisions, which apply where a party 'deals as a consumer'. For a customer to qualify as a consumer, the customer must not enter into the contract in the course of a business and the other party must do so, but there is a third test in that the goods or services supplied are of a type ordinarily supplied for private use or consumption (1893 Act, s 3). Subsection (3) provides that the burden of proof rests with the supplier to show the customer does not deal as consumer.

18.2.3   IMPLIED CONDITIONS AND WARRANTIES

18.2.3.1   Title

Section 12 (1) of the 1893 Act provides that in every contract of sale of goods there is:

• an implied *condition* that the seller has the right to sell the goods; and

• an implied *warranty* that the goods are free from any charge or encumbrance not disclosed to the buyer.

18.2.3.2   Sale by description

Section 13 of the 1893 Act provides that there is an implied *condition* that the goods will correspond with the description, where there is a contract for the sale of goods by description. If the goods are sold by description and by sample, it is not sufficient that the bulk of the goods corresponds with the sample, if the goods do not also correspond with the description.

18.2.3.3   Sale by sample

Section 15 of the 1893 Act defines a contract of sale as a contract for sale by sample where there is a term in the contract expressed or implied to that effect. In the case of such a contract, there are three implied conditions;

• that the bulk shall correspond with the sample in quality;

• that the buyer shall have a reasonable opportunity of comparing the bulk with the sample; and

• that the goods shall be free from any defect rendering them unmerchantable which would not be apparent on reasonable examination of the sample.

18.2.3.4   Merchantable quality

Where the seller sells goods in the course of a business there is an implied condition that the goods supplied are of merchantable quality (1893 Act, s 14 (2)) This condition is displaced:

• as regards defects specifically drawn to the buyer's attention before the contract is made; or

• if the buyer examines the goods before the contract, as regards defects which that examination ought to have revealed.

Merchantable quality is defined in s 14 (3), which states that goods are of merchantable quality if they are as fit for the purpose or purposes for which goods of that kind are commonly bought and they are as durable as it is reasonable to expect having regard to:

• any description applied to them;

- the price (if relevant); and

- all other relevant circumstances.

18.2.3.5   Fitness for particular purpose

Where the seller sells goods in the course of a business and the buyer expressly or by implication makes known to the seller any particular purpose for which the goods are being bought, there is an implied condition that the goods supplied under the contract are reasonably fit for that purpose (1983 Act, s 14 (4)). It is not necessary that the particular purpose should be a purpose for which such goods are commonly supplied. The condition is not implied where the circumstances show that the buyer does not rely, or that it is unreasonable for him to rely, on the seller's skill or judgement.

18.2.3.6   Spare parts and servicing

Section 12 of the 1980 Act implies in any contract for the sale of goods a *warranty* that the spare parts and an adequate after sale service will be made available by the seller in such circumstances as are stated in an offer, description, or advertisement by the seller and for such period as is so stated. If no period is stated then it must be for a reasonable period.

18.2.3.7   Motor vehicles

Section 13 of the 1890 Act provides for a *condition* in every contract for sale of a motor vehicle that at the time of the delivery it is free from any defect which would render it a danger to the public including persons travelling in the vehicle. This condition is, however, not implied where the buyer is a person whose business it is to deal in motor vehicles. The condition implied under s 13 of the 1980 Act is in addition to any other terms such as conditions as to merchantable quality. Section 13 (3) 1980 Act provides that the condition set out in the section shall not apply where:

- it is agreed that the vehicle is not intended for use in the condition in which it is to be delivered to the buyer under the contract;

- the statement to that effect is signed by or on behalf of the seller and the buyer and given to the buyer on or before delivery; and

- it is shown that the agreement is fair and reasonable.

18.2.4   EXCLUSION CLAUSES

18.2.4.1   Introduction

Section 55 of the 1893 Act permitted the negativing or variation of implied terms by express agreement. The 1980 Act amended and restated s 55, limiting the effectiveness of exclusion clauses. Of course, the restrictions in the 1980 Act are in addition to the common law and rules regulating specific sectors.

18.2.4.2   Condition as to title

Section 55 (3) of the 1893 Act now provides that any provision exempting any of the provisions of s 12 of the 1893 Act shall be void.

18.2.4.3   Sale by sample, sale by description, condition as to quality or fitness

Where the buyer deals as consumer, any term exempting any of the provisions of s 13, 14, or 15 of the 1893 Act shall be void where the buyer deals as a consumer. In any other case, such a term will not be enforceable unless it is shown that it is fair and reasonable (1893 Act, s 55 (4)). Section 2 (3) of 1980 Act requires regard to be had to the criteria set out in the Schedule to the 1980 Act in deciding whether or not a term is fair and reasonable.

18.2.4.4   Warranty as to spare parts and servicing

Section 12 (3) of the 1980 Act provides that any term of a contract exempting from all or any of the provisions of s 12 of the 1980 Act shall be void.

18.2.4.5   International sales

Special rules apply to international sales of goods. In the case of such sales, any of the implied terms set out in ss 12–15 of the 1893 Act (including the condition as to title) may be negatived or varied (1893 Act s 61 (6)).

However, this provision does not affect s 12 (3) of the 1980 Act (warranty as to spare parts and servicing) or s 13 of the 1980 Act (motor vehicles)

A contract for the international sale of goods means a contract of sale of goods made by parties whose place of business (or habitual residences) are in different States and which satisfies one of the following conditions:

• the goods are being or will be carried from one State to another;

• offer and acceptance have been effected in different States; and

• delivery of the goods will be made in a State other than that in which the offer and acceptance have been effected.

18.2.5   REMEDIES FOR NON-CONFORMITY

Breach of a condition gives rise to a right to treat the contract as repudiated. Accordingly, non-conformity with any of the conditions set out in ss 12–15 inclusive of the 1893 Act or s 13 of the 1980 Act affords the buyer the primary remedy of the right to reject the goods and to demand a refund and/or damages under the general law of contract. However, where the buyer has accepted the goods or part of them, that right of rejection is lost and the condition is treated as a warranty (1893 Act, s 11 (3)) in the absence of agreement to the contrary. However, where the buyer deals as consumer, even though he may be deemed to have accepted the goods, the right to reject is resuscitated in the circumstances set out in s 53 (2) of the 1893 Act.

18.3   Sale of Goods—The Sales Directive

18.3.1   INTRODUCTION

The European Communities (Certain Aspects of the Sale of Consumer Goods and Associated Guarantees) Regulations 2003 (SI 11/2003) (the '2003 Regulations') give effect to Directive 1999/44/EC of the European Parliament and of the Council of 25 May 1999, on certain aspects of the sale of consumer goods and associated guarantees. The 2003 Regulations substantially overlap with the 1980 Act. Both provisions set out what is required to demonstrate conformity of the goods with the contract. The 2003 Regulations establish a hierarchy of remedies which differs from that of general contract law. However, the regimes run in parallel.

18.3.2 KEY CONCEPTS

'Consumer' means a natural person who is acting for purposes which are outside that person's trade, business, or profession. 'Seller' means any natural or legal person who under contract sells consumer goods in the course of his/her trade, business, or profession. 'Consumer Goods' means any tangible moveable item other than:

- goods sold by way of execution or otherwise by authority of the law;
- water or gas where it is not put up for sale in a limited volume or set quantity; and
- electricity.

18.3.3 GOODS TO BE IN CONFORMITY WITH CONTRACT

Regulation 5 (1) sets out the mandatory rule that the goods delivered under a contract between a seller and consumer must be in conformity with that contract. The regulation sets out the circumstances where the consumer goods are presumed to be in conformity. These circumstances cover substantially the same ground as the terms implied by ss 12–15 of the 1893 Act. However, the lack of conformity is excused if at the time the contract was concluded, the consumer was aware or ought reasonably to have been aware of the lack of conformity or if the lack of conformity has its origins in materials supplied by the consumer.

18.3.4 BURDEN OF PROOF OF LACK OF CONFORMITY

Regulation 8 assists the consumer by establishing a presumption that any lack of conformity which becomes apparent within six months of the date of delivery of the goods is deemed to have existed at the time of delivery of the goods. The burden of proof accordingly rests on the seller to prove the contrary. However, this presumption does not apply if it would not be a reasonable inference that the lack of conformity existed at the time of delivery by reason of the nature of the goods concerned or the nature of the lack of conformity concerned.

18.3.5 REMEDIES

The seller is liable to the consumer for any lack of conformity as described above which exists at the time the goods were delivered. If the goods do not conform the consumer may in the first place require the seller to repair the goods or to replace them free of charge. However if either of those remedies is impossible or disproportionate the consumer may require an appropriate reduction of the price or have the contract rescinded. The consumer is also entitled to a reduction or rescission if the seller has not completed the repair or replacement within a reasonable time or without significant inconvenience to the consumer. However, the consumer is not entitled to rescission if the lack of conformity is minor.

18.4 Sale of Goods–Guarantees

Guarantees given in connection with the sale of goods are regulated by:

- the general law of contract;
- ss 15–19 of the 1980 Act; and
- the 2003 Regulations.

Section 15 of the 1980 Act deals with a guarantee supplied by a manufacturer or supplier (other than the retailer). The 2003 Regulations include a guarantee given by a retailer.

However, under the 1980 Act, where a seller delivers a guarantee to the buyer, the seller shall be liable to the buyer for the observance of the terms of the guarantee as if he were the guarantor unless he expressly stipulates to the contrary at the time of delivery (1980 Act, s 17). The 2003 Regulations require that consumer guarantees are legally binding upon the offeror of the goods and that the guarantee should state that the consumer's statutory rights are not affected by the guarantee.

18.5   Supply of Services

18.5.1   INTRODUCTION

The 1980 Act introduced for the first time a set of implied terms in contracts for the supply of a services (1980 Act, s 39) where the supplier is acting in the course of a business.

Section 39 does not make it clear (as the Act does in relation to the sale of goods) whether the implied terms amount to a condition or a warranty. The issue will, accordingly, fall to be determined in accordance with general contract law.

18.5.2   IMPLIED TERMS

Section 39 of the 1980 Act provides that in every contract for the supply of a service where the supplier is acting in the course of a business, the following terms are implied:

(a)   that the supplier has necessary skills to render the service;

(b)   that he will supply the service with due skill, care, and diligence;

(c)   where materials are used, they will be sound and reasonably fit for the purpose for which they are required; and

(d)   where goods are supplied under the contract, they will be of merchantable quality.

The distinction, as to whether a contract is for the sale of goods or for the supply of services, can frequently be very fine. A lottery ticket has been held to be a contract of sale of goods and not a supply of services (*Carroll v An Post National Lottery Company* [1996] 1 IR 443). Software has been held to be goods, if sold in physical form (*St Albans Council v International Computers Ltd* [1996] 4 ALL ER 481). Where materials are used, or goods are supplied, the implied terms as to merchantability and fitness of purpose are extended to them.

18.5.3   EXCLUSION CAUSES

Save where the customer deals as consumer, the terms implied into a contract for supply for services under s 39 of the 1980 Act can be negatived or varied by an express term of the contract or by the course of dealing between the parties or by usage, if the usage be such as to bind both parties to the contract (1980 Act, s 40 (1)). Where the recipient of a service deals as consumer, it must be shown that the express term is fair and reasonable and has been specifically drawn to his attention. The criteria set out in the Schedule to the 1890 Act must be taken into account in determining what is fair and reasonable (s 2 (3) 1980 Act). The restriction on exclusion clauses under s 40 does not apply to the international carriage of passengers or goods. Section 39 does not apply to a contract for the carriage of passengers or goods within the State (s 40 (6)).

18.6   European Communities (Unfair Terms in Consumer Contracts) Regulations 1995 and 2000

18.6.1   OVERVIEW

The European Communities (Unfair Terms in Consumer Contracts) Regulations 1995 and 2000 (the 'Regulations') implement the Unfair Terms in Consumer Contracts Directive (Council Directive 93/13/EEC) ('UTCCD'). The purpose of the UTCCD is to ensure that consumers are protected against an abuse of power by a seller or supplier, particularly in relation to one-sided standard contracts or unfair exclusions of essential rights which the consumer does not have the opportunity to negotiate. A contract or a contract term will not be unfair just because it represents a bad bargain. The UTCCD sets out general criteria for assessing whether a contract term is unfair. Regulation 6 provides that an unfair term in a contract concluded with a consumer by a seller or supplier will not be binding on the consumer. The contract will continue to bind the parties if it is capable of continuing in existence without the unfair term.

18.6.2   KEY DEFINITIONS

Consumer means 'a natural person who is acting for purposes which are outside his business'. Seller means 'a person who, acting for purposes related to his business sells goods'. Supplier means 'a person who, acting for purposes related to his business, supplies services'.

18.6.3   WHAT CONTRACTS ARE INCLUDED?

Any contract between a consumer and a seller or supplier is covered by the Regulations. The following types of contract are specifically excluded:

- individually negotiated contracts;

- contracts of employment;

- contracts relating to succession rights;

- contracts relating to rights under family law; and

- contracts relating to the incorporation or organisation of companies or partnerships or terms which reflect mandatory, statutory, or regulatory provisions of Irish law or international conventions.

18.6.4   EXCLUDED TERMS

A contract term which has been individually negotiated with the seller or supplier will not be caught by the Regulations. However, the Regulations may still apply to the remainder of the contact. The onus of proving that a contract or contract term was individually negotiated rests with the seller or supplier. The Regulations only apply to ancillary terms of a contract. Terms that are core to the contract relating to its main subject matter, such as quality or price of the goods or services to be supplied, do not come within the scope of Regulations provided they are set out in plain and intelligible language. However, these terms may be taken into consideration when assessing the unfairness of other terms in the contract.

18.6.5   DEFINITION OF AN UNFAIR TERM

A term will be regarded as unfair if:

> *contrary to the requirement of good faith, it causes a significant imbalance in the parties' rights and obligations under the contract to the detriment of the consumer, taking into account the nature of*

the goods or services for which the contract was concluded and all circumstances attending the con-clusion of the contract and all other terms of the contract or of another contract on which it is dependent.

It is clear that the fairness of a term cannot be looked at in isolation but must be assessed in the context of the contract as a whole and the circumstances under which it was con-cluded. The Regulations do set out some guidelines in this regard.

18.6.6   GOOD FAITH

Under sch 2 of the Regulations the following factors should be taken into account in as-sessing good faith:

- the strength and bargaining position of the parties;
- whether the consumer had an inducement to agree to the term;
- whether the goods or services were sold or supplied to the special order of the con-sumer; and
- the extent to which the seller or supplier has dealt fairly and equitably with the con-sumer whose legitimate interest he has to take into account

18.6.7   INDICATIVE LIST OF UNFAIR TERMS

Schedule 3 of the Regulations sets out an indicative non-exhaustive list of terms which *may* be regarded as unfair. This includes any attempt to exclude or limit liability for the death or personal injury of a consumer resulting from an act or omission of the seller or supplier.

18.6.8   INTERPRETATION AND APPLICATION

Where there is any doubt as to the meaning of the term, interpretation in favour of the consumer shall prevail. The effect of including an unfair term is that that term will not be effective and will not bind the consumer. The remainder of the contract, to the extent possible, will continue to apply. The Regulations apply even in circumstances where a contract purports to apply the law of a country other than a Member State. Accordingly, sellers and suppliers are prevented from evading their obligations by nominating the law of a non-EU jurisdiction.

18.6.9   ENFORCEMENT

Consumers are entitled to rely on the provisions of the Regulations in any case before a court of competent jurisdiction but powers are also given to the National Consumer Agency ('NCA') and other authorised persons to enforce the provisions of the Regulations, including the powers to search premises, to inspect records, and to require the giving of information.

18.7   Consumer Protection Act 2007

18.7.1   INTRODUCTION

The Consumer Protection Act 2007 (the 'CPA') implements the Unfair Commercial Prac-tices Directive ('UPCD') (Directive 2005/29/EC of 11 May 2005). The purpose of the direc-tive is to set out a general prohibition covering unfair commercial practices which distort consumers' economic behaviour. The general prohibition is elaborated by rules on the two types of most common unfair commercial practices, namely misleading commercial practices and aggressive commercial practices. Thus where issues arise which are not covered by specific rules the general principles are available to resolve the matter.

The CPA is enacted for the purpose of implementing the Directive. Accordingly a word or expression that is used in the CPA and which is also used in the Directive is to have the same meaning as in the Directive and the courts are directed to construe the CPA in a manner that gives effect to the Directive. The courts are to have regard to the provisions of the Directive including its preambles.

18.7.2   UNFAIR COMMERCIAL PRACTICES

The overarching principle of the CPA is that a trader shall not engage in an unfair commercial practice (CPA, s 41). The CPA follows the scheme of the UCPD by then going on to describe two types of unfair commercial practice: 'misleading commercial practices' and 'aggressive commercial practices'. Finally, a black list of prohibited commercial practices is set out in s 55. The practices on the black list are deemed to be unfair without any proof of their being misleading or aggressive, or otherwise unfair.

18.7.3   KEY CONCEPTS

Section 2 of the CPA defines the key concepts that are referred to throughout the Act:

- 'Commercial practice' means any conduct (whether an act or omission), course of conduct, or representation by the trader in relation to a consumer transaction. It can be seen from this language that whereas the bulk of consumer practices with which the legislation may be concerned will relate to advertising or marketing, it is not in any way confined in that way. The legislation also makes it clear that it makes no difference whether the practice takes place before, during, or after the consumer transaction.

- 'Consumer'. This definition has been amended by s 75 of the Competition and Consumer Protection Act 2014 which provides that 'consumer' means a natural person (whether in the State or not) who is acting wholly or mainly for purposes unrelated to the person's trade, business, or profession.

- A 'consumer transaction' is a promotion or supply of a product to a consumer.

- A 'trader' is a person who is acting for purposes related to the person's trade, business, or profession.

- 'Product' means goods or services.

- 'Goods' are widely defined as meaning real or personal property of any nature or description. The meaning of 'goods' for the purposes of the CPA is much wider than would normally be understood by that term. It includes real property. Section 2 also specifically includes within the definition a wide range of items the categorisation of which would otherwise be uncertain.

- 'Services' is also very widely cast. It embraces any service or facility provided for gain or reward or otherwise than free of charge. Again, there is a specific list of items in s 2 that are included. However, services do not include services provided under a contract of employment.

18.7.4   UNFAIR COMMERCIAL PRACTICE – THE GENERAL RULE

18.7.4.1   Two essential elements

The essential elements of an unfair commercial practice involve:

- a breach of professional diligence; and

- the causing of a material distortion in decision making of an average consumer.

Section 41 (2) provides that a commercial practice is unfair if it:

(a) is contrary to one or both of the following (the requirements of professional diligence):

(i)   the general principle of good faith in the trader's field of activity;

(ii) the standard of skill and care that the trader may be reasonably be expected to exercise in respect of consumers; and

(b) would be likely to:

(i)   cause appreciable impairment of the average consumer's ability to make an informed choice in relation to the product concerned; and

(ii) cause the average consumer to make a transactional decision that the average consumer would not otherwise make.

In determining whether or not a commercial practice is unfair, the practice shall be considered in its factual context, taking account of all of its features and circumstances (CPA s 41 (3)).

18.7.4.2   Breach of professional diligence

Professional diligence calls for two things: (1) observance of the general principle of good faith. This, however, is confined to the trader's field of activity; and (2) the standard of skill and care reasonably to be expected of a trader. It is, accordingly, not sufficient for a trader to be honest. The trader must also be competent. This obligation is analogous to the common law concept of duty of care.

18.7.4.3   Material distortion

The requirements of professional diligence deal with the standards that are expected of the trader. It is not sufficient that the practice fall below those standards. It must also be demonstrated that it causes material distortion of the decision-making process of the average consumer. However, it is notable that it is not necessary under s 41 (2)(b) to show that the practice is likely to cause loss, damage, or injury to consumers. In some cases, consumers may well have suffered a loss as a result of an unfair commercial practice. However, a practice may be unfair even though no transaction has as yet occurred or loss incurred. The distortion must pass a double-headed test: that it is likely to cause (i) an appreciable impairment of the average consumer's ability to make an informed choice; and (ii) the average consumer to make a transactional decision that he would not otherwise make. There is, accordingly, an inbuilt de minimis aspect to the provision. The impairment must be appreciable before it is of legislative importance.

18.7.4.4   Average consumer

There may be consumers who could be led to believe that a Mars bar is indeed a confection from the red planet, but clearly a regulation which required business to guard against such foolishness, would be excessive. The notion of the average consumer has been developed by the European Court of Justice. The Court takes as its benchmark the average consumer who is reasonably well informed and reasonably observant and circumspect taking into account social, cultural, and linguistic factors. There may be circumstances, however, where the perspective of an average consumer needs to be refined. The legislation does this in two circumstances. Where a practice is directed at a particular group of consumers, the average consumer is taken to be the average member of that group. In circumstances where the commercial practice or product would be likely to materially distort the economic behaviour only of a clearly identifiable group of consumers the trader could reasonably be expected to foresee as being particularly vulnerable, the average consumer is then deemed to be the average member of that vulnerable group.

The Directive makes it clear however, that even in relation to the average members of a vulnerable group, its provisions are without prejudice to what it describes as the common and legitimate advertising practices of making exaggerated statements or statements which are not meant to be taken literally.

18.7.5 LIMITS OF SCOPE

The CPA is only concerned with the practices of a trader in relation to a consumer transaction. Business-to-business transactions are, accordingly, not the focus of the legislation (UCPD, Recital 6). Questions of taste and decency are not regulated by the Directive (unless of course the practice included misleading information in relation to such matters) (UCPD, Recital 7). Health and safety rules are not affected unless, again, misleading information is furnished as part of the practice (UCPD, Art 3.3).

Unfair commercial practices are focused on the distortion of the economic preferences of a consumer. The law is not concerned with the economic effect on a trader's competitors, although an unfair commercial practice could have an indirect effect on a competitor. Accordingly, practices which are unfair to business rivals would continue to be regulated by other areas of the law, such as competition law (UCPD, Recital 6). A contract for supply of products is not to be void or unenforceable by reason of any contravention of the CPA (except in relation to pyramid selling schemes).

18.7.6 MISLEADING PRACTICES

We have seen that the CPA distinguishes between two areas of unfair commercial practices, namely misleading commercial practices and aggressive commercial practices. Chapter 2 of the Act sets out those practices regarded as misleading. Under s 43 a commercial practice is misleading if:

- it includes false information in relation to any matter set out in s 43 (3) and that information is likely to cause the average consumer to make a transactional decision that the average consumer would not otherwise make, or

- it is likely to cause the average consumer to be deceived or misled in relation to any matters set out in s 43 (3) and to make a transactional decision that the average consumer would not otherwise make.

There is a lengthy list of matters set out in s 43 (3). Examples include the main characteristics of the product, the price of the product, and the existence of any approval or sponsorship of the product. The determination of whether a practice is misleading is to be considered in its factual context, taking into account all its features in the circumstances. There are specific provisions dealing with representations as to price reduction or recommended retail prices.

18.7.6.1 Confusing marketing or advertising

Marketing or advertising which is likely to cause the average consumer to confuse a competitor's product or trade mark etc. with the advertiser's product, trade mark etc. and to make a transaction decision that the average consumer would not otherwise make, is misleading (CPA, s 44). This provision extends to a consumer protections akin to that afforded to a rival trader by the law of passing off.

18.7.6.2 Compliance with a code of practice

A commercial practice is misleading if it involves a representation that the trader abides or is bound by a code of practice, that representation is likely to cause the average consumer to make a transaction decision the average consumer would not otherwise make, and the trader fails to comply with a firm commitment in that code of practice (CPA, s 45).

18.7.6.3   Omitting or concealing material information

Section 46 (3) of the CPA specifies what constitutes material information in the context of the purchase of products. This includes the main characteristics of the product, the address of the trader, and the price.

18.7.6.4   Surcharge for credit card or other forms of payment

A surcharge imposed by a trader for payment by one method (such as credit card or debit card) which is not imposed for other methods of payment (such as cash payment) is prohibited. Where such surcharge is imposed on all methods of payments the trader is required is to quote the total price inclusive of the surcharge (CPA, s 48 and s 49, but not yet commenced).

18.7.7   AGGRESSIVE COMMERCIAL PRACTICES

Whereas most of the focus of the legislation is on misleading commercial practices and on the black list that we will deal with below, aggressive commercial practices are also prohibited. A commercial practice is aggressive if by harassment, coercion, or undue influence it would be likely to (i) cause significant impairment of the average consumer's freedom of choice or conduct in relation to the product concerned and (ii) cause the average consumer to make a transactional decision that the average consumer would not otherwise make (CPA, s 53). The CPA sets out matters to be taken into account in determining whether the commercial practice employs harassment, coercion, or undue influence (CPA, s 53 (3) and s 54). This includes the use of threatening or abusive language or behaviour.

18.7.8   PROHIBITED COMMERCIAL PRACTICES—THE BLACK LIST

Section 55 sets out a formidable list of practices which are prohibited without any evidence that they are misleading or in any way unfair. It includes obvious cases such as a representation that a product is legal when it is not. It also includes more subtle techniques such as using editorial content that has been paid for to promote a product, if that is not made clear, or the inclusion of an invoice in marketing material for a product that has not been ordered.

18.7.9   PROHIBITION OF PYRAMID PROMOTIONAL SCHEMES

Part 4 of the CPA modernises the law relating to pyramid promotional schemes. The Pyramid Selling Act 1980 is repealed. The definition of a pyramid promotional scheme is very wide and there are a number of ancillary provisions included in order to frustrate efforts to cloak a pyramid scheme as something else. An agreement, to the extent that it requires or provides for a payment of money or monies worth in respect of a pyramid promotional scheme, is void.

18.7.10   CIVIL REMEDIES

Any person, including a trader and the National Consumer Agency (the 'Agency'), can apply to the Circuit Court or High Court for an order prohibiting a trader from committing or engaging in a prohibited act or practice (CPA, s 71). A prohibited act or practice includes unfair commercial practices and certain other practices specified in s 67.

The Agency can accept an *undertaking* from a trader in lieu of s 71 proceedings for a prohibition order. An aggrieved consumer has a statutory right of action for relief by way of damages including exemplary damages (CPA, s 74).

Where the trader is a body corporate, not only is the body corporate liable, but also any director, manager, secretary, or other officer of the trader who authorised or consented to the doing of the prohibited act or practice is also liable. There is a presumption of consent by each director or employee whose duties included making decisions that could have affected the management of the body corporate, to a significant extent. It is notable that there is no defence of due diligence available to any director or other officer who is deemed to have consented in this fashion (CPA, s 74 (5)).

A *compliance notice* can be issued by the Agency specifying the contravention and requiring remediation (CPA, s 75). The compliance notice can be appealed to the District Court. Failure to comply constitutes an offence and compliance orders are to be published.

18.7.11   CRIMINAL PENALTIES

Criminal proceedings can be commenced for an offence under the CPA (CPA, s 76). The defence of due diligence is available in relation to criminal proceedings (CPA, s 78). A *body corporate* can be prosecuted under the Act (CPA, s 77). However, where an offence has been committed by a body corporate, and where that offence has been committed with the consent, connivance, or approval of, or due to the neglect of a director, manager, secretary, or other officer of the body corporate, that director, etc. is also guilty of an offence.

Upon a conviction, in addition to any fine or penalty imposed, the court is required unless special and substantial reasons for not doing so are shown, to order the convicted person to pay to the Agency the costs and expenses incurred by the Agency in relation to the investigation, detection, and prosecution of the offence.

The Agency on behalf of an aggrieved consumer who has consented, may apply for an order, which is ancillary to a criminal conviction, for compensation for the loss or damages incurred by that consumer.

The court has jurisdiction ancillary to the conviction for an offence to order the convicted person to publish a corrective statement and to prescribe the content of that statement.

Instead of initiating prosecution in relation to offences under the Price Display Regulations, Price Display Orders or regulations requiring product prices to be indicated, the Agency can issue a fixed payment notice.

18.7.12   CONSUMER PROTECTION LIST

The Agency maintains a consumer protection list of persons against whom the measures specified in s 86 have been taken.

18.7.13   WHISTLE-BLOWERS' CHARTER

Section 87 of the CPA provides for a whistle-blowers' charter. A person who, apart from that section, would be so liable, shall not be liable in damages in respect of the communication to the Agency of that person's opinion that an offence has, or is being committed, or that there is not compliance with the provisions prohibiting various acts and things under the statute. However, this exemption does not apply if it is proven that the person has not acted reasonably and in good faith in forming that opinion and communicating it to the Agency. The section also provides that an employer shall not penalise an employee for having formed such an opinion and having communicated it to the Agency, again subject to the same proviso in relation to acting reasonably and in good faith. However, the making of such a report to the Agency knowing it to be false constitutes an offence.

18.8 Liability for Defective Products Act 1991 and European Communities (Liability for Defective Products) Regulations 2000

18.8.1   OVERVIEW

The Liability for Defective Products Act 1991 and the European Communities (Liability for Defective Products) Regulations 2000 (together the 'DPA') were enacted to give effect to the provisions of the Council Directive on the Approximation of the Laws, Regulations and Administrative provisions of the Member States concerning Liability for Defective Products and Directive 99/34/EC (which amended the 1985 directive) respectively (together the 'Defective Products Directives'). The Defective Products Directives and the DPA introduced the principle of strict liability on the part of a producer for damage caused by defective products, subject to that producer being able to prove certain exonerating circumstances. No contractual derogation is permitted from the provisions of the DPA. Prior to the introduction of the DPA, liability was imposed upon manufacturers of defective goods in negligence, contract, and/or pursuant to statute. The DPA does not replace these remedies but rather introduced an additional remedy. Pursuant to the DPA it is not necessary to prove negligence or recklessness but merely that there was a causal relationship between the damage and the defect. It is therefore common for a claim under the DPA to be made in conjunction with a claim for negligence or breach of contract.

18.8.2   CORE PRINCIPLE

Section 2 (1) of the DPA sets out the core principle and states that 'the producer shall be liable in damages in tort for damage caused wholly or partly by a defect in his product'.

18.8.3   WHO IS A PRODUCER?

Producer is defined in s 2 (2) of the DPA and includes:

    (a)   the manufacturer of a finished product; or

    (b)   the manufacturer or producer of any raw material or the manufacturer or producer of a component part of a product; or

    (c)   in the case of products of the soil, stock farming, and of fisheries or game, which have undergone initial processing, the person who carried out such processing; or

    (d)   any person who, by putting his name, trade mark or other distinguishing feature on the product or using his name or any such mark or feature in relation to the product, has held himself out to be the producer of the product; or

    (e)   any person who imported the product into a Member State from outside the EU; or

    (f)   in certain circumstances where the producer of a product cannot be identified, the supplier of the product may be deemed to be the producer for the purposes of the DPA.

18.8.4   WHAT IS A PRODUCT?

A product is defined in s 1 (ii) as all moveables, including primary agricultural products which have not undergone initial processing and includes:

    (a)   all moveables even though incorporated into another product or into an immoveable whether by virtue of being a component part or raw material or otherwise, and

(b)   electricity where damage is caused as a result of failure in the process of generation of electricity.

While real property is excluded, products, which have been incorporated into real property, such as materials used in building, still fall within the meaning of the DPA.

18.8.5   PROVING A CAUSE OF ACTION

In order to demonstrate the cause of action the injured person must prove the damage, the defect, and the causal relationship between the two (DPA, s 4).

18.8.6   WHAT IS DAMAGE?

The DPA defines damage as death or personal injury or loss or damage to or destruction of any item of property other than the defective product itself (DPA, s 1). There are, however, certain qualifications which apply. The property must be property which is of a type ordinarily intended for private use and consumption and which was used by the injured person mainly for its own private use and consumption. In order for the DPA to apply, where damage is to property, the damage must be in excess of €440, exclusive of the value of damage to the product itself. Damages will only be awarded on any amount in excess of that limit.

Where the damage is solely to the defective product the DPA will not apply.

18.8.7   WHAT IS A DEFECTIVE PRODUCT?

The defectiveness of a product is not determined by reference to its fitness for use. A product is defective under s 5 of the DPA if it fails to provide the safety which a person would be entitled to expect taking all circumstances into account including:

(a)   the presentation of the product;

(b)   the use that it would be expected to be put; and

(c)   the time it was put into circulation.

The DPA provides that a product will not be defective just because a better product has been put into circulation.

18.8.8   DEFENCES

Section 6 of the DPA provides that a producer will not be liable if he can show that:

(a)   he did not put the product into circulation;

(b)   having regard to the circumstances it is probable that the defect which caused the damage, did not exist at the time the product was put into circulation by him or that defect came into being afterwards;

(c)   the product was neither manufactured by him for sale or any form of distribution for an economic purpose nor manufactured or distributed by him in the course of his business;

(d)   the defect concerned is due to compliance by the product with a statutory or EU requirement;

(e)   when the product was put into circulation the state of scientific and technical knowledge was such that the existence of the defect could not have been discovered (known as the 'state of the art' defence). In other words if the product was manufactured in accordance with the 'state of the art' at the time and the 'state of the art' was such that the particular defect could not have been discovered; or

(f)   in the case of a manufacturer of a component or raw material, that the defect was attributable to the design of the product in which the component was fitted or the raw material incorporated or to the instructions given by the manufacturer.

18.8.9   PERIODS OF LIMITATION

Under s 7 of the DPA an action for damages may not be brought after three years from the date from which the cause of action accrued or, if later, the date on which the plaintiff became aware or should reasonably have become aware of the damage, the defect, and the identity of the producer. No action may be brought after ten years from the date the producer put the product into circulation unless proceedings have already been instituted.

18.9   European Communities (General Product Safety) Regulations 2004

18.9.1   OVERVIEW

The European Communities (General Product Safety) Regulations 2004 (the 'Regulations') give effect to Directive 2001/95/EC (the 'Directive') on general product safety. The 2004 Regulations revoked and replaced 1997 Regulations of the same name which had implemented an earlier Directive. The purpose of the Directive is to provide consistency across Member States in relation to product safety standards by imposing a general standard of safety to apply to all products where there are no specific standards in place. It imposes a general obligation on producers not to put dangerous products on the market. It further seeks to improve safety monitoring and to ensure rapid intervention in the event of dangerous products coming onto the market.

18.9.2   KEY DEFINITIONS

18.9.2.1   Consumer

'Consumer' means 'any natural person who in respect of a product covered by the Directive is acting for purposes which are outside his or her trade, business or profession'.

18.9.2.2   Product

'Product' means 'any product intended for consumers or likely to be used by consumers supplied in the course of a commercial activity. Products can be new, used or reconditioned'.

18.9.2.3   Dangerous product

'Dangerous product' means 'any product which is not a safe product'.

18.9.2.4   Safe product

'Safe product' means 'any product which under normal or reasonably foreseeable conditions of use including duration and where applicable putting into service, installation and maintenance requirements, does not present any risk or only the minimum of risks compatible with the product's use, considered to be acceptable and consistent with the high level of protection for the safety and health of persons'.

18.9.2.5 Producer

'Producer' means:

- the manufacturer of a product, when the manufacturer is established in the Community, and any other person presenting himself or herself as the manufacturer by affixing to the product his or her name, trade mark or other distinctive mark, or the person who reconditions the product;

- the manufacturer's representative, when the manufacturer is not established in the Community or, if there is no representative established in the Community, the importer of the product; or

- other professionals in the supply chain, in so far as their activities may affect the safety properties of the product.

18.9.3 APPLICABLE PRODUCTS

The Regulations apply to all products other than products which are subject to specific safety requirements or second-hand products (including antiques and reconditioned products) provided the consumer has been informed.

18.9.4 PRINCIPAL TERMS

18.9.4.1 General prohibition

Regulation 4 (1) sets out a general prohibition that 'a producer shall not place or attempt to place on the market a product unless it is a safe product'.

18.9.4.2 Safety of products

The safety of the product will be assessed by taking all relevant circumstances into consideration and Regulation 5 sets out circumstances in which a product will be presumed safe.

18.9.4.3 Duties of producers

Producers are required to provide consumers with all relevant information required to enable the consumer to assess the risk inherent in the product. Producers are also required to adopt measures enabling rapid identification of specific products should rapid recall or withdrawal of specific products from the market become necessary and carry out sample testing.

18.9.4.4 Duties of distributors

Distributors are required to act with due care to ensure products supplied are safe and provide all information required to assist in tracing products and give full cooperation in relation to any product investigation.

18.9.4.5 General duty

Any producer and/or distributor who knows or, being a professional, ought to know that a product poses a risk to consumers which is incompatible with the Regulations shall immediately inform the National Consumer Agency (the 'NCA') of the risk and give details of any action to prevent the risk. There are specific criteria set out in relation to the information required in the event that the risk posed is serious.

18.9.5   NATIONAL CONSUMER AGENCY

The duties of the NCA in relation to product safety are set out in regs 9, 10, 11, and 13 and include:

- setting appropriate product checks;

- setting labelling requirements;

- issuing directions prohibiting certain products from being put on the market;

- informing the Commission of any measures being taken or proposed to be taken which restricts, recalls, or withdraws a product from the market; and

- enforcement of the Regulations.

18.10   The European Union (Consumer Information, Cancellation and Other Rights) Regulations 2013

18.10.1   INTRODUCTION

The Consumer Rights Directive (2011/83/EU) (the 'Directive') was finally adopted in 2011 after many years of extensive debate. The European Union (Consumer Information, Cancellation and Other Rights) Regulations 2013 (the 'Regulations') transpose the Directive into Irish law and makes ancillary provisions. The Regulations came into operation on 14 June 2014.

The Directive started life as an ambitious proposal to consolidate and reform four major directives into one single instrument. Those directives were the Distance Selling Directive, the Off Premises Directive (also known as the Doorstep Selling Directive), the Unfair Contract Terms Directive, and the Consumer Sales Directive. The objective was to enact an overarching, comprehensive, and cohesive piece of legislation that would deal with inconsistencies and gaps in the existing structure.

It was also intended that the Directive would be on a full harmonisation basis. Full harmonisation means that a Member State must not maintain or introduce, in its national laws, provisions diverging from those laid down in the Directive in relation to matters within the scope of the Directive. That would mean that Member States would not be entitled to introduce levels of consumer protection that are different from that in the Directive.

The Directive hit very heavy opposition. In order to progress it, the ambition of the Directive is much reduced. Only the Doorstop Selling Directive and the Distance Selling Directive are replaced. The directives on Consumer Sales and Unfair Contract Terms have not been repealed.

Within the scope of the Directive, the principle of maximum harmonisation applies. However, the Directive allows Member States a certain level of discretion in relation to certain issues. The Regulations transpose the Directive within the permitted variations as chosen by the Government and also sets out a regime for enforcement.

18.10.2   SCOPE OF THE REGULATIONS

The Regulations deal with:

(a)   the information rights of consumers in respect of certain on-premises contracts and in respect of off- premises and distance contracts;

(b)   right of cancellation for off-premises and distance contracts;

(c)   prevention of hidden costs; and

(d)   transfer of risk to the consumer.

The Regulations apply to sales contracts concluded after 14 June 2014 between a trader and a consumer. This includes contracts for the sale of digital content, service contracts, contracts for the supply of digital content not supplied on a tangible medium, and contracts for the supply of certain utilities. There is a long list of contracts to which the Regulations do not apply (reg 3 (2)). Thus, for example, the following types of contract are excluded:

(a) healthcare;

(b) financial services;

(c) sale of removable property;

(d) residential property rental;

(e) package holidays; and

(f) timeshare.

There are also exceptions and refinements specific to particular provisions. It is essential that reference is made to the detailed text of the Regulations to check the position in relation to any particular case.

18.10.3 KEY DEFINITIONS

18.10.3.1 Distance contract

Regulation 2 defines a distance contract as:

(a) a contract between a trader and a consumer;

(b) concluded under an organised distance sales or services-provision scheme;

(c) without the simultaneous physical presence of the trader and the consumer; and

(d) with the exclusive use of one or more means of distance communication up to and including the time at which the contract is concluded.

A distance contract would, for example, include an online transaction using a trading website. Distance contracts are discussed in more detail in **chapter 22, 'Information Technology'**. This chapter will discuss the Regulations as they apply to on-premises and off-premises contracts.

18.10.3.2 Off-premises contract

Under Regulation 2, an off-premises contract captures a contract:

(a) concluded in the presence of the consumer and trader away from the business premises of the trader (e.g. an agreement concluded with a door-to-door salesperson);

(b) where the offer was made by the consumer in the presence of the consumer and trader, away from the business premises of the trader;

(c) where the contract is concluded on the trader's premises or by distance communication immediately after the consumer has been individually addressed, away from the trader's premises in the presence of the trader (e.g. a proposal put to a consumer at the consumer's doorstep, but finalised online); or

(d) concluded during a sales or promotion excursion organised by the trader.

18.10.3.3 On-premises contract

An on-premises contract is a contract which is not a distance or off-premises contract.

18.10.3.4 Consumer

A consumer is defined in Regulation 2 as a natural person, who is acting for purposes which are outside the person's trade, business, craft, or profession.

18.10.3.5 Trader

A trader is a natural or legal person who is acting for purposes related to the person's trade, business, craft, or profession, and includes any person acting in the name, or on behalf, of the trader (reg 2).

18.10.4 PRE-CONTRACT INFORMATION FOR CONSUMERS

The Regulations require certain pre-contract information to be given to consumers. The extent of the information depends on whether the transaction is off-premises, distance, or on-premises.

18.10.4.1 On-premises contracts

As one would expect, the range of information required for on-premises contracts is more limited than that which applies to the other categories and then only to the extent that it is not apparent from the context. Moreover, the requirements do not apply to contracts of a day-to-day nature that are performed immediately (for example, a haircut).

The information to be provided is set out in Schedule 1 of the Regulations. These include:

(a)   the main characteristics of the goods or services;

(b)   the identity and contact details of the trader;

(c)   the price and additional charges,

(d)   payment and delivery arrangements,

(e)   complaints-handling policy,

(f)   after-sales and guarantees, and

(g)   the duration of the contract.

In relation to digital content, information on the functionality and inter-operability of digital content with hardware and software must be furnished.

18.10.4.2 Off-premises contracts

In addition to the requirements in relation to on-premises contracts, a number of further information headings is imposed in relation to off-premises contracts. These include:

(a)   the right of cancellation;

(b)   the cost of returning the goods;

(c)   deposits to be furnished by the consumer; and

(d)   the cost (other than basic rate) of using distance communication (i.e. telephone) for the conclusion of the contract.

This pre-contract information forms part of the contract and cannot be altered without the express agreement of both parties (reg 7(6) and reg 10(5)). Moreover, a trader cannot recover the additional costs that are required to be disclosed, if he has not given the relevant information on those costs (reg 7(7) and reg 10(6)).

18.10.4.3 Off-premises contracts for repair or maintenance

For small jobs (less than €200) for repair and maintenance carried out immediately, where the consumer has requested the service, the pre-contract information rules are substantially relaxed (see reg 8).

18.10.4.4 Confirmation of off-premises contracts

A trader must provide a copy of the contract, or confirmation of its terms, to the consumer

18.10.5 RIGHT OF CANCELLATION – OFF-PREMISES CONTRACTS

Under the existing directives, consumers have a cooling-off period within which the consumer can decide to cancel the contract. This cooling-off period is now extended to 14 days and the manner of exercise of the right is clearly set out.

There is a substantial range of contracts to which the right of cancellation does not apply (reg 13 (2)). These include contracts for supply of digital content online or services where the supply/service has begun at the request of the consumer, contracts for personalised goods, perishable goods, or contracts where the price is subject to fluctuation.

The cooling-off period is 14 days from the date of the conclusion of the contract, save for sales contracts, where the period begins from the date the consumer gets the goods (reg 15 (2) and (3)). If the pre-contract information obligations in relation to cancellation have not been observed, the period is extended to 12 months (reg 16).

The Regulations set out a format of the Model Cancellation Form that may be used by the consumer. However, the consumer may cancel by other unequivocal statement to that effect (reg 17).

Upon cancellation, the trader's obligation to perform is terminated, the trader must reimburse the consumer within 14 days, and the consumer must return the goods within 14 days, unless the trader has agreed to collect them. There are specific provisions dealing with the provision of services, certain utilities, or digital content online during the cancellation period at the request of the consumer (reg 21 and reg 22).

18.10.6 PREVENTION OF HIDDEN COSTS – OFF-PREMISES AND ON-PREMISES CONTRACTS

18.10.6.1 Payment surcharges

A trader cannot charge a fee in excess of the cost to the trader for the use of the payment method. The burden of proof rests on the trader (reg 24).

18.10.6.2 Express consent for additional payments

The express consent of the consumer must be obtained to any payment additional to the payment of the main obligation of the contract. The use of a default setting (such as a pre-ticked box), which the consumer is required to reject, does not constitute consent. Again, the burden of proof rests on the trader (reg 26).

18.10.6.3 Telephone charges

A trader cannot charge more than the basic rate for use of a line to contact a trader about a contract concluded with the trader (reg 27). This applies to a help-line after the contract is concluded. It does not apply to calls for the conclusion of the contract. The only obligation on the trader in relation to such calls arises under sch 2, which requires information on any surcharge applied to such calls to be communicated to the consumer pre-contract.

18.10.7 DELIVERY AND RISK

18.10.7.1 Risk

The Regulations introduce a new regime in relation to when risk passes and when delivery is required to be made in business-to-consumer contracts, while the existing law will continue to apply to business-to-business contracts.

This new regime only applies to contracts for sale where the buyer deals as consumer.

The definition of 'consumer', however, is the definition under the 1980 Act (Sale of Goods and Supply of Services Act 1980, whereby 'a party to a contract is said to deal as consumer in relation to another party if— (a) he neither makes the contract in the course of a business nor holds himself out as doing so, and (b) the other party does make the contract in the course of a business, and (c) the goods or services supplied under or in pursuance of the contract are of a type ordinarily supplied for private use or consumption').

The position under s 20 of the Sale of Goods Act 1893 is that the passing of risk is linked to the passing of title in goods, unless otherwise agreed and the goods remain at the seller's risk until the property therein is transferred to the buyer, but when the property is transferred to the buyer, the goods are at the buyer's risk whether delivery has been made or not). This can disadvantage a consumer, as the property in the goods may pass to the consumer before the goods have been delivered to him.

The Regulations restate the general rules, but disapply them where the buyer deals as consumer and the seller dispatches the goods to the buyer. In those circumstances, risk passes when the buyer acquires physical possession of the goods or the goods are delivered to a carrier commissioned by the buyer, which had not been proposed by the seller (reg 28).

18.10.7.2 Time for delivery

Section 29 of the 1893 Act provides that where the seller is bound to send the goods but no time is fixed, the seller is bound to send them within a reasonable time. At common law, there is a presumption that time is of the essence. Thus, in the event of late delivery the buyer may reject the goods and demand a refund: *Hartley v Hymans* [1920] KB 475.

The Regulations apply new rules where the buyer deals as consumer. These rules require that, unless the parties have agreed otherwise, the seller shall deliver the goods by transferring physical possession or control to the buyer without undue delay and not later than 30 days from the conclusion of the contract (reg 30). In the event of default, the buyer may require the seller to deliver within an additional appropriate period, to be specified by the buyer.

Where the seller has further failed to deliver within this additional period, the buyer may repudiate the contract. However, the buyer does not need to go through this additional step of giving additional time, if delivery within the original period is essential in the circumstances or the seller has been informed pre-contract that it is essential.

Regulation 30 supplements these rules. Where the buyer deals as consumer, it disapplies the rule that delivery of the goods to the carrier is deemed to be delivery to the buyer (1893 Act, s 32).

18.10.7.3 Unsolicited goods

Unsolicited goods or services provided to a consumer by a trader are treated as an unconditional gift (reg 32 amending s 47 of the 1980 Act).

18.10.8 ENFORCEMENT

The Regulations are brought within the suite of consumer legislation to which the civil and administrative sanctions under the Consumer Protection Act 2007 apply.

Breaches of the provisions in relation to information, the obligations of the trader in the event of cancellation, payment fees, additional charges, and telephone surcharges are criminal offences. The consumer is entitled to rights under contract and in certain cases to an action for breach of statutory duty (reg 20(8)).

The rights of a consumer cannot be waived nor can any contractual provision trump the consumer rights (reg 39).

18.11   Consumer Credit Act 1995

18.11.1   OVERVIEW

The Consumer Credit Act (the 'CCA') gives effect to Directive 87/102/EEC as amended by Directive 90/88/EEC concerning consumer credit. The CCA regulates most types of consumer credit arrangements including mortgages, bank loans, consumer hire, and hire purchase agreements. The principal exceptions to the type of lenders covered by the CCA are pawn-brokers and credit unions. The purpose of the CCA is to harmonise the manner in which consumers credit agreements are administered across the EU and to ensure transparency in credit transactions for consumers. Set out below is an overview of the key general provisions. However, it should be noted that the CCA is an extensive piece of legislation with detailed provisions relating to the various specific types of credit agreement.

18.11.2   ADVERTISING AND MARKETING OF CREDIT ARRANGEMENTS

The CCA sets out certain rules relating to the advertisements offering:

- to provide or to arrange to provide credit;
- to enter into a hire purchase or consumer hire purchase agreement for the letting of goods by the advertiser; or
- to arrange the letting of goods under a hire purchase or consumer hire agreement by another person by a consumer, and provides that full information as to the nature of the arrangement must be given including the amount and frequency of payments, details of any deposit, and details of any interest or other charges applicable.

18.11.3   MINORS

The CCA prohibits disseminating documentation to minors which invites a minor to borrow credit, obtain goods or services on credit, or apply for information or advice on getting credit.

18.11.4   REQUIREMENTS RELATING TO THE FORM OF CREDIT AGREEMENTS

All credit agreements with consumers must be in writing and be delivered personally to the consumer. The agreement must fully set out the terms of the arrangement. The CAA details the minimum information that must be included in each type of credit agreement with a consumer including the rate of interest, the APR, the amount, frequency, and number of repayment instalments, the date of expiry, and the cost to the consumer of early termination.

18.11.5   COOLING-OFF PERIOD

Consumer must be given a ten-day 'cooling-off' period during which they can withdraw from the arrangement without penalty. This cooling-off period does not apply to credit card or overdraft transactions or housing loans.

18.11.6 WITHOUT PREJUDICE TO OTHER RIGHTS

The existence of a credit arrangement shall not affect the rights of the consumers under other consumer legislation with regard to any products purchased by means of a credit arrangement.

18.11.7 COMMUNICATION WITH CONSUMERS

The CCA set outs restrictions regarding communication with consumers in relation to credit agreements. There is a prohibition on visiting or telephoning a consumer at work or from contacting the consumer at home between 9pm and 9am or on Sundays or public holidays without consent. The CCA also sets out restrictions regarding written communication.

18.11.8 ENFORCEMENT

The CCA imposes limitations on the right to enforce a credit agreement. At least ten days' notice must be served on the consumer. Such notice must give details of the action proposed to be taken and setting out how any breach may be remedied. Where the breach is remedied within the period prescribed, it is prohibited to keep any record of the fact that the breach had occurred. Where a breach cannot be remedied no action may be taken before the expiry of 21 days from the initial notice.

18.11.9 MORTGAGE WARNING

Mortgages are required to carry a warning:

- that the borrower's home may be at risk in the event of default of the mortgage arrangements; and

- in the event of a variable interest rate, that the payment rates may be adjusted from time to time.

18.12   Competition and Consumer Protection Act 2014

18.12.1 OVERVIEW

The Competition and Consumer Protection Act ('CCPA') was enacted on 28 July 2014 and came into force on 31 October 2014. The CCPA makes a number of changes to consumer law.

18.12.2 COMPETITION AND CONSUMER PROTECTION COMMISSION ('CCPC')

The functions of the National Consumer Agency ('NCA') have been transferred to a new body, the CCPC. The CCPA, in Chapter 3, provides for the dissolution of the NCA and the Competition Authority and for the transfer of all functions, which were vested in these dissolved bodies, to the CCPC. The CCPC has the same functions of these existing bodies with enhanced powers of investigation.

18.12.3 NEW DEFINITIONS

Section 75 of the CCPA provides some new definitions of 'authorised officer', 'consumer', 'goods', and 'transactional decision' to replace those in the CPA.

18.12.4 SPEAKING YOUR LANGUAGE

A trader is prohibited, under s 77 of the CCPA, which amends s 55 of the CPA, from undertaking to provide an after-sales service to a consumer if that after-sales service is only available in another language, which is not an official language of the relevant State in which the trader is located, unless this is clearly disclosed to the consumer.

18.12.5 REPORTING A BREACH

The 'whistle-blowers' protection' provided in the CPA no longer requires that the report of a breach to the former NCA, now CCPC, is made in 'good faith'. Instead, a person making such a report must have acted 'reasonably',

18.12.6 GROCERY GOODS

Part 6 of the CCPA introduces new provisions, which allows the Minister to regulate certain practices between relevant grocery goods undertaking and other grocery goods undertakings.

A relevant grocery goods undertaking is defined in the CCPA as 'a grocery goods undertaking engaged in the production, supply, distribution, wholesale or retail of grocery goods in the State, that has, or is a member of a group of related undertakings that has, an annual worldwide turnover of more than €50 million'.

18.13 Other Consumer Protection Legislation

There is a wide range of other consumer protection legislation such as:

- Food Safety Authority of Ireland Act 1998 (as amended);
- National Standards Authority of Ireland Act 1996 (as amended);
- Occasional Trading Act 1979 (as amended);
- Package Holidays and Travel Trade Act 1995 (as amended);
- Pawnbrokers Act 1964 (as amended); and
- European Communities (Cooperation between National Authorities responsible for the enforcement of Consumer Protection Laws) Regulations 2006.

In addition, legislation governing regulated areas of the economy contains provisions for the protection of consumers or sections of the general public.

CHAPTER 19

COMMERCIAL DRAFTING

The difficult task, after one learns how to think like a lawyer, is relearning how to write like a human being.

(Floyd Abrams)

19.1 Introduction

The purpose of good drafting is the same in commercial law as in any field. It is to set out as clearly as possible what the parties intend to occur. You are aiming to record their rights and duties. Your clients may be as technically proficient as any legal expert in reviewing these agreements, or they may be entering into a commercial contract which is more complex than any they have negotiated in the past. Irrespective of who your client is, whether a large multinational corporation with a team of in-house lawyers, or a small family-owned business, many of them will believe that most lawyers simply are not capable of reducing their agreement to writing. Or that they can do so well.

They may be right. Many lawyers cannot write well. Simple ideas get lost in a fog of over-complex drafting and poor grammar. If the lawyer drafting the agreement cannot reduce it concisely to writing then what chance have the parties of finding it useful in their ongoing relationship? What happens when one of the parties has a different interpretation of the terms of the agreement to the other and seeks the aid of the courts as a result of a disagreement? What if one party is purchased by another entity? How will the new owner view the legacy agreement they have succeeded to?

The purpose of this chapter is to provide some useful tips to ensure clarity in your commercial drafting. Drafting is one of the primary skills you will develop as a lawyer. You should not expect that your first piece of drafting gets reviewed by the senior partner you work for without amendment. Retain early drafts if you believe that the comments noted on them may be of use to you in future similar exercises.

19.2 Instructions and Objectives

It is critically important that you receive and record clear instructions from a client on what the purpose of an agreement is before you commence drafting. You may have a very clear email from the client setting out the background, timing requirements, etc. but it is often useful to call a client to elicit additional information. People are often more candid in a telephone call than in an email. Has the client, for example, found that a previous agreement had certain weaknesses that it would like addressed in the new draft? Perhaps the earlier agreement was drafted in another jurisdiction and needs to be localised in greater depth than before. Are there commercial reasons why the agreement needs to be changed—your client may be moving to a different business model (for example franchising) and all of this information may not have been included in the original set of instructions. Nevertheless, it may enable you to prepare a draft more precisely tailored to the business needs of your client.

There may be changes outside your client's business which may have an impact on the draft. For example, including a certain kind of provision may be becoming more widespread in the industry in which the client operates and, while not yet legally required, your client may wish their contracts to be more in tune with those trends.

If your client has an in-house lawyer, then instructions will be likely to come from him or her. The in-house lawyer's area of work may be different from yours and so you are being engaged to provide specialist advice. If the instructions are coming from a non-lawyer, you need to take care that you do not assume that their understanding of legal terms is the same as yours—there may be cultural differences if you are in two different jurisdictions, or a word may have a slightly different nuance of meaning in their industry to the strict legal interpretation.

Do not be afraid to ask the client to clarify what a term means in their industry. Many professions, other than law, use jargon and some of it may be highly technical, though second-nature to your client. You, however, may not know what they are talking about. Most people are quite happy to give a short explanation to you or email over a chart or memo which gives you more background. This is especially so in the scientific, medical, and technological fields.

19.3   Legal and Other Constraints

A client may ask you to prepare a document which, unbeknown to the client, is illegal. This is extremely rare and most people are well aware that for example, one cannot enter into an agreement with competitors to fix prices or selling conditions. If you suspect that there may be legal constraints on what your client wishes to achieve, then you should alert him or her to the nature of these constraints as soon as possible. There is an increasingly strong compliance culture across the globe and most organisations are extremely risk-averse and do not wish there to be the slightest doubt about the enforceability of their agreements. In the unlikely event of a client insisting on the preparation of a document which you know to be illegal, then you should decline to act.

Similarly, you may be of the view that entering into an agreement, no matter how clear the instructions, seems not to be in the best interests of your client. You can (diplomatically of course) query the purpose of the agreement and draft it so as to best protect your client's interests if he or she wants to proceed. You should ensure that your reservations as to the commercial terms are noted by the client so put them in writing if you remain concerned.

19.4   Organisation

If you find you write better with a tidy desk, clear it and begin. If you have a complex structure in terms of numbers of parties, draw up a structure chart and have it to hand when drafting. Get the mechanics out of the way—how will each party sign—under seal? By hand? Under a power of attorney? Insert the appropriate signing clauses, names, addresses, and then begin with the recitals. The recitals should express in three or four paragraphs why the agreement is being entered into.

19.5   Timing

You will need to estimate, in advance, how long it will take for you to produce a first draft. This will have implications for cost and practicality and your client will need to communicate this to their opposite number in the company/business with which they are contracting.

Sometimes unforeseen complications arise, which make the deadline impossible to reach. However, estimating the time needed is a drafting skill in itself with which you will become more accurate.

You should remember that not all drafting is actually writing and time can be spent on initial research, precedent hunting, and considering the structure. The law relating to the contract may be unclear or changing. You may need to factor this into timing estimates. Does the contract relate in part to aspects of the law with which you are not familiar? If yes, then, if possible, have it reviewed by a colleague who is familiar with that area of law. It may be necessary for you to brief an external expert such as an environmental consultant before finalising your draft. Factor this into your time estimate if needed.

All these are an integral part of the drafting process so try not to underestimate the time you will need for these tasks. Also, the time taken will, to a large degree, depend on how many of these types of agreements you have prepared before. Most clients understand that larger-value agreements will involve negotiation with the other party at every stage at which they may have a lawyer's input. More simple or lower-value arrangements may only need one or two drafts.

19.6   Using Precedents

You will rarely come across an agreement that no one else has had to draft before. If your office does not have a good set of precedents, you should consider investing in a loose-leaf set from reputable local legal publishers. There are many available and while they will not provide wording for every eventuality they will cover very many areas and will save you time. Do not use them slavishly, non-Irish precedents may not work in Irish law or there may be reasons, particular to your transaction, why they are inappropriate.

Ensure consistency between your own document and the precedent. For example, if the precedent uses the word 'factory' and you use the word 'premises', then you should use only one of those terms to avoid confusion.

Has the client ever done a transaction like this before? He may have prepared working notes or an internal memorandum which will greatly assist your drafting. A client will rarely object to his lawyer asking him for more background information in order to ensure that the first draft is as close to the client's needs as possible, so do not be afraid to ask.

19.7   Style

Whether or not we write well, we all write with a particular style. Try to develop your own voice in drafting and keep it constant. You may find that reading your drafting aloud helps you pick up errors. Absorb as much as possible from your colleagues—war stories may make it easier for you to avoid drafting errors than any chapter on drafting ever will.

19.7.1   AUDIENCE

Will your drafting be reviewed by an in-house lawyer or a non-lawyer? What jurisdiction are they based in? Bear this in mind when drafting.

Once you have determined the above information, you can proceed to the detail of the drafting.

19.7.2 PLAIN ENGLISH

Try to use clear and plain English in your drafting. You may need to use a Latin term for which there is no short English equivalent, but keep Latinisms to a minimum as they can be off-putting. If you are writing a set of terms and conditions for use in dealings with consumers then you should take special care to use readable, immediately clear language. Short sentences and the use of the word 'you' rather than 'the hirer' or 'the consumer' will add greatly to the clarity of your drafting.

19.7.3 CROSS-REFERENCES

Check cross-references to ensure that they are correct before sending the draft out. If possible, minimise the use of cross-references as checking and rechecking that they remain accurate through several drafts is time-consuming and therefore expensive for the client.

19.8 Outline and Structure

Prepare an outline agreement based on your structure chart, if you have used one. It will make the drafting seem less daunting if the agreement is complex. Insert your boilerplate provisions, such as choice of law etc., in square brackets so that you can fine-tune them later on if needed.

The structure of an agreement is critical to its clarity. It should include some or all of the items detailed below.

19.8.1 TITLE

What is the name of the agreement to be? You should include a drafting date on all drafts to assist you if the agreement goes through a large number of drafts.

19.8.2 DATE

The date of the agreement is the date on which it is entered into. If your client wants to include an earlier effective date there is generally nothing wrong with that (for example, an agreement may have in practice been assigned to another company and they are only now getting around to formalising that transfer). Nonetheless, you will still need your agreement to be dated when it is signed, in case of disputes as to its validity. For clarity, write dates and numbers in digits and in words and have your clients check them.

19.8.3 PARTIES

Are both entities companies as we understand that term in Irish law? If an agreement is entered into by a company before it is properly incorporated, the promoter will be personally liable for the contract. Will the parent or subsidiary be entering into the agreement if your client forms part of a group? Will anyone else be guaranteeing the obligations of one of the parties under the agreement? If so, then they need to be included as a party. Do searches against the parties. People erroneously believe their registered business name to be a legal entity in its own right.

19.8.4   PRE-CONDITIONS

Are there any conditions precedent to be satisfied before the agreement comes into effect? If so they need to be included. For example, the agreement may be subject to regulatory approval (such as that of the Competition Authority or the Financial Services Regulator). Alternatively, your client may want to ensure that certain consents are obtained first—for example, shareholder consents, environmental licences, or planning permissions may be required.

19.8.5   SCHEDULES

You may wish maps, drawings, lists, and technical descriptions to be included in a schedule to the agreement. If these are technical in nature (a common example is the specification for a computer system) then you as the lawyer may not be involved in drafting them. You should ensure, if they are being prepared in parallel, that those drafting them are aware of the deadlines to avoid any last-minute delays. You should read these schedules, when produced, to ensure that nothing in them is at odds with what you have drafted in the main agreement.

19.8.6   BLANKS

You may be asked to produce a first draft while there are terms still being negotiated and there will therefore be blanks in your agreement. These should be square-bracketed and closed off with your client as the negotiations progress.

19.8.7   DEFINITIONS

If you are using certain terms repeatedly, then having a list of definitions will shorten and simplify your agreement. If a term is only used once, it may not be necessary to include it in a definitions list. Many Acts have cumbersome titles and it may be simpler to define the Act to which you refer as the 'Principal Act' rather than repeating its full title each time it is referred to.

It is a matter of personal or firm style as to where the list of definitions is placed. Generally, they appear at the front of the document and are always alphabetical.

19.9   Execution Clauses

Decide in what way each party will execute the agreement and provide for that in the execution clause. It may be necessary to execute the agreement under seal in certain instances (for example, if there is no consideration in the contract or if local law requires it). If the contract is being entered into by a company, it is important to refer to the articles of association for details as to how the contract should be executed.

19.10   Limitation of Liability

It is common for parties to try and exclude or limit their liability for breach of contract to a particular sum. Limiting liability is likely to be viewed more favourably by the courts than excluding liability so it is more commonly used for this reason. Of course, you should consider whether you can exclude or limit liability at all, particularly in consumer-facing contracts where such limitations and exclusions may not be enforceable.

If there is an ambiguity in an exclusion clause, the ambiguity is generally construed against the party who is seeking to rely on the exclusion. This is known as the *contra proferentem* rule. A limitation of liability clause should, therefore, be clearly drafted to avoid any ambiguity whatsoever.

Bear in mind when drafting such a clause that excluding liability may impact on the consideration being paid as it makes the contract less valuable from the point of view of the party against whom it may be enforced.

There are statutory constraints over what you can exclude or limit liability for. For example, the Unfair Terms in Consumer Contracts Regulations 1995 state that you cannot exclude liability in negligence for death or personal injury.

Often, in a business-to-business contract, you may decide that different types of liability have different applicable caps on liability (e.g. property damage may have a cap of its own). It isn't a one-size-fits-all approach, and requires careful consideration. Insurance advices may be required as liability should not be accepted for your client where they are uninsured for it, unless they are very clearly informed about such risks, and can therefore factor them into price.

19.11 Boilerplate Provisions

The term 'boilerplate' refers to frequently used provisions in agreements that do not vary much from agreement to agreement. As with precedents, you need to take care that you are not just dropping such clauses into your agreement without any thought as to whether they fit in well to the rest of the agreement. You should constantly review other lawyers' boilerplate terms to see whether they include useful provisions. Legal developments may mean a boilerplate term becomes obsolete, so they should be read by you fully each time you draft.

Boilerplate provisions can deal with interpretation issues. For example, you may have a clause saying the male includes the female, headings are for reference only, schedules form part of the agreements, reference to an Act mean that Act as it is amended, etc.

Commonly used boilerplate provisions include those detailed below.

19.11.1 TERMINATION

The parties set out detailed provisions dealing with how the agreement is to be terminated. You may need to provide for fault-based as well as no-fault termination.

19.11.2 NO PARTNERSHIP

You may wish it to be explicit that the parties are not carrying on a partnership. Be careful of dropping in long lists of boilerplate clauses—'no partnership' clauses have been dropped into partnership agreements where they are plainly inappropriate!

19.11.3 FURTHER ASSURANCES

The parties agree to execute anything additional requested by the other party to give effect to the agreement.

19.11.4 WAIVER AND FORBEARANCE

The parties may wish to provide in the agreement that if they decide, once, to give a concession to the other party, that does not compel them to continue to do so in the future.

19.11.5 SEVERABILITY

The parties may wish to provide that if a clause is unenforceable then it can be dropped without the entire agreement failing, unless it goes to the root of the contract. A court may or may not choose to follow this, but such terms are common and may be useful.

19.11.6 COUNTERPARTS

If an agreement is to be executed in several counterparts, this should be stated and the clause should confirm that any one of those counterparts shall be an original.

19.11.7 NOTICES

The parties should provide how notices should be given to each other under the contract and to whom. If an organisation has job titles for its senior roles, then those should be used, not the name of individuals in case those persons move on and their post is not passed quickly to their successor.

19.11.8 GOVERNING LAW/JURISDICTION/ARBITRATION

These are separate fields of law in their own right but you should check their desirability before finalising your contract. You also need to ensure you take the governing law into account—for example, there is no point providing for Irish governing law if your client's customers are located all across Europe and may, under the Rome Convention, have the protection of their own mandatory rules. Irish law may still be, for the most part, the governing law, but your clients may need to instruct lawyers in the other jurisdictions in which consumer customers reside to get advice from those lawyers on what mandatory laws apply there.

19.11.9 NO DEDUCTIONS

Many agreements provide that any payments made under them are to be made without deduction for withholding tax or any other charges. You should either check the taxation aspects of the contract yourself or ask your clients to ensure that their own in-house or external tax experts approve the drafting. Make sure that if you are advising on tax that you are being paid for that separate advice.

19.11.10 JOINT AND SEVERAL OBLIGATIONS

You may wish to provide that any warranties, indemnities, and obligations given or entered into by more than one person are given jointly and severally.

19.12   Problems in Drafting

19.12.1 ERRORS

Spelling errors and other typos may cause confusion—do not rely on computer spellcheck programs to catch errors—the typo may itself be a proper word and so may not be caught. Reread—if possible the next day—as you may pick up errors more easily after a rest. Have someone else read your draft if you think this will help pick up either errors or ambiguities in what you have drafted.

If the grammar you use in the document is inaccurate your client may not trust the rest of the content! The rules of grammar are there to ensure readability and accuracy and you should ensure that your use of English is correct at all times.

Good punctuation will mean that when you cannot avoid a long sentence now and then, at least it will be readable. Use grammar and structure to your advantage. Break down complex ideas into paragraphs to make them more readable. Do not use more than one idea per paragraph or clarity will be lost. Use sub-paragraphs if necessary. Use headings to signpost ideas.

19.12.2 INCONSISTENCIES

Reread what you have drafted to ensure that where you use a term, that its use is consistent throughout. Any reader who picks up inconsistencies will find your draft difficult to read and will doubt the accuracy of what is there. A common error is to have excellent definitions and then use those defined words in the agreement as if they were undefined. Capitalise defined words if possible to minimise the risk of this happening.

Have you used the wrong word—for example, if you wish to convey an obligation to do something as opposed to the option to do it, then use the word 'must' not 'may'.

19.12.3 UNUSUAL USE OF WORDS

A key to clear drafting is to use words in their normal meaning. If a term has become outdated (all the more so if it now may cause offence and may not have in the past) then you should use an alternative word or expression.

19.13   Managing the Contractual Documentation

Place 'discussion draft' on the front of your first draft of the contract and if you do not wish your client to send it to the other side, tell him or her so. Often business people believe that they are speeding things up (especially in the age of email) by sending first drafts to all concerned. This is rarely efficient especially if you need your client's input on technical and business issues in the agreement before providing him with a more advanced second draft. Explain to your client what you think is best in terms of who processes changes to the document. Should you meet after the first draft has been sent out or make a call if a meeting is not possible? Decide these things with your client before you begin drafting and it will give you more time to complete your task and you will both be aware of when the client can expect to receive the draft.

After your client has reviewed the first draft, it is usual, assuming no great travel is involved, to have a meeting to 'turn the pages' on it together before proceeding to the next draft. The agreement can then be fine-tuned and re-sent to the client. You should emphasise to your client that generally a first draft should not be sent to the other side's lawyers if it is in very rough form. Both sides do not need to spend legal fees until the draft is more advanced. Often, time constraints may mean that this is not possible, but you should aim for it if at all practicable, as it will save time and money all round in the long run.

19.14   The Negotiation Process

Now that your draft is prepared, you will need to take your client through the process of getting it finalised with the other side. If you think that there will be a lengthy time gap between this and your client's original negotiations, then there should be a letter of intent in place to govern the gap period or at least a confidentiality agreement to protect your client if negotiations break down. The letter of intent (sometimes called a memorandum of understanding) may be binding or non-binding as provided for in the letter and may have a short exclusivity period built into it. If it is binding then you should endeavour to finalise the written contract as quickly as possible and try to ensure that your client does not commence performance under the contract until it is signed.

When the other side's lawyers have reviewed the contract, they will invariably send you comments for you and your client to discuss. Part of the negotiation process will be for you and your client to accept what changes you can, while maximising your client's protection under the agreement. Not all of the other side's changes will be unreasonable so you should try at all times to ensure good relations with the other lawyers. Many clients fear 'over-lawyering' in business, so you should represent your profession as being commercial, helpful, and expert and remain aloof from any petty squabbling that you may be drawn into. Indeed it may suit the respective parties to the deal to portray the lawyers as the 'bad guys', as a justification for making certain contractual demands on one another. Within limits this can be unavoidable; however, you should make sure that your position is represented accurately.

A common bone of contention in the negotiation of commercial agreements is risk allocation. Your client may be investing a great deal of money in the purchase of a business in which it has a limited chance to carry out due diligence enquiries. In that scenario, it would be usual to expect the sellers of the business to provide extensive warranties to your client, the purchaser. These will naturally be contested by the seller's lawyers and so the extent of the risk allocation should be made clear to all parties at initial meetings.

Before negotiations begin, you should take the opportunity to discuss alternative plans with your client should negotiations fail. If negotiations become heated, and you want your client to have the benefit of your advice at an all-parties meeting without the others being present, you should ask to park certain points and revert to them at the end of the meeting after a short chat with the client. Often other points will by then have been negotiated and the parties will be more willing to compromise as they can see that progress is being made towards concluding the agreement.

19.15   Conclusion

Keep up to date with case law on the meaning of contractual terms, both in Ireland and abroad. These terms are often the subject of high-value litigation and an awareness of the legal trends is part of what your client is paying for. This is especially so when in changed economic times, it suits parties to revisit their former bargain, or to seek to rely on a meaning that the other party may not have intended. Learn from your colleagues' good drafting where you notice it, but respect copyright laws, your client is not paying for your 'cutting-and-pasting' skills! Conversely, protect your own intellectual property and recognise the financial worth of what you write for your clients. Many firms now have a policy of sending out documents only in PDF format for this reason (and others); however, this practice is not yet widespread.

CHAPTER 20

TERMS AND CONDITIONS OF TRADING

20.1 Introduction

20.1.1 GENERAL

One of the most important things for any business is the number of sales being made and the resulting cashflow. However, it is equally critical for a business to ensure that the terms and conditions upon which such sales are being made ('Terms and Conditions') protect the business' interest in an appropriate manner.

The purpose of this chapter is to provide background as to why it is advisable to ensure standard Terms and Conditions are adopted by trading businesses, to set out the principal legislation governing this area of business, and to highlight the key areas and issues that often arise in connection with drafting standard Terms and Conditions. **Chapter 18, 'Consumer Law'** has already set out the main provisions of the Sale of Goods Act 1893 (as amended) ('the 1893 Act') and the Sale of Goods and Supply of Services Act 1980 (as amended) ('the 1980 Act') and accordingly, this chapter will concentrate on the main areas which standard Terms and Conditions should cover when one is acting for a business that is supplying goods and/or services to another business. In addition, we will touch on certain relevant provisions of the European Union (Consumer Information, Cancellation and Other Rights) Regulations 2013 ('EUCICORR') that came into operation on 14 June 2014 and which apply solely to contracts with consumers (as opposed to business-to-business contracts) concluded after that date.

20.1.2 WHY HAVE STANDARD TERMS AND CONDITIONS?

Many businesses sell goods and/or supply services on the basis of ad hoc informal arrangements and this is generally fine until a dispute arises. In such circumstances, arguments often arise, for example, in relation to what or whose Terms and Conditions apply or whether any specific Terms and Conditions have in fact even been agreed.

Accordingly, it is important that solicitors are familiar with the law governing Terms and Conditions generally, in addition to the specific areas which all such Terms and Conditions should seek to cover. Having appropriate standard Terms and Conditions may minimise or prevent bad debts and exposure to potential liabilities for a client business.

The preparation or the revision of standard Terms and Conditions does not only require input from a solicitor, but also from the business in question, given that such terms will need to reflect the commercial needs and operations of the business. For example, the nature of the goods being sold and/or the services being provided may require bespoke provisions surrounding the payment terms or delivery.

The main advantage of having standard Terms and Conditions of trading is that they should enable a business to have clear contractual terms favourable to it in a readily available format which discourages protracted negotiation and the time and expense that may be involved in having bespoke Terms and Conditions for each customer (i.e. equivalent to a separate contract for each customer). Of course, the use of standard Terms and Conditions may not be appropriate in all circumstances and one common safeguard which businesses often seek to implement is to establish procedures whereby contracts over a certain value must be referred to their solicitor prior to the standard Terms and Conditions being issued. Standard Terms and Conditions may also provide that they are subject to any specific written agreement in place between the parties concerning any particular sale.

20.2   Whose Terms and Conditions Apply?

A frequent dispute which can often arise relates to what is commonly referred to as the 'battle of the forms', whereby both the supplier and the customer argue that their own Terms and Conditions apply exclusively to the commercial arrangements between them. The courts will apply the traditional offer and acceptance analysis when dealing with any such 'battle of the forms' such that a contract will be deemed to have been formed when an offer is made by one party that is clearly accepted by the other party, whether in writing, in words, or by conduct.

To avoid this, it is critical that a supplier's Terms and Conditions are properly incorporated into the contract with the customer. To seek to ensure this is effectively carried out, the following steps should be implemented by the supplier:

(a)   ensure that any pre-contractual correspondence, such as brochures, catalogues, etc. state that the standard Terms and Conditions of the supplier will apply;

(b)   ensure that an express reference to the supplier's standard Terms and Conditions is included:

(i)   on any quotation to the customer (and supply a copy of the standard Terms and Conditions referenced in the quotation);

(ii)   on purchase order forms (if applicable) and on any acknowledgement or confirmation of the purchase order form by the customer (again, a copy of the standard Terms and Conditions should be supplied);

(iii)   on any delivery docket and/or invoices; and

(c)   require that customers submit an executed supplier purchase order form which can then be accepted by the supplier by issuing an acknowledgement stating a contract has come into existence upon the standard Terms and Conditions attached to (or printed on the back of) the purchase order form.

It should be noted that simply having standard Terms and Conditions printed on the back of an invoice will generally not be sufficient to incorporate such terms into the contract given the invoice is unlikely to be sent to the customer until after the contract has been entered into and/or the goods/services delivered.

Ideally, the standard Terms and Conditions should contain an execution block for the parties to sign so that no argument could be made by the customer that their standard Terms and Conditions apply. In practical terms, this may prove difficult to effect and accordingly, the steps outlined above at (a) to (c) should be followed insofar as they can be in the circumstances. In addition, specific provisions should be included in the standard Terms and Conditions of the business in question to ensure maximum protection in relation to the 'battle of the forms'. An example of such an 'entire agreement' clause is set out below:

This contract constitutes the entire agreement between the parties relating to its subject matter. The Customer acknowledges and agrees that it has not relied on any statement, promise or representation (whether written, oral, or implied) made or given by or on behalf of the Supplier which is not set out in the contract. Any samples, drawings, descriptive matter, or advertising issued by the Supplier and any descriptions contained in the Supplier's promotional material are issued or published for the sole purpose of giving an approximate idea of the goods described in them and they shall not form part of the contract or any other contract between the Supplier and the Customer for the sale and/or the supply of the Goods. Nothing in this clause excludes or limits the Supplier's liability for misrepresentation.

It should be noted that the final sentence in the above sample clause is included given that, under s 46 of the 1980 Act, one cannot exclude liability in a contract for the supply of goods or services for misrepresentation unless the provision seeking to do so is shown to be fair and reasonable.

Another 'battle of the forms' clause which is intended to help the supplier establish that its standard terms prevail in the event of a 'battle of the forms' is set out below:

The terms and conditions set out herein are the only ones on which the Seller will supply the goods and prevail over any terms and conditions put forward by the Customer, including any terms or conditions which the Customer purports to apply which are endorsed on, delivered with or contained in the Customer's order, confirmation of order, specification or other document forming part of the Contract.

20.3   General Terms and Conditions of Sale/Supply

Standard Terms and Conditions typically include the standard provisions under which the contractual relationship between the supplier and the customer will operate such that, if the customer breaches these terms, the supplier can take steps to enforce the Terms and Conditions as a contractual matter against the customer. Set out below are examples of the type of provisions which one would expect to be included.

20.3.1   BASIS OF CONTRACT

This clause will set out the legal basis upon which the contract is formed (for example, the order constitutes the customer's offer to purchase the goods and/or services on the basis of these Terms and Conditions).

20.3.2   ORDERS AND SPECIFICATIONS

The Terms and Conditions should make it clear that it is the customer's responsibility rather than the supplier's responsibility, to make sure that the order and/or the specifications (if applicable) are correct.

20.3.3   PRICE OF THE GOODS/SERVICES

Price is obviously a vital provision for the supplier and is dealt with in more detail below. At a minimum, the supplier must decide whether the price is to be exclusive of the cost of packaging, carriage, insurance, and unloading (in the event that the goods need to be delivered) and whether the price is to be exclusive of VAT. Equally important from the supplier's perspective are the terms of payment (i.e. credit terms and how the payment is to be made). Furthermore, it should be noted that late payment by a customer does not automatically entitle a supplier to terminate a contract with the customer and if such a termination right is required by the supplier, an express provision should be included in the Terms and Conditions in this regard (see 'Payment' below at **20.4.3.2**).

20.3.4   INTELLECTUAL PROPERTY

The Terms and Conditions should make it clear that title in any intellectual property rights in the goods will at all times remain vested with the supplier (or the relevant third party licensor) and also set out the procedure to be followed where it is alleged that the goods sold infringe intellectual property rights of any third party (e.g. supplier shall be notified and the customer will not admit liability etc.).

20.3.5   FORCE MAJEURE

An appropriate force majeure clause should be included so as to ensure that events which are beyond the reasonable control of the supplier (e.g. floods, fires, etc.) do not give rise to any liability on behalf of the supplier if it cannot perform the contract. Given the supplier is responsible for the main obligations under the contract (i.e. delivery of goods/services), the supplier should seek to ensure that the force majeure clause is drafted as widely as possible.

20.3.6   GOVERNING LAW

It is critical that the standard Terms and Conditions expressly state the governing law applicable to the trade. In the case of a supplier resident in Ireland this should be the laws of Ireland with any disputes being subject to the exclusive jurisdiction of the Irish courts.

20.3.7   GENERAL BOILERPLATE CLAUSES

Standard boilerplate clauses should also be incorporated into Terms and Conditions of trading, for example, restriction on assignment by the customer, variation, notices, etc. (see **chapter 19 on 'Commercial Drafting'**).

20.3.8   CONSUMER INFORMATION REQUIREMENTS

Parts 2 and 3 of EUCICORR set out the substance and form of the information that must be provided to consumers before they will be bound by a contract. There are variations in the criteria required for on-premises, off-premises, and distance contracts. Schedules 1 and 2 detail the information required including information relating to the goods, the provider, pricing, delivery, payment, complaints handling, after-sales services, duration of contract, and functionality or interoperability (in the case of digital products).

20.4   Key Provisions

There are several provisions in the context of standard Terms and Conditions which solicitors acting for suppliers need to pay particular attention to, details of which are set out below.

20.4.1   TITLE

The supplier and the customer are free to agree between themselves as to when ownership of the goods being sold shall pass from the supplier to the customer. The transfer of title is crucial in every sale of goods contract and can be particularly important if issues regarding payment arise, especially if the customer subsequently becomes insolvent.

Given that a supplier of goods will generally rank at, or very near to, the bottom of the list of creditors upon the insolvency of a customer, one mechanism that suppliers can take advantage of is a 'Retention of Title' clause. The basic premise of such a clause is that the supplier never releases title to the products sold to the customer unless payment has been received for such goods and/or no monies are owing from the customer in question to the supplier. If the Retention of Title clause is effective, the customer's secured and unsecured creditors have no right to the relevant goods and the supplier will be entitled to collect its goods, which never enter the liquidator's pool of assets.

There are two main types of 'Retention of Title' clauses which we shall call the 'standard' clause and the 'all monies' clause.

20.4.1.1   Standard clause

The standard clause seeks to provide that the supplier will retain title until it has received full payment for the goods. This clause should be supplemented by provisions which deal with repossession mechanics when the customer is in an insolvent situation, for example, a right for the supplier to enter the premises and repossess the goods. The clause should also list the insolvency events that will trigger the right for the supplier to demand payment and/or repossess the goods.

20.4.1.2   All monies clause

Under this variation of a Retention of Title clause, the supplier maintains ownership of the goods supplied until the customer has paid not only for the particular goods in question but also for any outstanding indebtedness owed by the customer to the supplier. The advantage of this clause over the standard clause is that all goods supplied to the customer remain the property of the supplier until all indebtedness owing by the customer has been repaid (as opposed to the standard clause where the customer gets title to those goods it has already paid for).

It should be noted that there remains uncertainty as to whether such an 'all monies' clause would be void as against a liquidator and any creditor of the customer unless it has been registered at the Companies Registration Office within 21 days of its creation (the 2014 Act, s 409). Although such registration is possible in theory, the reality is that it is not practical in the context of standard Terms and Conditions and so it is advisable that such an 'all monies' clause be incorporated as a separate sub-clause from the standard clause so that it could be severed if it was ever held invalid by the Irish courts for lack of registration as a charge.

Retention of Title clauses have been subject to changing interpretations by the courts and although it is advisable that they are included, clients should be aware that specific advice would need to be taken in the event that they seek to rely on and enforce such provisions (given that the nature of the goods being sold changes from business to business).

In addition to Retention of Title, the issue of when risk in the goods passes to the customer should also be expressly addressed in the standard Terms and Conditions. Section 20 of the 1893 Act provides that the goods remain at the supplier's risk until title in the goods has been transferred. Where delivery has been delayed through the fault of either the buyer or the seller, the goods are at the risk of the party at fault as regards any loss which might not have occurred but for the fault. Even if title has not passed, the supplier will generally want to ensure that the risk in the goods will pass at the time of delivery to the customer. In addition, it is advisable that the supplier protects itself from the risk of the goods being destroyed by requiring that the customer insures the goods against all risks from date of delivery to the date of sale.

In consumer contracts, the goods remain at the seller's risk until the consumer acquires physical possession of the goods or the goods are delivered to a carrier that has been commissioned by the buyer.

20.4.1.3   Sample title provisions

1. The risk in the Goods shall pass to the Customer on completion of delivery.

2. The legal and beneficial ownership of the Goods will not pass to the Customer until the Seller has received payment in full for:

    (a)   the Goods; and

    (b)   any other goods or services that the Supplier has supplied to the Customer [in respect of which payment has become due].

3. Until the legal and beneficial ownership of the Goods has passed to the Customer, the Customer shall:

    (a)   hold the Goods on trust as the Supplier's bailee;

    (b)   store the Goods (at no cost to the Supplier) separately from all other goods held by the Customer so that they remain identifiable as the Supplier's property;

    (c)   not remove any identifying mark relating to the Goods;

    (d)   not encumber or in any way charge any of the Goods;

    (e)   maintain the Goods in satisfactory condition and keep them insured against all risks for their full price from the date of delivery and provide evidence of such insurance to the Supplier upon request;

    (f)   notify the Supplier immediately if the Customer becomes subject to any of the events listed in Clause [X] (Termination Events); and

    (g)   provide the Supplier with such information relating to the Goods as the Supplier may require from time to time.

4. The Customer may resell or use the Goods before the legal and beneficial title has passed to it solely on the condition that any sale is effected in the ordinary course of the Customer's business.

5. If, before legal and beneficial title to the Goods passes to the Customer, the Customer becomes subject to any of the Termination Events, then, provided that the Goods have not been resold, or irrevocably incorporated into another product, the Supplier may at any time require that the Customer delivers up the Goods and if the Customer fails to do so promptly, enter any premises of the Customer where the Goods are stored in order to recover them.

20.4.2   DELIVERY

Unless specific provisions in connection with delivery of goods are provided for in standard Terms and Conditions of trading, delivery will be deemed to take place at the supplier's place of business or if there is no place of business, the supplier's residence (s 29 (1) of the 1893 Act). Given that the 1893 Act contains rules as to delivery, it is advisable that express provisions regarding delivery are included in standard Terms and Conditions which reflect the nature of the supplier's business. For example, the supplier's goods may be delivered via a third party carrier or collected from the supplier's premises. As delivery is typically linked to the transfer of the risk in the products, it should be clear when delivery occurs.

20.4.2.1   Delivery mechanics

Provisions should be included as to the location, date, and costs for the delivery of the supplier's goods, dependent on the nature of the business in question. If the supplier's business is set up to make deliveries, a provision will need to be included to the effect that the supplier will deliver the goods to the location set out in the purchaser order form or as otherwise agreed between the supplier and customer. If the customer collects the goods, a provision should be included to the effect that the customer shall collect the goods from the supplier's premises or such other location as notified by the supplier. The delivery date and time may, where practicable and possible, also be expressly provided for, although it will be largely dependent on the nature of the goods being supplied. Unless otherwise provided for, the supplier is only required to deliver goods within a reasonable time (s 29 (2) of the 1893 Act). From the supplier's perspective, it would be preferable to have a date range for the delivery of the goods so as to have flexibility and make it clear that time of delivery is not of the essence nor should the supplier be liable for any delay in the delivery of goods caused by a force majeure event or as a result of any failure by the customer to provide adequate delivery instructions (see below for commentary on late delivery and time of the essence). The supplier will also seek to ensure that costs in connection with any delivery are the customer's responsibility and that the Terms and Conditions expressly reference this.

20.4.2.2 Completion of delivery

Due to the fact that delivery is generally linked to the transfer of risk in goods and the payment obligation on behalf of the customer, it is very important to ensure the Terms and Conditions are clear as to when delivery has or is deemed to have taken place. The supplier will prefer that delivery is deemed to have taken place at the first possible opportunity and so would want to ensure that delivery of the goods is deemed to have taken place upon (i) the goods arrival at the delivery point or (ii) where the supplier is using a carrier to deliver the goods, that delivery takes place upon delivery of goods to the carrier's premises.

20.4.2.3 Late delivery/Time of the essence

The supplier should always ensure that its Terms and Conditions make it expressly clear that time of delivery is not of the essence due to the common law rule that delivery of goods under a sale of goods contract is deemed to be 'of the essence', which could allow a customer to terminate a contract in the event of a delayed delivery. There should also be an express provision which provides that late delivery does not entitle the customer to reject the goods and terminate the contract nor is the supplier liable for any damages that may have been incurred by late delivery. However, the enforceability of such a provision may be a matter of debate as it could be deemed not to be 'fair and reasonable' and hence unenforceable. Accordingly, a prudent approach may be that such clauses should remain silent on the issue of damages but limit the period under which a customer will be entitled to reject the goods and terminate the contract as a result of late delivery (i.e. 30 days after the delivery date range provided, save in the case of a force majeure event or delay as a result of failure by customer to provide adequate delivery instructions).

One should also consider including an express provision to the effect that where the supplier fails to deliver the goods at all (outside of a force majeure event), its liability shall be limited to the costs and expenses incurred by the customer in obtaining replacement goods of a similar description and quality. Again, such a provision would be subject to a test of reasonableness to ensure enforceability and will largely depend on the nature of the goods being sold and whether, for example, excluding liability for loss of profits is reasonable in the circumstances.

20.4.2.4 Customer fails to take delivery

Section 37 of the 1893 Act provides that where the supplier is ready and willing to deliver goods and requests the buyer to take delivery and the buyer does not do so within a reasonable time, the buyer is liable to the supplier for any loss occasioned by his neglect or refusal to take delivery and also for a reasonable charge for the custody of the goods.

Notwithstanding the above statutory protection, the supplier should ensure that there are express provisions in connection with the customer's failure to take delivery which (i) make it clear as to when delivery of the goods shall be deemed to have taken place; (ii) make the customer liable for all costs and expenses (including insurance) in connection with the storage of such goods; and (iii) allow the supplier (after a specific time period depending on the nature of the goods i.e. whether perishable or not) to dispose of such goods and recover from the customer any loss and additional costs incurred from the date of delivery as a result of their failure or refusal.

20.4.2.5   Quantity of goods being supplied

To the extent the supplier's goods are difficult to measure precisely, the supplier should ensure that there is an express clause which provides that the customer shall not be entitled to reject the goods if the supplier delivers an amount within a certain percentage range e.g. up to 3% more or less than the actual quantity ordered. In order to ensure that such a clause is not challenged as unreasonable, it would be prudent to include language such that a pro rata adjustment shall be made to the price of the order upon receipt of notice from the customer that the wrong quantity of goods was delivered.

20.4.2.6   Cancellation of a sales contract and subsequent return of goods

Regulations 14 to 19 of EUCICORR provide, subject to a number of specific exclusions, for consumers to have the right to cancel off-premises and distance contracts within 14 calendar days (an increase from seven working days under the Distance Selling Directive (97/7/EC)). In such consumer contracts, in the event of the goods already having been delivered, the supplier shall bear the cost of returning the goods unless they have included a term informing the consumer that they will bear this cost (reg 20 of EUCICORR). Further, if the goods are particularly difficult to transport, it is also necessary to provide the consumer in advance with an estimate of return costs. Where the right to cancel exists, the model cancellation form in Part B of sch 3 of EUCICORR must be distributed to consumers.

20.4.2.7   Instalments

Pursuant to s 31 (1) of the 1893 Act, unless otherwise agreed, a buyer of goods is not bound to accept delivery thereof by instalments. To the extent the supplier may wish to deliver goods by instalments, it should therefore ensure that this is made expressly clear in its Terms and Conditions. In addition, given that s 31 (2) of the 1893 Act potentially allows for a customer (depending on circumstances of the case) to terminate an entire contract where the supplier makes defective deliveries, the supplier should ensure to include express language to the effect that each instalment constitutes a separate contract and that any delay or defect in an instalment shall not entitle the customer to cancel any other instalment (or the entire order).

20.4.3   PRICE AND PAYMENT

Clear express terms in connection with price and payment are obviously critical matters for any supplier of goods and/or services. As a general point, detailed instructions should be sought from a supplier in relation to what their standard credit terms (if any) are and what is included in the price of their goods/services (e.g. packaging, delivery costs).

20.4.3.1   Price

Section 29(5) of the 1893 Act provides that: *unless otherwise agreed, the expenses of and incidental to putting the goods into a deliverable state must be borne by the supplier.*

Accordingly, express provisions need to be included in standard Terms and Conditions which set out what items are to be included in the price or what items are extra costs, for example, insurance costs, packaging costs, and/or delivery costs. It would generally be the case that the cost of packaging would be included in the price although, depending on the nature of goods being supplied, a supplier may wish to reserve the right to charge additionally for packaging to the extent a customer requires special packaging. Delivery costs are something that would normally be expressly stated to be an extra cost for the account of the customer.

Unless the Terms and Conditions state otherwise, the price of goods will normally be deemed to be inclusive of VAT. In business-to-business contracts, prices would normally exclude VAT given that businesses can generally recover all or part of amounts paid in respect of VAT as input tax.

To the extent that a supplier provides a quotation prior to an order being made, such a quotation should be stated to be subject to expiry after a certain period of time, for example 14 days from the date of the quotation. If a supplier's price is not set out in the purchase order, express provisions should be included such that the price published in the supplier's latest price list shall apply.

For consumers, reg 26 of EUCICORR provides that a consumer's express consent has to be obtained in order for any additional services included to be binding (thus banning hidden fees and the use of pre-ticked boxes on websites). Schedules 1 and 2 of EUCICORR also require the total price of the goods or services inclusive of tax to be provided prior to the conclusion of contracts and where applicable all additional delivery charges and any other costs that may be payable.

20.4.3.2   Payment

The credit terms for payment will generally depend on the existing practices of the supplier in question but it should always be expressly provided for in standard Terms and Conditions.

From the supplier's perspective, it is preferable to set the payment period by reference to either the date of the invoice or the deemed delivery of the goods (as opposed to when the goods were actually received by the customer). The supplier will also want to ensure that the time for payment is 'of the essence' such that it gives the supplier the right to terminate the contract if the customer fails to pay on time.

The supplier will also want to ensure that there are sufficient provisions to incentivise the customer into making their payments on time. This can be done in a variety of ways, with the most common provision being the application of interest on any late payments. It should be noted that suppliers have an existing statutory right (with regard to commercial but not consumer transactions) to add interest on late payments pursuant to the Late Payments in Commercial Transactions Regulations 2012 (the '2012 Regulations'). From 1 July 2014, the late payment interest rate is 8.15% (that is based on the ECB rate of 0.15% plus the 8% margin applied pursuant to the 2012 Regulations). However, in the interest of certainty, it is advisable to state expressly the right to charge interest pursuant to the Terms and Conditions. Care should be taken not to apply an interest rate which could be deemed excessive and held invalid as amounting to a penalty. *Dunlop Pneumatic Tyre Co v New Garage and Motor* [1915] AC 79 established that a sum will be held to be a penalty if it is 'extravagant and unconscionable in comparison with the greatest loss that could conceivably be proved to have followed from the breach'. It is generally accepted that anything over 15% is likely to be unenforceable and that the normal practice would be to have an interest rate of anything between 2% and 4% over the base lending rate of a major bank. Accordingly, a prudent course of action could be (in commercial transactions) simply to reflect the interest rate as provided for under the 2012 Regulations (i.e. ECB rate plus 8%).

Where goods are being delivered by instalments, the supplier should seek to include provisions providing that where any instalment is not paid on the due date, the remaining outstanding balance of the price for the goods will automatically become due for payment and that further deliveries will be withheld pending payment.

Regulation 25 of EUCICORR provides that suppliers are prohibited from charging fees to consumers that exceed the actual cost to the supplier of processing the means of payment provided (e.g. credit or debit card fees).

20.4.3.3　Set-off

The supplier should seek to ensure express provisions are included which exclude any right the customer may have to deduct or withhold any sums owing from them to the supplier. The customer may look to withhold sums owing in a variety of different circumstances. For example, where the supplier owes the customer monies, the customer may seek to set off the amount owing as against the monies they owe the supplier. Alternatively, the customer may seek to withhold monies for goods purchased on the basis that the customer has a claim for damages where the goods supplied were defective. Accordingly, the Terms and Conditions for the supplier should have express provisions which exclude any deduction, discount, or set-off by the customer in connection with any payments owing by the supplier.

20.4.4　WARRANTIES/QUALITY

As set out in **chapter 19, 'Consumer Law'**, ss 12 to 15 of the 1893 Act, as amended by s 10 of the 1980 Act, provide that in every contract for the sale of goods, there are implied conditions, namely that:

(a)　the seller has the right to sell the goods in question and there are no undisclosed encumbrances on the goods and the purchaser will enjoy quiet possession of them (s 12);

(b)　the goods will correspond with their description (s 13);

(c)　there is an implied condition of merchantable quality except where defects are specifically brought to the buyer's attention prior to the contract or there are defects which ought to have been noticed in an examination of the goods by the buyer before the contract was made (s 14); and

(d)　in the case of a contract for sale by sample, there is an implied condition that the bulk will correspond with the sample in quality (s 15).

In the case of a contract for the sale of goods, any term excluding the implied terms and conditions in sections 13, 14, and 15 of the 1893 Act will be void where the buyer deals as consumer and in any other case (i.e. business-to-business contracts), will not be enforceable unless it is shown that it is fair and reasonable (see **20.4.5.1** in connection with assessing what is 'fair and reasonable'). This is also largely the case with the implied terms pursuant to s 39 of the 1980 Act which apply to any contract for services as detailed in **chapter 18, 'Consumer Law'**. However, it should be noted that it is not possible in any circumstances for standard Terms and Conditions to exclude the implied terms as to title and quiet possession. Any term seeking to do so will be void and unenforceable.

The key assessment when seeking to exclude such implied terms in business-to-business contracts is that they will only be deemed enforceable to the extent that they are reasonable. It is therefore important when drafting standard Terms and Conditions which expressly exclude all terms implied by statute or common law (to the fullest extent permitted by law) to provide the customer with specific limited rights in the event that they receive defective goods. For example, it is much more preferable for the supplier to have the option of repairing or replacing the goods instead of offering a refund, although offering the option of either a refund or replacement to the customer is a safer course of action to ensure such exclusions are not deemed to be unreasonable and hence unenforceable.

In the context of seeking to ensure that exclusions are deemed reasonable (and hence enforceable), a prudent course of action would be to have limited warranties included in the standard Terms and Conditions which relate to the goods: (i) conforming in all material respects with their description and any applicable specification, and (ii) being free from material defects in design, material, and workmanship. Such warranties should be limited in time (e.g. 12 months from delivery). The remedies for breach of any such warranties should be limited to those discussed above (i.e. refund and/or replacement) and damages, loss of profits, indirect, or consequential losses should be specifically excluded.

Express provisions should also be included to ensure not only the contractual remedies available to the customer but also the circumstances in which the customer may reject the goods and the procedures that must be followed in connection with such a rejection. For example, express provisions should require the customer to give notice in writing within a reasonable time period of any defect in connection with the goods. Furthermore, the supplier should ensure there are provisions excluding the remedies available to the customer where:

(a) the customer continues to use the goods after giving notice of the defect;

(b) the defect only arose as a result of the customer not following the instructions of the supplier in relation to use of the goods;

(c) the customer alters or repairs the goods without the written consent of the supplier;

(d) the defect only arose as a result of fair wear and tear or negligence by the customer; or

(e) the defect arose because of the specifications supplied by the customer to the supplier.

20.4.5 LIMITATION OF LIABILITY

A supplier will always look to ensure that any potential liability it may have in connection with the goods/services it offers is limited to the fullest extent possible by law. However, as noted above, there are statutory and common law controls which render provisions which seek to limit the supplier's liability for certain matters unenforceable which a supplier will need to be aware of. The drafting of provisions which seek to limit liability must not be too prohibitive in order to ensure that such provisions are enforceable and not in breach of statutory or common law rules. As referenced above, the ability to limit liability under business-to-business arrangements (e.g. implied terms pursuant to s 13 to 15 of the 1893 Act) is far greater than that pursuant to a contract between a supplier and a consumer.

Set out below is an example of a wide-ranging provision which seeks to limit liability under several headings, whilst expressly acknowledging that nothing in the Terms and Conditions seeks to exclude any liability which would be unenforceable as a matter of law.

20.4.5.1 Sample exclusion/limitation of liability

1. Nothing in these Terms and Conditions shall limit or exclude the Supplier's liability for:

   (a) death or personal injury caused by the Supplier's negligence; or

   (b) fraud or fraudulent misrepresentation; or

   (c) breach of the terms implied by s 12 of the Sale of Goods Act 1893 (as amended); or

   (d) for any matter in respect of which it would be unlawful for the Supplier to exclude or restrict liability.

2. Subject to clause 1 above, the Supplier shall not be liable to the Customer, whether in contract, tort (including negligence), breach of statutory duty, or otherwise, for any loss of profit or indirect or consequential loss arising under or in connection with the Contract.

In connection with any clause which seeks to exclude indirect or consequential losses, care must be taken to ensure that all headings of loss which the supplier wants excluded are expressly referenced given that, for example, a loss of profits can in certain instances be deemed a direct loss and so the exclusion of indirect losses would potentially not cover loss of profits in certain instances. Other specific headings should be considered depending on the nature of goods/services being provided, e.g. loss of reputation, loss of business.

When drafting exclusion clauses in connection with other matters, for example, excluding those terms implied by s 13 to s 15 of the 1893 Act, one needs to be cognisant that it will only be valid to the extent it can be shown to be reasonable. Accordingly, it is important when drafting such Terms and Conditions to be mindful of the matters which a court would likely look at in connection with assessing what is 'fair and reasonable', including:

(a) the strength of the bargaining position of the respective parties (including alternatives open to customers);

(b) whether the customer receives an inducement to agree to the terms;

(c) whether the customer knew, or ought reasonably to have known, of the existence of the term (having regard to, inter alia, any custom of trade and any previous course of dealings between the parties); and

(d) whether any goods involved were manufactured to the special order of the parties.

It should be noted that there is no guarantee that the 'fair and reasonable' test will be satisfied in any particular scenario given that the circumstances of contracts can differ greatly. However, the above guidelines should be of assistance in seeking to ensure exclusion provisions satisfy the 'fair and reasonable' test.

The prudent approach is not to just seek to exclude all matters which it is technically possible to exclude but to seek to adopt a balanced approach in conjunction with the instructions of the supplier. For example, limiting a customer's right to simply receiving a replacement product (as opposed to a refund) in addition to having wide-ranging exclusions is more likely to fall foul of the 'fair and reasonable' test than provisions which allow for a refund and put a cap on the supplier's liability for goods/services supplied. It is therefore generally preferable for a supplier to incorporate a clause which accepts a level of liability rather than including blanket provisions that seek to exclude all liability which, by virtue of not being deemed 'fair and reasonable', could expose the supplier for losses incurred by the customer on account of the provisions being unenforceable.

20.4.6 TERMINATION EVENTS

The supplier will want to ensure that express provisions are included in standard Terms and Conditions which allow the supplier to terminate the contract with the customer immediately in the event that the customer suffers an insolvency type event which would likely lead to the customer being unable to pay for the goods. Set out below is an example of insolvency type termination event provisions that could apply if they happened to a customer.

(a) An order has been made or petition presented or resolution passed for the winding up or dissolution of the Customer (being a company) or for the appointment of a liquidator or examiner to the Customer (being a company) or anything analogous to any of the aforementioned events occurs in any other jurisdiction (otherwise than for the purposes of amalgamation or reconstruction upon terms previously approved in writing by the Supplier); or

(b) a receiver and/or manager has been appointed by a person over the whole or any part of the business or assets of the Customer (being a company); or

(c) the Customer ceases or threatens to cease to trade or the Customer ceases, or threatens to suspend, payment of its debts or is unable to pay its debts as they fall due or admits inability to pay its debtors; or

(d) a meeting of the Customer's creditors is called pursuant to s 266 of the Companies Act 1963 (as amended) or the Customer commences negotiations with all or any class of its creditors with a view to rescheduling any of its debts, or makes a proposal for or enters into any compromise or arrangement with its creditors; or

(e) the Customer (being an individual) is the subject of a bankruptcy petition or order.

20.5   Conclusion

This chapter has sought to provide a summary of the key provisions that should be looked at when preparing standard Terms and Conditions for a trading business. It is crucial that input from the business in question is sought prior to drafting the Terms and Conditions. This is because vital parts of standard terms are driven by commercial realities and the mechanics that a business already has in operation in connection with, for example, payment terms or how delivery is to be effected. Whilst different businesses will have different needs, most of the above fundamentals should be of relevance.

CHAPTER 21

INTELLECTUAL PROPERTY

21.1 Introduction

21.1.1 GENERAL

Intellectual property is the bedrock of the information society and has enormous importance in every area of commercial life. It impinges on every aspect of business, indeed often it is the most valuable asset a business owns. As a result, it is vital that solicitors acquire at least a general knowledge of the area so as to recognise when their clients may require advice to protect this asset and so as to be able to give pragmatic and succinct advice.

21.1.2 WHAT IS INTELLECTUAL PROPERTY?

Intellectual property is that area of law, which has evolved to protect what is essentially the fruit of creative endeavour. Legal rights have been introduced and developed to protect this intangible property, upon which many businesses rely and which particularly in the information technology industry, may generate enormous profits for the proprietors of those businesses.

As with any piece of property, intangible or real or personal, intellectual property may be traded. It may be sold or assigned for monetary consideration. It may be licensed or bequeathed in a will. In short it may be exploited in precisely the same way as any piece of real or personal property.

It is vital that every business knows what intellectual property rights it owns, what should be done to achieve the best possible protection of those rights, whether those rights are being exploited as well as may be, and what to do if those rights are infringed. The solicitor should be in a position to advise in relation to all of these matters.

21.1.3 CATEGORIES OF INTELLECTUAL PROPERTY

The principal areas of intellectual property are protected by statute. These statutes, aside from the copyright legislation, make provision for a scheme of registration of various rights in order to assist in the clearer identification of those rights and of their ownership. The statutes grant the owner of an intellectual property right a clear monopoly in the property protected, which may be exploited as the owner decides. Intellectual property rights include the following categories:

(a) patents which protect inventions;

(b) trade marks which protect names used in the course of trade and in the provision of goods and/or services;

(c) passing off which protects, in common law, the goodwill and reputation of a business;

(d) copyright and design which protect the physical form of literary, dramatic, musical, and artistic endeavour; and

(e) confidential information in which under common law an obligation of confidentiality exists in relation to information imparted from one party to another.

It is extremely important, when advising clients, that the specific statute is carefully considered on each occasion. Frequently, cases in this area of the law fall to be decided on the precise wording of a particular section or subsection of the relevant Act.

21.1.4   INTELLECTUAL PROPERTY—CONTRACTUAL CONSIDERATIONS

All of the statutes and the common law, which protect intellectual property, allow the general rules to be changed by agreement between the parties concerned. It is, in almost every situation, prudent for a solicitor to advise the client that the intention of the parties should be clearly agreed and set out in writing, prior to any dealings between the parties relating to intellectual property rights. Thus, if one party has an idea, an invention which may be patentable, it is sensible for that person, prior to discussing the invention with anyone, to enter into an agreement in writing that the parties will keep any information exchanged confidential. The parties are thereby bound by contract not to reveal any information without consent.

Similarly, all of the relevant statutes and the common law provide rules in relation to the ownership of intellectual property in an employment contract. Nonetheless, it is sensible, for the avoidance of doubt to set out in writing what has been agreed between the parties to avoid arguments in the future.

Clearly, in any case where a person has an invention or a design, or an author has written a book, a play, or a film script, and wishes to agree with a third party to exploit it in any way, it is essential, for the avoidance of argument in the future, that the terms and the basis upon which the exploitation is to take place are clearly set out in writing prior to commencement of the exploitation. It is in these situations that the solicitor may provide vital assistance to the client.

21.1.5   INTELLECTUAL PROPERTY AND COMPETITION LAW

As intellectual property law confers an exclusive monopoly right on the owner and competition law seeks to ensure free and open competition, an obvious dichotomy may arise between the two areas of law. The Competition Act 2002 as amended (the 'Competition Act'), provides for domestic competition law provisions similar to Articles 101 and 102 of the Treaty on the Functioning of the European Union ('TFEU'). Unlike under the EU competition law regime, there is no de minimis provision in the Competition Act. The Competition Act is covered in **chapter 23, 'Competition law'**.

Patent, know-how, software copyright licences, and certain research and development licences are all covered by European Commission block exemptions, so that such agreements falling within the provisions of the relevant block exemption benefit from a presumption of compatibility with EU competition law. There are at present no specific declarations (the Irish equivalent of block exemptions) for licences of intellectual property under the Competition Act, although the Declaration in Respect of Vertical Agreements and Concerted Practices covers provisions governing the assignment or use by the buyer of intellectual property rights where such provisions are ancillary to agreements falling within its scope. Accordingly, it is up to each party to assess whether an agreement complies with the Competition Act. Care should be taken to ensure that protection under the Trade Marks Act 1996 or other intellectual property legislation should not be used as a vehicle for the operation of an anti-competitive agreement or to abuse a dominant position.

Articles 34–36 of the TFEU prohibit measures which impose quantitative restrictions on imports from other Member States or have equivalent effect. The doctrine of exhaustion of rights has been developed to accommodate, on the one hand, the monopoly right granted in intellectual property law and, on the other hand, the EU rules allowing free movement of goods within the Community.

A trader applying a trade mark to and selling goods in one part of the EU cannot prevent the sale of those goods which have been placed on the market with his consent, being sold in another EU country. This is the case even when the trade mark is registered in that other EU country. The trade mark rights are exhausted when the goods have first been placed on the market for sale in the EU.

This doctrine of exhaustion of rights does not however apply to goods which are imported from third countries outside the EU or the European Economic Area ('EEA'). Thus, goods which are imported from, for example, the US or the Far East, may not be sold in the EU or the EEA without the unequivocal consent of the owner of the trade mark in the EU. In *Levi Strauss & Co and another v Tesco Stores Limited and another* (2002) EWHC 1556 (Ch), the High Court in England, following a preliminary reference from the ECJ, confirmed that a trade mark owner was entitled to prevent goods bearing his trade mark from being imported into Europe without his express consent.

21.1.6   INFRINGEMENT REMEDIES

The remedies for infringement of intellectual property rights are in all cases damages, or an account of profits, an injunction to prohibit the infringement, and delivery up and destruction of the infringing property.

Damages will be calculated by reference to a reasonable royalty rate or licence fee, but may take into account various matters in mitigation. For example, if a defendant could show that he was unaware of or had no reasonable grounds for suspecting that an intellectual property right existed, the plaintiff may be precluded from being awarded damages.

Certain of the statutes provide specific remedies for seizure of goods and orders for delivery up. Some of these remedies may be enforced by the Garda Síochána.

Further, infringement of copyright, design, and of registered trade marks may constitute a criminal offence, the penalties for which are a fine and/or a term of imprisonment. The Directive on the Enforcement of Intellectual Property Rights (2004/48/EC) was passed on 29 April 2004 and is designed to ensure fair and equitable enforcement of intellectual property rights throughout the EU. The European Communities (Enforcement of Intellectual Property Rights) Regulations 2006 (SI 36/2006) transpose into Irish law those aspects of Directive 2004/48/EC which had not previously been part of Irish law.

21.2   Patents

21.2.1   INTRODUCTION

The law relating to patents is governed by the Patents Act 1992 (the '1992 Act'), the Intellectual Property (Miscellaneous Provisions) Act 1998, and the Patents (Amendment) Act 2006 which confusingly also contains changes to the trade marks, copyright, and designs legislation. These amendments were necessary to bring Ireland in line with the TRIPs agreement, which the World Trade Organization has agreed with most countries worldwide and with the European Patent Convention 2000, which came into force on 13 December 2007. The Patent Rules were also enacted in 1992 and have been amended over the intervening years to deal with the administration of patents by the Patents Office and with the powers of the Controller of Patents in relation to the regulation of the patent regime. The Patents (Amendment) Act 2012 brought into effect certain changes to ss 119 and 121 of the 1992 Act. Finally, the Intellectual Property (Miscellaneous Provisions) Act 2014 amends s 42 of the 1992 Act relating to the Bolar provision which exempts certain commercial experiments, done with a view to obtaining regulatory approval, from constituting patent infringement. This brings Ireland into line with a number of other European countries which had a wider provision, extending the exemption to sale outside the EU and by an originator/innovator.

A number of international conventions also exist with the objective of streamlining patent application, filing, and novelty search procedures throughout the world. These are the Paris Convention of 1883, the Patent Co-operation Treaty 1970, the European Patent Convention 1973, and the European Patent Convention 2000. Aside from licensing and transfer of patents, solicitors generally do not become involved in the area of patents until issues arise which must be decided by the courts. This is an extremely specialised area of the law and patent agents who are trained in scientific and engineering matters are expert in the drafting and processing of patents. It is important, however, for a solicitor to have some knowledge of the patent process in order to be able to advise properly when the matter reaches the stage of court proceedings.

21.2.2   PATENTABILITY

A patent may be obtained for any patentable invention and will grant the owner of the patent a monopoly protection in the invention for either a ten-year (short-term) or 20-year period. An invention is patentable if it is susceptible of industrial application, is new, and involves an inventive step (1992 Act, s 9 (1)). In the case of a short-term patent the invention must be new, susceptible of industrial application, and must not clearly lack an inventive step (1992 Act, s 63 (4)). There is no definition in the 1992 Act of 'invention'. However, the following shall *not* be regarded as an invention:

  (a)   a discovery;

  (b)   a scientific theory;

  (c)   a mathematical method;

  (d)   an aesthetic creation;

  (e)   a scheme, rule, or method for performing a mental act, playing a game, or doing business;

  (f)   a computer program; and

  (g)   the presentation of information.

The 1992 Act also provides that a method for treatment of the human or animal body by surgery or therapy and a diagnostic method practised on the human or animal body shall not be regarded as an invention susceptible of industrial application (1992 Act, s 9 (4)). However, it is provided that this provision shall not apply to a product and, in particular, a substance or composition for use in any such method.

An invention shall be considered to be new if it does not form part of the state of the art. This comprises everything made available or disclosed to the public (whether in the State or elsewhere) in any way before the date of filing of the patent application (1992 Act, s 11). Disclosure of an invention will be discounted if it happened within six months before the filing of the patent application as a result of a breach of confidence or, because the invention was displayed at an exhibition officially recognised under the Paris Convention on International Exhibitions, 1928 and the application makes a declaration to that effect when applying (1992 Act, s 12).

The invention will be considered as involving an inventive step if, having regard to the state of the art, it is not obvious to a person skilled in the art (1992 Act, s 13).

An invention is considered as susceptible of industrial application if it may be made or used in any kind of industry. Industry in this context includes agriculture (1992 Act, s 14).

There are certain exceptions to patentability under the Patents Act (1992 Act, s 10). A patent will not be granted in respect of:

(a)   an invention, the publication or exploitation of which will be contrary to public order or morality, provided that the exploitation will not be deemed to be so contrary only because it is prohibited by law; and

(b)   a plant or animal variety or an essentially biological process for the production of plants or animals other than a microbiological process or the products thereof.

The Biotechnology Directive (98/44/EC) was designed to harmonise the patenting of biotechnological inventions throughout the EU and to confirm that, inter alia, processes for cloning human beings are not patentable. The Directive was debated for some ten years before coming into force in 2000. It has been implemented in Ireland.

21.2.3   GRANT OF A PATENT

Patents are granted by the Patents Office to which a formal application is made. Of their nature such applications are extremely technical and the actual application will be made by a specialised patent agent. However, it is important for a solicitor to be able to give a client an idea of the procedure involved in obtaining protection.

21.2.3.1   Applications

A patent application may be made by any person alone or jointly with another person (1992 Act, s 15) but the right to a patent belongs to the inventor (1992 Act, s 16) who has a right to be mentioned in the application (1992 Act, s 17).

Under s 18 of the 1992 Act, a patent application for a 20-year patent must contain:

(a)   a request for the grant of a patent;

(b)   a specification containing a description of the invention to which the application relates, one or more claims, and any drawing referred to in the description or the claim; and

(c)   an abstract (a brief summary description).

The application must be accompanied by a filing fee (1992 Act, s 18), must clearly disclose the invention to which it relates (1992 Act, s 19), and the claim or claims must define the matter for which protection is sought and must be supported by the description (s 20). The application must relate to one invention only or at least to a group of inventions, which are so linked as to form a single inventive concept (s 21).

Under s 63 (7) of the 1992 Act, if application is being made for a short-term (ten-year) patent, the specification must:

(a)   describe the invention and the best method of performing it, which is known to the applicant;

(b)   incorporate one or more claims, which must not exceed five, defining the matter for which protection is sought; and

(c)   be accompanied by any necessary drawings and an abstract.

A full-term (20-year) patent and a short-term patent may not co-exist for the same invention (1992 Act, s 64). The threshold for obtaining a short-term patent is lower than that required for obtaining a 20-year patent (see **21.2.2**).

Under s 23 of the 1992 Act, the date of filing of a patent application is the earliest date upon which the applicant paid the filing fee and filed documents which contained:

(a)   an indication that a patent is sought;

(b)   information identifying the applicant; and

(c)   a description of the invention even though the description does not comply with the requirements of the Act or with any requirements that may be prescribed.

If an objection is raised, at the time during which the application is being examined, that the application relates to more than one invention, the applicant may amend the specification or delete the claims. The applicant may also file another application for the extra invention. This is known as a 'divisional application' which is in respect of subject matter, which must not extend beyond the content of an earlier application as filed and complies with the relevant requirements. Such an application will be deemed to have been filed on the date of filing of the earlier application and will have the benefit of any right to priority (1992 Act, s 24).

It is also possible to file an application and claim the priority of an earlier application in respect of the same invention, which has been filed either in the State or abroad (1992 Act, s 25).

21.2.3.2 Priority

The date of priority is the date of filing of the patent application (1992 Act, s 27) in the State or abroad. This is an important date as it fixes the time which is to be considered for the purpose of assessing whether the invention is new. It also fixes the date from which infringement proceedings may be taken. Often an inventor will instruct his patent agent to apply for a patent at the first opportunity. This is to ensure that no rivals make application for the same invention and to obtain as early as possible a priority date. A more detailed application may then be filed within a 12-month period. Once the application is received at the Patents Office, it is inspected by one of the Controller of Patents, Designs and Trade Marks' examiners (the 'Controller') to make sure that the application complies with the requirements of the 1992 Act. The applicant may request that a search be undertaken on behalf of the Controller in return for the appropriate fee to ensure that the invention complies with the requirement that it is new. Clearly, if the invention is not new, it is open to attack and will be invalid. The Controller must allow an applicant an opportunity to amend the application in light of the result of the search report within a prescribed period.

Alternatively, an applicant for a patent may submit a statement to the Controller to the effect that an application for a patent for the same invention has been made in a prescribed foreign State (UK or Germany) or under the provisions of any prescribed Convention or Treaty (the European Patent Convention 1973 or the Patent Cooperation Treaty 1970) (1992 Act, s 30; Patent Rules 1992, r 26).

In this case the applicant must submit evidence, either of the results of the search carried out on that application, or of the grant of a patent in pursuance of the application. Where the applicant has submitted the results of a search, the Controller shall allow an opportunity to amend the application in light of that evidence.

The patent application must then be published in the Patents Office Official Journal, which is published every fortnight and is available online on the Patents Office website, www. patentsoffice.ie. Publication must be as soon as practicable after the expiry of 18 months from the filing date or from the priority date, if claimed. If the applicant requests it may be published earlier (1992 Act, s 28). If no objections are received, the patent proceeds to grant, it is sealed and issued.

21.2.4 PROTECTION CONFERRED BY A PATENT

21.2.4.1 Generally

While a patent is in force, it confers upon the proprietor the right to prevent all third parties not having his consent from using the invention whether directly or indirectly (1992 Act, s 40). Direct use of the invention includes, for example, making, putting on the market, or using a product which is the subject matter of the patent, or importing or stocking the product for those purposes (1992 Act, s 40). The prevention of indirect use of the invention means that a proprietor may also prevent all third parties not having his consent from supplying or offering to supply in the State someone, other than a party entitled to exploit the patented invention (1992 Act, s 41).

21.2.4.2   Exception to monopoly

The following provisions are imported from the Community Patent Convention. The rights conferred by a patent do not extend to acts done privately for non-commercial purposes, or acts done for experimental purposes. These acts may be done without infringing the patent holder's rights. Nor do they extend to the extemporaneous preparation for individual cases in a pharmacy, of a medicine in accordance with a medical prescription. They do not extend either to use of the patented product on board vessels or aircraft or land vehicles, when such temporarily or accidentally enter territorial waters of the State or the State itself (1992 Act, s 42). This provision is presumably designed to assist in ensuring the safety of such vessels. The invention must be used exclusively for the needs of the vessel.

21.2.4.3   Rights on application

A patent application provisionally confers upon the applicant the same protection as that conferred on a granted patent from the date of its publication (1992 Act, s 44). In turn, infringement proceedings may be brought after a patent has been granted in respect of infringing acts committed between the date of publication of the application and the date of grant (1992 Act, s 56).

21.2.4.4   Extent of protection

The extent of the protection conferred by the patent or patent application is to be determined by the terms of the claims. A description and drawing submitted will be used to interpret the claims (1992 Act, s 45).

21.2.4.5   Short-term patents

The protection conferred by a short-term patent is the same as for a 20-year patent, subject to the provisions of the 1992 Act, s 66. This section attempts to strike a balance between the rights of a short-term patent holder and third parties. To this end it requires the holder of a short-term patent to request the Controller to establish a search report on the invention before he may initiate proceedings against a third party for alleged infringement of his patent. Any such proceedings may be brought in the Circuit Court irrespective of the amount of any claim.

21.2.5   OWNERSHIP

The owner of a patent is normally the inventor. In the case of joint inventors both parties may be named as the owners of the patent.

In the case of inventions made by an employee, these will belong to the employer if they are made in the course of the employee's employment. The 1992 Act does not specifically provide for this, so contracts of employment should stipulate that the inventions belong to the employer. If not stipulated in the contract, then the invention may still be deemed to belong to the employer if the court considers it should, because the invention was invented during the course of the employment of the employee or in circumstances where the employee was employed for the purposes of inventing. Section 16 of the 1992 Act states that if the inventor is an employee, the right to a patent shall be determined in accordance with the law of the State in which the employee is wholly or mainly employed.

21.2.6   SUPPLEMENTARY PROTECTION CERTIFICATES ('SPC')

Pharmaceuticals may not be sold to the public unless they have been granted a product authorisation. In order to obtain such an authorisation, the applicant must provide detailed technical information in relation to the testing of the product and its efficiency, all of which must be considered by the regulatory authorities, which in Ireland, is the Health Products Regulatory Authority (HPRA). The SPC was introduced at the behest of the pharmaceutical industry to compensate that industry for the lengthy regulatory delays which occur while a manufacturer of a new product is seeking approval for sale of it to the public. The European Council Regulation (EEC No 1768/92) introducing the SPC, was given effect in Irish law by the European Communities (Supplementary Protection Certificate) Regulations 1993 (SI 125/1993). The SPC has the effect of extending the 20-year life of a pharmaceutical patent by a period, which gives protection for 15 years from the date upon which it first received marketing approval in the EU. The maximum extension allowed over and above the usual 20-year patent is five years. A similar facility was introduced in respect of Plant Protection Products under Regulation (EC) No 1610/96 of the European Parliament and of the Council.

It is important to check whether an SPC exists in relation to both medicinal and plant protection products if the client is considering manufacturing the patented product, as the patent may have been extended and the client might be exposed to an infringement action.

21.2.7 INFRINGEMENT

A patent is infringed by anyone who, in the State without the consent of the proprietor, makes, offers, or puts on the market a product which is the subject matter of a patent or uses a process which is the subject matter of a patent, knowing (or it is obvious to a reasonable person in the circumstances) that the use of the process is prohibited.

Civil proceedings may be brought by the proprietor or licensee of a patent for alleged infringement of a patent (1992 Act, s 47). He may seek:

(a) an injunction restraining the defendant from any apprehended act of infringement;

(b) an order requiring the defendant to deliver up or destroy any product protected by the patent in relation to which the patent is alleged to have been infringed or any article in which the product is inextricably comprised;

(c) damages in respect of the alleged infringement;

(d) in the alternative, an account of profits derived by the defendant from the alleged infringement; and

(e) a declaration that the patent is valid and has been infringed by the defendant.

Damages will not be awarded, nor will an order be made for an account of profits against a defendant who proves that, at the date of infringement, he was unaware of, and had no reasonable grounds for supposing that the patent in question existed.

However, he will be deemed to have been aware or to have had reasonable grounds for so supposing where the number of the relevant patent had been applied to a product (1992 Act, s 49).

21.2.8 GROUNDLESS THREATS

In the normal course, where a property right is being infringed the owner will instruct a solicitor to send a strong letter demanding that the infringement be stopped. This is known as a 'cease and desist' letter. In the case of patents it is important to note that a person who has been threatened with proceedings for infringement of a patent (other than in relation to making or importing a product for disposal or of using a process) may bring his own proceedings to court for relief (1992 Act, s 53). He may seek:

(a) a declaration to the effect that the threats complained of were unjustifiable;

(b) an injunction against the continuance of the threats; and

(c) such damages if any as have been suffered.

It is for these reasons that, rather than the usual form of strongly-worded cease and desist letter being sent at the commencement of a patent action, a letter is sent simply drawing the attention of the alleged infringer to the existence of the patent. This is to avoid a claim for groundless threats being made against both the client and the solicitor.

21.2.9   REVOCATION

Any person may apply to the court or the Controller of Patents for revocation of a patent (1992 Act, s 57). The grounds for revocation are:

(a)   the subject matter of the patent is not patentable;

(b)   the specification of the patent does not properly disclose the invention so that it may be carried out by a person skilled in the art;

(c)   the matter disclosed in the specification extends beyond that disclosed in the application which was filed;

(d)   the protection conferred by the patent has been extended by an amendment of the patent or the specification of the patent; and

(e)   the proprietor of the patent is not the person who is entitled to the patent (1992 Act, s 58).

Thus, an employee who claims that an invention is not his employer's, might apply for revocation or the owner of an existing patent might apply, if the new patent is an obvious improvement of his patent. In cases where a claim for infringement is made, one of the standard defences is to seek revocation of the plaintiff's patent on one or all of the grounds (a) to (e) above. The Controller has the power to revoke patents on his own initiative if it appears that the patent which has been granted formed part of the state of the art. In such a case, the proprietor of the patent will have an opportunity of making observations and amending this specification of the patent in order to preserve it (1992 Act, s 60). In the event that proceedings for revocation are brought before the court, the Controller must be given notice in writing by the plaintiff of those proceedings (1992 Act, s 62). Section 94 provides that a communication between a person or person acting on his behalf and a solicitor or patent agent or person acting on his behalf, or for the purpose of obtaining, or in response to a request for information which a person is seeking for the purpose of instructing the solicitor or patent agent in relation to any matter concerning the protection of an invention, patent, design, or technical information, or any matter involving passing off shall be privileged to the same extent as a communication between client and solicitor in any proceeding before a court in the State (1992 Act, s 94).

21.2.10   INTERNATIONAL CONVENTIONS

21.2.10.1   The Patent Co-operation Treaty

The main object of the Patent Co-operation Treaty 1970 (the 'PCT') is the streamlining of patent application filing and novelty search procedures for an applicant wishing to obtain patent protection in a wide number of countries around the world. It was signed by Ireland in 1970 and has been ratified as a result of the Patents Act, 1992.

Under the PCT, the applicant makes one central application, usually to their local patent office, designating the countries in which patent protection is required. A novelty search is then carried out by an international searching authority and this search is then furnished to the national office of each country in which protection is sought. Further prosecution in each country is then in the hands of the local patent office in accordance with its normal procedure.

21.2.10.2   European Patent Convention

The European Patent Convention 1973 (the 'EPC') is more advanced than the PCT in that searching and examination are centralised in the European Patent Office in Munich.

The EPC was made effective in Ireland by the 1992 Act. The procedure under the EPC is that anyone seeking to protect an invention in several member countries of the Convention may do so by making just one application to the European Patent Office in Munich. The applicant must designate all of the countries in which protection is desired. This means he must specifically name the countries in which he seeks patent protection for his invention. Nationals of both member and non-member countries are entitled to take advantage of this arrangement. Under the 1992 Act, a European patent designating Ireland, granted by the European Patent Office, is treated as if it was granted by the Irish Patent Office (1992 Act, s 119). However, if the language of the specification of the European patent is not English, a translation in English of the specification must be filed with the Irish Patent Office and published here in order that the patent may have effect in Ireland (1992 Act, s 119 (6), (7)). Similarly, in the case of a European patent application designating Ireland, such an application must be treated as having the same legal status in Ireland as an application filed with the Irish Patents Office (1992 Act, s 120).

Section 122 of the 1992 Act permits a European patent application designating Ireland, which has been deemed to be withdrawn, to be proceeded with as a national application under the 1992 Act, subject to certain conditions.

Section 123 of the 1992 Act provides that the High Court is given jurisdiction to determine questions as to the right to be granted to a European patent and sets out the circumstances in which such jurisdiction is exercisable.

Section 124 of the 1992 Act provides for the recognition in Ireland of questions as to the right to a European patent to be determined by a court or competent authority of another Contracting State of the EPC, subject to certain conditions.

A decision as to whether to file a European patent application, specifying those European countries in which patent protection is sought or individual national applications, will depend on several factors. The European patent procedure is expensive, but if protection in several countries is required, it may still be cheaper than a corresponding series of individual country applications. The examination procedure carried out by the European Patent Office is well respected, so that if a European patent is granted, it is likely that such a patent would be subsequently upheld in the national courts. Another factor is that under Art 99 of the EPC, a European patent may be revoked in total only during the first nine months of grant; subsequently it may only be revoked country by country, by application to the appropriate national court.

Section 127 of the 1992 Act allows Ireland to be designated in an international application. This section also provides that an international application designating the State, for example, by an American client, shall be deemed to be an application for a European patent (under the EPC) designating the State. This means that functions concerning international applications, which would otherwise have to be performed by the Irish Patents Office, may instead be performed by the European Patent Office. The applicant will eventually receive a grant by the European Patent Office of a European patent designating Ireland if he has availed of this procedure.

21.2.10.3 Community Patent Convention

For many decades, there has been discussion seeking to bring in one patent EU wide to simplify the system and to reduce the cost of obtaining a patent. The Community Patent Convention (the 'CPC') was initially signed in 1989 but has never come into force. The 1992 Act does not itself mention the CPC although it includes a general provision allowing the Minister for Enterprise, Trade and Employment to make an order enabling effect to be given to 'any international treaty, convention or agreement relating to patents to which the State is or proposes to become a party' (1992 Act, s 128). This Convention was eventually abandoned and instead in December 2012 Regulation 1257/2012, implementing enhanced cooperation in the area of the creation of unitary protection, and Regulation 1260/2012, implementing enhanced cooperation in the area of the creation of unitary protection with regard to the applicable translation arrangements, came into force. Thus a new regime for patents is currently being implemented by the European Union which when ratified by 13 Member States including Germany, France, and the United Kingdom, will allow application for unitary patent protection by one application (http://www.epo.org/law-practice/unitary.html) and in a very far-reaching step will provide a unified patent court where patent holders may opt to have disputes resolved (http://www.unified-patent-court.org/).

It will be necessary for Ireland to hold a referendum and for the people to confirm their consent before Ireland can ratify. The new regime will allow three options in respect of a patent, a national one, a bundle of patents in a number of European countries, or a unitary patent which will have effect in all those countries which have ratified the regime. The new regime is illustrated below.

New Regime

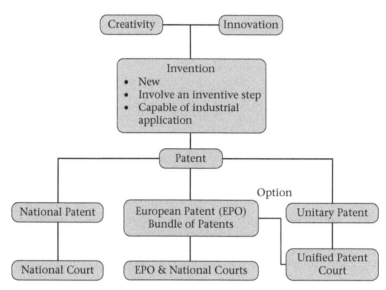

21.3   Trade Marks and Counterfeit Goods

21.3.1   INTRODUCTION

This section of the law was developed to prevent the public being deceived by a trader alleging that he had an association with goods which, in fact, he did not enjoy. The first Trade Marks Act was introduced in 1875 and brought in a system of registration of trade marks. Currently, this area is governed by the Trade Marks Act 1996 (the '1996 Act'), sections of the Patents Amendment Act 2006, and the regulations made thereunder. The Intellectual Property (Miscellaneous Provisions) Act 2014 also assists Ireland to ratify the Singapore treaty which harmonises certain aspects of trade mark offices procedure world wide.

21.3.2   WHAT IS A TRADE MARK?

21.3.2.1   Generally

Section 6 of the 1996 Act says that a 'trade mark' means:

> *any sign capable of being represented graphically which is capable of distinguishing goods or services of one undertaking from those of other undertakings.*

The 1996 Act goes on to say that a trade mark may, in particular, consist of words (including personal names), designs, letters, numerals, or the shape of goods or of their packaging.

A trade mark may be something as simple as a word or name, it can be written in a particular script or with a band of colour around it, or it can be as complicated as any designer can imagine. A trade mark does not have to be a name at all. It may be three stripes, it may be the shape of a bottle, and it may even be a smell, provided that the applicant has been able to represent the smell graphically and that it is distinguishable from other smells.

Once a trade mark has been registered under the 1996 Act, it is a property right and the proprietor of a registered trade mark is entitled to all the rights and remedies provided by the 1996 Act. A trade mark may be registered in one of 45 classes. The Nice Agreement, on the International Classification of goods and services for the purposes of the registration, provides an internationally recognised classification system of goods and services in respect of which trade marks may be registered. Ireland has signed up to the Nice Agreement and applies the classification system to the examination and registration of trade mark applications.

Under the Nice Agreement, goods and services are divided into various categories, for example food and drink, paper products, financial services, etc. When a trade mark is registered, it may be registered for a particular product or service within a class or for all of the goods or services within a class or, indeed, for goods and services in several different classes. The registration of a mark, in respect of a specific product or service or class of products/services, defines the extent of the protection afforded by that registration.

The Nice Agreement consists of 34 classes of goods (classes 1–34 inclusive) and 11 classes of services (35–45 inclusive).

21.3.2.2   Marks which may be refused registration

Sections 8–10 of the 1996 Act govern marks which may be refused registration. Signs which do not satisfy the requirements described above, which are devoid of any distinctive character, or which consist of signs or indications which may serve, in trade, to designate the kind, quality, quantity, intended purpose, value, geographical origin, time of production of goods or of rendering of services, or other characteristics of goods or services or which consist exclusively of signs or indications which have become customary in the practice of the trade will not be registered as trade marks.

However, if any of those trade marks has in fact acquired a distinctive character as a result of the use made of it, then registration will be permitted (for example, the Waterford Glass Mark is a mark indicating geographical origin, but is registered because of its distinctive character).

Pursuant to s 8 (2) of the 1996 Act, a sign will not be registered as a trade mark if it consists exclusively of the shape which results from the nature of the goods themselves, or the shape of goods which is necessary to obtain a technical result, or the shape which gives substantial value to the goods.

Pursuant to s 8 (3) of the 1996 Act, a trade mark will not be registered if it is contrary to public policy or morality or if it deceives the public, for example as to the nature, quality, or geographical origin of the goods or service.

A State emblem of Ireland, or one which resembles such an emblem, will not be registered unless the consent to its registration has been given by the Minister for Communications, the Marine and Natural Resources. The national flag of the State will not be registered if it would be misleading or grossly offensive and the Controller may refuse to register a mark which consists of any emblem of a public authority unless, as provided in s 9 of the 1996 Act, 'such consent as is required by rules is obtained'.

Pursuant to s 10 (1) of the 1996 Act, a trade mark will not be registered if it is identical with an earlier trade mark and the goods or services are identical. Pursuant to s 10 (2) of the 1996 Act, a trade mark will not be registered if it is identical to or similar to an earlier trade mark and the goods or services are identical or similar, or if there exists the likelihood of confusion, including the likelihood of association of the later trade mark with the earlier trade mark. Pursuant to s 10 (3) of the 1996 Act, a trade mark will not be registered if it is identical to or similar to an earlier trade mark and the earlier mark has a reputation and the use of the later trade mark would take unfair advantage of, or be detrimental to, the distinctive character or reputation of the earlier trade mark. A trade mark will not be registered if its use in the State is liable to be prevented because it is passing itself off as an unregistered mark already used in the course of trade or if it would infringe the copyright, registered design, or any other law relating to a right to a name, a right of personal portrayal, or an industrial property right unless the owner of the earlier trade mark consents. An 'earlier trade mark' is defined in the 1992 Act, s 11.

Pursuant to s 12 of the 1996 Act, however, if there has been what is called honest concurrent use of the trade mark, then the Controller is not allowed to refuse the application.

21.3.3   REGISTRATION OF A TRADE MARK

21.3.3.1   Application for a trade mark

Application for registration of a trade mark is made to the Controller and is made in respect of particular goods or services or in respect of particular classes of goods or services in one of the 45 separate classes or categories of goods and services. Each class or category is defined in relation to the nature or description of the goods or services.

The Controller examines the application to make sure that the requirements of the 1996 Act have been fulfilled and once the application for registration has been accepted, it is advertised in the official Patents Office Journal which is published fortnightly and can be viewed on the Patents Office website at www.patentsoffice.ie. Any person is entitled to give notice of opposition to the registration within one month of the advertisement and that period can be extended by two months. If the Controller receives no objection then he registers the trade mark, which lasts for ten years and may be renewed for further periods of ten years (minus one day) on payment of the requisite fee, forever.

Section 17 of the 1996 Act provides that a person who applies for registration of a trade mark may disclaim any right to the exclusive use of any part of the trade mark. Further, the Controller may refuse to accept the application, unless the applicant agrees to make a disclaimer in respect of a particular element of the mark. The registration which subsequently occurs therefore is restricted accordingly.

21.3.3.2   Non-use

Pursuant to s 51 of the 1996 Act, if a trade mark has not been put to genuine use in the State by, or with the consent of, the proprietor for a period of five years, then it may be revoked.

21.3.3.3   Community trade marks

The Community Trade Mark Office (Office for the Harmonisation of the Internal Market ('OHIM')) (www.OHIM.eu) opened in Alicante in Spain in April 1996 to give the applicants for trade marks the facility to apply to a Central Office for a trade mark which is applicable in all of the Member States of the EU. There is a right to claim priority for an application for a period of six months from the date of filing of the first convention application and any filing equivalent to a regular national filing shall be treated as giving rise to the right of priority (1996 Act, s 40).

21.3.3.4   Madrid Protocol

The Madrid Protocol is a system of registration of trade marks, administered by the World Intellectual Property Organization ('WIPO') which allows an applicant to apply for a trade mark in several different jurisdictions by filing one application in a single language, in one trade mark office. The Protocol became operative in Ireland on 19 October 2001. A list of countries which have joined the protocol is to be seen on the WIPO website www.wipo.int/madrid/en/index.html.

21.3.4   BUSINESS NAMES

It is possible to register a business name under the Registration of Business Names Act, 1963 (the '1963 Act'). However, registration does not confer an exclusive right to the name in the registered owner. The purpose of the 1963 Act is to provide a register of firms and individuals trading in the State under a name other than that of the owner or owners of the business.

Thus no exclusive protection is granted to the owner of a business name by registration of it. There may be several registrations for the same name each owned by a different party (see https://www.cro.ie/Registration/Business-Name and Information Leaflet 14 from the CRO regarding business name registration).

21.3.5 COUNTERFEIT AND PIRATED GOODS

Commission Regulation (EC) No. 608/2013 of 29 June 2013 amending previous regulations concerning customs enforcement of intellectual property rights came into force on 1 January 2014 replacing Council Regulation No.1383/2003. This remedy should not be forgotten as it provides a very effective and cheap method of protecting intellectual property in goods being imported from a third country outside the EU. Details of any intellectual property right are lodged with the Customs section of the Revenue Commissioners in Nenagh, along with a form setting out the name of the rights holder etc. Goods which are suspected of infringing intellectual property rights will be held by customs for investigation. A person in Ireland is nominated to inspect goods when they are seized by customs and identify whether they are counterfeit, following which (allowing for a period during which the importer may appeal), they will be destroyed. The form can be found on the Revenue Commissioners' website. There is no charge for this service and the customs personnel are very helpful so it is worthwhile advising clients to lodge the relevant paperwork to avail of this service.

See http://www.revenue.ie/en/customs/leaflets/counterfeit-pirated-goods.html

The procedure is very straightforward and, in comparison with the other remedy of court application for an injunction, for a one-off infringement is from a client's point of view just as useful and much more cost-effective.

21.3.6 INFRINGEMENT

21.3.6.1 Generally

The proprietor of a registered trade mark has exclusive rights in the trade mark and those rights are infringed if someone else uses (1) an identical mark in relation to identical goods or services; (2) an identical or similar mark in relation to similar or identical goods or services and there exists a likelihood of collusion; and (3) an identical or similar mark which has a reputation in the State, and the use being without due cause takes unfair advantage of, or is detrimental to, the distinctive character or the reputation of the trade mark (1996 Act, s 14). 'Use' includes in particular:

(a) affixing a sign to goods or the packaging thereof;

(b) offering or exposing goods for sale, putting them on the market, or stocking them for those purposes under the sign or offering or supplying services under the sign;

(c) importing or exporting goods under the sign; or

(d) using the sign on business papers or in advertising.

21.3.6.2 Exceptions to infringement

No one is prevented from using a registered trade mark to identify goods or services as those of the proprietor or licensee of that registered trade mark, but such use must be in accordance with honest practices. Otherwise it will be treated as infringing the registered trade mark if it takes unfair advantage of, or is detrimental to, the distinctive character or reputation of the trade mark (1996 Act, s 14 (6)).

A trade mark is not infringed by the use of a person of his own name or address or of indications concerning the kind, quality, quantity, intended purpose, value, geographical origin, time of production of goods or of rendering of the service, or other characteristics of goods or services, or where it is necessary to indicate the intended purpose of the product or service, in particular as accessories or spare parts. However, all of these uses must be in accordance with honest practices, industrial and commercial matters (1996 Act, s 15 (2)).

A trade mark will not be infringed by its use on goods which have been put on the market in the European Economic Area by the proprietor of the trade mark or with his consent. This is referred to as the exhaustion of rights of a registered trade mark and stems from EU law, confirming that the owner of a trade mark has exclusive right to use the mark and protect himself against competitors wishing to take advantage of the trade mark, while at the same time prohibiting the owner of the trade mark using his mark to limit the free movement of goods.

However, there may be grounds for preventing the goods being sold, if, for example, their condition has been changed or impaired after they have been put on the market (1996 Act, s 16). Further, a trade mark owner can prevent goods from outside the European Economic Area being sold without his consent even if he has affixed his trade mark to the goods (*Levi Strauss & Co and another v Tesco Stores Limited and another* [2002] EWHC 1556 (Ch)).

21.3.6.3   Remedies

When a mark is infringed, the court has the power to grant an injunction prohibiting the infringement and order the payment of damages and may require the infringer to remove the offending sign or, if that is not possible, to destroy the goods, materials, or articles in question (1996 Act, ss 18, 19).

Section 20 of the 1996 Act makes provision for the owner of a trade mark to apply for an order for the delivery up to him of infringing goods, materials, or articles. Section 23 of the 1996 Act says that the court may make an order destroying goods which have been seized under the 1996 Act, s 20. No rules of court have been made as to the service of notice on the infringer of this application to destroy but, in practice, the court will generally require that the infringer be notified of the application.

21.3.6.4   Seizure orders

Section 25 of the 1996 Act gives the District Court the power to request the Garda Síochána to seize goods, materials, or articles and to bring them before the court. On proof to the District Court that they are infringing goods, materials, or articles the court may make an order delivering them up to the owner of the registered trade mark, ordering them to be destroyed or dealt with in such other way as the court thinks fit. This is an extremely useful remedy if the client's trade marks are being infringed by the sale of counterfeit goods at, for example, a street market or concert. This section also means that an application may be made to the District Court *ex parte*, which provides a cheap and effective remedy for the client.

21.3.6.5   Groundless threats

Section 24 provides that, if proceedings are threatened for an infringement of a registered trade mark when it is not in relation to the application of the mark to goods or the importation of goods to which the mark has been applied or the supply of services under the mark, then the person who receives the threat of the proceedings may seek a declaration that the threats are unjustifiable and may look for an injunction prohibiting the threat and for damages.

21.3.7   ASSIGNMENT AND CHARGES OF REGISTERED TRADE MARKS

Trade marks are transferable by assignment, testamentary disposition, or operation of law in exactly the same way as any personal property may be transferred with either the goodwill of the business or independently. An unregistered trade mark may only be transferred with the benefit of the goodwill of a business. Any assignment must be in writing, signed by the assignor, and sealed, if the assignor is a body corporate.

Registered trade marks may also be charged in the same way as any other personal property. Where a trade mark has been assigned or mortgaged or licensed, particulars of the transaction should be registered with the Controller. If this is not done then the transaction is ineffective as against a third party acquiring a conflicting interest and being unaware of the transfer or mortgage or licence (1996 Act, s 29). Furthermore, unless the application for registration is made within six months of the transaction, or at least as soon as is practicable, the assignee/mortgagee will not be entitled to damages or an award of costs in proceedings in respect of any infringement of the mark occurring after the date of the transaction and before the application for registration of the prescribed participators is made.

21.3.8 LICENSING

Licences of registered trade marks may be granted but they must be in writing and signed by and on behalf of the grantor to be valid. It is wise also to put a notice of the licence on the Register of Trade Marks. If this is not done the owner of the trade mark may be exposed to a claim to expunge the trade mark for non-use.

21.3.9 DOMAIN NAMES

A domain name or Internet protocol address is the name used to identify a website, in the same way as the address of a premises identifies it. The name corresponds to a series of numbers, but for convenience, the addresses have been converted into a more legible form and consist now of two names. Although these names often incorporate trade marks, a domain name will not necessarily become a trade mark, unless it is used to denote origin of goods or services and not merely as part of the website address. A domain name consists of two parts: the top level domain ('TLD') and the second level name. There are two types of TLDs. These are the generic TLDs which are .aero, .biz, .com, .coop, .edu, .gov, .info, .int, .mil, .museum, .name, .net, .org, and .pro plus a special top-level domain (.arpa) for Internet infrastructure and over 200 country code TLDs ('ccTLD'). The ccTLD for Ireland is ie. The second level name is a unique name chosen by its owner.

Since the Internet at its inception was completely unregulated and the Internet Corporation for Assigned Names and Numbers ('ICANN'), which manages top level domains, allowed registration of any name on a first come, first served basis, numerous disputes have arisen in relation to so called 'cybersquatting'. This is the registration of well-known names of businesses of people, or of registered trade marks by third parties who do not own the names, in the hope that the owners will wish to purchase the domain names in order to protect their property right. ICANN administers, through approved dispute resolution providers, a uniform domain name dispute resolution policy, which can be used by parties as an alternative to court proceedings. If a domain name is being used in the course of business, it is sensible for the proprietor to apply to register it as a trade mark. In so doing, it is possible for a monopoly to be held in the name in those jurisdictions in which the trade mark is registered. Applications for registration of a domain name are made for the generic TLDs to an ICANN accredited registrar or to the registrar with responsibility for the relevant ccTLD. A list of accredited registrars worldwide can be viewed on the InterNIC site at www.icann.org. In Ireland, the registrar is the ie domain registry which can be found at www.iedr.ie. Fees for registration vary from registrar to registrar. On 10 December 2009, the European Commission introduced a .eu top level domain name. Over 3.3 million .eu domain names were registered within the first year of its introduction.

21.4 Passing Off

21.4.1 MEANING OF PASSING OFF

Passing off is a tort actionable at common law. It recognises the right of a person to seek to protect the goodwill of his business from unfair trading. It prohibits a third party from selling goods or carrying on business under a name, mark, description, or otherwise in such a manner as is likely to mislead the public or likely to deceive or confuse them into believing that the merchandise or business is that belonging to another person. The most succinct description of passing off is that of Lord Parker in *A. G. Spalding & Brothers v A. W. Gamage Ltd* (1915) 32 RPC 273, a case which involved a stock of the plaintiff's footballs which they had discontinued and which the defendant bought and advertised for sale at very low prices as the latest model.

Lord Parker described the tort of passing off as follows:

> 'Trader A cannot without infringing the rights of Trader B represent goods which are not B's goods or B's goods of a particular class or quality to be B's goods or B's goods of that particular class or quality.'

The right of protection which the plaintiff has is not just to protect a particular mark applied to goods or to protect a reputation but rather to give a trader a property right in the goodwill built up in the business. The courts have accepted that both the word 'trader' and the word 'goodwill' are very broad in meaning and whiskey and champagne makers, actors, and writers have all been granted relief in passing off. So, A cannot without infringing the rights of B represent goods, which are not B's goods, to be B's goods. This, then, is the essence of passing off.

Passing off is now regarded as having been categorically defined in the *Advocaat* case, *Erven Warnink BV v J. Townsend & Sons (Hull) Ltd* [1979] AC 731, where Lord Diplock decreed that there were five characteristics, which must be present in order to create a valid cause of action for passing off:

(a)   a misrepresentation;

(b)   made by a trader in the course of trade;

(c)   to prospective customers of his or ultimate consumers of goods or services supplied by him;

(d)   which is calculated to injure the business or goodwill or another trader (in the sense that this is a reasonably foreseeable consequence); and

(e)   which causes actual damage to a business or goodwill of the trader by whom the action is brought; or (in a *quia timet* action) will probably do so.

All of these characteristics have been endorsed by Clarke J in *Jacob Fruitfield Food Group Ltd v United Biscuits* [2007] IEHC 368.

21.4.2   A MISREPRESENTATION

It should be understood that passing off does not confer a monopoly right in either the name in a trade mark or in the get-up of goods. The action may only succeed if use of any of those things is calculated to mislead or may mislead. The defendant may use any part of the plaintiff's property, provided that he does not do it in a way which will deceive. The basis of the action is that a false representation is made by the defendant so that an association with another person (the plaintiff) is made in the minds of the public. This representation must be material in that there must be a proper risk of damage to the plaintiff.

21.4.3   MADE BY A TRADER IN THE COURSE OF TRADE

Although the *Advocaat* case expressly required the plaintiff to be a trader, this requirement is in fact an unnecessary one. If the plaintiff is not trading, then he cannot suffer damage to his business or to his goodwill. Having said that, what constitutes a trader is, as far as the law of passing off is concerned, extremely wide. Basically, anyone who makes an income from the provision of goods or services may be said to be a trader. Trade associations have been successful in bringing actions for passing off, including, for example, the BBC and the British Medical Association. Charities such as Dr Barnado's Homes have been granted injunctions. In these cases the court accepted the contention that in spite of the fact that the BBC, the British Medical Association, and Dr Barnardo's are non-profit-making organisations they could nonetheless be regarded as trading. On the other hand, a political party was not considered to be a trader on the basis that it was involved in non-commercial activities: *British Medical Association v Marsh* (1931) 48 RPC 565 and *Dean v McGivan* [1982] FSR 119.

21.4.4 TO PROSPECTIVE CUSTOMERS OF HIS

On the face of it evidence of actual deception will be useful examples to persuade a judge that a passing off has occurred. However, at the end of the day, it is settled that the court's decision will not depend solely on the evaluation of such evidence and that 'the court must in the end trust to its own perception into the mind of the reasonable man'. This view has been approved by Laffoy J in the High Court in the interlocutory application in *Symonds Cider & English Wine Co Ltd v Showerings (Ireland) Ltd* 1997 1 ILRM 481, High Court, (unreported), when she did not take into account the surveys of the opinion of the public which had been carried out by both parties as to confusion. Laffoy J was strongly of the view that she was able to decide whether a passing off had occurred without such survey evidence and that it was more appropriate that she should do so.

21.4.5 BUSINESS OR GOODWILL

Goodwill is created by trading. Originally this meant that the plaintiff had to satisfy the court that his business was within the jurisdiction and that he had been trading for some time. However, over the past 20 years or so, the courts have accepted that goodwill may be created in different ways, aside from simply trading within the jurisdiction. In *C&A Modes Ltd v C&A Waterford Ltd* [1978] FSR 126, the Court accepted that even though C&A had no store in the Republic of Ireland, there was a very regular custom from the south to the north of Ireland where C&A had a store in Belfast and a substantial amount of advertising was carried out by C&A in the Sunday magazine supplements, in women's magazines, and on television, all of which was received in the Republic of Ireland. This was the first case where a court accepted that goodwill could be built up from foreign trading.

In *O'Neills Irish International Sports Co Ltd and Charles O'Neill & Co Ltd v O'Neill's Footwear Dryer Co Ltd*, 30 April 1997, High Court, (unreported), Barron J appears to have decided in favour of the plaintiff more on the basis of their reputation than the goodwill they had built up in the name O'Neill. The defendant was a company owned by Mr John O'Neill who had obtained a patent for an electrically-operated shoe dryer. As he could not find any support from sports manufacturers, including the plaintiffs, for his invention and not having sufficient financial resources to manufacture it himself, he decided he would import a similar product from the Far East with a view to encouraging interest from manufacturers in his own product. He sold the imported product in a box similar to a normal shoe box with pictures of different types of shoe and of the dryer on it. The label on the box said that the product was an O'Neill's footwear dryer and referred to Celbridge Ireland and also said 'made in China'. The plaintiffs sought an injunction on the basis of passing off, claiming that they had a reputation in the name O'Neill's and that the defendant was trading on that reputation. It was held that the defendant was deliberately trading upon the plaintiff's reputation and the court found that the defendant was wrong in the belief that he could use his own name and market his product under that name. While a person may use his own name in the course of trade, this does not entitle him to use it in such a way as is calculated to lead others to believe his goods are those of another.

Bayerische Moteren Werke AG v Ronayne t/a BMWCare [2013] IEHC 612 involved a claim for infringement of trade marks and passing off by Mr Ronayne of the BMW roundel logo, BMW word mark, and Original BMW Care Products Natural Care mark. Mr Ronayne who has a small garage in Cloonfad, Co. Roscommon was not an authorised dealer. He was an excellent mechanic and particularly knowledgeable of BMW motor cars. He arranged for a website to be made advertising his skills and using the tag line BMWcare.

The plan was always to ensure that people did not think he was connected to BMW. He did so by always saying he was independent. The website included phrases like; 'Independent advice and assessment'; 'We are proud to be independent' and 'Beholden to no one'. The website designer had wanted to get an alternative logo that looked 'BMW-ish' in case the roundel could not be used.

Mr Ronayne was aware of the decision in *Deenik*, a judgment of the ECJ (*BMW and BMW Nederland v Deenik*, Case C-63/97) which he said meant he could use the BMW marks to make his website look like a BMW site. He was convinced he could use the name provided he made it clear he was not associated with official BMW. He was convinced that BMW could not say he infringed their brand when he always said he was not affiliated to them.

However, the Court found that Mr Ronayne was not a man looking for a name for his business but making a business out of a name. He was not advertising services but creating an identity. He had used the plaintiff's name and merely added a common descriptive word, which amounted to taking on the plaintiff's identity. The distinguishing feature of Mr Ronayne's brand was the plaintiff's trademarked name. His activities were not authorised by any judgments of the European Court of Justice.

21.4.6   DAMAGE

The plaintiff must satisfy the court that the action of a defendant has or is likely to cause the plaintiff damage. The first of these requirements, that is where the plaintiff has already suffered damage, is straightforward in that if confusion in the minds of the public may be proved as to ownership of the goods and it may be argued that the defendant's goods are inferior, then the court may be satisfied that both the goodwill and the reputation of the plaintiff are being damaged. The second category, that is that the action is likely to cause damage, is in practice generally not a difficult proof to overcome. If goodwill and reputation may be shown and if, which is almost always the case, the defendant's products or the services offered are inferior, the court will accept that damage is likely to be caused. In *Falcon Travel v Falcon Leisure Group* [1991] IHR 175 Murphy J took a novel approach to the issue of damage. The plaintiffs had been trading in Dublin for three or four years when Falcon Leisure, the UK tour operator, began trading as well. The plaintiffs were able to show that they were receiving numerous phone calls which should have been for the defendants and that they were losing business from people ringing the defendants when they intended to ring the plaintiffs. The defendants argued that there could be no likelihood of confusion to the public as they were a tour operator and the plaintiff was a travel agency. The defendant also argued that the plaintiff had actually benefited from the confusion rather than having suffered damage. Murphy J agreed that a passing off had occurred and that the plaintiff's reputation had become entirely submerged with that of the defendant. The court found that goodwill, which was appropriated, could constitute damage in itself, without proof of loss of custom. In this case the court awarded damages to the plaintiffs rather than an injunction so that Falcon Travel could launch an advertising campaign to make sure that the public was aware of the difference between the plaintiffs and the defendants.

In *McCambridge Ltd v Joseph Brennan Bakeries* [2011] IEHC 433 the plaintiff succeeded in persuading both the High Court and the Supreme Court that the defendant had passed off their packaging as that of the plaintiff's. The matter came back to the High Court for an assessment of damages and was settled following a full hearing. Mr Justice Charleton decided in any event to deliver the judgment he had written on 27 May 2014 (see http://www.courts.ie/Judgments.nsf/0/825F1316814F0D1280257CE6002B3149). He set out 12 guiding principles.

1) If through legislation a wronged plaintiff in an intellectual property case is enabled to choose either damages or an account of profits, or if that choice is left to the court on making a finding of liability, it is a matter of statutory construction as to how the court proceeds as to the choice of remedy (*Hollister Incorporated and Another v Medik Ostomy Supplies Ltd* [2012] EWCA Civ 1419).

2) Since an account of profits is an equitable remedy, restorative rather than punitive, it may be refused by the court if the result is unfair (*Walsh v Shanahan* [2013] EWCA Civ 411) but at common law a wronged plaintiff in intellectual property actions, particularly passing off, retains the right to seek an account of profits as opposed to damages though, as a separate equitable principle, damages may be declared the proper remedy by a court in refusing an injunction application(*Falcon Travel Ltd v Owners Abroad Group plc trading as Falcon Leisure Group* [1991] 1 IR 175).

3) The form of account of profits in trade mark cases is ordinarily for the entirety of the profits made on articles or services wrongly bearing the mark (*Hollister Incorporated and Another v Medik Ostomy Supplies Ltd* [2012] EWCA Civ 1419, *Cartier v Carlile* (1861) 31 Beav 292), though instances exist where even a trade mark owner cannot fairly claim the entirety of profits (*Hotel Cipriani SLR v Cipriani (Grosvenor Street) Ltd* [2010] EWHC 628).

4) Some passing off cases are close to trade mark cases as to their colourable nature and the blatant approach of the tortfeasor, hence, in those circumstances there is little warrant for seeking a nuanced approach of division of profits (*Woolley and Timesource Limited v UP Global Sourcing UK Limited and The Lacmanda Group Limited* [2014] EWHC 493, *My Kinda Town v Soll* [1983] RPC).

5) Where in patent cases the profit results only partially from the use of the process as part of a wider manufacturing or production system, only the portion of profits properly attributable to that wrongful misuse are recoverable as an account of profits (*Celanese International Corporation v BP Chemicals Ltd* [1990] RPC 203, *Imperial Oil v Lubrizol* [1996] 71 CPR (3d) 26).

6) Copyright mandates a similar approach. The reasoning of basic fairness underpinning this equitable remedy of an account of profit generates that nuanced approach (*House of Spring Gardens Ltd v Point Blank Ltd* [1984] IR 611, *Sheldon v Metro-Goldwyn Pictures Corporation* (1940) 309 UK 390, *Zupanovich v B&N Beale Nominees Pty Ltd* (1995) 59 FCR 49).

7) Ordinarily, where a new product is put on the market and passed off by a defendant who has never produced that product before as that of the plaintiff, or where the expiry of a licence to use indicia of goodwill has been deliberately ignored, the measurement of an account tends to be all profits (*Woolley and Timesource Limited v UP Global Sourcing UK Limited and The Lacmanda Group Limited* [2014] EWHC 493).

8) There are neither reasons of policy or of legal analysis which enables the proper approach to an account of profit in passing off to be treated differently from patent, copyright or trade mark cases, though the statutory foundation on which each of these is based may require particular cases to be treated differently. It would offend common sense to claim, for instance, that because a hotel used a name associated with a protected mark that all the profits of everyone who stayed there are those of the owner of that goodwill and it is to be noted in relation to passing off that such a claim was not made in *Hotel Cipriani SLR v Cipriani (Grosvenor Street) Ltd* [2010] EWHC 628.

9) Depending of the facts, passing off may be approached differently as to a product already made by the defendant and then got up so that it may be seen as calculated to deceive or where it is clear that only a proportion of the customers switching to the product passed off in infringement of the plaintiff's entitlement to its goodwill

and there the approach may be a nuanced one of part of the profits only (*My Kinda Town v Soll* [1983] RPC 15).

10)   Though intention has long since ceased to be part of the ingredients of the tort of passing off, provable malice may make it more worthwhile for a plaintiff to seek damages than the equitable remedy of an account of profit because damages in those circumstances can be, but need not be, aggravated or exemplary.

11)   A broad approach to apportioning profits should be taken by a court, remembering that the plaintiff is the wronged party and that obscure argument by economists is not what drives consumption in the marketplace.

12)   Apportioning profits is not an impossible task. Jobs as hard in damages are done every day by the courts. Primarily, profit levels before and after should be considered as should the make up of the offending goods and the probability of the confusion resulting as to what proportion of customers.

These cases therefore are the latest law on the Irish approach to the assessment of damages in a passing off claim and presumably also influential in all intellectual property cases.

21.5   Copyright and Designs

21.5.1   INTRODUCTION

Copyright subsists in the physical material of a wide variety of work. The protection does not extend to ideas or principles, which underlie any element of a work. Thus copyright is a negative right to prevent the reproduction, including copying, of physical material.

21.5.2   COPYRIGHT AND DESIGN PROTECTION

21.5.2.1   Statutory regulation

Copyright is now governed by the Copyright and Related Rights Act 2000, the Copyright and Related Rights (Amendment) Act 2004, the Copyright and Related Rights (Amendment) Act 2007, and sections of the Patents (Amendment) Act 2006 (the '2000 Act'). Designs are protected by the Industrial Designs Act, 2001 (the '2001 Act').

In 2013, the Copyright Review Committee published its report; identifying areas of the legislation that might be deemed to create barriers to innovation; and making recommendations to resolve problems identified. The Committee was chaired by Dr Eoin O'Dell of Trinity College. A draft Bill accompanies the report (see http://www.djei.ie/science/ipr/crc_index.htm).

The European Union (Copyright and Related Rights) Regulations 2012, provide a legal basis for the owners of the copyright in a work to seek an injunction in certain circumstances against Internet Service Providers ('ISPs'). The legislation is intended to address a gap in the 2000 Act which was highlighted by the High Court in October 2010 in the case of *EMI Records Ireland Ltd & Others v UPC Communications Ireland Ltd* [2010] IEHC 377. In that case, Charleton J held that as he was constrained by the wording of the 2000 Act, he could not grant an injunction to prevent infringement of copyright against an ISP in the circumstances of a 'mere conduit' (transient communications).

21.5.2.2   Subsistence of copyright

Copyright is a property right, like any other, which permits the owner of the copyright to authorise third parties to do certain things in relation to a work which would, except for the existence of the 2000 Act, be prohibited or, to use the word used in the 2000 Act, restricted.

Copyright subsists in:

(a) original literary, dramatic, musical, or artistic works;

(b) sound recordings, films, broadcasts, or cable programmes;

(c) the typographical arrangement of published editions; and

(d) original databases (s 17(2)).

21.5.2.3   Designs

The 2001 Act provides that a design is registrable if it is new and has individual character. A design 'means the appearance of the whole or a part of a product resulting from the features of, in particular, the lines, contours, colour, shape, texture or materials of the product itself or its ornamentation' (2001 Act, s 2). Thus, any part of a product which is decorative constitutes a design. A product 'means any industrial or handicraft item, including parts intended to be assembled into a complex product, packaging, get-up, graphic symbols and typographical typefaces, but not including computer programs' (2001 Act, s 2).

A design which is new and has individual character on a worldwide basis is registrable under the 2001 Act, in a register maintained by the Controller. However there is a provision, which allows a design to be made available to the public for a period of up to one year before filing for a design registration. The author of a design shall be treated as the first proprietor, unless the design is made in the course of employment in which case the employer is the first proprietor. The provisions for registration and rectification of the register are similar to those for registration of a trade mark and designs are classified in a prescribed system of classification. There is a priority right of six months in respect of an application made in a country which is a signatory to the Paris Convention for the Protection of Industrial Property 1883.

Both an application for registration and a registered design constitute a property right. A registration lasts for a period of five years and may be renewed upon payment of a fee for four subsequent periods of five years, resulting in a total period of registration of 25 years (s 43). The 2000 Act, in addition, provides that copyright in a registered design expires after a period of 25 years (s 31A). The provisions relating to licensing, infringement, offences, remedies, search and seizure, exhaustion of rights, and groundless threats are all similar to those of trade marks. Section 78 of the 2000 Act provides that copyright in a work is not infringed by anything done pursuant to an assignment or licence from a person registered under the 2001 Act and in good faith and in reliance on such registration without notice of any proceedings for the cancellation of the registration.

Council Regulation (EC) No. 6/2002 on Community designs establishes a system for registration of industrial designs providing protection throughout the Community in the same manner as the system for trade marks. The system came into operation in 2003 and is administered by OHIM. The European Communities (Community Designs) Regulations 2003 give effect in Ireland to the provisions of the Regulations (SI 27/2003).

The Irish Court considered the Design Regulations in *Karen Millen Ltd v Dunnes Stores and others* [2007] IEHC 449. The case concerned a shirt which was not a registered design but benefited from the unregistered design right. The court found that the shirt had individual character and granted an order against *Dunnes Stores*. The case was appealed to the Supreme Court which made a reference to the ECJ, which ruled on 19 June 2014 that for a design to have individual character, the overall impression which the design produces must be different from earlier designs and that it is not up to the right holder to prove the individual character of a design to benefit from the unregistered Community design right. Dunnes Stores' appeal was as a consequence dismissed by the Supreme Court [2014] IESC 23 in July 2014.

Section 79 of the 2000 Act provides that the making of any object which is in three dimensions will not be an infringement of copyright in a two-dimensional work if the object would not appear to a person who is not an expert in relation to objects of that description to be a reproduction of it.

21.5.3   OWNERSHIP: MEANING OF AUTHOR

Section 21 of the 2000 Act defines the term author by reference to different circumstances. Author means the person who creates a work. In the case of a sound recording, this is the producer. In the case of a film, the producer and the principal director are the authors. In the case of a broadcast, the person making the broadcast is the author. In the case of a cable programme, the person providing the cable programme service in which the programme is included is the author. In the case of a typographical arrangement or a published edition, the publisher is the author. In the case of a work which is computer generated, the person by whom the arrangement necessary for the creation of the work is undertaken is the author. In the case of an original database, the individual or group of individuals who made the database is the author. In the case of a photograph, the photographer is the author (2000 Act, s 21).

Section 23 provides that the author of the work is the first owner of the copyright. However, there are three exceptions to this rule:

(a) where the work is made by an employee in the course of employment, the employer is the first owner of any copyright in the work subject to any agreement to the contrary;

(b) where the work is the subject of government or Oireachtas copyright then the author is not regarded as the first owner. If the work is the subject of the copyright of a prescribed international organisation or the copyright in the work is conferred on some other person by an enactment, then the author will not be the first owner of the copyright; and

(c) where a work, except a computer program, is made by an author in the course of employment by the proprietor of a newspaper or periodicals, the author may use the work for any purpose except for making it available to newspapers or periodicals without infringing the copyright.

21.5.4   DURATION OF COPYRIGHT

21.5.4.1   Literary, dramatic, musical, or artistic work

Section 24 of the 2000 Act provides that copyright in a literary, dramatic, musical, or artistic work or in an original database lasts for 70 years after the death of the author. In the case of such a work, which is anonymous or pseudonymous, copyright will expire 70 years after the date on which the work is first lawfully made available to the public. Where the author becomes known during that seventy-year period, copyright will expire 70 years after the death of that author.

21.5.4.2   Films

Section 25 of the 2000 Act states that copyright in a film lasts for 70 years after the last of the following people dies: (a) the principal director of the film; (b) the author of the screenplay of the film; (c) the author of the dialogue of the film; or (d) the author of music specifically composed for use in the film.

In a case where a film is first made available to the public during the period of 70 years following the death of the last of these people, copyright will expire 70 years after the date of such making available.

21.5.4.3   Sound recordings

Section 26 of the 2000 Act states that copyright in a sound recording lasts for 50 years after the sound recording is made or, where it is first made available to the public during that 50-fifty-year period, for 50 years from the date of such making available to the public.

21.5.4.4   Broadcasts

Section 27 of the 2000 Act provides that copyright in a broadcast lasts for 50 years after the broadcast is first lawfully transmitted. Copyright in every repeat broadcast expires at the same time as the original broadcast.

21.5.4.5   Cable programme

Section 28 of the 2000 Act provides that copyright in a cable programme will expire 50 years after the cable programme is first lawfully included in a cable programme service. Again, copyright in a repeat cable programme expires at the same time as the original one.

21.5.4.6   Typographical arrangements

Section 29 of the 2000 Act provides that copyright in a typographical arrangement of a published edition lasts for 50 years from the date it is first made available to the public.

21.5.4.7   Computer-generated works

Section 30 of the 2000 Act provides that copyright in a work which is computer generated lasts for 70 years after the date on which the work is first lawfully made available.

21.5.4.8   Copyright in works in volumes, parts, etc.

Section 31 of the 2000 Act provides that where a work is made available to the public in volumes, parts, instalments, issues, or episodes and the copyright subsists from the date on which the work is so made available, copyright subsists in each separate item.

21.5.4.9   Works not previously available

Where a work is made available to the public for the first time after the expiration of the copyright, the person who makes it available will have the same rights as the author, except for moral rights, for 25 years from the date the work is made available.

21.5.5   INFRINGEMENT

21.5.5.1   Rights restricted

Under the provisions of s 37 of the 2000 Act, the owner of copyright in a work has the exclusive right to undertake or authorise others to undertake all of the following acts, namely:

(a)   to copy the work;

(b)   to make available to the public the work; and

(c)   to make an adaptation of the work.

Each of those acts is called 'acts restricted by copyright'. Copyright is infringed if any of the acts restricted is done by any person without the consent of the owner/author of a copyright. The Copyright and Related Rights (Amendment) Act, 2004 (entitled 'an act to remove doubt in relation to the lawfulness under the Copyright and Related Rights Act, 2000, of displaying certain works in public') inserted a new subsection 7(A) into s 40. The amendment provides that 'for the avoidance of doubt, no infringement of any right . . . in relation to an artistic or literary work occurs by reason of the placing on display the work, or a copy thereof, in a place or premises to which members of the public have access'. The amendment arose as a result of the centenary celebration of James Joyce's Bloomsday. An exhibition of original manuscripts of Joyce's works by the National Library was to be held as part of the celebration. However, the press reported threats of legal action for breach of copyright if the works were exhibited. The Oireachtas passed this legislation and as a result the display by the National Library of the original manuscripts, copy manuscripts, and first editions of Joycean works were no longer a restricted act under s 37 of the 2000 Act and there was no infringement.

21.5.5.2 Secondary infringement

Secondary infringement comprises a number of dealings with a work without the permission of the copyright owner, including selling, importing, making, or having in his or her possession, custody, or control a copy of the work knowing it to be an infringing copy, or having an article specifically designed or adapted for making copies of that work knowing that it has been or is to be used to make infringing copies.

21.5.5.3 Acts permitted in relation to copyright works

Chapter 6 of the 2000 Act sets out certain acts, which are exempted from infringement (2000 Act, ss 49–106).

These include such matters as fair dealing, that is, making use of a work for a purpose and to an extent reasonably justified by the non-commercial purpose to be achieved. For example, fair dealing may be for research or for private study, for criticism, or for review (2000 Act, ss 50, 51).

Copyright in a work is not infringed if it is copied in the course of educational instruction or in preparation for education and instruction (2000 Act, s 53). Librarians or archivists are permitted to make copies of a work for various purposes, again of a non-commercial nature (2000 Act, ss 61–70).

Copyright is not infringed in a work by anything done for the purpose of parliamentary or judicial proceedings or for the purpose of reporting those proceedings, nor is it infringed for the purposes of a statutory enquiry (2000 Act, s 71).

Any material comprised in records, which are open to public inspection, may be copied and a copy may be supplied to anyone without infringing copyright (2000 Act, s 73).

A back-up copy of a computer program may be made without infringing copyright (2000 Act, s 80). Copyright is not infringed when anything is done for the purposes of reconstructing a building (2000 Act, s 96).

21.5.6 MORAL RIGHTS

The Berne Convention on copyright requires that, independently of the author's economic rights and even after transfer of the said rights, the author shall have the right to claim authorship of the work and to object to any distortion, mutilation, or other modification of or other derogatory action in relation to the said work which 'would be prejudicial to his honour or reputation'. These were introduced into Irish law for the first time in the 2000 Act.

Section 107 of the 2000 Act provides the paternity right. This is the right of the author to be identified as such. There are certain exceptions to these rules, including where copyright in the work originally vested in an employer, where the work is made for the purposes of a newspaper or periodical, or where government or Oireachtas copyright subsists in the work.

Section 109 of the 2000 Act recognises the integrity right. This is the right of the author of a work to object to any distortion, mutilation or other modification of or other derogatory action in relation to the work, which would prejudice his reputation. The integrity right does not apply to a work made for the purpose of reporting current events or of a newspaper or periodical. The integrity right is qualified in respect of works in which the copyright originally vested in the author's employer.

Pursuant to the 2000 Act, s 116 moral rights may be waived. Moral rights are not capable of assignment or alienation (2000 Act, s 118). Moral rights may be passed on the death of the person entitled to the right (s 119).

21.5.7 PERFORMER'S RIGHTS

A performer is granted rights by the 2000 Act for the first time in Irish law. The rights granted under s 203 are the exclusive right to authorise or to prohibit:

(a) the making of a recording of the whole or any substantial part of a qualifying performance directly from the live performance;

(b) the broadcasting live, or including live in a cable programme service, of the whole or any substantial part of a qualifying performance; or

(c) the making of a recording of the whole or any substantial part of a qualifying performance directly from a broadcast or a cable programme including the live performance.

21.5.8 DATABASE RIGHT

The 2000 Act introduces for the first time in Irish law a property right in a database, which consists of the creation of a mechanical collection or arrangement of facts or information which does not require skill or judgement to compile. This is a separate or '*sui generis*' right, which lasts for a period of 15 years and exists in addition to copyright subsisting in original databases referred to at **21.5.2.2** above. The Database Right was introduced by Directive 96/9 of the European Parliament and of the Council, to ensure uniform protection throughout EU Member States. To date there has only been one significant case relating to the interpretation of this Directive. This case is the *British Horseracing Board Limited and others v William Hill Organisation Limited* [2001] All ER (D) 431. Judgment in this matter was given by Laddie J on 9 February 2001. This case was concerned with the extent to which the plaintiffs could prevent the defendant from using, without their licence, certain data, which according to the plaintiff had been derived indirectly from them.

In this case it was argued, that the indirect capture of data (i.e. through a third party) from a database was not an extraction as it merely replicated the data. This argument was rejected. It was also argued that in the case of the database that was consistently updated, repeated and systematic taking of minor data could not be considered to be cumulative and therefore could not be considered to be an infringement, as the data was taken from different databases. This argument was also rejected. The case was appealed and the Court of Appeal referred a number of questions to the European Court of Justice ('ECJ'). The judgment of the ECJ was handed down on 9 November 2004. The ECJ agreed that the British Horseracing Board's central database fell within the criteria for protection by Directive 96/9. The Court held that as the data extracted and used by William Hill did not involve a substantial investment, independent of the costs of creating the data, the data did not constitute a substantial part of the contents of the database. Therefore William Hill's activities did not amount to an infringement of those rights.

21.5.9 LICENSING

As with any property right, copyright may be licensed. A range of copyright may subsist in, for example, a song, where there is copyright in the lyrics, in the music, in the sound recording, and in the performance, or in a book, where copyright may subsist in the text and in the typographical arrangement. Chapters 16 and 17 of Part II of the 2000 Act contain detailed provisions as to licensing bodies which administer schemes for the licensing of copyright in works in which rights are held by more than one owner. Section 175 of the 2000 Act provides for the establishment of a register of copyright licensing bodies who collect fees or royalty payments for use of this copyright. The Copyright and Related Rights (Register of Copyright Licensing Bodies) Regulations 2002 set up this register and several collection agencies have been registered.

21.5.10   DELIVERY UP AND SEIZURE

Section 256 of the 2000 Act provides, that the owner of rights in a recording of a performance may apply to the District Court for a seizure order addressed to the Garda Síochána to seize illicit recordings, articles used to make illicit recordings, or protection-defeating devices, where such items are being hawked, carried about, or marketed and, subsequently, for such items to be destroyed or delivered up to the rights owner. Hearsay evidence will be permitted in any such application and the witness will not be required to reveal the source of his information. However, the applicant exposes himself to a claim in damages if, at the end of the day, no infringement is established or the application was made maliciously.

Section 257 of the 2000 Act introduces a novel application allowing a rights owner to seize recordings, articles, or devices without the protection of a court order where it is impractical to seek an order first and subsequently to seek an order for destruction or for delivery up. Notice must first be given to the Garda Síochána for the district and the items may not be seized at a permanent or regular place of business. The section is clearly designed to assist rights owners at concerts and similar occasions.

21.6   Confidential Information

21.6.1   INTRODUCTION

This branch of intellectual property law deals with the protection of 'know-how'. Know-how may be secret formulae, secret processes as used in the manufacture of a product, or something as simple as the names of customers and other sales information which, if disclosed to the competing business, would cause significant harm to the owner.

In certain cases an employer will impose an obligation of confidentiality on an employee in relation to proprietary information rather than apply for patent protection for a secret invention. This may operate as a more effective protection, since a patent has to be published and put into the public domain. This gives competitors the opportunity to improve upon the invention to such an extent that they may produce the second generation of product or a product entirely different, which is also patentable and does not infringe the first product. On the other hand, if employees are bound by contract to keep their employers' invention secret then it may never come into the public domain like, for example, the secret formula for the manufacture of Coca-Cola.

The court, in a case of confidential information, is being asked to enforce a moral obligation. An equitable principle is invoked, that a person to whom something was made known in confidence cannot use the knowledge to the detriment of the informant.

21.6.2   RELATIONSHIPS IMPOSING CONFIDENTIALITY

In order to assess whether a relationship is one which imposes confidentiality, the court must first decide whether there exists from the relationship between the parties an obligation of confidence regarding the information which had been imparted and it must then decide whether the information which was communicated could properly be regarded as confidential. Once it is established that an obligation of confidence exists and that the information is confidential, then the person to whom it is given has the duty to act in good faith and this means that he must use the information for the purpose for which it is imparted to him and cannot use it to the detriment of the informant. The explanation of what constitutes confidential information was given by Costello J in *House of Spring Gardens Ltd v Point Blank Ltd* [1984] IR 611. This case is the leading case in the area of confidential information in Ireland and largely follows the English dicta on the subject.

In general, the areas where an obligation of confidence would be imposed may be divided into two sections:

(a)   the protection of trade secrets/confidential information in non-employment cases. Thus, for example, where a plaintiff has employed a third party company to carry out a project on the plaintiff's behalf, an obligation of confidence will be imposed upon that third party and upon the plaintiff, not to use the information without consent; and

(b)   the protection of trade secrets in the master and servant situation. (In the course of employment, an employee has a duty to do nothing, which would conflict with the business interests of their employer. It is always safest, where at all possible, to avoid argument in this area and to insert in an employee's contract of employment in clear terms an obligation to keep information including trade secrets and skill and experience gained during the employment confidential.)

Once the contract of employment has concluded and an employee has left the employment, there is nonetheless a duty not to use confidential information. The leading case in this area is *Faccenda Chicken Ltd v Fowler* [1986] 1 All ER 617. In this case Neill LJ found that there were three types of information acquired by a servant in the course of employment:

(1)   trivia/public information which is not protected;

(2)   skill and experience which is not protected, although it could be restricted by contract in restriction of trade clause. (This type of information is protected during the course of the employment under the duty of fidelity owed by the employee to his employer.) After the employment ends, subject to any competitive restraints, the employee is free to use his skills and experience elsewhere; and

(3)   trade secrets so confidential that, even though they have been learned by heart, cannot be used for anyone's benefit but that of the employer and are protected even after the employee leaves employment.

21.6.3   REMEDIES

The remedies for breach of confidential information are an injunction to restrain the breach of confidential information and damages or an account of profits. In *Nu glue Adhesives v Burgess Galvin*, 23 March 1982, High Court, (unreported), McWilliam J found that if there had been an abuse of confidential information, damages would be limited to an amount equal to six weeks' salary for a chemist. He considered that the defendants could have come up with the formula themselves within a six-week period.

Where the court is asked to award an injunction, that injunction must be capable of being framed with sufficient precision to enable the enjoined party to know what it is he may not do (*Lawrence David Ltd v Ashton* [1991] 1 All ER 385).

In *Terrapin v Builders' Supply Co (Hayes) Ltd* [1960] RPC 128, Roxburgh J defined what he called the 'springboard' formula. He said:

'As I understand it, the essence of this branch of the law, whatever the origin of it may be, is that a person who has obtained information in confidence is not allowed to use it as a spring-board for activities detrimental to the person who made the confidential communication, and spring-board it remains even when all the features have been published or can be ascertained by actual inspection by members of the public. The possessor of such information must be placed under a special disability in the field of competition in order to ensure that he does not get an unfair start.'

Roxburgh J granted the plaintiff an injunction.

The courts, however, have found difficulties with the 'springboard' doctrine and have in some instances suggested that rather than an injunction being granted, the correct course is to compensate the plaintiff in damages (*Coco v A. N. Clark (Engineers) Ltd* [1969] RPC 41).

In some cases, in order to overcome the advantage gained by an employee in using confidential information, the court will impose an injunction for a period of time that it considers sufficient to enable a member of the public to come up with the formula themselves.

Moreover, it should be noted that overall it is often extremely difficult to prove a plaintiff employer's case to a degree sufficient to persuade a court to grant an injunction and the importance of ensuring the employers put in place properly drafted and reasonable contractual terms dealing with confidential information cannot be over-emphasised.

CHAPTER 22

INFORMATION TECHNOLOGY

22.1   What is Technology Law?

Information technology, in its various guises, is crucial for modern business. A modern business may establish a website or social media profile as a form of marketing. It may keep a database of its customers. It may send marketing emails or sell its products online. Its staff may use computers or handheld devices to do their job. It may contract through its website. These activities give rise to novel legal issues, and there are specific rules that apply to the use of information technology by business. This chapter explores some of the most important, including data protection, electronic marketing, online sales (also known as 'ecommerce'), the electronic execution and storage of documents, and the monitoring of employees' use of workplace computers.

While this chapter considers these specific rules, solicitors advising in this area should remember that, in most circumstances, the same legal rules apply online and offline. For example, an online contract still needs to comply with the basic rules of offer and acceptance, and online advertising still needs to comply with the usual rules set out in the Consumer Protection Act 2007.

22.2   Data Protection Law and Practice

The Data Protection Acts, 1988 and 2003 apply to any business which 'processes' or uses 'personal data' (i.e. information relating to an identifiable person such as its customers or employees). In practical terms, these rules apply to virtually every business operating in Ireland.

22.2.1   INTRODUCTION

Governments and businesses have historically held and processed information about their citizens and customers. However, the development of computers revolutionised the processing of data. Computers allow huge amounts of personal information to be held in any one place and in relation to any one individual. The development of computer networks, particularly the Internet, allows vast quantities of data to be transferred between physical locations. In addition, much of modern commercial life and government activities involve the capture and use of information about individuals. The proliferation of smartphones and other smart devices coupled with modern analytics tools has resulted in an exponential increase in recent years in the amount of personal data that is captured and processed.

Performing daily activities, such as opening bank accounts, taking out insurance policies, using credit cards and debit cards, applying for store 'loyalty cards', all enable information to be gathered about a person's spending and leisure habits. Even browsing the Internet can enable information to be gathered in respect of website visitors. The use of sophisticated information capturing devices, such as 'cookies' and similar technologies, permit website and app owners to gather information on visitors.

In Ireland, these activities are primarily regulated by the Data Protection Act 1988 (the '1988 Act') and the Data Protection (Amendment) Act 2003 (the '2003 Act') which are construed together as one Act (the 'Acts'). The 2003 Act transposed the provisions of Directive 95/46/EC on the protection of individuals with regard to the processing of personal data and on the free movement of data (usually known as the Data Protection Directive) into Irish law and significantly amended many of the provisions of the 1988 Act.

In addition to the Acts, Irish law also recognises a broad 'right to privacy' that is protected by the Constitution, the Charter of Fundamental Rights, and the European Convention on Human Rights.

22.2.2   KEY DEFINITIONS

The Acts use a number of technical terms. Solicitors need to understand how these terms are defined.

(a) *'Data Controllers'* are persons who either alone or with others control the content and use of personal data.

(b) *'Data Processors'* are persons that process data on behalf of Data Controllers (excluding employees of Data Controllers).

(c) *'Personal data'* includes automated (i.e. computerised) and manual data (data that is recorded as part of a structured filing system) relating to a living individual who is or can be identified from the data or from the data in conjunction with other information which is in the Data Controller's possession or which is likely to come into such possession. In simple terms, personal data is information about a living person stored electronically or on a structured manual file.

(d) The *'Data Subject'* is the person who is the subject of the personal data.

'Processing' is given a very broad definition in the Acts. It is defined as performing any operation or set of operations on the information or data, whether or not by automatic means. The definition goes on to give a non-exhaustive list of examples of processing which includes obtaining data, recording data, collecting data, storing data, altering or adapting data, retrieving data, consulting data, using data, disclosing data, or blocking, erasing, or destroying data. In practical terms, doing almost anything with personal data may well constitute the processing of that personal data.

These definitions may be made clearer with an example:

Example:

Bank A collects information about its customers to operate those customers' accounts. This information is processed on behalf of Bank A in computer servers operated by a Technology Company B.

In this simple example, Bank A is the Data Controller. Technology Company B is the Data Processor. The Bank's customers are the Data Subjects. The information relating to the Bank's customers is 'personal data' and the various things that are done to that personal data, including collecting it and storing it on the computer systems constitutes the 'processing' of that data.

22.2.3 DUTIES OF DATA CONTROLLERS

Section 2 of the Acts, read in conjunction with ss 2C and 2D of the Acts, imposes a number of obligations on Data Controllers. These are discussed below.

(a) Individuals should be made fully aware at the time they provide personal information of:

   (i) the identity of the persons who are collecting it (though this may often be implied);

   (ii) to what use the information will be put; and

   (iii) the persons or category of persons to whom the information will be disclosed.

(b) Secondary or future uses, which might not be obvious to individuals, should be brought to their attention at the time their personal data is obtained. Individuals should be given the option of saying whether or not they wish their information to be used in these other ways.

(c) If a Data Controller has information about people and wishes to use it for a new purpose (which was not disclosed and perhaps not even contemplated at the time the information was collected), he or she is obliged to give an option to individuals to indicate whether or not they wish their information to be used for the new purpose.

These first three requirements are generally understood as representing the requirement to process data fairly. From a practical perspective, in order to ensure compliance with these fair processing requirements, companies regularly issue notices to their employees and their customers describing how they process their data. Similarly website privacy policies describe how companies obtain and process personal data from web users fairly.

It should be noted that a stricter test of 'fairness' may be applied where the data subject is a minor. The Data Protection Commissioner has suggested that when dealing with the personal data of minors, the standard of fairness in the obtaining and use of the data may be more onerous than when dealing with data relating to an adult. The Article 29 Working Party (the European Commission's data protection advisory body) has made similar observations, arguing that the duty to process personal data fairly must be interpreted strictly when the data subject is under age. As a result, Data Controllers must exercise utmost good faith when processing a child's data.

(d) Personal data shall be accurate, complete, and, where necessary, kept up to date. Section 1(2) of the Acts clarifies this obligation somewhat by defining inaccurate data as data that is incorrect or misleading as to any matter of fact.

(e) Personal data shall be held only for one or more specified, explicit, and legitimate purposes. Thus, collecting information about people routinely and indiscriminately, without having a sound, clear, and legitimate purpose for doing so, will result in a breach of this obligation. When collecting personal data, Data Controllers should clearly and explicitly specify to the Data Subject the purpose for which the personal data is being collected and stored.

(f) Personal data shall not be further processed in a manner incompatible with that purpose or those purposes. According to guidelines issued by the Data Protection Commissioner, a key test of compatibility is whether you use and disclose the data in a way in which those who supplied the information would expect it to be used and disclosed. This test was failed by Westwood Swimming Ltd. in circumstances where it used its CCTV system to monitor an employee. It was held that the leisure centre contravened the Acts by using CCTV images, which were stated to have been obtained for security purposes, for the separate, and incompatible, purpose of employee monitoring. (Case Study 9 of the 2011 Report of the Data Protection Commissioner).

(g)   Personal data shall be adequate, relevant, and not excessive in relation to that purpose or those purposes for which they were collected or further processed. This requirement is often breached where a business seeks more information from a consumer than is strictly necessary to provide the good or service sought. For example, property management companies have been found in default where they seek excessive information about residents (e.g. a copy of passport/driving licence, PPS Number, emergency contact details, vehicle details, employment details, copy of a current lease/tenancy agreement, etc.) which is not necessary for the installation of a new keypad access system (Case Study 4 of the 2013 Report of the Data Protection Commissioner).

(h)   Personal data shall not be kept for longer than is necessary for that purpose or those purposes. This obligation may have been broken by the Public Appointments Service when the organisation retained the files of applicants for positions in the Civil Service for a period of 30 years (Case Study 11 of the 2011 Report of the Data Protection Commissioner).

(i)   Appropriate security measures shall be taken against unauthorised access to or unauthorised alteration, disclosure, or destruction of personal data, particularly where the processing involves the transmission of data over a network and against all other forms of processing.

Section 2C of the Acts expands upon this obligation concerning security measures and provides that Data Controllers must put in place appropriate security provisions for the protection of personal data, having regard to: (i) the current state of technological development; (ii) the cost of implementing security measures; (iii) the nature of the personal data; and (iv) the harm that might result from unauthorised processing or loss of the data concerned. Data Controllers and Data Processors are also obliged to take all reasonable steps to ensure that their employees, and other persons at the place of work concerned are aware of and comply with the relevant security measures.

Section 2C goes on to provide that if a Data Controller uses a third party to process data (i.e. if the Data Controller engages a Data Processor), the processing of such data should be covered by a contract which contains certain prescribed terms. This contract should stipulate at least the following:

(a)   the conditions under which data may be processed;

(b)   the minimum security measures that the Data Processors must have in place; and

(c)   some mechanism or provision that will enable the Data Controller to ensure that the Data Processor is compliant with the security requirement (this might include a right of inspection or independent audit).

Since various commercial arrangements entail a personal data processing component, an increasing number of commercial contracts need to have provisions along the lines set out above.

22.2.4   PRE-CONDITIONS TO PROCESSING

Sections 2A and 2B of the Acts lay down the pre-conditions that must be met before personal data can be lawfully processed.

Section 2A contains the general rule that personal data shall not be processed by a Data Controller unless the Data Controller complies with its obligations under s 2 (outlined in **22.2.3** above) *and* at least one of the pre-conditions contained in s 2A (1) is satisfied (i.e. these obligations are cumulative). Section 2A goes on to set out a series of pre-conditions to the processing of personal data.

When this broad definition of processing (discussed above in **22.2.2** above) is read in the context of the rule that processing cannot take place unless one of the pre-conditions in s 2A (1) is satisfied, it transpires that virtually no dealings in personal data can be carried out by a Data Controller unless one of the pre-conditions contained in this section is satisfied.

22.2.4.1 Consent

The first and most important pre-condition, contained in s 2A, provides that data may be processed where the Data Subject has given his or her consent to such processing. The Data Protection Directive gives us some guidance as to the meaning of 'consent' by indicating that a Data Subject's consent must be freely given, specific, and informed. The minimum age at which consent can be legitimately obtained was not defined in the Acts. Section 2A (1) of the Acts states that consent cannot be obtained from a person who, by reason of age is likely to be unable to appreciate the nature and effect of such consent. Judging maturity will vary from case to case. The Data Protection Commissioner has indicated that in the marketing area, where sensitive data is involved, including on websites, it is a matter for the Data Controller to judge if a person of a certain age can appreciate the issues surrounding consent and to be able to demonstrate that a person of that age can understand the information supplied and the implications of giving consent.

There exists an ongoing debate in the EU as to what precisely constitutes consent. From a Data Controller's perspective, it is always easier to ascertain an individual's consent by asking the individual to indicate if he or she objects to his or her data being processed (the 'opt-out procedure'). On the other hand, advocates of privacy rights have argued that in order for a consent to be valid, the Data Subject is required to indicate expressly that he or she consents to his or her data being processed (the 'opt in procedure').

Certain Member States have sought to clarify this issue in transposing Directive 95/46/EC. On the other hand, the Irish legislature has not provided any particularly clear guidance in this regard. However, it is notable that the earlier drafts of the Data Protection Bill, 2002, which was ultimately enacted as the 2003 Act, did provide that the consent should be 'explicit'. This requirement was dropped from the final version of the Bill that was enacted and thus, in the absence of any requirement of 'explicit' consent in s 2A (1)(a), it can be argued that use of the 'opt-out' procedure or implied consent may in certain circumstances be sufficient in order to ascertain consent under the Irish legislation. However, it remains to be seen how the judiciary will interpret this requirement.

22.2.4.2 Other pre-conditions

Section 2A (1) goes on to contain a number of other pre-conditions, which must be carefully considered if a Data Controller proposes to process data without the consent of the relevant Data Subjects. These pre-conditions include where the processing is necessary for the performance of a contract to which the data subject is a party, where the processing is necessary to prevent an injury or other damage to the health of the Data Subject, where the processing is necessary to protect an individual's vital interests, where the processing is necessary for the administration of justice, or where the processing is necessary for the purposes of the legitimate interests pursued by a Data Controller or a third party recipient of the data.

22.2.5 THE PROCESSING OF SENSITIVE PERSONAL DATA

Section 2B contains an additional set of pre-conditions one of which must be satisfied prior to the processing of sensitive personal data. Sensitive personal data is defined as including data concerning racial or ethnic origin, political opinion, religious belief, trade union membership, mental or physical health, sexual life, or data concerning the committing of an offence or proceedings in relation to an offence.

Without going into detail in relation to the pre-conditions for the processing of sensitive data, it should be noted that one of the first of these pre-conditions is that the 'explicit' consent of the Data Subject is given, before a Data Controller can process sensitive personal data. In other words, the use of some type of an 'opt-out' procedure would not appear to be adequate in these circumstances as it is unlikely to be treated as explicit consent.

22.2.6   NON-COMPLIANCE WITH DUTIES

It must be stressed that non-compliance with the principles set out in s 2 (1) of the Acts, or a failure to ensure that pre-condition under s 2A or 2B has been met, does not automatically constitute a criminal offence. However, it may lead to a complaint being made by a Data Subject to the Data Protection Commissioner who may take action by issuing an Enforcement Notice (pursuant to s 10 (2) of the Acts). In addition, the Data Controller may be liable under ordinary common law principles (e.g. the law of confidence, the law of contract, or the law of tort), where the Data Controller fails to comply with its obligations as set out in s 2 of the Acts.

A Data Controller may also be in breach of its duty of care under s 7 of the Acts where it fails to adhere to its obligations in the Acts. Section 7 creates a general duty of care for the Data Controller to the Data Subject. Subject to certain limitations, a person who has suffered loss as a result of non-compliance with the Acts may recover damages in tort against the Data Controller.

The decision of the High Court in *Collins v FBD Insurance plc* [2013] IEHC 137 clarified the extent to which a Data Subject may be entitled to damages for a breach of their data protection rights. The plaintiff in this case sought damages in the Circuit Court following a formal decision of the Data Protection Commissioner that the defendant company had breached the requirements of the Acts when it failed to provide all the information it held about the plaintiff following a subject access request.

The Circuit Court awarded Mr Collins general damages of €15,000 on foot of this breach. FBD appealed the award of damages to the High Court. Overturning the award of damages, the High Court held that a Data Subject has no entitlement to automatic compensation for a technical breach of his rights under the Data Protection Acts where he cannot prove that he has suffered loss or damages as a result of the breach.

22.2.7   THE USE OF PERSONAL DATA FOR DIRECT MARKETING PURPOSES

Section 2 (7) of the Acts contains particular and detailed rules concerning the use of personal data for direct marketing purposes. Section 2 (7) provides that where personal data is kept for the purpose of direct marketing and the relevant Data Subject requests in writing that the relevant Data Controller cease processing the data for that purpose, then, generally, the Data Controller has 40 days to accede to such request.

Section 2 (8) creates an additional burden on Data Controllers that intend to process personal data for the purposes of direct marketing. This provision provides that where a Data Controller intends to process personal data which it holds for the purposes of direct marketing, then the Data Controller shall inform the relevant Data Subjects that they may object, by means of a request in writing to the Data Controller and free of charge, to such processing. This provision appears to create a positive obligation on all Data Controllers to inform Data Subjects that are being targeted for direct marketing purposes of their right to object to such use of their personal data.

Regulation 13 of the Electronic Communications Regulations (outlined in **22.2.13** below) sets out further restrictions on the use of personal data for direct marketing purposes.

22.2.8   RIGHTS OF DATA SUBJECTS

In parallel with setting out a series of obligations for Data Controllers, the Acts create a number of important rights for Data Subjects.

22.2.8.1   The right to be informed of data being kept

Section 3 of the Acts provides that where a person suspects that another is keeping personal data, he or she may write to that person requesting that he or she be informed as to whether any such data is being kept. If it is, then the individual must be given a description of the data and of the purpose for which it is kept. This must be done within 21 days of the request being made.

22.2.8.2 The right to prevent data being used for the purposes of direct marketing

This right is discussed in **22.2.7** and **22.2.13?**.

22.2.8.3 Right of access

Section 4 of the Acts confers upon the Data Subject a right of access to the data in the Data Controller's possession. It provides that if the Data Subject makes a written request, the Data Controller must inform the Data Subject whether he or she holds personal data relating to the Data Subject and, within 40 days, supply him or her with a detailed description of such data and additional information concerning the data.

There exist a number of exceptions to this right in s 5 of the Acts, which ought to be considered prior to advising a client to exercise his or her s 4 rights. It must be stressed that the Data Protection Commissioner and the courts are of the view that CCTV footage of an individual amounts to personal data for the purposes of the Acts and can be the subject of an access request. In *Bus Átha Cliatha/Dublin Bus v Data Protection Commissioner* [2012] IEHC 339, the High Court upheld the decision of the Circuit Court affirming a decision of the Data Protection Commissioner to issue an Enforcement Notice, requiring the appellant, Dublin Bus to provide a copy of CCTV footage to a passenger who allegedly fell on a bus and commenced personal injury proceedings arising out of her alleged fall.

22.2.8.4 Right of blocking of erasure

Section 6 of the Acts give the Data Subject a right to have his or her personal data in the Data Controller's possession rectified, erased, or blocked if the Data Controller fails to comply with its duties under the Act. Generally the Data Controller has 40 days to accede to such request.

22.2.8.5 Right to prevent processing where it might cause damage or distress

Section 6A of the Acts provides that generally an individual is entitled at any time, by notice in writing served on a Data Controller, to request the Data Controller to cease or not to commence processing of that individual's personal data where such processing is likely to cause substantial damage or distress which is or would be unwarranted. There are certain public interest exceptions to this right.

22.2.8.6 Rights of Data Subjects concerning automatic processing of data

Section 6B of the Acts provides that a decision which produces legal effects concerning a Data Subject or otherwise significantly affects a Data Subject may not be based solely on the processing by automatic means of personal data where such processing aims to evaluate personal matters such as work performance, creditworthiness, reliability, or conduct. This right is subject to a number of exceptions.

22.2.8.7 Right to be forgotten

The decision of the Court of Justice of the European Union in Case C-131/12 *Google Spain SL and Google Inc. v Agencia Española de Protección de Datos (AEPD) and Mario Costeja González* established the so-called right of data subjects 'to be forgotten' by Internet search engines. In this case, the Court of Justice of the European Union considered whether Google could be obliged to remove links to a formal public notice in a Spanish newspaper, published in 1998, which truthfully stated that a certain individual's assets were being auctioned off for non-payment of social security debts.

Drawing on the fact that data protection is a fundamental right under European law, and the fact the Data Subject had not consented to the processing of their information by Google, the Court inferred a 'right to be forgotten' from the general rights to deletion and objection discussed above (see **22.2.8.4** and **22.2.8.5**). This right arises where returning the search results is deemed to be excessive or where a balancing exercise suggests that the content should be removed. Crucially, the CJEU found:

(a)   that a Data Subject does not need to show any prejudice to invoke this right to be forgotten;

(b)   the right to be forgotten generally takes precedence over other rights, including the right to free expression; and

(c)   content which could lawfully be returned on one day may need to later be removed due to the passage of time.

The Court did accept that, in certain cases, content would not need to be removed if it could be shown that keeping this content accessible was in the public interest.

22.2.9   THE TRANSFER OF PERSONAL DATA OUTSIDE THE STATE

Section 11 of the Acts contains a number of restrictions on the transfer of personal data by a Data Controller to a country or territory outside of the EEA. It provides that such a transfer may not take place unless that particular country or territory ensures an adequate level of protection for the privacy of its Data Subjects in relation to the processing of personal data. This provision enables the European Commission to make findings as to when a particular country or territory satisfies this adequacy requirement.

There also exists a number of exceptions, to this general prohibition on the transfer of data outside of the EEA, which include (i) where the Data Subject has consented to the transfer; (ii) where the transfer is necessary for the performance of a contract between the Data Subject and the Data Controller; (iii) where the transfer is necessary for reasons of public interest; or (iv) under some international obligation of the State, or where the transfer is necessary in order to prevent personal injury or damage to the health of the Data Subject. This provision gives the Data Protection Commissioner wide powers to prohibit the transfer of personal data from the State to a place outside of the State.

The European Commission has made a number of Decisions permitting the transfer of data to Switzerland, Canada, New Zealand, Argentina, Uruguay, Andorra, Israel, the Faroe Isles, and the UK territories of Jersey, Guernsey, and the Isle of Man. These jurisdictions are regarded by the Commission as offering adequate levels of data protection. Note that the United States is not an approved jurisdiction for transfers. Due to the varying standards of data protection in the US, transfers of data from Europe to the US may only take place (in the absence of fulfilling one of the exceptions above, or using special model contracts clauses, discussed below) where the recipient in the US has signed up to the Safe Harbour Scheme. This is a voluntary scheme to which US companies may sign up, whereby they adopt standards of data protection comparable to EU standards. In the absence of participation in the Safe Harbour Scheme, data exporters to the USA may need to obtain consent from the Data Subject to the data transfer or use the approved model contractual terms produced by the EU Commission.

Solicitors advising clients who rely on the Safe Harbour Scheme need to be alert to the fact that the effectiveness of this arrangement has been queried by the courts.

In *Schrems v Data Protection Commissioner* [2014] IEHC 310 the Irish High Court queried whether, in light of recent allegations concerning the activities of the US National Security Agency, the Safe Harbour Scheme afforded appropriate protection to EU citizens. Given that the rights of privacy and data protection are now protected as fundamental rights under the EU Charter of Fundamental Rights, and given that the Safe Harbour Decision is an EU law instrument, the High Court referred this issue to the Court of Justice of the European Union.

The European Commission has approved a set of standard contractual clauses which offer companies and other organisations a straightforward means of complying with their obligation to ensure 'adequate protection' for personal data transferred outside of the EEA. These clauses allow Data Controllers to export personal data either to another Data Controller or to a Data Processor outside the EEA. The most recent version of these clauses, issued in February 2010, is specifically designed to cover the situation, increasingly found in practice, where a Data Controller in Europe outsources the processing of the data to a Data Processor which in turn outsources some of this processing to a 'sub-processor'.

While model contractual clauses may provide an acceptable approach to ad hoc international data transfers, they are a cumbersome and unappealing solution for a multinational business that wishes to transfer personal data seamlessly throughout its entire organisation. In such circumstances, a multinational corporation may seek to comply with its data protection requirements through the adoption of binding corporate rules ('BCRs'). BCRs are binding internal codes of conduct requiring that the company and its employees comply with data protection norms. Such codes of conduct are approved by a lead national data protection authority and may then be circulated to other relevant national data protection authorities, as appropriate, for comment and consideration. While a regulator ensures that the corporation complies with data protection law, the manner in which the rules operate lies at the discretion of the organisation.

In January 2012, the Data Protection Commissioner approved Intel Corporation's Binding Corporate Rules ('BCRs'). Approval followed an intense analysis of Intel Corporation's application for approval in conjunction with other EU Data Protection Authorities. The approval process was led by the Data Protection Commissioner due to the location of Intel's European Manufacturing Centre in Ireland which is Intel Corporation's biggest single location in Europe.

The Commissioner believes BCRs are a valuable tool for corporations that recognise the corporate benefit in striving to embed privacy principles into their business practices on a daily basis and to comply with EU data protection requirements.

22.2.10 DATA BREACHES

The Data Protection Acts do not explicitly oblige a Data Controller to inform a Data Subject when their personal data is lost, stolen, or compromised. However, in 2010, the Data Protection Commissioner issued the 'Data Security Breach Code of Practice'. This Code stipulates that where an incident occurs which 'gives rise to a risk' of unauthorised disclosure, the Data Controller must 'give immediate consideration' to informing the Data Subject and any other relevant authority (e.g. the Gardaí). In addition, the Data Protection Commissioner must generally be informed of any data breach.

There is no obligation to inform the DPC where (i) the Data Subjects have been notified; (ii) the breach affects no more than 100 Data Subjects; *and* (iii) the breach does not involve information of a sensitive or financial nature.

22.2.11 REGISTRATION WITH THE DATA PROTECTION COMMISSIONER

Section 16 of the Acts and the Data Protection Act 1988 (Section 16 (1)) Regulations 2007 (the '2007 Regulations') set down who has to register with the Data Protection Commissioner. Broadly speaking, Data Controllers and Processors fall into three categories for the purpose of registration. First, certain prescribed categories of Controllers and Processors are required to register under all circumstances. Second, Data Controllers and Processors falling under expressly set out exemptions are not required to register. Third, any Data Controllers or Processors that do not fall into either of the express inclusion or exclusion categories are still required to register.

Regulation 4 of the Data Protection Act 1988 (Section 16(1)) Regulations 2007 sets out the categories of persons who are always obliged to register with the Commissioner.

In broad terms, they include:

    (a)   banks and financial/credit institutions which are Data Controllers;

    (b)   insurance undertakings (not including brokers) which are Data Controllers;

    (c)   Data Controllers whose business consists wholly or mainly in direct marketing, providing credit references, or collecting debts;

    (d)   Internet service providers which are Data Controllers;

    (e)   authorised providers of electronic communications networks or services who are Data Controllers;

    (f)   Data Controllers who process genetic data; and

    (g)   Data Processors that process personal data on behalf of any of the above Data Controllers.

In addition, Regulation 3 of the 2007 Regulations suggests that Data Controllers and Processors who process personal data relating to mental or physical health may be required to register.

Section 16 of the Acts and Regulation 3 of the 2007 Regulations set out certain categories of Data Processors and Controllers who, provided that they do not fall under one of the mandatory registration categories set out above, are excluded from the requirement to register. However, it should be noted that this exclusion will only apply where the Controller or Processor only processes data for an excluded purpose and the process is limited to that necessary for the excluded purpose.

Broadly speaking, these categories include:

    (a)   Data Controllers that are not-for-profit organisations;

    (b)   Data Controllers that only process 'manual data';

    (c)   Data Controllers who are elected representatives or candidates for electoral office;

    (d)   Data Controllers who only process data in relation to past, existing, or prospective employees in the ordinary course of personnel administration;

    (e)   solicitors and barristers who are Data Controllers and process data for the purpose of providing professional legal services;

    (f)   Data Controllers who process personal data relating to their past, existing, or prospective customers, suppliers, shareholders, directors, or officers in the ordinary course of their business;

    (g)   Data Controllers who process personal data with a view to publishing journalistic, literary, or artistic material; and

    (h)   Data Processors that only process personal data on behalf of Data Controllers falling under one of the above exceptions.

Any Data Controller or Data Processor who is required to register but fails to do so is guilty of an offence.

Members of the public can inspect the register free of charge and may copy entries in the register. Applications for registration can either be made in writing or online on the Commissioner's website. Registrations last for a period of one year and, at the end of the year, the entry must be renewed or removed from the register.

In recent years, the Data Protection Commissioner has taken a number of cases against companies for failing to register as either Data Controllers or Data Processors. In February 2012, three insurance companies, Zurich Insurance Plc, FBD Insurance Plc, and Travelers Insurance Company Limited appeared in the Dublin District Court on charges relating to the processing of personal data by them in contravention of s 19 of the Data Protection Acts. This section sets out the effects of registration and certain related offences.

Each company had employed a firm of private investigators which had illegally obtained details of individuals' social welfare records and payments. While each of the three companies was registered with the Data Protection Commissioner under s 16, the Commissioner noted that a description of personal data in the form of social welfare data was not recorded on any of the register entries. It also noted that the purpose for which personal data in the form of social welfare data was processed by the insurance companies was not recorded on the register entry.

Each of the three companies pleaded guilty before the Dublin District Court in February 2012. The Court applied the Probation Act to each of the defendant companies. Each company also made a voluntary charitable donation of €20,000.

22.2.12 CONDUCTING A DATA PROTECTION ANALYSIS

Data protection issues are best analysed in a structured manner. The following list of questions provides a way to think through these issues:

(a)   Is any 'personal data' being 'processed'? (See definitions in **22.2.2**.)

(b)   If so, who is doing the processing? Are they acting as a data controller or a data processor? (See definitions in **22.2.2**.)

(c)   Is the data controller complying with the general data protection principles? E.g. is excessive information being collected, is appropriate security in place, etc? (See discussion in **22.2.3**.)

(d)   If there is a data processor, has an appropriate contract been put in place? (See discussion in **22.2.3**.)

(e)   Has one of the pre-conditions for processing been fulfilled? (See discussion in **22.2.4**.)

(f)   Is any *sensitive* personal data being processed? If so, has one of the pre-conditions for processing *sensitive* personal data been fulfilled? (See discussion in **22.2.5**.)

(g)   Is the personal data being used for marketing purposes? If so, have the specific opt-out rules been respected? (See discussion in **22.2.7**.)

(h)   Have any data subject rights (e.g. the right to access, erasure, to be forgotten etc) been invoked? Or does the client need to be advised about these rights? (See discussion in **22.2.8**.)

(i)   Is the personal data being transferred outside of the european economic area? If so, have safeguards been put in place? (See discussion in **22.2.9**.)

(j)   Has a data breach taken place? (See **22.2.10**.)

(k)   Is registration with the DPC required? (See **22.2.11**.)

(l)   Is there a risk of enforcement action or litigation? What form might it take? (See **22.2.6**.)

22.2.13 ELECTRONIC COMMUNICATIONS REGULATIONS 2011

Directive 2002/58/EC (as amended by Directive 2009/136/EC) concerning the processing of personal data and the protection of privacy in the electronic communications sector (known as the 'Communications Data Protection Directive' or the 'CDPD') was transposed into national law by the European Communities (Electronic Communications Networks and Services) (Data Protection and Privacy) Regulations 2011 (SI 336/2011) ('Electronic Communications Regulations') which came into effect on 1 July 2011.

The Electronic Communications Regulations strengthen the rules concerning direct marketing and accordingly have been given substantial media attention since they endeavour, inter alia, to tackle the nuisance of SPAM mail. Other issues addressed by the Regulations include the retention of telephone records, processing of location data, the creation of telephone directories, 'caller ID', and the storage and access to information on terminal equipment, i.e. 'cookies'.

22.2.13.1 Restrictions on directing marketing

Regulation 13 of the Electronic Communications Regulations restricts the ability to use publicly available electronic communications services to send unsolicited communications or to make unsolicited calls for the purpose of direct marketing. These rules, which are enforced via criminal prosecutions brought by the DPC, are important legal tools in tackling individuals and businesses that send unwanted and unsolicited marketing communications by SMS or by email. In particular, it provides that:

(a)   the use of automatic dialing machines, fax, email or SMS text messaging for direct marketing to individuals is prohibited, unless the subscriber's or user's consent has been obtained in advance (an exception is made for email to an address used for business purposes);

(b)   the use of automatic dialing machines, fax, email or SMS text messaging for direct marketing to a non-natural person (i.e. a body corporate) is prohibited, if that subscriber or user has recorded its objection in the National Directory Database or has informed the sender that it does not consent to such messages;

(c)   the making of telephone calls for direct marketing to the line of a subscriber or user is prohibited, if the subscriber or user has recorded its objection in the National Directory Database or has informed the sender that it does not consent to such messages;

(d)   the use of automatic dialing machines or telephone calls to the mobile telephone of a subscriber or user is prohibited, unless the subscriber or user has consented to such calls (i.e. an opt in);

(e)   the placing of direct marketing information in an SMS sent for non-marketing purposes (e.g. to confirm a reservation) is prohibited (a practice known as tagging), unless the subscriber or user has consented to such direct marketing.

Regulation 13 (10) provides that the person making an unsolicited call for purposes of direct marketing shall include in the call their name and on request their address and telephone number. Similarly, the sender of an unsolicited email or SMS for direct marketing purposes shall include in the message their name and a valid address at which they can be contacted.

Regulation 13 (11) provides that where the subscriber's electronic contact details are obtained from a customer in the context of the sale of a product or service, email and SMS text messaging can be used for direct marketing purposes if an easy to use, free of charge opportunity is given to object to these marketing messages and provided that the SMS text or email concerns similar products or services.

The Data Protection Commissioner has taken a broad view as to what constitutes 'direct marking' for the purpose of this Regulation. Unsolicited emails requesting support in an election have been found to amount to unlawful direct marketing (Case Study 5 of the 2004 Report of the Data Protection Commissioner). This broad interpretation should be noted as, unlike much of data protection law, a breach of reg 13 is a criminal offence, and prosecutions are actively brought by the DPC. For example, in March 2011, the Commissioner brought a series of high profile and successful prosecutions against leading telecommunications firms including O2, Eircom, UPC, and Vodafone for sending their subscribers unsolicited marketing text messages and making unwanted phone calls.

Careful advice on this Regulation should be given to any client considering on embarking on an electronic direct marketing campaign.

Regulation 14 sets out the rules for recording subscribers' indications that they do not wish to receive unsolicited telephone calls on an 'opt-out' register in the National Directory Database. Subscribers with unlisted numbers will automatically be included on this 'opt-out' register.

22.2.13.2 Location data

Regulation 9 deals with location data. Location data created by mobile phones enables mobile phone companies and third party companies to whom they disclose such information to know the precise whereabouts of an individual in possession of a powered on mobile phone.

Regulation 9 provides that generally, location data can only be processed if made anonymous or with the consent of the individual for the provision of a value added service. Regulation 9 requires that full information must be given to users or subscribers, prior to obtaining such consent, in relation to the type of location data that will be processed and of the purposes and duration of the processing as well as the transmission of the data to any third parties. Consent to the processing of the location data can be withdrawn at any time by simply making a request that the processing be stopped. There are public interest exceptions in Regulation 10 with regard to the use of location data.

22.2.13.3 Storage and access to information on terminal equipment

Regulation 5 provides that information can only be stored on or retrieved from a user or subscriber's terminal equipment, e.g. computer or phone, provided that user consent is given and that clear and comprehensive information is provided. The information to be provided includes the purpose of storing or retrieving the information. This regulation covers the use of 'cookies' on websites among other things.

22.2.14 USEFUL LINKS

The Office of the Data Protection Commissioner has an excellent website which contains all the relevant legislation, reports of the Commissioner, examples of cases which the Commissioner has had to consider, and guidance notes on the Acts and the responsibilities of Data Controllers and Data Processors. The website's address is www.dataprotection.ie.

22.3 Electronic Contracts

22.3.1 BACKGROUND

Since 1999, European and Irish law have evolved to provide varying degrees of legal support and protections for online sellers and buyers. Initially the focus was on ensuring that contracts concluded electronically were not at an enforceability risk simply because they did not exist in paper format. Subsequently, the law has developed to address the more specific legal issues and challenges that arise in the context of contracts concluded remotely, with a particular focus on ensuring that consumers are not unduly disadvantaged in their dealings with online retailers. The laws governing electronic signatures and electronic identities have also been updated by means of an EU Regulation.

This overview is intended to act as a guide to these key pieces of e-commerce legislation but you should always check the particular facts of each case carefully against the text of the legislation. Readers should also be alive to the fact that while this chapter focuses on contracts concluded online, the full range of contract, sale of goods, and consumer protection laws that apply to 'in person' transactions will also usually apply to online transactions to the extent they are subject to Irish law.

22.3.2 KEY LEGISLATION

The first major statutory development in Ireland was the enactment of the Electronic Commerce Act, 2000 (the '2000 Act') and the law has continually evolved since. The 2000 Act implemented Directive 1999/93/EC on electronic signatures, and some of the provisions of Directive 2000/31/EC on electronic commerce. The remaining provisions of the

Electronic Commerce Directive were enacted in the European Communities (Directive 2000/31/EC) Regulations 2003. Subsequently a succession of European Directives were adopted in relation to distance contracts with consumers and these were transcribed into Irish law primarily by means of the European Communities (Protection of Consumers in Respect of Contracts Made by Means of Distance Communication) Regulations 2001 (since repealed), the European Communities (Distance Marketing of Consumer Financial Services) Regulations 2004, and the European Union (Consumer Information, Cancellation and Other Rights) Regulations 2013.

Most recently, at EU level, Regulation (EU) No. 910/2014 of the European Parliament and of the Council of 23 July 2014 adopts a single pan-European law on electronic identification and trust services for electronic transactions in the internal market. This Regulation will repeal the Signatures Directive 1999/93/EC with effect from 1 July 2016 when most of its provisions are due to become effective.

22.3.3   EXCLUDED LAWS

The 2000 Act, and its provisions, do not apply to the law relating to the transfer of land or to the execution of documents such as wills, trusts, or enduring powers of attorney, which will still have to be evidenced in traditional forms of writing (s 10). Interestingly, a contract for the sale of land can be in electronic form while the conveyance itself must be in a traditional form of writing. However, the vast majority of day-to-day online business-to-business and business-to-consumer contracts benefit from the provisions of the 2000 Act.

22.3.4   ADMISSIBILITY OF ELECTRONIC CONTRACTS

Section 19 of the 2000 Act confirms that an electronic contract shall not be denied legal effect, validity, or enforceability solely on the grounds that it is wholly or partly in electronic form, or has been concluded wholly or partly by way of an electronic communication. In the formation of a contract, an offer, acceptance of an offer, or any related communication (including any subsequent amendment, cancellation, or revocation of the offer or acceptance of the offer) may, unless otherwise agreed by the parties, be communicated by means of an electronic communication.

Section 21 deals with the time and place of dispatch and receipt of electronic communications. Under the so-called 'postal rule' acceptance is deemed by the law to occur at the time the letter of acceptance is posted by the offeree and not the time at which it is received or read by the offeror. Prior to the implementation of the 2000 Act, it was not clear whether the rule applied to electronic communications. Section 21 provides that where an electronic communication enters an information system, or the first information system, outside the control of the originator, then, unless otherwise agreed between the originator and the addressee, it is taken to have been sent when it enters such information system or first information system. Therefore, in the case of an email, an emailed acceptance of a contract would be deemed to be sent once it passes outside the sender's email system. Note that reg 910 of 2014 proposes to introduce new specific measures under Art 41 whereby a qualified electronic time stamp shall enjoy the presumption of the accuracy of the date and the time it indicates and the integrity of the data to which the date and time are bound.

Where the recipient has designated an information system for the purpose of receiving electronic communications (e.g. an email address), then, unless otherwise agreed or the law otherwise provides, the electronic communication is taken to have been received when it enters that information system. Where the addressee of an electronic communication has not designated an information system the electronic communication is taken to have been received when it 'comes to the attention of the addressee'.

In practice, this would include circumstances where a recipient of an email does not actually open the email when he knows that it contains an acceptance of his contract offer. He will not be entitled to rely upon his failure to open the email to claim that the acceptance was not received by him. Provided the sender of the acceptance has sent the email to the correct email address and the email has been successfully sent, the fact that the recipient refuses to open the email does not prevent the communication having been received by him.

The places of dispatch and receipt of an electronic communication are deemed to be the places of business of the parties or, if there is no such place of business, the place where they ordinarily reside.

22.3.5   ELECTRONIC SIGNATURES AND ADVANCED ELECTRONIC SIGNATURES

Before looking at the requirements in the 2000 Act governing electronic signatures, it is important to bear in mind that most contracts do not actually require a signature (electronic or otherwise) in order to be valid. Many day-to-day contracts are executed without any signature formality but are equally as binding as those which have. The benefit of capturing a signature on a contract is to avoid repudiation by a party claiming not to have agreed to the terms.

The 2000 Act makes an important distinction between 'electronic signatures' and 'advanced electronic signatures'.

An 'electronic signature' means:

> data in electronic form attached to, incorporated in or logically associated with other electronic data and which serves as a method of authenticating the purported originator, and includes an advanced electronic signature.

This definition would seem to encompass, for example, a scanned version of a handwritten signature or, in certain cases, a typed name at the foot of an email.

The issue of whether or not an email address can constitute an electronic signature arose in the UK decision, *Nilesh Mehtha v J Pereira Fernandes SA* [2006] EWHC 813 (Ch), 7 April 2006. In this case, the defendant stated in an email that he would give a personal guarantee in the amount of £25,000. The English High Court had to decide whether, for the purposes of s 4 of the Statute of Frauds 1677, the presence of an automatically inserted email address at the top of the email constituted a signature by, or on behalf of, the defendant.

In this case, the email was not 'signed', but the header of the email showed that it came from the defendant's email address, which was the same email address that had appeared on other emails sent by him to the plaintiff's solicitors, which he had signed. The wording of the email in question was such that it contained an offer and contemplated that formal documents would be entered into in relation to the personal guarantee. Notwithstanding that the terms of the guarantee had been subsequently agreed orally by the defendant and the plaintiff's solicitors, the defendant argued that he was not bound to honour the terms of the guarantee on the basis that it had not been 'signed' for the purposes of s 4 of the Statute of Frauds.

The English High Court held that the contents of the email constituted a sufficient note or memorandum for the purpose of s 4 of the Statute of Frauds, as it contained an offer in writing made by the guarantor which contained the essential terms of what was offered, and the offer had been accepted unconditionally by the plaintiff's solicitors (albeit orally). However, the court held that the email did not bear a signature, within the meaning of s 4 of the Statute of Frauds, of either the guarantor or his authorised agent, as the automatic insertion of an email address was not intended as a signature. The inclusion of the email address, in the absence of contrary intention, was incidental, in that the signature or name just happened to appear somewhere rather than being inserted into the document in order to give, and with the intention of giving, authenticity to it.

As an aside, the judge stated that if a party, or a party's agent, sending an email types his or his principal's name, that would be a sufficient signature, subject to other legal requirements and providing always that the name was inserted into the document in order to give, and with the intention of giving, authenticity to it.

The Statute of Frauds issue also arose in the case of *In WS Tankship II BV* v *The Kwangju Bank* Ltd and another [2011] EWHC 3103, where the English High Court accepted that a communication made through the secure SWIFT system used by banks had been signed for the purposes of the Statute of Frauds. By sending the SWIFT message in this case the defendant had caused its name to be inserted into the message and this constituted a sufficient signature for the purposes of the Statute of Frauds. The method of transmission also provided sufficient authentication to enable the message recipient to identify that the message was from the defendant. The following extract from Blair J's judgment provides a useful summary of the legal position:

> 'It is said on behalf of Kwangju Bank that this is not text which it typed in, but an output message header, that is, text generated by the SWIFT messaging system. That may be correct, but the name appears, and in my opinion it is a sufficient signature for the purposes of the Statute of Frauds. The words "Kwangju Bank Ltd" appear in the header, because the bank caused them to be there by sending the message. They were "voluntarily affixed" in the words of the old cases (c.f. *J Pereira Fernandes SA v. Mehta* [2006] 1 WLR 1543 dealing with email addresses). Whether or not automatically generated by the system, and whether or not stated in whole, or abbreviated (in fact the name of the bank appeared here in complete form), this is in my judgment a sufficient signature for the purposes of the Statute of Frauds. The position is analogous to that considered by Christopher Clarke J in *Golden Ocean Group Ltd v. Salgaocar Mining Industries Pvt Ltd* [2011] EWHC 56 (Comm) who at [103] observed that "an e-mail, the text of which begins 'Paul/Peter', may be regarded as signed by Peter because by that form of wording Peter signifies that he is addressing Paul and authenticates the content of the whole of what follows". Therefore, I reject Kwangju Bank's submissions in this regard.'

In another UK example, *PNC Telecom plc v Thomas and another* ([2002] EWHC 2848 (Ch)), the court held that a fax transmittal and its incorporated signature were valid as shareholder notification under the UK Companies Act 1985 and the UK Electronic Communication Act 2000.

In contrast to the broad interpretation of an 'electronic signature', an 'advanced electronic signature' means an electronic signature which is:

(a)   *uniquely* linked to the signatory;

(b)   capable of identifying the signatory;

(c)   created using means that are capable of being maintained by the signatory under his, her or its sole control; and

(d)   linked to the data to which it relates in such a manner that any subsequent change of the data is detectable.

An example of an advanced electronic signature would be an encrypted 'digital' signature using what is called Public Key Infrastructure ('PKI'). In simple terms, the use of PKI technology allows the sender of the information to encrypt the contents of the electronic communication so that (i) the recipient can be sure that the email has come from the purported sender, and (ii) no other party has altered the data prior to it being received. If a sender of an email encrypts his email using his unique advanced electronic signature based on qualified certificate technology the email can only be opened and read by the individual to whom it was sent. The recipient can be sure that it has been signed by the sender since only he has the means of encrypting the message with his advanced electronic signature based on a qualified certificate as defined in the 2000 Act.

The use of advanced electronic signatures significantly reduces the inherent confidentiality and integrity risks that are associated with an open network such as the worldwide web.

Section 13 of the 2000 Act provides that, if by law or otherwise, the signature of a person or public body is required (whether the requirement is in the form of an obligation or consequences flow from there being no signature) or permitted, then, subject to meeting the requirements of s 13 (2), either an electronic signature or an advanced electronic signature may be used.

In other words, in most circumstances, an electronic signature will be given functional equivalence to a handwritten signature.

However, an electronic signature does not suffice in every case. For example, where a signature is required to be witnessed, s 14 provides that, the signature to be witnessed must be an advanced electronic signature. In addition, the document must contain an indication that the signature is required to be witnessed and the witness must also sign using an advanced electronic signature which meets the requirements of Annex 1 (i.e. the advanced electronic signature both meets the definition in the 2000 Act and in addition in based on a 'qualified certificate'). The requirement to use advanced electronic signatures also applies where documents are required to be executed under seal (s 16).

Readers should bear in mind that the above legislative provisions governing electronic signatures and advanced electronic signatures will be impacted by the coming into force of EU Regulation 910 of 2014 which will, with effect from 1 July 2016, update the laws governing e-signatures and electronic seals while also addressing new concepts such as electronic time stamps and electronic identity services.

22.3.6 PROVIDERS OF CERTIFICATION, ELECTRONIC IDENTITY, AND ELECTRONIC TRUST SERVICES

Part 3 of the 2000 Act deals with certification services. If the use of an advanced electronic signature practically guarantees the identity of the sender of an electronic communication, from where does one obtain an advanced electronic signature? The PKI system depends on the integrity of trusted third parties who are prepared to effectively guarantee the identity of persons to whom they issue advanced electronic signatures. If an advanced electronic signature is not unique or is capable of being used by a third party, it will not meet the definition in the 2000 Act.

Part 3 of the 2000 Act provides for the accreditation and supervision of 'Certification Service Providers' ('CSPs') who provide certification of electronic signatures.

Section 29 provides that CSPs can operate without prior authorisation. This may seem odd. If it is so important that a CSP acts with the utmost integrity and security to protect the confidentiality of the advanced electronic signatures it issues, why are there no national or EU standards to apply to it? The answer lies in the fact that the EU did not wish to hinder the emergence of CSPs through heavy regulation. As CSPs who issue 'qualified certificates' will have liability to those who rely on any certification services they provide, then the market will determine the standards appropriate to such an emerging technology. For example, if a CSP were to lose the private keys of its customers, this would potentially ruin its business, as the fundamental trust required of a CSP would be lost and its customers would be likely to revoke their existing private keys and seek alternative CSP services elsewhere.

Notwithstanding the previous paragraph, it is open to the Minister for Enterprise, Trade and Innovation to establish a scheme of voluntary accreditation of CSPs to enhance the levels of certification service provision in the State and in May 2010, the Minister adopted the Electronic Commerce (Certification Service Providers Supervision Scheme) Regulations 2010 (SI 233/2010). These Regulations require that CSPs established in the State who issue qualified certificates must notify the Minister of Communications, Energy and Natural Resources within one year that they issue qualified certificates to the public. The Regulations enable the Minister to be satisfied that the requirements of Annex I and II of the Electronic Commerce Act 2000 have been met (including by requiring conformity to ISO/IEC standard 17021 (entitled 'Conformity assessment—requirements of bodies providing audit and certification of management systems') and ISO standard 27006 (entitled 'Information technology—security techniques—Requirements for bodies providing audit and certification of information security management systems'). Based on the notifications and evidence of certification forwarded the Minister now maintains lists of CSPs established in the State who issue qualified certificates to the public.

EU Regulation 910 of 2014 will further update the position as it will introduce a new regime governing electronic identification and trust services when it becomes law on 1 July 2016.

22.3.7   ELECTRONIC ORIGINALS

Section 17 of the 2000 Act facilitates the retention and presentation of electronic forms of 'original' information. Information may be presented or retained in electronic form, provided:

(a)   there exists a reliable assurance as to the integrity of the information from the time when it was first generated in its final form;

(b)   the information is capable of being displayed in intelligible form to a person or public body to whom it is to be presented; and

(c)   at the time the information was generated in its final form, it was reasonable to expect that it would be readily accessible so as to be useable for subsequent reference.

The 'consent' requirements discussed below also apply to the holding of electronic originals. In most cases, where an electronic document is stored in a secure file (e.g. a Microsoft Word, Google docs, or Adobe pdf file or an archived email) and it can be shown that the document has not been altered since the day it was stored (e.g. by checking the 'properties' of the document), the standards listed in s 17 will be met. However, if the document was stored on an open network where many people had access to it, it may be more difficult to assert that there was a reliable assurance as to the document's integrity.

22.3.8   ELECTRONIC COMMUNICATIONS

Broadly speaking, the 2000 Act gives legal recognition to communications and information in electronic form. Therefore electronic communications, information, signatures, and contracts cannot be denied legal effect or be discriminated against simply because they are in electronic form.

22.3.9   CONSENT REQUIREMENT

However, while the 2000 Act does go some way to remove some of the legal ambiguities previously associated with electronic communications, it does not compel people to communicate or conduct business in electronic form. Therefore, in order for an electronic communication to obtain full legal recognition, it is a requirement of the 2000 Act that the parties to the communication must consent to the information being provided in electronic form.

Where information is required or permitted to be given to a public body and the public body consents to the giving of the information in electronic form, but requires that the information be given in accordance with particular information technology and procedural requirements, or that a particular action be taken by way of verifying the receipt of the information, these requirements must be met. However, any public body which introduces IT and procedural requirements must ensure that those requirements have been made public and are objective, transparent, proportionate, and non-discriminatory. For example, the Companies Registration Office ('CRO') may agree to accept the registration of certain forms on their website but the CRO will be entitled to require that the electronic forms be filled out and submitted in the manner described on the website. Another example, the Revenue Online Service (www.ROS.ie), enables the electronic filing of certain tax returns.

Where the recipient of an electronic communication is a non-public body, that person must consent to receiving the information in electronic form. The Act is not intended to force people to transact electronically (s 24).

22.3.10   ELECTRONIC EVIDENCE

Evidence will not be denied admissibility in legal proceedings solely because it is in electronic form (2000 Act, s 22). However, this is not to say that electronic evidence will always be admitted and the normal rules of evidence will continue to apply.

In this regard, it should be noted that the Law Reform Commission issued a detailed Consultation Paper in 2009 entitled 'Documentary and Electronic Evidence' (LRC CP 57—2009) which reviews in detail the evidential issues that arise in respect of electronic documentation.

22.4   Selling Online

22.4.1   INTRODUCTION

While the 2000 Act established a baseline for the legal recognition of electronic contracts, there have been several legislative developments since which have been designed to provide an enhanced and harmonised level of legal support and protection for e-commerce businesses operating within the EU and their customers.

22.4.2   LEGISLATIVE DEVELOPMENTS

The first major development was the adoption of the European Communities (Protection of Consumers in Respect of Contracts Made by Means of Distance Communication) Regulations 2001 (the 'Distance Contracts Regulations') which were implemented into Irish law with effect from 15 May 2001.

The Distance Contracts Regulations introduced new standards for any business supplying goods or services to consumers (i.e. persons acting for purposes which are outside their trade, business, or profession) under distance contracts. Businesses covered by the Regulations were required to adopt terms and conditions of sale and appropriate contractual procedures to comply with the Regulations or run the risk of being guilty of one of the many offences listed under the Regulations.

The Distance Contracts Regulations implemented European Directive 97/7/EC. This Directive aimed to harmonise the laws in respect of distance contracts for consumers throughout the Member States of the EU, substantially increasing protection for consumers. The 1997 Directive was replaced in 2011 by the Consumer Rights Directive (2011/83/EU) which in turn has been transposed into Irish law by the European Union (Consumer Information, Cancellation and Other Rights) Regulations 2013 (the 'Consumer Information Regulations'). The Consumer Information Regulations came into force in June 2014 and therefore represent the current principal law governing distance contracts with consumers.

22.4.3   THE CONSUMER INFORMATION REGULATIONS 2013

While certain categories of contracts are excluded from the scope of the Consumer Information Regulations, there is an emphasis in the Regulations on off-premises, distance selling, and contracts concluded by electronic means. While echoing many of the requirements of their predecessor, the Distance Contracts Regulations, the Consumer Information Regulations are more detailed and prescriptive. For example, in addition to covering distance contracts of goods and services they expressly extend to contracts for 'digital content' and to 'off-premises' contracts.

22.4.3.1   Transparency and consumer information

The Consumer Information Regulations stipulate that contracts will not be binding on consumers unless the content and display of information provided to the consumer meets certain criteria. Schedule 2 of the Regulations sets out 24 different categories of information which are required to be provided to consumers in plain and intelligible language and in a way appropriate to the means of communication used. For example, the initial display for concluding the contract must contain, at a minimum, the main characteristics of the goods; the identity of the trader; the total price; the existence of the right to cancel;

information regarding auto-renewal of the contract; and conditions for termination (if applicable). However, the merchant must also ensure that the full suite of sch 2 information is also provided to the consumer 'in an appropriate way' before the consumer is bound by the contract.

In the case of mobile devices, reg 10 (7) acknowledges that limited space or time may be a factor in which case the seller must still include minimal information 'on that means of communication'. In addition, the Regulations require that descriptions of goods, their cost, and the duration of the contract must be provided in a 'clear and prominent manner, and directly before the consumer places his order'. Order buttons must be labelled 'order with obligation to pay' or a 'corresponding unambiguous formulation'.

In addition to the pre-sales information requirements, reg 12 of the Consumer Information Regulations requires that consumers be provided with much of the same information again in durable medium (which includes email) unless the consumer has already been provided with it on a durable medium prior to conclusion of the contract. Online merchants must include details of the existence of a right to cancellation and how it can be exercised (see further below).

22.4.3.2   'Cooling-off period'

One of the most notable changes to the 2001 Distance Contracts Regulations is the increase from seven to 14 days in the duration of the 'cooling-off' period in which a customer can unilaterally decide to withdraw from any obligations under the relevant contract.

The 'cooling-off period' provision does not apply to contracts for the following goods and services:

- goods whose price depends on fluctuations in financial markets;
- non-prefabricated or personalised goods made on the specifications of the consumer;
- goods which will deteriorate rapidly;
- goods which are by their nature inseparably mixed with other items;
- the supply of alcoholic beverages whose price has been agreed in advance;
- repair or maintenance specifically requested by the consumer;
- sealed health or hygienic goods;
- public auction contracts;
- passenger transport services;
- non-residential accommodation, goods transport, car rental, catering, or leisure with a specified date or period of performance.

If information on the right to cancel the contract is not included as required under the Commercial Information Regulations then the cancellation period will be extended such that it will expire 12 months following the expiration of the 14-day period which would have been applicable had the trader been compliant with the Consumer Information Regulations in the first instance.

The Consumer Information Regulations include a Model Cancellation Form to be used by merchants unless they provide another 'unequivocal statement' of cancellation.

22.4.3.3   Return and reimbursement

If the right to cancel the contract is exercised, the merchant must reimburse all payments, including delivery charges, received from the customer. If the merchant does not collect returned goods from a consumer, the merchant may withhold such reimbursement provided that reimbursement occurs within 14 days of receipt of the goods. The direct costs of the return will be borne by the consumer unless the trader has agreed to bear those costs. If the trader has not agreed to bear return costs and the item cannot, owing to its nature, be returned by post, an estimate of the return costs should be included in the information provided to the consumer relating to cancellation and return.

22.4.3.4 Case law

There have been a number of European Court of Justice decisions where the transparency and 'cooling-off' provisions of the original Distance Contracts Regulations have fallen for consideration. In Case C-49/11 *Content Services Limited v Bundesarbeitskammer*, the Austrian consumer protection agency challenged Content Services' business practices on the basis that such practices infringed the original Distance Selling Directive (which had similar transparency requirements to those under the Consumer Information Regulations). Customers of Content Services were required to submit their order forms online, where they were required to tick a box confirming that they had read the relevant terms and conditions. The terms required them to waive right of withdrawal in respect of the software purchased and the prior information required by the Distance Contracts Directive was only available via a hyperlink. The Court held that the provision of a hyperlink was not sufficient to meet the requirements under Art 5 of the Distance Selling Directive as information requiring consumers to actively click to was neither 'given' to consumers nor 'received' by them. The Court of Justice also found that a website and the information which was accessible to consumers via a hyperlink could not be regarded as having been provided in a 'durable medium' as required by the Directive. While *Content Services* was decided on the basis of the now repealed Distance Selling Directive (97/7/EC), given the transparency requirements in the Consumer Information Regulations are even more prescriptive, it is likely to be followed in future cases where merchants do not fully embrace the transparency requirements of the Regulations.

22.4.3.5 Digital downloads and services already completed

In the case of the supply of digital content, a consumer who exercises the right to cancel the contract is not liable for the cost of that supply, provided that the user has not already expressly consented to the delivery/download of the content before the expiry of the cancellation period in the knowledge that the cancellation right would be lost by consenting to such download. Similarly, the cooling-off period will not apply to services which have been performed with the express prior consent of the consumer in the knowledge that consent to the performance of the service would deprive the consumer of the right to cancel.

While contravention of the Consumer Information Regulations constitutes the commission of an offence, in the case of a dispute, the burden of proving that the cancellation right was exercised in compliance with the Regulations falls on the consumer.

22.4.3.6 Fees for means of payment

The Regulations prevent the charging of fees for the use of a particular means of payment, which exceed the cost borne by the provider for the use of such means of payment. This provision is targeted at situations where higher payment mechanisms are used to drive down the headline price for the product or service. In the event of a dispute the burden of proving compliance with the Consumer Information Regulations lies with the seller. Where such excessive fees are found to have been charged, the customer is entitled to a refund of the excess amount. It has been clarified with the European Commission that price rebates for payment by direct debit are not covered by this Regulation.

22.4.3.7 Prohibition of 'pre-ticked consent' for additional payments

Regulation 26 of the Consumer Information Regulations is aimed at preventing hidden extra charges on consumers by obtaining consent to additional charges by way of default or opt-out provisions, such as, for example, pre-ticked boxes. In the event of a dispute the burden of proving compliance with the Regulations is on the seller.

22.4.3.8   Enforcement and penalties

If found guilty of an offence a person will be liable to a fine, between €4,000 and €5,000, or up to 12 months' imprisonment, or both. Many of the Consumer Information Regulations are to be enforced by the National Consumer Agency.

22.5   Managing Employee and Contractor Use of Email, Internet and Computer Systems

22.5.1   INTRODUCTION

As electronic communications devices and platforms continually evolve, employers can be faced with a myriad of legal issues and challenges arising from unauthorised use of their systems and devices. The challenges extend across the sphere of employment laws (which are beyond the scope of this chapter) and data protection laws. The challenge for employers faced with investigating workplace malpractice is enhanced by the fact employees are increasingly able to establish a legal entitlement to privacy in relation to communications sent using company equipment or over company networks, typically by reference to the Data Protection Acts 1988 and 2003 and the right to private correspondence under Art 8 of the European Convention on Human Rights.

The typical fact patterns and legal issues arising for employers are perhaps best illustrated by a selection of Irish and UK case law.

22.5.2   EMPLOYEE MISCONDUCT

Kiernan v A-Wear UD 643/2007 is a typical case where an employee posted abusive comments about a manager on her social media account. The employer referred the link to the company's official social media account and asserted that the employee had made a damaging association which justified dismissal for gross misconduct. The Employment Appeals Tribunal held that whilst the company's disciplinary procedures were fair, the sanction applied was not. In the circumstances, the sanction of dismissal was disproportionate to the offence:

> 'Certainly the claimant's comments deserved strong censure and possible disciplinary action but they did not constitute gross misconduct in the circumstances. However the comments made by the claimant concerning her supervisor were indeed disrespectful, inappropriate and damaging the employment relationship and to that extent the claimant's contribution to her dismissal was not insignificant.'

Accordingly, the Tribunal awarded the claimant €4,000.00 under the Unfair Dismissals Acts.

In contrast, the Liverpool EAT case of *Preece v JD Wetherspoons plc* 2104806/10 related to a similar fact pattern where a pub manager made inappropriate comments on Facebook, while at work, about two customers who had verbally abused and threatened her. The employee believed that her privacy settings restricted access to close friends but her comments were in fact accessible to a wider audience (including relatives of the customers). In this case, the contract of employment provided that Wetherspoons could immediately terminate the employment contract if it found the employee to be guilty of gross misconduct and it also referred to the employee handbook. The handbook contained a disciplinary and dismissal procedure, including examples of gross misconduct which referred to acts committed outside work which either had an adverse bearing on the employee's suitability for the job, amounted to a serious breach of trust, affected employee or customer relations, or brought the Wetherspoons name into disrepute. The policy specifically referred to blogging and reserved Wetherspoons' right to take disciplinary action should the contents of any blog, including pages on sites such as MySpace or Facebook, 'be found to lower the reputation of the organisation, staff or customers and/or contravene the company's equal opportunity policy'. The Tribunal determined that while the employee had a right to freedom of expression under Art 10 of the European Convention on Human Rights, the action taken by Wetherspoons was justified under Art 10 (2) in view of the risk of damage to its reputation. Accordingly, the employee was deemed to have been fairly dismissed for gross misconduct and dismissal fell within the range of reasonable responses available to a reasonable employer.

22.5.3 OWNERSHIP OF INFORMATION

Another emerging area of law is the question of who 'owns' a customer relationship. In *Pennwell Publishing v Ornstien & Ors* [2007] IRLR 700, a journalist imported contacts from a previous employment into the employer's Outlook database and included long-term journalistic contacts that he later tried to argue were his own. The English High Court considered the case by reference to the EU Database Regulation, and confirmed that as the database was developed in the course of the journalist's employment, the intellectual property rights in the database of contacts more properly belonged to the former employer.

There have also been a number of reported cases in relation to LinkedIn accounts. In *Hays v Ions* [2008] EWHC 745 (Ch), the English High Court considered a case of an employee of a recruitment agency who allegedly used his LinkedIn network to approach clients for his own rival agency, three weeks before resigning. The employee argued that the employer encouraged use of LinkedIn and that once contacts accepted his invitation to join his network they ceased to be confidential as they could be contacted by anyone in his personal network. Mr Justice Richards in the English High Court held that the employee must disclose the LinkedIn business contacts requested by Hays and all emails sent to or received by his LinkedIn account from his former employer's computer network. In contrast with Pennwell, which was determined on intellectual property grounds, the court determined this case on the grounds that the employee had taken confidential information from his employer.

22.5.4 PRIVACY CASES

In the case of *Copland v United Kingdom* ([2007] ECHR 253) the European Court of Human Rights ('ECtHR') ruled that a college had violated an employee's right to respect for her private life and correspondence under Art 8 of the Convention, by the way in which it monitored her telephone calls, email correspondence, and Internet use. Case law has established that telephone calls from business premises attract rights of privacy and fall within the recognised notions of 'private life' and 'correspondence'. It followed logically that emails and Internet usage should also be similarly protected.

The European Court of Human Rights found it to be of particular significance here that the employee had been given no warning that her communications and Internet usage would be monitored. The Court concluded that the collection and storage of personal information relating to her telephone, email, and Internet usage, without her knowledge, amounted to an interference with her right to respect for her private life and correspondence, in breach of the Convention.

The Court reasoned that:

(a) the fact that the data might have been legitimately obtained by her employer (in the form of telephone bills) was no bar to finding an interference with rights guaranteed under the Convention; and

(b) the storage of personal data relating to the private life of an individual also fell within the application of the Convention.

It was irrelevant that the data held by her employer was not disclosed or used against her in disciplinary or other proceedings.

The Convention was implemented in Ireland in the form of the European Convention on Human Rights Act 2003 (the 'HRA'). Therefore, employees can now pursue actions for alleged breaches of the HRA through the Irish courts. In light of this case, employers wishing to monitor their employees should be clear about the purpose for so doing and be satisfied that the particular monitoring arrangement is justified by real benefits that will be delivered. Furthermore, employees should be made aware of the nature, extent, and reasons for any monitoring, unless (exceptionally) covert monitoring is justified.

The Data Protection Commissioner has published on her website guidance in relation to the monitoring of employees which in turn refers to the Article 29 Working Party Document (WP55) on the surveillance of electronic communications in the workplace. These documents provide insight into the potential data protection arguments that can be made by employees in the context of workplace monitoring of communications.

22.5.5   DRAFTING AN ACCEPTABLE USAGE POLICY

Most businesses in Ireland that have a human resources section have a wide range of workplace policies to deal with all aspects of the employment relationship, for example, disciplinary procedure, grievance procedure, equal opportunities policy, and confidentiality policy.

Organisations take varying approaches to the use of company email and Internet facilities. However, some of the key points to be contained in a typical Acceptable Usage Policy might be summarised as follows:

(a)   The extent (if any) to which email may be used for private purposes. Some companies tolerate limited personal use or allow personal email accounts so that the company's name is not associated with personal messages. However, the company's technical ability to monitor such accounts is limited.

(b)   Email may be accessed and intercepted by company managers and the IT department to review all messages which are sent and received on the email system for whatever purposes.

(c)   Internet use is only for business-related activities and web-surfing for personal use is prohibited. If limited personal use of email and Internet is tolerated by the company, the policy should lay down the ground rules as to the extent of permitted use, prohibited categories of sites, etc.

(d)   Do not send emails which are obscene or may cause offence or annoyance to others.

(e)   Staff should be careful to ensure that any software, files, or any other documentation is not copied or retransmitted in breach of copyright or other intellectual property rights.

(f)   By sending an email message the company may be contractually bound and therefore it should always be ensured that the sending of information via email is authorised by the appropriate senior personnel.

(g)   Always double check the addressees of external emails.

(h)   Personal data contained in emails and by which a person may be identified may be accessed as of right by those persons under the Data Protection Acts, 1988 and 2003, the Freedom of Information Act 2014, and in the context of discovery.

(i)   Never open an email or an email attachment from an unknown source unless certain as to the integrity of the source.

(j)   Any breaches of the email or Internet policy may lead to disciplinary action up to and including dismissal.

(k)   Social media tools and their use now need to be addressed in such policies also with limitations and principles being articulated in these policies which clarify how an employee might effectively use such tools in the context of his or her employment.

CHAPTER 23

COMPETITION LAW

23.1 Introduction

Solicitors practising in Ireland often have to advise on competition law issues. This chapter is an overview of how competition law arises in practice.

The topic of competition law can arise, for example, whenever businesses:

(a) make arrangements (however informal) with other businesses which could distort competition (e.g. price-fixing);

(b) engage in practices which involve abusing market power (e.g. unjustifiably refusing to supply goods or services);

(c) participate in mergers, acquisitions, or joint ventures; or

(d) receive, directly or indirectly, State aid from any of the EU Member States.

A failure to advise properly on this area can expose the lawyer to claims of negligence but the consequences for the clients can be even more dramatic because the penalties for breaching competition law include imprisonment, fines, damages, exemplary damages, injunctions, declarations, and voidness (i.e. legal unenforceability) of arrangements. So, it is important to be able to identify areas in which competition law arises in practice and then to know how to source and apply the rules. This chapter is designed to help solicitors perform these tasks.

This chapter begins by explaining the concept of competition law, which is the body of legal rules designed to ensure rivalry in the market. Examples of competition law in practice are then considered. How competition law is applied in practice, in particular the conduct of 'undertakings' is discussed. The sources of competition law are then considered.

For completeness, it should be noted that merger control law is another area of competition law. It is the area of law which regulates mergers, acquisitions, and joint ventures on competition grounds. Solicitors in Ireland often need to advise on EU and Irish merger control law. This topic is not however dealt with in this chapter.

23.2 Concept of Competition Law

Competition is another name for rivalry. So competition law is the body of legal rules designed to ensure rivalry in the market. The topic of competition law is known in the USA as 'antitrust' law because it was designed in the 1890s to challenge the economic power of various businesses which were organised as trusts (e.g. the oil trusts). The topic has been traditionally known as 'restrictive practices law' in Britain and Ireland because it dealt with arrangements which restricted competition such as non-compete covenants in business agreements (e.g. sale of businesses and apprenticeship contracts). The term 'competition law' is now the more common term for the subject.

It is worth noting that EU and Irish competition laws are both much broader in terms of their content than US antitrust law or the common law rules on restrictive practices law. This is because EU and Irish competition laws cover many forms of anti-competitive arrangement, abuse of dominance (i.e. not just monopolisation as in US antitrust law) but also merger control, State aid, and how Member States engage in the marketplace.

23.3 Example of Competition Law in the Practice of Solicitors

Competition law can arise in various contexts and it is useful to review some examples.

Solicitors have to advise on *arrangements* such as distribution agreements, franchises, purchasing agreements, price-fixing between competitors, intellectual property licences, joint ventures, and the behaviour of trade associations. There could also be 'soft' agreements (e.g. understandings which are undocumented or documented incompletely) such as where a supplier tries to insist on the reseller selling goods at a particular resale price. All of these could potentially have competition law consequences. In these situations, the solicitor is trying to establish whether (a) the arrangement is anti-competitive but (b) if it is anti-competitive whether the arrangement could be permissible because it is, on balance, beneficial to the economy despite its anti-competitive elements.

It is also possible that solicitors may have to advise on *practices* by market participants which are suspected of abusing their 'dominant position' in the market. Such practices could include refusals to supply, predatory pricing, exclusionary practices, excessive pricing, and refusals to license. In these situations, the solicitor is trying to establish whether (a) the business has a 'dominant position' and (b) whether the business is 'abusing' the 'dominant position. Merely having a dominant position is not a problem under competition law but abusing it is not permissible.

Equally, solicitors may have to advise on the competition law aspects of mergers, acquisitions, and joint ventures. Essentially, the solicitor is trying to establish whether the proposed transaction would 'substantially lessen competition'.

Ultimately, there is no finite list of possible breaches of competition law. The rules are very general in nature and therefore somewhat elastic in their application. It is also possible that solicitors may find it challenging to advise in this area because some practices are well hidden from view because participants go to great lengths to prevent detection (e.g. price-fixing or market-sharing cartels). It is equally possible that there can be complex economic issues involved in the cases.

23.4 The Application of Competition Law in Practice to Control the Behaviour of 'Undertakings'

The EU and Irish competition rules apply to 'undertakings' and, in the case of Irish competition law, to the behaviour of certain individuals (e.g. directors, company secretaries, and officers) connected with undertakings.

The term 'undertaking' is not defined in EU competition legislation but was understood by the Court of Justice of the European Union ('CJEU') in Case C-41/1990 *Klaus Höfner and Fritz Elser v Macrotron GmbH* [1991] ECR 1-1979, paragraph 21, to mean 'every entity engaged in an economic activity, regardless of the legal status of the entity and the way in which it is financed'. The term is defined by s 3 (1) of the Competition Act 2002 (the '2002 Act') (as substituted by s 47 (f) of the Competition and Consumer Protection Act 2014 (the '2014 Act')) as meaning 'a person being an individual, a body corporate or an unincorporated body of persons engaged for gain in the production, supply or distribution of goods or the provision of a service and, where the context so admits, shall include an association of undertakings'. The same definition applies to both s 4 and s 5 of the 2002 Act. The Supreme Court defined the concept of 'engaged for gain' in *Deane v Voluntary Health Insurance* [1992] 2 IR 319 as being wider than 'engaged for profit' and said that the words 'for gain' 'connote merely an activity carried on or a service supplied...which is done in return for a charge or payment...'. Hence, the entity does not have to be profit-making to qualify as an undertaking.

In both EU and Irish competition law, an undertaking could be, for example, a company, a State-owned company engaged for gain, an equity partner, a trade association, or a sole trader but not an employee (who does not have a substantial equity interest in the business). Plaintiff solicitors in competition litigation will have to prove that the defendant is an undertaking while defendant solicitors would seek to establish that the defendant is not an undertaking. In practice, in commercial disputes, the parties are usually undertakings but this may not be so, for example, in cases where an entity is operating as a regulator.

23.5   Sources of Competition Law

23.5.1   INTRODUCTION

The sources of competition law are both geographical and legal in nature. European Union ('EU') competition law is available at http://ec.europa.eu/competition/antitrust/legislation/legislation.html. EU court cases on competition law are available at www.curia.eu. Irish competition law is available at www.oireachtas.ie and www.ccpc.ie.

23.5.2   GEOGRAPHICAL SOURCES OF COMPETITION LAW

In terms of the geographical sources of competition law, it is clear that in practising in Ireland, one has to consider at least two sources of competition: the EU and the Irish competition rules.

If there is a conflict between the EU and the Irish rules then the EU ones prevail over the Irish ones. However, the Irish rules may be more extensive and onerous than the EU ones provided the Irish ones do not undermine the objectives of the EU rules (see, e.g. Case 14/68 *Walt Wilhelm and Others v Bundeskartellamt* [1969] ECR 1 and Case C-344/98 *Masterfoods* [2000] ECR I-11369).

It is also possible that other competition rules may also be relevant such as those of the UK, the US, or any other country where the arrangement or practice being reviewed by the solicitor has an impact on trade.

In practice, the Irish and the EU rules are the most relevant. The Irish ones apply whenever there is an effect on trade in Ireland; this is almost invariably the case if the arrangement or practice relates to Ireland. The EU rules apply whenever there is an effect on trade between EU Member States; this requirement is easy to satisfy such as when trade is potentially affected cross-border even if the level of that trade is low (e.g. sales of the *RTE Guide* (the television listings magazine of the Irish broadcaster RTE) in the UK (including Northern Ireland) were relatively low but still sufficient to trigger an effect on trade between Member States) (see Cases C-241/91P & C-242/91P *Radio Telefís Eireann (RTE) and Independent Television Publications Ltd (ITP) v Commission* [1995] ECR I-743). If there is no effect on trade between Member States then EU competition law is not applicable and one then turns to Member State competition law. (On the effect on trade between Member States, see also the Commission Notice entitled 'Guidelines on the effect on trade concept contained in Arts 81 and 82 of the Treaty' (2004) OJ C 101/81.) (Arts 81 and 82 of the Treaty establishing the European Community are now numbered Arts 101 and 102 of the Treaty on the Functioning of the European Union (the 'TFEU')).

23.5.3   LEGAL SOURCES OF COMPETITION LAW

In terms of the legal nature of the sources of competition law, there are differences in the type of sources used in EU and Irish competition law.

EU competition law is mainly found in: (a) the TFEU (in particular, Arts 101–109); (b) various regulations (which are binding legal instruments which do not need to be implemented into Irish law) including, in particular, Regulation 1/2003 (OJ 2004 L1/1); (c) a few directives but they are rare in competition law; (d) a very large number of decisions because the Commission takes its formal decisions in the area of competition law by way of decisions; and (e) the case law of the CJEU and the Commission. There are also many other examples of 'soft law' (i.e. sources of inspiration as to what is EU law but not amounting to law) including, for example, communications, notices, opinions, and recommendations. These soft sources can be very important in practice because they indicate the likely approach of the European Commission in many cases.

Irish competition law is mainly found in: (a) statutes of the Oireachtas (e.g. the 2002 Act, the Competition (Amendment) Act 2006 (the '2006 Act'); the Competition (Amendment) Act 2012; and the 2014 Act); (b) statutory instruments; and (c) the case law of the courts. However, the decisions of the Competition and Consumer Protection Commission ('CCPC') (which administers Irish competition law subject to supervision by the court) do not constitute laws as such but its decisions and communications are important sources of how Irish competition law applies in practice.

EU and Irish competition laws are very similar but they are not identical. Nor should they be. It is better that they are compatible but they do not have to be identical because the two systems have similar but not identical aims. Irish competition law is modelled largely on EU competition law in terms of the substantive rules but the procedural regimes are different due mainly to the Irish Constitution which reserves to courts the power to make decisions which can punish or impose penalties. (Thus, for example, the European Commission may impose fines in its decisions but the CCPC may not do so because that is a function reserved to the courts.)

There are a few areas of EU and Irish competition law where only one of the two regimes applies: for example, in the area of merger control, a transaction is subject either to EU or Irish competition law but not both. So, for example, the sale of Telefonica's O2 Ireland to Hutchison Whampoa's Three Ireland was supervised by the European Commission under the EU's Merger Control Regulation but not the Irish authority (i.e. the then Competition Authority or, now, the CCPC). Equally, a transaction such as the sale of a medium-sized Irish business to another Irish medium-sized business would be regulated by the Irish but not the EU regime. Occasionally, there can be a transaction transferred from the EU to the Irish authorities (or vice versa) but that is rare (an example of such a transfer was the transfer from the European Commission to the Irish agency of Heineken's purchase of Beamish & Crawford (see http://www.tca.ie/images/uploaded/documents/M08011%20 Heineken-Scottish%20and%20Newcastle%20Determination%20public.pdf)).

There are also a few areas of competition law which are only dealt with by EU competition law and they include State aid and the law on public undertakings (see Arts 107–109 and 106 of the TFEU respectively). Conversely, Irish competition law has specific rules on grocery goods which are not shared by the EU (e.g. Ireland's 2006 and 2014 Acts).

The Irish courts may apply all of the Irish competition laws and most of the EU ones. Equally, the Commission and the CJEU apply EU competition law only. The CJEU may give a preliminary ruling on the compatibility or relationship of Irish competition law with EU law pursuant to Art 267 of the TFEU but it does not opine on national law.

The 2002 Act is the principal Irish statute on competition matters. It largely entered into force on 1 July 2002 but the merger control provisions entered into force on 1 January 2003 and all of it is now in force but it has not been amended or repealed by later legislation.

The CCPC and Irish courts have regard to EU practice including EU case law, notices, and communications.

23.5.4 THE NATURE OF BREACHES OF COMPETITION LAW

In EU law, a breach of EU competition law is not classified as a criminal offence but the penalties can be very severe with very heavy fines imposed on undertakings. (Examples of fines include those fines imposed totaling €1.7 billion for interest rate derivative agreements, €1.47 billion for cartels in regard to cathode ray tubes, and €799 million for price-fixing in the air cargo sector.)

A breach of Irish competition law can be civil or criminal or both. Curiously, Ireland's Competition Acts impose criminal and civil penalties for breaching not only Irish competition law but EU competition law as well. Therefore, solicitors have to be more than usually careful to advise clients on the implications of breaching competition law because there can be breaches of civil and criminal law.

23.6 Rationale of Competition Law

Why does competition law exist? The short answer is: to enhance consumer welfare. Fennelly J said in the Supreme Court in the *ILCU* case [2004] IEHC 330, paragraph 109 that 'the entire aim and object of competition law is consumer welfare'.

Markets which are efficient tend to be more beneficial to consumers because they can benefit from lower prices, higher service standards, more innovation, and greater choice. This is because businesses have to compete strongly for the custom of consumers in competitive markets and therefore businesses tend to allocate resources efficiently and produce what consumers will buy.

While the rationale of competition law might seem an abstract issue for many solicitors, it is useful to ask the rationale of the particular practice or arrangement. This is often done by testing it by asking the question 'does this help or harm consumer welfare?' The answer to the question will often help fashion the advice as to whether the practice or arrangement is lawful or not.

23.7 The Market: Market Definition and Market Assessment

23.7.1 INTRODUCTION

Competition does not exist in the abstract. It exists, or does not exist, in a market. Any solicitor advising on a case should consider the 'market' carefully by examining two issues: (a) the definition of the relevant market; and (b) establishing the level of competition in the market.

23.7.2 DEFINING THE MARKET

The first task is to define the market which is relevant to the case at hand. There may be several markets in the one case (e.g. the Determination in Merger Notification M/08/009

Kerry/Breeo: Proposed acquisition by Kerry Group plc of Breeo Foods Limited and Breeo Brands Limited, 28 August 2008 where rashers, sausages, hams, and so on were separate markets). Not every case requires detailed economic analysis of the relevant market but court cases almost invariably do and many serious or complex complaints or merger notifications would also do so. Solicitors should therefore instruct micro-economists to examine the relevant product, geographical, and temporal markets in the context of the particular case if market definition is likely to be an issue. Some guidance on the concept of 'market definition' can be found in the European Commission's Notice on the Definition of relevant markets for the purposes of Community competition law ((1997) OJ C372/5) (the 'Market Definition Notice'). It is worth noting that findings of market definition are not precedent: for example, technological changes can alter the definition of the relevant market – the case of recorded music would be a good example of how the market definition can change (e.g. records to tapes to CDs to Internet downloads).

Markets are usually defined on three levels: the product market; the geographical market; and the temporal market. The first two levels are the most relevant in practice.

The product market is the market comprising all those products and/or services which are regarded as interchangeable or substitutable by the consumer by reason of the products' characteristics, prices, and intended use (see Market Definition Notice, paragraph 7). Put simply, between which products would a consumer switch if one was not available or the price rose significantly? Occasionally, supply-side substitutability is also used.

The geographic market comprises the physical area in which the undertakings concerned are involved in the supply and demand of goods or services in which the conditions of competition are sufficiently homogenous and which can be distinguished from neighbouring areas because the conditions of competition are appreciably different in other areas (see Market Definition Notice, paragraph 8). Pricing, regulatory, linguistic, consumer behaviour patterns, and so on all help give guidance on the geographic market definition.

The temporal market relates to the time element or factor in the market. For example, products can be sold on a seasonal basis and there can be a larger market at one time of the year than another, i.e. turkeys could be more expensive at Christmas time than at other times of the year.

One examines the relevant market by paying attention to both the demand-side substitutability and the supply-side substitutability. Demand-side substitutability refers to the degree of willingness of a consumer to replace one product with another product if there is a change in price: for example, a consumer might replace one can of soft drink with another where the price of the former product rose by, say, 5 or 10% so the two drinks are said to be 'substitutable' (in the demand sense) but as the consumer would be unlikely to switch to buying a newspaper instead of the soft drink can, those two products (i.e. the can and the newspaper) are not substitutes for each other. More technically, if the price increase results in consumers switching from one product to another thereby rendering the price increase unprofitable for the supplier because of the resulting loss of sales then the products are substitutable and this is known as the SSNIP (small but significant and non-transitory increase in price) test. Supply-side substitution is also often relevant. Supply-side substitution examines whether suppliers are able to switch production in the short term without incurring significant additional costs or risks in response to small and permanent changes in relative prices. If the new products can be put on the markets relatively easily then those products could be substitutable.

A market can typically be defined broadly or narrowly. A broad product definition might be all fruit but a narrow one might be tomatoes. A broad geographical definition would be 'the world' but a narrow one might be ferry port services in a particular port serving a particular route. A wide or narrow market definition can have a decisive impact on the outcome of a case. If the market is defined narrowly then an arrangement is more likely to have a negative impact on competition and an undertaking is more likely to be dominant than if the market is defined broadly. Conversely, if the market is defined broadly, it is less likely that an arrangement would have a negative impact on competition or an undertaking is dominant. Hence, in abuse of dominance cases, plaintiffs tend to want to define the market narrowly (e.g. in *Ballina Mineral Water Company v Murphy Brewery*, High Court, Kearns J, unreported, 31 May 2002, where the plaintiffs argued that the defendants were involved in the draught lager market and even then of just one brand of lager thereby increasing the chances of dominance, while defendants usually take the opposite approach (in the same case, the defendants argued successfully that they were in the beer market and not the narrower lager market)).

What factors are taken into account in market definition? There is no finite catalogue. Examples include pricing data (e.g. what happened to the demand for Product X when the price of Product Y rose by, say, 5%?), legislative or regulatory requirements, evidence of substitution (e.g. in a shock scenario where Product X was not available due to a strike then to which products did consumers switch?), the recorded beliefs of executives (e.g. in emails or marketing plans), taxation rules, the views of customers, and so on. It is worth noting that much of this type of evidence can be difficult to find and may not be entirely reliable in every case.

23.7.3 CONSIDERING THE LEVEL OF COMPETITION IN THE MARKET

The second task, after defining the market, is to consider the level of competition in the market (i.e. how dynamic is the market?). Who competes in the market? How many competitors are active in the market? Could other competitors enter the market? Are there high barriers to entry, expansion, or exit in the market? What are the market shares of the market participants? (Market share is not equivalent to market power but market share is a useful proxy for market power.) How easy could such market shares change? How likely are new competitors to enter, or existing ones to expand, in response to a change in prices? The market is likely to be more competitive if it is easy to enter, expand, and exit the market.

If there are many competitors each with low market shares in a market characterised by low barriers to entry, expansion, and exit then one is typically not so concerned with the level of competition in the market because it is easy to compete and if someone is behaving anti-competitively (e.g. by charging excessive prices) then others could enter or expand easily so as to compete. By contrast, if there are few competitors or a small number of competitors have high market shares and considerable market power in a context where the barriers to entry, expansion, or exit are high, one would potentially be dealing with a less than competitive market.

23.8 Anti-Competitive Arrangements

23.8.1 INTRODUCTION

The first rule of competition law relates to anti-competitive arrangements. It is sometimes referred to as the 'rule on cartels' but that is misleading because the rule covers many other arrangements and not just cartels. It is the most common competition rule encountered in practice by solicitors advising on the area in Ireland.

The rule is embodied in s 4 of the 2002 Act and Art 101 of the TFEU. (Art 101 was numbered, at various times, Art 85 of the Treaty establishing the European Economic Community ('EEC Treaty') and Art 81 of the Treaty establishing the European Community ('TEC'). For all intents and purposes, the wording has not changed over time – just the words 'common market' were changed by the Treaty of Lisbon to 'internal market'). Both s 4 and Art 101 prohibit anti-competitive arrangements between undertakings unless, on balance, the anti-competitive arrangement is beneficial to the economy generally because of some other indispensable benefits which it brings to the economy.

Section 4 (1) of the 2002 Act provides:

Subject to the provisions of this section, all agreements between undertakings, decisions by associations of undertakings and concerted practices which have as their object or effect the prevention, restriction or distortion of competition in trade in any goods or services in the State or in any part of the State are prohibited and void, including in particular, without prejudice to the generality of this subsection, those which—

 (a) *directly or indirectly fix purchase or selling prices or any other trading conditions,*

 (b) *limit or control production, markets, technical development or investment,*

 (c) *share markets or sources of supply,*

 (d) *apply dissimilar conditions to equivalent transactions with other trading parties thereby placing them at a competitive disadvantage,*

 (e) *make the conclusion of contracts subject to acceptance by the other parties of supplementary obligations which by their nature or according to commercial usage have no connection with the subject of such contracts.*

Section 4 (5) of the 2002 Act provides:

The conditions mentioned in subsections (2) and (3) are that the agreement, decision or concerted practice or category of agreement, decision or concerted practice, having regard to all relevant market conditions, contributes to improving the production or distribution of goods or provision of services or to promoting technical or economic progress, while allowing consumers a fair share of the resulting benefit and does not—

 (a) *impose on the undertakings concerned terms which are not indispensable to the attainment of those objectives,*

 (b) *afford undertakings the possibility of eliminating competition in respect of a substantial part of the products or services in question.*

Section 4 (6) of the 2002 Act provides:

The prohibition in subsection (1) shall not prevent the court, in exercising any jurisdiction conferred on it by this Act concerning an agreement, decision or concerted practice which contravenes that prohibition and which creates or, but for this Act, would have created legal relations between the parties thereto, from applying, where appropriate, any relevant rules of law as to the severance of those terms of that agreement, decision or concerted practice which contravene that prohibition from those which do not.

Article 101 of the TFEU provides:

The following shall be prohibited as incompatible with the internal market: all agreements between undertakings, decisions by associations of undertakings and concerted practices which may affect trade between Member States and which have as their object or effect the prevention, restriction or distortion of competition within the internal market, and in particular those which:

 (a) *directly or indirectly fix purchase or selling prices or any other trading conditions;*

 (b) *limit or control production, markets, technical development, or investment;*

 (c) *share markets or sources of supply;*

 (d) *apply dissimilar conditions to equivalent transactions with other trading parties, thereby placing them at a competitive disadvantage;*

 (e) *make the conclusion of contracts subject to acceptance by the other parties of supplementary obligations which, by their nature or according to commercial usage, have no connection with the subject of such contracts.*

It is clear that the two provisions are comparable but apply in a different geographical sphere: the 2002 Act relates to trade in Ireland while the TFEU applies to cross-border EU trade. It is also clear that the framework is the same: there is a general prohibition (i.e. s. 4 (1) and Art 101 (1)) and then an exemption mechanism (s 4 (5) and Art 101 (3)).

23.8.2 AGREEMENTS BETWEEN UNDERTAKINGS, DECISIONS BY ASSOCIATIONS OF UNDERTAKINGS, AND CONCERTED PRACTICES

23.8.2.1 Form of arrangement

The rule on anti-competitive arrangements (whether in s 4 or art 101) relates to what might be termed 'arrangements'. In legal terms, these arrangements are agreements between undertakings, decisions by associations of undertakings, or concerted practices involving undertakings. The concepts are construed widely.

In the case of 'agreements', they could be arrangements which are legally enforceable (or not) whether written or oral. They could be contracts or even so-called 'gentlemen's agreements' (see Case 41/69 *ACF Chemiefarma NV v Commission* [1970] ECR 661). It could also involve mere interaction between competitors at meetings (see Case C-8/08 *T-Mobile Netherlands* [2009] ECR I-4529). Contact between competitors can therefore be problematical but there must be some element of consensus or agreement (however informal or loose). Solicitors should advise clients about the risks of too much interaction with their competitors.

In the case of 'decisions by associations of undertakings', this can include decisions of associations, decisions by an ad hoc or chance meeting of competitors, bye laws of an association, or any other arrangement. This is to avoid undertakings seeking to circumvent the rules but not agreeing something themselves but doing so using the conduit of a trade association. It is often easier to prove a cartel or other anti-competitive arrangement using the minutes or a trade association than trying to find the intentions of individual market participants. Indeed, solicitors advising trade associations or participants should have regard to the Competition Authority's 'Notice on Activities of Trade Associations and Compliance with Competition Law' (N/09/002) which would still apply to the CCPC. Indeed, competition agencies worldwide are very focused on the competition law activities of trade associations so it is worth bearing that in mind in advising trade associations and clients who attend meetings of such groupings.

The term 'concerted practice' is the catch-all phrase to encompass a variety of arrangements which are not already caught by the terms 'agreements between undertakings' or 'concerted practices'. The CJEU has always taken a wide view of the concept but there must still be an element of consensus or agreement. The CJEU defined a concerted practice in Case 48/69 *ICI v Commission (Dyestuffs)* [1972] ECR 619 as:

> 'a form of coordination between undertakings which, without having reached the stage where an agreement properly so-called has been concluded, knowingly substitutes practical cooperation between them for the risks of competition.'

23.8.2.2 'Object' or 'effect' of preventing, restricting or distorting competition

The rule controls those arrangements which have the 'object' *or* 'effect' of 'preventing, restricting or distorting competition'.

Article 101 captures arrangements which have as their object *or* effect the prevention, restriction or distortion of competition; this means that there can be a breach of Article 101 irrespective of whether (a) the parties had intended to distort competition (i.e. they had the 'object' of distorting competition) or (b) the parties never intended breaching competition but the consequences of their arrangement was to distort competition (i.e. they did not have the 'object' of distorting competition but there was an 'effect' on competition). This means that Article 101 is a very broad provision capturing intentional and unintentional distortions of competition. The CJEU has made it clear in Case C-67/13P *Groupement des cartes bancaires v Commission* on 11 September 2014 that a narrow construction of 'object' is needed.

Equally, the arrangement must have the object or effect of preventing, restricting, or distorting competition and any one of those three phenomena would suffice (but one must exist).

23.8.2.3   Form of arrangement: horizontal or vertical

Arrangements can be described as either horizontal or vertical in nature. They are horizontal when they are concluded between two or more parties at the same level of the economic chain (e.g. between two distributors). They are vertical when they are between parties at different levels of the economic chain (e.g. between a manufacturer and a distributor). Solicitors need to be cautious about both types of arrangement but need to be particularly careful about horizontal ones because they are more likely to raise competition concerns.

23.8.2.4   Two or more undertakings are party to the arrangement

Before s 4 or art 101 may apply, there must be an arrangement involving two or more undertakings. Therefore the provisions do not typically apply to intra-group transactions or arrangements within a group because they involve just one undertaking so solicitors do not usually have to advise that there is a s 4 or art 101 issue with such arrangements. The same applies to agreements between employers and employees because again there is typically only one undertaking party to such arrangements. (In such circumstances, the common law on restraint of trade may still apply; see the Competition Authority's Notice on 'Employment Agreements and the Competition Act' of September 1992 (now revoked but interesting in setting out the thinking on the topic.))

23.8.3   SANCTIONS FOR BREACHING THE PROHIBITION ON ANTI-COMPETITIVE ARRANGEMENTS

An anti-competitive arrangement contrary to s 4 (1) or Art 101 (1) is prohibited and void by virtue of s 4 (1) or Art 101 (2). Solicitors advising plaintiffs seeking to enforce an arrangement (and solicitors advising defendants in such claims) should check to see if there is any possible defence to a claim that the arrangement is unenforceable (e.g. if an exclusive distribution agreement did not benefit from an exemption then it would be void and unenforceable).

There can be severe penalties. If it is a hard core cartel (e.g. a price-fixing or market-sharing arrangement) then there can be more severe penalties than for breaches of competition law generally. Under s 8 of the 2002 Act (as amended) the penalties are up to ten years in jail and/or fines of up to 10% of worldwide turnover in the case of undertakings or €5,000,000 in the case of individuals. Under EU competition law, the fines can be up to 10% of worldwide turnover but there are no penalties on individuals (who are not undertakings).

It is also possible that those aggrieved persons who have suffered loss because of the anti-competitive arrangements may, under s 14 of the 2002 Act, sue the parties to the anti-competitive activity for damages, exemplary damages, injunctions, and/or declarations. There is also the possibility of suing for, at least, damages under EU law as well.

23.8.4   EXEMPTIONS FOR SOME ANTI-COMPETITIVE ARRANGEMENTS

It is possible that there could be an anti-competitive arrangement which is, when viewed in the round, pro-competitive because of the various benefits which it brings to the marketplace. For example, an exclusive distribution agreement may be anti-competitive on its face but, on balance, because the exclusive distributor has some degree of protection from competition, the distributor will devote a great deal of energy and enthusiasm to promoting the products.

EU and Irish competition law therefore permit some form of exemption for arrangements which would otherwise be void because they are anti-competitive.

Article 101 (3) of the TFEU provides:

The provisions of paragraph 1 may, however, be declared inapplicable in the case of:

– any agreement or category of agreements between undertakings,

– any decision or category of decisions by associations of undertakings,

– any concerted practice or category of concerted practices,

which contributes to improving the production or distribution of goods or to promoting technical or economic progress, while allowing consumers a fair share of the resulting benefit, and which does not:

> (a) *impose on the undertakings concerned restrictions which are not indispensable to the attainment of these objectives;*

> (b) *afford such undertakings the possibility of eliminating competition in respect of a substantial part of the products in question.*

In respect of Irish competition law, a comparable provision is contained in s 4 (5) of the 2002 Act (as amended).

Solicitors practising in this area used to be able to notify arrangements to the Competition Authority or the European Commission to determine whether or not the arrangement was anti-competitive and whether it could be exempted. Since 1 January 2003, when the relevant provisions of the 2002 Act entered into force, and 1 May 2004, when Regulation 1/2003 entered into force, it has not been possible to notify arrangements to the Irish or EU authorities respectively. Instead, solicitors have to conduct a so-called 'self-assessment' of the arrangement to determine if it is compatible with the section or article. To assist that process, if the arrangement fits within an EU 'Block Exemption' or Irish Declaration then it benefits from the exemption. There are various block exemptions and declarations; for example, in regard to distribution agreements, one would review the EU block exemption on vertical agreements (i.e. Commission Regulation (EU) No. 330/2010 of 20 April 2010 on the application of Art 101 (3) of the Treaty on the Functioning of the European Union to categories of vertical agreements and concerted practices: http://eur-lex.europa.eu/legal-content/EN/TXT/HTML/?uri=CELEX:320 10R0330&from=EN) and the Irish Declaration in respect of Vertical Agreements and Concerted Practices (http://www.tca.ie/images/uploaded/documents/Verticals%20Declaration% 202010.PDF). Indeed, solicitors often find it helpful to draft an agreement to fit within the scope of the block exemption/declaration so as to reduce the risk of a breach of Art 101 or s 4.

23.9 Abuse of Dominance

23.9.1 INTRODUCTION

The second rule of competition law relates to the abuse of dominance. The rule is embodied in s 5 of the 2002 Act and Art 102 of the TFEU. (Art 102 was numbered, at various times, Art 86 of the EEC Treaty and Art 82 of the TEC.)

The rule relates to undertakings which have a dominant position (i.e. are dominant). This term, dominance, is not defined in the TFEU or the Irish competition legislation.

The rule does *not* outlaw an undertaking having a dominant position. Instead, it outlaws the *abuse of dominance* but not the dominant position itself.

Article 102 of the TFEU provides:

Any abuse by one or more undertakings of a dominant position within the internal market or in a substantial part of it shall be prohibited as incompatible with the internal market in so far as it may affect trade between Member States.

Such abuse may, in particular, consist in:

> (a) *directly or indirectly imposing unfair purchase or selling prices or other unfair trading conditions;*

> (b)   limiting production, markets or technical development to the prejudice of consumers;
>
> (c)   applying dissimilar conditions to equivalent transactions with other trading parties, thereby placing them at a competitive disadvantage;
>
> (d)   making the conclusion of contracts subject to acceptance by the other parties of supplementary obligations which, by their nature or according to commercial usage, have no connection with the subject of such contracts.

Section 5 of the 2002 Act provides:

> (1)   Any abuse by one or more undertakings of a dominant position in trade for any goods or services in the State or in any part of the State is prohibited.
>
> (2)   Without prejudice to the generality of subsection (1), such abuse may, in particular, consist in—
>
> > (a)   directly or indirectly imposing unfair purchase or selling prices or other unfair trading conditions,
> >
> > (b)   limiting production, markets or technical development to the prejudice of consumers,
> >
> > (c)   applying dissimilar conditions to equivalent transactions with other trading parties, thereby placing them at a competitive disadvantage,
> >
> > (d)   making the conclusion of contracts subject to the acceptance by other parties of supplementary obligations which by their nature or according to commercial usage have no connection with the subject of such contracts.
>
> (3)   The putting into effect of a merger or acquisition in accordance with the provisions of Part 3 of this Act, together with any arrangements constituting restrictions which are directly related and necessary to the implementation of the merger or acquisition and are referred to in the notification of the merger or acquisition under subsection (1) or (3) of section 18, shall not be prohibited under subsection (1).

There are several conditions which must be satisfied for Art 102/s 5 to apply: (1) the conduct must be by an undertaking or undertakings; (2) the undertaking(s) must have a dominant position (i.e. dominance); (3) the dominance must exist in a particular market; (4) the dominant position must exist in, for the purposes of Art 102, the internal market or in a substantial part of the internal market or, for the purposes of s 5, the State or any part of the State; (5) there must be an abuse of that dominance (i.e. the conduct must amount to an abuse of dominance); and (6) trade between Member States must be affected for Art 102 to apply.

23.9.2   CONCEPT OF DOMINANCE

Dominance does not exist in the abstract. It exists in the context of a particular market. Dominance is therefore said to be a 'relational' concept because it is not an abstract one. Dominance must exist in regard to a particular market and there are, quite simply, billions of markets which could fall within the scope of Art 102. The CJEU defined 'dominance' in Case 85/76 *Hoffmann-La Roche* [1979] ECR 461:

> '38. Article [102]...prohibits any abuse by an undertaking of a dominant position....The dominant position...referred to relates to a position of economic strength enjoyed by an undertaking which enables it to prevent effective competition being maintained on the relevant market by affording it the power to behave to an appreciable extent independently of its competitors, its customers and ultimately of the consumers.
>
> 39. Such a position does not preclude some competition, which it does where there is a monopoly or a quasi-monopoly, but enables the undertaking which profits by it, if not to determine, at least to have an appreciable influence on the conditions under which that competition will develop, and in any case to act largely in disregard of it so long as such conduct does not operate to its detriment.

A dominant position must also be distinguished from parallel courses of conduct which are peculiar to oligopolies in that in an oligopoly the courses of conduct interact, while in the case of an undertaking occupying a dominant position the conduct of the undertaking which derives profits from that position is to a great extent determined unilaterally.

The existence of a dominant position may derive from several factors which, taken separately, are not necessarily determinative but among these factors a highly important one is the existence of very large market shares.

40. A substantial market share as evidence of the existence of a dominant position is not a constant factor and its importance varies from market to market according to the structure of these markets, especially as far as production, supply and demand are concerned.

Even though each group of vitamins constitutes a separate market, these different markets, as has emerged from the examination of their structure, nevertheless have a sufficient number of features in common to make it possible for the same criteria to be applied to them as far as concerns the importance of the market shares for the purpose of determining whether there is a dominant position or not.

41. Furthermore although the importance of the market shares may vary from one market to another the view may legitimately be taken that very large shares are in themselves, and save in exceptional circumstances, evidence of the existence of a dominant position.

An undertaking which has a very large market share and holds it for some time, by means of the volume of production and the scale of the supply which it stands for – without those having much smaller market shares being able to meet rapidly the demand from those who would like to break away from the undertaking which has the largest market share – is by virtue of that share in a position of strength which makes it an unavoidable trading partner and which, already because of this secures for it, at the very least during relatively long periods, that freedom of action which is the special feature of a dominant position.'

It is possible for one undertaking acting alone to be dominant. (This distinguishes this provision from the prohibition on anti-competitive arrangements because to breach that prohibition, there must be two or more undertakings involved.) However, the dominant position could also be 'joint dominance' – as the CJEU stated in the Cases T-68/69 etc *Società Italiano Vetro SpA v Commission* [1992] II-ECR 1403:

'There is nothing, in principle, to prevent two or more independent economic entities from being, on a specific market, united by such economic links that, by virtue of that fact, together they hold a dominant position vis-à-vis the other operators on the same market.'

23.9.3 CONCEPT OF ABUSE OF DOMINANCE

There is no legislative definition of 'abuse' of dominance. It is generally understood to mean an unfair or exploitative misuse or abuse of the power which the dominance has conferred on the undertaking. Examples include predatory pricing, excessive pricing, unjustifiable refusals to supply, and unfair pricing.

23.9.4 PENALTIES FOR ABUSING DOMINANCE

A breach of the EU or Irish rules on abuse of dominance can result in fines. Indeed, the highest EU fine (to date) on a single undertaking has been related to the abuse of dominance by Intel – a fine of €1.06 billion was imposed where the Commission found that Intel had engaged in two practices which the Commission described as:

'[first], Intel gave wholly or partially hidden rebates to computer manufacturers on condition that they bought all, or almost all, their x86 central processing units (CPUs) from Intel. Intel also made direct payments to a major retailer on condition it stock only computers with Intel x86 CPUs. Second, Intel made direct payments to computer manufacturers to halt or delay the launch of specific products containing a competitor's x86

CPUs and to limit the sales channels available to these products. Intel is obliged to desist from the specific practices identified in this case and not to engage in these or equivalent practices in the future.'

23.9.5   NO EXEMPTION MECHANISM

Unlike Art 101 or s 4, there is no exemption mechanism to permit an abuse of dominance.

23.9.6   PENALTIES

Undertakings breaching Art 102 or s 5 may be fined up to 10% of the undertaking's previous year's worldwide turnover. It is also possible that those aggrieved persons who have suffered loss because of the anti-competitive arrangements may, under s 14 of the 2002 Act, sue the parties to the anti-competitive activity for damages, exemplary damages, injunctions, and/or declarations. There is also the possibility of suing for, at least, damages under EU law as well.

23.10   Administration of Competition Law

23.10.1   INTRODUCTION

There is no point in having substantive competition law rules if there is not an effective administration or enforcement mechanism.

23.10.2   EU COMPETITION LAW

23.10.2.1   European Commission

EU competition law is primarily administered by the European Commission with appeals going to the CJEU (in particular, the General Court in the first instance). The Commission has a special directorate general (DG Competition) which deals with competition law. Sometimes, solicitors may wish to contact (even on a no-names basis) officials in DG Competition who may be able direct the solicitors to particular areas of law but will not usually give specific advice. (It is worth recalling that the Commission is not infallible on competition law issues and some of its decisions have been annulled by the CJEU.)

The rules on the administration of EU competition law are primarily contained in Regulation 1/2003 (the so-called 'Modernisation Regulation') which entered into force on 1 May 2004. It also decentralised aspects of EU competition law and conferred various powers on National Competition Authorities (e.g. Ireland's CCPC, courts, and, in its field, the Commission for Communications Regulation); for example, the Irish courts may apply Art 101 (3) of the TFEU even though that power was reserved to the European Commission solely between 1962 and 2004. (Ireland's designation of national competition agencies was embodied in the European Communities (Implementation of the Rules on Competition laid down in Arts 81 and 82) Regulation 2004 (SI 195/2004) as amended by SI 525/2007.) More generally, designated national competition authorities may require an infringement to be brought to an end, order interim measures, accept commitments as well as impose fines, periodic penalties, or other national penalties (see Art 5 of Regulation 1/2003).

The European Commission and the Member State competition agencies must cooperate with each other in their work. This avoids inconsistent application of EU competition law between the EU and Member State systems. For this reason, there is the European Competition Network ('ECN') which is a forum for discussion, debate, and cooperation. (See the Commission Notice on cooperation within the Network of Competition Authorities ((2004) OJ C 101/43).) This need for cooperation also extends to the Member State courts so the Commission can assist the courts. (See the Commission Notice on the cooperation between the Commission and the courts of the EU Member States in the application of Arts 81 and 82 EC ((2004) OJ 101/54).)

If a Member State competition agency is acting on the basis of Art 101 or 102 of the TFEU then it must, under Art 11 of Regulation 1/2003, inform the Commission in writing before (or without delay after) commencing its first formal investigative measure. A national competition authority must inform the European Commission, no later than 30 days before making a decision requiring termination of an infringement, accepting commitments, or withdrawing the benefit of a block exemption regulation. In any event, a national competition agency may consult with the European Commission; as such, an agency could be a court. This is almost a second form of preliminary reference 'to Europe' (the other, and the only formal one, being a preliminary reference under Art 267 of the TFEU by a Member State court to the CJEU).

Cases can come to the attention of the European Commission by various means. For example, the Commission hears about cases by virtue of complaints from competitors, customers, and others (e.g. former employees), leniency applications by cartelists seeking immunity from fines, and 'own initiative' cases where the European Commission decides to investigate a particular issue (e.g. because of media reports, cases in the same sector before other regulators, or general reviews of the sector).

The European Commission is entitled, by virtue of Regulation 1/2003, to impose penalties on undertakings which breach competition law. These penalties can be onerous. In principle, they can include fines of up to 10% of the previous year's worldwide turnover of the undertaking.

23.10.2.2 European courts

The EU's courts are also involved in the administration of EU competition law. Appeals from decisions of the European Commission (e.g. decisions to impose fines) are made to the General Court and, in turn, to the CJEU. Equally, Member State courts hearing cases concerning EU competition law may sometimes refer questions of EU competition law to the CJEU under Art 267 of the TFEU where the question needs to be answered to decide the case and relates to an issue of EU law which is unclear (an example would be the reference by the Supreme Court in Case C-209/07 *Competition Authority v Beef Industry Development Society Ltd and Barry Brothers (Carrigmore) Meats Ltd* [2008] ECR I-08637).

23.10.3   IRISH COMPETITION LAW

23.10.3.1 Introduction

The administration of Irish competition law is comparable to the administration of EU competition law. The principal exception relates to the fact that the Irish Constitution provides that only courts (i.e. not administrative agencies) may impose penalties such as fines.

23.10.3.2 Competition and Consumer Protection Commission)

Irish competition law is primarily administered by the Ireland's Competition and Consumer Protection Commission ('CCPC') which is the successor institution to the Competition Authority (first established under the Competition Act 1991 and re-established under the 2002 Act) and the National Consumer Agency (established under the Consumer Protection Act 2007). The CCPC is a very largely independent statutory body which acts under the supervision of the courts. The CCPC investigates potential breaches of Irish competition law (which includes some provisions of EU competition law insofar as they are referred to in the 2002 Act (namely, Arts 101 and 102 of the TFEU)). In that respect, the CCPC has powers to interview witnesses, conduct searches of premises (including homes) when authorised to do so by a court, and to institute certain types of civil and criminal cases in the courts.

The imposition of penalties (whether civil or criminal) for breach of Irish competition law is reserved to the courts because the Irish Constitution provides that only the courts may administer justice. This means that, unlike the European Commission which may impose fines, the CCPC may not do so. Instead, the CCPC may either bring some criminal prosecutions itself in the courts or, more likely, refer the possible breach to the Director of Public Prosecutions who then may (or may not) bring the matter before the courts.

One area where the CCPC is very much involved in making competition decisions is the area of merger control.

The CCPC also has an important role in the advocacy of competition policy and suggesting ways in which competition can be included in government policy as well as legislation.

The CCPC has cooperation agreements with a variety of regulatory and government bodies such as the Commission for Communications Regulation, the Broadcasting Authority of Ireland, and the Commission for Energy Regulation. Such agreements facilitate cooperation, avoid duplication of activities, and ensure consistency of decision-making.

23.10.3.3   Minister for Jobs, Enterprise and Innovation

The Minister for Jobs, Enterprise and Innovation has an important role in promoting competition policy and proposing competition legislation. The Minister may also ask the CCPC to conduct a study of any practice or method of competition affecting the supply of goods or services.

The Minister for Communications and the Broadcasting Authority of Ireland also have a role to play in regard to media mergers under the 2014 Act. Their role relates to merger control and so falls outside the scope of this chapter.

23.10.3.4   Courts

The entire Irish competition law regime is ultimately under the supervision of the courts. The Irish courts have a role to play in regard to EU competition law because of the direct effect of, for example, Arts 101 and 102 of the TFEU as well as Arts 3 and 6 of Regulation 1/2003. If an Irish court is acting as a competition authority in applying Arts 101 and 102 then it may have to, in certain circumstances, refer its draft judgment to the European Commission for comment. The latter does not have to comment (e.g. it did not do so in the *ILCU* case). Such a review process can be absolutely confidential. Court judgments on EU competition law must, under Art 15 (2) of Regulation 1/2003, be sent to the European Commission 'without delay after the full written judgment is notified to the parties' and are then added to the latter's website, which contains a database of judgments (http://ec.europa.eu/competition/elojade/antitrust/nationalcourts/). It is also possible for the European Commission and the CCPC to submit comments to a court hearing a case which involves Arts 101 and 102 by way of an *amicus curiae* brief (see the Commission Notice on the cooperation between the Commission and the courts ((2004) OJ C101/04)).

23.11   Conclusions

Of all the areas of EU law, competition law is probably the most significant in practice because more EU lawyers practise competition law than probably any other area of EU law. The CJEU stated in Case 6/72 *Europemballage and Continental Can v Commission* [1973] ECR 215, paragraph 24 that the competition laws are 'so essential that without [them] numerous provisions of the Treaty would be pointless'. Equally, the CJEU stated in Case C-126/97 *Eco Swiss China Time v Benetton International* [1999] ECR I-3055, paragraph 36 that the competition rules are 'essential to the accomplishment of the tasks entrusted to the [EU] and, in particular, the functioning of the internal market'.

INDEX